Virginia

HIKING THE OLD DOMINION

Allen de Hart

THE UNIVERSITY OF NORTH CAROLINA PRESS

Chapel Hill & London

© 1995 The University

of North Carolina Press

All rights reserved

Manufactured in the

United States of America

Original edition published in 1984 by Sierra Club Books.

The paper in this book meets the guidelines for permanence

and durability of the Committee on Production Guidelines

for Book Longevity of the Council on Library Resources.

Library of Congress Cataloging-in-Publication Data

De Hart, Allen.

   The trails of Virginia: hiking the Old Dominion / Allen de

Hart.—New and rev. ed.

     p.   cm.

   Rev. ed. of: Hiking the Old Dominion. c1984.

   Includes bibliographical references and index.

   ISBN 0-8078-4508-6 (pbk. : alk. paper)

   1. Hiking—Virginia—Guidebooks. 2. Trails—Virginia—

Guidebooks. 3. National parks and reserves—Virginia—

Guidebooks. 4. Virginia—Guidebooks. I. De Hart, Allen.

Hiking the Old Dominion. II. Title

GV199.42.V8D4   1995

917.55′0443—dc20   94-33818

             CIP

99 98 97 96 95   5 4 3 2 1

Contents

Acknowledgments, ix

Abbreviations, xiii

Introduction, 1

PART I. NATIONAL FOREST TRAILS, 25

Chapter 1. Jefferson National Forest, 28

    Blacksburg Ranger District, 30

    Clinch Ranger District, 38

    Glenwood Ranger District, 46

    Mount Rogers National Recreation Area, 53

    New Castle Ranger District, 69

    Wythe Ranger District, 78

Chapter 2. George Washington National Forest, 83

    Deerfield Ranger District, 85

    Dry Run Ranger District, 97

    James River Ranger District, 107

    Lee Ranger District, 115

    Pedlar Ranger District, 128

    Warm Springs Ranger District, 139

PART II. NATIONAL PARK SYSTEM TRAILS, 149

Chapter 3. Appalachian National Scenic Trail, 151

Chapter 4. Blue Ridge Parkway, 160

Chapter 5. Shenandoah National Park, 172

Chapter 6. National Battlefield Parks, 188

Chapter 7. National Historical Parks, 200

Chapter 8. National Wildlife Refuges, 204

Chapter 9. Other Trails in the National Park System, 212

PART III. STATE MANAGED TRAILS, 223

Chapter 10. Wildlife Management Areas, 225

Chapter 11. Parklands, 236

    Mountain Division, 238

    Piedmont Division, 253

    Coastal Division, 262

PART IV. COUNTY AND MUNICIPALITY TRAILS, 279

Chapter 12. County Parks and Recreation Areas, 281

Chapter 13. Municipal Parks and Recreation Areas, 301

PART V. REGIONAL, MILITARY, COLLEGE,
AND PRIVATE TRAILS, 329

Chapter 14. Regional Parks, 331

Chapter 15. U.S. Army Corps of Engineers and Military Areas, 341

Chapter 16. Colleges and Universities, 347

Chapter 17. Private and Special Holdings, 350

Maps, 359

Appendix A. Sources of Information, 379

Appendix B. Federal and State Endangered and Threatened
Species in Virginia, 387

Appendix C. Trails for Special People, 391

Bibliography, 393

General Index, 399

Trail Index, 409

Illustrations

Beartown Wilderness Area, JNF, 2

Cascades Trail, JNF, 32

Fenwick Wetlands Trail, JNF, 74

Hardscrabble Trail, GWNF, 93

Panther Falls Trail, GWNF, 130

Appalachian Trail, Mount Rogers, JNF, 153

Blue Ridge Parkway, Roanoke, 161

Mountain Industry Trail, Mabry Mill, BRP, 170

Shenandoah National Park from Old Rag Mountain, 173

Petersburg National Battlefield Park, 197

Cumberland Gap National Historical Park, 201

Great Dismal Swamp National Wildlife Refuge, 209

Great Falls Park, George Washington Memorial Parkway, 217

New River State Park Trail, 249

False Cape State Park, 265

York River State Park, 275

Echo Lake Park, Henrico County, 294

White Oak Trail, Newport News Park, 316

Belle Isle Trail, Richmond, 322

Noland Trail, Mariners' Museum Park, 353

Acknowledgments

In the 1980s I began an intensive effort to hike all the trails in Virginia for a comprehensive guidebook, but the fieldwork was only part of the task. I needed assistance from the offices of each ranger district in the Jefferson and George Washington national forests, from the Blue Ridge Parkway and Shenandoah National Park staffs, from state parks and recreation officials, and from the offices of all county and municipal parks. In addition, I needed information from professors and forestry specialists from colleges and universities, owners of private lands with trails, leaders of trail organizations, and a cadre of hikers to help with logistics.

When *Hiking the Old Dominion: The Trails of Virginia* was published by Sierra Club Books (and distributed by Random House) in 1984, there were more than ninety individuals listed on the acknowledgments pages. Some of them are acknowledged again among those who have assisted in making a second edition possible. Jim Cohee, editor of Sierra Club Books, agreed in 1994 to release our contract arrangements to the University of North Carolina Press because the new manuscript was too comprehensive for the small size of the Sierra Club Totebooks series. David Perry, regional editor of the UNC Press, became responsible for projecting this edition into an entirely new size and format.

During the three years of rehiking the trails of Virginia I again depended on the stewards of the trails. Assisting from the Jefferson National Forest were Joy E. Berg, forest supervisor; Bill Sweet, fire and recreation staff officer; David Olson, public affairs officer; Arlene Fields, administrative officer; and Harry T. Fisher, forester. District assistance was provided by David Collins, district ranger of the Blacksburg Ranger District; Raoul W. Gagne, district ranger, and John Stallard, forest technician, of the Clinch Ranger District; Joseph H. Hendrick, district ranger, and William Baggett, supervisory forester, of the Glenwood Ranger District; Steve Sherwood, district ranger, and Lew W. Purcell, supervisory forester, of the Mount Rogers National Recreation Area; Robert W. Boardwine, district ranger of the New Castle Ranger District; and Louis E. Brossy, district ranger of the Wythe Ranger District.

In the George Washington National Forest headquarters were George W. Kelly, forest supervisor; W. Terry Smith, public affairs officer; and Mary H. Otman, recreation clerk. District assistants were David Rhodes, district ranger, and Michael Gallegly, forester, of the Deerfield Ranger District; Bud Risner, district ranger, and Bob Tennyson, forester, of the Dry River Ranger District; Cynthia Snow, district ranger, and James Mattox, land use assistant, of the James River Ranger District; John Coleman, district ranger, and Bill Kruszka, recreation technician, of the Lee Ranger District; James A. Hunt, district ranger of the Pedlar Ranger District; and Vick Gaines, district ranger of the Warm Springs Ranger District.

Harry L. Baker, landscape architect, and Jim Fox, resources planner, of the Blue Ridge Parkway headquarters, and Deanne Adams, chief of interpretative and visitor services, and Janet Stombock, park manager, of the Shenandoah National Park assisted in verifying trail distances and connections under their supervision. John R. Davy Jr., chief of planning of the Commission of Outdoor Recreation for Virginia assisted in providing resource information on the state park system, and James W. Garner, state forester of the Department of Forestry helped with information on the state forests. Wayne Bowman, forester, assisted in the absence of a supervisor for the Cumberland State Forest.

Without the help of Wayne Cottrill, maintenance service supervisor of the Fairfax County Park Authority, and Darrell Winslow, executive director of the Northern Virginia Regional Park Authority, I would not have been able to select the parks with trails from among the hundreds in the area. David Leatherwood of the Upper Valley Regional Park Authority also assisted in the Shenandoah Valley trails information.

Other assistance was available from Clarke Slaymaker, park planner of the city of Alexandria; Lloyd Culp Jr., refuge manager of the Great Dismal Swamp National Wildlife Refuge; Michael Shaver, acting chief of visitor services at Prince William Forest Park; Jack Collier, chief ranger at Cumberland Gap Memorial Park; Ann Fuqua, site manager of the George Washington Memorial Parkway; Jean Cashin of the Appalachian Trail Conference's *Appalachian Trailway News*; Terry Ramsey of the John H. Kerr Dam and Reservoir; Bob Simpson of the forest products public relations staff of the Chesapeake Forest Products Company; Louise Dooley, assistant vice president of VMI Foundation; Carolyn Faubion, forest technician of Westvaco; Michelle St. Clair of the science and stewardship office of the Nature Conservancy (Virginia chapter); Henry Harman of the Old Dominion Appalachian Trail Club; Kenneth E. Apschnikat, superintendent of Manassas National Battlefield Park; and Larry Miller, citywide activities superintendent of Richmond's Department of Recreation and Parks.

Contributing information on the state's flora and fauna was Steve Croy, professor of biology at Virginia Polytechnic Institute and State University and director of the Virginia Natural Diversity Information Program of the Nature Conservancy. Other support information came from Ed Page, former president of the National Bridge Appalachian Trail Club and the Virginia Trails Association; Gerald L. Baliles, former state attorney general and governor; Walter Cowen, director of the University Press of Virginia; Ed Garvey, author of *Hiking Trails in the Mid-Atlantic States*; Jeannette Fitzwilliams, founder of the Virginia Trails Association and former president of the National Trails Council; and David A. Tice, specialist in forest management and environmental planning, who assisted in the first edition. Special thanks go to the staff of the UNC Press for making this revised edition possible, and particularly to Pamela Upton, assistant managing editor, who supervised the editing process.

Several families opened their homes to me as bases for many of the field trips. Among them are Dr. and Mrs. Raymond Shultz, Mr. and Mrs. Lawrence Pitt, Mr. and Mrs. John Bowman, Mr. and Mrs. Atlas Parker, Mr. and Mrs. Emmett Snead III, Mr. and Mrs. Steve Belcher, Dr. and Mrs. Francis Giles, and Mr. and Mrs. Robert Dillon. Throughout the years of hiking, backpacking, and camping on the trails of Virginia, I have had many faithful companions. They provided transportation, arranged schedules and appointments, prepared food, pushed the measuring wheel, and stayed with me through adversity and unexpected research. In this dedicated team are Todd Adcock, Chris Addison, Jeff Ayscue, Scott Bailey, Robert Ballance, Joyce Barbare, Steve Bass, Mike Batts, Steve and Kim Belcher, Kim Bendheim, Tom Bond, John and Jimbo Borum, Dale Bowman, Chris Bracknell, Jason Burgess, Richard Byrd, Lori Clark, Noel Copeland, Steven Cosby, Flora de Hart, Rob Dillon, Robert Dillon, Lindy Eagle, Ronnie Echols, Craig Eller, Greg Frederick, Nancy Freeman, Paul Girard, Steve Guyton, Bernd and Jorn Haneke, Rudy Hauser, David Hicks, Rocky Holloway, Barry Jackson, Heather Jakeway, Becky Johnson, Mike Johnson, Billy Jones, Johnny King, Steve King, Terrel Knutson, Michael Lambert, Sarah Lancaster, John LeMay Jr., Jack Lewis, Mike Lewis, Ed Liberatore, John Lohmeyer, Chad McLane, Jason Mason, John Matthews, Walter May, Matt Morgan, Win Neagle, Robert Old, Debe Pacher, Kevin Parker, Dennis Parrish, Todd Phillips, Lawrence Pitt, Julia Pope, John Rohme, Bill Ross, Virginia Rynk, Chuck Satterwhite, Sandy Satterwhite, Todd Shearon, Brad Shuler, Emmett Snead, Eric Springer, David Stinchfield, Kenneth Tippette, Jon Toppen, Ed and Seth Washburn, Ryan Watts, Dan Watson, Buster White, Charlotte Wicks, Rob Wilfong, Meredith Wilkins, Mary Willete, Darrell Williams, Chuck Wilson, and Autumn Wright.

In addition to this team of hikers, some of whom have hiked with me regularly for fifty years, I am grateful for the support of my parents, brothers, and sister. My oldest brother, Moir (who died in 1979), was a personal inspiration. Twelve years my senior, he took me on my first hiking and camping trip near Smith River Falls in Patrick County when I was five, and he taught me in my childhood to appreciate and care for the natural environment. My middle brother, Willie Lee (who died in 1953), and my youngest brother, Richard, followed me into the forests to build and hike trails, canoe the rivers, hunt and fish, and explore. We all must have had a great influence on the youngest in the family, Virginia. She has taught her children and grandchildren to appreciate the beauty of nature, something our beloved parents and Moir taught us.

Abbreviations

AT	*Appalachian National Scenic Trail*
ATV	all-terrain vehicle
BRP	Blue Ridge Parkway
BSA	Boy Scouts of America
CCC	Civilian Conservation Corps
CO	county road in West Virginia (e.g., CO 636)
FR	forest road (e.g., FR 186)
GWNF	George Washington National Forest
I	interstate highway (e.g., I-81)
JNF	Jefferson National Forest
KY	major Kentucky primary road (e.g., KY 80)
mp	milepost (usually on the BRP or in Shenandoah National Park)
NPS	National Park Service
NVRPA	Northern Virginia Regional Park Authority
NWR	National Wildlife Refuge
PATC	Potomac Appalachian Trail Club
SR	state secondary or county road (e.g., SR 635)
TIS	Transportation Inventory Survey
TN	major Tennessee primary road (e.g., TN 91)
US	federal highway (e.g., US 11)
USFS	United States Forest Service
USGS	United States Geological Survey
VA	major Virginia primary road (e.g., VA 41)
WMA	Wildlife Management Area
WV	major West Virginia primary road (e.g., WV 17)
YACC	Young Adult Conservation Corps
YCC	Youth Conservation Corps
4WD	four-wheel drive vehicle

The Trails of Virginia

Introduction

Of all the exercises walking is the best.
—*Thomas Jefferson*

The purpose of this book is to provide the public with a descriptive catalog of Virginia's hiking trails. The words *hiking trail* are used broadly to define a pathway with an official name. This designation includes trails as diverse as floral garden walks (Meadowlark Gardens in Vienna), trails for the physically impaired (Fenwick Mines near New Castle), and long and wide multiple-use routes (*Virginia Creeper Trail* through Damascus). There are long and rocky backpacking trails (*Cumberland Mountain Trail*) on the remote Kentucky/Virginia state line, trails only a few yards long on a scenic bed of wildflowers (Big Spy Mountain), and damp, winding, mysterious boardwalk routes (Dismal Town) in the Great Dismal Swamp National Wildlife Refuge.

Virginia has more than 4,500 outdoor recreational areas comprising 3,159,450 acres of land and water. Private outdoor recreational areas account for another 2,500 places with 329,101 acres. Within these properties (according to the state's Department of Conservation and Development) are 5,167 miles of foot trails. There are 1,890 miles of bicycle trails and 1,895 miles of horse trails, some of which are described in this book. In addition the state has 2,976 miles of canoe trails. With this remarkable mileage, Virginia is for trail lovers.

Virginia's longest trail is the 544-mile *Appalachian National Scenic Trail* (from the Tennessee/Virginia state line near Damascus to the West Virginia/Virginia state line near Harpers Ferry). The second and third longest are the *New River State Park Trail* (55.3 mi.) and *Big Blue Trail* (55 mi.). The *Virginia Highlands Horse Trail* (66.3 mi.) and the *Glenwood Horse Trail* (65 mi.) are the longest equestrian trails. The largest network of bicycle trails is in the city of Alexandria and Fairfax/Arlington counties area. There are many short trails. For example, the leg stretchers on the Blue Ridge Parkway (the *Priest Trail*, the *Boston Knob Trail*, the *White Oak Flats Trail*, and the *Thunder Ridge Trail*), are all 0.1 mile or less. Virginia's highest trail is the *Mount Rogers Spur Trail* (0.4 mi., 5,729 ft. in elevation) off the *Appalachian Trail*. Among the lowest trails is the *Grandview Preserve Trail* (2.2 mi., 8 ft. in elevation) in Hampton. One of the trails with the most stream fordings is the *Lick Branch Trail* with 26 crossings in 2.8 miles. The trail with the highest cascades is the *Crabtree Falls Trail* (2.8 mi.) near Montebello. There are trails with natural duff and moss and rocks. Some are graded, manicured, and landscaped. Others are neglected, abandoned, eroded, and dangerous. Still others are grassy, carpeted with ferns and flowers, or covered with wood chips, sawdust, asphalt, or cement. Some are traversed over swinging bridges, around cliffs, or through virgin forests or over sand dunes. They all provide a natural

Beartown Wilderness Area, JNF. (Photograph by Milton Grubb)

science education for us. Each has its secrets: Who constructed it? What wildlife follows it? What rare plant is near its treadway? How old is it? Will the trail provide a "warm harmonious glow of mind and body," a feature claimed to be significant for the pleasure of walking by Christopher Morley in his 1917 essay "The Art of Walking"? Virginia has many rarely used trails. They await your footsteps. Think of yourself as an adventurer, a discoverer. "You never know when an adventure is going to happen," said Morley, and Walter Teller, in "Country Walks," a section of his book *Area Code 215*, says, "To be a discoverer you must go looking for something." Such is my invitation to you as you explore the trails of Virginia.

Native Americans may have been in the area of what is now Virginia and North Carolina as early as 5000 B.C. during the Archaic Period. But archaeological study is more specific for the Woodland Period, the first around A.D. 1600, and particularly the Late Woodland Period after A.D. 900. During this period Indian settlements were more stable, with agriculture, ceramic ware, domestic crafts, and ceremonies. By the time the English settled at Jamestown in 1607, the entire Chesapeake Bay area was the Powhatan chiefdom. This vast territory for about 13,000 indigenous inhabitants extended from the Potomac River south to the Nansemond River. The westward boundary was along the fall line, the James River Falls at Richmond being an example. The eastern territory included the southern half of the Eastern Shore.

Powhatan's (Wahunsonacock in the native language) area probably included thirty-one territorial units, each with a chief (*weroance*). All the chiefs were at least partially subject to Powhatan, and most of the units were Algonquian speaking. Some of the groups were captured by Powhatan; others, such as the Werowocomocos and the Chiskiacks on the York River, were likely inherited. West of the fall line were hostile Monacans and Mannahoacs, whose language was Siouan. Iroquoian-speaking groups such as the Nottoways and the Meherrins were on the southern side of Powhatan's claim, and farther south into present-day North Carolina were Algonquian-speaking groups such as the Chowanocs and the Roanokes. Communication between the diverse groups was by canoeing (some dugouts were large enough for forty people) and on land trails. The width and usage of the forest trails depended on the degree of trade and social exchanges between the chiefdoms.

In 1612 William Strachey wrote about the network of trails among the Powhatans in *The Historie of Travell into Virginia Britania*. John Smith also wrote about the trails not only along the riverside but across the necks between rivers (James, York, Chickahominy, and Rappahannock). Pocahontas (Matoaca in the native language, but Rebecca after her marriage to John Rolfe) at the age of twelve or thirteen was familiar with the trails between Jamestown and the Powhatan village because she escorted John Smith (after his release from Powhatan) through Paspahegh Indian territory to Jamestown.

Trail design was "dry, level, and direct" and sometimes wide enough for sociable groups. The English called them "plain roads." The Indians regularly removed brush and stones from the trails but left the large logs. It was traditional courtesy among the Indians to welcome travelers and give them food and drink. The hosts would also pick out briars and thorns from the travelers if the journey had been on a rough trail. Salves were used for bruises and sores. Whether a family encampment or a settlement, the rules were for the hosts to be hospitable. If the traveler was on a business trip or representing a diplomatic mission, the settlement chief would meet the guests. This could mean pipe smoking, banquets, and dancing. A few Indian units, such as the Nottoways, had thatched guest houses. (Siouan-speaking Indians provided female companionship ["trading girls"] for the male travelers.) Forerunners of a modern lean-to were bark shelters, observed and described by a number of the European writers. But not all Indian travelers used shelters. One writer, Benjamin Hawkins, described seeing healthy, athletic Indians sleeping through a storm with rain falling on their faces.

Travelers carried their own bedding and knives. Warriors and hunters packed leather for moccasin repair and weapons for food foraging. Among foods frequently carried were chinaroot bread and parched cornmeal. They also ate sap and cambium from trees such as maple, birch, beech, poplar, and willow. Other foods in season were berries, wild potatoes (*wapatos; Saggittaria spp*) and roasted ground nuts (*Apios americana*). Trail markings indicated trail conditions, food sources, threat of enemies, and assurances of the right path.

Long-distance trails, particularly for traders, were never well maintained; they were narrow but usually as straight as possible. It was customary for Europeans to have local or experienced guides for risky explorations into the backcountry to settlements of other groups or tribes. Traveling traders transported mica, cooper, flint, hides, dried fish, pearls, medical roots, salt, shells for gorgets, and steatite (soft stone for carving bowls). Also on the market was a poisonous root (*Cicuta maculata*, probably harvested on the Eastern Shore), which could be used for death to an enemy. Color pigments came from plants such as the red puccoon (*Lithospermum caroliniense*), likely from the Nottoway Indians in current Sussex County. White pigments from the hoary puccoon (*Lithospermum canescens*) came from the Blue Ridge Mountains, or farther away.

The Powhatan chiefdom first met Europeans when Spaniards attempted to build a settlement in the Chesapeake Bay area in 1566. In 1570 Spanish Jesuit priests sailed up the James River to what is now Chippokes and crossed the peninsula to the York River to settle. They were killed, except for a boy who escaped, in 1571. When Pedro Menendez arrived with a supply ship in 1572, he retrieved the boy and vengefully executed a number of Powhatans (see *Powhatan Foreign Relations, 1500–1722*, by Helen C. Rountree). Friend and foe to the English, the Powhatans could have killed all the English settlers the first year, but instead they shared enough food to keep some of the disease-ridden colonists alive. After Powhatan's death in 1618, a year after a peace treaty had been signed, his younger brother, Opechancanough, took command. Less friendly to the English, he conspired the Massacre of 1622, which killed 347 men, women, and children. For the next ten years the trails of tidewater Virginia were stained with blood as the English and Powhatans fought and the Indian groups fought and raided one another. Again in 1644 Opechancanough plotted another slaughter of more than 500 English settlers. Opechancanough was captured and brought to Jamestown by a group of soldiers led by Governor William Berkeley. While under confinement Opechancanough was shot by a soldier assigned to guard the chief's quarters. The Powhatans appealed for peace. In a treaty settlement the Indians were granted the "hunting grounds north of the York River," and no Indian "was to come south of it, except as a messenger." Trails from Jamestown upriver to the falls (Richmond), downriver to the Chesapeake Bay, and across the peninsula to the York and Pamunkey Rivers would be safer for English settlers. Five years later a colonist wrote an essay titled "A Perfect Description of Virginia," which was published in London. "Virginia is the earthly Paradise. It is full of trees and the hum of bees . . . and a bird we call the *mockbird*. . . . In this happy Virginia there is nothing wanting to produce plenty, health and wealth."

By 1648 there were 15,000 English settlers in the quiet and prosperous colony, and they lacked great concern about the civil war that had begun in England in 1642. Although Charles I was condemned for treason and beheaded in 1649, not until 1652 did parliamentary commissioners come from England to demand the colony's surrender to Oliver Cromwell. Governor Berkeley bitterly signed the decree, left the state house in Jamestown, and retired to his manor in Greenspring to sulk in his silk and lace. Not completely silent during the Cromwellian years, he supported the Cavalierian cause (of church and king) by inviting Cavalier immigrants to Virginia. When Charles II was returned to the English throne in 1660, the Virginia House of Burgesses reinstated Berkeley as Virginia's governor. During the 1660s the population continued to increase, farms and plantations expanded, and old trails became better roads for horses and carriages on the Virginia Peninsula. Occasionally there were attacks by Doeg and Ricahecrian Indians on the frontier.

The trail routes beyond tidewater Virginia had long been of interest to the English. They were intrigued by a "China boxe" lined with taffeta, which chief Patawomeck said came from a trader south of the mountains (Blue Ridge Mountains). There was speculation that the item came from Spanish ocean traffic in Mobile Bay, a southern trailhead with trade routes to the *Lower Cherokee Trading Path*, the *Saponi Trail*, and the *Occoneechi Path*. By 1650 not only were the routes of interest to the English, but there were plans to explore the frontier with packhorses and Indian guides where trails did not exist. Some of these early explorers were Edward Bland and Abraham Wood in the 1650s; John Lederer, a former German physician, in the late 1660s and early 1670s; and Captain Thomas Batts and Robert Fallam, and James Needham and Gabriel Arthur in the early 1670s. But credit for opening the frontier goes to Abraham Wood, who under the governorship of Sir William Berkeley spent much of his life as commander of a large trading post at Fort Henry (Petersburg) and who discovered and named the New River in 1654. He also financed and sent Batts and Fallam in 1671 to explore north and west of what is now Radford. Their expedition went as far west as Tug Fork (Kentucky state line), a tributary to Big Sandy and the Ohio River.

Lederer, who made three excursions to the Blue Ridge Mountains (climbing to the top for views of the Shenandoah Valley in 1669), was the first to travel mainly alone for a two-month loop to include part of North Carolina. Sent and financed by Governor Berkeley in the summer of 1670, Lederer probably went west to the base of the Blue Ridge Mountains between Charlottesville and Lynchburg, then south to Sapon at the Staunton/Roanoke River (near Brookneal). His travels continued south to Occoneechee (Clarksville) and into North Carolina near Oxford and to Sara (Durham). A place called Wesacky is likely to be near the confluence of the Haw and Cape Fear Rivers. His course turned east to Katearas (Rocky Mount) and north to current Weldon for a return to Fort Henry. Lederer's survival convinced Abraham Wood that it was time to send trading representatives to Indians never before contacted.

In 1673 Wood sent Needham and Arthur to discover the "south or west sea," which Wood believed was not far beyond the Blue Ridge Mountains. With Appomattox Indian guides, they left Fort Henry, followed the *Occoneechi Path* and other trails to the Catawba River and Hickory Nut Gap (east of Asheville) in North Carolina, and southwest to the village of the Tomahitan Indians (near Rome, Ga.). Later Needham returned with a report to Fort Henry, but on his return to Arthur he was slain by Indian John, an Occoneechee guide, near the Yadkin River. Indian John also laid plans to murder Arthur. Arthur was safe as long as he stayed with the king of the Tomahitans, a friend to the English. For nearly a year Arthur roamed the Southeast with the Tomahitans, learned their language fluently, and faced death on at least three adventurous occasions. In May 1674 the king of the Tomahitans began a journey to Fort Henry with a trading team, Arthur, and a boy of Spanish/Indian heritage. Near Sara, Indian John was waiting to murder Arthur and other associates. But Arthur and the boy escaped. They continued to the village on Occoneechee Island in the Staunton/Roanoke River and in the cover of darkness crossed safely. In their flight on the *Occoneechi Path* for a week they had only huckleberries for food. They arrived at Wood's home in mid-June 1674. Nearly a month later the king of the Tomahitans, who also had escaped and taken the *Saponi Trail*, arrived to visit Wood. The young Arthur, who did not read or write, had walked 2,500 miles (and canoed 1,000 mi.) from Virginia to Mobile Bay, to Port Royal on the Atlantic, to the Ohio River, and back to General Wood, to whom he was indentured. Historians would record him as Virginia's most adventurous English hiker of the seventeenth century.

Virginia's population increased to 40,000 in 1670; of this number 6,000 were white servants and 2,000 were black slaves. Commerce increased, and tobacco remained the colony's chief export. In May 1676 a party of Doeg Indians attacked and killed some of the settlers on an estate owned by Nathaniel Bacon near the Falls (Richmond). Bacon requested a commission from Governor Berkeley to head a team for a retaliation attack. The governor refused, but Bacon defied him by leading a party of settlers to rouse the Doegs in a bloody fight near what became known as Bacon Quarter Branch in eastern Richmond. This was the first act of what became Bacon's Rebellion for five dramatic months. Bacon was a member of the Governor's Council; therefore his rebellious behavior came to the attention of the House of Burgesses. The twenty-eight-year-old Bacon was a graduate of Cambridge University and a tempestuous orator. His opposition to the governor's restricted franchise and high taxes on the farmers was shared by the majority of the population. He persuaded the burgesses to appoint him general and commander in chief against the Indians. Governor Berkeley was helpless and furious. The governor soon fled to Accomack on the Eastern Shore.

During the summer, Bacon's forces crossed the James River at Curles (near Hatcher Island) and followed the Indian trails to kill or disperse the Appomattox Indians (near Petersburg). They also followed the *Occoneechi Path* and other trails to kill and disperse the Nottoway Indians and the Occoneechee Indians at the Roanoke River (near Clarksville). Governor Berkeley returned on a flimsy fleet to recapture Jamestown in September but was defeated by Bacon's troops, who in the fight burned the colony's government headquarters. In late October, Bacon died of a fever at Gloucester and was secretly buried by his friends. Governor Berkeley returned and tyrannically killed enough Virginians to cause Charles II to say, "That old fool has hanged more men in that naked country than I have for the murder of my father." Recalled to England by Charles II, Governor Berkeley died of natural causes in 1677.

The early trails of Virginia west of the James River were becoming roads for expanding settlements, and new trails were developing beyond the fall line toward the Blue Ridge Mountains. In 1716 Governor Alexander Spotswood led an expedition of sixty-three men and seventy-four horses to the Shenandoah Valley. Later known as the Knights of the Golden Horseshoe, they left from the Mattaponi River and traveled northwest to the Rapidan River. From there they followed rough paths to and wilderness routes over the Blue Ridge Mountains (probably at Milam Gap) to the Shenandoah River (near the current community of Alma). Their one-month expedition exposed them at worst to rattlesnakes and hornets (plus an attack of measles). They claimed the area for King George's health and camped, fished, hunted (and had bear steaks), and drank at least ten varieties of liquor, plus punch and cider.

Not until the eighteenth century did Virginians explore the colony's longest trail, the *Great Indian Warpath* through the length of the Shenandoah Valley. In the southwest it connected with the *Warrior's Path* (later known as the *Wilderness Trail* through the Cumberland Gap into Kentucky). It also extended to trails in the Northeast (Pennsylvania, for example). The 1928 trail map by W. E. Myer shows a similarity in this and other Virginia trails to current highway routes. Examples are I-81 (and US 11) for the *Great Indian Warpath*; I-85 for the *Occoneechi Path* from Charlotte to Petersburg; and part of the *Saponi Trail* from Greensboro to Charlottesville on US 29.

HOW TO USE THIS BOOK

This book is divided into seventeen chapters. They cover national forests and parks, battlefield and historical parks, the *Appalachian National Scenic Trail*, national wildlife refuges, state parks and wildlife management areas, state historic sites, county and municipal recreation areas, regional park systems, military and U.S. Army Corps of Engineers installations, colleges and universities, and private holdings. Each chapter has an introduction to acquaint you with the area's natural and cultural environment, major features and topographical location, and support facilities such as campgrounds. There are addresses and telephone numbers listed at the conclusion of each description of a forest, park, refuge, recreation area, or privately owned site. You will find references to other guidebooks throughout this book, and a bibliography is provided. Addresses and telephone numbers of public and citizens' organizations are also listed in Appendix A. There is a trail number-ing system to assist you in determining the general location on the maps.

Format for Trail Descriptions: In the chapters on national forests (Chapters 1 and 2) the districts are arranged alphabetically, but the trails are not. Instead, each trail or group of trails is described from the southwest to the northeast, or as close to this arrangement as possible. This follows the slanted directions of the mountains and valleys and allows you to maintain the same orientation in all descriptions. The trail, or group of trails, is set in pockets or areas likely to be near campgrounds of that particular district. The description will also refer to the proximity or bound-ary to other districts. For the Blue Ridge Parkway and the Shenandoah National Park (Chapters 4 and 5) the format is the opposite. The trails are numbered with descriptions from north to south because the mileposts in both parks are in that order. The *Appalachian Trail* description format is either north or south. The *Allegheny Trail* is described from south to north, though the West Virginia Scenic Trail Association has organized the descriptive routing in the opposite order. There is not a format pattern for state parks, with the exception of the *New River State Park Trail*. Its description is from south to north, though the former rail-road markers may be opposite. (In consistency with this description the *Virginia Creeper Trail* in Chapter 1 is also described south to north.) In all the other chapters the parks and refuges are listed alphabetically, just like the districts in the national forests. Trails are not listed alphabetically in the description; instead they are described according to trailhead and connections in order of trail routing. On all trails throughout the book, the descriptions usually begin at the most accessible trailhead. Parentheses are used to indicate side trails or connecting trails from a main trail.

Title and Number: The trail name is from the most current source, but references may indicate that it was formerly known by another name. Some trails will carry a double name because two trails run together for a distance. An example is where the *Appalachian Trail* may follow the *Virginia Creeper Trail*. The USFS trail num-bers listed at the close of a trail or trails description are from the TIS, on the USGS topographical maps modified for USFS boundaries, and the USFS district maps. On these maps the *Appalachian Trail* is always number 1. The other numbers in each district are not consistent (and may follow the age of the trail rather than a pattern of proximity). In this book the USFS trail numbers are listed in order of their appearance in the description. For example, in the Little Wilson Creek Wilderness Area the first two trails listed are in Grayson Highlands State Park, thus without forest numbers. The *Scales Trail* number is 4523, the *First Peak Trail* is 4524, the *Kabel Trail* is 4606, and the *Big Wilson Creek Trail* is 4607. You may not need to use these numbers, but if you do, they will be there as a reference point for your study of the USFS maps. There is another number assigned to each trail solely for the purpose of having a numerical order in the book and for cross-referencing with the book's maps. The first trail is the *Dickinson Gap Trail* (no. 1), and the last trail is the *Troy Creek Trail* (no. 1035). These numbers are included after the trail title(s), and they are in bold type in the outside margin of the page. They are also listed in the index to serve as an easy location reference.

Length: The trail length is always within the nearest 0.1 mile (with the exception of short trails that may be described in feet or yards). All numbers followed by *miles* or *mi.* indicate the distance from one trailhead to the other of each trail. If the mileage is followed by *round-trip*, the distance is doubled as either backtracking or forming a loop. If the word *combined* is used, the main trail and other trails are combined as a group. Some trail networks offer a hiker a diversity of distances and even backtracking to choose a shorter or longer trail in the group, but altogether you will have an idea of the total distance. If neither *round-trip* or *combined* is used, the trail distance is linear with trailheads accessible by vehicle at both ends. I have used a 400 Rolatape measuring wheel (which registers each foot) on all the trails.

Difficulty: Trails are described as *easy* (has a gentle grade, may be short, and does not require rest stops); *moderate* (has a greater change in elevation or rough treadway that requires some exertion and likely rest stops); and *strenuous* (has high or steep elevation change and requires exertion and perhaps frequent rest stops; requires some skill over rough treadway). Elevation changes on some of the strenuous trails are listed.

Connecting Trails: Where a single trail is listed with a number of connecting trails, some of the trails may be covered in more detail under another heading. If so, they will be enclosed in parentheses. Although reading about a connecting trail may create a temporary break in your chain of thought, a return to the main description usually will start with the words *to continue* or *continuing ahead.* The objective is to give you an option on how far you wish to hike before backtracking, making a loop, or staying on the main trail. If continuing, you can ignore the paragraphs in parentheses, but the information is there if you change your mind.

Features: Some of the trails have features that are more distinctive, rare, or outstanding than trails in general. I found something attractive or scenic about all the trails, but I have made an effort to avoid repetitive superlatives. Appendix C contains a brief list of suggested trails for special populations such as adventurous backpackers, families with young children on short trips, and people with disabilities. (Disabled hunters should contact the district rangers in the usfs for information on special hunting roads.)

Trailheads: Where possible, access to a trailhead is described from the Virginia official highway map. But in a number of places a county map or city map will almost be essential for you to find your way if there are multiple trailheads. Also, I recommend the *Virginia Atlas and Gazetteer* by DeLorme Mapping Company, P.O.

Box 298, Freeport, ME 04032 (phone: 207-865-4171). This map is usually available at bookstores and convenience stores. (See other maps listed under Maps, below.) An identifiable place on the regular maps is listed, an intersection is named (usually with road junction numbers), and the distance from that point to the trailhead is given. Access may also be described from the opposite direction. If the trailhead has more than one access point, the easiest and nearest to an identifiable place is described first.

Roads: Virginians call every road, even an interstate, a *route* (not to be confused with a rural mail route, or RFD). A single word for all roads can be confusing to outsiders and to some Virginians who depend on many types of road systems when driving to trailheads. Road conditions affect your decision on what type of vehicle to drive. In this book, roads are described according to the systems used by the Department of Highways and Transportation as follows: *I* denotes an interstate highway, with red, white, and blue shield. (A green shield is an alternate or business route.) *US* indicates a federal/state arterial system, with black and white shield. *VA* is used for the major state primary system, with black and white, rounded, three-corner shield, numbered from 1 to 599. (Numbers generally do not duplicate a US route number.) *SR* indicates a state secondary or county road (the bulk of the state's road system), paved or gravel, with black and white round signs (but rectangles are used on the official highway map), numbered from 600 up, with numbers often repeated in other counties. *T* is for town and county combinations in towns with populations of 3,500 or less; these are rectangular, may be blue, and are numbered 1000 and above. In addition the USFS has its own numbering system on forest roads open to the public (but sometimes gated, depending on hunting season). The road sign is usually rectangular in brown and yellow and is listed in this book as *FR*. The USFS roads are not shown on the state's official highway map. County roads in West Virginia are listed with a *CO*.

Once you have located the trailhead, the next decision is where to park. Parking areas are described in the book, but a relocation may have occurred between my visit and yours. Some trailheads do not have parking areas; only roadside parking is available at these locations. Unfortunately, there are parking areas with a high rate of vandalism and theft. Always lock your vehicle doors, and lock your valuables in the trunk or leave them at home.

Introduction: A long trail or a group of trails may need an introduction to provide more information than is usual for the description. This may include history, an expanded description of the features, or physiographics. For example, under Salt Pond Mountain Area, the introduction covers information on the geology, altitude, and human history.

Description: This is the heart of the trail focus. It begins at the trailhead and guides you across the ridges, over the streams, and into the wonderland and mystery of the forests, fields, and plateaus. It offers milepoints, sometimes frequently to reaffirm that you are on track. References may be made to the plant and animal life along the way. Spur trails to overlooks and grand views are listed at milepoints. Sometimes campsites are suggested, and I have made an effort to make you feel part of an adventure. You will have individual experiences with plant and animal life, weather, and a sense of comfort in the woods, but the description (though you are not likely to have a measuring wheel) is supposed to chart your passage from every significant point to the next.

Descriptions include the value of trail connections, frequency of usage, and the change in elevation. Most of the trails are described as *main* or *primary* (blazed, marked, or maintained); some are *primitive* (the opposite of primary). Others are as follows: A *side* or *spur* offers a shorter route or a path to a point of interest. A *multiple* trail is used by equestrians, bicyclists, or hikers. *Jeep* indicates mainly old forest or hunting roads used by 4WDS. A *manway* or *wilderness* trail is exceptionally primitive, overgrown, or obscure. *Special* indicates a trail used for special populations, such as the physically impaired. A *gated trail* may be a foot trail only for pedestrians during a protected season for wildlife, but may be open to both hikers and vehicles at other times. A *seeded trail* is usually a former logging road planted with grass for soil stabilization. There are numerous paths used by hunters and fishermen that may be called *fisherman's trails* or *hunter's trails* on both public and private lands. Some mountain trails are used as *ski trails* in winter. Other trails may be described as *recreational* (for jogging, exercise, and fitness); *historic* (emphasizing heritage or historical districts or sites); and *nature* (including interpretive, botanical displays). Any or all of these trails may be described as ascents or descents to creeks and ridge saddles and to easy points to highways in the event of an emergency. At the end of the descriptions are listings of the USGS map for the trails and the USFS trail number.

Address and Information: This is found at the end of all districts, parks, or administrative organizations responsible for a single trail or group of trails. The "available are" listing enables you to have an idea of what to ask for when you write or call. Telephone numbers are the most recently known at press time.

NOTICE: On July 15, 1995, some areas of Virginia's current 703 telephone area code will become part of a new 540 area code. Because this book is going to press before the change takes place, however, only the 703 area code is listed throughout. After July 1995 the following northern Virginia exchanges will remain in the 703 district: Alexandria, Arcola, Arlington, Braddock, Dale City, Dulles, Engleside, Fairfax, Falls Church, Haymarket, Herndon, Independence Hill, Lorton, Manassas, McLean, Nokesville, Occoquan, Stafford, Triangle, and Vienna; other exchanges will switch to 504. The telephone companies will honor a twelve-month permissive dialing period until mid-July 1996, during which time callers may use either the old 703 or the new 540 area code.

Support Facilities: Information about campgrounds and their facilities are usually described in the introductory section of the district, park, or recreation area. At other times a store or shopping center is listed. Restaurants, telephones, and service stations may also be mentioned.

Signs, Blazes, and Markers: Virginia's Native Americans left hatchet marks on the trees to guide themselves home. Today trailblazers leave ax marks, painted logos, and plastic, diamond-shaped cards. But not all of Virginia's trails are currently blazed or signed. Examples are in the national forests.

The flagship of all Virginia trails, the *Appalachian Trail* is overall the most blazed, marked, signed, and manicured (see Chapter 3). The *AT* mark is always a white 2×6-inch vertical blaze, with side/spur trails (usually for water) painted blue. An exception is where it joins other primary trails, such as the yellow-blazed *Allegheny Trail.* It is maintained primarily by volunteer clubs of the Appalachian Trail Conference with help from the forest and park staffs. Neither of the national forests has a policy or guidelines for consistency in trail blazes, colors, or signage in the districts. The most likely colors are yellow, blue, and orange. Occasionally there will be other colors or a white/gray on such trails as the *Wild Oak Trail* in the Deerfield District. (The USFS boundary marks are red and should not be confused with trail blazes. Also, some trees slated for timbering may have a variety of color markings, even color banding.)

Do not expect to see blazes in the wilderness, but you may see trailhead signage. Vandalism of signs in the national forests is a problem especially in isolated areas. Signs and trailhead outdoor boardmaps are frequent and clearly designed in the Shenandoah National Park. The Blue Ridge Parkway also has good signage and trail directions. State parks have well-marked trails, and some are color coded. In areas where blazes are faint, I have made an effort to emphasize natural markers—rock formations, flora, streams, viewpoints, bridges, roads, and power lines. If the blazes disappear, I recommend that you backtrack to the last blaze seen to determine if a sharp turn or other change in the trail went unnoticed.

Maps: An official Virginia highway map is essential. It is available at service stations, convenience stores, drug stores, and newsstands. It can also be ordered (free) from the Virginia Department of Highways and Transportation (phone: 800-367-7623 in Virginia, or 804-786-3181; see Appendix A for address), or the Virginia Division of Tourism (phone: 800-847-4882 [for ordering free travel guide only] or 804-786-2051; see Appendix A for address). The tourism office will send you an annual travel guide that covers the state's attractions, activities, and accommodations, plus brochures on horse trails, hiking trails, and bicycle trails. The *Virginia Atlas and Gazetteer* (cited under Trailheads, above) is exceptionally valuable, with many details. Detailed county maps are available from county courthouses, local chambers of commerce, and statewide from the Department of Highways and Transportation at a nominal cost. City maps are available from city newsstands, bookstores, and chambers of commerce for a small charge. Other significant maps are *ADC's Street Maps* of the cities and metropolitan suburbs. Such a map of northern Virginia, for example, is necessary to hike or bike on a labyrinth of trails in a megalopolis. Colorful and detailed, it shows all streets, parks, town/city boundaries, streams, lakes, streets/roads/interstates, airports, shopping centers, schools, hospitals, churches, zip code numbers, and much more. Contact the ADC Map People, 6440 General Green Way, Alexandria, VA 22312 (phone: 703-750-0510). The map/magazine is available at convenience stores and newsstands.

If you plan to hike in a wilderness area, a topographical map and compass are recommended to prevent disorientation. The USGS maps most commonly used and referred to in this guidebook are on the scale of 1:24,000 (1 in. = 2,000 ft.); they are of considerable assistance in locating roads, residences, lakes, forests, and streams and, with the contour line, in determining elevation. The USGS maps used by the national forests have a modified printing that shows all forest boundaries. For each trail or group of trails described in this guidebook there is a USGS map noted at the end of the description. If your local blueprint store or outdoor sports store does not have the map you desire, you can order from Branch of Distribution, USGS, Box 25286 Federal Center, Denver, CO 80225. Because you must pay in advance, write for a free Virginia map index and order form. Expect two to four weeks for delivery. You may also contact the national forest headquarters.

There are two other sources of maps for your hikes. On the *Appalachian Trail*, the best map to use is the one numbered for a particular district and supported by the *Appalachian Trail* guidebooks of that area (see Chapter 3). These may be ordered from the Appalachian Trail Conference in Harpers Ferry, West Virginia. For other areas, you can obtain a contour map from each of the forest ranger districts. Some of the maps are outdated and have titles such as "Map" or "Sportsman's Guide." They are supposed to show all the trails by name and number, forest roads and number, and all secondary and primary roads and number. They cut off trails at their boundaries and rarely show their continuation or connection in the adjoining district. They can be purchased (for a small fee) at the district office or at forest headquarters. Call or write for a list of these and other maps (some free) of the districts. The maps also list and describe all the recreation areas, including campgrounds.

Wilderness: The Jefferson National Forest and the George Washington National Forest have seventeen wilderness areas, described in the introductions and narratives of Chapters 1 and 2. Not all have trail networks, but trail life in these areas is different from all the other areas. Wilderness management is guided by the Wilderness Act of 1964, whose purpose is to preserve and protect natural ecosystems and values. A basic factor in wilderness guidelines is the provision of a unique experience for the visitors without evidence that anyone has visited. Therefore, when planning trips into the backcountry, remember that a trip to a wilderness area is considerably demanding.

In wilderness areas no timber is harvested, and no roads, dams, or reservoirs are constructed; there are no power projects with transmission lines and no developed recreational facilities. Recreational usage is not promoted, and facilities, if any, are not designed for comfort. Maintenance occurs only when users are adversely affecting the soil or vegetation on the treadway. Shelters may be absent or in the process of being phased out. Signage and blazes are kept to the minimum; only ax blazes may give some direction, or signage may be of metal or unpainted routed wood. Where there are roads, they usually serve the USFS for safety reasons, fire suppression, and the treatment of diseased trees.

A few set policies are prescribed for hikers and campers. Basics include no-trace planning, no-trace travel, and no-trace camping. The regular backpacking rule of "pack it in, pack it out" applies. The maximum group size is ten. Camp stoves are strongly encouraged, and campfires must be from only dead and down wood. Topographical maps, compass, first-aid kit, and water purifier are essential. Use of horses is not encouraged because of limited trail maintenance. Hunting, fishing, and trapping may occur but are subject to appropriate state and federal laws. Law enforcement personnel check for litter, vehicle usage, and adherence to fire regulations. For information, consult the district ranger and request the "Leave No Trace Land Ethics" brochure. You may also wish to purchase *Field Guide to Wilderness Survival* by Tom Brown and the *Wilderness Guide* by Peter Simer and John Sullivan for the National Outdoor Leadership School. The contents cover the impact of camping on the environment, how to dress and what equipment is necessary for the backcountry, cooking, maps, first aid, weather, and more.

PLANTS, ANIMALS, AND MINERALS

This book does not attempt to describe in detail any of the plants, animals, or minerals seen on the trails. References are made in general terms, but more specific details are given for places where I encountered unusual or impressive scenery. Hikers may see the same thing, or something entirely different during a different season. Therefore, I have used common names for a single or multiple species. For example, *oak* may be used to name any of the twenty-six species of oaks. If there are exclusive groves such as chestnut oak (*Quercus prinus*), I may be more specific and give the botanical name. The same is true for the eleven species of rhododendron, except for outstanding displays of rosebay, great laurel (*Rhododendron maximum*), purple (*Rhododendron catawbiense*), flame (*Rhododendron calendulaceum*), or the rose (fragrant) (*Rhododendron roseum*). The latter is unforgettable on the *Appalachian Trail* in Nelson County during May. Residents of the Appalachian Mountains usually call rhododendron "laurel," and mountain laurel (*Kalmia latifolia*) "ivy." To save space, I frequently refer to "wildflowers" rather than describe all the various flowers in a given location. Sometimes one wildflower will be more profuse, and I include it specifically. An example is the beds of lily-of-the-valley (*Convallaria majalis*) on North Mountain near New Castle. Once the botanical names are given, only the common names are used thereafter.

Virginia has more than 85 species of ferns and more than 3,400 species and varieties of other vascular plants. Some occur statewide, while others occur in only one or a few areas. Among the books for serious examination are *Atlas of Virginia*

Flora, volumes 1 and 2, by Harvill, Stevens, Ware, and Bradley (contains maps showing county-by-county occurrences of the known species); and two scholarly sources, *Flora of West Virginia*, volumes 1–4, by Strausbaugh and Core, and the *Manual of the Vascular Flora of the Carolinas* by Radford, Ahles, and Bell. These books have most of the plants found in Virginia. Otherwise, for basic information, use Lawrence Newcomb's *Wildflower Guide*, the *Peterson Field Guide*, or the *Audubon Society Field Guide for North American Wildflowers*. All are concise, colorful, and easy to carry. The nonvascular plants in Virginia consist of more than 25,000 species and include algae, lichens, fungi, liverworts, and mosses. Again, consult with the field guide books for basic use. If you are interested in the wild plants for food, read the *Field Guide to Edible Wild Plants* by Bradford Angier. For medical usage, try Mannfried Pahlow's *Living Medicine*. (For a book on the poisonous plants, see Health and Safety, below.)

From among the 75 species of terrestrial mammals known in Virginia, you will be lucky to see a dozen in one day or hear the nocturnal ones at night. Your chances of seeing birds is better because of their daily activity. There are approximately 400 species, with some overwintering in Virginia during the migratory periods. On trails where I have seen an unusual number of bird species, I have indicated the information in the description. Two excellent books for birding are *Virginia's Birdlife*, published by the Virginia Society of Ornithology, and *Birds of the Blue Ridge Mountains* by Marcus B. Simpson Jr. The state's herptofauna consists of 144 species and subspecies almost equally divided: 75 amphibians and 69 reptiles. Some occur statewide, but most have a rather limited distribution. The remaining vertebrate animals in the state, the fish, are known to occur in more than 200 freshwater species and in an almost equal number of marine and estuarine species. Additionally, invertebrates represent at least 90 percent of the animals in the state. They include insects and mollusks. A few of many recommended books for the hiker interested in wildlife are *Amphibians and Reptiles of the Carolinas and Virginia* by Martof, Palmer, Bailey, Harrison, and Dermid; *Mammals of Virginia* by John W. Bailey; *Snakes of Virginia* by D. W. Linzey; *Mammals of the Carolinas, Virginia, and Maryland* by Webster, Parnell, and Biggs; and the popular Audubon field guides on butterflies, mammals, fish, insects and spiders, and others. Virginia has a number of rare plants and animals, some of which I have referred to in the trail descriptions. Most are rare because of habitat destruction, not natural occurrence. A good overview of this subject is found in *Endangered and Threatened Plants and Animals of Virginia*, edited by D. W. Linzey. Another book, by Christopher White, is *Endangered and Threatened Wildlife of the Chesapeake Bay Region* (of Delaware, Maryland, and Virginia). A list of Virginia's endangered species is in Appendix B of this book.

White-tailed deer (*Odocoileus virginianus*) and wild turkey (*Meleagris gallopavo silvestris*) are perhaps the most likely seen game animal and nonmigratory game bird in the forests and parks. Other game species frequently sighted are squirrel, fox, rabbit, and raccoon. Black bear (*Ursus americanus*) and bobcat are elusive and rarely seen by hikers. The state's deer population in 1993 was about 900,000, with

200,000 harvested by hunters. The highest density was in Bedford, Botetourt, and Loudoun counties. The black bear population is about 3,000, with about 450 killed each year. (The Virginia Department of Game and Inland Fisheries restricts hunting of the bear to one per person per year.) The turkey flock is about 95,000, with 11,000 harvested annually.

If you hike in the mountains of southwestern Virginia, you will become aware of the seven counties with bituminous coal on the Appalachian plateau, and layers of sandstone and limestone. Many of the valleys are underlaid with shales and carbonates. Faulted rock formations are prominent. The state's highest concentrations of oil and gas are also in this area. Farther northeast the geological makeup of the Blue Ridge Mountains includes more metamorphic and igneous rock. Limestone is noticeable throughout the Shenandoah Valley, and shale is sometimes found in mountainside slides in both the Allegheny and the Blue Ridge Mountains. Slate is prominent in central counties of the state, particularly Buckingham. Other rock formations in the state are of feldspar, granite, quartz, greenstone (both in the Blue Ridge Mountains and near the fall line in Prince William County), gneiss, schist, and soapstone. Virginia is the only state in the nation that produces aplite, an acidic granite of quartz and feldspar. In a number of areas along the Blue Ridge Mountains you will see the remains of old iron mines and furnaces, which were prominent before the turn of the century. The state has three physical geographical divisions: mountains (from the Blue Ridge Mountains west to other Appalachian Mountain chains at the borders of Kentucky and West Virginia); piedmont (between the fall line and west to the Blue Ridge Mountains, about 40 mi. in the northeast to 185 mi. along the southern border); and tidewater (coastal and level plain of alluvial soil). The fall line runs from Alexandria slightly southwest to Fredericksburg, Richmond, Petersburg, and Clarksville/South Hill (a factor in Native American and European settlements for navigation). Unique to the fall line is a distinctive break in the piedmont's crystalline rock formation. For a book on minerals, consult *Mineral Resources of Virginia* by Thomas Watson.

HEALTH AND SAFETY

Trails may appear to be a safe retreat from the dangers of an industrial world, except on the trails are precipitous rocks, streams to be forded, falling tree limbs, poisonous plants and animals, and stormy weather. Hikers must go prepared. Even a minor injury or bacterial disorder can ruin an otherwise pleasant trip. Although veteran hikers know how to prepare for a journey and how to face emergencies, there are some commonsense suggestions for the novice: Do not take chances at dangerous places. Observe official regulations and guidelines. Use care in the use of fires, knives, tin or glass cans, and fishhooks. Do not go swimming in unfamiliar waters. Avoid unfiltered or unapproved drinking water. Make certain you have enough warm clothes and that your boots fit properly. Take a first-class first-aid kit. Do not hike at night. Do not become overexhausted. Avoid getting cold and wet. Do not carry firearms unless you are hunting wild game. Be prepared for stormy weather. Take precautions against getting lost. For overnight or long hikes always have an emergency plan. You may wish to take your first backpacking trip with trained or seasoned hikers who can give you additional suggestions.

First-Aid Kit: The following items are recommended for your first-aid kit: adhesive bandages (a variety of shapes and sizes for small or large wounds, fingertip cuts, and scraped knuckles); sterile gauze pads and tapes; cleaning pads (water may not be available); antibiotic cream; cortisone cream; phenol for insect bite or blister relief; lotion or cream for chapped skin and cold sores; sunscreen; tweezers; elastic bandage for twisted ankle or knee; acetaminophen or aspirin (ask your doctor about stronger pain killers); repellents against ticks, mosquitoes, and other biting insects; antihistamines for allergic rhinitis/hay fever; tablets for stomach upsets or acidity; moleskin; and your personal medical prescription. One rule is to not take something you do not know how to use. Although you may think this list is long, properly packaged it should not take up much space. You may wish to have a professional first-aid kit instead of making a kit for yourself. If so, contact Chinook Medical Gear, Inc., 2805 Wilderness Place, Suite 700, Boulder, CO 80301 (phone: 800-766-1365), or Adventure Medical Kits, P.O. Box 2586, Berkeley, CA 94702 (phone: 800-324-3517). You may also wish to check with your local outdoor sports store for a kit to suit your needs. (See Planning Your Trip, below.)

Safety Equipment: In addition to the first-aid kit, there are other important safety items. Take a Swiss army knife (which should have scissors if you have not included a pair in the first-aid kit); waterproof matches (this is also a good storage place for first-aid needles); maps, pencil and note paper, compass, and flashlight (preferably one with krypton bulbs); batteries; whistle (for SOS calls); 75 to 100 feet of nylon rope; biodegradable soap; safety pins; and water filter. The day has passed when you could dip your Sierra cup in any bubbling mountain stream without fear of acquiring *Giardia* (bacteria causing severe diarrhea). Water purification is necessary unless you are at campgrounds or recreational areas where water is officially tested safe. Boiling water is still one method (a full boil for three to five minutes), and iodine crystals may help against some pollutants, but not against *Giardia*. Inexpensive filters are available from your outdoor sports shops. The snakebite kit, recommended in the past as being essential, is no longer preferred for treatment of poisonous snakebites. Immediate transportation to a hospital emergency clinic is considered the best response. If you are hiking in a poisonous snake environment, have a hiking companion and wear protective legwear.

Poisonous Plants and Animals: Virginia has three types of poisonous snakes: rattlesnakes (habitat mainly in the mountains); copperheads (general locations); and cottonmouth moccasins (chiefly in state's southeastern swamps and backwater). The rattlesnake is thought by some to be the most deadly, and its bite requires immediate treatment.

The female black widow spider (*Latrodectus mactans*) is usually under benches, picnic tables, and around old stumps and logs. Her bite may go unnoticed until the victim experiences severe abdominal pain (much like appendicitis) and profuse sweating. Treatment should be at an emergency clinic. Black widows can be identified by their red underbelly.

Bites from yellow jackets, wasps, bees, and hornets can cause pain and swelling. To some hikers with allergies a single sting can be serious, and multiple stings life-threatening. A pharmacist can recommend an effective product for quick insect bite relief, or take an emergency insect-sting allergy kit obtained with a doctor's prescription.

Most common among poisonous plants are poison ivy, oak, and sumac, with ivy (*Toxicodendron radicans*) being the most profuse. Its oil, urushiol, is colorless and may not show its effect until hours or days after contact. Treat with cortisone or calamine lotion or medication prescribed by a doctor. Remember, "leaves of three, leave it be." To avoid this nuisance, be able to identify the leaves and berries.

The berries of the Virginia creeper and the American holly are poisonous when ingested. Also toxic are buckeye, wild cherry, jimsonweed, white snakeroot, ground cherry (except the ripe fruit), lupine, nightshade, and lily-of-the-valley.

Among the toxic mushrooms are the destroying angel and the greengill. Avoid eating mushrooms unless you know them with certainty. A recommended book is *Plants That Poison* by Ervin M. Schmutz and Lucretia B. Hamilton.

Lyme disease, for many years difficult to diagnose, is contracted only through the bite of an infected deer tick (the deer being the carrier). Currently, the disease is more serious in a few states outside Virginia, but caution should be taken. At first a large circular red rash may appear with stages of lesion expansion. After a few months or years, aches and pains and paralysis develop. It is treatable with doxycycline or amoxicillin, but prevention is simple: use a repellent with deet or permethrin, and check yourself daily.

Coping with other bugs such as mosquitoes, black flies, deerflies, no-see-ums, and red-bugs (chiggers) requires knowing their habitats, wearing long and light-colored clothes, and using repellents.

Hypothermia: Fatalities are rare on Virginia's more than 5,000 miles of trails, but when they occur, the causes are mainly drowning, falling, or hypothermia. The latter occurs when the body core temperature falls below normal. It can develop unexpectedly in weather temperature up to 40–50°F when the hiker has wet, cold clothes and may be physically exhausted. Usually the first sign is uncontrolled shivering, which consumes an already low energy reserve. The result is a lack of reasoning, and the victim seems to be unaware of a loss of control. Without immediate treatment the hiker can collapse, unable to speak, and may become unconscious. Companions should be aware of symptoms other than shivering, such as slurred speech, memory loss, and stumbling. Avoid the causes by staying dry and out of wind and rain or snow, and wear adequate clothes and rain or snow gear. Treatment must be immediate with a change into warm, dry clothes and sleeping bag, a warm drink (no alcohol), warmth to face and head, gentle handling, and evacuation to an emergency hospital.

Weather: The Old Dominion has moderate weather conditions with average temperatures for Norfolk in winter 42°F, in spring 58°F, in summer 77°F, and in fall 62°F. Farther west in Roanoke the temperature in winter averages 37°F, in spring 56°F, in summer 74°F, and in fall 57°F. Temperatures are always lower in the state's higher elevations, such as at Mount Rogers (the state's highest).

Snow is most likely from January through March in the western half of the state but infrequent in the Chesapeake Bay area. Without warning there can be rapid changes in the weather and in temperatures on Mount Rogers and in the Allegheny Mountains and Shenandoah Mountains bordering West Virginia. Hikers should be prepared with proper clothing and equipment and calls to the local ranger districts or local weather stations.

Lightning is the most serious threat in the summer months. (It strikes about 1,800 people, of whom 300 are killed, each year in the United States.) Lightning may strike directly, when you are the primary target, or indirectly, when it bounces from a tree or other object. Safety suggestions are to stay away from conductive materials such as water, metal boats, carbon fishing rods, and even metal framed backpacks. Do not stand under a single tree or stand (or lie flat) in open areas or in rock crevices. If in a group, do not cluster. If possible choose a shrubby area, squat low, balanced on the balls of your feet with feet together. Some guides suggest you choose this position on your sleeping bag or foam mattress. Even though a victim of a lightning strike may appear unconscious, a persistent effort using CPR or mouth-to-mouth breathing may resuscitate the person.

Search and Rescue: One way to avoid being lost in the forest is to not venture off the trail unless you have adequate maps or are familiar with the territory. However, if you get lost, the following is recommended: Do not panic; rest and examine your maps with a compass. If you are lost on a trail, try to remember directions to where you saw the last blaze or sign; otherwise, stay in place. Make a fire and keep warm. Use an SOS of three sounds. Conserve your food and water. If you are able to walk and if after a reasonable number of hours or days you are not rescued, follow a stream to a road and perhaps a house or store with a telephone. Leave a message at the site you left and indicate your intended plans or route. (You could carry a walkie-talkie or cellular phone with you, but most hikers feel this compromises the wilderness experience. Furthermore, rescue teams are complaining that they are receiving trivial calls from the inexperienced.)

If you are in a group when another hiker is seriously injured, a litter may be the best method of transport. A pole litter can be made with two seven-foot poles and two thirty-inch poles for a rectangular frame. Use rope interloops. Remember, do not create additional victims by careless or risky evacuation. Helpful in search and rescue plans are Bernard Shanks's *Wilderness Survival* and Paul Gill's *Pocket Guide to Wilderness Medicine.*

Getting started is as simple as having the interest in going, but the distance and length of time on the trails will determine, and delay, your preparation. If you plan to hike all of the *Appalachian Trail* in Virginia (544 mi.), you may need five to six weeks (plus time for diversions). If you are in a group (more than two), expect to take longer because groups usually slow the pace, and the housekeeping of camping becomes cumbersome. You may plan for other activities besides hiking, such as bicycling, horseback riding, fishing and hunting, long-term camping, water sports, or mountain climbing. Or you may wish to take only a daypack from your vehicle and, like John Muir, just pack some bread and tea in a sack, or a modern prepacked luncheon. Whatever your plans as an outdoors aficionado, there are some basic guidelines. Below are some examples of what to take, mainly recommended by the writers and guides of the trail community.

Decide on who and how many are going; what are their limitations and special considerations? Are you taking grandparents, children, or a physically impaired relative or friend? If you are on a challenge backtracking trip into the wilderness, will you go alone or take a companion or companions? If you are going into the wilderness with others, choose only pleasant and agreeable companions, those you can trust to finish the journey and support you in a crisis or emergency. In your planning, contact forest or park officials for information on maps, permits, restrictions, accessibility, weather conditions, rank of trail traffic, campgrounds, shelters, water, and trail hazards. Determine your objective and who is the leader in the trek. Make a checklist, which you will probably change a number of times: the essentials (must-have items); partially needed items (may decide on after you see how heavy your backpack is); and optionals (frills, extra comforts, or perhaps a heavy zoom lens). Do not take firearms (unless for hunting) or portable radios (unless for weather channels), and do not take a portable television set or pets.

Basic items to take are sleeping bag; tent; hiking boots (with insoles and socks); backpack or daypack; food (if freeze-dried, take some onions and bell peppers or sauce mix for improved flavor); canteen; cookware; stove; mattress; water purifier; first-aid kit with other items listed under *Health and Safety* (above); clothing (prepare for stable to radical weather); pen/pencil and note paper; and personal hygiene kit. Do not forget to service your vehicle, one that will certainly get you to and from the trailheads but, if stolen, will not cost four years of mortgage payments to replace. Dress realistically; dealing with stinging bugs and bees and poisonous snakes and spiders requires more the Daniel Boone type than a tennis player in lederhosen (though you may see *Appalachian Trail* through-hikers in only boots, shorts, and a pack). If your trip is to include canoeing and bicycling and you plan to take the equipment on top of your car, take extra time for long-range planning. Of help will be *The Campers Companion* by Rick Greenspan and Hal L. Kahn. Experienced hikers know of *The Complete Walker III* by Colin Fletcher. If you are a beginner, his book is worthwhile for what *Field and Stream* has called "The Hiker's Bible." His thorough checklist covers every subject on which you are likely to have a question.

Trail Courtesy: As the trail population increases (40 million in the United States in 1995), so does the need for standards in trail relationships with others. If you insist on using a portable TV or a two-way radio or cellular phone (solar-powered satellite phone and computer hookups are on the market also), be courteous to other hikers who feel such gadgets undermine the traditional trail experience and disrupt the tranquility of the trails.

Another less serious subject is the scramble to have sleeping space at the *Appalachian Trail* shelters. The through-hikers feel the shelters should be reserved for them. Be prepared to set up camp outside the shelter if it is filled. Whether you are in or out, respect privacy and the unwritten curfew.

On some of the long trails you may wish to share conversation, supplies, and food with strangers. In contrast, on some of the municipal trails you may watch strangers suspiciously without speaking. Again, you should think of trail courtesy, but be alert and aware of any dangers. Bikers should sound a warning bell if passing a hiker from the back, and the ethics of good horsemanship demand that you not gallop or fail to dismount at the bridges. Follow the "carry in, carry out" principle, and always camp at least 100 feet from streams. Of concern to all hikers is the increase in crime on the trail system in general. Trail courtesy is seriously tested as a result. While through-hiking the *Appalachian Trail* in Pennsylvania in 1978, I was robbed by two armed motorcyclists, and I feel lucky I was not shot. Hikers are encouraged to have companionship in high risk areas and to report all violations of property or persons to the proper authorities. If you encounter a poacher, make an effort to remember as much as possible about identity, but allow the law enforcement officers to respond to your report.

Contemporary Market: In your trail planning be alert to all the new items on the market. Begin with a study of *Backpacker* magazine's annual "Budget Guide," usually published in March. There are departments or lists of new items in magazines such as *Walking, Sports Afield, Popular Science, Outdoor Life,* and *Natural Health.* Among the items are a handheld global positioning system unit that displays latitude and longitude, plus direction and distance back to your base camp (GPS, 960 Overland Ct., San Dimas, CA 91773). If fishing, you may wish innovative waders and backpacks with space for fly and lure boxes. Other items are a blaze orange and waterproof compass, battery-warmed gloves, and new first-aid supplies. For health and food items and books, check *A Consumer's Dictionary of Medicines* by Ruth Winter, which concerns over-the-counter medicine and herbal medications, and *The Doctor's Sore Foot Book* by Daniel M. McGann, which is about keeping your feet in walking order. For herbal health care, ask for a catalog from Health Center for Better Living (813-566-2611). *Prevention* magazine has articles on health foods and how to stay healthy. One example is from research about the value of taking apples, onions, and tea on the trail. They have flavonoids, natural components that are claimed to reduce the risk of heart disease. One of the oldest suggestions (Hippocrates, 400 B.C.) is to take vinegar on your trip (for infections, pain relief, and indigestion). Environmentally minded hikers should check out *E*, the environmental magazine (P.O. Box 699, Mt. Morris, IL 61054) and *The Modern Backpacker's Handbook: An Environmental Guide* by Glenn Randall.

TRAILS FOR THE FUTURE

The Virginia Division of Parks and Recreation reported in 1994 that overall trail mileage in the past decade had increased by nearly 2,000 miles. The growth in greenways—linear parks for jogging, biking, hiking, and walking—among municipalities has been the greatest. There is an increase of hiker traffic on the *Appalachian Trail*, particularly on the Blue Ridge Parkway and in Shenandoah National Park. At least thirty new trails have been opened in the national forests, and the state opened its longest trail, the *New River State Park Trail*, in southwestern Virginia. The state's most expensive trail from private funds, the five-mile *Noland Trail*, was constructed in Newport News. The National Park Service released an overview of *Trails of the Mid-Atlantic Region* to show expansion options.

This expansion is national. In 1993 the National Park Service reported that more than 273 million Americans had visited the national parks that year. In 1994 Tom Cove, spokesperson for the Sporting Goods Manufacturing Association in Washington, D.C., stated that Americans may be spending up to $5 billion annually for camping and backpacking equipment and supplies. What does this mean for trails of the future in Virginia and the nation? Trail experts say the increase of interest, usage, and funding problems is not a surprise. Addressing the subject are organizations such as the Outdoor Recreation Coalition of America, the International Association of Fish and Wildlife Agencies, the American Hiking Society, the Appalachian Mountain Club, and others. With the increase in popularity of trail usage comes more maintenance, supervision, security, and facilities. Some agencies, such as national forests and parks, claim they are neither staffed nor financed for maintenance of the current trails, much less the demand for more. Some managers for city and county parks in Virginia have reported that a few parks and trails have been closed because of a lack of funding. In response to these needs individual hikers with thousands of other volunteers should help preserve the trails. Those not already active can begin by becoming informed. One approach is to join hiking organizations such as the Appalachian Trail clubs and the American Hiking Society. Additional information is available from the publications of the trail organizations.

In addition to being informed, hikers can follow the example of Ed Garvey, author and international hiker, who for many years picked up trash left by others on the *Appalachian Trail*. We can follow that example with volunteerism and assume some responsibility for the trails—our trails. In the December 1993 edition of *Backpacker* magazine, John Viehman, executive editor, said, "Backpackers should embrace the idea of a user tax," and he gave three reasons why. One was that we needed to "forget the notion that public land is there for our enjoyment as a right of citizenship." In response to the editorial, hikers said, "We are buying responsibility which should always be our main concern" and "A user fee degrades the wilderness." The issue of user fees has been around for more than twenty years; it will be part of future plans for trails for many years to come. An example of the continuing discussion is covered in an article by Kimberly Ridley, associate editor of AMC *Outdoors*. In the July/August 1994 edition she states, "Despite the range of opinion, almost everyone stresses that safeguards need to be developed to ensure that funds raised are dedicated to the protection of land for conservation and recreation purposes."

For Virginians, and those who visit the cherished commonwealth, there is more than history and beauty from the mountains to the sea; there are plans for the future. The scope of the program is described in the 1994 *Virginia Outdoors Plan* by the Department of Conservation and Economic Development. (The outdoor plan is revised every four years.) While we can enjoy such a progressive and challenging study, we can also appreciate those who design, construct, and maintain the pathways for us. Welcome to the trails of Virginia.

1 : **National Forest Trails**

I plan to implement ecosystem management, develop
new knowledge, synthesize research, and apply it to
management of natural resources.
—Jack Ward Thomas

There are two national forests in Virginia with a total of 1,765,311 acres: Jefferson (JNF) (704,231), and George Washington (GWNF) (1,061,080). The forests are among the nation's 156, and among 35 in the Southern Region's (Region 8) 14 states from Texas to Virginia. Unlike the 5 North Carolina forests with one supervisor and one headquarters in Asheville, the Virginia forest headquarters are separate, with the JNF in Roanoke and the GWNF in Harrisonburg. Virginia's national forests border each other at the James River, and both have boundaries that spill over into West Virginia. The JNF also extends into Kentucky and borders the Cherokee National Forest at the Tennessee state line. The GWNF also shares a state line boundary with the Monongahela National Forest in West Virginia.

National forests and national grasslands are under the management of the USFS, a federal agency, in the Department of Agriculture. Additionally, the Department of Agriculture administers programs such as the Agricultural Stabilization and Conservation Service, the Animal and Plant Health Inspection Service, the Economic Research Service, the Science and Education Service (for watershed, soil, and air research), and the Soil Conservation Service.

The purpose and management of the USFS have been controversial from the beginning in 1905 when President Theodore Roosevelt appointed conservationist Gifford Pinchot as the agency's first chief of staff. Considered to be the founder of professional forestry, Pinchot said that to make the national forests "accomplish the most good the people themselves must make clear how they want them run." (His observations led eventually to the National Forest Management Act of 1976, which requires forest supervisory staff to hold public forums and respond to thousands of letters before a long written plan among alternatives is approved.) Another conservationist, John Muir, attempted to convince President Roosevelt that all national forests (as with national parks, begun in 1872) should be preserved. How the silviculturists interpreted the federal policies has remained a major part of the public controversy.

Since 1905 more than twenty-five congressional acts have been passed that affect the national forests. Among them is the Weeks Law (1911). It authorized the purchase of lands for timber production. In 1960 the Multiple Use–Sustained Yield Act reemphasized the basic purposes of forests for outdoor recreation, watershed, range, mineral resources, wildlife and fish, and timber production. The Wilderness Act of 1964 established a system for preserving rare areas from timber harvesting, mining, or other development. The National Trails System Act (1968) established a protective system for national recreational and scenic trails. (An example is the *Appalachian National Scenic Trail*, which passes through both the JNF and the

GWNF in Virginia. The act is administered by the National Park Service of the Department of the Interior.) The National Environmental Policy Act (1970) requires all federal agencies to prepare formal environmental impact statements on the environmental effects of all planned programs and actions. In 1974 the Forest and Rangeland Renewable Resources Planning Act required the USFS to prepare long-range programs concerning forest administration, roads and trails, research, and cooperative ventures. It was amended by the National Forest Management Act of 1976, which requires full public participation in the development and revision of land management plans and periodic proposal of a Land and Resource Management Plan (hereafter referred to as the Forest Plan). The environmental impact statements and the Forest Plan are the most revealing documents for hikers who wish to know about the stewardship of the USFS.

The most recent JNF Forest Plan was distributed in October 1985, but at the time of this writing a new edition is in process. In the 1985 documents there were a statement of purpose, an analysis of management, responses to issues (there are only 14 percent as many letters from the public as in the GWNF Forest Plan), remarks on concerns and opportunities, a statement of management direction, and a number of appendixes, tables, and maps. The public issues concerned ATVs, access needs, development of mines and energy resources, below-cost timber sales and timber roads, clear-cutting, multiple-use trails, and wilderness areas with mineral rights.

In comparison the 1986 GWNF Forest Plan did not gain public acceptance and was subjected to eighteen appeals filed with the USFS. Because the appeals could not be resolved, the chief of the USFS remanded the study to the regional office in Atlanta for complete revision. After six years the documents were printed January 1993. One of the volumes, Appendix I, contained 755 pages of letters from the public and the GWNF officials' responses. Public issues were ecosystem diversity, below-cost timber sales, forest access, ATV users, roadless area management, resource sustainability, gypsy moth damage, and legal and procedural adequacy of the 1986 environmental impact statement and Forest Plan. Hundreds of letters stated ATVs were destructive, disruptive, and "not compatible with USFS preservation." There were also arguments against the "share-the-trail" concept of the USFS, a policy that seemed to please none of the opposing sides. Representing the feelings of many hikers was the Potomac Appalachian Trail Club's statement that "multiple recreational use of trails where such endangers the safety of the users and seriously threatens the viability of the treadway" is unacceptable. On the complaints about a lack of trail maintenance, the GWNF staff replied it depended on user traffic. Proposals for new trail construction were defended with "priorities for trail construction will be set on an annual basis as funding allows." Trail diversity and maintenance in the Lee Ranger District appears to many hikers to be a model for the other districts (see GWNF, Chapter 2).

Nationally many of the complaints from the public arise from the traditional management of selling timber below cost. The USFS responds with an explanation for economic benefits other than timber sales and the advantages for additional forest access. In 1992 the Wilderness Society reported that only 19 of 120 national forests made a profit and that the loss to taxpayers was at least $244 million. Other complaints were that the USFS had evaded or broken environmental regulations, and in 1993 a congressional investigation reported unexplained timber thefts of $100 million.

The new USFS chief, Jack Wood Thomas, has stated that he believes in the ecosystem management style promoted by Jerry Franklin, a veteran scientist of the USFS and of the University of Washington. Thomas, a former USFS chief wildlife biologist, is the first scientist ever appointed to head the top office of the USFS. "It will take decades for the beneficial effects of ecosystem management to be clearly seen," he said. The management policy would gradually phase out clear-cutting, balance multiple uses, emphasize environmental protection of water and soil, and protect the endangered species. Outlining Thomas's concepts is an article, "Can This Man Save Our Forests?" by Paul Raeburn in *Popular Science*, June 1994.

There are 2,000 miles of trails listed on Virginia's national forests TIS. The USFS does not have the staff or the money to keep them all maintained, blazed, and signed. To understand the needs of the USFS, its position in the cross fire of public demands, its adaptation to the new management policies, and its future plans, the following is suggested to trail users: Study the Forest Plan and environmental impact statements. Become active in a hiking/maintenance organization (or form a new one). Subscribe to magazines such as *American Hiker* (published by the American Hiking Society, phone: 703-255-9304; see organizations in Appendix A). Finally, make an appointment to meet a district ranger or staff specialist to receive on-site information.

1 : Jefferson National Forest

Mountains, they fill the soul with awe.
—*Charles Kuralt*

The Jefferson National Forest (JNF) was created by Congress in 1936. It received part of the Natural Bridge National Forest, which had been absorbed by the GWNF in 1933. The two forests cover 1.7 million acres. The JNF has 704,231 acres in five ranger districts (Blacksburg, Clinch, Glenwood, New Castle, and Wythe) and one national recreation area (Mount Rogers).

Located in the Appalachian geological fold belt of ridges and valleys in southwestern Virginia, southeastern West Virginia, and southeastern Kentucky, the JNF extends 220 miles southwest from Glasgow to Pennington Gap. It includes portions of 19 counties in Virginia, Letcher and Pike counties (961 acres) in Kentucky, and Monroe County (18,211 acres) in West Virginia. The forest boundaries touch Tennessee and North Carolina in the southwest, where Mount Rogers, the state's highest peak, rises 5,729 feet. The Blacksburg, New Castle, and Glenwood districts border the GWNF, but the Glenwood district is the only one through which the BRP passes. The JNF has 11 wilderness areas: Beartown, Kimberling Creek, Lewis Fork, Little Dry Run, Little Wilson Creek, Mountain Lake, Peters Mountain, James River Face, Thunder Ridge, Barbours Creek, and Shawvers Run, totaling 58,047 acres. There are 500 miles of trout streams, 1,132 miles of forest roads, and 2,350 miles of boundary lines in the entire forest.

The JNF is in three physiographic provinces. The most western rock strata are plateaus with flat-topped ridges and narrow valleys. Soils are derived from sedimentary rocks. Coal seams occur mainly in Dickerson, Lee, Wise, and Scott counties. In the valleys and ridges province, which is most of the forest, the ridges are sandstone, and the valleys are underlain with shales and carbonates. Many of the rock formations are heavily faulted. There is natural gas throughout this province; about 55 percent of the JNF is under lease for oil or natural gas. In the most eastern province, the Blue Ridge Mountains have mainly metamorphic and igneous rock. Numerous ridgelines, coves, and toeslopes have rich soil as a result.

In plans to protect or provide additional habitat for wildlife, the forest service has implemented management programs to increase the areas for grass and forb and browse acreage, to retain den tree clumps and hard mast for terrestrial and arboreal wildlife, and to emphasize the featured species system. Another emphasis is placed on special management areas of the Recreation Opportunity Spectrum for a total of 7,275 acres in the districts. Roaring Branch, in the Clinch district, has a clear, cascading stream and rock outcrops. Hipes Branch, in the New Castle district, contains a cascading trout stream and remote slopes to rocky cliffs for bear, deer, and turkey habitat. Rush Creek includes old growth hemlock, Whitetop

Laurel Gorge and rock walls by a trout stream (protecting 16 species of salamanders on Whitetop Mountain), and old growth hardwood in Little Laurel Creek, all within Mount Rogers National Recreation Area. Apple Orchard Falls has falls and old growth hemlock in the Glenwood district; Mill Creek contains a wilderness-type area with Angel's Rest in the Blacksburg district; and Little Wolf Creek has an isolated area for wildlife observation in the Wythe district. On the list of endangered, threatened, and sensitive species list in the 1985 *Land and Resource Management Plan* there are 39 animal and 23 plant species. The 2 endangered plants are the Virginia round-leaf birch (*Betula uber*) and the lesser whorled pogonia (*Isoleria medeoloides*). Endangered mammals are the eastern cougar (*Felis concolor couguar*), the Virginia big-eared bat (*Plecotus townsendi virginianus*), the gray bat (*Myotis grisescens*), and the Indiana bat (*Myotis sodalis*). The bald eagle (*Haliaetus leucocephalus*) and the peregrine falcon (*Falco peregrinus anatum*) are endangered birds.

The JNF has 35 recreational areas in which 11 have developed campgrounds. Mount Rogers National Recreation Area has five, with a total of 277 campsites; all the other districts together have 328 campsites. Fishing, hiking, and picnicking are the most popular activities associated with the campgrounds. Other sports are boating, swimming, cross-country skiing, bicycling, horseback riding, and hunting. For ATVs there are more than 300 miles of roads available. In association with the International Mountain Bicycling Association, the USFS distributes a brochure, *A Guide to Responsible Trail Riding*. Unless marked otherwise, such as the *AT*, or trails for the disabled, all trails are open to bikers. The JNF has not forgotten people with disabilities. One of the finest examples of outdoor facilities for the disabled is the Fenwick Mines area of the New Castle Ranger District.

There are more than 1,000 miles of trails in the forest, with the *AT* being the longest (278 mi.) and the most famous. Trail descriptions below will show frequent connections with it and other trails. Other long-distance trails are two equestrian trails: the *Virginia Highlands Horse Trail* (66.3 mi.) in the Mount Rogers National Recreation Area and the *Glenwood Horse Trail* (65 mi.) in the Glenwood Ranger District. Another long trail is the *Iron Mountain Trail* (57 mi.) in the Mount Rogers area, which also has the most trails (127), but nearly 50 percent are not maintained or up to USFS standards. During the 1980s almost all trail systems in the JNF received inadequate attention due to limited funding and staffing. Volunteers, particularly the Appalachian Trail clubs, worked to fill the void. The projected recreation demand table of the 1985 *Final Environmental Impact Statement* of the JNF shows a need for more campsites, hiking trails, and ATV accommodation in the 1990s.

Address and Information: JNF Headquarters, USFS, 210 Franklin Rd., S.W. Roanoke, VA 24001; phone: 703-265-6054. Available for free are JNF newsletter, JNF map with recreation locations, wilderness brochures, and campground and dispersed camping brochures and flyers. JNF map, sportsman district maps, *AT* map, topographical map, and Mount Rogers map have small fees.

Blacksburg Ranger District

Although the district is geographically segmented into three areas, the *AT* connects them by crossing the New River between Narrows and Pearisburg, and Sinking Creek Valley east of Newport. The district's southwestern section, southwest of Pearisburg, extends from Brushy Mountain north to Wolf Creek Mountain and includes two nonfee campgrounds by Dismal Creek: Walnut Flats and White Pine Horse Camp (neither of which have showers). Peters Mountain, the boundary between Virginia and West Virginia, plus a southwestern corner of Monroe County in West Virginia, and south to Johns Creek Mountain comprise the northern section. In this section are White Rocks Campground, which has a fee but no showers. It also has the district's two wilderness areas: Peters Mountain (3,325 acres) on the southeastern slope of Peters Mountain, and Mountain Lake (11,113 acres) on a highland plateau of the Eastern Continental Divide north of Johns Creek to Little Mountain. In addition, this section has the Interior Picnic Area by Big Stony Creek and the Cascades Recreation Area near Pembroke. Forming the southeastern section, northeast of Blacksburg, is a long strip of Brush Mountain and Sinking Creek Mountain. It, as with the northern section, has an eastern boundary with the New Castle Ranger District. All sections of the district have large and small game animals, and the best trout streams are Big Stony Creek, Craig Creek, and Dismal Creek. The district has 176 miles of forest roads.

Through the 110,100-acre district passes 83.2 miles of the *AT*. It enters from the west at SR 608 (the Wythe Ranger District border) northeast of Crandon, and from the east at SR 620 (the New Castle Ranger District border) west of Catawba (see Chapter 3). Other than the *AT* there are 67 miles of trails—16 miles of which are equestrian. Annual trail traffic volume is 86 percent low to medium, with a percentage that is high at the *Pandapas Pond Trail* and very high at the *Cascades Trail*.

The USFS does not recognize or have on its TIS trail listing trail names such as *Bear Cliff*, *Bald Knob*, *George's Cut*, *Harvey Hollow*, *Mill Creek*, *Bailey Gap*, *War Branch*, and *North Fork*—all abandoned, on private property, or locally titled. The *Dickinson Gap Trail*, also called the *Ronk Trail*, is not on the inventory or maintained, but it can be used as a 1.3-mile connector to the *AT* on Peters Mountain from SR 635 (7.5 mi. east from US 460 southeast of Pearisburg). Two ridgeline trails are listed on the TIS but are not maintained. Nonblazed *Potts Mountain Trail* (4.7 mi.) trailheads are at a junction with the *AT* (east of Wind Rock) and east to SR 636 between Waiteville north and Maggie south. Difficult to follow, the trail is partly in the Mountain Lake Wilderness Area. The other ridgeline trail, blue-blazed *Niday Trail* (2 mi.) on Sinking Creek Mountain, is accessible from FR 209, 1.5 miles south from VA 42 in the community of Sinking Creek. Its western trailhead is an *AT* junction. Farther west, 3.6 miles on the *AT* is maintained and blue-blazed *Sarver Trail*, a 0.3-mile connector trail to a shelter and spring, and another 0.7-mile descent to SR 630 (north of SR 621 at Caldwell Fields). Trails at the University of Virginia Biological Station on SR 613 are not open to the public except by advance permission. Mountain Lake resort trails, also on SR 613 and near the station, require permission from the management at the time of visitation. There is not a trail to Mann's Bog, and the USFS discourages unscientific usage of its sensitive environment.

1–4

Information: Blacksburg Ranger District, 3089 Pandapas Pond Rd., Blacksburg, VA 24060; phone: 703-552-4641; on US 460, 1 mile west of Blacksburg). Available are district map with trails, flyers on recreational and wilderness areas, and hunting and fishing brochures.

DISMAL CREEK AREA
Giles County

Ribble Trail

5–8

Length and Difficulty: 2.3 miles (3.7 km); moderate to strenuous
Features: spring, wildflowers
Trailheads: From Mechanicsburg it is 3 miles east on VA 42 to SR 606. Turn left on SR 606, go 1 mile, and turn right on FR 201. Pass Dismal Falls, White Pines Horse Camp, and Walnut Flats campgrounds. Continue upstream to junction with trailhead (and a 0.4-mi. connector to the *AT*) on the right side of a curve.
Description: The blue-blazed trail ascends north, parallel to FR 201 before crossing it twice in the ascent. Wildflowers, woodferns, and cinnamon ferns are in the two stream areas. There are sections of rhododendron, mountain laurel, and white pine. The trail junction with the *AT* and FR 612 is near Honey Spring Picnic Area at the summit of Flat Top Mountain (4,066 ft.) in Big Horse Gap. A spring is near a small pond. Backtrack or make a 9-mile loop on the *AT*. Other loops can be made by using the horse trails. At White Pines Horse Camp are three equestrian trails: the *Pearis Thompson Horse Trail* (2.5 mi.), the *Standrock Branch Horse Trail* (2.5 mi.), and the *Hoof and Hill Trail* (0.8 mi.), which is a connector halfway up the mountain. Both main trails join FR 612 on Flat Top Mountain 1 mile apart. By using FR 612 east to the junction with the *Ribble Trail* and the *AT*, loops can be made of 11 miles or 15 miles.
USGS maps: Mechanicsburg, White Gate; *USFS trail nos.*: 62, 1059, 1060, 1061

CASCADES RECREATION AREA
Giles County

Cascades Trail (3.8 mi.), Conservancy Trail (7.6 mi.)

9–10

Length and Difficulty: 11.6 miles (18.8 km) combined, round-trip; moderate to strenuous
Features: waterfall, cliffs, trout stream, scenic views
Trailhead: From Pembroke on US 460 take SR 623 for 3.5 miles to the parking lot at Cascades Recreation Area, a day-use facility.
Introduction: At the parking lot are rest rooms, a picnic ground, a host's cabin, and short trails to the creekside for mobility impaired populations. The major attraction here is the Cascades. The *Cascades Trail* (1.9 mi. one way) is a national recreation trail, designated in 1979. Popular and spectacular, the Cascades

Cascades Trail, JNF. (Photograph by Allen de Hart)

has a claim to being one of Virginia's most photographed waterfalls. Making a dramatic 66-foot drop into an oval pool, it is one of two major falls on Little Stony Creek. Its headwaters are 7 miles upstream in a red spruce bog near Lone Pine Peak in the Mountain Lake Wilderness Area and are fed by eight other significant streams from Big and Butt Mountains. (Although the *Conservancy Trail's* western trailhead can be reached by vehicle on SR 714, it is included as a backtracking trail here because SR 714 may be rough and muddy in inclement weather. Also, the eastern trailhead is not on SR 714 but makes an easy connection with the *Cascades Trail*.)

Description: From the parking area the inviting trail goes 0.2 miles to a junction. Take the right route, cross the footbridge over Little Stony Creek (which is stocked with rainbow and brook trout). The trail ascends over rocks and webs of tree roots by rare wildflowers. Cross another footbridge at 1.6 miles, turn right, and reach the Cascades at 1.9 miles. On the western wall is an observation deck. (Climbing the sidewalls in the gorge is prohibited.) Backtrack, but for a different return do not cross the footbridge after 0.2 miles. Instead take the first right from the waterfalls, ascend 100 yards to an old wagon road, and turn left to follow its descent to the parking lot.

At the junction with the wagon road the *Conservancy Trail* (3.8 mi. one way) begins. It goes up the old road in an archway of rhododendron for 0.6 miles to a fork; turn left. (The jeep road on the right descends to the Upper Cascades.) Immediately after this fork is a second fork. The wagon road goes ahead, but the *Conservancy Trail* turns left up the ridge on an older road and through hardwoods. After another 0.3 miles turn left (old road on right goes to SR 714), cross a stream in a rhododendron and hemlock thicket, and continue the ascent to a fork at 1.7 miles. Turn left and after 0.4 miles is a precipitous outcropping with magnificent vistas of the gorge and beyond to the New River Valley. The trail continues west, first near the rim, then in a cove, and finally onto a plateau with a field and outlooks from large cliffs. A closed fire tower is nearby. Panoramic views are of Pearis Mountain in Virginia and the Peters Mountain range on the Virginia/West Virginia boundary. Backtrack. (There is a 0.3-mi. access road on the east to SR 714. On SR 714 it is 6.4 mi. to SR 613, 1.2 mi. southwest of Mountain Lake Resort.)

USGS map: Eggleston; *USFS trail nos.*: 70, 7013

PETERS MOUNTAIN AREA
Giles County (Va.) and Monroe County (W.Va.)

Allegheny Trail
11–12

Length and Difficulty: 12.7 miles (20.3 km); moderate to strenuous

Features: Hanging Rock, wildlife, wildflowers

Trailheads: Access to the northeastern trailhead from Waiteville, West Virginia, is 0.8 miles on WV 17 northeast to CO 636 (Gap Mills Rd.), where it is 3.5 miles left (north) to a parking area on the left at the top of Peters Mountain. (Access here from the northern side of Peters Mountain is on CO 15, 5.4 mi. southwest from Gap Mills at WV 3). The southwestern trailhead can be reached via the *AT* from SR 635 in Virginia. From US 460, southeast of Pearisburg, it is 10 miles on SR 635 to Stony Creek bridge (1 mi. west of Interior Picnic Area). From a small parking space it is 40 yards to the *AT* and a left turn. Pass Pine Swamp Branch Shelter at 0.4 miles and ascend steeply to the top of Peters Mountain, where at 1.9 miles is a blue-blazed 0.2-mile connector to the *Allegheny Trail*. (Or continue on the *AT* for 0.2 mi. to the yellow-blazed *Allegheny Trail* on the right.) The southwestern access from West Virginia is from Sugar Camp Farm parking area. It is accessible from the junction of US 219 and Painters Run Road (CO 219/21) 2.4 miles southwest of Lindside on US 219. After 1.2 miles on Painters Run Road turn left at junction with Green Valley Road (CO 219/24) and go 0.5 miles to the parking area. Access from the parking area is on 1.8-mile blue-blazed *Ground Hog Trail*, which ascends the northern side of Peters Mountain with switchbacks to junction with the *AT*. It is 3.3 miles northeast on the *AT* to the *Allegheny Trail*.

Introduction: The *Allegheny Trail* in this district is the southwestern terminus of a 300-mile footpath that extends from here to the West Virginia/Pennsylvania state line, near Bruceton Mills. Administrative management is by the West Virginia Scenic Trails Association, and the trail is divided into four corridor sections. This part of the trail is in Section IV; at least 50 miles are planned to connect with Section III at Meadow Creek on Lake Sherwood Road near Neola, West Virginia. Planning and construction are under way to complete the trail through Alleghany County, Virginia, south from Jerry's Run at I-64, and into the northeastern area of Craig County near Paint Bank in Virginia. (See New Castle Ranger District in this chapter.)

Description: In an open hardwood forest the trail begins as a footpath, but after 0.7 miles it becomes a forest road for 4WDs, used mainly by hunters. Here and throughout the traverse you are likely to see or hear deer, turkeys, grouse, hawks, and chipmunks. The trail passes a private cottage on the northern side and a dirt road that descends on private property on the northern side. At 4.3 miles the old road becomes a foot trail. To the left is a private grassy field with apple trees and deer blinds. There is a scenic rock formation at 5.6 miles, after which the foot trail becomes an old road again in a hardwood forest. White snakeroot and fern patches are frequent. At 8.1 miles the trail crosses from Virginia into West Virginia. After 9.3 miles there is a gradual descent on a scenic old road to a damp area among mountain laurel. At 10.1 miles, on the right is a locked gated road near a spring. Soon the trail becomes a path to a field with dewberries and shooting stars (*Dodecatheon meadia*). The trail leaves the leeward side and crosses to a rocky area at 11.5 miles in its approach to Hanging Rock Raptor Migration Observatory (3,812 ft.). Formerly a fire tower, it has a railed deck for a 360° view of Peters Mountain and the valleys below in both states. The descent continues to the parking area at Mill Gap Rd (CO 15). The area is good for birdwatching.

USGS maps: Interior, Waiteville; *USFS trail no*: 65, 701

WHITE ROCK BRANCH AREA
Giles and Monroe Counties

13   **Virginias' Walk**
Length and Difficulty: 1.5 miles (2.4 km) round-trip; easy
Features: nature study
Trailhead: From US 460, southeast of Pearisburg, travel on SR 635 for 16 miles to Kire intersection. Turn right on SR 613 for 1 mile, and turn left on FR 645 to White Rocks Campground.

Description: The campground has 49 camping units with drinking water, rest rooms, and grills. You can begin the nonblazed trail loop at the upper camping driveway. The trail crosses tributaries of White Rock Branch and twice crosses the Virginia/West Virginia state line in and out of the Mountain Lake Wilderness Area. Vascular plants include oak, maple, birch, hemlock, haw, orchid, wild phlox, and itchweed (*Lygodium palmatum*). The poisonous roots of the latter can be made commercially into an insecticide powder. You are likely to see deer, raccoons, birds, and salamanders.

USGS maps: Interior, Waiteville; *USFS trail no.*: 71

HUCKLEBERRY RIDGE AREA
Giles County

Huckleberry Loop Trail   14
Length and Difficulty: 8 miles (12.8 km); moderate
Features: old growth hemlock, wildlife
Trailhead: From US 460, southeast of Pearisburg, travel on SR 635 for 13.5 miles to FR 772 on the left. (A sign, "Glen Alton," should be here.) After 0.2 miles is a parking area for gated Kelly Flats Road (FR 942).
Description: Formerly called the *Flat Peter Loop Trail*, it is an excellent loop for the study of flora and fauna and Peters Mountain tributaries to Stony Creek. From the gate the yellow-blazed trail continues up the road and after 0.5 miles leaves the road on the right in a young hardwood forest. It rock-hops North Fork Creek, follows upstream for 1 mile to a clearing, crosses the creek again to the former *Dixon Branch Trail* north of Huckleberry Ridge to rock-hop 1.7 miles upstream. At the headwaters is a virgin stand of hemlock. At 3.3 miles the trail crosses a saddle on Huckleberry Ridge for a left turn on former *Dismal Branch Trail*. It proceeds downstream, sometimes in the middle of the creek bed, among rhododendron slicks. Its junction with old Kelly Flats logging road, P 1040, is at 5.5 miles. A turn left followed by crossing Laurel Branch at 6.5 miles brings the hiker to a field of wildflowers, birds, butterflies, and, occasionally, grazing deer. The loop is completed at a gate near the parking area.

USGS map: Interior; *USFS trail no.*: 52

SALT POND MOUNTAIN AREA
Giles County

Chestnut Trail (1.3 mi.), War Spur Trail (1.1 mi.), War Spur Connector Trail (1.1 mi.)   15–18
Length and Difficulty: 4.4 miles (7 km) combined, round-trip; easy
Features: overlook, old growth hemlock, wilderness
Trailhead: From US 460 at Hodges Chapel, west of Newport, travel on SR 613 for 7.2 miles (along the way is Mountain Lake Resort and a junction with SR 700 at 4.8 miles, and University of Virginia Biological Station at 5.7 miles). Access from SR 635, coming south on SR 613, is 5.2 miles.

Introduction: Salt Pond Mountain, on the Eastern Continental Divide, may be the district's most diverse and significant natural environment. For nearly 7 miles from Bald Knob (4,363 ft.) near Mountain Lake in the southwest, to Wind Rock (4,128 ft.) and Potts Mountain in the northeast, the mountain plateau is a master field trip for biologists and geologists. There are cliffs and jumbled mounds of Tuscarora sandstone, swales, bogs, virgin forests, rare plants and animals, and a 25-acre natural lake (3,875 ft., the highest in the state). More than 20 streams have their headwaters in this natural showplace. One stream, Little Stony Creek, with its headwaters in a red spruce bog, is the source of Cascade Falls.

Humans have been kind to the region. Native Americans, English and German explorers and settlers, and a Civil War supply route have left no impact on the area. Only the road across the mountain, Salt Sulphur Turnpike (sr 613) remains. Even the historic and quaint Mountain Lake Hotel continues to support the natural value and beauty of the mountain. The history of the turnpike begins in the 1820s when as a stage coach route it connected the resort communities of Mountain Lake and Salt Sulphur Springs, a healing mineral spring, in West Virginia. For a number of years guests were transported daily on the rough and narrow road over Peters Mountain and Salt Pond Mountain. Enter the U.S. government. In 1960 the usfs set aside a 1,583-acre tract for preservation. It became part of the 6,900 acres included in the Wilderness Study Area in 1975. In 1984 and 1988 Congress approved the Mountain Lake Wilderness with 11,113 acres, 2,500 of which are in West Virginia.

Description: From the parking area the *Chestnut Trail* goes to the right through a mixed forest with an understory of striped green maples, azaleas, ferns, and carpets of wintergreen. At its junction with the *War Spur Trail* there is a short side trail to an overlook (3,650 ft.) with impressive views of War Spur Hollow, Johns Creek Valley, and other parts of the wilderness area. The *War Spur Trail* descends to War Spur Branch and a stand of virgin hemlock and red spruce at 1.8 miles. After an ascent and junction with the *War Spur Connector Trail*, it is 0.9 miles right on a grassy treadway to the *AT*. Backtrack to the parking area on the connector. (A loop of 6.2 mi. can be made by hiking the *AT* north and west [past Wind Rock] to sr 613 for a return on the road, right, to the parking area.) (At Wind Rock there is 1.9-mi. *Mountain Lake Horse Trail*, which parallels the *AT* from sr 613 along Potts Mountain ridge.)

USGS maps: Eggleston, Interior, Waiteville; *USFS trail nos.*: 56, 68, 69, 1004

JOHNS CREEK AND MOUNTAIN AREA
Giles and Craig Counties

19   **Johns Creek Mountain Trail**
Length and Difficulty: 2.9 miles (4.6 km); moderate
Features: rock outcrops
Trailheads: From Newport go east on va 42 for 1.1 miles, turning left on sr 601 for 6 miles to Rocky Gap parking area. The eastern trailhead is on Maggie Road (sr

658), 1.5 miles south to VA 24 near Simmonsville, and 2.7 miles north to SR 632 near Maggie.

Description: From the parking area the 0.5 miles is a southeastern access route on the *AT* up the old Kelly Knob fire tower road. On the way are views of Salt Pond Mountain, Potts Mountain, and Johns Creek Valley. The trail turns left from the *AT* on the ridge crest. At 0.6 miles the trail crosses a forest road, and again at 2.2 miles. There are rock outcrops and other scenic spots along the ridge in an oak/hickory forest. Views from the ridge include Sinking Creek and Sinking Creek Mountain to the south.

USGS maps: Waiteville, Newport; *USFS trail no*: 57

Sartain Trail   20

Length and Difficulty: 8.4 miles (13.4 km) round-trip; moderate
Features: walnut grove, wildflowers, wildlife
Trailhead: From Newport go east on VA 42 for 1.1 miles, turning left on SR 601 for 8.1 miles to SR 632. After a turn left on SR 632 (becomes FR 156) proceed 0.8 miles to the parking area. Going west on VA 42, turn right on SR 658, past Simmonsville, and drive 4.1 miles to SR 632, where a left turn is 4.9 miles from the parking area.
Description: Formerly the *Johns Creek Trail*, the new name is from Sartain Branch, one of a number of Salt Pond Mountain drains that cross the trail. The trail is in the Mountain Lake Wilderness Area, and the trailhead is near the *AT* crossing of FR 156. At first the trail goes north to skirt an inholding, but after 1 mile it returns to the old Johns Creek wagon road where gold star (*Hypoxis hirsuta*) are prominent. After 9 stream crossings there is a campsite at 2.5 miles near a double white oak and the mouth of Sartain Branch. At 3.2 miles is an open black walnut grove with some trees 8.5 feet in circumference. The trail ends at patches of blackberries and flame azaleas under a power line at 4.2 miles. Views of the cliffs on Salt Pond Mountain are of the northwest. Backtrack.
USGS maps: Waiteville, Newport; *USFS trail no*.: 1060

PANDAPAS POND AREA
Montgomery County

Pandapas Pond Trail   21–23

Length and Difficulty: 1 mile (1.6 km) round-trip; easy
Connecting Trails: *Poverty Creek Horse Trail* (4.5 mi.), *Brush Mountain Horse Trail* (3.8 mi.)
Features: fishing, wildflowers
Trailhead: From the ranger station 1 mile north of Blacksburg, it is 2.7 miles on US 460 northwest to FR 808 on the left, and the parking area.
Description: This is a popular area for fishing, picnicking, and nature study. The trail follows the lake's perimeter, partly on a steep hillside with wildflowers, oaks, flame azaleas, and pines. Cardinal flowers and wild geraniums (*Geranium maculatum*) grow near the upstream area near the boardwalk. (Extended hik-

ing is on the *Poverty Creek Horse Trail*, downstream from the parking area to SR 708, and the *Brush Mountain Horse Trail*, of which the first 1.3 mi. ascend to FR 188.)

USGS map: Newport; *USFS trail nos.*: 74, 1002, 1001

Clinch Ranger District

The Clinch is the JNF's most western ranger district. Its 90,000 acres are in three major sections. The largest section is south of the towns of Big Stone Gap, Norton, and Coeburn to the Clinch River Valley. It has two campgrounds, Bark Camp (4.1 mi. south of the junction with US 58A in Tacoma on SR 706, and left on SR 699 for 0.3 mi. to SR 822 and 1.7 mi.) and High Knob (3.5 mi. south of Norton on VA 619, and left on FR 238 for 1.6 mi.). The smallest section is scenic, windswept Stone Mountain, west of Big Stone Gap and Appalachia between the northern fork of the Powell River Valley and the Powell River. Cave Springs Recreation Area is near the western end of the section (off US 58A west of Big Stone Gap on SR 621 for 6.6 mi.). The most northern section extends from the Pound River Valley up to the high boundary line of Kentucky and Virginia. To the northeast of this section is Breaks Interstate Park and to the southwest in Kentucky is a tract with the headwaters of the famous Cumberland River. Nearby is Cane Patch Campground (6.5 mi. west of Pound on SR 671). The district's forest is mainly southern and northern hardwoods with a mixture of white pine, hemlock, and other pines. Because of a geological environment different from the other JNF districts, the Clinch is unique in mineral development. Although coal is not mined on its properties, it does have 20 gas wells, some of which are pumping into an interstate system. An additional 80 wells may be drilled by the turn of the century.

Although a major highway through the district, US 58A follows the *Trail of the Lonesome Pine*, a pioneer route to Kentucky. The route was made famous by John Fox Jr.'s 1908 classic novel of the same name about mountain railroads and feuding families. It was made into a movie in 1915 and in 1936 was the first outdoor technicolor film, starring Sylvia Sidney and Henry Fonda. In Big Stone Gap at the June Tolliver Playhouse the story is an outdoor drama from June to September. But the centerpiece of each section in this rugged mountain area is a long backpacking trail of physical challenge and natural beauty. Other trails have unique distinctions also. An example is the district's only Kentucky trail, the remote 4.7-mile *Mayking Loop Trail* west of Cane Patch on SR 671 to the state border, or east from Oven Fork, Kentucky, on CO 932. Another trail, the *Little Stony Creek Trail*, is the district's only national recreation trail. It passes the district's highest waterfalls. A new and historic trail is the distinct 5.8-mile *Guest River Gorge Trail* (2.3 mi. south of Coeburn on VA 72 across the road from the Flatwoods Group Picnic Area). This trail follows the former Louisville and Nashville railroad grade through a tunnel, over a high trestle, and into the ragged walls of the gorge. Limited to day use, a

1.5-mile section is paved for the physically disabled. There is also an access for kayakers and canoeists. The river is stocked with trout.

24–25

Information: Clinch Ranger District, 9416 Darden Dr., Wise, VA 24293; phone: 703-328-2931. Available are district map with trails, recreation flyers, and hunting and fishing brochures.

PINE MOUNTAIN AREA
Wise and Dickenson Counties

Cumberland Mountain Trail

26–29

Length and Difficulty: 22.8 miles (36.5 km); moderate to strenuous
Connecting Trails: Austin Gap Trail (4.1 mi.), *Bobs Gap Trail* (1.5 mi.), *Counts Cabin Trail* (1.8 mi.)
Features: solitude, scenic rock outcrops, wildlife
Trailheads: Access to the southwestern trailhead is at Pound Gap at the state line on US 23, 2 miles northwest of the city of Pound and 6 miles south of Jenkins, Kentucky. From the southern side of the gap the trail follows a road (paved in the beginning) northeast up the ridge on private land to the WIFX radio tower. The yellow-blazed trail begins at the wood's edge on the ridge. The northeastern trailhead, for hikers, is at a parking area above Pool Point Tunnel on KY 80, 1.5 miles east of Elkhorn City and 5 miles west of Breaks Interstate Park entrance. (Another access, mainly for equestrian traffic, is at the gauging station near Spur Pine Island in Elkhorn City.)
Introduction: Formerly called the *Pine Mountain Trail*, the *Cumberland Mountain Trail* is listed by the USFS as a horse and hiking trail, but there are steep and rocky sections over which horses cannot go, such as the large rock outcrops near the southwestern trailhead and at the northern trailhead railroad bridge over Russell River. (An easier access route for equestrians in both directions is about halfway on the trail at Mullins Road, FR 616, off SR 611 between Isom and Blowing Rock.) The trail is an exceptionally challenging and desirable trail along the wild, dry crest of Pine Mountain, a priority area for the USFS purchase of inholdings on the trail route. Hikers and equestrians should respect the current posted areas of private property. Trail organizations and some government agencies hope eventually to connect this trail in the southwest to the Cumberland National Memorial Park, a distance of about 60 miles. In an oak/hickory and pine forest the wildlife includes bears, deer, foxes, turkeys, bobcats, squirrels, rattlesnakes, and many species of songbirds. There is no water source on the main trail.
Description: Backpacking from the southwestern trailhead, follow the ridge through hardwoods with rock outcrops and wildflowers. (In July there are dense and wide beds of yellow loosestrife.) After 1 mile the trail reaches Austin Gap and a junction with the *Austin Gap Trail* on the Virginia side of the ridge. (The *Austin Gap Trail* has two points of descent, right and left, and reconnects on a spur ridge for a singular descent of 1 mi. to SR 630, 4 mi. east of US 23 in

Pound. The loop part of the trail crosses Bad Creek twice and follows a beautiful level ridge through rhododendron and witch hazel.)

On the *Cumberland Mountain Trail* it is another 1 mile to Tucker Gap, and another 6.1 miles to the *Bobs Gap Trail*. (The *Bobs Gap Trail* descends on the Virginia side for 1.5 mi. to SR 622 at Cutler Creek, 1.8 mi. west of the community of Isom.) After another 1.9 miles the trail connects with Mullins Road (FR 616), an access road for horse traffic, 1.8 miles from SR 611 on the Virginia side, north of Isom. For the next 2 miles the trail follows FR 616 on the ridgeline to Jesse Gap, followed by an old woods road to pass Blowing Rock Gap and arrive at the *Counts Cabin Trail* after another 1.3 miles (for a total of 13.3 mi. from the southwestern trailhead).

(The blue-blazed *Counts Cabin Trail* descends 1.8 mi. on the Virginia side to SR 611, 1 mi. east of the community of Blowing Rock. There is a parking area with signage at the SR 611 trailhead.) For the next 5 miles the *Cumberland Mountain Trail* undulates on Pine Mountain in a mixture of Virginia pine, hardwoods, and mountain laurel. Spectacular views exist north of the Elkhorn Creek Valley in Kentucky, and south to the John W. Flanagan Reservoir on the Virginia side.

In a strip mining area the trail leaves the national forest boundary and descends for 3 miles to a trail junction. On the descent the trail reaches Skegg Gap on the southeastern side of Pinnacle Rock. At an old road junction the trail turns left and goes 0.5 miles to another old road junction. Equestrians turn left here to exit at Elkhorn City, and hikers turn right for a descent of 0.9 miles to the Clinchfield railroad in Potter Flats at 22.2 miles. At the railroad the trail turns left and approaches the high railroad trestle over Russell River. Across the trestle at the railroad tunnel the trail ascends to the right on a steep, narrow footpath to a parking area in the curve of Pool Point, KY 80.

USGS maps: Jenkins East, Hellier, Elkhorn City, Clintwood; *USFS trail nos.*: 201, 201A, 201B, 201C.

30   **Red Fox Trail**

Length and Difficulty: 2.2 miles (3.5 km) round-trip; moderate

Feature: historic site

Trailhead: From northern Pound on US 23, go west on SR 667 (old US 23) and ascend 0.6 miles to a parking area and trail sign.

Description: The trail begins at a gate near an old railroad grade. It turns left and after 0.3 miles turns right into the forest and begins an ascent on the original wagon road to Pound Gap. Along the way and at the end of the 1.1-mile trail, Killing Rock, are interpretive markers. (Killing Rock is where Marshall Taylor "Red Fox," preacher and U.S. marshal, and his cohorts ambushed a wagon carrying the Ira Mullins family, May 14, 1892. Five in the wagon were killed, but two escaped. Red Fox was hanged October 27, 1893, at the Wise County Courthouse in Wise.) Backtrack.

USGS map: Jenkins West; *USFS trail no.*: 205

Laurel Fork Trail

Length and Difficulty: 3 miles (4.8 km) round-trip; moderate

Feature: primitive lakeside camping

Trailhead: On us 23 in Pound, near western junction with us 23B, turn at signed entrance to the North Fork of Pound Reservoir. After 0.6 miles is a parking lot and a boat ramp.

Introduction: The 4,500-acre reservoir area was authorized by Congress in 1960 to be constructed by the U.S. Army Corps of Engineers; it became operational in 1966. Operated for flood control, it also offers many recreational activities—fishing and boating at a 154-acre lake, picnicking, hiking, camping, and nature study—originally in nine locations. One attraction is to explore the old roads and logging trams on the mountainside of Cumberland Mountain. There are two areas that have trails: Laurel Fork and Phillips Creek. (Across the dam is the 0.5-mi. *Lakeside Trail*, a short walk to an overlook of the lake. It is maintained by the Corps of Engineers.)

Description: The trail begins on the western slope of the ridge near the rest rooms. At 0.7 miles it ascends through a weedy old field with poison ivy to a ridge crossing at 1 mile. Among dogwood, hickory, and hemlock it descends to cross a small stream and enter a large grassy meadow at the lake and boat ramp at 1.5 miles. Backtrack.

USGS map: Flat Gap, Jenkins West; *USFS trail no.*: 206

Phillips Creek Trail

Length and Difficulty: 1 mile (1.6 km) round-trip; easy

Feature: historic site

Trailhead: In Pound, from us 23, go west 5.7 miles on sr 671 to entrance, right, on sr 834 for the Cane Patch Campground.

Description: A former day-use facility, the area is now a campground with showers and a bathhouse and is near Phillips Creek swimming area. The interpretive trail begins at the end of the camping area and makes a 1-mile loop through a wildlife food plot and continues by an old homesite, a whiskey-still site, waterfalls, an Indian history area, and a narrow-gauge railroad bed.

USGS map: Flat Gap; *USFS trail no.*: 202

STONE MOUNTAIN AND WALLEN RIDGE AREA
Lee and Wise Counties

Stone Mountain Trail

Length and Difficulty: 13.5 miles (21.6 km); strenuous

Connecting Trails: *Olinger Gap Trail* (1.1 mi.), *Lake Keokee Loop Trail* (3.7 mi.), *Payne Branch Trail* (2.3 mi.)

Features: outstanding views, wildlife, cascades, rock formations, old growth hemlock

Trailheads: Reach the southwestern trailhead at Cave Springs Recreation Area from the junction of us 58A and us 23 in downtown Big Stone Gap. It is 4.1

miles west on US 58A to SR 621; turn right. Follow SR 621 along Powell River for 6.6 miles to FR 845. A right turn leads 0.3 miles to the campground entrance. Another route is from US 58A at Ely. Turn north on SR 676, go 1 mile to SR 621 and turn right; then go 4.4 miles to turn left on FR 845. The northeastern trailhead is on US 23 on the western side of Roaring Branch bridge, 1.4 miles north of downtown US 58A in Big Stone Gap, and 1.3 miles south of the VA 68/160 junction in Appalachia. Park 0.2 miles north of the trailhead on US 23 at a dumpster and flea market site.

Introduction: The *Stone Mountain Trail* is the district's third longest trail and equals or surpasses the scenic quality of the *Cumberland Mountain Trail*. One of its appeals is Cave Springs Recreation Area, where vehicles can be safely parked for an extended backpacking trip. Other factors are the beauty of Roaring Run, the magnificent views of Black Mountain in Kentucky and mountain ridges in southwestern Virginia, and fishing in Lake Keokee from a short connector trail. Because of the deep, damp gorge and the dry rock outcroppings, there is a wide range of trees, flowers, ferns, mosses, and lichens. Among the wildlife are deer, turkeys, raccoons, owls, and hawks. The peak of fall color for maple, sassafras, blueberry, and black gum is in mid-October. The unique masonry at Cave Springs was constructed by the USFS in the 1960s, and the many stone steps in Roaring Run were installed by the CCC in the 1930s.

Description: If beginning at the Roaring Branch trailhead, ascend the moss-covered stone steps parallel to the cascading stream for 0.6 miles to rock-hop the branch. Towering old growth hemlock, some over 300 years old, and dense rhododendron keep the gorge deeply shaded. After crossing the branch twice more, follow the ascending trail through hardwoods and mountain laurel to a ridge crest and knoll at 3 miles. At 4 miles is High Butte (3,050 ft.), with superb views of Powell River Valley, Powell Mountain, Wallen Ridge South, and the North Fork of the Powell River Valley North. The Black Mountain range in Kentucky is to the northwest. The trail descends, passes a sheer rock formation, and undulates over knolls for the next 1.9 miles for a gentle descent to Olinger Gap.

(Here the blue-blazed *Olinger Gap Trail* descends north to join the *Lake Keokee Loop Trail*. To the right is 2.5 mi. and to the left is 1.2 mi. to the parking area and boat ramp of Lake Keokee Recreation Area. The 92-acre lake is stocked with bass, sunfish, and muskie. Camping is prohibited, but there are picnic tables and rest rooms. In a hardwood forest with mountain laurel, wintergreen, galax, wild orchids, and ferns, the trail passage is easy to moderate. Access by highway is 8 mi. southwest from Appalachia [4.6 mi. on VA 68 from the junction with US 23; 1.9 mi. on SR 606; 0.6 mi. south on SR 623; and 0.9 mi. south on SR 876].)

From Olinger Gap the *Stone Mountain Trail* ascends and passes right of an old cabin at 6.3 miles and left of a clear-cut at 7 miles, undulates for 1 mile before reaching a dangerous cliff overlook at 8 miles, and makes a steep descent to Low Gap at 8.4 miles. After the sag, the trail ascends through an expansive mountainside of ferns and reaches the crest of the ridge at an old fire tower site at 10 miles. After 0.2 miles on the old road, the trail turns left on a footpath.

(Ahead on the old road is the blue-blazed *Payne Branch Trail*. It descends on a remote, rocky, and hydric passage to parallel Payne Branch in rhododendron slicks and groves of fetter-bush and sweet pepperbush. A small parking area is near a large oak tree, opposite a white and green house trailer in the community of Sigma. It is 1.3 mi. out on sr 625 to sr 606, where northeast on sr 606 it is 4.6 mi. to sr 623, the access route to Lake Keokee.)

At 10.8 miles the *Stone Mountain Trail* leaves the high ridge, passes beside a spectacular rock wall and overhangs, and begins a long descent. After 26 switchbacks in an open hardwood forest, the trail reaches an overlook above the subterranean stream of Cave Springs at 13.3 miles. The remaining 0.2 miles leads to the campground or parking area by a small lake fed by the springs.

USGS maps: Appalachia, Big Stone Gap, Keokee; *USFS trail nos.*: 207, 327, 402, 213

Wallen Ridge Trail   38

Length and Difficulty: 6.6 miles (10.6 km); easy to moderate

Features: wildlife, wildflowers

Trailheads: From west on us 58a in Dryden, turn south on sr 737 (or sr 629) for a few yards; turn left on sr 619 and follow it 1.6 miles to sr 642. Turn left on sr 642 for 0.2 miles and turn right on sr 619, Lovelady Road. It is 2.6 miles to Lovelady Gap, a parking area for four vehicles and the western trailhead. (Access is also from us 23 in Jasper, 3.9 mi. west on sr 611 to sr 619 and right 1.1 mi. to Lovelady Gap.) The eastern trailhead is on FR 641, 6.5 miles northeast from sr 611, and 3.1 miles southwest from us 23 (opposite sr 844, Wildcat Rd.) and 2.1 miles south on us 23 from the us 58a junction in Big Stone Gap.

Description: Hiking east on the yellow-blazed trail, follow the forest boundary on pleasant Wallen Ridge, which has an average elevation of 2,800 feet. Turkeys and squirrels may be seen in an open hardwood forest of mainly maple, oak, and hickory. Dense patches of sweet cicely (*Osmorhiza claytonii*) are prominent. Other wildflowers are black cohosh, puttyroot, and jewelweed. Views of Stone Mountain (nw), Powell and Jasper Mountains (se), and the valleys in between are visible in the winter. At 1 mile is a large tree growing in a rock formation, and at 4.9 miles is a saddle where a blue-blazed spur trail descends steeply for 0.4 miles to FR 641 (5.1 mi. from sr 611 east and 1.4 mi. west from the main trailhead). The trail ascends a knob before dropping to Turkey Cove Gap at 5.4 miles. After 1 mile it crosses a small stream and joins a rocky road for its final 0.2-mile descent to FR 641.

USGS maps: Big Stone Gap, Keokee; *USFS trail no.*: 329

Appalachia Trail   39

Length and Difficulty: 2.2 miles (3.5 km) round-trip; moderate

Features: rhododendron slicks, outcrop

Trailhead: Access is from the junction of us 23 (W. Main St.) and Inman Street (opposite VA 68/160) in Appalachia. Follow Inman Street across the bridge 0.2 miles to Spruce Street, turn left, then right on Roberts Street, which becomes Cold Springs Drive for 0.7 miles to a dead end. There is space for parking one or two cars at the USFS gate.

Description: The yellow-blazed trail follows an old forest road through a cool and dark channel of rhododendron and hemlock to a fork at 0.6 miles. It turns right to follow a power line on the left before switching to another power line. The trail ends at 1.1 miles beside an outcropping with impressive views of Stone Mountain and Powell River. Backtrack.

USGS map: Appalachia; *USFS trail no.*: 214

HIGH KNOB AND LITTLE STONY CREEK AREA
Wise and Scott Counties

40–44   **Chief Benge Scout Trail**
Length and Difficulty: 16.4 miles (26.2 km); moderate to strenuous
Connecting Trails: *High Knob Lake Shore Trail* (1 mi.), *Bark Camp Lake Trail* (3.5 mi.), *Kitchen Rock Trail* (0.6 mi.), *Little Stony Creek Trail* (2.9 mi.)
Features: panoramic High Knob, lakes, wildlife, wildflowers, waterfalls
Trailheads: The western trailhead is at the parking lot of High Knob Tower (4,162 ft.). From US 58A and SR 619 in Norton, travel on SR 619 for 4.5 miles to junction with FR 238 on the left. After 0.6 miles, turn right to High Knob Tower parking area. To reach the eastern trailhead from Coeburn, go 3.2 miles south on VA 72 to SR 664, 1.1 miles west on SR 664, 1.3 miles south on FR 700, and 0.9 miles south on FR 701 to Falls of Little Stony parking area. (Central access points are described below.)
Introduction: The *Chief Benge Scout Trail* is partly new and partly the former *Mountain Fork Trail* and *High Knob Trail*. It passes through two campgrounds (no hookups): High Knob Recreation Area with camping, picnicking, swimming (with bathhouse and warm showers May 1 to October 31), and fishing facilities; and Bark Camp Recreation Area with camping (no showers), picnicking, and fishing (electric motors only). Excellent for backpacking the entire distance, the trail also allows convenient day hikes from three road crossings. It follows sections of streamsides, old railroad grades, and logging roads through a botanical display of rosebay rhododendron, mountain laurel, gentian, orchids, and beds of fern, galax, and wintergreen. Wildlife includes deer, turkeys, raccoons, beavers, and owls.
Description: If beginning at High Knob Tower parking area, views include Tennessee, Kentucky, and a vast expanse of southwestern Virginia. The yellow-blazed trail descends 1.3 miles to High Knob campground, joins the *Lake Shore Trail* loop near the bathhouse, and crosses Mountain Fork footbridge. It passes large rock formations before reaching FR 704 at 3.9 miles. From here the trail curves on a spur ridge, crosses Bark Camp Branch, and ascends on an old road to a beautiful grazing field at 6.8 miles. (Deer and turkey frequent the area.) At the end of the field the trail turns sharply left and follows an old road in a

hardwood forest to Edith Gap, where it crosses SR 706 at 7.5 miles. (Access on SR 706 is 0.7 mi. north to FR 704, and right to FR 238, which leads left to High Knob.) The trail begins a descent to cross the headwaters of Little Stony Creek. It follows the northeastern side of the creek until it makes a junction with the *Bark Camp Lake Trail* at 9.6 miles. It continues on the southern side of the lake and across the dam at 11.3 miles.

(The *Bark Camp Lake Trail* circles the lake. It provides a tranquil walk on a well-designed path where hemlock is frequent and fragrant. Beds of ferns and running cedar are prominent. Wood ducks fly over a lake that has bass, sunfish, and muskies. The campground has a paved trail from the parking area to a fishing deck for the physically handicapped. Also, on the northern side of the parking area is the *Kitchen Rock Trail,* a 0.5-mile loop in a hardwood forest. One access to the camp is from the junction of US 58A and SR 706 in Tacoma [halfway between Norton and Coeburn]. Drive south 4 miles to SR 699, turn left for 0.2 miles on SR 699, and turn right on SR 822. It is 1.6 miles on SR 822 to FR 933 on the right, the entrance road to the campground.)

From the dam the *Chief Benge Scout Trail* descends on the northern side of the stream to SR 822, where it crosses at 11.8 miles. For the next 4.6 miles the trail follows sections of an old railroad grade, rock-hops Little Stony Creek a number of times, and passes through tulip poplar and rhododendron groves. It exits to the eastern trailhead at the Falls of Little Stony parking area at 16.4 miles on SR 701.

(At the end of the parking area the yellow-blazed *Little Stony Creek Trail* [a national recreation trail] descends through a deep gorge with spectacular scenery. Three falls [25, 12, and 30 ft.] are within the first 0.5 mi. Two high footbridges and a spur trail to the first fall also offer exciting views. The trail serves as a 2.9-mi. extension of the *Chief Benge Scout Trail* to Hanging Rock Picnic Area on FR 805, off a curve from VA 72, 2.1 mi. north of Dungannon and 9.2 mi. south of Coeburn.)

USGS *maps:* Coeburn, Dungannon, Fort Blackmore, Wise, Norton; USFS *trail nos.:* 401, 401A, 211, 209, 331

DEVIL'S FORK AREA
Scott County

Devil's Fork Loop Trail   45–46
Length and Difficulty: 7.3 miles (11.7 km) round-trip; strenuous
Connecting Trail: Straight Fork Ridge Trail (1.8 mi.)
Features: cascades, pools, old growth hemlock
Trailhead: From VA 72 (0.3 mi. north of Dungannon), go 8.9 miles west on SR 653 to SR 619. Turn right on SR 619, and after 1.1 miles turn left on FR 619 in a curve (beside a fenced-in white house). (Also, from VA 72/65 in Fort Blackmore, it is 2.9 mi. north on paved SR 619 to junction with SR 653.) From High Knob it is a continuous 7.4-mile descent on SR 619 to FR 619, right at the white house.
Description: From the parking area the trail goes 0.3 miles to Y Bottom, the

conjunction of Straight Fork, right, and Devil's Fork, left, the beginning of the loop. If hiking left, the trail follows an old railroad grade (difficult to recognize in some rough areas) beside cascades, flumes, and pools. At 1.6 miles is a pool sculpted by rushing water to form the Devil's Bathtub. With the shade of old growth hemlocks, the treadway is rocky, mossy, and damp. After 2.4 miles and 11 stream crossings, the trail turns north at Three Forks to ascend on a narrow ridge between Deep and Corder Hollows. For the next 3 miles the trail is in a hardwood forest, crossing spur ridges of Little Mountain, and dipping into hollows with small streams. At 5 miles is a good campsite, and at 5.7 miles is the junction on the left with the *Straight Fork Ridge Trail*. (The *Straight Fork Ridge Trail* ascends steeply 1.8 mi. to FR 237. Access at the top of the mountain is 3.9 mi. from SR 619 at High Knob.) The trail loop turns right and descends on an old and steep road to the parking area at 7.3 miles.

USGS maps: East Stone Gap, Fort Blackmore; *USFS trail nos.*: 212, 204

47–50   ## Glenwood Ranger District

The most northeastern district of the JNF is the 72,300-acre Glenwood Ranger District. It is on the Blue Ridge Mountains, northeast of Troutville to the James River between Glasgow and Big Island, where it borders the Pedlar Ranger District of the GWNF. For the first 13 miles the forest is a corridor, mainly on the northern side, along the BRP. At Bearwallow Gap the forest boundaries expand north to the James River near Buchanan and south to the Peaks of Otter in the BRP (see Chapter 4). The width is about the same for the remainder of the distance. Major natural attractions are the wilderness areas and the high peaks of the northeast, and the man-made attractions are the *AT* and the BRP, which parallel each other through the district. Separated from the main forest are a few dissected tracks of rough terrain. They are on the southern slope of North Mountain at the boundary of the James River District of the GWNF.

There are two wilderness areas: James River Face (8,886 acres), Virginia's first, made possible by the Congressional Wilderness Act of 1975; and adjoining Thunder Ridge (2,344 acres). Both represent some of the most geologically rugged and botanically diverse areas in the state. The more adverse terrain is on the steep river face of the gorge, where dense vegetation discourages exploration. Impressive views of the gorge, river, and mountain are from the overlooks on US 501/VA 130 southeast of Glasgow. Access into the interior of the preserve is by the *AT*, the *Sulphur Spring Trail*, the *Piney Ridge Trail*, the *Belfast Trail*, the *Gunter Ridge Trail*, and the *Balcony Falls Trail*. Cave Mountain Lake Campground (with access from Natural Bridge Station across the James River on SR 759 and SR 781) is the largest and most used of the district's campgrounds. A fee area, it has flush toilets, electrical and water hookups, trailer waste disposal station, and showers at the bathhouse near the lake and beach. The *Wildcat Mountain Trail*, a 4-mile loop trail, was developed primarily for the use of campers at the campground. Over rough terrain, its elevation gain is about 1,500 feet. Counterclockwise it follows a tributary of Back Run to the ridge, descends, crosses FR 3103, and returns by more tributaries.

47

The North Creek Campground (with access from I-81, exit 168, near Buchanan on SR 614 to Arcadia and FR 59) is more primitive. It has a hand pump, vault toilets, and trailer waste disposal unit. It also has a loop trail, the *Whitetail Trail* (2.6 mi.), primarily developed for users of the campground. The yellow-blazed trail is easy to moderate, with a short loop of 0.9 miles within the longer loop. On the longer route is a wildlife waterhole and wildlife clearing, an excellent spot for bird-watchers. Another district camp is Hopper Creek Group Camp, where reservations are necessary from the district office. Access is off SR 759 from Natural Bridge Station. In addition to the picnic area at Cave Mountain Lake, there is Middle Creek Picnic Area on SR 614, south of Arcadia. The district's rainbow trout streams are North Creek, Middle Creek, and Jenning's Creek—all flowing toward Arcadia to become Jenning's Creek. On the eastern side of the district is Hunting Creek near VA 122.

48

Two outstanding projects in the district during the early 1990s have been the North Creek Special Management Plan, east of Arcadia, and the 65-mile *Glenwood Horse Trail*, which runs the entire length of the district. The North Creek project is special because the emphasis is decidedly in favor of preservation and recreation instead of timber harvesting in the 7,400-acre holding. Significant characteristics are the preservation of 1,825 acres in the Apple Orchard Falls area, an emphasis on songbirds as the featured wildlife species, protection of wildlife habitat waterholes, erosion prevention in the trout streams, and increased trail mileage. In the trail project there are plans to elevate the *Cornelius Creek Trail* to national recreation trail status and to form the *Backbone Ridge Trail* into a loop in the North Creek area. Trails for the disabled are also planned.

49–50

The district's 65-mile *Glenwood Horse Trail* is the finest equestrian trail in central Virginia. Its existence is the work of the USFS, horsemen's associations, and riding clubs. There are four trailheads. The southern trailhead is at Day Creek parking lot near Camp Virginia Jaycee. From the junction of US 460/221 and SR 697 (1.5 mi. between Villamont and Montvale west of Bedford), drive north on SR 697 for 0.6 miles and turn left on FR 186 for 0.4 miles to FR 3082. At this trailhead there is a spur, which goes west on FR 3082. The main trail goes north (right), and an alternate trail loop through Blackhorse Gap goes north on FR 186. The Buchanan trailhead is off VA 43. Take exit 162 (or 167 if coming from the north) on I-81 to US 11 in Buchanan. Take VA 43 south 1.7 miles and turn right on SR 625 for 0.3 miles. The Hunting Creek trailhead is west of Big Island. Off US 501, stay on VA 122 for 3 miles south. Turn right on SR 602, and after 0.5 miles fork left to continue 3.4 miles to the parking lot on the left. (If coming from Roanoke, turn north on VA 122 in Bedford.) The northern trailhead, Hellgate Creek, is south of Natural Bridge Station. From I-81 take exit 175 or 180 to US 11 at Natural Bridge; follow VA 130 for 3.2 miles. Turn right on SR 759, go 0.7 miles, and turn left on SR 702. After 1 mile turn right on SR 815 for 0.3 miles to the parking lot. It is recommended that riders unfamiliar

with the orange-blazed main trail (and brown for alternate routes) request information from the district office. Until the trail becomes more refined and mapped,
you may have some questions about campsites, use of support vehicles, advance
storage of feed and supplies, and restrictions.

The district's TIS trail inventory indicates trail traffic volume is low on all trails
except the 51.5 miles of the *AT*. The *AT*'s highest elevation is on Apple Orchard
Mountain (4,225 ft.), and its lowest point is at the James River bridge (660 ft.). In
the Apple Orchard Mountain area are a number of rare plants and animals.
Examples are the oak fern (*Gynocarpium dryopteris*) and the giant snail-eating
ground beetle (*Scaphinotus webbi*). Some trails are not blazed; others are blue,
orange, or yellow. Most of the trails form networks; 12 connect with the *AT*. Three
separate trails, rarely used, are on the southwestern corridor of the BRP and the *AT*.
All trails except the *Hunting Creek Trail* are on the western side of the BRP. On the
wilderness trails, look for the Carolina hemlock (*Tsuga caroliniana*) in its most
northern range limit and the paper birch (*Betula papyrifera*) in its most southern
range limit.

Address and Information: Glenwood Ranger District, P.O. Box 10, Natural
Bridge Station, VA 24579; phone: 703-291-2188; on VA 130, 0.5 miles west of Natural
Bridge Station. Available are district map with trails; brochures on recreation
opportunities and Glenwood horse trails; flyers on hiking, camping, and wilderness areas.

CURRY CREEK AND HAMMOND HOLLOW AREAS
Botetourt County

Curry Creek Trail (0.7 mi.), **Spec Mines Trail** (2.8 mi.),
Hammond Hollow Trail (3.3 mi.), AT (10 mi.)

51–53

Length and Difficulty: 6.2 miles to 11.4 miles (9.9 km to 18.2 km) combined, round-
trip; moderate to strenuous
Features: scenic views, wildlife, wildflowers, streams
Trailheads: The most southern terminus is on the *AT* at Salt Pond (1.1 mi. west
from gated FR 191 at BRP mp 101.5). The most northern is at Bobblets Gap (BRP
mp 93.2 and FR 4008). Other accesses are described below.
Introduction: All three of the spur trails run northwest off the *AT* and descend
separately and end separately, but they are connected by the *AT*, which parallels
the BRP at the top of the mountain, and by FR 634, which is a comparable
parallel farther down the mountainside. By using the *AT* and the roads, multiple circuits can be made. Except for the first 3.5 miles on FR 634, all other
roadway is part of the *Glenwood Horse Trail* system. Wildlife in the areas includes deer, turkeys, grouse, raccoons, squirrels, owls, hawks, songbirds, and
snakes, including the timber rattlesnake. Vascular plants are mainly southern
hardwoods, pines, rhododendron, mountain laurel, wildflowers, and ferns.
There are more than 10 different stream crossings and 6 scenic overlooks.
Description: If hiking northeast on the *AT* at Curry Creek, a 11.4-mile loop can be
made by descending on the blue-blazed *Curry Creek Trail* for 0.7 miles to right

on FR 634-1 for 3.5 miles to FR 186 and joining the *Glenwood Horse Trail* (FR 186 becomes SR 606 out to US 11, north of Troutville). Turn right and ascend FR 186 for 2.2 miles to the *AT* at Black Horse Gap at 6.4 miles. Return right on the *AT* for 5 miles, passing Wilson Creek Shelter, to point of origin.

Another 8-mile circuit on the *AT* is at Iron Mine Hollow Overlook at the BRP. Descend on the *Spec Mines Trail* (planned yellow blazing) 2.1 miles and turn left on FR 634. (The trail continues another 0.7 mi. to SR 645, which accesses SR 640 to US 11.) Follow FR 634 2.4 miles to FR 186, turn left, and ascend 2.2 miles on FR 186 to the *AT* at Black Horse Gap. Turn left on the *AT* for 1.3 miles to point of origin at Iron Mine Hollow Overlook, and Taylors Mountain Overlook along the way. (The *Spec Mines Trail* can also be used to turn right on FR 634-2 for 3 mi. to a right turn on the *Hammond Hollow Trail*. Ascend 1.4 mi. to the *AT* at 6.8 mi. Turn right on the *AT* for 2.8 mi. for a return to Iron Mine Hollow Overlook at 9.6 mi. Along the *AT* is Harveys Knob Overlook.)

For an additional use of the *Hammond Hollow Trail*, after the 1.4-mile descent from the *AT* to FR 634-3, turn right (which is both the *Hammond Hollow Trail* and the *Glenwood Horse Trail*) for 1.9 miles. Turn right for 0.1 mile and turn right again on FR 4008 at 3.4 miles. (At FR 4008 junction with SR 617, there is an access north on SR 617 to SR 625 and US 11 south of Buchanan.) Ascend on FR 4008 1 mile to main route of the *Glenwood Horse Trail*, and another 1 mile up to the *AT* and the BRP at Bobblets Gap. A return right on the *AT* passes Bobblets Gap Shelter en route to the *Hammond Hollow Trail* for 0.8 miles and a total of 6.2 miles.

USGS maps: Villamont, Montvale; *USFS trail nos.*: 20, 28, 27, 1

JENNINGS CREEK AND NORTH CREEK AREAS
Botetourt County

Buchanan Trail (1.5 mi.), **Cove Mountain Trail** (1.8 mi.)   54–55
Length and Difficulty: 3.3 miles (5.3 km) combined, round-trip; easy to moderate
Features: scenic views, wildlife, spring
Trailheads: For the *Buchanan Trail*, go east 1.2 miles on VA 43 from Buchanan, turn left on Quarry Road, and after 1 mile look for trail on right. For the *Cove Mountain Trail*, take I-81 exit 168, follow SR 614 to Arcadia, turn right on SR 622 at Arcadia Store and go 0.1 mile for parking.
Description: These trails have different entrances into the forest but meet 100 yards down the slope from the *AT*. The *Buchanan Trail* ascends from an old quarry to a logging road at 0.8 miles. At 1.3 miles is a spring. The *Cove Mountain Trail* ascends steeply to an old logging road. At 0.9 miles and 1.4 miles are wildlife waterholes. Dappled with sunlight, the wide trail is exceptionally scenic with autumn colors. At 1.8 miles it joins the *Buchanan Trail*. (A loop of 7.9 mi. can be made by hiking the *AT* southwest 3 mi. [Cove Mountain Shelter is at 1.7 mi.] to blue-blazed *Little Cove Mountain Trail*. Turn left sharply, descend, and follow the trail 2.8 mi. to Jennings Creek and SR 614. Turn left on SR 614 and after 0.7 mi. make a junction with the *AT* at a parking area, where a left on the *AT*

provides a return to Cove Mountain and Buchanan trails after 1.4 mi.) (The *Glenwood Horse Trail* partially follows the *Buchanan Trail* and the *Cove Mountain Trail*.)

USGS maps: Arnold Valley, Buchanan; *USFS trail nos.*: 24, 23

56 **Little Cove Mountain Trail** (2.8 mi.), **AT** (1.7 mi.)
Length and Difficulty: 4.5 miles (7.2 km) combined; moderate
Features: wildlife, stream, scenic views
Trailhead: From I-81, exit 168, take SR 614 through Arcadia (see *Cove Mountain Trail*, above, for connection options), past junctions with FR 59 (North Creek Rd.) and SR 618 (Middle Creek Rd.), and after 0.5 miles on SR 614 park at trail sign by Jennings Creek, on the right.
Description: The trail crosses Jennings Creek on a footbridge and three times on Little Cove Creek. It ascends and reaches a ridge at 1 mile. It crosses two forest roads, the *Glenwood Horse Trail*, and reaches the *AT* at 2.8 miles. Here are views of Purgatory Mountain and Buchanan. Backtrack or continue left on the *AT* for 1.7 miles to mp 90.9 at the BRP for a support vehicle at VA 43, or turn right on the *AT* and follow it back to SR 614 at Jennings Creek for a 7.9-mile loop.
USGS map: Buchanan, Montvale; *USFS trail no.*: 25

Apple Orchard Falls Trail (West) (3.2 mi.), **Cornelius Creek Trail** (2.9 mi.),
57–58 **AT** (1.2 mi.)
Length and Difficulty: 6.4 miles or 7.3 miles (10.2 km or 11.7 km) combined, round-trip; strenuous
Features: wildflowers, wildlife, waterfall, scenic views
Trailheads: From I-81, north of Buchanan, exit 168, follow SR 614 for 3.3 miles, past Arcadia, and turn left on FR 59, which leads to North Creek Campground. Pass the camp and reach road's end and parking area after 7.5 miles from I-81. Access is also from mp 78.7 on the BRP, Sunset Field Overlook. See Chapter 4 for *Apple Orchard Falls Trail (East)*.
Description: Both trails begin at the end of FR 59 for the northern trailheads, the *Apple Orchard Falls Trail* left and the *Cornelius Creek Trail* right. They both join the *AT* 1.2 miles apart, and their elevation change is about the same, 2,000 feet. Backtracking is 6.4 miles round-trip on the *Apple Orchard Falls Trail* and the *Cornelius Creek Trail*, or making a loop with the *AT* is 7.3 miles. On the blue-blazed *Apple Orchard Falls Trail* there are steep sections and a number of stream crossings. At 2 miles it reaches the spectacular 200-foot Apple Orchard Falls. Ascend to a large overhanging rock at 2.3 miles. Continue the steep ascent to the *AT* crossing at 3.2 miles, where a 0.2-mile spur connects to the BRP. The *Cornelius Creek Trail* follows Cornelius Creek and up the western side of Backbone Ridge on old logging roads. It makes a sharp left turn over Backbone Ridge to descend, then ascend, for its junction with the *AT* at 2.9 miles. After a turn left, go 1.2 miles to connect with the *Apple Orchard Falls Trail*.
USGS map: Arnold Valley; *USFS trail nos.*: 17, 18, 1

THUNDER RIDGE AREA
Bedford County

Hunting Creek Trail 59
Length and Difficulty: 1 mile (1.6 km); moderate to strenuous
Features: scenic views, wildflowers, stream
Trailheads: The western trailhead is at mp 74.9 of the BRP where the *AT* crosses. To reach the eastern trailhead, from the Big Island junction of US 501 and VA 122 go 3 miles on VA 122. Turn right on SR 602 for 1.5 miles, where it becomes FR 45. Drive 3.5 miles to an extreme left curve; trailhead is on the right.
Description: This deluxe leg-stretcher is the only USFS trail in the district that goes east of the BRP. Blue-blazed, short, and switchy, it drops 1,000 feet out of the sky at Thunder Ridge (3,485 ft.) to riparian fern beds and the headwaters of trout-stocked Hunting Creek. Its eastern trailhead at FR 45 is also a junction with the *Glenwood Horse Trail*.
USGS map: Snowden; *USFS trail no.*: 3

JAMES RIVER FACE WILDERNESS AREA
Rockbridge County

Balcony Falls Trail (4.1 mi.), Sulphur Spring Trail (6.6 mi.) 60–61
Length and Difficulty: 10.7 miles (17.1 km) combined; strenuous
Features: wilderness, scenic views, wildlife, wildflowers, sulphur spring
Trailheads: From junction of VA 130 and SR 759 near Natural Bridge Station, take SR 759 for 0.9 miles, turn east on paved SR 782, pass James River Recreation Area, and continue straight on gravel road to FR 3093 for 1.5 miles to northern trailhead parking area. To reach the southern trailhead, continue on SR 759 for 2.3 miles, then turn east on SR 781 (which becomes FR 35) for 3.2 miles to the parking area at Sulphur Spring Hollow.
Description: These trails connect with other trails in the James River Face and Thunder Ridge wilderness areas, but the arms go in such opposite directions it is difficult to form circuits. These trails are also used for horse traffic. Begin the *Balcony Falls Trail* on a gradual contour for the first 1.6 miles, after which the trail ascends steeply on switchbacks into the James River Face Wilderness. At 2.5 miles is a major scenic view of the James River Gorge and the town of Glasgow. (Balcony Falls is a rapids in the James River near the confluence of Maury River.) Following a former old fire road the trail becomes the *Sulphur Spring Trail* at 4.1 miles, with an altitude gain of 1,450 feet.

Continuing ahead the trail skirts west of the main ridge, then returns to the main ridge for a junction with the *AT* at 5.5 miles. (A turn right on the *AT* is 0.5 mi. from a junction with the *Belfast Trail*.) Cross the *AT*, follow an easy grade, and at 5.7 miles there is an excellent view of James River Gorge. At 7.8 miles join the *Piney Ridge Trail* on the left. (The *Piney Ridge Trail* descends 3.7 mi. south to FR 54.) After 70 yards the trail crosses the *AT* and begins its descent to Sulphur

Spring Hollow. Pass Sulphur Spring on the right at 10.4 miles and reach the southern trailhead on FR 35 at 10.7 miles. Total elevation change is 1,175 feet.

USGS map: Snowden; *USFS trail nos.*: 7, 3001

62–63   **Belfast Trail** (2.8 mi.), **Gunter Ridge Trail** (4.7 mi.)

Length and Difficulty: 7.5 miles (12 km) combined; strenuous

Features: geological formations, scenic views, wildlife, stream

Trailheads: The northwestern trailheads are separate. The southeastern trailhead is a merge with the *AT*. To access the northwestern trailheads from VA 130 near Natural Bridge Station drive southwest on SR 759 for 1.5 miles to the *Gunter Ridge Trail* across the Elk Creek bridge on the left. Continue ahead on SR 759 for 1.7 miles, turn left on SR 781, and reach the *Belfast Trail* trailhead after another 1.3 miles.

Description: If beginning with the *Belfast Trail*, cross a footbridge over Elk Creek, meet the *Glenwood Horse Trail*, pass the site of a former Boy Scout Camp, and begin to ascend on the northern side of Belfast Creek. At 0.6 miles enter the James River Face Wilderness. Leave the creek and at 1.4 miles arrive at Devil's Marbleyard, a unique pile of blocky rubble of sandstone, part of a fold that happened about 200 million years ago. Holes in the blocks were bored by worms, known as *Skolithus*, when the rocks were sand, according to geologist Edgar Spencer of Washington and Lee University. Reach a ridge crest at 2 miles, join the *Gunter Ridge Trail* on the left at 2.4 miles, and join the *AT* at 2.8 miles. Backtrack, or follow the *Gunter Ridge Trail*. (Make a loop by turning right on the *AT* and following it 1.8 mi. Turn right and descend on the *Sulphur Spring Trail* for 2.8 mi. to FR 35. Turn right on FR 35 and follow it 1.9 mi. to the *Belfast Trail* for a circuit of 9.2 mi.)

On the blue-blazed *Gunter Ridge Trail* from the *Belfast Trail*, stay in the slight hollow to a saddle and follow it out to a knoll at 0.9 miles on Gunter Ridge. Begin a descent in hardwoods with mountain laurel and blueberries as an understory. Follow 20 switchbacks to the leaving edge of the wilderness at Little Hellgate Creek. Cross the *Glenwood Horse Trail* at 3.8 miles on FR 3015. (To the right on FR 3015 is 1.3 mi. to *Glenwood Horse Trail* trailhead at Big Hellgate Creek.) Leave the forest and follow a road to exit at SR 759 at 4.7 miles.

USGS map: Snowden; *USFS trail nos.*: 9, 8 (no number for *Glenwood Horse Trail*)

64   **Piney Ridge Trail**

Length and Difficulty: 3.7 miles (5.9 km) one way; strenuous

Features: wilderness, wildlife, wildflowers

Trailheads: To reach the southern trailhead from the BRP, go west on US 501 for 1.8 miles to FR 54 on the left. Drive 0.6 miles on a narrow road past Big Island Hunt and Fish Club to park near the trailhead on the right. The northern trailhead is at the *AT* (2.9 mi. north on the *AT* from Petites Gap on the BRP, mp 71).

Description: At the southern trailhead by yucca follow Piney Ridge between Snow

Creek and Peters Creek among hardwoods, Virginia pine, and mountain laurel. Enter the James River Face Wilderness at 1.5 miles. Reach the junction with the *Sulphur Spring Trail* 70 yards north of the *AT* at 3.7 miles. Backtrack. (If planning for a potential loop, turn right on the *AT*, follow it through Hickory Stand, down the mountain to Matts Creek Shelter, by super scenic views of the James River Gorge, and to US 501 at the James River bridge for 7.6 mi. Turn right on US 501, hike 1.3 mi. to FR 54, turn right, and go 0.6 mi. to southern trailhead of the *Piney Ridge Trail* for a total of 13.2 mi.) Elevation gain, 1,550 feet.
USGS map: Snowden; *USFS trail no.*: 2

Mount Rogers National Recreation Area

Virginia's highest and most spectacular land mass is a 60-mile series of mountain ranges from Damascus to the New River. Easily a star attraction, it is between the Great Valley on the north and North Carolina on the south. It is Mount Rogers National Recreation Area, Virginia's unique national forest district. It is unique because its scenic beauty and potential for varied recreation prompted Congress to designate this natural wonder a national recreation area in 1966. Like a diamond in Mount Rogers's crown of jewels is Grayson Highlands State Park, centrally adjoining on the southern side. Within the recreation area's 117,000 acres are six campgrounds, three wildernesses, four special management areas, and a vast network of trails. Although the Mount Rogers area is particularly scenic throughout, what most significantly sets it apart from other Virginia mountain areas is the boreal crest zone. The zone frames Whitetop Mountain (5,530 ft.) in the west, Mount Rogers (5,729 ft.) in the center, and the three peaks of Pine Mountain (4,859 ft.) in the east. Inside are extensive alpine mountain balds, dense red spruce (*Picea rubens*), oleoresin fragrant Fraser's fir (*Abies franseri*), dazzling displays of purple rhododendron, and matchless views from rocky crags. The weather is typically cool and moist, but it can change suddenly into fierce thunderstorms in the summer and blizzards in the winter. These storms and the more frequent whiteouts from fog in any season can be a dangerous risk for hikers unprepared and inexperienced.

Habitat for wildlife varies widely because of the low valleys and remote coves in comparison with high, open, windswept plateaus, a 3,700-foot elevation change. At least 156 species of birds have been sighted, some of which may be seen in any season: sparrow hawk, ruffed grouse, downy woodpecker, white-breasted nuthatch, junco, song sparrow, and more. Among the most common mammals are deer, fox, raccoon, gray squirrel, woodchuck, and chipmunk. The bear population, once hunted to near extinction, is being restocked by the state's Department of Game and Inland Fisheries. Deer hunting is popular, and its season is usually mid-November to early December. Classified as sensitive on the endangered and threatened species list are the sharp-shinned hawk (*Falco peregrinus anatum*) and the golden pigmy salamander (*Desmognathus wrighti*). Populations of pintos, paints, bays, and other kinds of ponies have been introduced as grazing animals to keep the high meadows open. They are most noticeable between Grayson Highlands State Park and Rhododendron Gap, or as far east as the peaks of Pine Mountain. Fishing is permitted in the national recreation area's trout-stocked lakes and streams. There are also four streams capable of maintaining a trout population without artificial stocking. They are Big Wilson Creek, Whitetop Laurel Creek, Fox Creek, and Helton Creek.

Wilderness areas are designated to maintain some of the natural regions. They are Lewis Fork (5,618 acres), Little Wilson Creek (3,613 acres), and Little Dry Run (2,858 acres). The first two are in the central area of the district, but Little Dry Run is in the northeast, south of Speedwell on US 21. In addition to the wilderness areas are four special management areas, part of the USFS's Recreation Opportunity Spectrum. The purpose of the agency is to "protect and maintain the qualities that make [the special areas] stand out." They are Whitetop Mountain (1,115 acres), Rush Creek (85 acres), Whitetop Laurel Creek (800 acres), and Little Laurel Creek (200 acres).

The district's human history, after the Native Americans, included first the hunter, trapper, and pioneer settlers with herdsmen. With the growth of railroads and the timber industry at the turn of the century, towns such as Troutdale and Konnarock developed. Timber harvesting stripped the valleys and high mountain-sides of prime hardwoods and conifers. Until 1883 Mount Rogers had been called Balsam Mountain, rich with large spruce and fir forests, but Virginia's legislature memorialized its first state geologist, William Barton Rogers, by renaming the mountain. Since 1966 the USFS, new steward of the area, has built forest roads, lakes, and recreational facilities to serve the public. But none of this development outshines the trail system. The longest trail is the 66.3-mile *Virginia Highlands Horse Trail* from Whitetop Mountain east to VA 94 near the New River. The second longest is 64 miles of the *AT*, whose maintenance is chiefly by Piedmont Appalachian Trail Hikers, Mount Rogers AT Club, and the Appalachian Trail Conference's Konnarock Crew stationed in Sugar Grove. Other long trails are the 50.6-mile *Iron Mountain Trail* (of which 16.8 mi. was the *AT* until 1972) and multipurpose 34-mile *Virginia Creeper Trail*, with 16.5 miles of its length in the national forest. In a labyrinth of trail options hikers and backpackers can use loops within loops. The ultimate in scenic beauty and diversity of topography is a 56.7-mile combination loop of the *AT* and the *Iron Mountain Trail*. Some of the trails and roads are described below in circuit sections where campgrounds can serve as a base camp. The district's TIS trail inventory lists 128 trails, but 61 are no longer trails, are not recommended for usage, or are not maintained. The district's trails are color-coded: blazes on the *AT* are white, light blue is used on connector or spur trails leading directly to the *AT*, and dark blue or raspberry appears on other trails connecting to main trails. Orange is for horse trails, and yellow is for the *Iron Mountain Trail*. This system helps users in forming loop hikes. Many trails do not have a blaze. Traffic volume is highest on the *Virginia Creeper Trail*, the *AT*, the *Mount Rogers Trail*, the *Wilburn Ridge Trail*, and the trails near Beartree Recreation Area.

The major campgrounds are described below. For equestrian camps there are Fox Creek on VA 603, 4 miles west of Troutdale; Hussy Mountain off US 21, 3 miles south of Speedwell on FR 14; and Raven Cliff, 6 miles east of Speedwell on SR 619. Special picnic areas are Shepherds Corner on VA 94, 5 miles south of Ivanhoe; Skulls Gap on SR 762, 4 miles south of Chilhowie; and Whitetop (go 13.8 mi. east of Damascus on US 58 to SR 600, turn left, and continue 1.6 mi. to FR 89 on the left). The national recreation area also has Mount Rogers Scenic Byway. It extends from Troutdale west to Konnarock for 13.2 miles on SR 603, and from Damascus to Volney for 32.5 miles on US 58. Emphasis is on farms, forests, stores, schools, mountain history, and folklore.

The future development of the national recreation area is controversial. Although the area is used year round for outdoor activities, including snow skiing in the winter, there are commercial interests in expanding the routes for snow sports and off-road vehicles. Other groups maintain that the area is already overcrowded (though it has not attained its projected visitor count). One group, Mount Rogers Planning District, has a mission to localize investment in future development, and another group, Graysonites for Progressive Change, opposes expanding US 58 to four lanes on the southern side of the main mountain.

Since 1990 the Virginia Department of Transportation has been considering two proposals: Option 2A would be for a four-lane highway to bisect the area along Comers Creek and destroy a natural area of the *AT*. Option 2B would use existing I-77 and I-81 for heavy traffic (such as double-unit trucking). Some of the major opposing groups to Option 2A are the Appalachian Trail Conference, Mountain Heritage Alliance, and the Sierra Club. "This is one of the few places on the entire *AT* where one can hike for days without crossing a paved road," says Melissa De Vaughn in "Paving the 'Rooftop of Virginia' " in the September/October 1994 issue of *Appalachian Trailway News*.

Meanwhile, the USFS is planning a 100-acre campground with swimming pool near the New River in Carroll County. Opponents claim the present facilities need better maintenance before there is new construction. Preservationists fear it is a matter of time before commercial convoys with condo blueprints, dreams of theme parks, and money for malls will destroy the area near Virginia's natural grandstand in the sky.

Address and Information: Mount Rogers National Recreation Area, Rt. 1, Box 303, Marion, VA 24354; phone: 703-783-5196; on VA 16, 7 miles south of Marion, I-81 exit 45. The headquarters office is a museum and visitor center. Available are maps of Mount Rogers area and wilderness areas, sportsman map and *AT* map—all for a small fee. Free material includes maps and brochures on the *Virginia Creeper Trail*, some circuit routes, recreational facilities, horse trails, the Scenic Byway, and cross-country skiing, and flyers on wildernesses and specific campgrounds.

65   **Virginia Creeper Trail**

Length and Difficulty: 34.1 miles (54.6 km); easy

Features: waterfalls, trout and bass streams, historic sites, trestles, farmland, wildlife, wildflowers

Trailheads: To reach the eastern trailhead, travel 15.2 miles on US 58 from the junction with VA 91 in Damascus. Take SR 726 for 1.7 miles to Whitetop Station parking area. The western trailhead is near the corner of Green Springs Road and A Street (1 block south on Pecan St. from Main St.) in Abingdon.

Introduction: The most southwestern area of the Mount Rogers National Recreation Area is at the Tennessee state line, adjoining the Cherokee National Forest. At the western corner, and at the foot of Iron Mountain, is the town of Damascus, known nationally for its hospitality. From the town and east to the base of Whitetop Mountain is the *AT*, US 58, Whitetop Laurel Creek, and Green Cove Creek, all winding and twisting and partially parallel to each other. Even Straight Branch is not straight. Following the creeks is the curving *Virginia Creeper Trail*, straighter than the *AT* and the roads because its design is based on an old railroad bed. There are points of brilliant fusion when streams, trails, and roads converge, intersect, or simply tease one another. In this setting of natural and human history are options for weeks of multiple backpacking circuits combining the *AT*, the *Virginia Creeper Trail*, and the *Iron Mountain Trail*. Although separate from these routes, the *Daniel Boone Auto Trail* touches this area. The area is also part of the Mount Rogers Scenic Byway, with 32.5 miles of US 58 from Damascus east to Volney. The nearest developed campground is Beartree Recreation Area on FR 837, 3 miles west on US 58 from its junction with SR 603, and 6.6 miles east on US 58 from its junction with VA 91.

The *Virginia Creeper Trail*, a national recreation trail, extends from the Virginia/North Carolina state line, in the community of Whitetop, northwest to Abingdon. The first 16.5 miles are in the Mount Rogers National Recreation Area. The other mileage is supervised by the Washington County Park Authority but is described here for continuity. (An extension of the trail into North Carolina is being studied by North Carolina Rails-Trails, Inc.) Its history is as exciting as its recreational opportunities. Hundreds of years ago the route was a Native American trace from North Carolina to the Ohio Valley. Daniel Boone used part of the trace on his westward explorations. In 1887 a railroad company was chartered, first to haul iron ore and later to transport timber. It became the Virginia-Carolina Railroad by 1900 and the Norfolk & Western Railroad by 1918, with a 75-mile route from Abingdon to Elkland, North Carolina. Usage and distance declined after the Great Depression, but supply and passenger services continued until the final run March 31, 1977, from West Jefferson, North Carolina, to Abingdon. Called the V-C railroad, it acquired the sobriquet of Virginia Creeper. According to one legend, the name comes from the five-leafed, red (in autumn), high climbing, woody vine (*Parthenocisus quinque-*

folia) common in the area. According to another legend, the slow speed on the gorge curves and the incline of 1,650 feet in elevation from Damascus to White-top Station give the trail its name.

Users of the trail will cross many trestles and bridges, pass waterfalls, follow stocked fishing streams, go through farmlands and residential areas, and may see a diversity of mammals, birds (at least 50 species), wildflowers (at least 170 species), and historic sites. The USFS ranks traffic volume on the trail as high. On a typical weekend are equestrians (sometimes as many as 25 in a convoy), bicyclists, walkers, joggers, strollers (particularly near Abingdon), and back-packers. All vehicular traffic (except bicycles) is prohibited. Campsites are infre-quent outside the forest property. (The USFS recommends camping 100 feet from streams.) For campsite information on private lands, users are requested to contact the Virginia Creeper Trail Club. Guidelines for bikers require a warning passing bell, and bikers as well as equestrians must dismount for trestle crossings. Food supplies and restaurants are in Damascus and Abingdon. For anglers a Virginia fishing license is necessary. Shuttle service is provided by Blue Blaze Shuttle Service, Rt. 2, Box 105, Damascus, VA 24235; phone: 703-388-3875. In addition to the USFS, contact the Virginia Creeper Trail Club, P.O. Box 2382, Abingdon, VA 24210; phone: 703-628-4790.

Description: If beginning at the eastern trailhead, look for the Whitetop Station sign at the junction of US 58 and SR 726 (15.2 mi. from US 58 and VA 91 junction at Damascus, and 9.6 mi. west on US 58 from Grayson Highlands State Park). (There is another SR 726, 2.2 mi. farther west on US 58, which leads to Taylors Valley.) Follow SR 726 for 1.7 miles to parking area at Whitetop Station. This is 1 mile northwest of the Virginia/North Carolina state line. (If beginning at the state line, the nearest road access can be reached by continuing 0.8 mi. farther on SR 726 to a left turn on SR 753 and crossing Big Horse Creek. To the right it is 0.3 mi. to the state line, from which backtracking is necessary.) At 0.7 miles is the first bridge, near a beaver dam and with excellent views of Whitetop Moun-tain. The Whitetop Station parking area is reached at 1 mile, and at 1.1 miles the trail crosses SR 755/726, the trail's highest elevation (3,577 ft.). From here it begins a gentle descent for the next 24 miles. The trail passes by a commercial Christmas tree farm at 1.7 miles and over a 270-foot-long trestle at 1.9 miles. Green Cove Station, now a visitor center, is reached at 3.9 miles. Access here is on SR 600, 1 mile off US 58 (13.7 mi. east from VA 91). After two more bridges the trail enters an area of hemlock, old apple trees, and patches of wildflowers. At 5 miles cross gravel road, SR 726. Pass a cattle pasture on rolling hills with ferns and blackberries at 5.6 miles. More bridges and cascades follow in the Green Cove Creek gorge. At 6.3 miles SR 859 crosses the trail. Access is 2 miles off US 58 (9.2 mi. east from VA 91). There are good campsites in this vicinity. From 7.2 miles to 7.4 miles is an exceptionally scenic place. The *AT* joins the trail to cross the 540-foot-long Luther Hassinger Memorial Bridge (trestle). Underneath is the confluence of the Whitetop Laurel Creek and Green Cove Creek. At 7.9 miles is a parking area for the *AT* and the *Virginia Creeper Trail* at historic railroad site of Creek Junction. Access is 1.3 miles off US 58 on SR 728 (8.8 mi. east from VA 91). The *AT* leaves the *Virginia Creeper Trail* at 8 miles. For the next 3.3 miles there are 10 bridges and trestles, waterfalls, hardwoods and rhododendron, and a section with 1,000-foot-high rock walls on the northern side of the gorge. There are good campsites at 9.1 miles. At 11.2 miles the trail passes through private property and a cattle farm to reach the village of Taylors Valley at 11.7 miles. Access is on SR 725, 2.6 miles out to NT 91 in Tennessee (2.3 mi. south of the US 58 and VA 91 junction). The *Virginia Creeper Trail* remains east of the creek to a parking area and to a gate. Near the gate is a 0.4-mile spur trail up Straight Mountain to the *AT*. (A right turn on the *AT* is an ascent to the crest of Straight Mountain for scenic views of area mountains and the Whitetop Laurel gorge at 1.8 miles. Saunders Shelter is 0.3 miles farther.) At 13.9 miles, at Straight Branch, is a signboard about Mount Rogers National Recreation Area. Beyond is an access to a parking area, picnic tables, fireplaces, the *AT*, and US 58 (3 mi. east of junction with VA 91). There is a good campsite at 14.1 miles. For the next 2.7 miles the trail parallels US 58; passes waterfalls, bluffs, and rhododendron thickets; and crosses four bridges. The last of the latter is Iron Bridge in sight of US 58. After crossing VA 91 at 16.8 miles the trail joins the *AT* at 17.2 miles; there is a spring on the northern side of US 58. At 17.6 miles the *AT* stays with US 58, and the *Virginia Creeper Trail* forks left to cross bridges over Laurel Creek and Beaverdam Creek in Damascus. The *Virginia Creeper Trail* reaches the corner of Laurel and Beaverdam avenues at 18.2 miles. Here is an information display and caboose near a parking area. (Damascus has restaurants, a post office, grocery stores, campsites, and an *AT* hostel.)

For the next 3.4 miles the trail runs parallel between US 58 and Laurel Creek, whose mouth is at the South Fork of the Holston River. Along the way are residential houses, an abandoned warehouse, and crossings of SR 718, SR 715, and SR 1230. The trail goes under US 58 bridge at 21.6 miles and parallels South Fork through cow pastures and gates to reach SR 712 at 23.6 miles. (It is 93 yards left to SR 711, accessible from US 58 on SR 907.) Access from US 58 on SR 712 is 1.2 miles (6.5 mi. from I-81, exit 19, in Abingdon). More pastures and a bridge over Rockhouse Run lead to Alvarado Bible Church on SR 710 at 25.4 miles. Access to US 58 is 2.8 miles east on SR 710 and SR 722 (5 mi. south from I-81). After three farm gates the trail crosses a long curved bridge (618 ft.) over South Holston Lake at the confluence of South Fork and Middle Fork at 26.7 miles. Views are outstanding of the South Holston Lake and rivers. More gates, bridges, and trestles follow up the Middle Fork gorge in a forest of large oak, poplar, and hemlock. At 28.2 miles is the trail's longest trestle (645 ft.). After passing through River Knobs and leaving the Middle Fork the trail crosses SR 677 (near Watagua Station) at a parking area at 30.3 miles. Access is 2.1 miles off US 58 on SR 677 (1.5 mi. south of I-81).

The character of the *Virginia Creeper Trail* changes for the final 3.8 miles. Horse traffic is prohibited, bicycle traffic increases, and urban views appear. Following three trestles through the Great Knobs, the trail crosses a golf cause-walk at 32.5 miles in the Winterham golf community. At 32.6 miles is the beginning (or end) of a 1.5-mile self-guided nature walk. Along the *Virginia Creeper Trail* are numbered markers to match a brochure on the plant species. Two historic markers indicate an old sawmill site and train turnaround. Pass under I-81, and at 34 miles is probably the largest white oak on the entire *Virginia Creeper Trail.* The final trestle (253 ft. long), over Town Creek, is at the trailhead on Green Springs Road. Across the street is a parking lot, and in this area is the site of pre–Revolutionary War Black's Fort. Now there is a small museum and information center with sheltered V-C Locomotive #433, a symbol of why this trail exists.

USGS maps: Abingdon, Damascus, Grayson, Konnarock, Park; *USFS trail nos.*: 4575, 1

IRON MOUNTAIN AREA (SOUTHWEST)
Washington and Smyth Counties

Straight Branch Trail (1.5 mi.), **Lum Trail** (1 mi.), **Iron Mountain Trail** (11.1 mi.), **Shaw Gap Trail** (1 mi.), **Beartree Gap Trail** (3.1 mi.),
Beartree Lake Trail (1 mi.), **AT** (2 mi.), **Feathercamp Branch Trail** (1.9 mi.)   66–77
Length and Difficulty: 20.8 miles (33.4 km) combined, circuit; moderate
Connecting Trails: *Chestnut Ridge Trail* (1.8 mi.), *Rush Trail* (1.5 mi.), *Feathercamp Ridge Trail* (0.4 mi.), *Wright Hollow Trail* (2.7 mi.), *Beech Grove Trail* (3.5 mi.)
Features: geology, historic site, wildlife, wildflowers
Trailheads: Access to Beartree Recreation Area is off US 58 on FR 837 at Beartree Gap (6.6 mi. east from US 58 and VA 91 junction at Damascus, or 3 miles west from US 58 and SR 603 junction). Drive 1.5 miles on FR 837 to group campground, and another 2.3 miles to the family campground.
Introduction: The Iron Mountain southwestern area of the Mount Rogers National Recreation Area includes the southwestern range from Damascus northeast to Skulls Gap on Iron Mountain at SR 600. The area is bordered on the southern side by US 58 and the Whitetop Laurel Creek area and extends upstream to the Konnarock vicinity. The base camp is Beartree campgrounds, which have rest rooms, warm showers, and waste disposal stations. The picnic area has 20 picnic pavilions, a grassy area for sports, and a lake with a 300-foot swimming beach and bathhouse. Beartree Lake is stocked with trout, and there is a fishing pier for the disabled. The group campground is open all year, but reservations are necessary from the district office. The family campground is usually open from March to September (and during deer season in late November and early December). For the purpose of grouping trails for circuits near campgrounds, the descriptions are divided into three sections of the *Iron Mountain* (southwest, central, and northeast) *Trail.* Three circuits are described here, but hikers will find other options with district maps.
Description: The first loop is 5 miles, the second option is 13.9 miles, and the third is 20.8 miles. Begin the first loop counterclockwise on the *Straight Branch Trail,* near the gate of Chipmunk Circle at the family campground. It follows the old

gated road 1.5 miles to SR 600. Along the way are stands of wild orchids at the gravel pits and wildlife among the hardwoods and hemlock. Turn left on SR 600 and ascend 1 mile to the *Iron Mountain Trail* at Skulls Gap. Keep left here on both road and trail for 0.7 miles to leave SR 600 and follow the *Iron Mountain Trail* on the left. Reach Straight Branch Shelter and spring at 4 miles. To the left is violet-blazed *Lum Trail*. Descend on it through rhododendron and black birch along Straight Branch for a return to the campground at 5 miles.

The second loop begins at Chipmunk Circle at the campground on the *Lum Trail*. Follow it up to Straight Branch Shelter and turn left on the *Iron Mountain Trail*. Descend easily and follow a level ridgeline before a slight descent to Shaw Gap at a clearing at 4.1 miles. En route there are views of Mount Rogers and Whitetop Mountain. At Shaw Gap, the *Shaw Gap Trail* and the *Beartree Gap Trail* descend left. To the right is unmaintained *Chestnut Ridge Trail*. (It goes 1.8 mi. to FR 615, which after 2.5 mi. reaches SR 730.) The *Iron Mountain Trail* stays on the ridgeline. For the second loop, turn left on the *Shaw Gap Trail*, which immediately forks left of raspberry-blazed *Beartree Gap Trail*.

If choosing the *Beartree Gap Trail*, descend gradually to switchbacks, pass through a gap, pass right of a small lake, and cross a stream after 1.9 miles. Descend alongside the stream to cross campground entrance road after another 0.7 miles. Intersect with the *Beartree Lake Trail* near the dam. (The *Beartree Lake Trail* circles the lake for 1 mi.) Turn right at the dam, cross US 58 and intersect with the *AT* after 0.2 miles for a total of 7.2 miles since leaving the campground. (To the right on the *AT* it is 8.2 mi. to the junction with the *Iron Mountain Trail*. To the left on the *AT* it is 31.3 mi. to the northern junction with the *Iron Mountain Trail*.) Backtrack to the lake, take either side upstream, pass through the picnic areas, and arrive at the group campground off FR 837 at 8.8 miles. Go to the end of group tent camping for the trailhead of the *Shaw Gap Trail*. Follow the dark blue-blazed trail upstream through rhododendron and on a mossy treadway to Shaw Gap at 9.8 miles. Turn right on the *Iron Mountain Trail* and backtrack to Straight Branch Shelter for a return on the *Lum Trail*, a distance of 13.9 miles.

For the third and longest loop, continue on the *Iron Mountain Trail* from Shaw Gap. Reach a grassy summit with panoramic views at 4.7 miles. At 5.9 miles reach a junction with FR 90. (On the left FR 90 descends 1.3 mi. to US 58, and on the right it ascends 1.4 mi. to former Feathercamp Mountain fire tower. The *Rush Trail* is also right for 1.5 mi. off FR 90.) At 6.1 miles the circuit reaches a spring and Sandy Flats Shelter. From here cross Feathercamp Branch and intersect with blue-blazed *Feathercamp Branch Trail* on the left. (It descends 2 mi. to US 58.) Skirt southern slope of former Feathercamp Mountain fire tower. (The *Feathercamp Ridge Trail* ascends right for 0.2 mi. to FR 90 and fire tower site with scenic views. Also from the *Iron Mountain Trail* at this point the *Wright Hollow Trail* is on the right. (It is 2.7 mi. to Sawmill Road and Creasy Hollow.) Continue ahead on the *Iron Mountain Trail* and descend gradually to cross the *Beech Grove Trail* at 9.4 miles. (The *Beech Grove Trail*, for motorcycles, goes right for 2.4 mi. to SR 605 and 1 mi. left to US 58.) Ascending, the *Iron Mountain Trail* continues ahead to 10.6 miles and a junction with the *AT*. (To the right the *AT* goes 3.5 mi. to downtown Damascus.) Turn left on the graded *AT* and descend. At 12.1 miles cross the *Beech Grove Trail,* and at 12.6 miles intersect with blue-blazed *Feathercamp Branch Trail* on the left. (The *AT* continues ahead to cross US 58 after 0.1 mi. and reach the *Beartree Gap Trail* after another 6.1 mi.) Turn left on the *Feathercamp Branch Trail* and follow upstream through rhododendron, hemlock, and maple. At 13.1 miles cross old logging road, and at 14.5 miles intersect with the *Iron Mountain Trail.* Turn right and return to the campground on the *Iron Mountain Trail* and the *Lum Trail* for a total of 20.8 miles.

USGS maps: Damascus, Konnarock, Whitetop Mountain; *USFS trail nos.*: 168, 4544, 301–6, 4545, 4551, 4563, 1, 169

LEWIS FORK WILDERNESS AREA
Smyth and Grayson Counties

Mount Rogers Trail (4 mi.), **AT** (2.9 mi.), **Pine Mountain Trail** (2 mi.), **Cliffside Trail** (1.4 mi.), **Lewis Fork Trail** (5 mi.)   78–86

Length and Difficulty: 12.3 miles (19.7 km) combined, circuit; strenuous
Connecting Trails: Flattop Trail (1 mi.), *Mountain Rogers Spur Trail* (0.5 mi.)
Features: wilderness, scenic views, Mount Rogers summit, wildflowers, wildlife
Trailhead: Mount Rogers trailhead parking area is 0.4 miles east of Grindstone Campground on SR 603, 5.9 miles west of Troutdale, and VA 16, or on a 0.3-mile spur trail in the campground.
Introduction: The 5,730-acre Lewis Fork Wilderness is between the Grindstone Campground on SR 603 (part of Mount Rogers Scenic Byway) in the north and Grayson Highlands State Park in the southeast. It rises 2,450 feet in elevation from near Big Laurel Creek to the summit of Mount Rogers (5,729 ft.), the state's highest point. The wilderness extends west to SR 600 near Elk Garden and east to Pine Mountain. In the northeast it is near Fox Creek parking area. A forest within a forest, its diversity of plant and animal life is part of its allure. Other appeals are its wild hollows with tucked away bubbling streams, open, high, flowery meadows, dense spruce and fir stands, and awesome views of the area's vastness. In the highest areas of the wilderness it is uncommonly wet— fog, mist, and rain in summer and snow, sleet, ice, and rime in winter—an overture to hypothermia and disorientation.

There are two base camps with developed facilities. Grindstone Campground has warm showers, flush toilets, and excellent campsites for trailers and tents. At the campground's southwestern corner is an interpretive 0.5-mile trail, the *Whispering Water Trail.* The campground is usually open from May to November. The other base camp is Grayson Highlands State Park, with similar facilities. It is open from Memorial Day to late October. Trailwise it is about 4 miles southeast of the wilderness edge but is accessible on the *AT.* In addition to this loop, there are connector trails that make ideal short or long loops with or without the *AT*. Also, from the parking area for the *Mount Rogers Trail* is the *Flattop Trail*, an access route to the trails of Iron Mountain.

Description: Blue-blazed *Mount Rogers Trail*, a national recreation trail since 1979, has high traffic volume. Begin either at the Mount Rogers trailhead parking area on SR 603 or from a 0.3-mile blue-blazed spur trail in Grindstone Campground. Ascend on switchbacks for 1.1 miles and reach the top of Broad Ridge, where the trail is flat and straight. At 2.3 miles intersect with dark blue-blazed *Lewis Fork Trail* on the left. (It descends 5 mi. to cross Lewis Fork and end at SR 603. Along the way it intersects with raspberry-blazed *Cliffside Trail* and other connecting trails east to both the *Virginia Highlands Horse Trail* and the *AT*.) Continue the ascent, pass a large outcrop, and enter a red spruce and yellow birch stand at 3.3 miles. Meet with white-blazed *AT* at 4 miles. (To the right the *AT* descends 2.1 mi. to a parking lot at SR 600, Elk Garden gap.) Turn left on the *AT*, follow an easy grade to an open meadow with views at 4.9 miles. Begin a slight ascent into stands of Fraser fir to the *Mount Rogers Spur Trail* at 5.7 miles. (The spur trail goes left 0.5 mi. one way, in dense and dark fir and spruce to the summit of aromatic Mount Rogers.) Continue on the *AT*, leave the wilderness at 6 miles, and pass Thomas Knob Shelter. Arrive at Rhododendron Gap with views to the left from the cliffs at 6.9 miles. (Here the *AT* turns right and parallels the *Wilburn Ridge Trail* for outstanding views into North Carolina and Tennessee. Rhododendron patches provide a colorful garden in June. After 1.4 mi. the *AT* enters Grayson Highlands State Park, where there are more banks of rhododendron, grassy plateaus with lichen-covered boulders, and grazing ponies in alpine meadows. From here the *AT* continues into Little Wilson Creek Wilderness, crosses Pine Mountain [East], and descends to SR 603, after 10.5 mi. from the state park.)

For a continuation of the circuit, go straight ahead at Rhododendron Gap on blue-blazed *Pine Mountain Trail* (the former *AT*), which is above 5,000 feet in elevation. After 1.1 miles turn left and begin a steep descent on the *Cliffside Trail*. (The *Pine Mountain Trail* continues another 1 mi. to intersect with the *AT*.) After 0.7 miles on the *Cliffside Trail*, meet the *Lewis Fork Trail* at 8.7 miles and turn left. (To the right the trail is 3.7 mi. to an intersection with the *Old Orchard Trail* and the *AT* before turning west and descending to follow Lewis Fork out to SR 603.) Ascend slightly to cross Lewis Fork in a cool hollow with tall trees. Return to the *Mount Rogers Trail* at 10 miles. Turn right and descend to the point of origin.

USGS map: Whitetop Mountain; *USFS trail nos.*: 166, 1, 4595, 4533.2, 4533

Sugar Maple Trail (2.3 mi.), **Helton Creek Trail** (3.5 mi.),
87–90   **Helton Creek Spur Trail** (1.2 mi.), **Virginia Highlands Horse Trail** (0.8 mi.)

Length and Difficulty: 4.7 miles or 6.5 miles (7.5 km or 10.4 km) combined, circuit; moderate

Features: wilderness, wildlife, wildflowers, stream, historic site

Trailhead: From US 58 (6 mi. west of Grayson Highlands State Park, and 1.5 mi. east of SR 600) turn on SR 783 and go 1.5 miles to where road becomes FR 4032 at parking lot.

Description: Park in a meadow where camping is allowed. Begin on the *Sugar Maple Trail* on the right, at first gate near old cement trough; ascend and pass sites of old houses. At 0.3 miles turn right through fields of asters and gold-enrod; pass another gate, and at 0.8 miles enter woods. Ascend on switchbacks to a contour grade. Reach junction with the *Helton Creek Trail* at 2.3 miles, the end of the *Sugar Maple Trail*. (An option here for a loop of 4.7 mi. is a left turn on the *Helton Creek Trail* for a descent to Helton Creek and a return to the parking lot.) Continue ahead on a gentle grade of an old tram road for 1.1 miles to the *Virginia Highlands Horse Trail* beyond the headwaters of Helton Creek. Turn left on the horse trail and after 0.8 miles arrive at a field where the *Helton Creek Spur Trail* turns left. (The *Virginia Highlands Horse Trail* continues ahead 0.5 mi. to its western trailhead at SR 600 at the gap of Elk Garden.) Descend on the spur trail, an old logging road, cross Helton Creek, and intersect with the *Helton Creek Trail*. Turn right and parallel the creek to the point of origin for a loop of 6.5 miles.

USGS map: Whitetop Mountain; *USFS trail nos.*: 4572, 4538, 4538A

LITTLE WILSON CREEK WILDERNESS AREA
Grayson County

Wilson Creek Trail (1.8 mi.), **Wilson Creek Horse Trail** (4.8 mi.), **Scales Trail** (2.7 mi.), **First Peak Trail** (4 mi.), **Kabel Trail** (2.1 mi.), **Big Wilson Creek Trail** (1.7 mi.)

91–102

Length and Difficulty: 11.5 miles (18.4 km) circuit; moderate to strenuous

Connecting Trails: *Bearpen Trail* (3 mi.), *Virginia Highlands Horse Trail* (junction), *AT* (junction), *Crest Trail* (3.9 mi.), *Third Peak Trail* (1.6 mi.), *Shapiro Trail* (1.5 mi.), *Hightree Rock Trail* (4.9 mi.), *Little Wilson Creek Trail* (1.7 mi.)

Features: cascades, balds, wildflowers, wilderness

Trailhead: The circuit begins in the Grayson Highlands State Park, the closest access to the wilderness, at the campground. Access is off US 58 at the park sign 7.7 miles west from Volney and VA 16 junction. (A rough and primitive route for 4WDS is on FR 613, off SR 603, 2.6 mi. west from VA 16 in Troutdale. The road is closed in winter, has turnaround problems, and is 4 mi. from SR 603 to gate or summit of Pine Mountain.)

Introduction: High on the open balds of Pine Mountain and down the slopes to cascading Big Wilson and Little Wilson Creeks is the 3,855-acre Little Wilson Creek Wilderness. It is adjacent to Grayson Highlands State Park on the west, where Big Wilson Creek is the boundary, and extends east to the mountain-side of Hightree Rock. From the wilderness headwaters are two Little Wilson Creeks, one on each side of First Peak. Both streams drain separately to Big Wilson, whose mouth is at the New River by US 58. Big Wilson is a native trout stream. Stands of red spruce and Fraser fir grow in the higher elevations, and the heath balds have hawthorne, white yarrow, and loosestrife. Old trails and roads and new trails provide loops within loops and make enough connections to go anywhere in the recreation area. The Grayson Highlands Campground is the ideal location for a base camp. It has all facilities, including hot showers. (See Grayson Highlands State Park, Chapter 11.)

Description: On entrance to the campground's grassy field, look for the *Wilson Creek Trail* sign on the left. The trail descends to Big Wilson Creek, where there are waterfalls and cascades in dense rhododendron at 1 mile. At 1.2 miles the trail returns to a primitive road, which also serves as the *Wilson Creek Horse Trail*. After a right turn, cross Quebec Branch, pass a meadow, and reach the park boundary at 1.8 miles. The old road now becomes the *Scales Trail*. Continue and after 0.1 mile cross the *AT* where a bridge is over Big Wilson Creek. (To the right the *AT* makes a crescent and returns to the old road at the crest of Pine Mountain after 2.5 mi.) At 2.7 miles there is a junction on the right with the *Bearpen Trail*. (On an easy contour, it goes 3.2 mi., mostly through the wilderness, crosses the *AT*, intersects with the *Big Wilson Creek Trail*, and ends at a junction with the *First Peak Trail*.) Continue ascent to The Scales, a wide saddle whose name comes from a former weighing and loading dock for summer-grazing cattle. Today there is a corral, mainly for horses. Here is also an intersection where the *AT*, the *Virginia Highlands Horse Trail*, and the *Scales Trail* cross one another. Approaching from the west is the *Crest Trail*, which ends here; the *First Peak Trail* ends here from the east.

Continuing the circuit, take the *First Peak Trail*, ascend a bald slope with blueberries, gooseberries, ferns, and wildflowers, and observe the Big Wilson Creek Valley. Scattered hardwoods are sugar maple and beech. At 4 miles is a junction on the left with the *Third Peak Trail*. (It descends 1.6 mi. to rough FR 613.) After 0.4 miles farther, reach the flat summit of Third Peak (4,920 ft.). Enter Little Wilson Creek Wilderness at 4.7 miles, ascend gently to Second Peak (4,857 ft.) at 5 miles. Descend to a junction with the *Shapiro Trail* on the left, and the *Bearpen Trail* on the right. (The *Shapiro Trail* descends steeply 1.5 mi. to a forest road and follows it 1 mi. to a gate and exit at SR 739 [Rocky Hollow Rd.]. Turn left for 1 mi. to SR 603, where a right turn on SR 603 is 1.2 mi. to Troutdale and VA 16.) (The *Bearpen Trail* goes west to end at the *Scales Trail*. It can be used as a return to the campground for a total of 11 mi.)

Pass over forested First Peak (about 4,600 ft.) and descend on rocky treadway to a junction on the left (east) with the *Hightree Rock Trail* (also called the *Mill Creek Trail*). (It is partially relocated, has switchbacks, crosses the headwaters of the other Little Wilson Creek, and skirts the cliffs of Hightree Rock. It descends to a hollow, crosses Mill Creek, and enters Rocky Hollow for its eastern trailhead on SR 739. It is 2.4 mi. left [north] on SR 739 to SR 603, where a right is 1.2 mi. from Troutdale and VA 16.)

On the circuit, turn right on the *Kabel Trail* to follow an old railroad grade. After curving north from Bearpen Ridge, cross a small stream that flows into Little Wilson Creek. At 8 miles the trail leaves the old railroad grade for a steep and rocky route. At 8.4 miles the *Kabel Trail* ends at a junction with the *Big*

Wilson Creek Trail. (It goes right 0.7 mi. to intersect with the *Bearpen Trail,* and ahead to Big Wilson Creek.) Descend ahead on a rough passage, partially eroded, to the wilderness boundary at 9.2 miles and Big Wilson Creek at 9.5 miles. Rock-hop or wade the creek and arrive at a primitive road, usable for horses and 4WDs in the Grayson Highlands State Park. (Downstream the road is gated at SR 817, which leads to SR 806 out to US 58.) Turn right and ascend steeply on switchbacks; at 10.7 miles is a large cascade, the site of a former footbridge over the creek. The road turns left and reaches the junction with the state park's *Wilson Creek Trail* at 11.3 miles. If ascending left here, it is 0.2 miles to the campground; if continuing to the horse trail on the left, it is 0.9 miles to the campground.

USGS map: Troutdale; *USFS trail nos.:* (first two trails in state park; no USFS trail numbers), 4523, 4524, 4606, 4607

IRON MOUNTAIN AREA (CENTRAL)
Smyth and Grayson Counties

Dickey Gap Trail (0.4 mi.), **AT** (5.9 mi.), **Hurricane Creek Trail** (0.5 mi.), **Iron Mountain Trail** (4.4 mi.), **Comers Creek Fall Trail** (0.3 mi.), **Comers Creek Trail** (0.7 mi.), **Virginia Highlands Horse Trail** (3.8 mi.)   103–7

Length and Difficulty: 11.8 miles (18.9 km) combined, circuit; moderate

Features: fishing, waterfall, wildflowers, scenic views

Trailhead: Access to Hurricane Campground is from VA 16, 2.3 miles north of Troutdale, to SR 650. On SR 650 go 1.5 miles to FR 84, turn left, and go 0.3 miles to campground entrance.

Introduction: Exciting circuit hikes are possible in the central area of Iron Mountain by using only trails, trails and forest roads, or only forest roads. These combinations are listed as having low traffic volume by the USFS. Described below are circuit options for 5.6 miles, 5.7 miles, 11.8 miles, 5.9 miles, and 8.3 miles. A good base camp for these hikes is Hurricane Campground. (For the Raccoon Branch trails, Raccoon Campground is a good base camp.) The Hurricane Campground has trailer and tent campsites, warm showers, flush toilets, and waste disposal. Attractions include trout fishing in Hurricane and Comers Creeks, and nature study. The *Hurricane Knob Nature Trail* is a scenic 1-mile loop within the campground. Access to the trail is across the road from the bulletin board at the left side of the rest rooms or by a large white pine tree near site #5. The fee campground is open from mid-March to mid-September.

Description: From the campground entrance, at junction of FR 84 bridge (confluence of Comers and Hurricane Creeks), take the blue-blazed *Dickey Gap Trail* through hemlock, birch, maple, and rhododendron for 0.4 miles to junction with the *AT.* Turn right, follow the *AT,* and at 2.1 miles cross a stream. At 2.9 miles meet an old logging road on the right and left. (To the right the *Hurricane Creek Trail* descends 0.5 mi. to intersect with FR 84 [Hurricane Creek Rd.], where a right turn leads 2.2 mi. downstream by picturesque Hurricane Creek to the campground for a loop of 5.6 mi.) Continue on the *AT,* ascend on switchbacks near a stream, and reach Chestnut Flats at 4.4 miles. Here is a junction with yellow-blazed *Iron Mountain Trail*, left and right.

(The *AT* follows left on the *Iron Mountain Trail* for a few yards, then turns right to ascend and descend Iron Mountain 2.3 mi. to Fox Creek trailhead parking area at SR 630. It is 3.9 mi. east on SR 603 to Troutdale and a store on VA 16.) (To the left on the *Iron Mountain Trail* follow a ridgeline with a steep mountain drop on the northern side for 2.4 mi. Begin a descent to reach Comers Creek at 2.8 mi., and intersect with the *Comers Creek Fall Trail* on the left. [The *Iron Mountain Trail* goes another 0.5 mi. to its eastern terminus at VA 16, near FR 741, and 1.8 mi. north of Troutdale.] Follow the *Comers Creek Fall Trail* 0.3 mi. to the fall and a junction with the *AT*. From here complete the circuit of 5.7 mi. by following the *Comers Creek Trail* 0.7 mi. to the campground.)

Continue right on the *Iron Mountain Trail* for the longest circuit, and arrive at the crest of Flat Top Mountain (4,451 ft.) at 5.4 miles from the campground. Descend to a dirt road, turn right, and after 0.1 mile turn left into the forest. At 6 miles reach a junction with primitive FR 828, Flat Top Gap. (Ahead is Cherry Tree Shelter and spring on the *Iron Mountain Trail* after 0.3 mi.) (To the left FR 828 descends for 3.2 mi. to SR 603 near Grindstone Campground. Along the way is 1-mi. *Flat Top Trail*, which descends to Mount Rogers trailhead parking area at SR 603.) Leave the *Iron Mountain Trail* at the junction with FR 828, turn right, and follow the *Virginia Highlands Horse Trail*. After 1.8 miles reach Hurricane Gap and intersection with FR 84. Turn right on FR 84 and for 4 miles follow alongside Hurricane Creek to the campground for a total of 11.8 miles.

Another moderate, shorter loop follows the *Dickey Gap Trail* as described above to the *AT*. But take the left this time, and pass Comers Creek fall and cascades at 1.3 miles. Enter a thicket of rhododendron and then a stand of open hardwoods. Reach SR 650/VA 16 junction at 2.5 miles. Cross SR 650 and after 0.8 miles on the *AT* reach a junction with the *Virginia Highlands Horse Trail*. Turn left and follow the horse trail for 2 miles to SR 650. Turn left on SR 650 for 0.1 mile to FR 84. Turn right and go 0.3 miles to entrance of the campground for a total of 5.7 miles. For a scenic forest roadway circuit that is particularly beautiful with autumn leaf colors, begin downstream of Comers Creek on an unmarked route. Tall trees, mosses, ferns, and wildflowers make this an excellent nature study walk. At the junction with FR 643, after 0.7 miles, turn left on the road away from the creek. Follow the gravel road around Bear Ridge for 2.3 miles to Barton Branch. Go upstream for 1 mile to a junction with FR 870. Turn left on FR 870, go 1.8 miles between Seng Mountain and Bear Ridge to FR 84. Turn left again, and after 2 miles return to the campground for a total of 8.3 miles.

USGS maps: Troutdale, Whitetop Mountain; *USFS trail nos.*: 4518, 1, 4530, 301, 4576, 4526, 337

Dickey Knob Trail (2 mi.), **Raccoon Branch Trail** (3.3 mi.), **AT** (about 1.3 mi.), **Mullins Branch Trail** (2.5 mi.)

108–10

Length and Difficulty: 10.6 miles or 18.2 miles (17.0 km or 29.1 km) combined, round-trip; moderate to strenuous

Features: fishing, spring, wildlife, solitude, orienteering

Trailhead: The trailhead is in Raccoon Branch Campground on VA 16, 2.3 miles south of Sugar Grove (and 11 mi. south of I-81, exit 45).

Introduction: This combination of trails provide fewer options for short loops in comparison with Hurricane Campground. The longer routes are also more isolated, though the campground is near a busy highway. Raccoon Branch Campground has trailer and tent sites, flush toilets (no showers), and waste disposal station. Interesting attractions include trout fishing at Dickey Creek and Raccoon Branch and backcountry exploring. The fee campground is open year round.

Description: At Raccoon Branch Campground, the *Dickey Knob Trail* and the *Raccoon Branch Trail* begin near campsite #4 and cross a wooden footbridge at the confluence of Dickey Creek and Raccoon Branch. Turn right to hike the 4-mile round-trip *Dickey Knob Trail*. Back at the confluence again, this time take the left, proceeding upstream on the *Raccoon Branch Trail* to AT spring and shelter, and up to the AT at 3.3 miles. Backtrack, or consider exploring the *Mullins Branch Trail* (a former part of the AT) for an experience in orienteering. (A topographical map, Atkins, is recommended.) Turn right on the AT, and after 0.5 miles there is a blue-blazed spur left to High Point (4,040 ft.), for partial views of Mount Rogers to the southwest. Continue on the AT curve left and descend, and after about 0.8 miles from High Point look for the *Mullins Branch Trail* on the right. The trail is unmaintained and unmarked by the USFS. Leave the AT and descend to locate Mullins Branch, where there should be an old wagon road. Follow it through tall hardwoods, hemlocks, and rhododendrons and crisscross the branch. At 2.5 miles reach the boundary of the forest and the edge of a farm, which leads to SR 673 and SR 672. Backtrack to the AT and on the *Raccoon Branch Trail*.

USGS maps: Troutdale, Atkins; *USFS trail nos.*: 346, 4610, 1, 4513

IRON MOUNTAIN AREA (NORTHEAST)
Smyth, Grayson, Wythe, and Carroll Counties

Iron Mountain Trail (2.5 mi.), **Hale Lake Trail** (0.6 mi.),
Unaka Nature Trail (1 mi.)   111–17

Length and Difficulty: 6.6 miles (10.6 km) combined, round-trip; moderate

Features: scenic views, fishing, solitude, wildlife, endangered species

Trailhead: On US 21, 17 miles south of US 11 in Wytheville (5 mi. south of Speedwell included) turn right on FR 57 and follow it for 3.5 miles to Comers Rock Recreation Area.

Introduction: This area is more remote and less used than other sections of the national recreation area. The potential for solitude is high. There are two lengthy trails that carry over from the southern sections; 40 of 66.3 miles of the *Virginia Highlands Horse Trail*, and 26.5 of 50.6 miles of the *Iron Mountain Trail*. Some portions of the *Iron Mountain Trail* are unmarked, overgrown, and unmaintained, and other sections are on private land. The equestrian trail is more up to standard. A few of the short side trails and singular trails are maintained. Examples are the *Henley Hollow Trail*, the *Little Dry Run Trail*, the *Divide Trail*, and the *Hale Lake Trail*. In this area is an endangered tree species, the round-leaf birch (*Betula uber*), found nowhere else in the world. It is protected by both state and federal laws. In a primitive environment the campgrounds are generally primitive. Comers Rock has nine campsites, vault toilets, and a hand water pump. Camping is on a breezy, dry ridge with an observation stand. Nearby is Hale Lake for trout fishing. Another campground is Raven Cliff on Cripple Creek. It has 20 campsites, picnic shelters for groups, and flush toilets. Cripple Creek is noted for its smallmouth bass and red-eye fishing. The remains of Raven Cliff Iron Furnace are accessible from the campground. To reach it from Comers Rock Campground, go 5 miles north on US 21 to Speedwell, where a right turn (northeast) on SR 619 is 6 miles from a sign on the right. Both campgrounds are nonfee for campers and are open year round.

Description: Begin at campsite #7 and go 100 yards to an *Iron Mountain Trail* sign. Turn left on the Comers Rock Overlook spur trail. (The trail on the right descends a slope to the West Fork of Dry Run and a junction with the *Virginia Highlands Horse Trail* at 1.2 mi.) After 0.5 miles, reach the panoramic views of Iron Mountain Range, Point Lookout Mountain, and Comers Rock Valley. Thick understories of striped maple and witch hazel are on the trail. Backtrack to the trail junction near the campsite and take a left turn on the *Iron Mountain Trail*. Hike through oak, white pine, hemlock, and rhododendron for 2.2 miles. Cross FR 57-B and descend to Hale Lake at 2.5 miles. Circle the lake on the *Hale Lake Trail* for 0.6 miles through pine, black gum, and tall sweet pepperbush. Backtrack for a total of 5.6 miles. The 1-mile *Unaka Nature Trail* begins right facing the picnic shelter in the campground and forms a loop through an outstanding range of botanical species.

A circuit could be made by taking the right fork at the campground and proceeding 1.2 miles to the *Virginia Highlands Horse Trail*. Then proceed right on an old wagon road for 3 miles to US 21. If not using another car for support, hike 1.2 miles right on US 21 to FR 57, and right on FR 57 back to camp for 9 miles. For a longer circuit and less road walking, follow the above, except at the junction with the *Virginia Highlands Horse Trail* at the West Fork of Dry Run take the *Little Dry Run Trail* for 3 miles to US 21. Cross the highway and enter *Henley Hollow Trail*. Ascend for 1.6 miles to the *Horse Heaven Trail*. Take a left, go 2 miles, turn right on FR 4009, hike 1.3 miles to a gate, cross FR 14, and take the *Divide Trail* for 0.8 miles to a junction with the *Iron Mountain Trail*. Take a right, and after 3 miles, exit at Dry Run Gap on US 21 across the road from FR 57. If a second car is waiting here, the hike would be 12.7 miles. Otherwise hike FR 57 back to camp.

USGS maps: Speedwell, Cedar Springs; *USFS trail nos.*: 301-2 (Iron Mountain), 337, 342, 4571, 305, 306, 307, 309, 301-1 (Iron Mountain)

New Castle Ranger District

The New Castle Ranger District is northwest of the city of Roanoke. It is bordered on the southwest by the Blacksburg Ranger District in the JNF, and on the north by the James River Ranger District in the GWNF. The western boundary is the state line of West Virginia, except a section of West Virginia between Peters and Potts mountain ranges in Monroe County. The mountain ranges are, as with the Wythe and Blacksburg districts, formed in a southwest to northeast direction. Johns Creek, the central drainage, flows northeast into Craig Creek, whose confluence is at the James River at Eagle Point. Sections of developed or maintained areas for trails and other recreational activities are Peters Mountain, Potts Mountain, North Mountain, Patterson and Price Mountains, Fenwick Mines, and Roaring Run.

The district has 140,000 acres in which are two wilderness areas. Both are north of New Castle, border the GWNF, and are rugged and remote. In Shawvers Run Wilderness Area (3,665 acres) the highest peak is Hanging Rock (3,800 ft.), a unique geological formation with panoramic views. There are no trails in this wilderness, but accessibility is on FR 177-1, on Potts Mountain off VA 311, 5.5 miles south of Paint Bank. In the center of Barbours Creek Wilderness Area (5,700 acres) is the *Lipes Branch Horse Trail* (2.3 mi.). It ascends to the eastern Potts Mountain ridgeline from The Pines, a compound with a corral on SR 617, 12 miles northeast from New Castle. *Cove Branch Trail* (1.7 mi.) connects the two wilderness areas from FR 275 in an ascent to FR 177-1, 1.8 miles north of Hanging Rock. This wilderness, as with Shawvers, has an abundance of wildlife.

118–19

There are three recreational areas for camping: Craig Creek, at Oriskany (11 mi. northeast of New Castle to SR 817); The Pines (12 mi. north of New Castle on SR 617); and Steel Bridge (3.5 mi. northeast of Paint Bank on SR 18). The campgrounds, open all year, have vault toilets, picnic tables, hand pumps for water (except Craig Creek), and streams for fishing.

There is a multiple-use trail system with diverse treadways. On USFS property is 6.8 miles of the *AT* from SR 620 at the Blacksburg Ranger District boundary to SR 624 off VA 11. Other trail mileage includes 84.4 miles of foot trails, all yellow-blazed except the *Dragon's Tooth Trail*, which is blue-blazed. The 8.3 miles of the *Allegheny Trail* also have a yellow-gold blaze. There are three horse trails (a total of 12 mi.), all east of New Castle off SR 606 on FRS 5012, 5061, and 267 on Caldwell and Switzer Mountains, with the exception of the *Lipes Branch Horse Trail* (2.3 mi.) at The Pines on SR 617. Old roads on Potts Mountain provide an excellent mountain bike trail. Each year the USFS has a cooperative program with biking organizations to have the 23-mile Great Craig County Escape Race on Potts Mountain. Only one motorcycle trail is listed by the district; it is the *Potts Arm Trail* (3.5 mi.) between FR 177-1 and FR 176, near the *Cove Branch Trail*. A few trails have been abandoned by the USFS and are no longer on the TIS. Examples are the *Tub Run Trail* and the *Caldwell Road Trail*, off VA 311 on FR 257, west of New Castle. During the 1990s the district is providing a model project in phases to serve people with disabilities. It is the Fenwick Mines Recreational Complex with specialized trails. If a short connector could be constructed between the *Price Mountain Horse Trail* on FR 5012 on Caldwell Mountain southwest to the *Lick Branch Trail* at Fr 183, there would be a linear foot trail of 35 miles from the western trailhead of Patterson Mountain to the *AT* near Dragon's Tooth. Another equestrian trail is the 2.8-mile *Lee's Creek Trail* from a parking lot on FR 183 (1 mi. north from SR 600) northwest to FR 5061, off SR 666.

120–23

Address and Information: New Castle Ranger District, P.O. Box 246, New Castle, VA 24127; phone: 703-864-5195; on SR 615, 1.5 miles east of New Castle. Available are district map with trails, camping flyers, wilderness area brochures with maps.

PETERS MOUNTAIN AREA
Monroe County, West Virginia

11 **Allegheny Trail**
Length and Difficulty: 8.3 miles (13.3 km); easy to moderate
Features: wildlife, wide grassy trail
Trailheads: To reach the southwestern trailhead from Waiteville, travel 0.8 miles northeast on CO 17 to CO 15 (Gap Mills Rd.) for 3.5 miles to the parking area on top of Peters Mountain. (Access here is also on CO 15, 5.4 mi. southwest from the village of Mills Gap at WV 3.) The northeastern trailhead is in the community of Laurel Branch; go 5.1 miles northeast to CO 20 (Crowder Rd.) on CO 17 from the junction of CO 15, and 5.5 miles southwest on SR 600 (which becomes CO 17 at the state line) from Paint Bank in Virginia.
Introduction: The *Allegheny Trail* is a 300-mile hiking trail from its junction with the *AT* in the Blacksburg Ranger District to the West Virginia/Pennsylvania state line, near Bruceton Mills. It is administered by the West Virginia Scenic Trails Association. Divided into four sections, this part is in section IV (from the *AT* to Meadow Creek on Lake Sherwood Rd. near Neola, W.Va.), with nearly 30 miles finished and another 25 miles planned or under construction. The area to be completed extends from Laurel Branch north to Jerry's Run junction with I-64 in the GWNF. The part north of there, 15 miles, is now open for an ascent to the state line and a descent to follow Laurel Run in the Monongahela National Forest. (See *Allegheny Trail* in the Blacksburg Ranger District in this chapter, in the James River District in Chapter 2, and in the index.)
Description: From the parking area on Gap Mills Road, CO 15, the trail passes a gate and descends south to parallel the road for 0.2 miles. It makes a sharp left onto a grassy forest fire road, FR 5057. On a gentle contour the trail descends from about 3,330 feet to 2,870 feet in more than 5 miles. At 2.3 miles the trail passes an open area near the crest of Peters Mountain. Although there are not any outcrops for views, this trail is most beautiful during mid-October, when leaf colors are at their peak. After curving around a few spur ridges and crossing tributaries that flow to Potts Creek, the trail reaches the end of FR 5057 at

5.6 miles. Here is a junction with abandoned Crowder Road, CO 20 (a former access road between Laurel Branch and Gap Mills). The trail turns right on Crowder Road and after 2.7 miles reaches a parking area near a gravel quarry, 0.2 miles before the road intersects with CO 17.

USGS Map: Ronceverte; *USFS trail no.*: 701

NORTH MOUNTAIN AND LICK BRANCH AREA
Botetourt, Craig, and Roanoke Counties

North Mountain Trail (South)   124–30

Length and Difficulty: 13.5 miles (21.6 km); moderate to strenuous

Connecting Trails: Dragon's Tooth Trail (1.2 mi.), Deer Trail (1.6 mi.), Grouse Trail (1.5 mi.), Turkey Trail (1.7 mi.), Catawba Creek Trail (AT connector) (3.7 mi.), Lick Branch Trail (4.4 mi.), which connects with Ferrier Trail (2.3 mi.)

Features: wildlife, solitude, wildflowers

Trailheads: The southwestern trailhead is 2.5 miles west of Catawba on the northern side of VA 311, halfway between the SR 624 junction and the *Dragon's Tooth Trail* parking area (and 0.1 mi. west of Catawba Grocery Store). To reach the northeastern trailhead, go 6.3 miles farther north on VA 311 to the junction with SR 618 at Broad Run Trading Post. Turn right on SR 618, which becomes FR 183, and cross rocky Broad Run, sans bridges, 10 times (or more if during rainy season). After 7.6 miles there is roadside parking only at Stone Coal Gap near a private property road entrance sign. Another access to this point from the southeast is 2.8 miles from SR 600 (1 mi. on SR 748 and 1.8 mi. on FR 183). There may be a state road sign indicating that SR 748 is the end of the road, but it is only the end of state maintenance; FR 183 is in good condition. The SR 748 junction with SR 600 is 0.2 miles west of its junction with SR 665 (1.5 mi. south to Haymakertown), and 10.9 miles west on SR 600 and SR 799 to VA 311 at Catawba.

Introduction: During the years of litigation for secure passageway of the AT on Catawba Mountain, the *North Mountain Trail* became a significant alternate route. Never had its knobby ridge had such foot traffic or been so well maintained—that is, the southwestern 9 miles before it left the ridge to cross Catawba Valley. The other 4.5 miles northeast to Stone Coal Gap remained secluded. Consequently it lost its identity, and when hikers heard of the *North Mountain Trail*, it was the 13.2-mile AT alternate, not the 13.5 miles entirely on top of North Mountain. (The AT alternate continues to be used with the AT, now a protected route over McAfee Knob, for a backpacking loop of 28.7 mi.) For the purpose of distinction, this *North Mountain Trail* has "South" in its title because it is the most southwestern of five trails in the state by the same name. The trail is high and dry, and water sources are unreliable. It has at least 30 knobs, some around the side and some over the top, and a few outcrops. In a diverse hardwood forest there are patches of huckleberries, mountain laurel, wildflowers, and families of Carolina towhee, grouse, and turkey.

Description: From the parking area on VA 311 near the trail sign, ascend switch-backs to an outcrop for views of Sinking Creek Mountain at 1.3 miles. At 2.4 miles is the *Deer Trail*, the first of three graded side trails that descend left (north) to FR 224. (The yellow-blazed *Deer Trail* descends 1.6 mi. to a parking area on FR 224, 1.7 mi. from VA 311 and 7.1 mi. southwest from SR 618.) At 3.4 miles is a junction with the *Grouse Trail*, on the left. (It descends on a yellow-blazed trail for 1.5 mi. to FR 224, 3.5 mi. from VA 311 and 5.4 mi. southwest from SR 618.) At 6.2 miles is a junction with the *Turkey Trail*, on the left. (It descends on a yellow-blazed trail for 1.7 mi. to FR 224, 7.2 mi. from VA 311 and 1.7 mi. southwest from SR 618.) (The FR 224 entrance from VA 311 is 2.1 mi. north on VA 311 from the *North Mountain Trail* southwestern trailhead and parking area.) On the *North Mountain Trail* between the *Grouse Trail* and the *Turkey Trail*, at 5.4 miles, is the trail's highest knob (3,062 ft.). At 7.4 miles on the right is a sign pointing to an intermittent spring about 200 yards down the mountainside. Usage of the trail abruptly changes at 9 miles, where the *Catawba Creek Trail* (*AT* connector) turns right.

(The 3.7-mi. *Catawba Creek Trail* descends mainly on an old road 1.4 mi. to SR 799. [Here it is 9 mi. left to Daleville and 8.3 mi. right to Catawba.] The trail crosses the road to a parking area, enters the forest, and crosses Little Catawba Creek and Catawba Creek, 0.3 mi. apart, to enter a meadow. At 2.4 mi. the trail leaves the valley and begins its ascent in a hollow, occasionally crossing a stream. Under the northern shadow of Tinker Cliffs Overlook, the trail steeply ascends to Scorched Earth Gap and a junction with the *AT*. A turn south on the *AT* provides the 28.7-mi. loop at SR 624 [0.2 mi. right] out to VA 311, the grocery store, and the southwestern trailhead of the *North Mountain Trail*.)

Continuing on the *North Mountain Trail*, which becomes more overgrown with summer foliage, the trail passes under a power line at 9.9 miles. On the ridgeline the sound of a cement industry can be heard to the south. The faint yellow-blazed trail passes through groves of mountain laurel, patches of lily-of-the-valley (at 11.8 mi.) and continuous stands of blueberries. At 12.3 miles the trail veers left on a mossy area to begin the descent on two switchbacks to FR 183 at Stone Coal Gap. Exit is on an embankment, and there may not be any signs. This is the northeastern trailhead (2,118 ft.).

Across the road and 100 feet right, a bearing tree on the left is the eastern trailhead of the *Lick Branch Trail*. Follow it under a power line past a private property sign on the left to enter a hardwood forest. Ascend through a huckle-berry patch. At 0.7 miles reach the ridgeline of Broad Run Mountain. Turn left at a cairn on a faint trail and faint blazes. (To the right is the abandoned *Price Mountain Trail*, which followed the ridge northeast to SR 606 and the northern section of the *Price Mountain Trail*, which is open. See Patterson and Price Mountains Area, below.) The *Lick Branch Trail* curves right, away from the main ridge, at 1.1 miles to descend on a spur ridge. At 1.6 miles it curves left (southwest) to the headwaters of Lick Branch and makes a junction with the *Ferrier Trail* on the right.

(The 2.3-mi. *Ferrier Trail* ascends on a slope to the thin ridgeline of Lick Mountain and follows it 1.3 mi. to a right curve on a spur ridge, parallel to Rolands Run Branch. It soon descends left and follows a grassy road to a locked gate, the end of the trail at FR 5026. A turn left here on FR 5026 will, after 1.1 mi., connect with the western trailhead of the *Lick Branch Trail*. Otherwise, a turn right on FR 5026 leads out 2.3 mi. to New Castle at the junction of SR 615/616.)

Continuing on the *Lick Branch Trail*, descend gradually for 2.8 miles and at least 26 rock-hoppings of the stream. There are tall hardwoods and hemlocks, rhododendron, ferns, and wildflowers such as goldstar and wild geraniums. Although the gorge is narrow, there are a number of desirable flat areas for campsites. At 4.4 miles the trail ends at FR 5026 cul-de-sac, immediately after crossing the branch and passing a locked gate. It is 1.1 miles on FR 5026 to the western terminus of the *Ferrier Trail* on the right. To reach these points from New Castle by vehicle, leave the junction of SR 615 and SR 616 at First National Bank in downtown New Castle and go 1.2 miles on SR 616; turn right on SR 690, and after 0.4 miles it becomes FR 182. It is 0.5 miles farther to FR 5026, on the right.

USGS maps: Looney, Catawba, New Castle: *USFS trail nos.*: 263, 5009, 186, 188, 187, (*Catawba Creek Trail*, unnumbered), 262, 189

FENWICK MINES AREA
Craig County

Fenwick Nature Walk (1 mi.), **Fenwick Wetlands Trail** (0.8 mi.)   131–32
Length and Difficulty: 1.8 miles (2.9 km) combined, partial round-trip; easy
Features: geological formations, facilities for disabled people, history
Trailhead: From the ranger station in New Castle go northeast on SR 615 for 3 miles to SR 611 (Barbours Creek Rd.) and turn left. Go 0.2 miles and turn right on SR 685, which leads into FR 181 and continues 1.8 miles on FR 181 to parking area. (Fenwick Mines Picnic Area is 0.5 mi. ahead on the right.)
Introduction: The Fenwick Mines Recreation Complex is another example of progressive leadership in the JNF not only to provide facilities to accommodate people with disabilities, but to include the general public also. The complex has a picnic area and a horse loading ramp. Overnight camping is allowed, and a model trail/picnic area with specific tables and rest rooms for the handicapped is provided.
Description: From the parking area walk left on the *Fenwick Wetlands Trail*, cross Mill Creek on a bridge shaded by hemlock, and advance to a grassy open area. Ahead, the 5-foot-wide trail of wood and crushed limestone winds around a stocked fishing pond, past an observation desk, and through a marsh for 0.8 miles to a picnic area. Sweet pepperbush, cattails, wild phlox, and Joe-Pye-weed (*Eupatorium fistulosum*) are near the trail. (In folk legend, Joe Pye was a Native American who taught the colonists the healing use of the plant for fevers.) Sounds of frogs and songbirds are prominent in the spring and summer.

Fenwick Wetlands Trail, JNF. (Photograph by Allen de Hart)

To the right of the parking area the self-guiding *Fenwick Nature Walk* crosses Mill Creek on a bridge and follows an old railroad grade. (From 1892 to 1923 the Low Moor Iron Company moved 938,000 tons of iron on the railroad to area furnaces.) After turning on the loop to descend, return along Mill Creek with its unique rock formations with slants, steps, flumes, and cascades. The exceptionally attractive area is shaded with tall oak, cherry, birch, and hemlock.
USGS map: New Castle; *USFS trail nos.*: 5003, 5007

Patterson Mountain Trail (5.7 mi.), **Tucker Trail** (1 mi.), **Helms Trail** (1.3 mi.), **Loop Trail** (1.3 mi.), **Elmore Trail** (1.6 mi.), **Price Mountain Trail** (5.8 mi.), **Kelly Trail** (2 mi.), **Sulphur Ridge Trail** (2.8 mi.)   133–40

Length and Difficulty: 21.5 miles (34.4 km) combined; easy to strenuous

Features: wildlife, wildflowers, solitude

Trailheads: There is access to two southwestern trailheads: For the *Patterson Mountain Trail*, take SR 606, 9 miles west from US 220 in Fincastle, to SR 614; go 0.7 miles and turn left on SR 612. After 0.3 miles turn right on FR 184. For the *Price Mountain Trail* the trailhead is 7 miles west from US 220 in Fincastle on SR 606 at the top of a ridge with a parking area. From New Castle ranger station, go northeast on SR 615 for 4.1 miles and turn right on SR 606. Go 1.7 miles to SR 614 and turn left. Go 0.7 miles and turn left on SR 612; turn right after 0.3 miles on FR 184 to the *Patterson Mountain Trail*.

    The northeastern trailheads are accessed from US 220 near Eagle Rock at the James River. Turn west from US 220 on SR 615 for 0.9 miles to SR 685. Follow it 0.5 miles to the junction with SR 818, and follow SR 818 6.6 miles (on old railroad grade) to FR 5020 on the left. After 3.3 miles be alert for space on the side of the road to park in a slight cove. To the right about 30 feet into the woods, ascending, is the nonmaintained *Patterson Mountain Trail*. Immediately to the right is its end, cut off with a steep road embankment. Ahead, 0.7 miles, is a parking space on the left. To the right is a clear-cut and the *Elmore Trail*. There is not a sign by the USFS as to where FR 5020 ends and FR 184 begins, but follow the road another 6.5 miles to approach the southwestern trailhead of the *Patterson Mountain Trail*.

Introduction: There are 8 potential loops, from 5 miles to 15 miles, and as many roadside trailheads in this network of trails when sections of FR 184 are used. The two main trails are on high mountain ridges with side trails descending into Patterson Valley, where there are frequent streams and hollows. Nearly all of the trails are signless, or signs are decayed. (The district ranger's office is planning a four-year project to bring the signs and blazes and maintenance up to standard.) Current blazes are faint yellow. Trail usage in this area is rated low. However, this charming and diverse area of hardwoods, scattered conifers, mountain laurel (in bloom the last two weeks of May), serviceberry, blueberry, and delicate trailing phlox on the steep slopes has an appeal to hikers, birders, and hunters. Deer, turkeys, owls, and songbirds are prominent. The elevation range is from 1,250 to 2,200 feet.

Description: Begin at the southwestern trailhead of the *Patterson Mountain Trail* (parking space is limited to the roadside). After 1.2 miles the trail is on a more gradual grade and on the right slope of the ridge. Hardwoods dominate, but mountain laurel and white and Virginia pine offer a contrast. At 2.6 miles is a junction with the *Tucker Trail* on the right. (It leads down the ridge, steeply at first, for 1 mi. to gated FR 5015 at FR 184.) Continue ahead on the *Patterson*

Mountain Trail for another 0.9 miles across a ridge spine to the *Helms Trail*, on the right, in a shallow sag.

(The *Helms Trail* descends on a scenic steep slope with well-graded switchbacks for 0.9 mi. to a junction with the *Loop Trail*. From here it continues 0.4 mi. to FR 184 at Patterson Creek. The *Loop Trail* goes east on a faint trail marked by yellow blazes for 0.1 mi. to a logging road. It goes downstream, and at a road fork it turns left. At a wildlife clearing it turns right on an old logging road at 0.7 mi. But after 50 ft. it turns left into blueberry bushes and a faint trail. It descends into a small gorge and follows right downstream. It then turns left up another ravine, but soon turns right to follow down another gorge to a junction with the *Elmore Trail* at 1.3 mi. To the right the *Elmore Trail* goes 0.4 mi. downstream to Patterson Creek, where it would have to be forded to reach FR 184 across the trailhead for the *Price Mountain Trail*. To the left the *Elmore Trail* ascends on the eastern slope of the gorge for 0.3 mi. to a large pine tree at FR 184. [To the right on the road it is 1.1 mi. down the mountain to the *Elmore Trail* trailhead at Patterson Creek.] After 0.1 mi. up the road, left, it leaves the road at the edge of a clear-cut [parking area is to the right] into the forest for its ascent of 0.7 mi. to the *Patterson Mountain Trail*.)

Continuing on the *Patterson Mountain Trail* from the junction with the *Helms Trail*, it is 1.5 miles on the ridge of open forest to the *Elmore Trail*. There are occasional glimpses through the foliage in the summertime of the Craig Creek Valley and Richpatch Mountains on the left (north) and Price Mountain to the right (south). In a low saddle the *Elmore Trail* is down the mountain on switchbacks to FR 184 (described above). The *Patterson Mountain Trail*, abandoned, continues on the ridge before descending on a slope to end at FR 5020/184 (also described above) at 5.7 miles.

If hiking the *Price Mountain Trail* from its northeastern trailhead, begin at the Patterson Creek Road. Here is a hiking logo but no blazes or other signs. It is across the road from the *Elmore Trail*'s southern trailhead, and is 4.8 miles east of the western trailhead of the *Patterson Mountain Trail* on FR 184. (There are two streams on this road: Little Patterson Creek, which flows west after about 1.5 miles; and Patterson Creek, which flows east for the remainder of the road in the valley.) Follow the *Price Mountain Trail* into the forest on a road to a wildlife clearing, but turn right before the clearing on a mossy road. Follow the road about 250 yards, and after crossing a small gully be alert for a footpath on the left up the slope. (An old sign to beware of the bears may be here.) Ascend to the ridgeline. After 3.1 miles is the junction with the *Kelly Trail*, on the right. (This trail descends 1.6 mi. down a steep slope to Patterson Creek. Rock-hop and pass through a flat area of tall trees to the road for 100 yds. There is neither parking space nor a sign. It is 2.4 mi. west to the trailhead of the *Patterson Mountain Trail*. It is also 0.3 mi. west of the *Tucker Trail* trailhead.)

Continuing on the *Price Mountain Trail*, the ridge crest has oak, locust, birch, and blueberry. At 4.6 miles reach a junction on the right with the *Sulphur Ridge Trail*. (At first it follows an old woods road in a 1.8-mi. descent to Sulphur

Springs Branch. It then turns left, heads upstream [but may be dry in the summer], and then for 1 mi. follows another old road with banks of blueberries and scrub pine to join the trail termini with the *Price Mountain Trail* at SR 606 parking area.) From the first connection with the *Sulphur Ridge Trail,* the *Price Mountain Trail* continues another 1.2 miles before reaching SR 606, as described above.

USGS maps: Oriskany, New Castle, Catawba; *USFS trail nos.*: 148, 191, 181, 153, 151, 334, 182, 149

ROARING RUN AND STONY RUN AREA
Botetourt County

Roaring Run Falls Trail (1.5 mi.), **Iron Ore Trail** (2.4 mi.),
Hoop Hole Trail (9 mi.)   141–43

Length and Difficulty: 12.9 miles (20.6 km) combined, partial round-trip; easy to strenuous

Features: waterfall, iron furnace ruins, wildlife, solitude

Trailheads: From the junction of US 220 and SR 615 at Eagle Rock by the James River, take SR 615 northwest along Craig Creek for 6 miles to SR 621. Proceed right on SR 621 for 0.9 miles to Roaring Run Furnace Recreation Area on the left, and 0.3 miles farther to a parking area for northeastern trailheads. From Low Moor at I-64/US 60/220 (between Covington and Clifton Forge), go south 5.8 miles on SR 616 and 3.3 miles on SR 621 to the parking area. For the southern trailhead, go 3.7 miles southwest from the Roaring Run parking area to Stony Run parking area on SR 621 and SR 615.

Description: All these trails are listed as national recreation trails. The *Roaring Run Falls Trail* makes a loop upstream with bridge crossings from the picnic area to cascades and an umbrella waterfall. There is a heavy canopy of hardwoods and hemlock, and the stream is stocked with trout. Across the creek from the picnic area are ruins of an iron furnace. Camping is not allowed on this trail.

The yellow-blazed *Iron Ore Trail* ascends from the *Roaring Run Falls Trail* southwest on an old wagon road. It passes between Iron Ore Knob and Shoemaker Knob. After passing under a power line at 0.4 miles it turns left at 0.8 miles at an old road junction. It crosses beneath a power line again at 0.9 miles in an area of young hardwoods and pines. Fragrant trailing arbutus (*Epigaea repens*) and white-pink mountain laurel border the old roadbed. At 1.4 miles it reaches a ridge crest to enter a stand of large oaks. It ascends to another ridge at 1.8 miles and bears sharply left. (There are good campsites here.) The trail ascends steeply in a rocky section to a summit where a forest fire has destroyed most of the mature trees. At 2.2 miles a descent begins, and a junction with the *Hoop Hole Trail* is reached at 2.4 miles. Backtrack or take the *Hoop Hole Trail* loop right or left to join a shorter loop at the southern end, where it ends at SR 615.

If hiking left, follow a steep and brushy slope for 0.7 miles to a spring. At 1.6 miles are tall trees with sparse understory. Cross a headwater stream of Crawford Branch and Stony Run before reaching a junction with the double loop at 2.2 miles. To the left the trail crosses the stream near excellent campsites. It then continues downstream along Stony Run by a treacherous ravine and towering hemlocks. After crossing the stream again, it reaches a display sign and a parking area near SR 615.

If hiking the larger loop, right from the *Iron Ore Trail*, the route is more strenuous, reclusive, and rarely maintained. It ascends and descends a knob to the eastern side of a sag and then climbs to Pine Mountain at 1 mile. On a rocky isolated ridge it ascends another knob (3,341 ft.) and at 2 miles curves to the southern side of a peak on Rich Patch Mountain. In a steep descent it veers west of Bald Knob to rapidly descend into the headwaters gorge of Hipes Branch. Rhododendron, hemlock, ferns, and wildflowers are here at 3.1 miles. After crossing the stream the trail turns east across the shoe of Bald Knob to a junction left and right at 3.8 miles with the shorter loop. A turn left is 0.3 miles east across a fork of Stony Run to complete the longer loop. To continue on the western side of the shorter loop, the trail parallels a fork and then the main stream of Hipes Run in a narrow gorge for nearly 1 mile. Abruptly it changes to a northeastern direction and slight ascent on its mountainside route to complete the loop at Stony Run and the parking area. There is a signboard 0.1 mile before the parking area.

USGS map: Strom; *USFS trail nos.*: 264, 5004, 5001

144   **Craig Creek Trail**
Length and Difficulty: 2.1 miles (3.4 km) round-trip; easy
Features: fishing, wildflowers
Trailheads: Craig Creek Recreation Area is 9 miles northeast of Fenwick Mines and
   10.6 miles southwest of Roaring Run on SR 615. From the junction of SR 615 and
   SR 817 in Oriskany it is 0.4 miles on SR 817 to FR 5075 for a right turn.
Description: This trail is within an oxbow of Craig Creek at the northern base of
   Patterson Mountain. Its termini are at the first trail sign and at the Craig Creek
   picnic area. On the left side of the slope the yellow-blazed trail ascends in a
   young hardwood forest with a ravine to the ridge top at 0.2 miles where the trail
   loop divides. There are mountain laurel, woodmint, and huckleberry. Turn
   right to reach a grassy and scenic field at 1 mile, where deer and woodchuck are
   among sundrops and other wildflowers. At the parking area, follow the creek
   downstream to an old woods road. Turn left and ascend to a ridge and to the
   trail origin.
USGS map: Oriskany; *USFS trail no.*: 5006

Wythe Ranger District

The 170,000-acre Wythe Ranger District has long, wide strips of mountain ranges. The two longest are Brushy and Walker Mountains in a northeast-southwest direction. Flowing between them are the North Fork of the Holston River, which flows southwest from the center of the district, and Walker Creek to the northeast. In the most southwestern corner of the district are shorter mountain ranges of Pond and Glade Mountains. Between them is the Mount Rogers National Recreation Area Headquarters and Visitor Center, 5 miles north of the boundary for the districts. The northeastern corner of the district adjoins Blacksburg Ranger District. On the district's edges are towns such as Tazewell, Marion, Wytheville, and Pulaski. Hungry Mother State Park, which adjoins the district, is 3 miles north of Marion. On the Brushy Mountain range are two wilderness areas: Beartown (5,109 acres), west of Burke's Garden; and Kimberling Creek (5,542 acres), northeast of the community of Bastian. Burke's Garden is an enormous, craterlike agricultural bowl whose ellipsoidal rim is district property. It reaches an elevation of 4,710 feet at the eastern edge of Beartown Mountain. On the southern rim are 8 miles of the *AT*. The garden was a Shawnee Indian hunting ground when Englishman James Burke discovered it in the 1750s. The easiest entrance route is on SR 623, from VA 61, east of Tazewell. Kimberling Creek Wilderness Area's main feature is its wildness with little evidence of human habitation. South of the major mountain ranges is I-81, which runs through the Great Valley, and north through the center is I-77, which passes through a 1-mile tunnel in Big Walker Mountain.

Stony Fork Campground is on SR 717, 4 miles west from I-77, exit 9, and 8 miles north on US 52 from I-81, exit 21. In a forest of hardwoods and rhododendron, this model facility has single and double units, flush toilets, showers, and trailer waste disposal station. From a nature trail is the western trailhead of the *Seven Sisters Trail*.

The district has three picnic areas: Dark Horse Hollow, 5.5 miles north of Wytheville on US 52; Big Bend, 12 miles farther north on US 52 and FR 206; and Wolf Creek, 3.5 miles west from I-77, exit 70, on SR 666 and SR 614.

Stocked trout streams include the East Fork of Stony Fork (see Stony Fork Campground, above); Reed Creek (see *Channel Rock Trail*, below), the South Fork of the Holston River, west of Sugar Grove; and Wolf Creek (see *Wolf Creek Trail*, below).

There are two special points of interest in the district. In Groseclose there is the 180-acre Settlers Museum of Southwest Virginia, a joint project with the USFS and Charles Phillippi, for a planned living history farm. The *AT* passes through it. The other unique feature is the Big Walker Mountain Scenic Byway. For 16.2 miles, beginning at the junction of I-77, exit on SR 717, the leisure motor route goes west, past the Stony Creek Campground, and ascends and descends Big Walker Mountain on US 52/21 to VA 42. There are stops along the way for observing wildflowers (and sometimes wildlife), history markers, an observation tower, and at the crest of Big Walker Mountain is a 1-mile trail on the former *AT* to Monster Rock.

The district has 72.6 miles of the *AT* from the boundary of the Mount Rogers National Recreation Area near the South Fork of the Holston River, west of Sugar Grove, to Crandon at the boundary of the Blacksburg Ranger District. In addition to the *AT* there are 20 miles of other foot trails, a variety of blue-blazed spur trails from the *AT*, and a 9-mile horse trail. Two blue-blazed alternates on the *AT* are the *Boss Trail* (2 mi.) (named in honor of Keith Smith of Virginia Tech Outing Club) and the *High Water Trail* (2.7 mi.) (used when Little Wolf Creek floods) at SR 615, off VA 42, west of Bland. The *Roaring Fork Trail* (1.3 mi.) is an unmaintained route to the confluence of Roaring Fork and Cove Branch gorge in remote Beartown Wilderness (accessible from FR 631 and FR 222 from SR 625, north of VA 42 at Ceres). Trails in long-range planning stages are the *Wolf Creek* (1-mi. extension from 1-mi. *Wolf Creek Nature Trail*), 3.5 miles west of I-77, exit 58, on SR 614; four trails at Peak Creek Opportunity Area (near Gatewood Reservoir west of Pulaski); and a horse trail in Currin Valley Opportunity Area (south of Marion, off VA 16 on SR 671). All trails in the district are well maintained, and all have low traffic volume, except the *Stony Fork Nature Trail*, which is moderate. The *Channel Rock Trail* (9 mi.) is an orange-blazed equestrian loop. It parallels Reed Creek in Crawfish Valley, crosses the Tennessee Valley Divide on Walker Mountain, follows part of Bear Creek and high ridges of Brushy Mountain, and passes through a gorge of Channel Rock Hollow. Access from I-81, exit 60, is north on SR 617 to Blacklick, left on SR 625, which becomes FR 727, and to a gate and parking lot.

146–50

Address and Information: Wythe Ranger District, 1626 West Lee Highway, Wytheville, VA 24382; phone: 703-228-5551; on US 11, west edge of Wytheville. Available are district map with trails, camping and scenic byway flyers, and wilderness areas brochure with maps.

STONY FORK AREA
Wythe County

151–52

Stony Fork Nature Trail (1 mi.), **Seven Sisters Trail** (4.8 mi.)

Length and Difficulty: 5.8 miles (9.3 km) combined, partial round-trip; easy to moderate

Features: nature study, trout stream, wildlife

Trailheads: From I-77, exit 47, on SR 717, go 1.3 miles to eastern trailhead, and 2.6 miles farther on SR 717 to Stony Fork Campground and western trailhead.

Description: Begin at campsite #32 and follow a yellow blaze through locust, Virginia pine, hemlock, and oak with understory of striped green maple and laurel in a loop. The *Stony Fork Nature Trail* continues right at 0.4 miles for a return to the campground; the *Seven Sisters Trail* begins on the left. It ascends on a ridge to curve in a hollow at 0.6 miles. Here the forest is filled with black cohosh, laurel, and maple. At 0.9 miles the trail enters another hollow with fragmented shale and continues on a ridge among chestnut oak. It reaches the crest of Little Walker Mountain at 1.1 miles, where it follows the ridgeline with oak, maple, wintergreen, and galax. At 1.7 miles is the highest peak (3,310 ft.) on the trail. From here the trail descends to other peaks at 2.5 miles and 2.9 miles. It reaches an old forest road at 3.8 miles, turns left to follow a wide mossy treadway, and

descends to the base of the mountain at East Fork at 4.7 miles. Here are tall white pines and dense rhododendron. It is 90 yards to the parking area at SR 717.
USGS maps: Big Bend, Crockett; *USFS trail nos.*: 6502, 6509

TRACK FORK AREA
Wythe and Pulaski Counties

Track Fork Trail (4 mi.), **Polecat Trail** (1.4 mi.)   153–54
Length and Difficulty: 5.4 miles (8.6 km) combined; easy to moderate
Features: stream, wildlife, historic site
Trailheads: There are three vehicular access routes to the *Track Fork Trail* and two
  to the *Polecat Trail*. The northern route from I-77, exit 47, begins on SR 717 (east
  from Stony Fork Campground) and goes east 2 miles to a junction with SR 601
  and 603. Continue east on SR 601 for 10.1 miles and turn right (south) on SR
  600. After 2.5 miles, reach the crest of Little Walker Mountain and the western
  trailhead on the left. This point can also be reached by turning right on SR 603
  (from SR 717 described above) for 4.6 miles to the junction on the left with SR
  600. Follow SR 600 through beautiful Crockett Cove Valley, pass FR 707 after 6.9
  miles, and ascend to the trailhead after another 1.3 miles. (From the FR 707
  junction, it is 2.8 mi. east to the *Polecat Trail* trailhead.) Another access to SR
  600 is from I-77 in Wytheville. After turning north from I-81, turn right on the
  first ramp, exit 41, to SR 610 (Peppers Ferry Rd.) and turn right again. Cross
  I-77, go under I-81, and after 0.3 miles turn right on SR 603 (Cove Rd.). Cross
  over I-81 and follow SR 603 for 4.2 miles to SR 600 on the right. (If coming east
  on I-81, take exit 72 and follow above directions.) The eastern trailhead for the
  Track Fork Trail can be reached from downtown Pulaski. At the junction of US 11
  and VA 99, go west on Third Street to Randolph Street. It becomes SR 738
  (Robinson Tract Rd.). After 4 miles turn left on narrow SR 641 (Cox Hollow
  Rd.). Follow it and FR 692 for 3.8 miles to the parking area and trailhead. The
  south approach to the *Polecat Trail* is from I-81/77 at Fort Chiswell. Drive 3
  miles north on VA 121 and SR 610 through Max Meadows to the junction with SR
  712. Follow SR 712 for 6 miles to FR 707 on the left; ascend and descend for 1.8
  miles to roadside parking on the left and trailhead on the right.
Description: These remote trails are frequented with turkeys, deer, raccoons,
  skunks, and songbirds. If entering *Track Fork Trail* from the eastern trailhead,
  proceed upstream on a wide old wagon road near a timber cut. The forest
  contains white pines, hemlocks, rhododendrons, hardwoods, and wildflowers
  among ferns. Near one of the Track Fork crossings at 1 mile is a junction with
  the *Polecat Trail* on the left. (It goes 1.4 mi. to FR 707.) At 1.3 miles the trail
  crosses into Wythe County from Pulaski County and ascends to a ridge saddle
  at 2.5 miles. Here is a sunny, grassy area for a good campsite. An old wagon road
  used by pioneers veers from the trail. From here the trail ascends on the
  southern slope of Little Walker Mountain, passes an old road, on the left, at 3.6
  miles, and reaches SR 600 at 4 miles.

If entering the *Polecat Trail* from FR 707, follow an old railroad grade to cross a tributary of Peak Creek at 0.6 miles. Cross the stream again at 0.8 miles. There are excellent campsites in this area of tall hardwoods and rhododendron patches. The trail abruptly climbs a ridge at 1 mile, then descends to cross a tributary of Track Fork. Among rhododendron and witch hazel the trail reaches the *Track Fork Trail* at 1.4 miles. (It is 1 mi. right to the parking area of FR 692, and 3 mi. left to SR 600.)

USGS map: Long Spur; *USFS trail nos.*: 6516, 6517

2 : George Washington National Forest

The Highlands . . . thickets harbor all
sorts of beasts of prey, as wolves, panthers,
leopards, lions . . . foxes and raccoons.
—John Lederer

The 1,061,080-acre George Washington National Forest (GWNF) celebrated its 75th birthday in 1992. Its history began six years after the Congressional Weeks Law authorized the purchase of land to form national forests. Shenandoah and Natural Bridge were two of the first forests, but President Herbert Hoover decreed in 1932 that the Shenandoah National Forest would henceforth be the George Washington National Forest. In 1933 the Natural Bridge National Forest was added to the GWNF, but part of it went to the JNF, which was formed in 1936.

The GWNF spreads from the James River and south of Covington in the south to near Winchester in the north. On its eastern boundary is the Shenandoah National Park and the BRP (which sometimes is in the forest). Its western boundary is the Monongahela National Forest in West Virginia. In the center of this vast and resplendent domain is the idyllic Shenandoah Valley, where pioneers settled to create their farms, and where battles were fought in the Revolutionary and Civil wars. The forest covers parts of 17 counties, including 4 in West Virginia. It has 1,287 miles of streams (called creeks, runs, forks, or branches) and rivers, and 3,190 acres of lakes, ponds, and tarns, the largest of which is Lake Moomaw. There are high, windswept peaks, knobs, and balds over 4,000 feet (Reddish Knob), cascading waterfalls (Crabtree), damp and dark drafts (Ramseys), natural springs (Wiggins), and native trout rivers (Jackson). The GWNF has six wilderness areas totaling more than 32,000 acres: Ramseys Draft, St. Mary's, Rich Hole, Rough Mountain, Barbours Creek, and Shawvers Run. There are six ranger districts.

At least 46 areas and about 51,000 acres of unique botanical and zoological habitats have been identified by the U.S. Fish and Game Wildlife Service and Natural Heritage. As a result, the forest service has set a primary goal of protecting the endangered, threatened, and sensitive species of flora and fauna. Examples of endangered vascular plants are swamp pink (*Helonias bullata*), usually found in mossy cold seeps; Virginia sneezeweed (*Helenium virginicum*), located near borders of dry ponds in only two counties; smooth rockcress (*Arabis serotina*), on shaley slopes; and northeastern bulrush (*Scirpus ancistrochaetus*). Paper birch, which grows only in the Dry River Ranger District, is listed as sensitive. American ginseng (*Panax quinquefolium*) is threatened, but harvesting is allowed with a license. It grows usually in rich, mesic coves. Two endangered mammals are the northern Virginia flying squirrel (*Glaucomys sabrinus fuscus*) and the Indiana bat (*Myotis sodalis*). Both are in the Warm Springs Ranger District. A complete status list of all flora and fauna is in Appendix F of the 1993 *Final Environmental Impact Statement* of the forest. There are about 1,400 species of plants in the forest, 70 species of trees, and 71 terrestrial mammal species. In the past few years large segments of hardwoods have been defoliated by the gypsy moth, the hemlock by woolly adelgid, and the dogwood by anthracnose, a fungal disease. The cost of treatment for the gypsy moth is exorbitant, and the only known enemy is the spores of a moth-killing fungus, *Entomophaga maimaiga*. Entire stands of Virginia pine and table mountain pine have been destroyed by the southern pine beetle. However, plant pathologists in the USFS have stated that recovery will occur through adaptation.

Because the GWNF is within a day's driving distance of 57 million people, the administrative policy of its managers is to provide a varied catalog of services to meet the diverse interests of the public. An example is the partnership between the forest and the Wildlife Center of Virginia to provide a 400-acre facility in the Pedlar Ranger District, south of Waynesboro. The environmental education center would provide classrooms, activity labs, universal interpretive trails, and learning stations. Another environmental awareness program is Eyes on Wildlife (also called Watchable Wildlife) in cooperation with Defenders of Wildlife. One of its purposes is to monitor healthy ecosystems for all plants. The GWNF is also active in providing accommodations for people with disabilities. Anglers, for example, have piers at Bealer's Ferry Pond (9 mi. north of Luray, off SR 684) in the Lee Ranger District, Elkhorn Lake (near Stokesville) in the Dry River Ranger District, and Bolar Flats Picnic Area (at the marina at Lake Moomaw). In the Warm Springs Ranger District, at Hidden Valley Recreation Area, is an ATV and motorcycle route for hunters with disabilities. Another special region is the Shady Mountain Disabled Hunter Area in the Pedlar Ranger District. The GWNF has cooperative programs with Ducks Unlimited, Trout Unlimited, and the Virginia Department of Game and Inland Fisheries. An example of these programs is Kids Fishing Day, usually held in late April. Some of the participating areas are Elkhorn Lake in the Dry River Ranger District, Sherando Lake in the Pedlar Ranger District, and Dunlop Creek in the James River Ranger District. In addition there is the Outdoor Classroom for young people at Augusta Springs in the Deerfield Ranger District. To help local rural areas with long-term economic development, the forest began a program in the early 1990s to obtain grants through the Rural Revitalization through Forest projects.

There are 98 recreation areas containing 27 developed campgrounds in the GWNF. From these areas are many trails that offer a variety of recreation. Of the more than 900 miles of trails, there are foot trails for backpackers and hikers, equestrian trails, bicycle trails, trails for motor vehicles, trails for the disabled, and multiple-use trails. Three long-distance trails pass through the forest: 57 miles of the *AT*, 36 miles of the *Big Blue Trail*, and 10 miles (with at least 18 more mi. planned) of the *Allegheny Trail*. Examples of long internal trails are the *Massanutten Mountain Trail* (East, South, and West), 60 miles in the Lee Ranger District; the *Shenandoah Mountain Trail* (South and North), 28 miles in the Deerfield Ranger District; and the *Wild Oak Trail* (circuit), 26 miles in the Dry River Ranger District. One of the long trails for motor vehicles is 12-mile *Rocky Run Trail* for ATVs and 4WDs in the Dry River Ranger District.

During the 1980s a large percentage of the trails lacked maintenance, signage, and blazing; improvements have begun in the 1990s. The Lee and Pedlar ranger districts, closest to metropolitan areas and volunteer groups, have a better record of trail upkeep. Maintenance is more difficult, and more commensurate with usage, in some of the rugged areas of other districts, termed "remote highlands," of which there are about 143,000 acres. But trails in these areas often appeal to the more experienced hikers who desire less manicuring of trails for a more wilderness atmosphere. Trail management policy is described on pages 3-141–142 of the 1993 *Final Revised Land and Resource Management Plan* (usually called *The Plan*). The GWNF management plans at least 225 miles of new trails, depending on funding, but with no time frame. Additionally, about 95 miles are planned in reconstruction of existing trails (see Appendix B in *The Plan*).

Address and Information: GWNF Headquarters, USFS, Harrison Plaza, 101 N. Main Street (P.O. Box 233), Harrisonburg, VA 22801; phone: 703-564-8300. Available for free are GWNF news information, brochures, and Forest Visitor Guide. GWNF map of Virginia and West Virginia, all district recreation maps, topographical maps, and wilderness maps of Ramseys Draft, St. Mary's, and Lake Moomaw have small fees.

Deerfield Ranger District

The 164,183-acre Deerfield Ranger District is flanked on the southwest by the Warm Springs Ranger District and a smaller area of the James River Ranger District. On the northeast is the Dry River Ranger District. On the western side is Cowpasture River and Highland WMA, and on the eastern side is VA 42, west of Staunton, and Goshen and Little Mountain WMAS. As with the JNF districts, this district's mountain ranges run southwest to northeast. On the west is the Shenandoah Mountain Range, and on the east is the Great North Mountain Range. In between them is Deerfield Valley, a bucolic channel of country roads, churches, farmlands, hollows, licks, drafts, and runs, with quaint stream names such as Danny Run, Body Lick, and Chair Draft feeding Calfpasture River. Walker Mountain, a narrow ridge in the valley's center, makes the valley the shape of a tuning fork. At the northern end of the valley, where US 250 cuts across the mountain passes, is Ramsey's Draft Wilderness (6,519 acres), with a network of rugged trails. Here is also Mountain House Picnic Area, a historic site of a former wayside station. Another picnic area is at Braley Pond, north of the junction of US 250 and SR 715. The district does not have developed campgrounds. For fishermen, trout are stocked at Mill Creek (by VA 39) and Braley Pond. The district has two state champion size trees: a black birch (*Betula lenta*) on top of Gwin Mountain (6 mi. south of US 250 on FR 396), and an Eastern hemlock (*Tsuga canadensis*) in Ramsey's Draft Wilderness (3 mi. upstream from US 250).

The longest trail in the district is the *Shenandoah Mountain Trail* (30.7 mi.). A major point of interest on the *North Mountain Trail* is Elliott Knob, listed by the

USFS as the highest peak in the GWNF. Some trails are used by motorized vehicles or are hunter access routes. An example is the former *Walker Mountain Trail* (13.7 mi.), now gated FR 387, which is open during hunting seasons. You can reach it from Yost at SR 640 and FR 61 junction. After 1.8 miles on FR 61 the southern roadhead is on the left. The northeastern access is at Bussard Hunter Access, off SR 600, 1.3 miles south from Deerfield. There are three trails, infrequently used, which access Walker Mountain from other roads. One is yellow-blazed *Back Draft Trail* (3 mi.); it crosses the mountain (9 mi. north from its southern roadhead) from SR 641 NW, and FR 61 (Clayton Mill Creek Rd.) east at Marble Valley on SR 600. On the western junction with SR 641 the trail becomes the *Brushy Ridge Trail* (0.9 mi.) to SR 629, and from here it becomes *Short Ridge Trail* (0.9 mi., mainly used by equestrians) to FR 399 (Jerkemtight Creek Rd.), a former 4.2-mile trail. It is 4 miles south of Deerfield on SR 629. Another hunter access trail is the *Sam Ramsey Hunter Access Trail* (3 mi.). It is between FR 61 and SR 692, 4 miles south of Marble Valley. The *Falls Hollow Trail* (3 mi.) is a combination road (FR 347, 657, and 448) and footpath. It is on VA 42, 3.2 miles southwest from the junction with VA 254. A steep and rocky route, its chief attraction is Elliott Knob (4,463 ft.). Part of the future trail plans are to reconstruct the *Benson Run Trail* and add 5 miles, and to reconstruct the *Shaws Ridge Trail* and the *Marshall Draft Trail*. The *Braley Pond Trail* would receive 2 miles of new trail, and 4 miles would be added at the Augusta Springs Conference Center.

155–61

Address and Information: Deerfield Ranger District, Rt. 6, Box 419, Staunton, VA 24401; phone: 703-885-8028/8029; on VA 254 at the western edge of the city. Available are district map with trails, Shenandoah Mountain Trail brochure, and wilderness area brochure with map.

MILL MOUNTAIN AND SIDLING HILL AREA
Bath, Rockbridge, and Augusta Counties

162 **Mill Mountain Trail**

Length and Difficulty: 8.3 miles (13.2 km); strenuous

Features: wildlife, scenic views

Trailheads: To reach the southern trailhead, go west 1.7 miles on VA 39/42 from Goshen, and turn right on SR 600. After 1 mile turn left near a forest sign. To reach the northern trailhead, continue north on SR 600 for 10.2 miles and turn left (at Marble Valley) for 4.8 miles on FR 61 (Clayton's Mill Creek Rd.) to trailhead on the left.

Description: From the roadside parking at SR 600 the trail follows a forest road for 0.6 miles, where it becomes an orange-blazed foot trail. It ascends and reaches the ridge of Mill Mountain for a right turn at 1.3 miles. For the next 1 mile there are excellent views from rock outcroppings. At 3.1 miles is a road junction: right leads down to scenic Ingram Draft; left leads to Panther Gap Draft. Continuing straight, the trail passes through former clear-cuts. At 3.8 miles it begins a steep climb and follows an old road to the top of Sidling Hill ridge. At 6 miles there is a footpath near the site of an old fire tower. At 6.7 miles it veers left at a fork. It then joins an old logging road from the left at 7.4 miles. Follow it in a descent to cross Little Mill Creek at FR 61 (Clayton's Mill Creek Rd.).

USGS maps: Green Valley, Craigsville; *USFS trail nos.*: 492

NORTH AND CRAWFORD MOUNTAINS AREA
Augusta County

North Mountain Trail (North)   163–66
Length and Difficulty: 14.5 miles (23.2 km); strenuous
Connecting Trails: *Crawford Mountain Trail* (7.8 mi.), *Cold Spring Trail* (2.2 mi.), *Chestnut Flat Spring Trail* (0.3 mi.), *Ferris Hollow Trail* (1.7 mi.)
Features: wildlife, scenic views, solitude
Trailheads: To reach the northeastern trailhead, travel 7 miles west of Staunton on VA 254 to the junction with VA 42. Turn left on VA 42, go 0.7 miles, and turn right at Buffalo Gap Presbyterian Church on SR 688 (Dry Branch Rd.). Cross a picturesque bridge after 2.7 miles, and reach Dry Branch Gap after another 1.2 miles; there is a small parking area. For the southwestern trailhead, turn off VA 42, 2 miles southwest of Craigsville on SR 687 (Ramsey Draft Rd.) and go 3 miles to the ridge top. If coming from the west off SR 600, it is 1 mile up the mountain to the trailhead. Another access to the trail is on FR 82, west from VA 42 at Miller Memorial Church (at Augusta Springs), and east from SR 600 at Rocky Spring Church.
Description: Begin at the northeastern trailhead (it is also the southern trailhead for the *Crawford Mountain Trail*, which goes north to US 250). The gated, yellow-blazed *North Mountain Trail (North)* follows the ridge crest of Great North Mountain. Several springs are close to the trail, but overall the ridge is dry; water should be carried. For the first 1.2 miles the trail is on and off an old logging road. (At 1.8 mi. a side trail leads right 0.2 mi. to Buffalo Spring.) Following a rocky ridge, hikers will likely see grouse or turkey. Oak, white pine, birch, and locust are the predominant trees.

At 4.2 miles is the junction with Elliott Knob road; turn right. (On the left at 0.1 mi. is a spring and small pond among larch and red spruce—a fine campsite. Farther down the mountain the road goes 2.5 mi. to VA 42.) The trail ascends 0.2 miles to Elliott Knob (4,463 ft., the highest peak in the district). At the top, turn right and go 0.1 mile. Here is an outstanding panoramic view near the TV relay station and old fire tower. Continue south on the ridge through red spruce; at 4.5 miles the *Cold Spring Trail* is on the right at the junction. (The *Cold Spring Trail* descends into Deerfield Valley, with scenic rock outcroppings. On this trail, after 1.8 mi. there is a spring, then a creek. It passes over earth mounds, and at 2.2 mi. reaches a parking area near an old woods road on FR 77 [Cold Spring Rd]. Access to the parking area from the northern trailhead of *North Mountain Trail* [North] is 2 mi. west on SR 688 [Dry Branch Rd.]; turn left on FR 77 and drive 3.3 mi. to trailhead.)

The trail continues ahead on the crest of Hogback Ridge and passes a junction on the right with the *Chestnut Flat Spring Trail*, a 0.3-mile old woods road. At 8.1 miles the trail crosses FR 82 (Hite Hollow Rd.). It is 6.5 miles right (west) to SR 600, and 4.8 miles left (east) to VA 42. Hiking over a number of knobs, reach an old woods road at 10.1 miles, which leads to FR 38, left (east). The *Ferris Hollow Trail* junction is on the right (west) at 11 miles. (The *Ferris Hollow Trail* descends 1.7 mi. to Calfpasture Creek near Marble Valley, partially on private land, to SR 600.) The trail enters an old road (a favorite passage for deer hunters) at 12.5 miles and follows its descent for the next 2 miles to reach the trailhead at SR 687 (Ramsey Draft Rd.).

USGS maps: Elliott Knob, Deerfield, Craigsville; *USFS trail nos.*: 443, 445, 491

Crawford Mountain Trail (2.6 mi.), **Chimney Hollow Trail** (3.5 mi.),
167–69   **Crawford Knob Trail** (3.5 mi.)

Length and Difficulty: 9.6 miles (15.4 km) combined; moderate to strenuous
Features: springs, bear oak grove, wildlife, stream
Trailheads: Directions to the southern trailhead of the *Crawford Mountain Trail* are the same as those given for the northern trailhead of *North Mountain Trail (North)* on SR 688, described above. For the *Chimney Hollow Trail*, go 9.5 miles west from Churchville on US 250; for the *Crawford Knob Trail*, go 2 miles west of Churchville on US 250 and turn south on SR 270 at Lone Fountain. After another 2 miles turn right on FR 1296.
Description: On the opposite side of the road from the northern trailhead of the *North Mountain Trail (North)*, the *Crawford Mountain Trail* ascends steeply over earth hummocks into a forest of oak, white pine, dogwood, haw, and sassafras. It reaches the top of Crawford Mountain ridgeline at 0.4 miles. After a gradual ascent, it reaches a junction with the *Chimney Hollow Trail* on the left. (The *Chimney Hollow Trail* leads 3.5 mi. north, passing over rock outcroppings, descending along a stream, entering stands of large white pine, and reaching its northern trailhead at a parking space on US 250. Across the road is the southern entrance to the *Dowells Draft Trail*. From here it is 15 mi. east on US 250 to Staunton.)

On the *Crawford Mountain Trail* it is 0.1 mile farther to a spur trail on the right (which leads 0.3 mi. through a wildlife clearing to a spring). At 2.6 miles is a junction with yellow-blazed *Crawford Knob Trail* on the right. (The *Crawford Knob Trail* enters a stand of bear oak, skirts the northern side of Crawford Knob [3,728 ft.], and descends on switchbacks. Along the way down the mountain are two springs. After following McKittrick's Branch and entering a timber regeneration area, it exits at FR 1296 [McKittrick's Rd.]. It is 0.4 mi. farther to SR 720 near Jerusalem Chapel.)

Although the *Crawford Mountain Trail* can be hiked farther north on the ridge, it is not maintained by the USFS because its former trailhead on private property has been closed. (Contact the district office for progress on establishment of a new public access.)

USGS maps: Elliott Knob, West Augusta, Stokesville; *USFS trail nos.*: 485, 489, 487

Dowells Draft Trail (4 mi.), **White Oak Draft Trail** (2.8 mi.)

Length and Difficulty: 6.8 miles (10.9 km) combined, partial round-trip; moderate

Connecting Trail: *Wild Oak Trail* (25.6 mi.)

Features: wildflowers, wildlife, solitude

Trailheads: The trailhead for the *Dowells Draft Trail* is across US 250 from the trailhead of the *Chimney Hollow Trail* (9.5 mi. west of Churchville on US 250). Its northern trailhead is at the *Wild Oak Trail* (see Dry River Ranger District in this chapter).

To reach the *White Oak Draft Trail* from the roadside parking of the *Dowells Draft Trail*, go 3.5 miles east on US 250 to FR 466 on the left. (If arriving from Churchville, it is 0.5 mi. west of White's Store to parking at gated FR 466 on the right [150 ft. from a small bridge on US 250]). Its northern trailhead is at the *Wild Oak Trail*.

Description: These two trails have trailheads on US 250, 3.5 miles apart, and they exit 1 mile apart on the *Wild Oak Trail* in the Dry River Ranger District. A loop of 7.8 miles can be made with two cars. The *Dowells Draft Trail* begins on an easy contour among young hardwoods, Indian pipe, and trailing arbutus. It enters a cove before descending to cross East Branch of Dowells Draft and a junction with FR 499 at 0.7 miles. After 0.2 miles to the right on the road, it leaves the road, on the left, and parallels Dowells Draft. At 2.1 miles it ascends away from the stream and gradually ascends to the *Wild Oak Trail* at 4 miles.

(To the left it is 2.1 mi. on the *Wild Oak Trail* to a crossing of FR 96 [FR 96 becomes SR 715 to the left in the Deerfield Ranger District, and to the right junctures with FR 95 near Elkhorn Lake in the Dry River Ranger District]. To the right on the *Wild Oak Trail* from the *Dowells Draft Trail* it is 0.2 miles to the first peak (3,407 ft.) and 0.8 miles to the second peak of Hankey Mountain. At the second peak it makes a junction with the *White Oak Draft Trail*. The *Wild Oak Trail* continues 3.4 miles on old FR 425 to FR 95B at North River Campground.)

At the US 250 parking space with gated FR 466 (old logging road) follow yellow-blazed *White Oak Draft Trail* to a fork on the right at 0.2 miles. Cross White Oak Draft at 0.7 miles and 0.8 miles, then follow the left fork of the old road. Cross a stream at 1 mile, and leave the road, left, at 1.2 miles. Ascend on a rocky area at 1.6 miles for views of Crawford Mountain, and reach the *Wild Oak Trail* at 2.8 miles.

USGS maps: West Augusta, Stokesville: *USFS trail nos.*: 650, 486

Braley Pond Trail (0.6 mi.), **Bald Ridge Trail** (8.3 mi.)

Length and Difficulty: 8.9 miles (14.2 km) combined, partial round-trip; easy to strenuous

Connecting Trails: *Bridge Hollow Trail* (1.8 mi.), *Wild Oak Trail* (25.6 mi.)

Features: lake, rugged area, peaks, wilderness, wildlife

Trailhead: From the junction of US 250 (0.2 mi. west from northern trailhead of the *Chimney Hollow Trail*) and SR 715 (with Elkhorn Lake sign), go 0.3 miles on SR 715 to FR 348-1 on the left, and go 0.6 miles.

Description: From the Braley Pond parking area the trail crosses a footbridge to the dam. It circles the 5-acre lake among a young forest of pine, oak, huckleberry, birdfoot violet, and false downy foxglove. Rainbow trout, sunfish, and large-mouth bass are stocked in the lake. Halfway around the lake the trail meets the southern trailhead of the *Bald Ridge Trail* at Johnson Draft.

The *Bald Ridge Trail* (formerly called the *West Augusta Trail*) ascends nearly 2,000 feet in elevation. As a result, it passes through different terrain and hardwood and conifer species. Deer, turkey, grouse, and bear are among the wildlife. This is an excellent trail for birders. The yellow-blazed trail begins on an extension of FR 348 (gated at US 250) used by motorized vehicles. It passes through two wildlife openings before leaving the road on the right at 1.1 miles. At 3.3 miles is an overview of Crawford Mountain and Elliott Knob, and at 3.6 miles it makes a junction with 1.8-mile *Bridge Hollow Trail*. (The *Bridge Hollow Trail* serves as a southern connector between the *Ramseys Draft Trail* and the *Bald Ridge Trail*.) From here to its end the trail stays on the high, rugged ridge. It crosses The Peak at 4.1 miles. It begins a climb near rock outcroppings at 5.5 miles and descends steeply at 6.1 miles to congested rock outcroppings. At 7.3 miles the trail starts its ascent of Gordons Peak on switchbacks and reaches the top (3,915 ft.) at 7.6 miles. After its descent on switchbacks, it passes through a laurel thicket and more outcrops to a junction with the *Wild Oak Trail*, right and left, at 8.3 miles.

Options here are to backtrack (a total of 17.2 mi.) or to extend the journey left (1.7 mi.) to the *Tearjacket Trail* for a connection to the *Ramseys Draft Trail* and downstream to US 250 (a total of 17.8 mi.), or right on the *Wild Oak Trail* (2.2 mi.) to SR 715/FR96 and 3.7 miles south on SR 715 to Braley Pond (a total of 15.2 mi.). A continuation of 2.1 miles on the *Wild Oak Trail* and 3.2 miles on the *Dowells Draft Trail* will create a total of 16.1 miles to FR 449. From FR 449 it is 1.3 miles to Braley Pond (right on FR 449 to SR 715, left on SR 715, and right on Braley Pond entrance road) for a 17.4-mile loop.

(Hikers may see a sign for the *Braley Branch Trail* [gated FR 254] at the picnic area of Braley Pond. The 1.9-mi. dead-end route is not maintained but offers a challenge to explore the upper reaches of Braley Branch at the base of Bald Ridge.)

USGS map: West Augusta; *USFS trail nos.*: 653, 496

RAMSEYS DRAFT WILDERNESS AND SHENANDOAH MOUNTAIN AREA
Augusta and Highland Counties

176–80 **Ramseys Draft Trail**
Length and Difficulty: 7.3 miles (11.7 km); moderate to strenuous
Connecting Trails: *Bridge Hollow Trail* (1.8 mi.), *Road Hollow Trail* (2.4 mi.), *Jerry's Run Trail* (2 mi.), *Tearjacket Trail* (1.3 mi.), *Hardscrabble Trail* (0.5 mi.), *Shenandoah Mountain Trail/North* (7.1 mi.)
Features: wilderness, historic site, wildlife, stream, hemlock forest

Trailheads: From SR 715, which figures in the preceding trail description, it is 5 miles west on US 250 to FR 68 and Mountain House Picnic Area, on the right, for the southern trailhead. The northern trailhead is the junction with the *Shenandoah Mountain Trail (North)* (3 mi. to FR 95).

Introduction: Ramseys Draft is the district's most publicized and popular area for hikers and allied adventurers. It is surrounded by wilderness and 10 high mountain knobs and peaks from 3,264 to 4,282 feet, except at a narrow southern opening at US 250. At this point is the historic site of Parkersburg Pike Lodge, a way station for travelers between West Virginia and Virginia. Some of the appealing features of Ramseys Draft are its wildness; its history; its stands of tall virgin hemlock, white pine, and tulip poplar; its diverse moss and fern ground covers; and its wildlife habitat for bear, bobcat, deer, turkey, and species of warblers unique to this area. Other features are its deep-shaded coolness in the summer (the temperature is as much as 10° to 15° lower than outside the canyon), its excellent campsites, and its tumbling stream with native trout.

After the pioneer settlers the timbermen came and logged part of the area, but they spared the virgin hemlock forests in the Left Prong of Ramseys Draft between Hardscrabble Knob and Freezeland Flat. Other stands of hemlock were left on the slopes and up the Right Prong. In 1913 the USFS purchased the property and by 1935 began to treat the Left Prong as a wilderness. During the early 1930s the West Augusta CCC Camp was established outside the canyon. In 1934 it was vacated for troops of Company 5449 from Fort Oglethorpe, Georgia, to train there. Men of the CCC camp constructed the *Ramseys Draft Trail* and *Jerry's Run Trail* (and probably the *Shenandoah Mountain Trail [North]*). In the mid-1980s the canyon and up to its rims became the Ramseys Draft Wilderness. In 1985 there was a flash flood in adjoining West Virginia that brought death and destruction to riverside towns and farm country. In this area the canyon was flooded and long sections of the wide old road were destroyed. Because of its wilderness character, the trail route has been left to nature by the USFS. The result is that hikers have formed a zigzagging route over rock piles, debris, and remaining pieces of the road to increase the original trail distance with 0.8 miles. Four loop hikes can be made with the use of connecting trails, two of which (*Bridge Hollow Trail* and *Road Hollow Trail*) are outside the wilderness boundary. (For longer hikes these circuit options can include the *Shenandoah Mountain Trail* for a 30.7-mi. linear trail and the *Wild Oak Trail* for another 25.6-mi. loop [in the Dry River District].)

Description: From the parking area, pass the signboard on the *Ramseys Draft Trail* and after 135 feet reach a junction with the *Bridge Hollow Trail* on the right. (The *Bridge Hollow Trail* crosses a footbridge and a small stream to begin a steep ascent, at first parallel with US 250. It curves in and out of coves among mossy trail banks and laurel to skirt the northern side of Bridge Hollow. It reaches the *Bald Ridge Trail* at 1.8 mi. From here, on the left, it is 7.7 mi. to connect with the *Ramseys Draft Trail* near its northern end—via the *Bald Ridge Trail*, the *Wild Oak Trail*, and the *Tearjacket Trail*.)

Ahead on the *Ramseys Draft Trail* after 35 yards is the *Road Hollow Trail* on the left. (The *Road Hollow Trail* ascends around a spur ridge to a cove at 0.4 mi. The remaining 2.1 mi. are narrow and not well designed; there are erratic ups and downs with slanted treadway. Dipping into dry stream beds of Road Hollow, the trail leaves a final cove at 2.3 mi. to ascend the ridge and join the *Shenandoah Mountain Trail* at 2.5 mi. From there it is 5.8 mi. right to connect with the *Ramseys Draft Trail*. To the left it is 1.3 mi. to US 250.)

Continuing on the *Ramseys Draft Trail*, the treadway is over rock flats, rock piles, part of a creek bed, and part of a road. At 0.3 miles on the left is an abandoned USFS building, and at 0.6 miles the trail enters the wilderness boundary. At 2.4 miles is a deep ravine at the confluence of Jerry's Run and Ramseys Draft. After ascending an embankment there is a junction with *Jerry's Run Trail* on the left. (*Jerry's Run Trail* goes upstream in a narrow canyon. It hugs the stream among tall hemlock and oaks until about 1.6 mi., where it leaves the stream on a sloping ascent to a junction with the *Shenandoah Mountain Trail*. From there, on the right, it connects with the *Ramseys Draft Trail* after 4.7 mi.)

On the *Ramseys Draft Trail* the old road ends at 4.3 miles at the Left Prong and Right Prong, and the trail enters a laurel thicket to ascend the Right Prong. In a steady, almost straight ascent for 1.9 miles the trail is among moss-covered rocks, tall hemlocks and hardwoods, and a cascading stream. At 6.2 miles the trail junctions with the *Tearjacket Trail* (formerly *Springhouse Ridge Trail*) on the right. At the junction is a beautiful camping area in a forest of maples, serviceberry, yellow birch, and fern beds. Ninety feet up the trail is Hiner Spring on the left. (The *Tearjacket Trail* [not named on the sign that instead indicates Bald Knob] goes 1.3 mi. east on a descending grade in dense laurel to an open forest for a junction with the *Wild Oak Trail* [white-blazed]. If the *Wild Oak Trail* is followed to the right for 1.7 mi., it will connect with the *Bald Ridge Trail*. [See *Bald Ridge Trail* previously described.])

Continue on the *Ramseys Draft Trail* for 0.2 miles to a ridge top where to the left the *Hardscrabble Trail* ascends 0.5 miles to a large boulder field. On the way is a continuous, dense bed of ferns. The best views of part of the canyon and peaks on the *Bald Ridge Trail* are from the southern edge of the boulders. Among the boulders are the remains of an old fire tower. Backtrack. The *Ramseys Draft Trail* now makes a 0.9-mile graded descent with two cove curves and ends in a flat saddle among old growth oaks. Backtrack, or choose one of the following options: (1) Continue northeast on the *Shenandoah Mountain Trail* for 3 miles to FR 95 (North River Rd.), accessible from Elkhorn Lake and farther south on FR 96 to SR 715 by vehicle; (2) backtrack to follow the *Tearjacket Trail* to the *Wild Oak Trail*, the *Bald Ridge Trail*, and the *Bridge Hollow Trail* for a 17.9-mile circuit; or (3) follow the *Shenandoah Mountain Trail*, left, for a return on *Jerry's Run Trail* for a circuit of 16.4 miles, or via the *Road Hollow Trail* for a circuit of 15.6 miles.

USGS maps: West Augusta, McDowell, Palo Alto; *USFS trail nos.*: (only main trail and connectors) 440, 442, 448, 441, 716, 440A, 447

Hardscrabble Trail, GWNF. (Photograph by Allen de Hart)

181–82   **Shenandoah Mountain Trail (North)**
Length and Difficulty: 7.1 miles (11.4 km); easy to moderate
Connecting Trails: *Road Hollow Trail* (2.5 mi.), *Jerry's Run Trail* (2 mi.), *Sinclair Hollow Trail* (1.6 mi.), *Ramseys Draft Trail* (7.3 mi.)
Features: wildlife, solitude, historic site, scenic view
Trailheads: Access south is at the Confederate Breastworks on US 250, 2.1 miles west from Mountain House Picnic Area at Ramseys Draft. The northern trailhead for trail connections is at the *Ramseys Draft Trail*, but for road access it is 3 miles farther north to FR 95 (North River Rd.) in the Dry River Ranger District. FR 95 can be accessed from SR 718 at Stokesville.
Description: This beautiful trail weaves in and out of the Ramseys Draft Wilderness boundary on Shenandoah Mountain and around spur ridges in West Virginia. Skillfully graded on a gentle ascent there are a number of views west to Shaws Ridge and Jack Mountain. It starts for the first 0.3 miles in the Civil War Confederate Breastworks in a forest of hardwoods, white pines, and hemlocks. At 1.3 miles the *Road Hollow Trail* makes a junction on the right. (It descends 2.5 mi. to connect with the *Ramseys Draft Trail* at its southern trailhead.) At 2.4 miles is *Jerry's Run Trail* on the right. (It descends 2 mi. to meet the *Ramseys Draft Trail*.) There is a thick hemlock grove at 3 miles. At 6 miles there is a grassy saddle with white snakeroot, white pines, and a junction with the *Sinclair Hollow Trail* on the left. (It descends 1.6 mi. to FR 64 [Shaws Fork Rd.] and SR 616, from which it is 6.9 mi. south to the village of Head Waters on US 250.) The main trail intersects with the *Ramseys Draft Trail* at 7.1 miles among old growth oaks. Hiking options here are to backtrack, make a circuit with the *Ramseys Draft Trail*, or continue 3 miles ahead to FR 95 in the Dry River Ranger District (see preceding descriptions and distances).
USGS maps: McDowell, West Augusta, Palo Alto; *USFS trail nos.*: 447, 448, 441, 447D

183   **Shaws Ridge Trail**
Length and Difficulty: 6.3 miles (10. km); moderate
Features: solitude, wildlife
Trailheads: To reach the southern trailhead, drive from the Confederate Breastworks parking area on US 250 west for 3.2 miles to the village of Head Waters and the junction with SR 616 on the right, to park at corner. To reach the northern trailhead, continue 0.9 miles farther west on US 250, where a turn right on SR 614 goes 5 miles to Jones Hunter Access and FR 501 on the right.
Description: This trail is mainly a hunter's trail, but it has potential for isolated camping, watching wildlife, and birding. Begin the trail in an ascent on the road embankment, and follow a yellow-blazed graded trail into a hollow with shagbark hickory and banks of stonecrop. After arriving on the ridgeline, the trail passes through Virginia pine, maple, and witch hazel. It descends to pass Mar-

tins Draft headwaters at 2 miles. Deer frequent this area. The trail gradually ascends Shaws Ridge, and at the end it merges into gated FR 501. It is about 1.5 miles to exit at Jones Hunter Access.

USGS maps: McDowell, Doe Hill, Palo Alto; *USFS trail no.*: 652

Shenandoah Mountain Trail (South)

184–86

Length and Difficulty: 23.6 miles (37.8 km); strenuous
Connecting Trails: *Nelson Draft Trail* (1 mi.), *Marshall Draft Trail* (1.3 mi.)
Features: historic site, solitude, wildlife, scenic views
Trailheads: The northern trailhead is on the southern side of US 250 at the Confederate Breastworks, 2.1 miles west from the Mountain House Picnic Area at Ramseys Draft. For the southern trailhead, take SR 627 (Scottstown Draft Rd.) 2.5 miles west from SR 629 (south of Deerfield), or 2.5 miles east from SR 678 (south of Williamsville).
Introduction: The trail was constructed by the CCC in the 1930s for isolated backcountry hiking. It follows the ridgeline of knobs and peaks between 3,000 and 3,900 feet in a forest of chestnut oak, maple, locust, pine, hemlock, rhododendron, and laurel. A few springs are near the trail, and more than 50 streams flow from the mountainside, either west to Cowpasture River or east to Calfpasture and Mill Creeks. The trail intersects with two forest roads and two short foot trails. There are options for exploring the Right Prong of Benson Run and historic points such as the Confederate Breastworks and Signal Corps Knob. Maps from the USFS may show the southern trailhead either ending at a private cabin on SR 678 at the Cowpasture River or dead-ending on a logging road between the cabin and SR 627. To avoid trespass, the USFS recommends the southern terminus be the ridge crossing of SR 627 (Scottstown Draft Rd.), thus making the trail distance 21.3 miles instead of 23.6 miles. Traffic volume is low on this trail, except during fall and spring hunting seasons.
Description: The trail begins at gated FR 396, 300 yards east of the Confederate Breastworks, and it follows the road on the ridgeline for the first 2.6 miles. Along the route it intersects with old logging roads, one at 0.9 miles, but at 1.4 miles FR 343 goes left for 1 mile to end near Signal Corps Knob (3,906 ft.). (At 2.6 mi. there is an alternate route of 3.3 mi, which leaves the ridge and turns right on an old road for a descent to the Right Prong of Benson Run. It passes waterfalls and good campsites and meets the western end of FR 173 on the eastern side of the stream. The road ascends on switchbacks to cross the main trail.) At 2.9 miles the trail is under a power line. At 3.1 miles the trail leaves the old road to skirt left of the ridge, but it returns to the top of the mountain at 3.9 miles. Here is one of a number of wildlife ponds found on the trail. For the next 3 miles are a few scenic views and rock outcroppings. At 7 miles there is a junction with FR 173. To the right is access to the alternate route (see above), and to the left it is 4.6 miles to SR 629. The main trail forks to the left at 7.1 miles. After 0.5 miles it reaches the ridgeline. Another 0.2 miles on the right is Phillips Spring, 300 yards down the hollow. The trail skirts west of The Bump (3,634 ft.)

at 9.5 miles. Reach the junction with the *Nelson Draft Trail* at 11.3 miles. (It leads 1.3 mi. down the western side of the mountain to end at FR 394 [Sugar Tree Rd.]. The road goes northwest along Nelson Draft for 2.5 mi. to SR 614 near Patna and north of Williamsville.) From 11.6 miles to 13.8 miles are a number of views west to Bullpasture Mountain and east to Walker Mountain.

There is a major intersection at 17.5 miles. Rough Jerkemtight Road descends east for 5 miles to SR 629, using part of FR 399 along Jerkemtight Creek. Another old road runs south 0.4 miles up to Wallace Peak (3,795 ft.), site of a former fire tower. There is a spring on the southern side of the peak, accessed by a short trail from the eastern side. A few yards ahead on the main trail is a junction with the *Marshall Draft Trail* near a large black cherry tree. (An orange-blazed foot trail, it descends steeply for 1.3 mi. to FR 394 [Sugar Tree Rd.]. On a dry ridge it has chestnut oak, Virginia pine, and blueberry patches. See description under *Wallace Tract Trail* for use of *Marshall Draft Trail* and 2 mi. of FR 394 to provide an extended distance from the *Shenandoah Mountain Trail*.)

Continue on the *Shenandoah Mountain Trail* to ascend and skirt east of North Sister Knob at 19.1 miles. The trail then goes back to the western side of the ridge to South Sister Knob for views of Cowpasture and Jackson river valleys at 20.7 miles. After a descent the trail reaches its southern terminus at SR 627 at 21.2 miles. (Across the road is the section of the *Shenandoah Mountain Trail* that has been abandoned because of private property near SR 678.)

USGS maps: McDowell, Deerfield, Williamsville, Green Valley; *USFS trail nos.*: 447, 393, 547

187   **Wallace Tract Trail**

Length and Difficulty: 2.5 miles (4 km); moderate

Features: solitude, wildlife, wildflowers, swinging bridge

Trailheads: The eastern trailhead is at a gated, signed, old logging road (FR 394-F) off FR 394 (Sugar Tree Rd.), 4.7 miles north from SR 627 (Scotchtown Draft Rd.), which is 0.6 miles east off SR 678, 3.4 miles south of Williamsville. The western trailhead is at the end of FR 282 (swinging footbridge over Cowpasture River), 0.8 miles off SR 678, 2.1 miles south of Williamsville.

Description: (This trail, plus 2 mi. of FR 394, north to 1.3-mi. *Marshall Draft Trail* is a 5.8-mi. route from the *Shenandoah Mountain Trail* [South and West] to Cowpasture River [see above]. If using this option, turn left [southwest] on FR 394 at the northern trailhead of the *Marshall Draft Trail*. Follow the scenic, infrequently used [except during hunting seasons] FR 394 for 2 mi. to the *Wallace Tract Trail*, right.) The *Wallace Tract Trail*, with sparse yellow blazes, descends gradually, first on the left slope of a ridge, then at 0.5 miles it switches to the right slope. With a grassy treadway it abruptly turns left on a side road at 1.1 miles among young pines and locust. It descends to a grove of locust and a damp, faint road to the left, where it crosses a stream (may be dry in the summer) at 1.5 miles. Enter a stand of large hemlocks and continue descent to exit from the forest into a hayfield at 1.9 miles. From there the trail may be unmarked; therefore, follow the right edge of the fertile hayfields of clover, lespedeza, and wildflowers such as bee balm and soapwort. The fields are woodchuck habitats. Pass a farm road that fords Cowpasture River, and turn right to the river edge before a break in the locust trees (which leads into another field). Continue downstream for 100 yards to the 170-foot-long swinging footbridge over Cowpasture River. Across the river is a grassy parking area, unless the gate 0.2 miles ahead on FR 282 is locked. Here is a parking area bordered with wildflowers, and it is 0.6 miles on FR 282 out to SR 678.

USGS map: Williamsville; *USFS trail no.*: 417

Dry Run Ranger District

The Dry Run Ranger District is a compact, almost rectangular tract of 227,123 acres (of which 49,106 are in West Virginia). Its southwestern border adjoins the Deerfield Ranger District and Ramseys Draft Wilderness Area; its northeastern corner adjoins the Lee Ranger District. From one district boundary to the other, Shenandoah Mountain forms a singular range. On the western side in West Virginia the creeks, runs, branches, and rivers drain to the South Branch of the Potomac River, and on the eastern side the drainage is to the forks of the Shenandoah River. On the high range are rugged and remote knobs with breathtaking scenery. Some windswept grassy knobs are Little Bald Knob, High Knob, and Flagpole Knob. The most dramatic is rocky Reddish Knob (4,397 ft.), with a parking area. From this range are views of North Fork Mountain in the Monongahela National Forest in West Virginia and the Shenandoah Valley and Blue Ridge Mountains in Virginia. The forest is mainly hardwoods, Virginia and white pines, and on the higher elevations, red spruce. Rhododendron slicks are throughout the district. Wildlife includes all the large and small game animals common to the Appalachian region. There is at least one rare animal, the Cow Knob salamander near Reddish Knob. Native trout are in many of the streams and lakes. Examples of stocked lakes are Elkhorn Lake, Todd Lake, and Brandywine Lake. Among the streams are North River, Dry River, and the North Fork of the Shenandoah River.

Only one major highway, US 33 between Harrisonburg and Brandywine, passes through the district. Some fantastic landscapes are viewed on the incline to High Knob. Comparable in scenic quality is the highway's forestry shroud alongside Dry River, at the base of Shenandoah Mountain. Campground and picnic areas with fee swimming facilities are Todd Lake (west of Stokesville on SR 718 and FR 95) in Virginia, and Brandywine (on US 33, 2 mi. east of Brandywine) in West Virginia. Both are open from May 15 to September 30. Nonfee campgrounds open year round are Hone Quarry (11 mi. west of Dayton on SR 257) in Virginia, and Camp Run (off WV 3 onto CO 3/1, northwest of Fort Seybert in West Virginia). Another campground and picnic area that has a smaller fee and fewer facilities is North River (west of Stokesville on SR 718, FR 95, FR 95B) in Virginia. There are two picnic-only recreation areas: Shenandoah Mountain (on rough FR 85 southwest of

Reddish Knob), and Bluehole (14 mi. west of Broadway on VA 259 to SR 820). Both are in Virginia.

The district's TIS trail inventory lists 164 miles of trails, 19 of which are in West Virginia. The longest in Virginia is 25.6-mile *Wild Oak Trail*; it makes a loop in the district's most southwestern section. A national recreation trail, it offers diversity of topography and flora and fauna, isolation, and backpacking challenge. During the 1980s many of the trails became overgrown and eroded and lacked signage and blazing and parking space. For some hikers, this was not a major inconvenience because they liked the wilderness characteristics. Others felt less secure because the trails appeared abandoned. However, in the 1990s maintenance has increased; signage and blazes have become standardized. In Appendix B of the 1992 Revised Forest Plan, the district lists plans to reconstruct a section of the *Shenandoah Mountain Trail*, the *California Ridge Trail*, the *Slate Springs Trail*, and the *Tear-jacket Gorge Trail*. New trail construction will include 3.6 miles added to the *North River Trail* and 1-mile *Elkhorn Lake Trail*. The *Little River Trail* (8 mi.) has been abandoned, but long-range plans are for its reconstruction. The *Slate Springs Trail*, with its five confusing trails of two As, two Bs, and a C, has been simplified somewhat by the assignment of two new names: *Pond Knob Trail* (2.4 mi.) and *Cliff*
188 *Trail* (4 mi.).

Address and Information: Dry River Ranger District, 112 N. River Rd., Bridgewater, VA 22812; phone: 703-828-2591; from the junction of VA 257 and VA 42, go north 0.3 miles to North River Road and turn left. Available are district map with trails; *Wild Oak Trail* and *North River Gorge Trail* brochures; Todd Lake Recreation Area map.

NORTH RIVER AREA
Augusta County

189–90   **Todd Lake Trail** (1 mi.), **Trimble Mountain Trail** (4 mi.)
Length and Difficulty: 5 miles (8 km) combined, round-trip; easy to moderate
Features: lake, wildflowers, wildlife, scenic views, geological formations
Trailhead: To reach Todd Lake Recreation Area from Bridgewater, travel west on SR 727, off VA 42 (southern end of Dry River bridge) for 6 miles and turn left on SR 730. Follow SR 730 for 6 miles and turn right on SR 718 at Stokesville. After 1 mile, turn left on FR 95 and go 3.1 miles to FR 523 on the right, to lake and entrance. If coming from Stanton, travel west on VA 250 for 7.9 miles. Turn right on VA 42 and go 5 miles to a left on SR 760. After 3.3 miles reach SR 749, turn left, go 1 mile, turn right, go 1.1 miles to SR 718 at Stokesville, and follow as above.
Introduction: Todd Lake Recreation Area is an excellent base camp for hikers in the North River Area. It has the best facilities on the Virginia side of the district. Activities include hiking, camping, fishing, and swimming. Facilities include camper and tent sites, flush toilets, warm showers, and waste disposal unit. If you are not camping, you will be charged a small fee for using the lake facilities. There is no parking space for hiking the *Trimble Mountain Trail*, but there is a small space to park outside the campground gate. The trail sign is across the road to the lake entrance for both trails.

Description: Follow the sign through a grassy field of wildflowers to the dam. Here are views of the lake and the mountains. American goldfinches frequent this area. Curve around the lake and at 0.7 miles descend and cross an arched bridge. Pass a drinking fountain and a picnic and beech area for a return to trail origin. For the *Trimble Mountain Trail* follow the same route, but turn right before crossing the dam. Parallel the road for 0.2 miles on a yellow-blazed access trail. Cross the paved road near the waste disposal unit to the sign for the *Trimble Mountain Trail*. After 0.1 mile the trail forks for a loop in a barrow area. Here are white and Virginia pine, and bristly locust (*Robinia hispida*). Turn right at the fork, ascend on an old road, and pass the site of a former sawmill at 0.3 miles. At 0.6 miles the trail levels off in an area of interest to birders. There are scenic views from a rock outcropping at 1.2 miles to see Broad Run and toward Elkhorn Mountain. Continue the circle through hardwoods and groves of mountain laurel around a slope to Trimble Mountain saddle. Here are more views, including views of North River Campground area. At 2.1 miles reach the highest point on the trail (2,476 ft.). (Trimble Mountain is 2,740 ft.) At 3 miles notice rocks along the trail with remnants of tree fossils. Gradually descend, and at 3.4 miles pass through a bed of maidenhair ferns in a hardwood cove. Return to fork in the loop and exit at highway. (The trail was adopted for maintenance by BSA troop 145 of Dayton, Virginia, in 1984.)

USGS map: Stokesville; *USFS trail nos.*: 376, 375

Wild Oak Trail

191–93

Length and Difficulty: 25.7 miles (41.1 km) round-trip; strenuous

Connecting Trails: *Grooms Ridge Trail* (4 mi.), *Tearjacket Trail* (1.3 mi.), *Bald Ridge Trail* (8.3 mi.), *Dowells Draft Trail* (4 mi.), *White Oak Draft Trail* (2.8 mi.), *Bear Draft Trail* (2 mi.)

Features: solitude, historic site, panoramic views, flora and fauna

Trailhead: From Stokesville go north 1 mile on SR 718 to junction with FR 101 and FR 95. Turn left on FR 95 for 0.1 mile to parking area on the right.

Introduction: The trail was designated a national recreation trail in 1979. Its name represents the prominence of oak species on its circuit. When formed, the *Wild Oak Trail* replaced such trails as the *Chestnut Ridge Trail*, the *Hankey Mountain Trail*, and the *Lookout Mountain Trail*. This is an excellent trail for backpacking and getting away from crowded campgrounds, but it is less remote during big-game hunting season from mid-October to the last of December. If you are hiking during that time, wear a blaze orange jacket and cap. Following mostly on ridge crests, trail elevation varies from 1,600 feet at its terminus to 4,351 feet on Little Bald Knob. Water sources are infrequent; hikers should plan accordingly. Passing through more than 40 species of trees, including 5 kinds of pines, the trail is bordered with more than 50 species of wildflowers. Wildlife includes bears, deer, raccoons, turkeys, grouse, owls, hawks, foxes, rattlesnakes, chipmunks, and a wide range of songbirds. There are three points of entry: one is the trailhead listed on FR 95 near SR 718; a second is Camp Todd (not Lake

Todd) on FR 95 in Horse Trough Hollow; and a third is on FR 96, west of Hankey Mountain and north of US 250 on SR 715. For the purpose of making this a circuit hike, the three sections reached by means of these entry points are combined.

Description: From parking area and signboard, pass gated road and into a meadow to follow the white-blazed trail. Ascend through hardwood forests, gradually reaching Grindstone Mountain. At 2.3 miles enter a stand of pitch pine and understory of mountain laurel. Pass a timber road, Little Skidmore, on the left at 2.6 miles. The trail now becomes steep and rocky to reach an overlook at 3.9 miles. At 4.6 miles is a junction with the *Grooms Ridge Trail*, also called the *Big Ridge Trail*, from the right. (It descends 4 mi. to FR 101, 1 mi. north of FR 95.) The main trail continues ahead on a wide trail, formerly the *Chestnut Ridge Trail*, and passes a steep and rocky section at 5.5 miles. It turns left at 6.9 miles to a junction with Bald Mountain Road. (Bald Mountain Rd. runs right for 5 mi. to FR 85, where the *Shenandoah Mountain Trail* intersects south of Reddish Knob. The *Buckwheat Mountain Jeep Trail* is also on the Bald Mountain Road, 2.5 mi. from the *Wild Oak Trail*.) At 7 miles is Little Bald Knob (4,351 ft.), the highest point on the trail. This area, particularly a few yards out on Bald Knob Road, provides magnificent views. Begin descent, sometimes on rocky terrain, to North River and Camp Todd on FR 95 at 10.2 miles. (This area is the site of a pioneer's cabin, fire guard station, and railroad tram for logging.)

After crossing the road near Camp Todd historical marker begin the exceptionally steep climb up Springhouse Ridge toward Big Bald Knob (4,100 ft.). At 11.5 miles pass a spring, and at 11.6 miles pass a junction with the *Tearjacket Trail*. (It goes 1.3 mi. west to the *Ramsey Draft Trail*, Hiner Spring, and 0.7 mi. beyond to Hardscrabble Knob at 4,282 ft.) Reach Big Bald Knob, a wide, flat wildlife clearing of mountain laurel, oaks, pitch pine, and blueberries at 12.4 miles. Pass a grassy open area at 12.6 miles and descend to a wildlife clearing with a pond at 13.1 miles. At 13.2 miles is a junction with the *Bald Ridge Trail* from the Deerfield Ranger District on the right. (It goes 8.3 mi. to Braley Pond off SR 715. Along the way it joins the *Bridge Hollow Trail* for a descent to the *Ramseys Draft Trail* and US 250.) Pass a stream in a rocky area at 13.8 miles, and at 15.4 miles reach FR 96 (2,312 ft.). (To the right is SR 715, which descends 4 mi. to US 250. To the left FR 96 descends to a junction with FR 95, Elkhorn Lake, Todd Lake, and point of trail origin.)

Cross the road and climb steeply through white pines and oaks. At 16.7 miles veer right from a side trail on the left. Join the *Dowells Draft Trail* on the right, at 17.5 miles. (It descends 4 mi. to near Braley Pond and to US 250 across the highway from the *Chimney Hollow Trail*, both in the Deerfield Ranger District.) Ascend to summit of Hankey Mountain (3,407 ft.) at 17.7 miles. Here is a wide, scenic area in a grassy field with wildflowers and scattered oaks. On the ridge crest pass two wildlife clearings and at 18.6 miles arrive at the second peak of Hankey Mountain (3,450 ft.). Here is a junction with an old forest road (FR 425) ahead, and the *White Oak Draft Trail* on the right. (It descends south to White

Oak Draft and out to US 250, 3.5 mi. east of the *Dowells Draft Trail* on US 250 in the Deerfield Ranger District.) Leave the wildlife clearing and for the next 2 miles pass through five wildlife clearings. White oak and chestnut oak are prominent along the trail. At 20.6 miles is an overlook near a wildlife field. Oak, locust, and wildflowers are noticeable. Pass under a power line at 21.5 miles and reach another wildlife field at 21.8 miles. At 22 miles reach a junction with the *Bear Draft Trail* on the right, and a road to North River Campground on the left. (The *Bear Draft Trail* goes 2 mi. southeast to a gated forest road and SR 535 near Stribling Springs and east on SR 728 to VA 42. The road on the left that goes to North River Campground connects with the *North River Gorge Trail.*) Proceed ahead on what was formerly called the *Lookout Mountain Trail.* At 22.8 miles and 23.3 miles there are overlooks along the ridge that provide panoramic views. At 24 miles is an area of table mountain pines, oaks, maples, and blueberries. Descend; the trail is at points steep and rocky. At 25.2 miles the trail passes a side trail on the right. (This trail leads to Girl Scout Camp May Flather and private property.) Turn left toward and then cross North River. Rock-hop or wade if a footbridge is not constructed. Cross FR 95 and return to point of origin at 25.7 miles.

USGS maps: Stokesville, Reddish Knob, Palo Alto, West Augusta; *USFS trail nos.*: 716, 424, 447, 535 (only numbers for the Dry River Ranger District)

North River Gorge Trail   194

Length and Difficulty: 5 miles (8 km); moderate

Features: scenic river gorge, wildflowers, fishing

Trailheads: To access the southern trailhead from the junction of FR 95 and FR 523 at Todd Lake, drive 1.5 miles south on FR 95 to FR 95B and turn left. Go 1 mile to the North River Campground across the bridge. For the northern trailhead, drive 1.6 miles east from Todd Lake on FR 95 to the trailhead, right or 1.5 miles west on FR 95 from junction with FR 101.

Description: Begin the hike downriver at a road gate at 0.2 miles. After 0.6 miles ford the river for the first of nine times. Descend through steep walls of Lookout Mountain and Trimble Mountain. Because the terrain is irregular and water depth uncertain, hikers should turn back if the crossings appear hazardous, particularly at rapids. Rocks can be slippery and mossy. Ford the river twice again by 0.9 mi. For the next 1.5 miles follow a large horseshoe curve on the northern side before fording again at 2.4 miles. Because of the mist and the moist earth the vegetation is lush and dense with willow, alder, and rhododendron. Stonecrop and ferns are on the river banks. Poplar, birch, oak, and maple are among the taller trees. Ford the river again at 2.7 miles, 3 miles, 3.2 miles, and 3.5 miles. On the right side of the river follow an old road to a crossing of the river at 4.5 miles. Cross, and follow road to a gate at FR 95. (A loop can be made of this trail and part of the *Wild Oak Trail* for about 10.5 mi. At the northern trailhead of the *North River Gorge Trail* go downstream about 1.1 mi. on FR 95 to crossing of the *Wild Oak Trail* [route may be under construction]. Turn right, cross the river on a pedestrian suspension bridge, and follow the *Wild Oak Trail* 3.4 mi. to the *Bear Draft Trail* junction. Turn right and descend to North River Campground after 1 mi.)

USGS map: Stokesville; *USFS trail no.*: 538

HEARTHSTONE LAKE AREA
Augusta County

195–201 **Timber Ridge Trail**
Length and Difficulty: 8 miles (12.8 km); strenuous
Connecting Trails: *Sand Spring Mountain Trail* (3 mi.), *Wolf Ridge Trail* (4.5 mi.), *California Ridge Trail* (3 mi.), *Little River Trail* (8 mi.)
Features: scenic views, wildlife, wildflowers, solitude
Trailheads: The southeastern trailhead (at a small roadside parking area) is on FR 101 (Tillman Rd.), 0.7 miles north of Hearthstone Lake entrance and 3.6 miles south on FR 101 from junction of SR 924 and VA 257. The northwestern trailhead is at Reddish Knob on FR 85, 2.5 miles south from SR 924 at the top of Shenandoah Mountain.
Introduction: Water on this trail is available only at the beginning, near the southeastern trailhead. The trail and all its connectors ascend steeply to focus on Reddish Knob and an elevation gain of 2,616 feet. (The trail would be easier to hike down the mountain from Reddish Knob.) Parts of the trails are old or recent logging roads. They are sparsely blazed, eroded in sections, damaged by vehicular traffic, and partly overgrown. Nevertheless, these backcountry routes have generous spaces for solitude (except during the hunting seasons), some wilderness atmosphere, and copious wildflowers. Examples are starry campion, milkweed, yarrow, mountain mint, gold star, bellflower, black cohosh, wild azalea, trillium, evening primrose, and mountain laurel. Most of the forest is hardwoods on a dry ridge. Circuit routes can be made on the lower half of the trail with use of FR 101, and also on the *Narrowback Trail*, east from FR 101.
Description: Begin the yellow-blazed trail in a forest of oak, maple, and white pine. Cross a stream after 0.2 miles and begin a steady ascent to reach the ridgeline of Hearthstone Ridge at 1.3 miles. Reach a small knoll at 1.8 miles, gently descend to a saddle, and pass a wildlife pond at 2.2 miles. Ascend to a knoll (3,182 ft.) at 2.5 miles, and continue to ascend until reaching a slope and junction with the *Sand Spring Mountain Trail* at 4.2 miles.

(The *Sand Spring Mountain Trail* descends steeply on an old road, frequently eroded by vehicular traffic, beside or under a power line. There is a wildlife pond after 0.2 mi. and trailing arbutus on the road banks. At 2.3 mi. pass a wildlife pond, on the right, with frogs, wildflowers, and butterflies. Ahead are some large anthills and another wildlife pond on the left. Turn right off the road at 2.6 mi. [may be difficult to find] and pass through a young forest of pines and hardwoods on a brushy trail. Reach FR 101 at 3 mi. [Across the road, east, is a good parking area and western trailhead for the *Narrowback Trail*.] To the right, down FR 101, it is 1.1 mi. to the *Timber Ridge Trail* for making this a loop of 8.3 mi.)

Continuing on the main trail, cross a saddle, and reach a junction with the *Wolf Ridge Trail* on a slope at 4.9 miles. (This trail descends on a ridge by the same name for 4.5 mi. The only semilevel areas are at 2.8 mi. and after crossing Wolf Run among rhododendron at 4.3 mi. The topography of this trail is similar to that of the *Sand Spring Mountain Trail*. At 4.5 mi. reach FR 101. If making a loop, turn right on FR 101, pass the *Sand Spring Mountain Trail* at 1.4 mi., and reach the *Timber Ridge Trail*, southeastern trailhead, for a loop of 11.9 mi.)

The main trail proceeds through a saddle of two small knobs and ascends on a sharp ridge with occasional knolls. At 7.5 miles is a junction with the *California Ridge Trail*. (It descends steeply and roughly on California Ridge with switchbacks. Tributaries are near the end at 3 mi. Here is private land, and the rough road downstream on Briery Branch is best used by 4WDs for 2.2 mi. to SR 924, which is 2.7 mi. west from junction of FR 101 and VA 257.) To complete the main trail ascend to junction with abandoned *Little River Trail* and FR 85 at Reddish Knob. Turn left on road for 0.1 mile to an overlook (4,397 ft.) and spectacular 360° views. Backtrack or have a second vehicle here.

If visiting the Hearthstone Lake for fishing or boating, turn off FR 101 on FR 1177 (Little River Rd.), which is steep and rough, to a parking area. Rough waters of Little River have left rock rubble in strands and among willows, obliterating all signs of the abandoned *Little River Trail*. If you are interested in additional hiking options for short loops, consider using the *Tillman Trail* (1.7 mi.) and the *Narrowback Trail* (1 mi.). Hikers are cautioned to wear blaze orange jackets and caps during hunting season. Both of the above trails are popular with hunters.

From the *Timber Ridge Trail*, walk south for 0.3 miles on FR 101 (toward Hearthstone Dam), and turn left in a curve to begin the *Tillman Trail* (formerly called the *Narrowback Trail*). Cross Big Run and ascend to Narrowback Mountain range at 1.2 miles. The trail continues ahead, down the mountain, but a hunter's path leads left on the ridge for bushwacking 1.6 miles to the *Narrowback Trail*. Turn left here, and after an easy route of 0.6 miles reach a parking area at FR 101, across the road from the entrance to the *Sand Spring Mountain Trail*, at 3.4 miles. Hike south on FR 101 and return to point of origin for loop of 4.5 miles. If not bushwacking on Narrowback Mountain, continue the descent on the *Tillman Trail* to FR 536 at 2 miles. Turn left on FR 536 and follow a crooked and narrow, but generally level, road for 2.7 miles to a junction with the *Narrowback Trail* in a cove on the left. Ascend 0.4 miles to crest of Narrowback Mountain, descend to FR 101, turn left on the road, and return to point of origin for a loop of 6.8 miles.

USGS map: Reddish Knob; *USFS trail nos.*: 431, 423, 378, 436, 646, 439, 432

Heartbreak Trail (1.2 mi.), **Hone Quarry Ridge Trail** (3.8 mi.),
202–4   **Big Hollow Trail** (1.5 mi.)

Length and Difficulty: 8.1 miles (13 km) combined, partial round-trip; moderate to strenuous

Features: geological formations, wildlife, wildflowers, scenic views

Trailheads: For eastern trailhead, from Hone Quarry Campground and Picnic Area walk up FR 62 to the bridge over Hone Quarry Run and make an immediate left. To access the western trailhead, drive up the mountain on SR 942 from the VA 257 junction, to the Virginia/West Virginia state line. Turn right on FR 85 and drive 0.8 miles to FR 539, which may be gated. Descend 2 miles to the trailhead for the *Hone Quarry Ridge Trail*.

Introduction: A loop, plus 1.7 miles of backtracking, makes this circuit worth considering from the Hone Quarry Campground. A more ambitious option is to follow the *Hone Quarry Ridge Trail* to FR 85, turn right, follow it to FR 85A, which leads to the *Slate Springs Trail*, and a descent on the *Cliff Trail* to the campground for approximately 14 miles. Inexperienced hikers unfamiliar with this option should carry Reddish Knob and Brandywine topographical maps because of the many side roads and hunting trails.

Description: From the campground, walk up FR 62, cross the bridge, and take the nearest trail left over boulders and under hemlock. (The blaze may be yellow or orange warped plastic.) This is the *Heartbreak Trail*, whose name should be ankle-break trail. After 0.2 miles the trail is clearly defined, and its graded construction gives purpose. Unless fallen trees have been removed, there is a difficult passage at 0.4 miles. Lichens and mosses are thick on the rocky terrain, and chunks of trailing arbutus grow in between the rocks. Sounds of the creek, and from campers and picnickers, rise from the left. Because of gypsy moth defoliation, there are a few open spaces for views of the Slate Springs Mountain and Hone Quarry Run. At 1.2 miles there is a junction with the *Hone Quarry Ridge Trail*, right and left. (To the left the trail descends steeply 1 mi. to private homes. Do not take this route.) Turn right on a wide jeep road used by ATVs and begin ascending the ridge. There are young hardwoods, mountain laurels, blueberries, and rabbits pea. Pass a flat knoll on the northern side at 2.2 miles, cross a narrow knoll, and reach the *Big Hollow Trail* on the right at 3.2 miles on a knoll. (Either turn right for a descent to the campground for a 4.6-mi. loop or continue left up the ridge to complete the *Hone Quarry Ridge Trail*.) If continuing, ascend 1.7 miles to the end of the trail at FR 539. Ahead, up the ridge for 2 miles is a junction with FR 85. Backtrack to the *Big Hollow Trail* and descend rapidly on an old woods road through hardwoods, rhododendrons, hemlocks, and pines. Exit in a hemlock grove only a few yards northwest of the *Heartbreak Trail*, near the bridge, for a circuit of 8.1 miles.

USGS map: Reddish Knob; *USFS trail nos.*: 435A, 435, 430

Length and Difficulty: 6.7 miles or 11.2 miles (10.7 km or 17.9 km) combined, round-trip; strenuous

Features: scenic views, remoteness, wildlife, wildflowers

Trailheads: Trailheads for all three trails are on the·northern side of FR 62: the *Cliff Trail* is across the road from the Hone Quarry Picnic Area; the *Pond Knob Trail* is 2.5 miles farther upstream; and the *Slate Springs Trail* is 0.3 miles farther upstream.

Introduction: An excellent circuit can be made with part of the *Slate Springs Trail*, all of the *Pond Knob Trail*, and 0.3 miles of FR 62 for a total of 6.7 miles. A longer and more scenic circuit can include 5.4 miles of the *Slate Springs Trail*, all of the *Cliff Trail*, and 2.8 miles of FR 62 for a total of 11.2 miles. A two-car arrangement makes the latter circuit 7.4 miles. Hikers will see carsonite posts with multiple-use signs on these trails. The section of the *Slate Springs Trail* shown on topographical and USFS maps from Oak Knob (junction with the *Cliff Trail* and the *Mud Pond Gap Trail*) to SR 604 (off VA 257) is not described here because of private property right-of-way. Trail users should avoid this route.

Description: At roadside parking on FR 62, begin the *Slate Springs Trail* in a hemlock grove and slope right of the ridge. Ascend on a steep, wide, and rocky treadway among a forest understory of dense mountain fetter-bush (*Pieris floribunda*) and blueberry. Gold star and pungent pennyroyal are part of the ground cover. There is evidence of gypsy moth damage to the oaks. At 0.7 miles the ridge becomes more defined, and at 1.6 miles the ridge is narrow and rocky. Here are views left to Hone Quarry Ridge. Snakeskin and wrinkled shield lichens are on the trail boulders. After curving right from the ridge, ascend steeply in a damp area to a junction with FR 85A at 2.3 miles. (To the left on the road it is 0.4 mi. to Flagpole Knob [4,302 ft.], and another 1.6 mi. to FR 85, where to the left it is 0.7 mi. to Hone Quarry Ridge, FR 539, and northwest access to the *Hone Quarry Ridge Trail*. Another 1 mi. leads to Briery Branch Gap and junction with SR 924.)

Turn right on the road, and after 0.1 mile keep right at the road fork. (There is a spring after 0.1 mi. on the left fork road.) Descend and arrive at Meadow Knob at 3.7 miles. Here is a large, flat, grassy bald with thistle, yarrow, and chickory. Locust, oak, and hemlock are at the forest edge. Scenic views are mainly north toward High Knob at the Virginia/West Virginia border. (At the eastern edge of the bald, a rough road follows Slate Springs Mountain ridgeline 1.8 mi. east to FR 225 [ahead is 0.2 mi. to natural Maple Spring], which descends right to Black Run, makes a junction on the right with the *Blueberry Trail* and the *Mud Pond Gap Trail*, and exits to SR 933. See *Blueberry Trail* description, below.) At the southeastern edge of the bald look for a yellow blaze and follow the trail for 0.7 miles to a small pond and grassy Pond Knob. Along the way are oaks and mountain fetter-bush. At the junction the *Slate Springs Trail* goes left and the *Pond Knob Trail* goes right. (It descends steeply on a ridge, but leaves it, left, on a switchback to a stream area among hemlocks to exit in a hollow at FR 62, 0.3 mi. downroad from trailhead of the *Slate Springs Trail*. Loop is 6.7 mi.)

If continuing on the *Slate Springs Trail*, descend from Pond Knob to a level area, and reach Oak Knob (3,500 ft.) after 1 mile. Here is the suggested end of the *Slate Springs Trail*. (To the left it is 0.3 mi. to beginning of the *Mud Pond Gap Trail*, which goes 2.6 mi. to FR 225.) Turn right on the *Cliff Trail* and descend south on the western slope of the ridge for 3 miles to FR 62, a drop of 1,520 feet in elevation. On the descent, pass the headwaters of a stream at 0.5 miles, pass views of the valley at spur ridge curves, enter a rocky cove at 1.7 miles, and reach the major cliff overlook at 2.5 miles. Along the way are oaks, black birch, and mountain laurel. The unforgettable views from the cliff are of Hone Quarry Lake upstream to Shenandoah Mountain, and the southern ridges of Slate Springs Mountain on the right, and Hone Quarry Ridge on the left and ahead. Continue descent on rocky switchbacks to FR 62, across the road from the picnic area of Hone Quarry Recreation Area for a total of 7.4 miles. A return to the origin of the loop is 2.8 miles upstream on FR 62.

USGS maps: Reddish Knob, Brandywine; *USFS trail nos.*: 428–428B, 429

208–9   **Blueberry Trail** (1.7 mi.), **Mud Pond Gap Trail** (2.6 mi.)
Length and Difficulty: 6 miles (9.6 km) round-trip; moderate
Features: wildlife, wildflowers, solitude
Trailheads: The western trailhead is at the junction with the *Slate Springs Trail*, and the eastern trailheads are on FR 225. Access is off VA 257 at Briery Branch on SR 731. Drive 1.6 miles to SR 742. Turn left, and drive 1.3 miles to SR 933. On SR 933 drive 1.3 miles to FR 225 (which is rocky in sections). It passes the site of the historic Union Spring mineral water health resort. After 1.8 miles on FR 225 is the *Mud Pond Gap Trail*, left. Another 0.7 miles up the road is the trailhead for the *Blueberry Trail*.
Description: The two trails can easily make a loop of 6 miles with 1 mile of backtracking on the *Mud Pond Gap Trail*, and 0.7 miles on FR 225. Begin at the *Blueberry Trail* because parking space is more adequate at the ridge crest than it is for the *Mud Pond Gap Trail*. Ascend to two knobs through oak, locust, birch, and blueberries. Descend into Mud Pond Gap at 1.1 miles, and then ascend to grassy openings, Mud Pond, and the junction with the *Mud Pond Gap Trail* at 1.7 miles. Wildflowers and honeybees are here. Deer frequent the pond. Ascending ahead it is 1 mile on the *Mud Pond Gap Trail* to Oak Knob and the junction with the *Slate Springs Trail* and the *Cliff Trail*. Return on the *Mud Pond Gap Trail* to the junction with the *Blueberry Trail* at 3.7 miles and keep right. Descend to a number of grassy spots with wildflowers and a more level area at 4.4 miles. Descend on a ridge slope where the trail meets a stream at 5.1 miles. In a damp area with hemlock, follow an old road to exit over hummocks at 5.3 miles. Turn left on FR 225 and ascend to point of origin at 6 miles.

USGS maps: Reddish Knob, Briery Branch; *USFS trail nos.*: 554A, 554

James River Ranger District

The 164,260-acre James River Ranger District is bordered by West Virginia and partly by the Monongahela National Forest on the west, the New Castle Ranger District in the JNF on the south, the Glenwood Ranger District in the JNF on the east, and the Warm Springs Range District of the GWNF on the north, where Douthat State Park is at the district border. The longest contiguous forest properties are North Mountain in the northeast, which adjoins the 9,200-acre Rich Hole Wilderness; Fore Mountain in the center; and Potts Mountain in the south, where 20 acres of the 5,700-acre Barbour's Creek Wilderness and 95 acres of the 3,665-acre Shawvers Run Wilderness are at the district line with the New Castle Ranger District. The James River begins here, from the confluence of Jackson River and Cowpasture River. Trout streams in the district are Jackson River, Smith Creek, and Jerry's Run. In the northwestern corner is a section of Lake Moomaw, a popular recreation area. Forest vascular plants include southern hardwoods, and conifers such as hemlock and white pine in the lower elevations and red spruce on the high peaks and ridges.

The district is in the process of developing a 19.6-mile Highlands Scenic Tour under the guidelines of the USFS Byways Program and a conceptual plan by the Commercial Design and Assistance Center of Virginia Polytechnic Institute and State University in Blacksburg. The circuit is composed of two segments: 11.3 miles of FR 447, named Top Drive, and SR 700 (Collierstown Rd.) on the western side of North Mountain; and 8.3 miles of SR 850 (formerly US 60, named North Mountain Rd.). The loop would cross I-64 at interchanges 35 (SR 269-850) and 43 (SR 780). Plans are to have a central interpretive center on the route, probably near Longdale.

Through the center of the district (east to west) is I-64, with ten access points to other main arteries for the backcountry. Many of the state roads and forest roads remain unchanged from past years and retain their tranquil character. On these routes visitors drive to the recreation areas, the largest of which is Morris Hill Recreation Area. It has campground and picnic facilities south of Gathright Dam at Lake Moomaw. High on a ridge in a hardwood forest, the campground receives the cool breeze from the lake. It has trailer and tent sites, waste disposal, and warm showers. Trails from the campground are gray-blazed *Fortney Branch Trail* (1.6 mi.), which switchbacks to Fortney Boat Ramp, and the *Morris Hill Trail* (1 mi.), which descends to the lake, opposite Coles Point. The camping fee includes use of the beach at Coles Point and boat ramp charge at Fortney Boat Ramp. Nearby is Coles Mountain Picnic Area on the northern side of the dam. Here are group picnic shelters, a swimming beach, and a bathhouse. It has a nature trail, the *Coles Trail* (0.7 mi.), by the lake. Also here at the southern side of the dam is a Corps of Engineers visitor center. It serves as an educational source for the history of the area, and for the dam and lake and its functions. Access to the campground and Coles Point can be reached by taking exit 10 off I-64, to Callaghan, and then proceeding north on SR 600 and SR 666. Another recreation area is Longdale, a picnic and lake area with cold showers. It is usually open from May 1 to September 30, in contrast to May 1 through October for Morris Hill Campground. For access to Longdale, take exit 35 off I-64 and go west 2.2 miles. Trails from here are described below.

Foot trails received little attention in the 1980s but have experienced a resurgence of interest by the district in the 1990s. The most famous trail is the developing *Allegheny Trail* at the western end of the district. It comes into the district south of Smith Knob on the Allegheny Mountain and descends to Jerry's Run at exit 1, on I-64. (Its proposed southern route would include part of the *McAllister Fields Trail* [2.5 mi.], a hunters' trail on Brushy Mountain.) At least six new trails are planned to be part of the Highlands Scenic Tour, and a new wildlife trail is planned at the 400-acre Evans Tract on Cowpasture River.

Address and Information: James River Ranger District, 810-A Madison Ave., Covington, VA 24426; phone: 703-962-2214; access is exit 24 from I-64 to Madison Ave., west of the Holiday Inn. Available are district map with trails, and brochures or flyers on recreation areas.

LONGDALE AREA
Alleghany, Botetourt, and Rockbridge Counties

North Mountain Trail (Central)
Length and Difficulty: 8.6 miles (13.8 km); strenuous
Connecting Trail: YACCer's Run Trail (3 mi.)
Trailheads: The western trailhead is accessible from Longdale Recreation Area. From the junction of I-81 and I-64 at Lexington, go west on I-64 for 21 miles to exit 35, and drive west on SR 850 for 2.2 miles to Longdale Recreation Area on the left. Trailhead is at the picnic parking area, to the left. To reach the northern trailhead, turn off I-64, exit 43 at the Goshen sign, on SR 780 and follow it south to FR 477 (Top Dr., Highlands Scenic Tour) for 7 miles to the junction with SR 770. Trailhead is a few yards left on SR 770.
Description: Elevation change is 2,055 feet. For the first 0.3 miles the *North Mountain Trail (Central)* and the *YACCer's Run Trail* are together, after which the *North Mountain Trail (Central)* goes straight and crosses FR 271 (Tri-County Rd.) at 0.4 miles. (To the right is a parking area for hunters and hikers.) Follow the orange-blazed trail over tank traps and ascend left of Downy Branch. At 2.6 miles is a primitive campsite and access to FR 333 (Simmon's Rd.), left, which is not maintained. The forest has both northern and southern hardwoods, white pine, and rhododendron. The ascent becomes steeper for the next 1.6 miles to the top of North Mountain. Turn left (northeast) on the crest and shift back and forth on the boundary of the JNF and the GWNF. Expansive views are from rock outcroppings at 6 miles, 7.5 miles, and 7.7 miles. Evergreens are dense in some sections of the trail, and the updraft from Longdale Valley is usually strong. At 8 miles skirt right of a knob (3,244 ft.), and exit at SR 770 (Collierstown Rd.) and parking area at 8.6 miles. To the left is a junction with FR 447 (Top Dr.). (SR 770 descends east on a narrow, crooked road to Collierstown, and

west 3.8 mi. to Longdale on an equally challenging road.) (One mile ahead on Top Dr. is a large parking area for a scenic overlook of the Shenandoah Valley and twin peaks, Big House and Little House mountains. After another 1.4 mi. is a parking area [east] for 0.3-mi. *Cock's Comb Trail* [west]. Here are great views of Rich Hole Wilderness and Mill Mountain. Ahead it is 4.6 mi. to I-64, exit 43.)
USGS map: Longdale; *USFS trail nos.*: 658, 467, 465

YACCer's Run Trail (3 mi.), Blue Suck Trail (2 mi.), Anthony Knobs Trail (2.9 mi.)

216–18

Length and Difficulty: 7.9 miles (12.6 km) combined, round-trip; moderate
Connecting Trail: *North Mountain Trail (Central)* (8.6 mi.)
Features: streams, wildlife, scenic views
Trailhead: Longdale Recreation Area parking lot (see directions for *North Mountain Trail (Central)*, above).
Description: These trails connect and form two loops, one of 3 miles on the *YACCer's Run Trail*; the other two trails form another 4.9-mile loop. Turkey, deer, and grouse are often seen by quiet hikers on these loops. Begin on the *North Mountain Trail (Central)* up the steps from the parking lot, and after 0.3 miles leave the *North Mountain Trail (Central)* by turning right on the gray-blazed *YACCer's Run Trail*. Cross Downy Branch, and ascend on a northern slope of the ridge to a clearing with silverberry. Make a sharp right at 0.2 miles, cross a small stream at 0.4 miles, and reach a knoll at 1 mile. Descend, and cross a ravine and Blue Suck Branch to a junction with an old road, the *Blue Suck Trail*, left and right, at 1.5 miles. (The road right leads back to the picnic area, but the *Blue Suck Trail* follows upstream for 1.7 mi. to FR 271 and a junction with the *Anthony Knobs Trail*.) At 1.8 miles the *YACCer's Run Trail* goes right and the *Anthony Knobs Trail* goes left. (If hiking back to the parking area at this point, follow right on a ridge of oaks and pines to scenic views at 2 mi. and 2.3 mi. At 2.7 mi. begin a descent, and at 3 mi. reach paved FR 172, 0.1 mi. from the parking lot, on the right.) If hiking the *Anthony Knobs Trail*, ascend and follow the ridge up and down knolls, but stay left of old woods roads. At 1.8 miles turn left, descend, cross Sinking Creek, and reach FR 271 and junction with the *Blue Suck Trail* at 2.9 miles. Return to other trails by ascending slightly and descending to a tributary of Blue Suck Branch.
USGS map: Longdale Furnace; *USFS trail nos.*: 467, 704, 666, 460

Rich Hole Trail (5.9 mi.), White Rock Tower Trail (6 mi.)

219–20

Length and Difficulty: 11.9 miles (19 km) combined; strenuous
Features: wilderness, scenic views, stream, wildlife, wildflowers
Trailheads: To reach the northern trailhead for the *Rich Hole Trail*, get off I-64 (west of Lexington) at exit 43 onto SR 850 and go west 2.8 miles to parking area on the right. (From I-64, exit 35 in Longdale, take SR 850 east for 5 mi. to parking area on the left.) For the southern trailhead of the *Rich Hole Trail* and the northern trailhead of the *White Rock Tower Trail*, take exit 35 off I-64 and

drive northeast on SR 850 for 1.3 miles. Turn left on narrow FR 108 and drive 1.3 miles to parking area. To reach the southern trailhead of the *White Rock Tower Trail*, drive southwest on SR 770, across the bridge from SR 850 at the northern side of I-64, exit 35. After 0.6 miles SR 770 becomes FR 333; follow it for 3.1 miles to parking area where trail is on the northern side.

Introduction: These contrasting trails can be hiked separately or as a single unit. In either choice a two-car arrangement is needed. There is an elevation change of 2,080 feet on the *Rich Hole Trail* and about 2,870 feet on the *White Rock Tower Trail*. The wilderness is covered with about 90 percent second growth mixed hardwoods and pitch and table mountain pines. There are a few old growth stands of northern red oak, basswood, and sugar maple. Hikers will notice damage to the dogwoods from anthracnose and to the hemlock by woolly adelgid. Rocky outcropping is on both Brushy and Mill Mountains. Deer and grouse are frequently seen.

Description: Beginning at the northern trailhead of the *Rich Hole Trail* there is a good view to the south after 0.5 miles on Brushy Mountain. At 0.8 miles the grade is steep and rocky until a saddle is reached on Mill Mountain near a large cliff at 1.2 miles. Dense laurel, rhododendron, azalea, blueberry, and fetterbush are common on the ridgeline. (To the north are the headwaters of Alum Creek, the site of most of the old growth hardwoods in the wilderness.) Turn left at the saddle and begin a long, graded descent into North Branch Hollow. At 1.8 miles North Branch begins among fern beds in rich, moist soil. At 2.3 miles make the first of 13 crossings of North Branch. The trail widens to an old road at 4.4 miles, and at 5.9 miles arrives at the junction with the *White Rock Tower Trail*. Here, at the edge of the wilderness, is a parking area on FR 108.

To continue the hike on unmarked and unblazed *White Rock Tower Trail*, turn right up a rocky and curvy FR 108 to a gate. Beyond the steep climb the road ends at 2.3 miles at White Rock on Mill Mountain (3,055 ft.). Along the old road is evidence of the popularity of deer hunting. White Rock is the site of former White Rock fire tower. A few red spruce and fragrant mountain mint are here. Views west are of Cowpasture Valley and beyond to Beards Mountain. From here follow the trail on the western slope of the ridge to a panoramic view at 2.8 miles. Pass other rock outcroppings among chestnut oak and laurel. (An occasional orange blaze may be seen.) At 4.8 miles curve left around the ridge and descend on switchbacks to an old road and timber cut at 5.3 miles. Leave the road and ridge and reach the cul-de-sac of FR 333 at 5.6 miles (1,761 ft.).

USGS map: Longdale Furnace; *USFS trail nos.*: 464, 466

POTTS VALLEY AREA
Alleghany County

221   **Eastern National Children's Forest Trail**
Length and Difficulty: 0.3 miles (0.5 km) round-trip; easy
Features: forest restoration, historic site, wildflowers
Trailhead: From Covington go south on VA 18 for 11.7 miles to SR 613 on the left. Go

3 miles on SR 613 to FR 351 on the right. After 0.8 miles is the parking area on the right.

Description: This is a unique trail. It is a paved loop nature trail in a young forest with wildflowers. It was created to honor more than 1,000 children from Virginia, West Virginia, Maryland, and Pennsylvania who reforested 177 acres with shortleaf pine after a Potts Mountain forest fire in 1971. The trail, with a stone monument and the names of the children in a time capsule to be opened in 2072, was dedicated in April 1972. From the parking area are excellent views of Potts Valley and Peters Mountain range. (This area is close to and northeast of Barbours Creek and Shawvers Run wildernesses in the New Castle Ranger District of the JNF. See Chapter 1.)

USGS map: Gordon Mines; *USFS trail no.*: 626

FORE MOUNTAIN AREA
Alleghany County

Fore Mountain Trail   222–23

Length and Difficulty: 13.3 miles (21.3 km); strenuous
Connecting Trails: *Dry Run Trail* (7.8 mi.), *Middle Mountain Trail* (8.8 mi.)
Features: scenic views, wildlife, wildflowers, trout stream
Trailheads: For the southwestern trailhead, turn off I-64, exit 16, north at intersection and traffic lights of US 60/220 (Madison St.) and SR 1104 (Valley Ridge Rd.). (District office is left on Madison St., 0.1 mi. to sign on right.) Descend right on Valley Ridge Road for 0.2 miles to sign of Dolly Ann Work Center. Turn left between a motel and a restaurant and go 0.3 miles to parking area on the left. The northeastern trailhead is actually in Douthat State Park, bordering the Warm Springs Ranger District, but parking is on SR 606, 4.3 miles north from the junction of VA 188 and US 60/220 in downtown Clifton Forge. (No I-64 exit here; take exit 27 from east or exit 24 from west to VA 188 in Clifton Forge.) To reach SR 606 from Covington, turn off US 60/220 (0.7 mi. west of district office) on SR 625 (Dolly Ann Dr.), which becomes FR 125, and follow FR 125 for 8.4 miles to SR 606. Turn right and go 1.1 miles to trail crossing.

Introduction: This trail is the district's longest and most publicized. It is multiple use, with the Bordernier Riding Club maintaining parts of the route. Because the northern trailhead is unaccessible to vehicular traffic, it is necessary to backtrack the 3.1 miles from the top of Middle Mountain to SR 606 at Smith Creek, or hike out in Douthat State Park. The trail is vulnerable to ATVs and 4WDs for at least 5 miles on Fore Mountain. *Dry Run Trail* is a road, partially gated, heavily used by 4WDs, and eroded in places.

Description: From the parking area at Dolly Ann Work Center, begin at the trail sign on a foot trail. One major switchback is at 1 mile in a forest of oak, hickory and maple. At 1.3 miles is a view of Covington. Reach the top of the mountain at 2 miles to follow a grassy timber road bordered with white snakeroot and azaleas. At 4 miles is a view to the east of Low Moor Valley and Rich Patch

Mountains. In a grazing field at 6 miles is a junction on the left with the *Dry Run Trail.*

(The *Dry Run Trail* descends on FR 448 for 0.5 mi. to cross FR 125. Along the way are chinquapin, mountain laurel, and Deptford pink. It descends from FR 125 to a wide saddle with a field of wildflowers and space to park. A gated timber road is on the right, but the *Dry Run Trail* ascends on an open and eroded road. At 2.6 mi. it reaches a view of Bald Knob to the right, and another view at 3.4 mi. of Big Knob [4,072 ft.]. After crossing Peters Ridge at 5 mi., the trail descends to Dry Run at 5.9 mi., where it parallels the stream to gated FR 339 at 7.8 mi. Space for parking is small. Access here is 0.3 mi. on Cypress Street from US 220 [N. Alleghany Ave.] in Covington, and 2.7 mi. west of district office.)

To continue on the *Fore Mountain Trail* (less used than the first 6 mi.), follow the mountain ridgeline. At 7.1 miles are views east to Clifton Forge. There are rock outcrops at 9 miles (2,823 ft.), after which the trail descends steeply to two major switchbacks. At 9.5 miles is a junction with FR 337 (it is an ungated dead-end road on the right, but 0.7 mi. to the left is SR 606). The trail descends 0.7 miles into a hardwood forest with beds of wintergreen to cross SR 606 (McGraw Gap Rd.) at 10.2 miles. Rock-hop or wade Smith Creek, a stocked trout stream, at 10.3 miles to begin an ascent of Pine Spur Ridge. After 1 mile there are views of Clifton Forge and Smith Creek Valley. Reach the ridge top at 13.3 miles, the end of the trail in the district, but the beginning of the *Middle Mountain Trail* in Warm Springs Ranger District (in this chapter) and a trail network in Douthat State Park. Backtrack for equestrians; for hikers, an extended hike can be another 8.8 miles (see Chapter 11).

USGS maps: Clifton Forge, Covington, Healing Springs; *USFS trail nos*.: 473, 471

JERRY'S RUN AREA
Alleghany County

224–25   **Jerry's Run Trail** (2.4 mi.), **Batlick Mountain Trail** (2.3 mi.)

Length and Difficulty: 9.4 miles (15 km) round-trip; easy to moderate

Features: trout stream, cascades, wildlife, seclusion

Trailhead: Access is 12 miles west of Covington and 2 miles east of the state line on I-64, exit 2; travel south on FR 198 for 0.6 miles, where the road becomes FR 69. The parking area is 0.4 miles ahead on the left.

Description: These two trails dead-end. *Jerry's Run Trail* has a high traffic volume, but the volume on the *Batlick Mountain Trail* is exceptionally low. Cross the road at the parking area to a 4WD road for *Jerry's Run Trail* and descend into a forest of white pine and hemlock to rock-hop Jerry's Run, a stocked trout stream, at 0.4 miles. At 0.5 miles on the right, at a white oak, is the *Batlick Mountain Trail* trailhead.

The *Batlick Mountain Trail* ascends at the base of a ridge and makes 11 switchbacks—all skillfully designed—in an open forest to the top of the mountain at 0.9 miles. After a turn left on the ridge there is a weathered bench at 1.1 miles. The trail now curves right, follows a flat ridge, makes a curve left, and halts at 2.3 miles near a USFS boundary marker (which may not be easy to detect). Here is the Virginia/West Virginia state line. Beyond the otherwise unmarked trail is private property. This is a good place for meditation. Backtrack.

To continue on *Jerry's Run Trail*, follow the 4WD road through a grand forest of beech, maple, oak, and hemlock with a rhododendron undercover. Rockhop Jerry's Run 8 times among cascades, rock piles, and pools to a dead end at 2.4 miles. Beyond is heavily posted private property. Backtrack.

USGS map: Jerry's Run; *USFS trail no.*: 659, 641

ALLEGHENY MOUNTAIN AREA
Alleghany County, Virginia, and Greenbrier County, West Virginia

Allegheny Trail

Length and Difficulty: 15.5 miles (24.8 km); strenuous
Features: scenic views, wildlife, isolation
Trailheads: From I-64, take exit 1 (12 mi. west of Covington); at Jerry's Run sign, turn north 0.2 miles to dead-end road and parking space for southern trailhead. For northern trailhead, from I-64, exit 7 (7.5 mi. west of Covington), at SR 661, turn north 10.4 miles on SR 661 and SR 781 to Rucker Gap and enter West Virginia. Descend 0.8 miles on CO 14 to Lake Sherwood Road, turn left, and proceed 1.3 miles to parking area on the left. (It is 2.5 mi. farther to Neola and WV 92.)
Introduction: The 300-mile *Allegheny Trail* is a foot trail from the Pennsylvania state line through West Virginia to north of Pearisburg, Virginia. Coming south, at milepost 253, it enters Virginia in this section, with 10.5 miles in the James River Ranger District. On its way it passes through pieces of private property. The other 5 miles are in the Monongahela National Forest in West Virginia. Constructed by the West Virginia Scenic Trails Association, the trail will be about 330 miles when completed. (The trail is an ongoing project and likely will cross Brushy Mountain from Jerry's Run, south of I-64, on its way to Peters Mountain. From there it will connect with its most southern section south of Paint Bank. See JNF, Chapter 1.)
Description: Begin at the southern trailhead and follow the yellow-blazed trail in a hardwood forest to the top of a ridge. Descend, cross a stream in Fox's Hollow at 0.9 miles, and pass left of a logging road at 1.1 miles. Ascend on a ridge spine to overlooks at 2.3 miles and 2.4 miles. Views southeast are of Brushy Mountain and Jerry's Run hollow (locally called Doe Lick), and north to Smith Knob. Follow the boundary between Virginia and West Virginia on an old woods road, but turn left onto private property and another road at 3.3 miles. Turn right at 3.7 miles. Cross a stream at 4.3 miles, and ascend on switchbacks. Leave private property at 4.6 miles. After following the ridge in and out of private property and USFS property, reach Smith Knob (3,400 ft.) at 8.1 miles. From a grassy bald there are outstanding views north to Laurel Run Valley and southeast to Panther Ridge. Descend in a rough area to junction with CO 15/3 (White's Draft Rd., which descends 5.2 mi. down the mountain in West Virginia to WV

92) at 9.7 miles. Curve around a ridge of Allegheny Mountain, leave Virginia, and descend on switchbacks to Laurel Run at 11.1 miles. For the next 4.4 miles the trail crosses Laurel Run six times, and passes by and through wildlife fields and forests of white pine, hemlock, hardwoods, and rhododendron to a parking area at CO 14 (Lake Sherwood Rd.). Along the way are excellent campsites.
USGS maps: Jerry's Run, Alvon, Rucker Gap; *USFS trail no.*: 701

OLIVER MOUNTAIN AREA
Alleghany and Bath Counties

226–30   **Oliver Mountain Trail**
Length and Difficulty: 8 miles or 9.6 miles (12.8 km or 15.4 km) round-trip; moderate to strenuous
Connecting Trails: *Brushy Lick Trail* (6.1 mi.), *Medden Hollow Trail* (1.8 mi.), *Jackson Trail* (1 mi.)
Features: lake, scenic area, wildlife, seclusion
Trailheads: From Covington at the junction of US 60/220, go north on US 220 for 3.7 miles to SR 687 and turn left. Go 3.3 miles to SR 641 and turn left. After 0.5 miles turn right on SR 666 and follow it 4.2 miles to its end and a junction with SR 600. At this junction it is 0.3 miles right to the northern trailhead at Lake Moomaw Fortney Branch Boat Ramp and parking area. To the left it is 0.7 miles on SR 600 to FR 192. It ascends 3.1 miles to the western trailhead.
Introduction: Topographical maps show the *Oliver Mountain Trail* to be approximately 10 miles, 3 miles of which are on private land. The trailheads would be from Lake Moomaw to Rucker Gap on SR 781 at the Virginia/West Virginia state line. In 1982 the USFS listed the trail as 7.5 miles, and in 1992 as 3.4 miles. Actually, the first 4.8 miles, from Lake Moomaw to Oliver Mountain, are on USFS property and can be easily followed. Because a backtrack of 3.2 miles is necessary to the FR 192 trailhead, the distance has been added for round-trip plans. For a period of years the USFS had permission for the entire distance through private property.
Description: A fee of $2 is required to park at the Lake Moomaw Fortney Branch Boat Ramp and parking area between May 1 and September 30. At the parking area's ramp edge, there is 0.3-mile *Fishing Access Trail* that hugs the mountainside to make a scenic route into a cove and exposed ridge. To begin the yellow-blazed *Oliver Mountain Trail* from the parking area, walk up the road 385 feet and climb over the right guardrail. Descend an embankment to a small stream. Ascend on a shale treadway with deer moss, turkey oak, and mountain laurel. At 0.7 miles is a wide cove and at 0.8 miles are views of the high parking area for the end of FR 192. After four other coves the trail reaches the ridge crest at 1.5 miles. Ahead it is 0.1 mile to the small parking area at the end of FR 192. To the right is the *Brushy Lick Trail*.
    (The *Brushy Lick Trail* is orange-blazed; it follows a dry ridge of hardwoods and Virginia pine, north. At 0.4 mi. is a junction, right, with the *Medden Hollow Trail*. [It is unmarked and unmaintained. It descends on a spur ridge for

0.8 mi. with views of Lake Moomaw. It then drops steeply into a hollow to follow an old logging road. It skirts the northern side of the ridge but curves around it at 1.3 mi. From here it descends into Medden Hollow, a narrow cove of Lake Moomaw at 1.8 mi. Backtrack.] Continuing on the *Brushy Lick Trail*, there are steep knobs, but at 1 mi. there is a saddle where the trail divides for a loop ahead and to the left. Ahead the trail ascends its steepest knob to 1.2 mi. It descends steeply and after a drop over some lesser knobs for 1,000 vertical ft. it reaches Hughes Draft. Here are the cove waters of Lake Moomaw at 2.6 mi. Turn left and follow a 4WD road upstream. [Abandoned tents and dead trees from beaver dams offer a ghostly hollow.] Rock-hop the stream [which may be dry in summer] four times, and turn left on a grassy old road at 3.7 mi. Follow upstream of shallow Brushy Lick, crossing it twice. At 4.6 mi. stay left among a few old apple trees near a campsite. Ascend steeply up a hollow to the saddle for rejoining the trail at 5.2 mi. Turn right and ascend on knobs to *Oliver Mountain Trail* at 6.1 mi.)

On the *Oliver Mountain Trail*, cross the parking space of FR 192 (considered the western trailhead because of the trail's dead end). Ascend on a narrow ridge, and stay close to the ridge's eastern edge for the next 0.8 miles. At 3.2 miles is a junction with the *Jackson Trail* on the left. (It descends steeply on a ridge to end after 1 mi. at a large parking area for FR 192. This space is useful if the other parking space is crowded or the gate to it is locked.) The *Oliver Mountain Trail* continues 0.2 miles to a low saddle on Oliver Mountain. For the next 1.4 miles to the private property boundary are four knolls on an average of 3,100 feet in elevation. The forest is open hardwood with trees such as oak, locust, ash, and hickory. Backtrack to FR 192, or to Lake Moomaw if only one vehicle is available. *USGS maps*: Rucker Gap, Falling Spring: *USFS trail nos.*: 438, 469, 502, 510, 469A

Lee Ranger District

231–33

Lee Ranger District has 189,082 acres about evenly divided in two segments. One is on both sides of Great North Mountain, where half of the segment (51,950 acres) is in West Virginia. The other segment is east of the Shenandoah Valley. Its topographical shape is like a gargantuan needle with the eye in Fort Valley. Surrounding the eye are Powell and Green Mountains on the west and Massanutten Mountain on the east and forming the needle point south to Harrisonburg. Snugly fitting the outside of the eye are oxbow forks of the Shenandoah River. On the southwestern corner the district adjoins Dry River Ranger District. On the eastern segment the boundary is within 2 miles of the Shenandoah National Park. Sandstone outcropping is frequent in both segments. Two of its highest peaks are along the Virginia/West Virginia border: Mill Mountain (3,293 ft.) and Devil's Hole Mountain (3,266 ft.). Other natural attractions are Big Schloss, a massive rock formation on Mill Mountain; Signal Knob, southeast of Strasburg; and Mountain Run, a cascading stream northeast of Harrisonburg. Drainage in the district is northeast, either to the Potomac or the Shenandoah River. Forests are mainly hardwood. Damage is extensive to pines from the southern pine beetle, and infestations by the gypsy moth on oaks and a fungal disease on dogwoods have also caused defoliation. Bear, deer, grouse, turkey, and raccoon are among the most prominent game animals.

Human history in the district is illustrated at Elizabeth Furnace Recreation Area, where there are remnants of the iron ore industry that flourished 150 years ago. Signal Knob had breastworks during the Civil War, and Sherman Gap Road, a Revolutionary War redeployment route for General Washington's army, is east of Fort Valley. There is archaeological evidence of an Indian village that existed between 3000 and 11500 B.C. at "The Point" of the South Fork of the Shenandoah River. Also on historic soil are two developed fee campgrounds, Elizabeth Furnace and Camp Roosevelt in Virginia, with the usual facilities. In West Virginia is Trout Pond Recreation Area with campground facilities including electrical hookups. Full service is provided usually from late April or early May to mid- or late September. There are four nonfee undeveloped campgrounds: Little Fort (open year round, near Woodstock); Hazard Mill (open April through November, near Bentonville); Hawk Camp (open April through December, near Capron Springs in West Virginia); and Wolf Camp (open year round, near Columbia Furnace). There are two canoe camps: Hazard Mill is accessible on SR 613 west from Bentonville, and High Cliff can be reached from Luray on SR 675 west and SR 684 north. Massanutten Visitor Center is on US 211, 3.8 miles east of New Market. On its staff is an interpretive specialist. Nearby are interpretive trails. The district estimates that it has about 2.5 million annual visitors who see or utilize the services of its total acreage.

Many visitors choose the district for its first-class trail network. There are 75 color-coded, paint-blazed, user-designated trails with a total of 245 miles for hikers and backpackers, equestrians, bicyclists, and the physically disabled. Additionally, there are trails designated for visitors who use motorized vehicles. Accounting for the popularity and quality of this trail system are the district's leadership in trail development, the volunteer assistance in planning and preservation of trails by the PATC and other volunteers, and the accessibility and proximity to metropolitan areas.

The district's longest trail is the *Massanutten Mountain Trail.* It has three connecting sections with a total of 60 miles. (The USFS plans to alter the connecting routes of east and west by relocations in the Waterfall Mountain area, and by completing new mileage on the western side with Short Mountain ridge, Gap Creek, and Kerns Mountain before the twenty-first century.) Another long trail, which connects with the *AT*, is the *Big Blue Trail*, with 55 miles in Virginia, of which 36 miles are in the district. A few isolated trails (the first two used mainly by hunters) are not described here. They are 2.7-mile *Orkney Springs Trail* (1 mi. north of Basyne on SR 717); 3.1-mile *Hunkerson Gap Trail* (at Tomahawk Pond Picnic Area, 3.5 mi. southwest of Orkney Springs on SR 610); and 1-mile *Canoe Camp Trail,* unblazed (at Hazard Mill Canoe Camp, west on SR 613 from Bentonville).

231–33

Address and Information: Lee Ranger District, Windsor Knit Rd., Rt. 4, Box 515, Edinburg, VA 22824; phone: 703-984-4101/4102; at junction of I-81, exit 279, SR 675/VA 185 E. Available are district map with trails, recreation flyers and brochures.

MASSANUTTEN MOUNTAIN (EAST) AREA
Shenandoah, Warren, and Page Counties

Massanutten Mountain East Trail   234–46
Length and Difficulty: 25.6 miles (40.9 km); moderate to strenuous
Connecting Trails: Big Blue Trail (9 mi.), Buzzard Rock Trail (3.9 mi.), Shawl Gap
   Trail (2.4 mi.), Veach Gap Trail (1.1 mi.), Milford Gap Trail (2.8 mi.), Tolliver
   Trail (2.3 mi.), Indian Grave Ridge Trail (2.5 mi.), Habron Gap Trail (1.5 mi.),
   Kennedy Peak Trail (0.3 mi.), Duncan Hollow Trail (9.1 mi.)
Features: historic site, old iron furnace, wildlife, scenic overlooks, solitude, wild-
   flowers
Trailheads: Access to the northern trailhead is officially from a parking area on SR
   619 south of the Front Royal Fish Cultural Center. It is also accessible on the *Big
   Blue Trail* from Elizabeth Furnace Recreation Area on SR 678. For either approach, turn south off VA 55 at Waterlick on SR 678 (5.2 mi. east of Strasburg and
   7.2 mi. west of Front Royal). Drive 1 mile to a junction with SR 619 on the left. It
   goes about 1.2 miles to a trailhead parking area on the right. To approach
   Elizabeth Furnace Recreation Area from the junction, continue straight on SR
   678 for 3 miles to the picnic parking area on the left (the campground is ahead
   on the left of SR 678). The southern trailhead is at Camp Roosevelt, farther
   upstream on SR 678 for 14.1 miles to junction with SR 675. Turn left, and after 4.2
   miles the campground is on the left.
Introduction: The Elizabeth Furnace Campground is an excellent base camp for
   hiking trails on both the Massanutten Mountain and adjoining ranges. The
   camping and picnic areas are open year round and have trailer and tent sites,
   flush toilets, warm showers, and waste disposal. At the picnic area are the *Pig
   Iron Trail*, a 0.2-mile interpretive loop trail explaining how pig iron was made at
   the furnace, and the *Charcoal-Passage Creek Trail*, a 0.4-mile interpretive loop
   trail explaining how charcoal was processed. In the nineteenth century the iron
   ore was mined, purified, and hauled by wagon over the Massanutten Mountain
   for barging on the Shenandoah River to Harpers Ferry. This old road is part of
   the *Big Blue Trail* described below. The *Big Blue Trail* (143 mi.) passes through
   the picnic area on its western route from the *AT* at Mathews Arm in the
   Shenandoah National Park to West Virginia for 55 miles, and on to Hancock,
   Maryland. (See *Mill Mountain Trail*, below, and Bibliography.)
Description: If using the *Big Blue Trail* to approach the *Massanutten Mountain East
   Trail*, hike from the picnic area, left of the furnace, downstream by Passage
   Creek for 0.4 miles. Vegetation includes basswoods, oaks, azaleas, phloxes,
   spicebushes, and asters. Here it ascends on graded switchbacks to an overlook
   at 1.5 miles, crossing the old wagon road occasionally. After a steep ascent, reach
   the ridge crest in Shawl Gap at 2.4 miles (1,700 ft.). Here is a junction with

orange-blazed *Massanutten Mountain East Trail* (left jointly with the *Buzzard Rock Trail*, and right jointly with the *Big Blue Trail*). Also to the left it is 0.1 mile to a junction, right, with the yellow-blazed *Shawl Gap Trail*. (It descends on an old forest road that switchbacks by clearcuts and wildlife clearings for 2.3 mi. Its eastern trailhead is at a parking area on SR 613, 1.8 mi. south from a junction with SR 619 [or 3.3 mi. from SR 678].)

To begin the *Massanutten Mountain East Trail* from SR 619, ascend on switchbacks to the rocky Buzzard Rock at 1.9 miles. Here are scenic views and the beginning of the *Buzzard Rock Trail* to Shawl Gap. Follow the ridgeline south and ascend to a knob, then descend to pass the junction with the *Shawl Gap Trail* at 3.8 miles. At 3.9 miles pass the junction with the *Big Blue Trail*, which runs jointly with the *Massanutten Mountain East Trail*. Ascend and descend on a rocky ridge on a narrow tread among hardwoods. After passing a number of overlooks, reach a junction with Sherman Gap Road at 6.2 miles. (This historic road may have been constructed at the request of General Washington during the American Revolution. The road is about 5 mi. from SR 613 at private property and crosses the mountain to descend and ford Passage Creek at SR 678. It may be overgrown and not easy for passage. The USFS plans to relocate part of the route and add it to its TIS.)

Reach Little Crease Mountain at 6.6 miles, and descend on switchbacks into Mill Creek Hollow. At 9.4 miles reach Veach Gap area, cross a stream, and turn left. To the right is yellow-blazed *Veach Gap Trail*. (It follows an old road 1.1 mi. along the stream among large hemlocks. It exits at the parking area of FR 409. From there it is 0.3 mi. to SR 744, and on SR 744 it is 0.5 mi. across Passage Creek to SR 678.)

At 9.5 miles is Little Crease Shelter, about 150 yards to the left. From here the trail ascends on a rocky road with legendary Revolutionary War history. (It is thought George Washington, who had surveyed the Massanutten Mountain in the 1750s, directed the road to be built in the 1780s for military redeployment if needed.) After 0.9 miles reach Veach Gap (1,800 ft.) at 10.6 miles. Here the *Big Blue Trail* goes east and leaves the *Massanutten Mountain East Trail*. (The *Big Blue Trail* descends 1.3 mi. to SR 613. From here it is 3.8 mi. to US 340 with a low-water crossing of the Shenandoah River along the way. After another 9 mi., part of which ascends steeply, the *Big Blue Trail* intersects with the *AT* near milepost 21 of the Skyline Drive.)

On the *Massanutten Mountain East Trail*, follow the ridge with successive ascents and descents on rocky conglomerate knolls; at 13.9 miles is Milford Gap and a junction with the *Milford Gap Trail*.

(The *Milford Gap Trail*, white-blazed, descends for 1.8 mi. right to Chalybeate Spring and continues 0.9 mi. to SR 758 near Passage Creek and out to Detrick. Also from this point, the *Milford Gap Trail* descends left for 2 mi. to Hazard Mill Campground near the South Fork of the Shenandoah River. A hike downstream on SR 613, 3.3 mi. farther, leads to the *Big Blue Trail* crossing. After 0.5 mi. on the *Milford Gap Trail* from the *Massanutten Mountain East Trail*, the

Tolliver Trail forks right, descending for 2.3 mi. to SR 717 at Burners Bottom near the South Fork of the Shenandoah River and east of the fire warden's home.)

At 15.3 miles on the *Massanutten Mountain East Trail* is a junction with the *Indian Grave Ridge Trail* on the left. (The purple-blazed trail descends for 2.5 mi. through oaks and pines to a parking area on SR 717, 3 mi. from SR 684 junction near Goods Mill Falls on the South Fork of the Shenandoah River.) At Habron Gap (1,927 ft.) at 18.8 miles, cross the *Habron Gap Trail.* (The eastern side is blazed blue; it descends by Keyser Path for 1.4 mi. in locust and walnut stand to SR 684 near Fosters Landing of the South Fork of the Shenandoah River. The unblazed western side descends to SR 684 off SR 769 near Mt. Zion Church.) The main trail continues on the ridge through numerous blueberry patches. At 20 miles it crosses the former *Stephens Trail.* There is a junction with the *Kennedy Peak Trail* at 22.4 miles on the left. (This 0.3-mi., white-blazed spur ascends to a former lookout tower [2,560 ft.] for an outstanding view of Page Valley.) The *Massanutten Mountain East Trail* skirts west of Kennedy Peak, but after 23.2 miles partially follows an old forest road to SR 675 (1,849 ft.) at 24.7 miles in Edith Gap. (On the road it is 6.5 mi. east to Luray and 1.4 miles west on SR 675 to Camp Roosevelt.) The trail does not cross the road, but turns right to descend on switchbacks through old iron mines. At 25.6 miles it reaches SR 675 and a small parking area at Camp Roosevelt. Across the road, 60 yards, is the northern trailhead of the *Duncan Hollow Trail.*

Historic Camp Roosevelt is the site of the first CCC camp in the nation, operating April 4, 1933, through May 1942. A sign here recognizes Henry Rich, the first CCC member. The fee campground has trailer and tent sites, flush toilets, and waste disposal. It is open from April 30 to September 30. There is a unique trail with Braille descriptions 0.9 miles south on FR 274 from the SR 675 junction at Camp Roosevelt. The 0.3-mile loop, the *Lion's Tale Trail* for the visually impaired, was designated a national recreation trail in 1979 and is maintained by area Lions Clubs.

USGS maps: Strasburg, Bentonville, Rileyville, Luray, Hamburg; *USFS trail nos.*: 483, 483A, 404, 405.1, 404B, 406, 484, 560, 560A, 567, 559, 404A, 410

Duncan Hollow Trail 247–51

Length and Difficulty: 9.2 miles (14.7 km); moderate
Connecting Trails: *Massanutten Mountain East Trail* (23.3 mi.), *Gap Creek Trail* (2.1 mi.), *Scothorn Gap Trail* (2.8 mi.), *Middle Mountain Trail* (0.6 mi.), *Waterfall Mountain Trail* (1.3 mi.), *Massanutten Mountain South Trail* (24.5 mi.)
Features: stream, wildlife, scenic forest road, wildflowers
Trailheads: Camp Roosevelt, across the road from the *Massanutten Mountain East Trail* (0.4 mi. south from junction of SR 675 and FR 274, Crisman Hollow Rd.) is the northern trailhead. Access to Camp Roosevelt from I-81, exit 269 (between New Market and Mt. Jackson), is 9.1 miles on SR 730 (Hider Spring Rd.), east to junction of SR 675 and FR 274. The southern trailhead is at parking lot on US 211, 1.4 miles west on US 211 to New Market Picnic Grounds, 2.2 miles west to the

Massanutten Visitor Center, and an additional 3.8 miles to New Market. Luray is 8 miles east on US 211.

Description: From the southern trailhead of the *Massanutten Mountain East Trail* at Camp Roosevelt, enter a graded, orange-blazed trail through an oak forest to Duncan Creek. Proceed 3 miles upstream, with Catback Mountain west and Massanutten Mountain east paralleling the trail, to blue-blazed *Gap Creek Trail*.

(The *Gap Creek Trail* ascends west on switchbacks to Peach Orchard Gap between Middle Mountain and Catback Mountain to descend for a junction with the *Scothorn Gap Trail* after 1 mi. [The *Scothorn Gap Trail* is a secluded route to the headwaters and bog of a stream, and between two knobs to end at FR 274 at Passage Creek. The red-blazed trail, the only red in the district, has several wildlife clearings, which are good for birding.] The *Gap Creek Trail* continues west to descend and join FR 274. A 5.6-mi. loop could be made by following FR 274, left, 1.7 mi. to a junction with the *Scothorn Gap Trail*.)

The *Duncan Hollow Trail* continues upstream on graded contours. It leaves the stream and hollow, right, at 4.6 miles to cross Middle Mountain at a saddle; it descends to the headwaters of Big Run at 5.2 miles. (Here yellow-blazed *Middle Mountain Trail* ascends right [north] for 0.6 mi. to a bog at the *Scothorn Gap Trail*, where it goes 1.5 mi. to the *Gap Creek Trail*, or southwest for 1.3 mi. to FR 724. At this point a circuit hike of 11.3 mi. can be made right to connect with the *Duncan Hollow Trail* and return to Camp Roosevelt.)

The main trail gradually descends; at 7.4 miles it passes a junction with the *Waterfall Mountain Trail*, a white-blazed trail on the right. (This trail ascends steeply over the mountain range that bears the trail name, and descends to FR 724. From here, southwest, it is 2.5 mi. on FR 724, which may be locked, to US 211 at New Market Gap.) The main trail descends, passes left of a relocation of the trail, and enters a wildlife opening at 7.9 miles. After the field, it descends to FR 415 (Big Run Rd.) on the right. For the next 1.3 miles the gated scenic road (good for birding and views north of Stricklen Knob and other knobs) passes through wildflowers and ferns. A parking lot at a barrow area is across the highway to a junction with the *Massanutten Mountain South Trail*.

USGS maps: Hamburg; *USFS trail nos.*: 410, 409, 555, 555A, 412, 416

MASSANUTTEN MOUNTAIN (SOUTH) AREA
Page, Shenandoah, and Rockingham Counties

252–61   **Massanutten Mountain South Trail**

Length and Difficulty: 19.5 miles (31.2 km); moderate to strenuous

Connecting Trails: Bird Knob Trail (2.2 mi.), *Roaring Run Trail* (3.8 mi.), *Pitt Springs Trail* (0.3 mi.), *Morgan Run Trail* (1.4 mi.), *Fridley Gap Trail* (3 mi.)

Features: wildlife, anthills, spring, stream, isolation, scenic views, wildflowers

Trailheads: The northern trailhead is at a parking lot across US 211 from the southern trailhead of the *Duncan Hollow Trail*, 1.4 miles east from the Massanutten Visitor Center on US 211, and 8 miles west of Luray. The southern trailhead is on SR 636, near gated FR 65 (Cub Run Rd.). From junction of US

33-A and SR 635 in Elkton, go north 0.8 miles to SR 636 on the left, and follow it 1.5 miles to SR 602 (Bethel Church). Turn right (north), go 0.7 miles, and turn left on SR 636. After 2.2 miles reach the parking lot, right.

Introduction: Before you hike the *Massanutten Mountain South Trail*, a visit to the Massanutten Visitor Center at the New Market Gap on US 211 is worthwhile. The *Discovery Way*, a 0.2-mile paved, self-guiding loop nature trail, begins at the southern end of the center's parking area. Another interpretive trail, the *Massanutten Story Book Trail* (0.3 mi.), is on FR 724 (Crisman Hollow Rd.), 1.5 miles north of the center. The paved trail for the physically disabled explains the geology of the mountains. The *Massanutten Mountain South Trail* is the district's second longest linear trail. (Combine it with the *Duncan Hollow Trail* and the *Massanutten Mountain East Trail* for a total of 52 mi. and an exciting backpacking experience.) There is not a shelter or campground at the northern trailhead, but there is a restaurant on US 211, near the New Market Gap Picnic Area. Boone Run Shelter is close to FR 65 at the southern trailhead.

Description: Descend from the parking lot on orange-blazed *Massanutten Mountain South Trail* to cross small streams draining into Big Run. At 0.4 miles pass under a power line, follow an old woods road to base of a spur ridge, and ascend an old skid road to 1.1 miles. After a clear-cut, cross an entrenched former turnpike, and join another old road to reach FR 70's loop at the New Market Gap Picnic Area (1,572 ft.). At the northern end of the loop road (125 yds. from US 211) the trail ascends to a spring at 2.2 miles. At 2.3 miles it passes a junction right with a path to the visitor center. The climb becomes steep in ascent to the ridgeline, which is at 2.5 miles. Follow the crest through hardwoods, scattered conifers, and berries. Pass a huge overhanging rock at 2.8 miles. On a rocky treadway reach an overlook at 3.1 miles. At 3.3 miles is a superb overlook. At 4.1 miles is a junction with white-blazed *Bird Knob Trail*. (This trail extends right 2.2 mi. to FR 375. It does not go to 2,684-ft. Bird Knob, but does go to a wildlife opening near it.) The *Massanutten Mountain South Trail* bears left onto a woods road, where for 0.7 miles there are large anthills. Wet weather springs are along this stretch. Reach FR 375 at 5.3 miles and bear right (FR 375 left ascends to WSVA TV towers). Pass the *Bird Knob Trail* right at 5.7 miles and meet purple-blazed *Roaring Run Trail* on the left at 6 miles. (This rocky and usually brushy trail first ascends Big Mountain, then descends for 3.7 mi. to Catherine Furnace on FR 65 near SR 685 and 2.2 mi. out to US 340.) The *Massanutten Mountain South Trail* runs jointly with FR 375 to Pitt Spring (1,751 ft.) at 8.7 miles. (Here FR 375 descends through Pitt Spring Gorge for 2 mi. to Catherine Furnace. Leave FR 375, and turn left on a grassy old road where a nice spring is just across the creek.) At 9.5 miles is white-blazed *Pitt Spring Lookout Trail*. (It extends as a spur 0.3 mi. to good views from an old lookout site.) At 12 miles the trail crosses Morgan Run and meets the *Morgan Run Trail*, which extends left. (This yellow-blazed trail descends along a rocky and sometimes boggy stream area to FR 65, Cub Run Rd.)

Ahead the *Massanutten Mountain South Trail* crosses a number of streams frequented by wildlife for the next 2 miles. There is also more solitude. It joins the *Fridley Gap Trail* at 14.4 miles. (The purple-blazed *Fridley Gap Trail* ascends left on an exceptionally rocky and boulder-strewn mountainside to cross Third Mountain. It descends to Cub Run and an old road at 0.8 mi. [To the left is 1-mi., yellow-blazed *Martin Bottom Trail*, whose eastern terminus is at FR 65.] The *Fridley Gap Trail* continues on an easy grade for 0.7 mi. to a grassy meadow and a junction with the *Massanutten Mountain South Trail*, right. From here the *Fridley Gap Trail* goes east 1.6 mi. on an old road bordered with wild azalea, mountain laurel, and turkey beard [*Xerophyllum asphodeloides*]. It descends from Second Mountain on a steep, rocky treadway to FR 65 [Cub Run Rd.]. On the road, right, it is 1.5 mi. to Runkles Gap, the southern trailhead of the *Massanutten Mountain South Trail*.)

Continuing on the *Massanutten Mountain South Trail*, it is 130 yards ahead to the confluence of Fridley Run and another stream in Fridley Gap. (To the right the *Fridley Gap Trail* descends in a hemlock grove to a large boulder field on the right and Mountain Run cascades on the left. It goes over large rocks to descend to a parking area at FR 1613, the trail's western trailhead. This point can be reached from I-81 by turning off at exit 251 on SR 608E. After 3.1 mi., at Athlone, turn right on SR 620 [KOA entrance is here], and travel another 3.1 mi. to SR 722. Turn left, and left again on SR 868. After 0.2 mi. look for gravel FR 1613 and follow it to its end.)

The *Massanutten Mountain South Trail* in Fridley Gap goes upstream 60 feet, crosses the stream, and ascends steeply on the side of a sharp ridge of Fourth Mountain. From 15.1 miles to 15.4 miles are rock outcroppings with views toward Harrisonburg. At 15.9 miles the trail descends to make a horse-shoe curve on a spur ridge before descending to Fridley Run. Here is a good campsite under hemlocks. The trail begins a gentle climb on the western side of Third Mountain, a dry area with trailing arbutus and blueberries and impressive views of Fourth Mountain and the Shenandoah Valley. At 17.3 miles the trail crosses Third Mountain to follow a grassy old road; it makes a junction with *Fridley Gap Trail* at 17.6 miles. Gypsy moth defoliation is substantial here. The *Massanutten Mountain South Trail* goes right to descend alongside Boone Run. Boone Run Shelter is on a spur trail, right, at 18.9 miles. The clean shelter is maintained by the PATC. Descend to cross the stream a number of times and reach FR 65 (Cub Run Rd.) at 19.5 miles. It is 0.2 miles farther down FR 65 to the gate and parking area.

USGS maps: Hamburg, 10th Legion, Elkton W., Stanley; *USFS trail nos.*: 416, 416B, 582, 584, 583, 419, 579

GREEN MOUNTAIN AREA
Shenandoah County

262–65   **Signal Knob Trail**
Length and Difficulty: 9 miles (14.4 km) round-trip; moderate to strenuous
Connecting Trails: *Blue Spur Trail* (0.5 mi.), *Massanutten Mountain West Trail* (17.1 mi.)

Features: Civil War lookout, spring, geological formations, wildflowers

Trailhead: From VA 55 at Waterlick, drive south on SR 678 for 3.4 miles to parking area on right (0.6 mi. north of Elizabeth Furnace picnic area).

Description: From the parking area a 10.6-mile circuit can be made by using the *Blue Spur Trail*, the *Big Blue/Bearwallow Trail*, and the *Massanutten Mountain West Trail*. If hiking counterclockwise, follow the yellow-blazed *Signal Knob Trail* on a graded tread through hardwoods, scattered conifers, azaleas, blueberries, filberts, and wildflowers. At 0.5 miles is a developed spring. Weave in and out of rocky coves to Buzzard Rock Overlook for an excellent view of Passage Creek Gorge at 1.5 miles. Turn left and ascend to Fort Valley Overlook at 2.2 miles, and to Shenandoah Valley Overlook on a short spur at 3 miles. Arrive at Signal Knob (2,106 ft.), a Confederate and Union Civil War lookout point, at 4.5 miles. Here is a junction with the northern trailhead of the *Massanutten Mountain West Trail*. Elevation gain is 1,334 feet. Views are of the North Fork of the Shenandoah River, Strasburg, and Winchester. Backtrack, or make a loop by descending on the *Massanutten Mountain West Trail* for 1.3 miles to a junction with the *Big Blue/Bearwallow Trail*, left, at Little Passage Creek. (The *Massanutten Mountain West Trail* continues south to Edinburg Gap and is described below.)

Ascend on switchbacks for 0.7 miles to the top of Green Mountain (2,080 ft.). Here are views west to the Shenandoah Valley and east to Massanutten Mountain and the Blue Ridge Mountains. Descend on switchbacks to a junction with the *Glass House Trail*, right, at 3.9 miles. (The 1.9-mi. blue-blazed *Glass House Trail* goes to the cottage by that name that is owned by the PATC.) At 5.3 miles there are iron pits on both sides of the trail, and at 5.6 miles the trail joins 0.5-mile blue-blazed *Big Blue Spur*, left. (The *Big Blue Trail* continues across SR 678 into the picnic area and joins the *Massanutten Mountain East Trail* as described above.) Follow the spur trail to the parking area for completion of the circuit.

USGS map: Strasburg; USFS trail nos.: 402, 563, 408, 405.2, 558

POWELL MOUNTAIN AND
THREE TOP MOUNTAIN AREA
Shenandoah County

Massanutten Mountain West Trail   266–71

Length and Difficulty: 17.1 miles (27.4 km); moderate

Connecting Trails: *Signal Knob Trail* (4.5 mi.), *Big Blue Trail* (3.3 mi.), *Wagon Road Trail* (1.3 mi.), *Mine Gap Trail* (1.1 mi.), *Lupton Trail* (0.5 mi.), *Seven Bar None Trail* (0.4 mi.), *Bear Trap Trail* (0.7 mi.)

Features: Signal Knob, stream, Woodstock Lookout, outcrops, springs, wildlife

Trailheads: The northern terminus is at Signal Knob, accessed by the *Signal Knob Trail* from Elizabeth Furnace. The southern trailhead is at Edinburg Gap on SR 675, 3.8 miles east of US 11 in Edinburg and 2.2 miles west on SR 675 from Kings Crossing.

Introduction: In the past 10 years there has been a major relocation of the *Massanutten Mountain West Trail*, and an addition of 5.6 miles. Except for the last 0.5 miles of the trail from Woodstock Lookout to SR 675, it is all new on the ridgeline of Powell Mountain. (Formerly this section was entirely on FR 1702, which is now a trail for ATVs and other motorized vehicles.) Three short spur trails have been added, and the *Big Blue Trail*, which ran conjointly for 2.9 miles, has been removed from Little Passage Creek to the northern ridge of Three Top Mountain. In addition a larger parking area has been constructed at Woodstock Lookout. (Under construction during the 1990s is an extension from Edinburg Gap, SR 675, south on Short Mountain and Kerns Mountain to New Market Gap, US 211.)

Description: From Signal Knob (2,106 ft.), which has splendid views of the North Fork of the Shenandoah River, follow the orange-blazed *Massanutten Mountain West Trail* south on an old road. Pass a spring at 0.8 miles and cross the *Big Blue/Bearwallow Trail* at 1.3 miles. (It ascends left over Green Mountain and descends to Elizabeth Furnace picnic area at 4.4 mi. It ascends right to Three Top Mountain and a junction again with the *Massanutten Mountain West Trail* after 3.3 mi.) Pass the Strasburg Reservoir right at 1.8 miles and gradually descend beside Little Passage Creek for the next 2.2 miles. At 2.3 miles is an abandoned manganese mine, left. Reach Powells Fort Camp at 4 miles. It is on the right, and a parking area is to the left. From here follow FR 66 for 0.3 miles, turn right after the gate, and ascend on switchbacks to within 0.1 mile from the top of Three Top Mountain (1,790 ft.) at 4.8 miles. From the right and ahead is the *Big Blue Trail*. Turn left on the *Massanutten Mountain West Trail*. (The *Big Blue* descends west to cross the Shenandoah River after 2.2 mi. After another 8.8 mi. it reenters the GWNF at Fetzer Gap, northwest of Mauretown.) At 5.9 miles is a spur trail on the left, purple-blazed *Mine Gap Trail*. (It descends 1.1 mi. east to FR 66 in Little Fort Valley.) Continue on the *Massanutten Mountain West Trail* in a hardwood forest with shallow sags and scattered rocky knolls. There is evidence of some forest damage by the gypsy moth. Reach SR 758 and parking area at Woodstock Gap at 9.3 miles. It is 5.6 miles west to Woodstock and US 11 on SR 758 and SR 665, and 3.9 miles east on SR 758 to Detrick and SR 678.

From parking area ascend steps and meet white-blazed *Wagon Road Trail*, left. (It descends as a steep loop to Little Fork Recreation Area on SR 758.) Reach the Woodstock Tower (1,893 ft.) after 275 yards from the parking area. There are grand views of seven bends of the North Fork of the Shenandoah River, west, and Woodstock Gap, east. Proceed on a rocky area. At 10.9 miles join purple-blazed *Lupton Trail*, left. (It descends sharply 0.5 mi. to Peters Mill Run and FR 1702, the old *Powell Mountain Trail*, now an ATV trail.) Pass a long rock pile at 11.5 miles, and a campsite at 12.4 miles. At 12.6 miles is blue-blazed *Seven Bar None Trail*. (It descends 0.4 mi. to Peters Mill Run and FR 1702.) Continue shifting from the ridgeline to the eastern side of rock formations and reach an excellent view of Edinburg and the Allegheny Mountains at 14.6 miles. Here, as elsewhere on the trail, are brilliant fall colors from maple, black gum, sassafras, and blueberry. There is a 0.4-mile pink-blazed trail, the *Bear Trap Trail*, left, at 14.7 miles. (It switchbacks to the headwaters of Peters Mill Run and FR 1702.) After another 0.2 miles the trail turns east to skirt Waonaze Peak (2,725 ft.) in dense rhododendron. (Summit is forested.) Switchbacks began at 16.1 miles on a rocky eastern face of Waonaze Peak. Pass a spring (a pleasant surprise) at 16.4 miles. After a left switchback, descend to FR 1702 in a curve at 16.6 miles. Turn right on the eroded road, pass a wildlife pond at 16.8 miles, and arrive at SR 675 in Edinburg Gap at 17.1 miles, the southern terminus of the *Massanutten Mountain West Trail*. Across the road is FR 374.

USGS maps: Edinburg, Rileyville, Strasburg, Toms Brook; *USFS trail nos.*: 408, 402, 405.2, 552, 550

NORTH MOUNTAIN (NORTH) AREA
Shenandoah County, Virginia, and Hardy County, West Virginia

Mill Mountain Trail (6 mi.), **Big Blue Trail** (5.6 mi.)   272–79

Length and Difficulty: 11.6 miles (18.6 km) combined; moderate to strenuous

Connecting Trails: Big Schloss (0.3 mi.), Peer Trail (3.3 mi.), Little Stony Creek Trail (3.7 mi.), Little Sluice Mountain Trail (4.8 mi.), Sulphur Springs Gap Trail (2.9 mi.), White Rock Trail (0.3 mi.), Cedar Creek Trail (3.8 mi.)

Features: scenic views, geological formations, springs, wildlife, wildflowers, isolation

Trailheads: The southwestern trailhead is at Wolf Gap Campground at the Virginia/West Virginia boundary on SR 675, 11.3 miles west of Edinburg. For the northeastern trailhead, travel west on SR 675 from Edinburg to a right turn on SR 608, 0.5 miles west of Columbia Furnace. After 1.2 miles on SR 608, the road becomes FR 88; travel 5.3 miles to its end.

Introduction: The *Mill Mountain Trail* is one of the district's most popular trails because of Big Schloss, a castlelike rock formation with panoramic views. Farther northeast on a network of trails in Virginia and West Virginia is remoteness among ridge trails and hollows. Only the Virginia trails are described. With a two-car arrangement, there are a number of partial or complete circuits. Nonfee Wolf Gap Campground has picnic tables and vault toilets.

Description: From the parking area begin the orange-blazed *Mill Mountain Trail* near campsite #9. Ascend on a wide woods road for 0.9 miles to ridge crest where the trail becomes more of a rocky footpath. At 1.9 miles join the *Big Schloss Trail*, right. It ascends 0.3 miles on a white-blazed trail to a massive rock formation (2,964 ft.). Views of Trout Run Valley in West Virginia and Great North Mountain and Little Schloss Mountain in Virginia are magnificent. After a return to the main trail, follow the ridgeline northeast. At 4.6 miles is Sandstone Spring in a stand of hemlock. Ascend through an oak and mountain laurel forest to the site of a former airway beacon (3,293 ft.). From here the trail descends gradually and reaches a junction with the *Big Blue Trail* at 6 miles. (To the left the *Big Blue Trail* goes 2.8 mi. to Waites Run Rd. and another 6 mi. to

Wardensville, West Virginia. Branching off from it are the *Halfmoon Trail* [3.2 mi.] and the *Halfmoon Lookout Trail* [0.8 mi.] in West Virginia.)

Turn right on the *Big Blue Trail* to follow an old woods road 0.6 miles to join purple-blazed *Peer Trail* on the left in West Virginia, and the yellow-blazed *Little Stony Creek Trail* on the right. Elevation at this point is 2,995 feet. (If you choose the *Little Stony Creek Trail* for a circuit, pass the locked Sugar Knob Cabin, owned and maintained by the PATC [user reservations are required]. Pass a spring here, and again at 1 mi. as the trail descends on the western slope of Stony Creek. An easy treadway, the trail passes through hemlock, white pine, oak, maple, tulip poplar, and rhododendron. There are a number of good campsites. Arrive at FR 92 after 3.7 mi. A continuing loop can be made right on FR 92 for 3.3 mi. to SR 675, and 1.5 mi. right on SR 675 to Wolf Gap, for a circuit of 14.5 mi. There is a steep, unmarked cutoff from FR 92 to SR 675 on the right 2.8 mi. from Little Stony Creek. It reduces the road walking by 1.5 mi.)

If continuing on the *Big Blue Trail*, go straight ahead over the broad ridge of Sugar Knob, and reach a junction with the *Little Sluice Trail* on the right after 1 mile from the *Little Stony Creek Trail*. Here too is a possible round-trip back to Wolf Gap by descending on purple-blazed *Little Sluice Trail* (primarily a hunter's dirt road) for 4.8 miles to FR 88. At FR 88 it is 0.5 miles right to FR 92, and another 3.4 miles to the *Little Stony Creek Trail* for a circuit of 20.5 miles. (If accessing the FR 88 trailhead for the *Little Sluice Trail* other than on FR 92, continue on FR 88 at the FR 92 junction, and it will become SR 608 into Columbia Furnace and SR 675 after 3.3 miles.)

Another long partial circuit with two-car assistance includes the *Cedar Creek Trail*. For this arrangement, continue on the *Big Blue Trail* from the *Little Sluice Trail*. Follow the trail past the wildlife pond and begin to ascend Little Sluice Mountain. Reach the ridge top at 1.1 miles and a junction right at 1.4 miles with the blue-blazed *White Rock Trail*. The 0.3-mile spur trail leads to a large cliff that provides outstanding southeastern views of Little North Mountain, Cedar Creek Valley, and Shenandoah Valley. The *Sulphur Springs Gap Trail* (an unmarked and unblazed woods road), left, connects at 2 miles. From here the *Big Blue Trail* descends on switchbacks and crosses small streams on its way to a junction with the *Cedar Creek Trail*, right, at 4.1 miles. (To the left is a wildlife clearing and Forest Service access road from the Van Buren Furnace ruins at SR 713. The *Big Blue Trail* continues straight ahead toward Little North Mountain.)

On an old road the *Cedar Creek Trail* ascends for 0.4 miles to make a left turn. Here it crosses the first of five streams on its way to a saddle between Little Sluice Mountain and Little North Mountain. It passes by a number of timber clear-cuts where wildlife are likely to be seen and birding is good. At 3.4 miles the trail begins a descent to gated FR 88, the southern trailhead. Total trail mileage from Wolf Gap is 15.4 miles; road distance on FR 88, FR 92, and SR 675 is 8.7 miles.

USGS maps: Wolf Gap, Woodstock; *USFS trail nos.*: 1004, 1004A, 1013, 1002, 571, 401, 514, 414, 573

Tibbet Knob Trail (2.4 mi.), **North Mountain Trail** (6.5 mi.)   280–86

Length and Difficulty: 8.9 miles (14.2 km) combined; strenuous

Connecting Trails: *Laurel Run Trail* (3.2 mi.), *Stackrock Trail* (1.5 mi.), *Falls Ridge Trail* (2.6 mi.)

Features: scenic views, wildlife, wildflowers

Trailheads: To reach the *Tibbet Knob Trail*, travel 11.3 miles west from Edinburg on SR 675 to Wolf Gap Campground at the Virginia/West Virginia border. For the *North Mountain Trail*'s southern trailhead travel 7.8 miles from Edinburg on SR 675 and turn left on SR 717. After 7.7 miles turn right (at Woodland Church) on SR 720, and follow it up the mountain 4.4 miles to the Virginia/West Virginia border. Trailhead is right (north).

Introduction: Trails described in this area are in Virginia or along the state line. (See Bibliography for trail guides on the West Virginia side of the mountains.) These trails, which do not have springs, follow the state line southwest and can be connected with 3.3 miles of SR 691 for a total of 12.2 miles. Circuits can be made by using the connecting trails listed above, which have springs.

Description: Begin at Wolf Gap Campground parking area or, across the road, at parking area for the yellow-blazed *Tibbet Knob Trail*. Through large oaks and pines with understory of sassafras, dogwood, azalea, and green striped maple go 0.4 miles to scenic overlook. After a steep climb reach Tibbet Knob (2,925 ft.) at 1.4 miles. Here is a splendid view of Trout Run and Long Mountain in West Virginia. Descend to SR 691 (Lost City Rd.) at 2.4 miles and the southern trailhead. (From here on SR 691 it is 1.5 mi. left to SR 789 and to SR 675 for a vehicular return to northern trailhead.) Turn right on SR 691 and hike, or drive, 3.3 miles to northern trailhead of the *North Mountain Trail* and the *Laurel Run Trail*, both on the left side at ridge saddle.

(Yellow-blazed *Laurel Run Trail*, an old road, descends left for 3.2 mi. through hardwoods, pines, hemlocks, and rosebay rhododendrons to gated FR 252. At this point blue-blazed *Laurel Spur Trail* goes southwest for 2.6 mi. on a trail–woods road combination to connect with the *Stack Rock Trail* and the *Falls Ridge Trail*, both of which ascend on different routes to the *North Mountain Trail*. From gated FR 252 it is 1.5 mi. on a gravel road to SR 691, and 0.5 mi. farther to historic Liberty Furnace on SR 717.)

The orange-blazed *North Mountain Trail* (3,005 ft.) ascends gradually for 0.8 miles to an overview of Massanutten and Blue Ridge Mountains across the Shenandoah Valley. At 2.1 miles reach purple-blazed *Stack Rock Trail*, left. (It descends 1.5 mi. to the *Laurel Spur Trail*.) At 2.3 miles join the *Falls Ridge Trail*, left. (It descends 2.6 mi. to a junction with the southern trailhead of the *Laurel Spur Trail*.)

(These two trails could make an excellent circuit hike partly using the *Laurel Spur Trail* for a total of 6.7 mi. Spring water and good campsites are along the way. There is also an easy access to these trails from the valley instead of the

North Mountain Trail. From the junction of the *Laurel Spur Trail* and the *Falls Ridge Trail* it is 0.4 mi. farther south to Falls Run and a junction with purple-blazed *Fat Mountain Trail.* To the left it is 0.1 mi. to a parking area at the end of SR 701. To reach this point by vehicle from Columbia Furnace, go 3.9 mi. west on SR 675, turn left on SR 717, go 4.4 mi., and at a church turn right on SR 701 for 2 mi. As for the *Fat Mountain Trail,* it is a 1.8-mi. woods road to Bull Gap. En route it ascends near Falls Run, crosses a saddle northwest of Fat Mountain, and descends along Bear Run to Bull Gap and a pipeline crossing, its southern terminus.)

Continue ahead on the *North Mountain Trail,* sometimes on a steep and rocky treadway. The trail is lined with huckleberry, mountain laurel, hawthorn, and bear oak. Deer, turkey, and grouse may be seen. At 2.7 miles, 3.9 miles, and 4.7 miles are rock outcrops for scenic views. At 5 miles the trail goes through a section of large, cone-shaped anthills. Pass the site of an old homestead at 6 miles, and reach the southern trailhead in a parking lot at SR 720 at 6.5 miles.
USGS maps: Wolf Gap, Orkney Springs, Lost City; *USFS trail nos.*: 578, 1009, 568, 568A, 572, 568B, 605

Pedlar Ranger District

Of its 144,906 acres, the Pedlar Ranger District has more territory east of the BRP than any of the state's districts. As with Glenwood Ranger District in the JNF, which adjoins the Pedlar Ranger District on the south, it is separated from the more western districts by the Shenandoah Valley. On its eastern boundary is the state's piedmont, and the northern area extends almost to Waynesboro and the Shenandoah National Park. The Maury River joins the James River on the district's southwestern corner, but the northwestern corner of the district drains into the South River, which flows into the North Fork of the Shenandoah River. Some of the state's most majestic mountain peaks are here: The Priest (4,063 ft.), Mt. Pleasant (4,071 ft.), and Cold Mountain (4,023 ft.). The district has the state's highest cascading waterfall, 1,200-vertical-foot Crabtree Falls in the South Fork of the Tye River gorge. On the western side of the district and east of Steeles Tavern is the 10,900-acre St. Mary's Wilderness, which ascends east to the BRP. Northern and southern hardwoods, hemlock, and Virginia pine are the district's dominant trees. Thousands of acres, particularly of oaks, have been defoliated by the gypsy moth. Of interest to anglers are the stocked streams of the North Fork of the Tye River, Irish Creek, the South Fork of the Piney River, and Pedlar River.

Among the man-made attractions in the district is Sherando Lake Recreation Area, a compound for camping, fishing, hiking, boating, and swimming. Showers for campers are available at the lake's bathhouse. It is open from April 1 to November 30. A popular retreat, it may be crowded; reservations can be made by calling 800-283-CAMP. Group camping reservations are arranged by the district office. The district's trail system has excellent options for day hikes or long backpacking circuits. Many of the forest trails connect with 56.9 miles of the *AT*, which tracks the entire length of the district, a distinction shared by three other districts of the state's twelve. Trails are color coded, mostly in blue, and are blazed with paint or plastic. Maintenance of the *AT* is provided by the Appalachian Trail clubs: Old Dominion, Tidewater, and Natural Bridge. Of the 37 trails listed in the district's TIS inventory, 13 connect with the *AT* or the BRP. A few trails are isolated. An example is 0.4-mile *Panther Falls Trail* on Pedlar River. Access is from US 60, 0.1 mile east of the BRP underpass, at FR 315 on the right. The crooked road descends 3.2 miles to a small parking area on the left. At a signboard a trail descends 0.1 mile to the upper level of Panther Falls. To reach the other access trail, which is more scenic, continue on FR 315 for 0.3 miles and turn left on FR 315A. After 0.5 miles is a large parking area. Walk down an old gated forest road for 0.2 miles and turn left in a meadow of wildflowers by Pedlar River. After 0.2 miles reach the falls, which begin in a flume, swirl into a deep pool (which has a deadly undertow), and foam in a sculptured hole before falling again into a pool. Other trails are short dead ends near mainstream traffic. An example is the *Mine Bank Mountain Trail*, a 0.6-mile walk from the BRP, mp 23.5 (the highest point, 3,333 ft., north of the James River on the BRP).

287–88

There are a number of gated or tank trap road-trails whose mysterious appearance invites browsing. Such a road is FR 42 and its side roads, 2.6 miles north on SR 664 from Lake Sherando Recreation Area. If followed its entire length, the road goes to a western entrance of St. Mary's Wilderness, but the first 4.9 miles have the hiking options, all on the left. After 0.5 miles there is a gated road (FR 1237), the former *Turkey Pen Ridge Trail*, which follows flat terrain to the *Mills Creek Trail* for 1.3 miles by Orebank Creek. At 1.5 miles on FR 42 is FR 1234 (Mills Creek Rd.), gated for traffic to Mill Creek Reservoir. A few yards ahead is a parking area on the left, where a 360-foot, blue-blazed spur trail leads to the road. Another 1.4 miles on FR 42 is Kennedy Creek and offroad campsites. One mile farther on FR 42 is the *Kennedy Ridge Trail*. It goes over a tank trap to ascend steeply on an old and rocky road for 3.1 miles, where it joins FR 162B, an access to St. Mary's Wilderness. Travel 0.2 miles farther on FR 42 for a gated road and a short walk to Coles Lake. As a finale, continue another 0.8 miles (passing the junction with FR 52 out to Stuarts Draft), and hike dead-end, 1.4-mile *Johns Run Trail*. Its mysteries are revealed in a deep, wet gorge.

289–90

Address and Information: Pedlar Ranger District, 2424 Magnolia Ave., Buena Vista, VA 24416; phone: 703-261-6105. Available are district map with trails, Lake Sherando map, wilderness flyer.

ROCKY ROW AREA
Rockbridge and Amherst Counties

Belle Cove Trail (4.6 mi.), **Saddle Gap Trail** (2.5 mi.),
Little Rocky Row Run Trail (2.7 mi.), **AT** (6.2 mi.)

291–93

Length and Difficulty: 13.5 miles (21.6 km) combined; strenuous
Features: rock outcrops, scenic views, wildlife, wildflowers

Panther Falls Trail, GWNF. (Photograph by Allen de Hart)

Trailheads: For the *Belle Cove Trail* drive 5.4 miles south on US 501 from the district office in Buena Vista to parking area at Belle Cove Branch bridge. For the *Little Rocky Row Run Trail* drive from US 501 and VA 130 junction (east of Glasgow) east 2.5 miles to parking area at James River Overlook at Rockbridge and Amherst county line. (Trail is 150 yds. back [west] on northern bank of US 501.)

To reach the *Saddle Gap Trail*, leave US 501/VA 130 (west of Snowden) on SR 812 and fork right on FR 36 to drive 2.8 miles to trail sign on left. For the *AT* follow the same route on FR 36, but stop 0.9 miles after leaving US 501/VA 130.

Description: *Belle Cove*, *Little Rocky Row Run*, and *Saddle Gap* trails are all blue-blazed and ascend to the *AT* within a 3.7-mile section. To avoid walking on busy highways, hikers should start north on the *AT* at FR 36 and after 5 miles turn right to descend on the *Saddle Gap Trail*. A hike downstream to the *AT* origin on FR 36 is a 9.4-mile circuit. An advantage of this loop is the *AT* shelter, Johns Hollow, 0.6 miles after leaving north on FR 36. (All other combinations need a two-car arrangement unless backtracking.) The most impressive feature on this section of the *AT* is Fullers Rocks (2,480 ft.), 0.1 mile north of its junction with the *Little Rocky Row Run Trail*. Here is a spectacular view of James River Gorge and James River Face Wilderness.

On the *Belle Cove Trail* from the parking area, enter the gated road and follow it through a former timber cut to cross Belle Cove Branch at 1.1 miles. Continue upstream into Belle Cove canyon, where wildflowers and ferns are abundant. Continue upstream with occasional crossings until crossing left at 4.1 miles for the approach toward Salt Log Gap and a junction with the *AT*. (It is 3.5 mi. north to BRP mp 51.7, and 1.1 mi. south to the *Saddle Gap Trail*. It is another 2.6 mi. to the *Little Rocky Row Run Trail*.) If ascending on the *Saddle Gap Trail* from FR 36, climb over a large tank trap into a forest of hemlocks and hardwoods near a stream. Leave the stream at 0.5 miles and follow switchbacks to the junction with the *AT*. When hiking the *Little Rocky Row Run Trail* from US 501/VA 130, look for a hiker's sign 150 yards west of the Rockbridge and Amherst county line. Ascend on switchbacks to the ridge crest. The trail is festooned with azalea, fern, and chinquapin. Rocks are laced with lichens and mosses. Pass under a power line at 0.6 miles where there are magnificent views of James River Gorge. Ascend switchbacks and follow ridge to a junction with the *AT* at 2.7 miles. To the left it is 0.1 mile to Fullers Rocks; to the right it is 1.9 miles to Johns Hollow Shelter, and another 0.6 miles to FR 36. From here it is 0.9 miles to US 501/VA 130 and 3.9 miles on the highway to the overlook and point of origin for the *Little Rocky Row Run Trail*.

USGS maps: Buena Vista, Glasgow, Snowden; *USFS trail nos.*: 511, 703, 512, 1

ELEPHANT MOUNTAIN AREA
Rockbridge County

Indian Gap Trail (2.6 mi.), **Reservoir Hollow Trail** (2.8 mi.),
Elephant Mountain Trail (1.2 mi.)   294–96

Length and Difficulty: 6.6 miles (10.6 km) combined; moderate to strenuous
Features: scenic views, wildflowers, streams
Trailheads: From the junction of US 501 and US 60 in Buena Vista, drive east 2.8 miles to a small parking area in a curve for the northeastern trailhead of the *Indian Gap Trail*. Its southwestern trailhead is at Laurel Park, the end of 21st Street. The eastern trailhead for the *Reservoir Hollow Trail* is the junction with

the *Indian Gap Trail*; its western trailhead is at the end of 12th Street via Pine Avenue and Woods Road in Buena Vista. The *Elephant Mountain* trailhead is on the *Reservoir Hollow Trail.*

Description: Ascend on the blue-blazed *Indian Gap Trail* and cross two small streams after crossing a ridge. At 0.9 miles is a side trail, left, to the BRP, and at 1.1 miles is a junction with the *Reservoir Hollow Trail.* Continuing on the *Indian Gap Trail,* descend through an area of hemlocks and cascades and regeneration hardwoods to Laurel Park at 2.6 miles. At junction with the *Reservoir Hollow Trail* continue ahead for 0.6 miles to a junction with the *Elephant Mountain Trail* on the right. A hike up Elephant Mountain (2,101 ft.) is strenuous on steep, rugged, and narrow sections of the route. Mountain laurels, pitch pines, chestnut sprouts, and blueberries are here. Reach the summit at 1.2 miles for outstanding views of Buena Vista and the Maury River Valley. Backtrack. To continue on the *Reservoir Hollow Trail* turn right after the descent, reach a primitive campsite at 1.9 miles, and descend to gate at Woods Road at 2.3 miles.

USGS map: Buena Vista; *USFS trail nos.*: 509, 509A, 509B

MT. PLEASANT AND COLD MOUNTAIN AREA
Amherst County

Henry Lanum Trail (6.2 mi.), **Mt. Pleasant Trail** (0.5 mi.),
Old Hotel Trail (3 mi.), **AT** (2.1 mi.)

297–99

Length and Difficulty: 12.3 miles (19.7 km) combined, round-trip; moderate to strenuous

Features: scenic views, wildflowers, stream, balds, historic site

Trailhead: From junction of US 60 and SR 634 (1 mi. west of Long Mountain Wayside; 16.9 mi. west of Amherst and 4 mi. east of BRP on US 60), drive north on SR 634 (Coffey Town Rd.) 1.7 miles. Turn right on SR 755, which becomes FR 48 after 1.4 miles, and follow it 1.3 miles to a parking area at Hog Camp Gap. Here is the intersection with the *AT*.

Introduction: These combined trails make two loops. The *Henry Lanum Trail* and the *Mt. Pleasant Trail* make a circuit of 7.2 miles; the *Old Hotel Trail* and the *AT* section provide a loop of 5.7 miles (to include a 0.6-mi. spur to the shelter). Formerly the *Pompey and Mt. Pleasant Loop Trail,* the trail was renamed by the USFS in honor of Henry (Hank) Lanum Jr. in 1991. For many years he was active in maintaining the *AT* for the Natural Bridge Appalachian Trail Club. The trail area is within the 5,900-acre Mt. Pleasant Special Management Area, designated in 1986. The *Old Hotel Trail* received its name from a Richerson family whose large home was the scene of social events and a hospitable respite for overnight guests. In a tract of about 700 acres the family kept slaves and raised cattle, sheep, and swine.

Description: From the parking area at Hog Camp Gap, FR 48 continues 0.3 miles to FR 51 and a parking area, but the Hog Camp Gap gate may be closed (particularly in the winter), and the road should be walked on the blue-blazed side. Begin on the blue-blazed *Henry Lanum Trail* and ascend on a wide treadway in a hardwood forest. Indian pipe (*Monotropa uniflora*) and starry campion (*Silene stellata*) are among the wildflowers. Reach a knoll at 1.5 miles; follow a more rocky and narrow footpath through mountain laurel and rhododendron; tiger lily and wild hydrangea are among the August flowers. At 2 miles arrive at Pompey Mountain (4,032 ft.) in a wooded area. From here the trail descends 0.7 miles to a wide saddle where flowers and filberts grow tall in moist and rich soil. To the right the *Henry Lanum Trail* continues, and to the left a 0.5-mile spur trail ascends to Mt. Pleasant. Also on the left is a spring, 125 yards from the spur. Ascend steeply to a rocky plateau (4,071 ft.) with magnificent scenery. Sweeping views are of Buffalo River drainage, Cold Mountain, Chestnut Ridge, and toward the east, Tye River Valley. In rock pockets and crevices are dense growths of mosses, sedum, blueberries, and scattered mountain ash (*Sorbus americana*). After returning to the *Henry Lanum Trail*, descend on a rocky road past a spring on the right at 3.3 miles, and another at 3.4 miles on the left. In a rocky area, cross a stream at 3.9 miles. Then gradually ascend in a forest of yellow birch for a return to the parking area and signboard at 5.2 miles (plus 1 mi. for the *Mt. Pleasant Trail*).

From the parking area at the *Henry Lanum Trail* cross the stile and enter blue-blazed *Old Hotel Trail*. Descend gradually in the forest. At 0.8 miles is a clearing with an eastern view of the North Fork of the Buffalo River Valley and Mt. Pleasant. There are thick patches of blueberries at 1.1 miles. At 1.5 miles is an ideal campsite in a grassy area with large white oaks. (Near, but east of here, is the site of the former Richerson home.) This area is also good for birding. Cross Little Cove Creek at 2.9 miles, ascend, and reach a junction at 3 miles with a left spur trail to the *AT*. Across the creek is Cow Camp Gap Shelter, maintained by the Natural Bridge Appalachian Trail Club. Ascend steeply for 0.6 miles to the *AT*. (To the left it is 3.8 mi. to us 60 and Long Mountain Wayside.) Turn right, ascend steeply, cross a rock wall, and reach the summit of Cold Mountain (4,022 ft.) at 4.4 miles. Here is a supreme panoramic view from a grassy and granite bald, excellent for stargazing. Reach the northern summit of Cold Mountain at 4.7 miles, where beyond the trail descends to the Hog Camp Gap parking area at 5.7 miles.

USGS maps: Montebello, Fork of Buffalo; *USFS trail nos.*: 702, 701, 515, 1

LOVINGSTON SPRING AREA
Amherst, Rockbridge, and Nelson Counties

Lovingston Spring Trail (3.1 mi.), **AT** (3.9 mi.)   300
Length and Difficulty: 7 miles (11.2 km) combined, round-trip; moderate
Features: springs, historic site, wildflowers, wildlife, isolation
Trailhead: From junction of us 60 and sr 634 (described above for Mt. Pleasant area), drive 4.9 miles on sr 634 to where it becomes FR 63. Ascend 2 miles on FR 63 to Salt Log Gap and turn left on FR 1176. After a 1-mile ascent, turn right at fork on FR 246 for a few yards and park in a level area opposite an old road, FR 1176A (Greasy Spring Rd.).

Description: This delightful double circuit has ridges and vales, lush vegetation, natural springs, remoteness, and a shelter. If hiking clockwise, descend on the rough road 0.2 miles to a junction with the *AT*. (Ahead on the road it is 0.2 mi. to Greasy Spring.) Turn left and ascend on blue-blazed *Lovingston Spring Trail* 0.6 miles to crest of the ridge, and near a parking area for 4WDS. (To the left it is 150 yds. to FR 1176, where a 0.2-mi. ascent reaches Rocky Mountain radio towers [4,072 ft.] and scenic views.) On the trail (formerly the *AT*), descend through tall dense ferns, spikemoss, clubmoss, and white snakeroot (*Eupatorium perfoliatum*) to Lovingston Spring at 0.9 miles. Past the spring there is an old road that forks right. (It descends 0.4 mi. past two cottage ruins and a small pond to a junction with the *AT* and the North Fork of the Piney River. A turn right on the *AT* makes a return circuit of 3.1 mi.)

To continue on the *Lovingston Spring Trail*, follow the old road (FR 1176B) among hardwoods, hemlocks, and rhododendrons to the crest of Elk Pond Mountain. After a slight descent among woodland sunflowers, reach Twin Springs at the *AT* at 3.1 miles. Here the *AT* passes between two natural springs. (Ahead on the *AT* it is 2.4 mi. to Spy Rock, noted for its supreme scenery.) To complete the circuit, turn right and follow the *AT*. At 3.5 miles is Seeley Woodworth Shelter on the left, with a capped spring. At 5.2 miles cross pioneer's road and rock-hop the North Fork of the Piney River. Deer and raccoon frequent this area. Ascend, and at 6.1 miles pass Wolf Rocks, which offers a view of Rocky Mountain and The Priest. Descend and complete circuit at 7 miles.

USGS map: Montebello; *USFS trail nos.*: 731, 1

TYE RIVER AREA
Nelson County

301–2   **Crabtree Falls Trail**
Length and Difficulty: 2.9 miles (4.6 km); strenuous
Features: cascading falls, scenic views, mosses
Trailheads: To reach the northern trailhead from the west, drive from the BRP (Tye River Gap, mp 27.2) on VA 56 east 6.6 miles to Crabtree Falls parking lot. From the east, at the junction with US 29 take VA 56 west to Massies Mill and about 12 miles to the parking lot. To reach the upper (southern) trailhead, use a 4WD or a high-axle vehicle on SR 826 (Crabtree Farm Rd.). It is 2.7 miles west on VA 56 from the Crabtree Falls parking area. Turn left on SR 826 and go 3.7 miles to a large parking lot.
Introduction: This is the district's most visited trail and also the most dangerous; more lives are lost here than in all the other districts in the GWNF. To be safe while experiencing its beauty, stay on the trail. The USFS has constructed a graded trail with sections of steps, overlooks, platforms, and guardrails for the first 2 miles. The trail features five major cascades and a number of smaller ones for 1,200 feet. (While in the Crabtree Falls area, hikers may find it worthwhile to visit Montebello State Fish Hatchery, which has excellent picnic facilities, 3 miles west on VA 56 from the falls, and the scenic *AT* suspension bridge over the Tye River 4.5 miles east from the falls on VA 56.)

Description: From the northern trailhead, pass the signboard and cross the arched bridge over the South Fork of the Tye River. The first constructed overlook is at 0.3 miles. Among switchbacks there are other rock or wood platforms for viewing. Ferns, wildflowers, and mosses are prominent. At 0.8 miles is a small cave, a favorite spot for children. Pass some memorial signs and at 1.7 miles reach the upper falls. Here is a rock wall for an overlook of Crabtree Creek and into the Tye River Valley. From here the remainder of the trail is on a wide woods road, parallel to Crabtree Creek, to the parking lot on SR 826 (Crabtree Farm Rd.). Camping is not allowed here, but a trail across the road leads to spacious meadows for tent camping.

(To reach the *AT* from here, hike the Crabtree Farm Road 0.5 mi. east to a junction. Ahead [south] is the *Shoe Creek Trail*, which descends 3.5 mi. to SR 827, an access west of Massies Mill. To the left on the *AT* it is 1.2 mi. to The Priest [4,063 ft.], a forested massif with outcrops for exceptional views. To the right on the *AT* it is 3.3 mi. west to Spy Rock for views of The Priest, Mt. Pleasant, Cold Mountain, Whetstone Ridge, and other summits.)

USGS maps: Montebello, Massies Mill; *USFS trail no.*: 526

WHETSTONE RIDGE AND SOUTH MOUNTAIN AREA
Rockbridge County

Whetstone Ridge Trail   303
Length and Difficulty: 11.4 miles (17.2 km); moderate to strenuous
Features: scenic views, isolation, wildflowers, wildlife
Trailheads: Access north is at the Whetstone Restaurant and Gift Shop parking area on the BRP, mp 29.1. Access to the southern trailhead is on SR 603 (Irish Creek Rd.), 2.5 miles east of the junction with SR 608 at Cornwall (north of Buena Vista), and 12 miles from the northern trailhead (across the BRP to SR 813, right, and 0.4 mi. to underpass of BRP for a descent on SR 603 to the parking area).
Description: This old trail has been restored with relocations and maintenance to make it the longest trail in the district, and one of the finest for viewing autumn colors. From the BRP parking lot, go north to enter the woods and parallel the BRP for 0.2 miles to Whetstone Ridge (3,080 ft.) and turn left. The easy treadway is through chestnut oak, striped maple, black gum, mountain laurel, flame azalea, and occasional white pine. Patches of blueberries are in sunny spots. Half of the first 2 miles of trail has been relocated, which opens new spaces for mosses and mushrooms. For a short section after 2.5 miles the trail switches back and forth on a woods road. At 4.4 miles the trail turns abruptly right on a different ridgeline. Rock outcroppings and overlooks are at 5 miles and 5.5 miles for views of Irish Creek Valley, The Priest, Rocky Mountain, and other summits. At the latter overlook is Adams Peak (2,976 ft.) to the northwest. Two other overlooks are at 6.3 miles (2,551 ft.). After 0.4 miles the trail skirts a flat knob to begin the remainder of the route on South Mountain. It undulates on five knolls, one as high as 2,800 feet, for the next 1.6 miles. After a descent from

the last knoll, the footpath becomes a woods road. On an easy treadway follow the ridgeline to 9.9 miles. From here begin a rapid descent, first on the mountain's western slope and later to the eastern slope, on a grassy and rocky road. Reach the parking area across SR 603 (near Irish Creek) at 11.4 miles.

USGS maps: Montebello, Cornwall; *USFS trail no.*: 523

SHERANDO LAKE AREA
Augusta County

Slacks Overlook Trail (2.6 mi.), **White Rock Falls Trail** (2.6 mi.),
304–6   **White Rock Gap Trail** (2.5 mi.)

Length and Difficulty: 4.8 miles (7.7 km) combined, round-trip; moderate

Features: waterfall, scenic overlook, historic site

Trailhead: Slacks Overlook, BRP, mp 19.9

Introduction: This circuit arrangement is one of at least five day options at or near Sherando Lake Recreation Area. All of the *White Rock Falls Trail* (see BRP, Chapter 4) is used in this circuit and connecting parts of the other two trails. Additionally, there are connecting trails in this area to the St. Mary's Wilderness.

Description: At the northwestern corner of the Slacks Overlook parking lot (2,787 ft.), descend 85 yards to the blue-blazed *Slacks Overlook Trail*. (To the left it goes 0.8 mi. to end at the *Torry Ridge Trail*.) Turn right, and follow an even contour in a forest of chestnut oak (greatly defoliated by the gypsy moth) and blueberries. At 1 mile curve to a cove for another ridge and then descend to a junction with the *White Rock Gap Trail* at 1.8 miles. (To the left the *White Rock Gap Trail* descends easily 2.2 mi. to FR 91 in the Sherando Lake campground.) From here the loop goes right on the *White Rock Gap Trail*, passes an old homesite, and crosses the BRP (mp 18.5) at 2.2 miles. Across the BRP the loop continues on yellow-blazed *White Rock Falls Trail*. Descend gradually, and follow an old woods road with switchbacks. At 3.9 miles reach the falls, right, and a rocky area of cascades and pools. (Here in the gorge is evidence of damage to the hemlocks by the woolly adelgid.) Ascend steeply among boulders and overlooks at 4.2 miles for views of The Priest and other mountains. Cross White Rock Creek at 4.5 miles and return to the BRP parking area at 4.8 miles.

USGS map: Big Levels; *USFS trail nos.*: 480A, (*White Rock Falls Trail* is mainly on BRP property), 480

White Rock Gap Trail (2.5 mi.), **Slacks Overlook Trail** (2.6 mi.),
307–11   **Torry Ridge Trail** (6 mi.), **Blue Loop Trail (A)** (0.9 mi.)

Length and Difficulty: 8.5 miles (13.6 km) combined, round-trip; moderate

Features: rock outcrop, scenic views, wildflowers, stream

Trailheads: At parking area near group camp in Sherando Lake Recreation Area. To reach Sherando Lake from the BRP, mp 16, travel 4.3 miles northeast on SR 814 and SR 664 to entrance, left. Drive 2 miles. (Access to this circuit is also at the Slacks Overlook, BRP, mp 19.9.)

Description: This circuit uses most of the *White Rock Gap Trail*, all of the *Slacks Overlook Trail*, part of the *Torry Ridge Trail*, and part of the *Blue Loop Trail (A)*. Begin the hike at the sign near the parking area at the group camp. Pass north of the lake, follow upstream, and cross a tributary to the North Fork of Buck Creek at 0.9 miles. Ascend gradually in a more narrow hollow, and at 2.2 miles turn right on blue-blazed *Slacks Overlook Trail*. Reach the overlook at 4 miles. From here the trail continues on the eastern slope of Torry Ridge, where gypsy moth damage has destroyed most of the oaks. At 4.8 miles meet the yellow-blazed *Torry Ridge Trail*. (To the left it goes 1 mi. to Bald Mountain [3,587 ft.], accessible on FR 162 from Bald Mountain Overlook, BRP, mp 22.2.) Turn right and follow a narrow ridge through small oaks, serviceberries, mountain laurels, blueberries, wildflowers, grasses, and gray-green lichens on rocks and trees. At 6.7 miles turn right at a junction with blue-blazed *Blue Loop Trail (A)*. Pass junction on the left with 0.3-mile *Dam Trail*. (It descends steeply to dam and parking area.) Here is a lookout. After a descent of another 0.4 miles, the trail passes a water tower and meets campsite #6-A in White Oak Campground. From here it is 0.9 miles through the campgrounds west to point of origin for a circuit of 8.5 miles.

(If a longer hike is desired, include the *Blue Loop Trail [C]*: continue on the rocky *Torry Ridge Trail*, which now shows both yellow and blue blazes, for 1 mi. to trail junction, and right on the *Blue Loop Trail [C]*. Descend 0.8 mi. to exit at the junction of FR 91 and FR 91B [fisherman's access road] at the bridge. On FR 91 it is 1.6 mi. to point of origin for a circuit of 10.1 miles.)

(There are two short and scenic trails at the lake. The *Lakeside Trail* circles the lake for 1 mi., and 0.7-mile *Cliff Trail* switchbacks on the eastern slope of the lake from and to the *Lakeside Trail*.)

USGS map: Big Levels; *USFS trail nos.*: 480, 480A, 507, 507A, 507C

Blue Loop Trail (A) (0.9 mi.), **Torry Ridge Trail** (6 mi.),
Mills Creek Trail (7 mi.)   312–13

Length and Difficulty: 15.3 miles (24.5 km) combined, round-trip; strenuous
Connecting Trails: *Blue Loop Trail (C)* (0.8 mi.), *Mills Creek Trail (A)* (0.8 mi.),
   Slacks Overlook Trail (2.6 mi.)
Features: rock outcrops, stream, isolation, wildlife, wildflowers
Trailhead: Near campsite #6-A in White Oak Campground at Sherando Lake.
Description: This circuit follows all but 1 mile of the *Torry Ridge Trail* and all of the *Mills Creek Trail*, the latter being the best choice for campsites and overnight backpacking trips. Ascend on the *Blue Loop Trail (A)* past the water tower and overlook in an ascent to the *Torry Ridge Trail* at 0.9 miles. Turn right, and pass rock formations and a junction with the *Blue Loop Trail (C)* at 1.9 miles. Ascend a long wide ridge to the summit of Torry Mountain (2,781 ft.) at 2.9 miles. Pass large boulders, descend, pass blueberry patches, and at 4.1 miles meet the *Mills Creek Trail*, left. (To the right the remainder of the *Torry Ridge Trail* descends on switchbacks to Mount Torry Furnace on SR 664, 1.3 mi. north of the entrance to

Sherando Lake.) Follow the *Mills Creek Trail* on a narrow treadway through blueberries and mountain laurels to a hollow and a junction with a woods road at 4.8 miles. Turn left, cross a stream, and reach Mills Creek at 5.6 miles. Cross Orebank Creek, turn left, and follow FR 1237 (formerly called the *Turkey Pen Ridge Trail*). After 0.6 miles the road fades out to a footpath in an ascent and descent to cross Mills Creek at 6.9 miles. (To the right the *Mills Creek Trail [A]* follows downstream to Mills Creek Reservoir at 0.8 miles.) The main trail turns left to follow a long, generally flat hollow. Occasionally crossing the stream, it passes through tall hardwoods and hemlocks. Rhododendrons and ferns are prominent near good campsites. At 9.9 miles the trail begins a steep ascent with switchbacks (about 1,000 ft. vertical gain in 1 mi.) to reach FR 162 (3,437 ft.) at 11.1 miles. (To the right, FR 162 descends on the ridge along the St. Mary's Wilderness border, 2.5 mi. to Green Pond and the western trailhead of the *St. Mary's Trail*.) Turn left, ascend, reach a junction with FR 162C at 11.4 miles, and turn left on it for about 0.1 mile to the summit of Bald Mountain (3,587 ft.). Turn left on the *Torry Ridge Trail* and follow it 2.9 miles to a junction with the *Blue Loop Trail (A)*. Turn right, descend, pass the *Dam Trail* and the lookout, which has views of the lake area, and return to point of origin at 15.3 miles.

USGS maps: Big Levels, Sherando; *USFS trail nos.*: 507A, 507, 518

314–17   **St. Mary's Trail**
Length and Difficulty: 6.5 miles (10.4 km); moderate to strenuous
Connecting Trails: St. Mary's Gorge Trail (0.5 mi.), Mine Bank Creek Trail (2 mi.)
Features: wilderness, river, waterfall, old mines, natural lake
Trailheads: From I-81, exit 205, drive east on VA 56 through Steeles Tavern for 2.5 miles. Turn left on SR 608 and go 3 miles (passing under railroad bridge) to FR 41 on right. Go 1.5 miles to parking area and gate. The northeastern trailhead is accessible on FR 162 at Green Pond, 3.8 miles down the mountain from BRP, mp 22.2, Bald Mountain Overlook. (Entrance gate to FR 162 may be closed.)
Description: These are unmaintained and unblazed wilderness trails with a potential circuit of 17.8 miles when forest roads outside the wilderness boundary are used. Begin the hike up the left side of St. Mary's River in an area of wildflowers, sumacs, ferns, hardwoods and pines. At 1.2 miles wade or rock-hop the river. (Crossing may be dangerous or impossible after heavy rain.) Near the confluence with Sugar Tree Branch, the *St. Mary's Trail* turns right and the *St. Mary's Gorge Trail* turns left. (It dead-ends after 0.5 mi. at the base of the gorge and at the beautiful St. Mary's Waterfall.) On the main trail, pass cascades and fern beds at 1.5 miles. Leave Sugar Tree Branch at 1.7 miles. For the next 6.5 miles the trail passes through relics of past manganese mining and near quartzite rock slides. At 3.7 miles reach a junction with the *Mine Bank Trail*, right.

(The *Mine Bank Trail* ascends in Mine Bank gorge under tall hardwoods and hemlocks, parallel with the stream. At 1.6 mi. the trail leaves the stream and ascends steeply to the BRP, mp 23, opposite Fork Mountain Overlook. To the left [northeast] it is 0.2 mi. to the western trailhead of the *Bald Mountain Trail*, which curves around the spur ridges for 2.5 mi. to exit at FR 162. Gypsy moth damage to the hardwoods is noticeable on the trail. If making a loop for the *St. Mary's Trail*, turn left on FR 162. Pass access to the *Torry Ridge Trail*, right, at 0.1 mi. and the *Mills Creek Trail*, right, at 0.4 mi., and descend to Green Pond and a junction with the *St. Mary's Trail* at 2.9 mi.)

Continuing on the *St. Mary's Trail*, at 3.7 miles cross small streams, and arrive at good campsites at 3.9 miles. At 4.9 miles the trail crosses St. Mary's River for the last time, but crosses other small streams, one near a forest of pitch pine at 5.3 miles. The trail ascends to a level area (Big Levels), passes old FR 162 and Green Pond, and ends at FR 162 opposite FR 162B (Kennedy Ridge Rd.) at 6.5 miles. (If making a circuit south on FR 162, as described above, it is 17.8 mi.)
USGS maps: Vesuvius, Big Levels; *USFS trail nos.*: 500, 500B, 500C, 500E

Cellar Mountain Trail (2.9 mi.), **Cold Spring Trail** (1.3 mi.)   318–19
Length and Difficulty: 8.4 miles (13.4 km) round-trip; strenuous
Features: rugged wilderness, spring, wildlife
Trailhead: From FR 42, go 1.2 miles north of FR 41 to small parking area (see *St. Mary's Trail* access directions to FR 41).
Description: These trails join near the dead end of FR 162A outside the northern edge of St. Mary's Wilderness. (A circuit of 14.2 mi. could be made by omitting the *Cold Spring Trail*, following FR 162A for 2.8 mi., and returning on the *St. Mary's Trail* to FR 41 and FR 42.) Begin on an old woods road and ascend on switchbacks in a mixed forest. The understory has chinquapins, berries, mountain laurels, and azaleas. Pass large anthills. At 1.7 miles reach the top of Cellar Mountain (3,640 ft.), and remain on the ridge to a junction with the *Cold Spring Trail* and FR 162A. (The *Cold Spring Trail* descends 1 mi. on switchbacks to a convergence of streams and springs. It ends 0.3 mi. farther at the wilderness boundary and private property.) Backtrack.
USGS maps: Vesuvius, Big Levels; *USFS trail nos.*: 501, 524

Warm Springs Ranger District

This is the only GWNF district that completely borders the Monongahela National Forest in West Virginia. As a result it provides added depth to wild and scenic places for exploring, hunting, fishing, hiking, camping, and cross-country skiing in its 171,526 acres. The forest properties rise to join each other with communal trails and roads such as the *Allegheny Mountain Trail* between popular Lake Sherwood in West Virginia and Lake Moomaw in Virginia. A section of this high boundary is 25 miles of remote FR 55. Its lofty, scenic drive is known mainly to hunters, explorers, and foresters. On its serpentine route is High Top, where deer forage in fertile meadows above the clouds, and Paddy Knob (4,477 ft.), with expansive views and tall asters and woodland sunflowers. At the northwestern corner of this long border is Locust Springs, a high plateau of northern hardwoods dappled with red spruce among bogs and beavers. There are more than 30 species of rare flora and fauna, rarely seen by humans except those adventuring into the web of trails. The district has more lake acreage than other GWNF districts. Lake Moomaw, for example, covers 2,530 acres and is a paradise for campers, fishermen, boaters, and hikers. It has a beach for swimming and a marina with 36 boat slips, luxuries in this backcountry free of expressways, malls, and billboards. Its streams are cold and fresh, and some are stocked with trout. Among them are Jackson River, Back Creek, Pads Creek, and Wilson Creek. It has one wilderness, Rough Mountain (9,300 acres), located in the southeastern corner, and it is close enough to the Rich Hole Wilderness in the James River Ranger District for an improved turkey and bear habitat.

One of its surprisingly appealing and secluded camping areas is Blowing Springs, set in Back Creek Gorge on VA 39, 9.5 miles west of Warm Springs. It receives its name from a forceful spring that releases strong air currents from beneath the earth's surface. It has a 1.3-mile enticing path downstream that allows views of rapids, geological formations, and wildflowers among the black walnuts and hemlocks. Anglers find the stream to be good for bass and trout. The campground is open usually from March 15 to November 30. Another campground, Hidden Valley, near Warm Springs, is also open at that time. In addition to the picnic areas at Bolar Mountain at Lake Moomaw, there are two others: Locust Springs, north of Thornwood, West Virginia, on WV 28, and Bubbling Springs, south of Millboro on SR 665.

A district with the history and charm of Hidden Valley deserves its share in the limelight. In 1992 Hollywood came to Hidden Valley to film *Sommersby*, a post–Civil War saga starring Richard Gere and Jodie Foster. Judge James W. Warwick's 1848 historic house quickly became a mansion, and the plantation fields became old town props for a swarming cast. Whatever the local excitement, it soon passed. After all, nearby is The Homestead in Hot Springs, with its glamorous 15,000-acre estate, known worldwide as a hotel and resort for the rich and famous. Tranquil and historic (since 1891), it blends with the pristine beauty of the district's rivers and mountains.

Among its trails none could be more appealing than the 28 miles at Locust Springs Recreation Area. They and all the other trails described in this district are listed in the TIS trail directory as having low traffic volume. During the 1980s 26 trails were dropped from the district's list as nonexistent, unknown, or not maintained. Included were *Claylick Draft, Mad Sheep, Lantz Mountain, Mill Mountain,* and *Paddy Knob.* Future plans for the trail system include construction of a 6-mile trail on the eastern side of Lake Moomaw, a trail to connect Lake Moomaw with Lake Sherwood, and, the most ambitious of all, part of a 75-mile connector between the *Big Blue Trail* (see Lee Ranger District) and the *Allegheny Trail* (see James River Ranger District).

Address and Information: Warm Springs Ranger District, Rt. 2, Box 30, Hot Springs, VA 24445; phone: 703-839-2521; on US 220 1.8 miles south of Hot Springs. Available for free are brochures and flyers on Lake Moomaw, Locust Springs,

Hidden Valley, campgrounds, and wilderness. There is a small fee for topographical maps and district map with trails.

ROUGH MOUNTAIN WILDERNESS AREA
Bath County

Crane Trail   320

Length and Difficulty: 3 miles (4.8 km); strenuous
Features: isolation, rugged, wildlife
Trailheads: From Millboro drive southeast on SR 633 to FR 129 and follow it 5 miles along the South Fork of Pads Creek to parking area and gate. The western trailhead is 8.8 miles north on VA 42 (right side) from I-64, exit 29.
Description: Follow an old road along the C&O railroad bed for 1 mile and turn left at second small hollow to cross railroad and Pads Creek. Ascend steeply by a small stream in the Rough Mountain Wilderness to the ridge crest (2,600 ft.) at 1.3 miles. Explore the rocky cliffs and look west to Cowpasture River and Beards Mountain. To the east are views of Short Mountain and Mill Mountain. Descend on switchbacks to gate at VA 42 at 3 miles. Backtrack or use a second vehicle.
USGS map: Nimrod Hall; *USFS trail no.*: 454

MIDDLE, LITTLE MARE, AND BEARDS MOUNTAINS AREA
Bath County

Middle Mountain Trail (5.5 mi.), **Brushy Ridge Trail** (3.9 mi.),
Salt Pond Ridge Trail (2.1 mi.), **Little Mare Mountain Trail** (6 mi.),
Gillam Run Trail (2.3 mi.), **Beards Mountain Trail** (6.4 mi.)   321–29
Length and Difficulty: 19.9 miles (31.8 km) combined, partial round-trip; moderate to strenuous
Connecting Trails: *Stony Run Trail* (4.5 mi.), *Blue Suck Trail* (3 mi.), *Sandy Gap Trail* (3.4 mi.), *Little Mare Mountain Spur Trail* (0.7 mi.), *Walton Tract Trail* (1.5 mi.), *Mountain Top Trail* (2.3 mi.)
Features: scenic views, outcrops, wildflowers, wildlife
Trailheads: Use Douthat State Park Campground for base camp. From I-64, exit 27, drive north 5.5 miles on SR 629 to visitor center. *Sandy Gap Trail* trailhead: from US 220 at Valley View, drive 2.5 miles on SR 606 to junction with SR 703 and go 3.3 miles to trailhead on right. *Little Mare Mountain Trail* trailhead: from VA 39, near Bath Alum, go 0.8 miles south on SR 683 (or north 0.9 mi. from SR 629). *Gillam Run Trail* trailhead: From northern entrance of Douthat State Park, drive 4.2 miles north on SR 629 to FR 361, right. *Walton Tract Trail* trailhead: from VA 39 at Millboro Springs, drive 5.2 miles south on VA 42 to SR 632 and turn right for 1 mile (also from I-64, exit 29, on VA 42, 10.5 mi. north to SR 632, left).
Introduction: With all the diversity of trails (10 in Warm Spring Ranger District and 24 in Douthat State Park), and base camp facilities for tired and hungry hikers in the park, this is a hiker's heaven. Although the 40 miles of park trails

George Washington National Forest 141

are for day hikes, they can be entrance trails to the 32 miles of linear trails in the forest for overnight camping. The nearest option for a circuit on the forest trails uses 2.3 miles on FR 194 and 1.7 miles on SR 629, explained below.

Description: Begin the hike in Douthat State Park (0.5 mi. south of the campground on SR 629) on orange-blazed *Stony Run Trail*. Ascend, and at 1.4 miles pass a junction with the *Locust Gap Trail* from the right. At 2.5 miles is Stony Run Falls on the left. For the next 2 miles ascend on switchbacks to a junction left with a short connector to the *Middle Mountain Trail* and right with yellow-blazed *Tuscarora Overlook Trail*. Access the *Middle Mountain Trail* or follow the *Tuscarora Overlook Trail* for scenic views. After 0.9 miles intersect on the ridge top with the blue-blazed *Blue Suck Trail* on the right, and the *Middle Mountain Trail* and the *Sandy Gap Trail* on the left.

(The *Blue Suck Trail* descends 3 mi. to just north of the visitor center in the park.) The *Middle Mountain Trail* goes 1.6 miles south to its end at the county line and district line, but its name is replaced by the continuing *Fore Mountain Trail* (see James River Ranger District).

(The *Sandy Gap Trail* descends for 0.6 mi. west to FR 125 [Smith Creek Rd.]. It then crosses Smith Creek at 0.8 mi., ascends to a large area of glacial rock slabs at 1.5 mi., and crosses a stream at 2.1 mi. Continuing, it ascends, crosses another stream near a spring at 2.4 mi., and reaches SR 703 [Homestead Skyline Dr.] through a channel of purple rhododendron at 3.4 mi. There is outstanding scenery with views west over the Jackson River. Flame azaleas, locust, and mountain laurel decorate the area. Bald Knob and Ingalls Airport are right, and SR 606 is 3.3 mi. left.)

Continue north on the ridge on the *Middle Mountain Trail*. Signs may show that the *Middle Mountain Trail* is also the *Salt Stump Trail* (which leads down the eastern side of Middle Mountain to SR 629 in the park). The main trail may have overgrowth, but it stays on the ridgeline, undulating among the oaks and sections of pitch pine. At 4.2 miles (on the *Middle Mountain Trail*) are excellent views. Begin to descend gradually along the ridge shoulder and reach FR 125 (Wilson Creek Rd.) at 5.5 miles. (To the right it is 1 mi. on FR 125 to SR 629 and Douthat State Park.) Turn left on FR 25 and go 0.3 miles to entrance of the *Brushy Ridge Trail* on the right. Begin by crossing tank traps on an old logging road, then cross a stream at 0.7 miles. Ascend gradually to a junction with the *Salt Pond Ridge Trail* on right at 2.5 miles.

(The *Salt Pond Ridge Trail* descends right to SR 629 and to Douthat State Park after 3.3 mi. In its descent it passes a number of large boulder outcroppings, streams, and tank traps to end at FR 194. [Some maps may show the trail continuing across the road and through private property to SR 629.] If attempting a loop, follow FR 194 for 2.3 mi. south to SR 629, turn left, and follow SR 629 for 1.7 mi. to the *Gillam Run Trail* on the right at FR 361. After 2.3 mi. on the *Gillam Run Trail*, reach the *Beards Mountain Trail*, where a right turn leads 2.2 mi. to the boundary of Douthat State Park. Here either the *Mountain Top Trail* or the *Mountain Side Trail* would lead to the *Brushy Hollow Trail* or the *Beards Gap Trail* for a return to the campground and a total of about 27 mi.)

At this point on the *Middle Mountain Trail* it is 12.5 miles from beginning on the *Stony Run Trail.* Keep left at the fork on the *Brushy Ridge Trail* and reach a junction with a private road at 13.9 miles in Brushy Mountain Gap near Trappers Lodge. (Access here is from near the front entrance of The Homestead in Hot Springs. Permission from office officials is necessary for hiking access.)

Continue on forest property and begin the *Little Mare Mountain Trail,* northeast, on a downgrade on the ridgeline. At 16.9 miles is a junction with the *Little Mare Mountain Spur* (which descends 0.7 mi. to a road, formerly called the *Mare Run Trail*). Continue descending on the ridge in a hardwood forest and exit from an old road to SR 683 at 19.9 miles. It is 0.8 miles left to VA 39 and the Bath Alum community.

The nearest access to the *Beards Mountain Trail* from Douthat State Park is from the lake parking area. Cross the road, enter the *Buck Lick Interpretive Trail,* and turn left on the *Wilson Creek Trail.* Pass right of cabins, and at the last cabin (#50) turn right on the *Ross Camp Hollow Trail.* Turn left on the *Mountain Side Trail* and ascend to the corner of the park to a junction left with the *Mountain Top Trail* at 2 miles. Turn left on the *Beards Mountain Trail* and for the next 2.2 miles in a hardwood forest gradually descend over six low knolls. The farther from the park, the more likely the overgrowth. At a narrow point on the ridge, join the *Gillam Run Trail,* left. (It descends steeply for the first 0.8 mi. to a junction with FR 361. Its other 1.5 mi. may be overgrown because it mainly parallels the forest road, which is easier to hike. Its northern trailhead is at gated FR 361 and SR 629, 4 mi. north of Douthat State Park.)

Continuing on the *Beards Mountain Trail,* there is a slight and easy decline to a junction with the *Walton Tract Trail* at 7 miles. To the left the *Beards Mountain Trail* descends in a low hollow to curve right at Hickman Draft. It dead-ends at the confluence with another stream at 5.8 miles. (The district plans to extend or connect the trail with FR 361.) The *Walton Tract Trail* follows a ridgeline before curving right at a bluff over Cowpasture River at 0.9 miles. It descends on the mountainside and crosses a high footbridge at an oxbow curve of the river at 1.5 miles. Canoe landings are on both sides of the access road. (See trailheads for access directions.)

USGS maps: Healing Spring, Warm Springs, Bath Alum, Nimrod Hall; *USFS trail nos.*: (forest trails only and in order of citing) 458 (Middle Mountain), 637 (Sandy Gap), 456 (Brushy Ridge), 620 (Salt Pond Ridge), 638 (Gillam Run), 459 (Beards Mountain), 714 (Little Mare Mountain), 714A (Little Mare Mountain Spur), 459A (Walton Tract)

PINEY MOUNTAIN AREA
Bath County

Bear Rock Trail (1.3 mi.), **Warm Springs Mountain Trail** (4.3 mi.), **Piney Mountain Trail** (7 mi.), **Tower Hill Mountain Trail** (1.3 mi.)   330–33
Length and Difficulty: 13.9 miles (22 km) combined; strenuous
Features: scenic views, wildlife, seclusion

Trailheads: There are three accesses to the Piney Mountain trails. To reach the first, from the junction of VA 39 and SR 609 at Bath Alum, drive north on SR 609 for 2.7 miles to fork left. After another 3.3 miles turn left on FR 465. Park here if road is gated; otherwise, drive 1.3 miles to the *Bear Rock Trail*, right. The second access is on FR 358, off VA 39, 2.4 miles east from US 220 (down the eastern side of Warm Springs Mountain), and 4.2 miles west of the VA 39 and SR 609 junction in Bath Alum. On gated FR 358 it is 2.2 miles to the southern terminus of *Piney Mountain Trail (South)* on the right side of the road. To reach the third access, for the northern trailhead of the *Piney Mountain Trail (North)*, drive north of Warm Springs on US 220 from VA 39 for 4 miles and turn right on SR 614. After 0.9 miles look for trailhead on right. For the *Tower Hill Mountain Trail*, use the same route as for the *Bear Rock Trail*, except turn right at the fork of SR 609 on SR 624 and go 0.6 miles to trailhead on the left.

Introduction: All forest roads to these trails are gated except the northern end of the *Piney Mountain Trail* on SR 614 and the southern end of the *Tower Hill Mountain Trail* on SR 624, which does not connect with the other three trails. Gates are likely to be open during late fall and spring hunting seasons. The *Warm Springs Mountain Trail* dead-ends in the north; the *Piney Mountain Trail* dead-ends in the south; and the *Tower Hill Mountain Trail* dead-ends in the north. As a result of gates and dead ends, hikers can expect to hike more miles and might need a second vehicle. If all gates are closed and all trails with backtracking are hiked, the shortest additional distance is 10.2 miles with the use of two vehicles. Map users will notice the trail locations on the GWNF map are different from those on the district map.

Description: If entering on the *Bear Rock Trail*, go 1.3 miles from the gate on FR 465 to a rocky ravine. (To the left a connector trail descends 0.3 mi. to SR 609.) Ascend by a small stream to the ridgeline of the *Warms Springs Mountain Trail* at 1.3 miles. (To the right it is 1.7 mi. to private property and a northern dead end. Backtrack.) Continue on the *Warm Springs Mountain Trail* to House Rock (3,600 ft.) at 1.5 miles from the *Bear Rock Trail*. On an easy contour continue and join the *Piney Mountain Trail (South)*, left at 2.6 miles from the *Bear Rock Trail*. Turn left on the *Piney Mountain Trail* and descend 1 mile on switchbacks to cross FR 453. Ascend to the ridgeline of Piney Mountain, which has both white and yellow pines. (To the left is a 1-mi. *Piney Mountain Trail* access trail to FR 465 in Walnut Tree Hollow.) Turn right, follow the ridge, descend, and switchback west to cross Jordan Run. Reach FR 453 at 4.2 miles, the trail's southern terminus. Either backtrack or follow the scenic and crooked FR 453 upstream for 2.5 miles to rejoin the trail. Ascend left to a junction with the *Warm Springs Mountain Trail*, but turn left and continue on the *Piney Mountain Trail (North)*. After 0.7 miles reach Bonner Mountain Knob. Turn right and descend 2.1 miles on a slender ridge between small streams to reach the northern trailhead at SR 614.

To hike the *Tower Hill Mountain Trail* follow the trailhead guide above and begin the ascent on a blue-blazed trail among oaks and white pines. After 0.5

miles is Chimney Rocks, with views of McClung Ridge. A turn right (northeast) leads to the forest boundary at 1.3 miles. (With the use of private property and USFS property this trail was formerly 14 mi. on Tower Hill Mountain to SR 614 near Williamsville.) Backtrack.

USGS maps: Warm Springs, Bath Alum, Burnsville; *USFS trail nos.*: 635, 451, 453, 452

HIDDEN VALLEY AREA
Bath County

Lower Lost Woman Trail (0.6 mi.), **Upper Lost Woman Trail** (1 mi.),
River Loop Trail (1 mi.), **Cobbler Mountain Trail** (2.4 mi.), **Muddy Run Trail**
(1.2 mi.), **Jackson River Gorge Trail** (1.8 mi.), **Bogan Run Trail** (7.5 mi.)   334–40

Length and Difficulty: 15.5 miles (24.8 km) combined, partial circuit; easy to moderate

Features: historic site, archaeological artifacts, fishing, wildlife

Trailheads: From junction of US 220 and VA 39 in Warm Springs, drive 3.2 miles west on VA 39 to SR 621 and turn right. After 1 mile turn left on FR 241 and go 1.3 miles to crossing of the *Cobbler Mountain Trail*, and 0.2 miles farther to the campground, left. The western trailhead of the *Bogan Run Trail* is 4 miles north on SR 600 from Mountain Grove on VA 39, west of Warm Springs.

Introduction: The fee campground has trailer and tent sites, vault toilets, and waste disposal unit in a white pine and hardwood forest. It has a double loop nature trail named to describe a campground worker who became lost nearby and was not found until the next day. Another nature trail is 1-mile *River Loop Trail*, accessible from the campground loop road. It is a good access for fishing in the Jackson River. The campground is usually open from March 15 to the end of November. A major feature of the valley is the Warwick House, built in 1848. It was the plantation home of Judge James W. Warwick. An example of Greek revival architecture, it was named to the National Register of Historic Places in 1973. In 1990 the GWNF signed a 30-year adaptive rehabilitation agreement with Ron and Pam Stidham to restore and operate the building as a bed and breakfast facility. Previously the home was used as a hunt club, a farmhouse, or a school. During the renovation a USFS archaeologist discovered prehistoric components dating to 7000 B.C.

Description: Circuit options are 0.6 miles, 1 mile, or 5.1 miles on all the trails except the *Bogan Run Trail*. If following the 5.1-mile loop, ascend from the *Lower Lost Woman Trail* trailhead, left, near campsite #28 in the campground. Stay left at the *Upper Lost Woman Trail*, and after 0.2 miles cross FR 241. Cross over a spur ridge of Cobbler Mountain and descend to cross a streamlet. At 1.7 miles pass right of a duck pond, and continue to cross a number of toeslopes of Cobbler Mountain. At 2.8 miles reach Muddy Run. (The *Muddy Run Trail* is a wide spur up a tributary where hemlock, pine, and birch form a canopy over cascades. Deer may be seen in the wildlife clearings and hawthorn thickets. It is 1 mi. to the end of government property.) Turn left and after 0.2 miles reach a junction with the *Jackson River Gorge Trail* (formerly the *Hidden Valley Trail*, which as a road/trail went upstream to SR 623 about 4.8 mi. from this point before the great flood of 1985). To the right, after 0.2 miles, is the end of the trail at the ford of the river. To the left, follow the trail downstream. On the banks of the trout-stocked river there are sycamore, hemlock, birch, and rhododendron. At 4.2 miles arrive at the parking lot near the bridge at FR 241. Follow the road left to the campground and point of origin at 5.1 miles.

For the *Bogan Run Trail*, begin at the bridge parking lot, cross the bridge on FR 241, pass the former *Rock Shelter Trail* (which paralleled the river to a swinging bridge at 3.4 mi.), and pass in front of the Warwick House, spring, and cemetery. Cross Limekiln Run, and at 1.5 miles turn left off FR 241. Ascend on the eastern slope of Back Creek Mountain, and at 3 miles begin to switchback. At 4 miles reach the top of the ridge (3,000 ft.) and FR 121 (Back Creek Mountain Rd.). From here the trail descends on switchbacks through hardwoods on an old logging road. At 5.5 miles leave forest property at the upper waters of Bogan Run. Pass a side trail on the right at 7.2 miles, and end the hike at the gate by SR 600. Backtrack or arrange a support vehicle.

USGS map: Warm Springs; *USFS trail nos.*: 612, 612A, 613, 611, 481B, 481D, 614

BOLAR MOUNTAIN AREA
Bath County

Greenwood Point Trail (4.4 mi.), **Sugar Hollow Trail** (1.4 mi.),
Loop Trail (1.8 mi.), **Fee Booth Spur Trail** (0.6 mi.), **Riverside Trail** (1.4 mi.),
Picnic Area Spur Trail (1.1 mi.), **Island Overlook Trail** (0.2 mi.),
341–48   **Campground #1 Spur Trail** (0.4 mi.) ·

Length and Difficulty: 15.7 miles (25.1 km) combined, round-trip; easy to moderate
Features: scenic views, lake, wildlife, fishing
Trailheads: Access from Warm Springs on VA 39 west is 2.7 miles to SR 687, left. Drive 2.6 miles to SR 603. Turn right and follow SR 603 for 6.6 miles to Bolar Mountain Recreation Area entrance. From Hot Springs, drive west on SR 615 for 2.7 miles to a right turn on SR 687. After 2.8 miles turn left on SR 603 and go 6.6 miles. From the Gathright Dam of Lake Moomaw, drive north as follows: on SR 605, 3.8 miles; on SR 687, 6.4 miles; turn left on SR 603 and continue 6.6 miles. If coming from West Virginia on VA 39, turn right on SR 600 and go 7 miles.
Introduction: Bolar Mountain Recreation Area has multiple campgrounds and picnic areas, a swimming beach and bathhouse, a boat ramp and marina, and a network of trails. One campground has electrical hookups. All have flush toilets. There are also group camps and picnic shelters for rent. Usually the open season is from Memorial Day to Labor Day or later into October or November for some facilities, such as boating and hiking. All the trails except the *Greenwood Point Trail* are in a compact unit near the facilities. Backtracking is necessary for the *Greenwood Point Trail*.
Description: For short hikes, park at the swimming area, cross the road to the trail sign, and choose a starting trail. All trails connect at different levels of the

mountainside in a forest of oaks, maples, and Virginia and white pines. The *Sugar Hollow Trail* goes over the mountain ridge to follow a small stream. There are scenic views of the lake from some of the trails, particularly the *Island Overlook Trail.* The longest trail, the *Greenwood Point Trail,* begins with the network of trails and parallels the highway past campgrounds #2 and #3 to the end of the road at 1.4 miles. (The trail can also be accessed here.) From here, cross the stream and ascend on switchbacks to a dry spur ridge in a thick forest. At 1.8 miles descend from a scenic view of the lake to a cove. At 2.7 miles reach a knoll, descend to a hollow, and ascend to a ridge. From this ridge the trail descends to Greenwood Point Campground at 4.4 miles. There is a vault toilet, but no drinking water. Lake reflections at sunrise or sunset and the sounds of waterfowl add to the excitement of camping here. Backtrack. (Long-range plans by the USFS call for reconstructing 2.5 mi. of the trail.)

USGS map: Falling Spring; *USFS trail nos.*: 720, 721, 722, 723, 724, 725, 726, 727

LAUREL FORK AREA
Highland County

Buck Run Trail (3.3 mi.), **Locust Spring Run Trail** (3.1 mi.),
Laurel Fork Trail (6.5 mi.), **Cold Springs Run Trail** (1.3 mi.),
Middle Mountain Trail (3.7 mi.), **Christian Run Trail** (1.3 mi.),
Buck Run Spur Trail (3.3 mi.), **Slabcamp Run Trail** (3 mi.),
Locust Spring Run Spur Trail (1.5 mi.), **Bearwallow Run Trail** (2.7 mi.)   349–58

Length and Difficulty: 28.2 miles (45.1 km) combined, multiple circuits; easy to moderate

Features: historic site, rare flora and fauna, high plateau, seclusion

Trailheads: From Bartow, West Virginia, drive northeast on WV 28 for 8.9 miles to FR 60/142 and turn right. From Monterey, Virginia, drive west on US 250 to junction with WV 28, turn north on WV 28, and after 6.7 miles turn right on FR 60/142. From US 33 at junction of WV 28, turn south on WV 28 and drive 16 miles to FR 60/142 and turn left. Another access is reached from the junction of US 220 in Virginia and Forks of Water, SR 642. Drive 10.3 miles on SR 642 (passing through Blue Grass community at 4.3 mi.), turning north on FR 457 to a parking area for the *Middle Mountain Trail* (not related to the *Middle Mountain Trail* near Douthat State Park).

Introduction: Laurel Fork, in the headwaters of the Potomac River, is an isolated high area, elevation 2,600 to 4,100 feet. The steep slopes in the area are circumvented by a network of easy, graded, and abandoned railroad beds and other trails. It is an ideal area for day hikes and overnight backpacking for nature study. The *Laurel Fork Trail* extends southwest to northeast somewhat centrally through the entire area, and a dozen trails branch from it. To fully experience this beautiful forest where regenerative power is demonstrated, multiple circuit hikes are recommended. Because of the high elevation there are red spruces and northern hardwoods. Orchids and ferns are trailside, and more than 30 species of rare flora and fauna thrive here. Among the animals are the snowshoe hare, the fisher, and the northern flying squirrel.

Description: From the parking area of the Locust Springs Picnic Area, begin on the *Buck Run Trail*, east (or the *Locust Spring Run Trail*, southeast for 3.1 mi.), to the central trail, the *Laurel Fork Trail*. (The *Buck Run Spur Trail* goes off to the right from the *Buck Run Trail* for 0.6 mi. to connect with the *Locust Spring Run Trail*.) Pass a beaver pond and meadows and stay on the southern side of the tributary along Buck Run, descending along the stream stocked with brook trout. Reach the *Laurel Fork Trail* at 3.3 miles; continue several miles on it, or take either of two options.

One option at this point is to turn left, cross a stream, and go 0.6 miles to the *Cold Spring Run Trail* on the right; follow it south for 1.3 miles, where it becomes the *Middle Mountain Trail*. At 2.9 miles is the *Christian Run Trail*, right. Follow it for a 1.5-mile hike looping back to the *Laurel Fork Trail* and a total of 8.3 miles. A right turn down the *Laurel Fork Trail* for 0.7 miles will connect with the *Buck Run Trail* or the *Locust Spring Run Trail* on the left. A return on either trail to the parking area would total 12.3 miles for the circuit.

Another option from the *Laurel Fork Trail* begins at the junction of the *Buck Run Trail*. Turn right, going upstream by Laurel Fork. At 3.6 miles (from the beginning at the parking area) reach the junction with the *Slabcamp Run Trail* on the right. This trail leads up the tributary for 3 miles to a junction with the *Locust Spring Run Spur Trail*, then continues 1.5 miles to the *Locust Spring Run Trail* (on which is a stand of red spruce and red pine) on the left for 1.5 miles and a return to parking area for a total circuit of 9.6 miles.

If continuing upstream on the *Laurel Fork Trail*, pass the *Christian Run Trail* on the left at 4 miles. Birch, oak, cherry, maple, beech, hemlock, and red spruce are on the trail. Wildflowers, ferns, and mosses are abundant. Animals in the area are bear, deer, turkey, grouse, raccoon, mink, and beaver. At 6.5 miles reach the *Bearwallow Run Trail* on the right. (Continuing up the stream for 1.4 mi. leads to SR 642 and limited parking space.) Bear right on scenic *Bearwallow Run Trail*, viewing beaver ponds and meadows, and after 2.7 miles on this trail reach FR 55 at 9.2 miles. Take a right on FR 55 to a junction with the *Locust Spring Run Spur Trail* at 11.2 miles. Go right on the *Locust Spring Run Spur Trail* for 1.5 miles to a junction with the *Locust Spring Run Trail*, bear left, and return to the parking and picnic area for a circuit total of 14.2 miles. (A route for a southern entrance to the *Middle Mountain Trail* starts at FR 457. This trail makes a connection with all the others. See trailheads above.)

USGS maps: Thornwood, Snowy Mountain, Hightown; *USFS trail nos.*: 598, 633, 450, 634A, 634, 599, 598A, 600, 623A, 601

II : National Park System Trails

3 : Appalachian National Scenic Trail

We need to tell the Appalachian Trail Story
again, again, and again, to insure the permanent
protection of this marvelous wilderness trail.
—Ed Garvey

The *Appalachian Trail (AT)* is the world's most famous hiking trail. Its history of challenge and adventure, its natural beauty, and its astonishing length have played a part in the idealization of the first of America's national scenic trails.

Many individuals dream of completing the trail's 2,145 miles as a through-hiker in one season; others are satisfied to finish sections as part of a long-term goal. Of the millions whose feet have touched its pathway at fleeting stops in parks and forests, only a few, less than 2,000, have taken the more than 5 million footsteps from Maine to Georgia. Some follow this continuous footpath through 14 states for physical endurance, spiritual achievement, educational encounters, therapeutic experiences, or a combination of reasons. Earl Shaffer, from York, Pennsylvania, in 1948 the first through-hiker, said he made the journey from Georgia to Maine to fulfill the wish and plans that he and his hiking friend, Walter Winemiller, had made to hike the entire *AT*. Then came World War II, and both men were in combat zones of the Pacific. Winemiller was killed on Iwo Jima. In 1965 Shaffer was also the first to traverse the *AT* in the opposite direction. At least one known hiker, Mary Kilpatrick of Philadelphia, had completed the *AT* in sections of unflagged and unblazed routes ten years earlier. But the first woman through-hiker was Emma Gatewood ("Grandma Gatewood") of Ohio, in 1955. The first person to document the distance of the *AT* with a measuring wheel was Myron Avery, first president of the PATC, founded in Washington, D.C., in 1927, and chairman of the Appalachian Trail Conference from 1930 to 1952.

Since the days of the early explorers the challenge and magnetic appeal have intensified among the young and the elderly, among the star athletes and the physically disabled, and among scientists to catalog the *AT*'s geology and biology. Setting a record for the number of through-hikes is Warren Doyle of Fairfax County, Virginia, who completed his tenth in 1995. His first was in 1973, and his eleventh is planned for 1997. For each hiker who has completed the *AT*, there is a different personal story of pain and pleasure, failure and fulfillment, and the kinetic drive to go back again. In Shaffer's *Walking with Spring* he wrote, "I knew that many times I would want to be back again . . . on the cloud-high hills where the whole world lies below and far away[,] . . . by the windworn cairn where admiring eyes first welcome newborn day."

The concept and name of the *AT* belong to Benton MacKaye, a forester and author from Shirley Center, Massachusetts. He has said that his thoughts of such a trail came early in the century, before the *Long Trail* in Vermont was begun in 1910. Among others who had long trail concepts was Allen Chamberlain, a Boston newspaper columnist and early president of the Appalachian Mountain Club (formed in 1876). By 1921, trail leaders in New England and in the Palisades Trail Conference (which later became part of the New York–New Jersey Trail Conference) planned connecting trails. An example of their efforts was the first and original section opened October 7, 1923, in the Harriman–Bear Mountain section of the Palisades Interstate Park. After 1926 the leadership of Arthur Perkins of Hartford, Connecticut, translated MacKaye's dream into reality, but it was Myron H. Avery of Lubec, Maine, who more than any other individual was instrumental in implementing and coordinating the agreements with government agencies (such as the CCC) and with volunteers to complete the AT.

The entire AT routing design was initially completed August 15, 1937, but considerable relocations were to follow. Trail mapping and maintenance nearly came to a standstill during World War II, and even when Shaffer began his journey, many sections of the AT were unblazed. A number of the Appalachian Trail Conference leaders considered his mission impossible. Today the AT is secure, with only a few miles unprotected or yet to be purchased as part of the NPS. Protection came by the National Trails System Act of 1968, to which supplemental amendments were made in 1970, 1978, and several times since. Its maintenance, however, depends on 32 organized clubs (and hundreds of volunteer workers in those clubs), whose chief purpose is assisting the Appalachian Trail Conference in planning and maintaining sections of the AT.

One-fourth (544.6 mi.) of the total AT mileage is in Virginia (including about 22 mi. that zigzag along the West Virginia state line in Jefferson and Monroe counties). The highest point for the trail is Mount Rogers (5,729 ft.), and the lowest is at the James River bridge (660 ft.). It passes through the JNF, the GWNF, part of the BRP, and almost all of the Shenandoah National Park. Ten volunteer clubs jointly assist the USFS and the NPS in planning and maintaining the AT. The Tennessee Eastman Hiking Club maintains 3.5 miles in Virginia (another 122.1 mi. are in Tennessee and North Carolina) from the state line to Damascus; Mount Rogers Appalachian Trail Club, 63.7 miles from Damascus to Brushy Mountain (VA 16); Piedmont Appalachian Trail Hikers, 42.2 miles from Brushy Mountain to Garden Mountain; Virginia Tech Outing Club, 28.1 miles from Garden Mountain to Brushy Mountain (SR 608); Kanawha Trail Club, 19.3 miles from New River to Stony Creek Valley; Roanoke Appalachian Trail Club, 113.4 miles from Brushy Mountain (SR 608) to New River and from Stony Creek Valley to Black Horse Gap; Natural Bridge Appalachian Trail Club, 88.4 miles from Black Horse Gap to Tye River; Tidewater Appalachian Trail Club, 10.5 miles from Tye River to Reeds Gap; Old Dominion Appalachian Trail Club, 16.7 miles from Reeds Gap to Rockfish Gap; and the PATC, 158.8 miles from Rockfish Gap to Loudoun Heights. (The PATC also maintains an additional 79.5 miles in West Virginia, Maryland, and part of Pennsylvania.) Because of relocations, the above mileages are subject to change.

The condensed listing of milepoints in this chapter is meant to emphasize major points of interest such as shelters, post offices, scenic views, highway crossings, food, amenities, and some trail connections. It is recommended the hiker acquire the guidebooks listed below. A number of trails that include parts of the AT

Appalachian Trail, Mount Rogers, JNF. (Photograph by Allen de Hart)

are described in Chapters 1, 2, 4, and 5. The USFS number for the *AT* is 1, the blaze is white, and side trails (leading to views, shelter, and water) are blue-blazed.

Address and Information: Appalachian Trail Conference, P.O. Box 807, Harpers Ferry, WV 25425; phone: 304-535-6331; office is located at the corner of Washington and Jackson streets. Available are free brochure and general information about the *AT*. If the following books and maps are not available at bookstores and outfitters, order from the Appalachian Trail Conference: *Appalachian Trail Guide, Maryland*

and Northern Virginia (and map); *Shenandoah National Park* (and map); *Central and Southwest Virginia* (and map). For information about huts and cabins rented by the PATC in the Shenandoah National Park, contact PATC, 118 Park St., SE, Vienna, VA 22180; phone: 703-242-0315 (for hikes, 703-242-0965).

Appalachian Trail

Milepoint 544.6 to milepoint 0.0

Milepoint		Location and Description
From N	From S	
544.6	0.0	Tennessee/Virginia state boundary (3,200 ft.), 11.3 mi. N of US 421
541.1	3.5	Damascus, Virginia (1,928 ft.), US 58; lodging, groceries, restaurant, post office 24236
537.6	7.0	Feathercamp Ridge, yellow-blazed *Iron Mtn. Trail* (extends 16.8 mi. to Chester Flats [4,200 ft.] junction with *AT*)
531.7	12.9	Saunders Shelter; water
527.1	17.5	Joint crossing with *Virginia Creeper Trail* on 0.1-mi. railroad trestle
524.2	20.4	Eastern crossing of US 58, near Summit Cut (3,160 ft.); groceries (2 mi. E and W)
517.3	27.3	Cross SR 600, Elk Garden (4,434 ft.); groceries (3.5 mi. E)
515.5	29.1	Deep Gap Shelter; water
513.5	31.1	Side trail (0.5 mi.) to thick forest summit of Mt. Rogers (5,729 ft.), state's highest point
507.9	36.7	Side trail (0.5 mi.) to Grayson Highlands State Park parking area, campground (1.2 mi. E)
502.1	42.5	Old Orchard Shelter; water
494.0	50.6	Side trail (0.5 mi. NW) to Hurricane Campground, Mt. Rogers National Recreation Area
491.9	52.7	Cross SR 650 (near VA 16 junction), Dickey Gap (3,313 ft.); Troutdale, groceries, restaurant, post office 24378 (2.6 mi. SE on VA 16)
490.4	54.2	Raccoon Branch Shelter; water
487.9	56.7	Trimpi Shelter; water
477.4	67.2	Mt. Rogers National Recreation Area visitor center and district ranger office, cross VA 16 (3,220 ft.); Sugar Grove, groceries, meals, post office 24375 (3 mi. S)
470.6	74.0	Chatfield Shelter; water
466.0	78.6	Groseclose, motel, restaurant, groceries at junction of US 11/I-81/VA 683; Atkins, laundry, groceries, post office 24311 (3.2 mi. W on US 11)
463.3	81.3	Davis Path Shelter; no water
454.1	90.5	Cross VA 42; Ceres, post office 24318 (5.2 mi. E)
452.2	92.4	Knot Maul Branch Shelter; water
444.2	101.4	Chestnut Knob Shelter (4,300 ft.); no water, views of Burke's Garden
435.1	109.5	Davis Farm Campsite; water (0.5 mi. W)
432.4	112.2	Jenkins Shelter; water

Milepoint		Location and Description
From N	From S	
427.6	117.0	Cross Little Wolf Creek and 11 other places within 2.5 mi.
420.4	124.2	Cross US 21/52 to SR 612; Bastian, groceries, meals, post office 24314 (1.8 mi. N); Bland, groceries, motel, meals, laundry, post office 24315 (2.5 mi. S)
419.6	124.8	Cross I-77 overpass
418.1	126.5	Helveys Mill Shelter; water
408.3	136.3	Jenny Knob Shelter; water
407.1	137.5	Cross SR 608, Lickskillet Hollow (2,200 ft.), 0.8 mi. N of VA 42 and Crandon; groceries
401.9	142.7	Cross SR 606; groceries (0.2 mi. W)
400.8	143.8	Side trail (0.3 mi.) to Dismal Creek Falls
395.0	149.6	Wapiti Shelter; water
386.6	158.0	Doc's Knob Shelter; water
381.2	163.4	Angels Rest (3,550 ft.), Pearis Mtn.; views
378.8	165.8	Pearisburg, VA 100 and US 460 junction; groceries, restaurants, lodging, laundry (1 mi. SE on VA 100)
364.7	179.9	Southernmost access in West Virginia to *Allegheny Trail* (2 mi. N on *Groundhog Trail* to county road 219/24)
361.6	183.0	*Allegheny Trail* junction on Pine Swamp Ridge
359.9	184.7	Pine Swamp Branch Shelter (2,530 ft.); water
355.9	188.7	Bailey Gap Shelter; water (seasonal)
348.0	196.6	War Spur Shelter; water
342.0	202.6	Laurel Creek Shelter; water
339.9	204.7	Sinking Creek Valley, cross VA 42; groceries (1.6 mi. W)
335.5	209.1	Sarver Cabin; water
329.5	215.1	Niday Shelter; water
319.6	225.0	Pickle Branch Shelter; water
316.1	228.5	Dragons Tooth on Cove Mtn. (3,050 ft.); views
307.7	236.9	Cross VA 311; Catawba, groceries, restaurant, post office 24070 (1 mi. W)
306.7	237.9	Boy Scout Shelter; water (seasonal)
305.7	238.9	Catawba Mtn. Shelter; water
304.2	240.4	McAfee Knob (3,197 ft.); cliffs, views
303.5	241.1	Campbell Shelter; water
298.6	246.0	Big Tinker Cliffs (3,000 ft.); views
297.5	247.1	Lamberts Meadow Shelter; water
292.1	252.5	Hay Rock, Tinker Ridge; views
288.3	256.3	Junction of US 220 and SR 816; Cloverdale, groceries, lodging, restaurant, laundry, post office 24077 (1.5 mi. S)
287.1	257.5	Cross under I-81 on SR 779 and across US 11; Troutville, groceries, lodging, post office 24175 (1 mi. N on US 11)
283.4	261.2	Fullhardt Knob Shelter; water (cistern)
277.0	267.6	Wilson Creek Shelter; water
274.6	270.0	Cross Black Horse Gap Rd., FR 186, near BRP mp 97.7

Milepoint		Location and Description
From N	From S	
269.7	274.9	Bobblets Gap Shelter; water
267.2	277.4	Bearwallow Gap (2,238 ft.), BRP mp 90.9, and junction with VA 43/SR 695; Buchanan, groceries, restaurant, lodging, post office 24066 (5 mi. NW)
264.0	280.6	Cove Mtn. Shelter; no water
257.9	286.7	Cross SR 714, Middle Creek/N. Creek Rd.; groceries (1.4 mi. E)
252.6	292.0	Cornelius Creek Shelter; water
251.6	293.0	Black Rock; views
249.9	294.7	Parkers Gap Rd. (3,380 ft.) FR 812, BRP mp 78.4
247.9	296.7	Thunder Hill Shelter; water (seasonal)
235.4	309.2	Matts Creek Shelter; water
232.8	311.8	James River, US 501; Big Island, groceries, restaurant, post office 24526 (4 mi. E)
230.5	314.1	Johns Hollow Shelter; water
228.5	316.1	Fullers Rocks (2,480 ft.); views
221.9	322.7	Punchbowl Shelter; water
217.2	327.4	Pedlar Dam
212.0	332.6	Brown Mtn. Creek Shelter; water
211.2	333.4	Cross US 60 at Long Mtn. Wayside (2,026 ft.); groceries (1 mi. W at junction with SR 634)
207.4	337.2	Cow Camp Gap Shelter; water (0.6 mi. SE on *Hotel Trail*)
206.6	338.0	Cole Mtn. (4,022 ft.); bald, views
205.3	339.3	Hog Camp Gap, FR 48; parking area, water at Wiggins Spring (0.5 mi. W)
203.1	341.5	Salt Log Gap (3,247 ft.), FR 63 (extension of SR 634), and junction with FR 48
197.7	346.9	Seeley-Woodworth Shelter; water
196.4	347.2	Twin Springs; water and campsites
195.5	349.1	Fish Hatchery Rd.; Montebello, groceries, meals, commercial campground, post office 24464 (1.9 mi. W, including SR 600 and VA 56)
195.1	349.5	Spy Rock; views (0.1 mi. E)
194.8	349.8	Maintop Mtn. (4,040 ft.); summit forested, but view on side trail 0.1 mi. S
191.9	352.7	Crabtree Farm Rd., SR 826, campsites (0.5 mi. W), 3.7 mi. farther W to VA 56
191.0	353.6	The Priest Shelter; water
190.6	354.0	The Priest (4,063 ft.); views
186.3	358.3	Cross VA 56 and Tye River suspension footbridge; Tyro, groceries, post office 22976 (1.4 mi. E), groceries (1.1 mi. W)
183.7	360.9	Harpers Creek Shelter; water
179.5	365.1	Hanging Rock; views
177.5	367.1	Maupin Field Shelter; water

Milepoint		Location and Description
From N	From S	
175.8	368.8	Reed Gap (2,645 ft.) near BRP and SR 664
171.0	373.6	Cedar Cliff; views
167.0	377.6	Humpback Rocks; views
166.2	378.4	Humpback Rocks parking area, BRP mp 6
164.4	380.2	Wolfe Shelter; water
159.1	385.5	Rockfish Gap (1,902 ft.), end of BRP and beginning of Skyline Dr.; lodging and restaurant; Waynesboro, lodging, groceries, restaurants, laundry, post office 22980 (4.5 mi. W), cross overpass of US 250 and I-64
158.3	386.3	Self-registration for hiking permits; side trail (0.2 mi. W) to Skyline Dr. entrance station
154.2	390.4	Bear Den Mtn. (2,885 ft.); views
152.8	391.8	Calf Mtn. (2,910 ft.); views
152.2	392.4	Calf Mtn. Shelter; water (maintained by PATC)
139.0	405.6	Blackrock Hut; water (for long-distance AT hikers only)
138.4	406.2	Blackrock (3,092 ft.); views
133.8	410.8	Doyles River Cabin; water (advance reservations required from PATC)
131.7	412.9	Loft Mtn. Campground, Skyline Drive mp 79.5; groceries, meals, camping, laundry, May through October
125.9	418.7	Pinefield Hut; water (for long-distance AT hikers only)
117.6	427.0	Hightop Hut; water (for long-distance AT hikers only)
111.2	433.4	South River Picnic Grounds; water
107.9	436.7	Pocosin Cabin; water (locked) (advance reservations required from PATC)
106.0	438.6	Lewis Mtn. Campground; water (seasonal), Skyline Drive mp 57.6, camping, groceries, lodging (0.1 mi. W)
105.1	439.5	Bearfence Mtn. Hut; water unreliable (for long-distance AT hikers only)
101.7	442.9	Hazeltop (3,812 ft.), highest point of AT in the Shenandoah National Park
98.0	446.6	Big Meadows Wayside and Visitor Center; lodging, meals, camping open all year (0.1 mi. E)
93.7	450.9	Rock Spring Cabin; water (locked) (advance reservations required from PATC); Rock Spring Hut (for long-distance AT hikers only)
93.4	451.2	Side trail (0.9 mi. E) to Hawksbill Mtn. (4,050 ft.); highest peak in Shenandoah National Park; Byrd's Nest #2 Picnic Shelter
92.0	452.6	Crescent Rock (0.1 mi. E); views
89.9	454.7	South service road to Skyland Lodge
89.1	455.5	North service road to Skyland Lodge (0.3 mi. W); lodging and restaurant
87.1	457.5	Stony Man Mtn. Overlook (3,097 ft.), Skyline Dr. mp 38.6; water (seasonal)
84.9	459.7	Pinnacles Picnic Ground, Skyline Dr. mp 36.7

Milepoint		Location and Description
From N	From S	
81.5	463.1	Mary's Rock (3,514 ft.); panoramic views (0.1-mi. side trail to summit)
79.8	464.8	Thornton Gap (2,307 ft.), US 211, Skyline Dr. mp 31.5; restaurant
77.8	466.8	Pass Mtn. Hut; water (for long-distance AT hikers only)
76.3	468.3	Byrd's Nest #4 Picnic Shelter (0.5 mi. E); water (May through October)
71.2	473.4	Elkwallow Gap, Skyline Dr. mp 23.9; groceries, meals (0.1 mi. E)
70.3	474.3	Range View Cabin; water (locked) (advance reservations required from PATC)
69.7	474.9	Rattlesnake Point Overlook, Skyline Dr. mp 23.9; Mathews Arm Campground (1 mi. W)
69.1	475.5	Junction with Big Blue Trail (W)
65.5	479.1	Gravel Springs Hut; water (for long-distance AT hikers only)
64.3	480.3	South Marshall Mtn. (3,212 ft.); views; North Marshall Mtn. (3,368 ft.); views at 481.5
58.7	485.9	Compton Peak (2,909 ft.); views
55.8	488.8	Possum's Rest; outcropping, N boundary of Shenandoah National Park
55.1	489.5	Tom Floyd Wayside (primitive camping for AT long-distance hikers only); no open fires, water
52.0	492.6	Cross US 522; Front Royal, groceries, restaurants, lodging, laundry, post office 22630 (3.2 mi. to 4.2 mi. W)
48.6	496.0	Mosby Campsite; primitive, water
46.7	497.9	Denton Shelter; water
43.6	501.0	Manassas Gap; cross VA 55 to SR 725 and under I-66; Linden, groceries, post office 22642 (1 mi. W on VA 55)
41.2	503.4	Manassas Gap Shelter; water
36.5	508.1	Dick's Dome Shelter; water
34.2	510.4	Sky Meadows State Park; steep side trail 1.3 mi. E to fee campsites and shelter, water
31.1	513.5	Ashby Gap, US 50; Paris, restaurant (0.1 mi. E), post office 22130 (1 mi. E), restaurant and lodging (1.2 mi. E)
27.6	517.0	Rod Hollow Shelter; water
17.9	526.7	Bear Den Rocks; views (Bears Den Hostel nearby, lodging)
17.3	527.3	Snickers Gap (1,060 ft.), junction of SR 601 and VA 7; Bluemont, restaurant and groceries (0.3 mi. to 1 mi. W), groceries, post office 22012 (1.8 mi. E)
14.8	529.8	Crescent Rock; views
14.1	530.5	Devils Racecourse (1,448 ft.); views
10.1	534.5	Blackburn Appalachian Trail Center; camping, water (0.1 mi. and 0.3 mi. E)
7.5	537.1	Buzzard Rocks; views
6.3	538.3	Lesser Shelter; water
3.9	540.7	Keys Gap; WV/VA 9, groceries (0.3 mi. W and 0.4 mi. E), 6 mi. E to Hillsboro, Virginia, and 7 mi. W to Charlestown, West Virginia
83.8	460.8	The Pinnacle (3,730 ft.); views
82.8	461.8	Byrd's Nest #3 Picnic Shelter; water (seasonal)

Milepoint		Location and Description
From N	From S	
0.0	544.6	Loudoun Heights, West Virginia/Virginia state line, and junction with 3.2-mi., blue-blazed *Loudoun Heights Trail* (from S to N the *AT* is 1.4 mi. left on a descent to US 340 and Shenandoah River Bridge, and it is 0.3 mi. farther to side trail and Appalachian Trail Conference headquarters); Harpers Ferry, restaurants, groceries, laundry, lodging, post office 25425
		(From S to N the *Loudoun Heights Trail* remains on the ridgeline, passes some Civil War infantry redoubts, and at 0.8 mi. offers a magnificent view of Harpers Ferry and the confluence of the Shenandoah and Potomac Rivers. The trail descends steeply to 2 mi., where it follows US 340 to the Maryland/Virginia state line at 2.5 mi. After crossing the Potomac River on the Sandy Hook Bridge, the trail reconnects with the *AT* at 3.2 mi. near the Harpers Ferry Hostel.)

360

4 : Blue Ridge Parkway

My daddy worked on the Parkway for 30 years; to him it was the
world's most important road. It was his heart, he loved it and lived it.
—Robert Dillon

America's most scenic highway, the Blue Ridge Parkway (BRP) traverses the ridgeline of the Southern Appalachians from Shenandoah National Park to the Great Smoky Mountains National Park. Initial funding for construction of the 469-mile ribbon of natural beauty was allocated by Congress in 1933 under the authority of the National Industrial Recovery Act. Three years later a bill introduced by North Carolina congressman Robert Lee Doughton authorized the administration and maintenance of the highway by the NPS. Many members of Congress opposed the bill on the belief that the federal government could not afford this luxury during the Great Depression. After a close favorable vote in the Senate, President Franklin D. Roosevelt signed the bill on June 22, 1936. Although most of the parkway was completed in the 1930s, its final 6.5 miles at Grandfather Mountain was not dedicated until September 11, 1987.

Credit for the BRP idea goes mainly to Harry F. Byrd, a U.S. senator from Virginia, but Theodore E. Straus of Maryland, a member of the Public Works Administration, gives himself credit. Senator Byrd accompanied President Roosevelt on an inspection tour of the CCC camps in the Shenandoah National Park in August 1933. At this occasion the president expressed his satisfaction with the corp's work and its potential. When Senator Byrd suggested the Skyline Drive be extended to the Great Smokies, the president replied that he liked the idea and that perhaps it should also include a route to New England. He instructed the senator to discuss the idea with Harold L. Ickes, Roosevelt's secretary of the interior. They later worked out a right-of-way. Initially the plans for the route were to include Tennessee, but political controversy, routing problems, and the influence of North Carolina ambassador Josephus Daniels, a close friend of Secretary Ickes, omitted the state. (Governors in the Northeast were contacted by Secretary Ickes, but the governors were not interested in the project.) Land purchases, over a narrow corridor in most places, included 81,536 acres in North Carolina and 30,887 in Virginia. Designed and engineered for leisure travel at no more than 45 mph, there are scores of overlooks, waysides, and parking areas for recreational purposes. Commercial vehicles are not allowed. A nonprofit citizens' group, Friends of the Blue Ridge Parkway, works to protect and preserve the BRP viewsheds from destruction by residential and commercial interests.

Flora on the parkway is diverse because of the elevation range from 646 feet at the James River (mp 63.2) to 3,950 feet at Apple Orchard Mountain (mp 76.7). Among the most common are rosebay and catawba rhododendron, mountain laurel, flame azalea, black-eyed Susan, aster, trillium, and wild geranium. Less common, but of exceptional fragrance, is rose azalea (*Rhododendron roseum*),

Blue Ridge Parkway, Roanoke. (Courtesy Virginia Division of Tourism)

usually in blossom in late May or early June. The hardwoods on the BRP are those common to the Southern Appalachian, and the conifers are hemlock, pine, and in high elevations, red spruce and Fraser fir. The gypsy moth on hardwoods and the sap-sucking woolly adelgid on hemlocks have caused damage or defoliation to hundreds of acres along the BRP. At best, because of the difficulty and expense of treatment, the NPS is trying to protect the immediate corridor of the BRP. At the visitor centers there is a free information brochure that lists the peak flowering species and the location of more than 545 wildflowers. Motorists, and particularly hikers, will see wildlife on the parkway and trails. More common species are chipmunk, woodchuck, opossum, raccoon, deer, and gray squirrel. Less likely to be seen are fox, bobcat, and black bear. At least 100 species of birds, including the spring migrators, have been identified.

The chief recreational areas in Virginia are at Humpback Rock, Whetstone Ridge, Otter Creek, Peaks of Otter, Roanoke Mountain, Smart View, Rocky Knob, and Mabry Mill. (In the early 1990s a joint planning project by Floyd and Patrick counties and the NPS calls for the enlargement of the Rocky Knob outdoor recreational facilities to include a lodge, folk art museum, and other amenities.) A popular tourist attraction, the BRP draws more than 21.5 million visitors annually, with the peak attendance in October, because of the kaleidoscope of forest colors, and in July. Activities include camping, fishing, bicycling, hiking, horseback riding, picnicking, cross-country skiing, and nature study. Hotel-type lodging is offered only at Peaks of Otter Lodge, open year round (and with special winter rates from the end of November to the end of March) at mp 84–87. Cabins (open June 1 through Labor Day) are available at Rock Castle Gap (mp 174), which is part of the Rocky Knob recreational area. Reservations are advised for either location (see Addresses and Information, below).

In addition to outdoor activities and lodging, there are historic exhibits, museums, cultural displays, arts and crafts shops, visitor centers, and restaurants. Food service is available at Whetstone Ridge (mp 29), Otter Creek (mp 68.8), Peaks of Otter (mp 85.6), and Mabry Mill (mp 176.2). Gasoline is available at Peaks of Otter. The nearest towns and cities along the parkway for support services and amenities are Waynesboro, Buena Vista, Roanoke, Floyd, Meadows of Dan, and Fancy Gap.

With such popularity and density of visitors, the NPS has a number of important regulations designed to protect the natural environment. Camping is allowed only at designated campgrounds. Fires are permitted only in campgrounds and picnic areas. All plants and animals are protected by law. Hunting and the carrying of firearms are prohibited. Pets must be on a leash or under physical control. Littering is prohibited. Quiet hours in campgrounds must be observed from 10 P.M. to 6 A.M. No swimming is allowed.

In Virginia the NPS lists 38 individual trails and seven short strips of the *AT* that connect to parking areas. Three trails, such as the *White Rock Falls Trail*, are mainly in a national forest but are accessible via the BRP. Although the NPS claims 18.5 miles for the *Roanoke Valley Horse Trail*, only 10.8 miles (from mp 110.6 to mp 121.4 at US 220) are defined. Crossing the Roanoke River is a major problem. Hikers may find the multiple-use *Chestnut Ridge Trail*, which connects with the *Roanoke Valley Horse Trail*, to be the most desirable. The longest foot trail is 10.8-mile *Rock Castle Gorge Trail* (mp 167.1), and the shortest are 0.1-mile round-trip trails such as *The Priest Overlook Trail* (mp 6) and the *Boston Knob Trail* (mp 10).

Topographically paralleling the parkway is 126.4 miles of the *AT* from Waynesboro at I-64/US 250 to near Troutville at SR 653. Sections of the *AT* farthest away in the parallel are The Priest and Bald Knob in the Pedlar Ranger District of the GWNF and Cove Mountain in the Glenwood Ranger District of the JNF.

The NPS advises hikers to leave information with a ranger when vehicles are left away from campgrounds overnight. Be prepared for any sudden change in weather. Do not hike on the parkway. Do not drink from the streams or springs unless the water is purified. Camp only at designated sites. Do not climb rocks at road cuts. Do not carry firearms. Do not damage or feed wildlife, or damage any flowering plants. For fishing, a state license is necessary for people 16 years or older.

Addresses and Information: Blue Ridge Parkway, 200 BB&T Building, One Pack Square, Asheville, NC 28801; phone: 704-298-0398 for recorded information and other telephone numbers; 704-271-4779 for road and weather conditions; 704-271-4744 for administration; and 800-727-5928 for accidents, fire, or other emergencies (callers with cellular telephone do not call CH). For ranger offices near the BRP, the districts and addresses are as follows: James River District (mp

0–69), Montebello Office, Rt. 1, Box 17, Vesuvius, VA 24483, phone: 703-377-2377; Big Island Office, P.O. Box 345, Big Island, VA 24526, phone: 804-299-5941; Peaks of Otter District (mp 69–106), Peaks of Otter Office, Rt. 2, Box 163, Bedford VA 24523, phone: 703-586-4357; Roanoke Valley District (mp 106–144), Vinton Office, 2551 Mountain View Rd., Vinton, VA 24179, phone: 703-857-2490; Rocky Knob District (mp 144–216), Rocky Knob Office, Rt. 1, Box 465, Floyd, VA 24179, phone: 703-745-9660; Fancy Gap Office, Rt. 2, Box 3, Fancy Gap, VA 24328, phone: 703-727-4511. Reservations for Peaks of Otter, phone: 703-586-1081 (800-542-5927 toll free in Virginia); for Rocky Knob Cabins, phone: 703-593-3503. Available for free are BRP brochure with map, BRP Virginia trails list, special locality trail maps, and flyers for services, campgrounds, lodge, and general information.

Mountain Farm Trail (mp 5.9)   361
An easy, 0.4-mile round-trip, self-guiding trail from Humpback Rocks Visitor Center, past pioneer Carter family homestead, to "kissin' gate."

Humpback Rock Trail (*AT*) (mp 6)   362
From Humpback Gap (2,360 ft.) parking area east to the *AT* is a strenuous ascent south for 0.8 miles to excellent views north and west. Continuing south, it is 1 mile to the northern crest of Humpback Mountain, with good views north and east, and to the south at the summit (3,650 ft). Descend 1.7 miles to 0.3-mile, blue-blazed spur trail, right, to large Humpback Rock Picnic Area (mp 8.4).

Cotoctin Trail (mp 8.4)   363
From farthest circle of Humpback Rock Picnic Area, this easy, 0.3-mile round-trip, unblazed path leads to a rock outcrop with sedum and a view of Rockfish Valley.

Greenstone Trail (mp 8.8)   364
From Greenstone parking area east, follow an easy, 0.2-mile round-trip, self-guiding trail around green volcanic chlorite and epidote of the northern Blue Ridge Mountains.

The Priest Trail (mp 17.6)   365
This is an easy, 0.1-mile round-trip walk for a southeastern view of The Priest (4,065 ft.).

White Rock Falls Trail (mp 18.5)   366
From a grassy parking area (west), cross the BRP to a moderately difficult GWNF orange-blazed trail. Follow it for 1.4 miles to beautiful cascades. Ahead are strenuous 1.3 miles to Slacks Overlook (mp 19.9). (Described in Chapter 2.)

White Rock Gap Trail (mp 18.5)   367
On the western side of the BRP. This is a moderate walk for 0.4 miles to a junction on the left with the *Slacks Overlook Trail*, partly in the GWNF. (Described in Chapter 2.)

368   **Big Spy Mountain Trail** (mp 26.3)
This grassy, easy trail extends 0.1 mile to a panoramic view (3,185 ft.) of the Shenandoah Valley, west, and Tye River Valley, east. The knoll has butter-and-eggs, lavender, bee balm, clover, and other wildflowers.

369   **Yankee Horse Trail** (mp 34.4)
An easy, 0.2-mile trail on the site of an old narrow-gauge logging railroad, where timber was harvested in the 1920s. Wigwam Falls is in a hemlock grove (2,140 ft.).

370   **Boston Knob Trail** (mp 38.8)
A graded, easy 0.1-mile trail under black birch and dogwood to a scenic view (2,523 ft.).

371   **Indian Gap Trail** (mp 47.5)
Within an easy, 0.3-mile loop trail are large balancing rocks, oaks, and mountain laurel (2,098 ft.).

372   **White Oak Flats Trail** (mp 55.2)
From the picnic table at White Oak Flats parking area (1,460 ft.), go south for an easy, 0.1-mile round-trip in open forest by a small stream.

OTTER CREEK/JAMES RIVER RECREATION AREA

This recreation area extends along Otter Creek from a parking overlook with picnic tables (mp 58.2) to a visitor center at the James River bridge (mp 63.6). In between is a campground with a restaurant and gift shop (mp 60.8) (phone: 804-299-5862). The area is bordered on both sides by the GWNF and is accessible from VA 130 on the northern side and from US 501 on the southern side of the James River, upriver from Lynchburg. One of the area's most popular activities is fishing in Otter Creek. The 67-unit campground has trailer and tent sites, flush rest rooms, and waste disposal system. Both the restaurant and the campground receive a high volume of visitors. The area has four trails.

373-74   **Otter Creek Trail** (3.4 mi.), **Otter Lake Trail** (0.8 mi.) (mp 60.8 to 63.6)
Length and Difficulty: 4.2 miles (6.7 km) combined; easy
Features: cascades, fishing, wildlife, wildflowers, historic sites
Trailheads: The northern trailhead is at Otter Creek restaurant parking lot, and the southern trailhead is at the visitor center.
Description: Follow downstream on the trout-stocked Otter Creek through a forest of oak, beech, hemlock, hornbeam, rhododendron, and mountain laurel. At 0.6 miles pass Terrapin Hill Overlook and go under the BRP and VA 130, crossing Otter Creek twice. Pass Lower Otter Creek Overlook at 1.9 miles and reach a junction with the *Otter Lake Trail* at 2.4 miles. (The *Otter Lake Trail* ascends left to switchbacks on the hillside. After 0.3 mi. there is a bench for resting and for

viewing the lake below. At 0.8 mi. the trail descends to steps below the dam to a junction with the *Otter Creek Trail.*) Continuing on the *Otter Creek Trail,* pass the 0.2-mile Otter Lake parking area to descend below the dam at 2.7 miles. After following part of an old railroad grade, arrive at the visitor center parking area at 3.4 miles.

USGS map: Big Island

James River Trail (0.2 mi.), **Trail of Trees** (0.5 mi.) (mp 63.6) 375–76
Length and Difficulty: 0.9 miles (1.5 km) combined, round-trip; easy
Features: elevated footbridge, canal lock, botanical tour, scenic view
Trailhead: Otter Creek Visitor Center parking area
Description: From the visitor center at the northern end of the James River Bridge, descend to a junction of trails under the bridge. Walk on a unique elevated footbridge under the James River Bridge for scenic river views. Descend on steps to an island at Battery Creek Lock in a grassy area with information exhibits at 0.2 miles. Here is the lowest point in elevation (about 600 ft.) of any trail on the BRP. Backtrack to the *Trail of Trees*, left, on a self-guiding botanical tour, which loops back to the visitor center.

USGS map: Big Island

Thunder Ridge Trail (*AT*) (mp 74.7) 377
An easy, 0.1-mile walk on the *AT* to views of Arnold Valley, west.

Apple Orchard Falls Trail (mp 78.7) 378
The access to the falls from Sunset Field Overlook (3,474 ft.) is in 0.2 miles of BRP property to the JNF, where the strenuous hike descends 1.2 miles. Backtrack. See Chapter 1 for details.

Onion Mountain Loop Trail (mp 79.7) 379
A short, easy, 0.2 mile trail in a deciduous forest with rhododendron and mountain laurel over lichen-covered rocks (3,195 ft.).

PEAKS OF OTTER RECREATION AREA
(mp 82.5 to 87.6)

The Peaks of Otter is a 4,200-acre recreational park on the BRP. There are no otters here. Three peaks (Flat Top, Sharp Top, and Harkening Hill) form a triangle, however, and a lake and visitor center are in the center of the triangle. Facilities include a trail system of 15 miles for viewing magnificent scenery and studying at least 55 species of trees and shrubs. Among them are tree of heaven, Carolina hemlock, minnie bush (*Menziesia pilosa*), mountain ash, and fragrant thimbleberry. At least 60 species of wildflowers have been found here as well as more than 45 species of birds and other wildlife. The park has a visitor center, a picnic area, a 24-acre lake stocked with brown and rainbow trout, and a large, 141-site campground (without hookups). A concessioner operates the 58-room Peaks of Otter

Lodge and restaurant, open all year. (Address for the lodge is Virginia Peaks of Otter Co, P.O. Box 489, Bedford, VA 24523; phone: 703-586-1081; visitor center phone: 703-586-9263.)

Fallingwater Cascades Trail (1.6 mi.), **Flat Top Trail** (4.4 mi.),
380–82   **Cross Rock Trail** (0.1 mi.) (mp 83.1 to 83.5)
Length and Difficulty: 6.1 miles (9.8 km) combined, partial round-trip; moderate to strenuous
Features: cascades, scenic views, geological formations
Trailheads: Fallingwater Cascades parking area, or Peaks of Otter picnic area
Description: The *Fallingwater Cascades Trail* and the *Flat Top Trail* were designated national recreation trails in 1982. Together they offer the scenic splendor of cascades in a gorge and of panoramic views from a high rocky peak. From Fallingwater Cascades parking area follow signs a few feet to the trail and turn right. Descend for 0.4 miles to the cascades, where hemlock, green striped maple, and rosebay rhododendron form a partial cover. Cross the falls four times, using care on slippery rocks in a flume area. After 0.3 miles by the cascades ascend to a junction with an access to the *Flat Top Trail*, right. Either turn left for completion of the *Fallingwater Cascades Trail*, or stay right to cross the BRP and reach the Flat Top parking area.

For the *Flat Top Trail* enter a forest of tall poplars and parallel the BRP to the first switchback. Here begins a 1,492-foot increase in elevation by switchbacks to Flat Top Mountain (4,001 ft.). On the way there is a steep, short, spur trail, *Cross Rock Trail*, to the left, at 2.2 miles. Pass The Pinnacle rock formation and reach Flat Top at 2.8 miles for panoramic views of the area. Southwest is a spectacular view of Sharp Top. Descend on switchbacks to the Peaks of Otter picnic area on VA 43, 0.6 miles east from the visitor center. Backtrack or use a second vehicle.
USGS map: Arnold Valley

Sharp Top Trail (1.5 mi.), **Elk Run Trail** (0.8 mi.), **Harkening Hill Trail**
383–86   (3.3 mi.), **Johnson Farm Loop Trail** (2.1 mi.) (mp 85.7 to 86)
Length and Difficulty: 10.7 miles (17.1 km) combined, round-trip; easy to strenuous
Features: scenic views, wildflowers, wildlife, historic sites, geological formations
Trailheads: The *Sharp Top Trail* begins at the camp store and bus station across the BRP from the visitor center; all other trails begin at the visitor center.
Description: The *Sharp Top Trail* (3 mi. round-trip) is the area's most popular trail peak. A strenuous ascent by foot, it can also be accessed by a BRP shuttle bus. At the top (3,875 ft.) are views of Bedford and the piedmont to the east, the Shenandoah Valley to the west, and the Blue Ridge Mountains north and south. Southwest on Sharp Top is a 0.4-mile spur trail among boulders to Buzzards Roost, also a site for scenic sights.

Another popular trail is the *Elk Run Trail*, an easy, 0.8-mile self-guiding loop nature trail near a stream. Its entrance is from the northern side of the parking area at the visitor center. (A brochure is available.) A much longer moderate to strenuous loop is the *Harkening Hill Trail*. It begins behind the visitor center near the amphitheater and ascends west on switchbacks to a ridgeline. The summit of Harkening Hill (3,364 ft.) is 1.8 miles. Descend and after 0.1 mile pass the Balanced Rock on a short side trail to the right. At 2.3 miles are views of former farmland and the current Johnson Farm trail area. After another 0.3 miles is a junction with the *Johnson Farm Loop Trail* on the left. Continue for 0.7 miles on the right for a return past an access trail to the lodge and on to the visitor center, or follow the *Johnson Farm Loop Trail* to leave the forest and enter the Johnson Farm area. There is a restored farmhouse and barn, outbuildings, and a garden. Follow the trail right, partially on an old road, cross a stream, and at 1.8 miles reach a junction with the *Harkening Hill Trail*, which returns to the parking lot at the visitor center. (There is also an easy, 1-mi. trail that circles Abbott Lake to the east of the visitor center and in front of Peaks of Otter Lodge.)

(Five miles south of the visitor center on the BRP begin a number of moderately difficult trails either on or connected by the *AT*. They range from 0.6 mi. to 2.9 mi. Hikers should look for these connections at mp 90.9, 92.5, 95.4, 95.9, 96.0, and 97.0, with a spur trail to Bobblets Gap lean-to from mp 93.1. See Glenwood Ranger District in Chapter 1.)

USGS map: Peaks of Otter

Stewarts Knob Trail (mp 110.7)   387

At the far end of the parking lot (1,275 ft.) is a 0.1-mile path, one way, leading up the embankment among oak, hickory, and sweet cicely. Keep right on all turns to a pedestrian overlook with a bench. Here is a magnificent view of the city of Roanoke.

Roanoke River Trail (mp 114.9)   388

From the parking area, the main trail leads to series of trails. One is a 0.6-mile loop beyond and underpassing the high bridge of the BRP. It passes through large stands of hemlock and wildflowers such as dwarf iris. A linear 0.1-mile trail, one way, descends to a river overlook. Other linear short trails (made by fishermen and explorers) descend to the river rocks and sandbars.

Roanoke Mountain Summit Trail (mp 120.4)   389

Access is on a winding, narrow loop road from the BRP to a parking lot at the summit of Roanoke Mountain. The access is 3.7 miles round-trip and restricted to vehicles without trailers. The 0.3-mile rocky trail offers good views of Roanoke Valley.

ROANOKE MOUNTAIN CAMPGROUND
(mp 120.5)

Leave the BRP and drive 1.1 miles on Mill Mountain Spur Road to Chestnut Ridge Overlook. The Roanoke Mountain Campground is 0.2 miles ahead. The campground has trailer and tent campsites (no hookups), flush rest rooms, and a waste disposal system. The *Chestnut Ridge Trail* makes a loop around the campground. The campground is open all year. One mile beyond the campground is Roanoke's Mill Mountain Zoological Park (phone: 703-343-3241).

390–91   **Chestnut Ridge Trail** (mp 120.5)
Length and Difficulty: 5.4 miles (8.6 km), round-trip; moderate
Features: historic site, wildflowers
Trailhead: Chestnut Ridge Overlook
Description: This trail is part of the *Roanoke Valley Horse Trail* system; hikers may find the trail rough, though well graded. It has gentle and moderate ascents and descents in a hardwood forest with mountain laurels and blueberries. Patches of galax, cat's claw, and woodland sunflowers are frequent. From the Mill Mountain Spur Road at Chestnut Ridge Overlook parking area follow the red-blazed trail left for 1.5 miles to SR 699 (Yellow Mountain Rd.). An access side trail to cross Mill Mountain Spur Road is on the left; otherwise cross under the bridge left and continue south through the woods. At 2.1 miles is a junction with a trail loop, left, around the campground, and again at 3.1 miles. At 4.5 miles reach SR 672. Across the road is a short access trail to the *Roanoke Valley Horse Trail*. It divides near Gum Spring Overlook. (From there it runs parallel to the BRP south to US 220 and north to cross SR 668.) Turn left on SR 672 and pass under the Mill Mountain Spur Road. Begin an ascent at 4.7 miles and reach the point of origin at 5.4 miles.
USGS map: Garden City

392   **Buck Mountain Trail** (mp 123.2)
From Buck Mountain Parking Overlook ascend moderately 0.5 miles through hardwoods, scattered pine, and mountain laurel to the summit of Buck Mountain. Here are scenic views of southern Roanoke Valley. Backtrack.

393   **Smart View Loop Trail** (mp 154.5)
The *Smart View Loop Trail* begins at the parking lot near the picnic entrance. Follow the sign across a field to picnic area access at 0.3 miles. Continue through cattle pasture to south of Smart View Parking Overlook and then descend to stream. Large deciduous trees, abundant wildflowers, and elderberry grace the trail. Cross Rennet Bag Branch, pass a dead-end spur trail on the right, and follow slope to eastern edge of park maintenance area. Complete the loop at 2.6 miles.

ROCKY KNOB RECREATION AREA
(mp 167–174)

The Rocky Knob Recreation Area has 4,200 acres, mainly east of the BRP; Rock Castle Gorge is its primary geographic feature. Major activities are camping, picnicking, hiking, fishing, and nature study. It has more than 150 species of birds, and among the mammals are deer, bear, bobcat, raccoon, and fox. Reptiles include rattlesnake and copperhead. Seasonal changes may vary as much as three weeks because of the altitude difference from the low country at the gorge. Heavily wooded with the usual Appalachian species, this area also has a large section of Carolina hemlock on the northern slopes of the gorge. Early settlers named the gorge from the octagon-shaped quartz crystals with pyramid tips.

Facilities at the recreation area include a visitor center, picnic grounds (with a 1.3-mi. yellow-blazed loop trail around the picnic area), housekeeping cabins, Rocky Knob Campground, and backcountry camping in Rock Castle Gorge. The developed campground is at mp 167. It has 92 trailer and tent sites (no hookups), flush rest rooms, and waste disposal system. Firewood is for sale. It is open usually from May 1 through October. At mp 169 is a picnic area and ballfield, and between the picnic area and the campground is an access trail to scenic Saddle Parking Overlook, mp 168. A spur trail also goes to the summit of Rocky Knob (3,572 ft.), with its twin knobs. The housekeeping cabins, at mp 174, are operated by the concessioner who operates the restaurant and gift shop at the popular Mabry Mill, mp 176. Backcountry camping is allowed only in the gorge, and permits from the ranger are necessary.

Rock Castle Gorge Trail (mp 167.1)   394–97

Length and Difficulty: 10.6 miles (16.9 km) round-trip; strenuous
Connecting Trails: *Woodland Trail* (0.8 mi.), *Black Ridge Trail* (3 mi.), *Hardwood Cove Trail* (0.8 mi.)
Features: scenic views, waterfalls, homesite history, fishing
Trailheads: Rocky Knob Campground, mp 167.1. (There is also vehicular access to the lowest level of the trail's descent near the end of SR 605, which is 0.7 mi. from VA 8, north of the Rock Castle Creek bridge.)
Description: This is a popular trail with diversity in plant and animal life, temperature, and terrain. It was designated a national recreation trail in 1982. From Rocky Knob Campground entrance, cross BRP to fence stile and begin to ascend on a grassy bald. Follow white blazes for 0.6 miles to Saddle Parking Overlook. The trail continues up the edge of the mountain, and the red-blazed, 0.8-mile *Woodland Trail* goes right to the parking lot and shelter in the picnic area. Ascend steeply and reach the summit of Rocky Knob at 0.8 miles. Here is a log shelter constructed by the CCC in the 1930s. The superb views are of Rock Castle Valley, VA 8, and on to Woolwine. At 1.2 miles is a junction with the *Woodland Trail*, which descends 0.3 miles to a picnic area across the parkway. Arrive at the Rock Castle Gorge Overlook (3,195 ft.) (mp 168.7) at 1.7 miles. Parallel the BRP in and out of woods and open grassy spaces. At 1.9 miles join the *Black Ridge Trail*, right. (It slightly ascends to the visitor center after 0.1 mi. From the visitor center the 3-mi., blue-blazed *Black Ridge Trail* follows moderately through forest and open pasture balds. It passes a scenic rock formation at 2 mi. and descends in an open pastoral setting. It loops back to the visitor center.)

Continuing on the *Rock Castle Gorge Trail*, pass a number of resting benches and arrive at Grassy Knoll (3,480 ft.) at 3.4 miles. Begin descent into a deep defile with a cascading stream. The forest canopy is composed of large sugar

Mountain Industry Trail, Mabry Mill, BRP. (Photograph by Allen de Hart)

maples, oaks, and virgin tulip poplar. After a number of switchbacks, reach the *Hardwood Cove Trail* at 4.3 miles. (It is a 0.8-mi. self-guiding nature trail that runs jointly with the *Rock Castle Gorge Trail*. Markers and brochures explain the geology and biology of the area.) Enter an enormous 12-acre jumble of boulders known locally as the Bear Rocks, a haven for wildlife. At the end of the nature trail, cross Rock Castle Creek at 4.9 miles. Turn left on the old Rock Castle Pike, a pioneer road for wagons and carriages transporting people and supplies from the foothills to the Great Valley through Rock Castle Gap (2,970 ft.). Descend among borders of rosebay rhododendron, cascades and flumes in the stream, and mossy treadway. Cross the creek a couple of times, pass a large vacant two-story clapboard house with an old-fashioned springhouse, and cross the creek again at 7.1 miles. At 7.4 miles reach a primitive campground (1,720 ft.), the site of a former CCC camp. (A permit from the ranger is necessary to camp here.) Continue on the old road to where the trail turns sharply left up a slope at 7.6 miles. (Ahead 100 yds. is a parking area and gate for access to VA 8. See trailheads, above.) From here the trail ascends gradually in and out of coves from Little Rock Castle Creek. In a mixed forest there are ferns, bloodroot, and trillium. Pass a number of resting benches, and at 9.5 miles the climb becomes more moderate. Enter a field and return to the fence stile at the point of origin at 10.6 miles.

USGS map: Woolwine

Mountain Industry Trail (mp 176.2)   398

This 0.4-mile round-trip walk passes through a reconstructed community showing mountain use of waterpower. E. B. Mabry's Mill (originally operated from 1910 to 1935) is probably the most photographed view of human history on the BRP. In addition to other buildings there is a modern restaurant and gift shop at the parking area. A highlight of the year is the arts and crafts festivals in October.

Round Meadow Creek Trail (mp 179.2)   399

From the Round Meadow Parking Overlook (2,800 ft.) descend steeply on a 0.5-mile loop trail into a gorge of rhododendron and tall hemlock.

5 : Shenandoah National Park

If you can see this National Park not as a thing but as a process, I
promise you a polyfaceted, multidimensional quality experience.
—Henry Heatwole

The 195,000-acre Shenandoah National Park is on the northern Blue Ridge
Mountains from Front Royal south to Waynesboro, where it connects with the BRP
at Rockfish Gap. Its ragged dimensions (it varies from 2 to 13 mi. wide), represent
the piecing together of 3,870 tracts acquired from private landowners in the 1920s
and early 1930s. Winding through the park's full length is the famous 105-mile
Skyline Drive, an engineering work of art. In its gentle weave from gaps to the
ridgeline, the scenic highway encounters 60 peaks that range from 2,000 feet to
4,000 feet in elevation. Almost halfway in the park, near Skyland, is Hawksbill
(4,051 ft.), the park's highest point, and to its east is the notable Old Rag (3,268 ft.),
a singular, granite-topped mountain. Paralleling the drive is 103 miles of the *AT*, to
which the *Big Blue Trail* connects at Mathews Arm Campground. In addition,
there are more than 500 miles of other trails in the park. Gracing the hollows and
canyons are 16 waterfalls with a range in height of 28 to 93 feet. For spectacular
views, visitors may choose among 75 overlooks to the historic Shenandoah Valley,
forks of the Shenandoah River and Massanutten Mountain range to the west, and
rolling piedmont to the east.

The park is easily accessible from I-66 at the northern end, I-64 at the southern
end, I-81 on the western side, and US 29 and US 522 on the eastern side. Two major
highways cross the park and divide it into three parts: North District from Front
Royal to US 211 in Thornton Gap, Central District from US 211 to US 33 in Swift Run
Gap, and South District to US 250/I-64 in Rockfish Gap.

Congress authorized the park in May 1926, after which the state purchased 280
square miles of land from private citizens. From state legislative appropriations
and private gifts the land was donated to the federal government—a gift from
Virginians to the nation. In December 1935 the park was fully established, and the
Skyline Drive, begun in 1931, was completed in 1939. Congress set aside 80,000
acres for wilderness areas in 1976.

Nearly 95 percent forested, mainly with hardwoods, the park contains more
than 100 species of trees. But vast areas of the forests were defoliated by the gypsy
moth in the late 1980s and early 1990s. Because of the cost and the lack of man-
power, treatment efforts by the park have been limited to a corridor of the Skyline
Drive. Springtime is the season to see many of the 1,200 species of flowering plants,
some of which are trillium, wild orchid, pink azalea, and mountain laurel. But
October (middle two weeks) is the month of the most brilliant colors, when the
maples and poplars of the coves turn orange and yellow, and the black gums and
oaks on the mountain tops are burgundy red and rust. Of the 2 million annual
visitors, more come in October than any other month. (July is the second most
popular month.)

Shenandoah National Park from Old Rag Mountain. (Photograph by Allen de Hart)

A sanctuary for wildlife, the park is home to 200 species of birds, of which 35 are warblers. Bear, deer, turkey, grouse, raccoon, squirrel, and chipmunk are the animals most likely seen. Timber rattlesnakes and copperheads are the only two poisonous snakes, and neither is likely to be seen from November through March. It is illegal to kill, harm, feed, or even frighten any wildlife in the park.

Visitor centers are at Dickey Ridge, 5 miles south from Front Royal, and Big Meadows, halfway through the park. There are four campgrounds: Mathews Arm (mp 22.2), Big Meadows (mp 51.2), Lewis Mountain (mp 57.5), and Loft Mountain (mp 79.5). Electricity and water hookups are not available. (Big Meadows is usually open all year except in January and February, and Mathews Arm may be closed the entire year, depending on the park's budget limitations.) Overnight lodging and restaurants are at Skyland Lodge (mp 41–43), and Big Meadows Lodge (mp 51.2). One or both may be open from early April to November. Cottages may be rented at Lewis Mountain (mp 57.5). Additionally, the PATC has six backcountry trail cabins for rent. (For information on location and fees, see PATC address, below.) There are five picnic areas, plus wayside tables along the highway. Gasoline and groceries are available at Elkwallow (mp 24.1), Big Meadows (mp 51.0), and Loft Mountain (mp 79.5).

A list of park regulations is presented when visitors enter the park on the Skyline Drive. Hikers entering from boundary trailheads pick up the list at self-registration display boards. Campers must follow the no-trace system of wilderness camping, and open fires are prohibited except at designated locations. Pets must be restrained, and except for seeing-eye dogs, none are allowed in public buildings or on some of the trails, such as the top section of Old Rag Mountain. Forbidden on the trails are ATVs, snowmobiles, and bicycles, but snow skiing is allowed on designated roads. Horseback riding is confined to equestrian trails. The usual speed limit for autos in the park is 35 mph.

Foot trails and equestrian trails form a network throughout the park. There are at least 43 designated short- and long-circuit hikes, but hikers with park maps, or observing any of the Skyline Drive's 30 trail-access signboards, can create more. Some of the trails with high traffic volume are the *White Oak Canyon* (5 mi.), the *Cedar Run* (3.5 mi.), the *Dark Hollow Falls* (0.9 mi.), the *South River Falls* (1.6 mi.), the *Doyles River* (4.7 mi.), the *Jeremys Run* (5.3 mi.), and the *Old Rag* (3.1.). Some basic information is provided in the pages ahead. Hikers with extensive plans are advised to have park trail maps and PATC's books and maps on the *AT* side trails and circuit trails. Because Old Rag Mountain is distinct from the main ridgeline of the park, its trails are described below in more detail.

There are two access roads and two access trails to the summit of Old Rag Mountain. Only day hikes are permitted. To avoid the crowds, go on a weekday. If accessing to the northern side from Skyline Drive at Thornton Gap, drive 8 miles east on US 211 to Sperryville. Turn right on US 522, and after 0.7 miles turn right on VA 231. Drive 8.1 miles to SR 602 at Hughes River bridge. Turn right, upstream, and continue for 3.4 miles (SR 602 becomes SR 707 and then SR 600) to a large overflow parking area on the left. Ahead it is 0.5 miles to the *Nicholson Hollow Trail*, right, and another 0.5 miles to a small parking area for the *Ridge Trail*. (Ahead is gated, yellow-blazed *Weakley Hollow Fire Road*.) Begin the 2,160-foot-in-elevation climb of the *Ridge Trail* at the trail sign. After 1.5 miles reach the ridge where the forest is less dense but the rock scramble becomes more intense. Crawl over, pass around, and twist through the granite fissures to reach the summit (3,268 ft.) at 2.7 miles. The panoramic views are of Berry and Weakley Hollows and Hawksbill (4,050 ft.) to the west; to the northwest is Stony Man Mountain (4,011 ft.); and to the east the horizon fades into piedmont farms and sky. Autumn is the most colorful season to visit. Within the boulders are sumac, goldenrod, maple, chestnut oak, and sassafras. The *Ridge Trail* ends 0.4 miles down the western side of the summit to join the *Saddle Trail*. Backtrack or follow the *Saddle Trail* on switchbacks 1.1 miles to the *Weakley Hollow Fire Road*. Turn right and follow its easy passageway of 2.5 miles to the *Ridge Trail* trailhead and point of origin.

400–401

The shorter and easier access to the summit is from Berry Hollow parking area. From the northern access trailhead, drive back to VA 231, turn right (south), and proceed 1.7 miles to Etlan. Turn right on SR 643 and drive 4.2 miles to a junction with SR 600. Turn right and continue upstream by Robinson River for 4.9 miles to end-of-road parking. Hike up the yellow-blazed *Berry Hollow Fire Road* for 0.9 miles to a junction with the *Weakley Hollow Fire Road* and the *Old Rag Fire Road*. Turn right, go 0.4 miles to Old Rag Shelter and spring to begin the *Saddle Trail*. Ascend on switchbacks and pass Byrd's Nest Shelter #1 on the right. (Tent camping is allowed with permits but must be outside the shelters. Camping on the summit of Old Rag Mountain is prohibited.) From here follow the *Ridge Trail* 0.4 miles to the summit. Backtrack or use a two-car shuttle. Hikers arriving from downtown Madison at US 29 should take VA 231 west 5.3 miles to Banco, where SR 670 goes left (VA 231 forks right to Etlan and SR 602 for the *Ridge Trail* access as described above). Follow SR 670 3.5 miles to Syria, turn right and stay on SR 643 for 0.3 miles, then turn left onto SR 600 for 4.1 miles to White Oak Canyon Falls access area, and another 1 mile to the *Saddle Trail* access parking area.

402

Addresses and Information: Shenandoah National Park, Rt. 4, Box 348, Luray, VA 22835; phone: 703-999-2243/2266/2229; on US 211, 4 miles west of Skyline Drive, and 5 miles east of Luray. Available are brochures and maps of the park, and recreation, accommodations, and trail information brochures and flyers. Books and maps may be ordered from the PATC, 118 Park St. SE, Vienna, VA 22180-4609; phone: 703-242-0693, or from the Appalachian Trail Conference, P.O. Box 807, Harpers Ferry, WV 25425; phone: 304-535-6331. Visitor centers on the Skyline Drive carry many of the publications and maps in stock. Suggested materials are *Appalachian Trail Guide to Shenandoah National Park* (with side trails) and maps, and *Circuit Hikes in the Shenandoah National Park*. Also recommended are *Shenandoah National Park: An Interpretive Guide* by John A. Conners, and *Guide to Shenandoah National Park and Skyline Drive* by the late Henry Heatwole.

Trail listings below are from north to south and include the following information: current trail name; distance in nearest 0.1 mile, one way; trailhead parking (P); direction (E if on eastern side and W if on the western side of the Skyline Drive); difficulty—easy, moderate, or strenuous, determined for the general public and not horse traffic; some major or unique features; connections with other trails (and some circuit options); and park boundary access (avoiding private property). Trail blazes are blue for foot trails and yellow for horse/foot trails (marked with an [h] at horse trail mileage).

The park has 522.2 miles in its trail system (142.2 mi. in the North District, 240.8

mi. in the Central District, and 139.5 mi. in the South District), of which 95.2 miles are the *AT*. The total includes all the short trails to huts, shelters, waysides, campgrounds, overlooks, walking paths in developed areas, and work centers. Most of these are unnamed and are not described below. Wilderness mileage is 175.3, and volunteers maintain 282.7 miles.

North District

403–45 Front Royal to US 211, beginning milepost to mp 31.5

mp	Trail Name	Mileage	Termini and Brief Description
0.1	Dickey Ridge Trail	9.2	Dickey Ridge to visitor center and *AT* at Compton Gap; easy to moderate; historic homesite
4.6	Fox Hollow Nature Trail	1.0	**Dickey Ridge trailhead (P)** connects with *Dickey Ridge Trail* near visitor center; easy; self-guiding to old farm
5.1	Snead Farm Loop Trail	0.8	From Skyline Dr. with use of *Dickey Ridge Trail*; easy; near visitor center, homesite
9.2	Lands Run Gap Trail	2.0(h)	**Lands Run Gap trailhead (P)** from Skyline Dr. to park boundary (W), gated at SR 622; moderate; cascades, falls; connects with *Dickey Ridge Trail* (E) to Fort Windham Rocks (lava flow 8 million years old), Springhouse Rd. and *Hickerson Hollow Trail* (E)
9.2	Hickerson Hollow Trail	1.0(h)	**Lands Run Gap trailhead (P)** from Skyline Dr. to park boundary (E); easy; historic homesite
10.4	Compton Peak Trails	0.4	**Compton Gap trailhead (P)** at *AT* crossing of Skyline Dr. N is 2.1 mi. to 0.2-mi. *Possum Rest Trail*, s is 0.8 mi. to two scenic spur trails (E and W) of Compton Peak (E trail has columnar basalt); easy to moderate
10.4	Compton Gap Fire Road	2.2(h)	From Skyline Dr. to park boundary (E) to SR 610; easy
12.3	Jenkins Gap Trail	0.8(h)	From Skyline Dr. to park boundary (W) to gated SR 634, has parking at Skyline Dr. and *AT* access; moderate
12.3	Bluff Trail	3.4(h)	Access (E) to *Mt. Marshall Trail* and to Gravel Springs Gap at 17.5 mp; moderate; 0.4-mi. wilderness
12.6	Mt. Marshall Trail	5.4(h)	From Skyline Dr. to park boundary (E); strenuous; 3.9 mi. in wilderness, access to The Peak (2,925 ft.)

mp	Trail Name	Mileage	Termini and Brief Description
17.6	Big Devils Stairs Trail	1.6	**Gravel Springs Gap trailhead (P)** at *AT* crossing of Skyline Dr., access on *Bluff Trail* to park boundary (E); moderate; canyon cascades; *Bluff Trail* connects with *Mt. Marshall Trail*, which connects with *Jordan River Trail*(h); *Harris Hollow Trail*(h) descends (E) from Gravel Springs Hut to park boundary for 1 mi.; moderate
17.6	Browntown Trail	2.3(h)	From Skyline Dr. to park boundary (W); strenuous
19.4	Keyser Run Trail	4.4(h)	**Keyser Run trailhead (P)** from Skyline Dr. to park boundary (E); moderate; connects with *Little Devils Stairs Trail* for access to SR 614 (E) and *Hull Branch Trail* (S)
19.4	Piney Branch Trail	4.2	**Keyser Run trailhead (P)** accessed from *Keyser Run Trail* to *Pole Bridge Link Trail*, descends to *Hull School Trail*; strenuous; waterfalls, 2.2 mi. in wilderness, historic homesite
19.4	Little Devils Stairs Trail	2.0	**Keyser Run trailhead (P)** from Skyline Dr. (E) on *Keyser Run Trail* to left turn and descent into canyon; strenuous; cascades, 1.5 mi. in wilderness; across Skyline Dr. is access to *AT* and Little Hogback Mtn.
20.4	Hogback Spur Trail	0.3	From Skyline Dr. (W) to *AT* to Hogback Mtn. (3,474 ft.); easy; scenic
20.8	Sugarloaf Trail	1.4	From *AT* (near Hogback Mtn. Overlook on Skyline Dr.) to *Pole Bridge Link Trail*; moderate; stream
21.1	Big Blue Trail	6.2	From *AT* parking lot (W 0.4 mi. on *AT*) near Hogback Overlook on Skyline Dr. to park boundary (W); moderate; streams, cascades, 3.9 mi. in wilderness
21.1	Thompson Hollow Trail	0.4	From *Big Blue Trail* to park boundary (W); easy; 0.3 mi. in wilderness
21.1	Overall Run Trail	0.7	At junction of *Big Blue Trail* and *Thompson Hollow Trail* (W) downstream to *Overall Run/Beecher Ridge Trail*; easy; stream, 0.7 mi. in wilderness
22.1	Piney Ridge Trail	3.2	From *AT* at Ranger View Cabin (E) to *Piney Branch Trail*; strenuous; historic homesite, waterfalls, 2.3 mi. in wilderness
22.1	Fork Mtn. Trail	1.1	From *Piney Ridge Trail* to *Hull School Trail* (E); moderate; 1.1 mi. in wilderness

mp	Trail Name	Mileage	Termini and Brief Description
22.2	Traces Nature Trail	1.7	Mathews Arm Campground Loop; easy; self-guiding for historic homesite (not blazed)
22.2	Elkwallow Trail	2.0	From Mathews Arm Campground to Elkwallow Wayside; easy; parallels Skyline Dr. on w side
22.2	Beecher Ridge Trail	3.1(h)	From *Mathews Arm Trail* to *Heiskell Hollow Trail* (W); moderate; ends at connector trail to Overall Run
22.2	Mathews Arm Trail	4.7(h)	From Mathews Arm Campground to park boundary (W); moderate; wilderness 3.2 mi., gated at road off SR 630 E of Bentonville
22.2	Heiskell Hollow Trail	3.3(h)	*Knob Mtn. Trail* to park boundary (W); strenuous; extends on private land to SR 697, 3.1 mi. in wilderness
22.2	Knob Mtn. Trail	7.1(h)	Mathews Arm Campground to *Jeremys Run Trail*; moderate; 6.6 mi. in wilderness; from s junction with *Knob Mtn. Trail*, *Jeremys Run Trail* is 0.8 mi. to park boundary (W); cascades
22.2	Weddlewood Trail	1.3(h)	*Mathews Arm Trail* to *Heiskell Hollow Trail*; easy; 0.6 mi. in wilderness
24.1	Jeremys Run Trail	5.3	From *AT* at Elkwallow to *Knob Mtn. Trail* (W); strenuous; stream, waterfalls, 5.2 mi. in wilderness, wildlife
24.1	Knob Mtn. Cutoff Trail	0.5	From *Knob Mtn. Trail* to *Jeremys Run Trail* (W); easy; 0.5 mi. in wilderness
25.5	Thornton River Trail	2.5	From Skyline Dr. parking area (E) to *Hull School Trail*; moderate; springs, wildflowers, stream, 2.2 mi. in wilderness; connects with 1.5-mi. *Thornton Hollow Trail*(h) to SR 612; on w side of Skyline Dr. is connection to *AT*
28.1	Hull School Trail	4.4(h)	From Skyline Dr. to Keyser Run Rd. (E); moderate; crosses North Fork of Thornton River and Piney River, wildlife, partly on fire roads, crosses streams and ridges, 4.1 mi. in wilderness
28.1	Rocky Branch Trail	3.0(h)	From Skyline Dr. parking area and from *Hull School Trail*, crosses *AT*, then Skyline Dr. and ends w at gate to SR 666; moderate; borders wilderness
28.1	Neighbor Mtn. Trail	6.6(h)	From Skyline Dr. parking area follow old road to Byrd's Nest #4 (W) and cross *AT* on ridgeline; strenuous; scenic, ends at gate on road off SR 611 near Vaughn, 6.2 mi. in wilderness

mp	Trail Name	Mileage	Termini and Brief Description
28.5	Pass Mtn. Trail	2.7	From Skyline Dr. at Beahms Gap parking overlook follow spur trail 0.1 mi. to AT and follow it s 2.1 mi. to Pass Mtn. Hut, descend E; strenuous; wilderness; exit is on US 211, 2.5 mi. E of Skyline Dr.
30.2	Pass Mtn. Nature Trail	0.1	On Skyline Dr. at Pass Mtn. Overlook; easy, leg-stretcher loop in forest and to rocky bluff

Central District

From US 211 to US 33, mp 31.5 to mp 65.5

446–522

mp	Trail Name	Mileage	Termini and Brief Description
33.5	Buck Hollow Trail	3.0	From Skyline Dr. Meadow Spring parking area to US 211 (2.6 mi. E of Skyline Dr.); easy; stream, 1.9 mi. in wilderness; access to AT (W) of Skyline Dr.
33.5	Hazel Mtn. Trail	4.6(h)	From Skyline Dr. (E) to *Pine Hill Gap Trail* and park boundary with exit to SR 681; moderate; 4.3 mi. in wilderness; connects with *Buck Ridge Trail*, *White Rocks Trail*(h), *Hazel River Trail*(h), *Pine Hill Gap Trail*(h)
33.5	Buck Ridge Trail	2.4	From Skyline Dr. on *Hazel Mtn. Trail* to *Buck Hollow Trail*; moderate; potential loop, 2.1 mi. in wilderness
33.5	White Rocks Trail	2.8(h)	From Skyline Dr. on *Hazel Mtn. Trail* to Hazel River; moderate; waterfall, cave, 2.8 mi. in wilderness
33.5	Hazel River Trail	3.1(h)	From Skyline Dr. on *Hazel Mtn. Trail* to park boundary (E); moderate; 2.6 mi. in wilderness, access to SR 600
33.5	Sams Ridge Trail	2.0	From Skyline Dr. on *Hazel Mtn. Trail* and *Broad Hollow Trail* to park boundary (E); strenuous; exit to SR 681; access to *Catlett Spur Trail* and *Catlett Mtn. Trail*
33.5	Meadow Spring Trail	0.5	From Skyline Dr. Meadow Spring parking (W) to AT; easy; AT (N) 0.7 mi. to spectacular views from Mary's Rock (3,514 ft.) and 1-billion-year-old granodiorite stone
35.1	Hannah Run Trail	3.7	At Pinnacle Overlook on Skyline Dr. (E) to *Nicholson Hollow Trail*, junction with *Catlett Spur Trail* (1.1 mi.) and *Catlett Mtn.*

mp	Trail Name	Mileage	Termini and Brief Description
			Trail (1.2 mi.); moderate; historic homesite, stream, 3.4 mi. in wilderness
35.1	Hot Mtn./ Short Mtn. Trail	2.2	From Skyline Dr. at Pinnacle Overlook descend (E) to *Hazel Mtn. Trail* and hike between two peaks to *Nicholson Hollow Trail*; moderate; stream, 2.2 mi. in wilderness
35.1	Pine Hill Gap Trail	1.9(h)	From *Hazel Mtn. Trail* to park boundary (E); moderate; 1.6 mi. in wilderness, access to SR 681 or SR 707
36.4	Leading Ridge Trail	1.5	From Skyline Dr. at Jewell Hollow Overlook N on *AT*, 0.3 mi. NW to trail; strenuous; dead end, secluded
37.8	Corbin Cabin Cutoff Trail	1.4	From Skyline Dr. W parking to *AT*, but E to PATC cabin and *Nicholson Hollow Trail* (E); moderate; 1.3 mi. wilderness
38.3	Nicholson Hollow Trail	5.5	From Skyline Dr. and *AT* (E) to Corbin Cabin and park boundary; moderate; stream, cascades, wildflowers, 4.9 mi. in wilderness, access to SR 600 and Old Rag Mtn., circuit potential
38.3	Crusher Ridge Trail	1.8	From Skyline Dr. (W) (N from Stony Man Overlook near *Nicholson Hollow Trail*); crosses *AT* after 0.1 mi.; follows NW on Crusher Ridge; descends on switchbacks to Shavers Hollow (no public access from SR 699); strenuous, secluded
39.1	Little Stony Man Trail	1.0	**Little Stony Man trailhead (P)** S on *AT* 0.3 mi. to trailhead for ascent to peak (4,011 ft.); easy; scenic geology, connects to 1.0-mi. *Stony Man Nature Trail* for cliffs, views
39.1	Passamaquoddy Trail	1.3	**Little Stony Man trailhead (P)** S on *AT* 0.3 mi. to right fork; easy; scenic, cliffs, and to Skyland developed area
41.7	Stony Man Horse Trail	0.9(h)	Near Stony Man parking area to Stony Man Mtn.; easy; parallels scenic nature trail (unblazed)
41.7	Skyland/ Big Meadows Horse Trail	11.2(h)	Skyland stables to Big Meadows stables at 51.2 mp; strenuous; crosses *White Oak Canyon Trail*, *Cedar Run Trail*, and Rose River fire road (E)
41.7	Skyland Trail	3.2(h)	From Skyland to park boundary (W); strenuous; access to SR 672, crosses *AT* at Furnace Spring, connects with *Furnace Spring Horse Trail* (0.4 mi.) to picnic area; easy

mp	Trail Name	Mileage	Termini and Brief Description
41.7	White Oak Canyon Horse Trail	1.8(h)	From stables at Skyland s to cross Skyline Dr. and to Old Rag Fire Rd.; easy
42.6	White Oak Canyon Trail	5.0	**White Oak Canyon trailhead (P)** (near entrance s of Skyland) to park boundary (E); moderate; outstanding scenery, waterfalls upper and lower, high traffic; access to SR 600 in Berry Hollow, circuit potential
42.6	Millers Head Trail	0.8	In Skyland from *AT* to Millers Head; easy; scenic views
43.0	Limberlost Nature Trail	1.3	**Limberlost trailhead (P)** off E side of Skyline Dr. on *Old Rag Fire Rd.*; easy; virgin hemlocks, wildflowers, stream (under construction, paved, for disabled), loop, no pets, connects with *Crescent Rocks Trail* and *White Oak Canyon Trail*
43.0	Old Rag Fire Rd.	5.1(h)	**Limberlost trailhead (P)** descends E; strenuous; scenic, 3.3 mi. in wilderness (see above for Old Rag Mtn. trails); connects with *Limberlost Nature Trail* (1.3 mi.), *White Oak Canyon Trail* (5 mi.), *White Oak Canyon Horse Trail* (h) (1.8 mi.), *Indian Run Trail* (2.3 mi.), which connects with *Corbin Mtn. Trail* (3.8 mi.), *Corbin Hollow Trail* (2 mi.), *Robertson Mtn. Trail* (2.4 mi.) (latter two trails are scenic routes to *Weakley Hollow Fire Rd.* [h], 2.3 mi.), *Saddle Trail* (1.1 mi.), *Berry Hollow Fire Rd.* (h) (0.8 mi.), circuit potential
44.4	Crescent Rocks Trail	1.1	Crescent Rock Overlook on Skyline Dr. to *Limberlost Nature Trail*; easy; hemlock grove; across Skyline Dr. (N) is 0.4-mi. spur to *Bettys Rock Trail* for scenic views w
45.6	Cedar Run Trail	3.1	**Hawksbill Gap trailhead (P)** crosses E over *Big Meadows Horse Trail*, descends to **White Oak Canyon trailhead** at SR 600; strenuous; waterfall, wildflowers 2.1 mi. wilderness, circuit potential (0.9-mi. Cedar Run Link is a connector near SR 600)
45.6	Hawksbill Trail	1.8	**Hawksbill Gap trailhead (P)** from Skyline Dr. w to Upper Hawksbill parking at 46.7 mp; moderate; summit of Hawksbill (4,050 ft.) observation deck, spectacular views, red spruce

mp	Trail Name	Mileage	Termini and Brief Description
46.7	Salamander Trail	0.7	From **Upper Hawksbill trailhead (P)** follow NW to *Hawksbill Trail*, left to *AT*, and right to near Rock Spring Hut (formerly *Nakedtop Trail*); moderate; rare Shenandoah salamander in area; access also from 47.8 mp
49.3	Rose River Fire Rd.	6.5(h)	From Skyline Dr. to park boundary (E); strenuous; former Gordonsville Pike, access to SR 670; scenic, wildlife; connects with *Skyland/Big Meadows Horse Trail* (11.2 mi.), *Rose River Loop Trail* (2.7 mi.), and *Stony Mtn. Trail*(h) (1.1 mi.), which goes to Rapidan Rd.; *Upper Dark Hollow Trail*(h) (2 mi.) connects *Stony Mtn. Trail* with *Rose River Fire Rd.*
49.3	Red Gate Fire Road	4.8(h)	Across Skyline Dr. from *Rose River Fire Rd.* to park boundary (W); moderate; portion of old Gordonsville Pike, gated near SR 611
50.7	Dark Hollow Falls Trail	0.8	**Dark Hollow Falls trailhead (P)** to falls at Hogcamp Branch; easy; falls, access to *Rose River Fire Rd.* and Rose River falls, circuit potential
51.1	Lewis Spring Falls Trail	1.8	From Skyline Dr. near Byrd Visitor Center to parking area at Big Meadow Lodge, near *AT*; moderate; waterfall, return on *AT* for loop; *Black Rock Trail* (0.2 mi.) is W of lodge to *AT* for scenic views; *Forest Nature Trail* (1 mi.) between visitor center and lodge/picnic area, forest succession
51.1	Rapidan Fire Rd.	7.4(h)	From Skyline Dr. to park boundary (E); strenuous; wildlife, headwaters of Rapidan River; connects with *Mill Prong Horse Trail* (1.6 mi.), *Stony Mtn. Trail*(h) (1.1 mi.), *Upper Dark Hollow Trail*(h) (2 mi.), *Charlie Thomas Trail* (unblazed in Rapidan WMA), *Camp Hoover Trail*(h) (1 mi.), circuit options N to *Rose River Fire Rd.* and S to *Laurel Prong Trail*(h) (0.6 mi.) and *Laurel Prong Trail* (2.3 mi.)
51.1	Tanners Ridge Horse Trail	2.5(h)	Big Meadows stables for loop S on Tanners Ridge; easy; crosses *AT* and Lewis Spring Rd.
51.6	Tanners Ridge Trail	1.4(h)	On Skyline Dr. near Tanners Ridge Overlook to park boundary (W); easy; access to SR 682

mp	Trail Name	Mileage	Termini and Brief Description
52.8	Mill Prong Trail	1.2	**Milam Gap trailhead (P)** at Milam Gap *AT* crossing to *Mill Prong Horse Trail*; moderate; Big Rock Falls; connects N with *Camp Hoover Trail*(h) (1 mi.) to *Rapidan Fire Rd.*; *Laurel Prong Trail*(h) S 0.6 mi. as horse trail to *Fork Mtn. Trail*(h) (1.3 mi.), which descends to *Staunton River Trail* (part horse and foot for 0.8 mi. and foot 3.9 mi. to Rapidan River access to SR 622); from Fork Mtn. Rd. is *Jones Mtn. Trail* (5.5 mi.), which leads to PATC cabin (locked) and *Staunton River Trail*, where *McDaniel Hollow Trail* (0.4 mi.) is second connector; circuit options
52.8	Fork Mtn. Fire Rd.	2.8(h)	*Rapidan Fire Rd.* to *Fork Mtn. Trail*; moderate; 2 mi. in Rapidan WMA; connections with Lower Rapidan Fire Rd.(h) (1.8 mi.), which joins *Graves Mill Trail*(h) (2.1 mi.) and access (E) to SR 649 (W of Criglersville) or SR 662 from Graves Mill (S)
None	West Naked Creek Trail	1.8(h)	Without trail connections to Skyline Dr. on a W arm of the park the access is on SR 607 (N of Jollett near PATC cabin [locked]) upstream to end of park boundary; easy; scenic, secluded
54.4	Powell Mtn. Trail	3.6	From Skyline Dr. at Hazeltop Ridge Overlook (SW) to park boundary; strenuous; scenic ridge trail; access at SR 759, NE of Jollett
55.1	Conway River Fire Rd.	1.4(h)	At parking lot and *AT* crossing at Bootens Gap on Skyline Dr. (E) to park boundary; moderate; connects to roads in Rapidan WMA and to SR 615; on *AT* (N) 0.4 mi. is S end of *Laurel Prong Trail*, which leads to *Cat Knob Trail* (0.5 mi.) and *Jones Mtn. Trail* (5.5 mi.) and Bear Church Rock with views
56.4	Bearfence Loop Trail	0.8	**Bearfence Mtn. trailhead (P)** S on *AT*; easy; geology, rock scramble (catoctin basalt), scenic
56.8	Meadow School Trail	1.5(h)	From Skyline Dr. parking (W) to park boundary; moderate; access to SR 759 E of Jollett
56.8	Slaughter Trail	4.2(h)	From Skyline Dr. parking (E) to park boundary; strenuous; cross *AT*, wildlife, wildflowers; access to SR 66, NW of Standardsville

mp	Trail Name	Mileage	Termini and Brief Description
57.5	Lewis Mtn. Trail	1.0	From s end of Lewis Mtn. Campground on Skyline Dr. to top of mountain and old farm site; easy; backtrack
59.5	Pocosin Hollow Fire Rd.	2.6(h)	From Skyline Dr. parking (small) E to *Pocosin Horse Trail* (1.3 mi.) and *Pocosin Hollow Trail* (2.8 mi.); moderate; remnants of old homesites, cascading stream, *AT* spring; circuit options by using South River Rd. to *AT*
62.8	South River Falls Trail	1.6	**South River Falls trailhead (P)** from picnic area to park boundary; moderate; waterfall; return on South River Fire Rd.(h) (2.3 mi.) (sw), road N is (1.4 mi.) through Rapidan WMA to *Pocosin Horse Trail*
62.8	Dry Run Fire Road	2.0(h)	From Skyline Dr. gated road w to park boundary; easy; access to SR 625, N of Elkton
62.8	Saddleback Mtn. Trail	1.4	**South River Falls trailhead (P)**, from picnic area follow *AT* s 0.5 mi.; easy; loop of 3.5 mi. with *AT*

South District

523–49   From US 33 to US 250/I-64, mp 65.5 to mp 105

mp	Trail Name	Mileage	Termini and Brief Description
68.6	Smith Roach Gap Trail	1.3(h)	From Skyline Dr. to park boundary (E); easy; gated SR 626
73.2	Simmons Gap Fire Rd.	3.7(h)	From Skyline Dr. both (E) and (W) to park boundaries (also called Beldor Rd.); easy; gated at SR 628
76.1	Rocky Mount Trail	5.4	From Skyline Dr. (near Two-Mile Run Overlook) (W) to *Gap Run Trail*; strenuous; geology, stream, peak (2,741 ft.); combine with *Gap Run Trail* (2.3 mi.) for 10-mi. loop; 5.2 mi. in wilderness
76.2	One Mile Run Trail	3.7	From Skyline Dr. (park at Two-Mile Run Overlook, w, and hike s 0.1 mi. to trailhead) to park boundary; moderate; stream, 2.7 mi. in wilderness, secluded, ends at private road
76.9	Brown Mtn. Trail	5.3	From Skyline Dr. at Brown Mtn. Overlook (W) to Big Run bridge; strenuous; scenic ridgeline, 5.2 mi. in wilderness, fossilized sandstone; can be loop with 1.3 mi. of *Big*

mp	Trail Name	Mileage	Termini and Brief Description
			Run Portal Trail(h) and *Rocky Mtn. Run Trail* (2.7 mi.) for 11 mi.; (trail also called *Rocky Mtn.–Brown Mtn. Trail*)
76.9	Rockytop Trail	5.7	From end of *Brown Mtn. Trail* (also called *Rocky Mtn.–Brown Mtn. Trail*) and *Big Run Portal Trail*(h) to *Big Run Loop Trail*; strenuous; splendid views, turkey beard, fossils; circuit option with *Brown Mtn. Trail*, *Big Run Loop Trail*, *Big Run Portal Trail*, and *Rocky Mtn. Run Trail* is about 18 mi.
79.4	Patterson Ridge Trail	3.1(h)	From Skyline Dr. in Loft Mtn. (W) to *Big Run Portal Trail*; moderate; follows sandstone ridgeline, 2.9 mi. in wilderness
79.4	Big Run Portal Trail	4.2(h)	From *Big Run Loop Trail* to *Brown Mtn. Trail* and *Rockytop Trail* (NW); easy to moderate; popular trail for equestrians and hikers; wildlife, wildflowers, 3.9 mi. in wilderness; no public access at NW end, but SW from *Patterson Ridge Trail* 79.4 mp, or Brown's Gap 82.9 mp on *Madison Run Fire Rd.*
79.5	Deadening Nature Trail	1.3	**Loft Mtn. trailhead (P)** at Loft Mtn. Wayside (gas and restaurant in summer); easy to moderate; self-guiding climb to peak (3,325 ft.) (E), partly on *AT*, loop can be made to Loft Mtn. Campground
81.1	Doyles River/ Jones River Trail	4.7	**Doyles River trailhead (P)** (200 ft. N of Big Run Overlook) (S) to Skyline Dr. 83.8 mp; moderate to strenuous; waterfalls, tall trees, crosses *Brown's Gap Fire Rd.*; (*Doyles River Trail*, 2.2 mi., *Jones River Trail*, 2.5 mi. all formerly *Doyles River Trail*); circuit with *AT* 8 mi.; popular
81.1	Big Run Loop Trail	4.2	**Big Run trailhead (P)** (W) (trail in 3 parts); moderate; 2.2 mi. to *Big Run Portal Trail*(h) (R), turn left on second part, horse and foot 1.3 mi. to *Rockytop Trail* (R), turn left on third part, 0.7 mi. to *AT*, turn L, after 1.6 mi. to **Doyles River trailhead (P)**; circuit of 5.8 mi.; popular
82.9	Madison Run Fire Rd.	5.6(h)	Brown's Gap on Skyline Dr. to park boundary (W) at SR 663, E of Grottoes; moderate; graded road with switchbacks, accesses *Austin Mtn. Trail* and *Furnace Mtn. Trail*; from SR 663 to junction with SR 659, L, is Stull Run Fire Rd.(h) (2.1 mi.) to dead end

mp	Trail Name	Mileage	Termini and Brief Description
82.9	Brown's Gap Fire Rd.	3.5(h)	Brown's Gap on Skyline Dr. to park boundary (E); strenuous; crosses *Doyles River Trail*, waterfalls, scenic, wildlife
82.9	Austin Mtn. Trail	3.2	Brown's Gap on fire road to spur right at *Rockeytop (W) Trail*, first L, exit to *Brown's Gap Fire Rd.*; moderate; loop if hiking back on fire road
82.9	Lewis Peak Trail	2.6	Brown's Gap on Skyline Dr. (W) to *Rockeytop Trail*, after 1.8 mi. turn left to park boundary (no public access); strenuous; 0.3 mi. to peak, scenic views, 2.5 mi. in wilderness
84.1	Doyles River/ Jones Run Trail	4.7	**Jones Run trailhead (P)** s end from 81.1 mp; (see **Doyles River trailhead [P]** above)
84.7	Furnace Mtn. Trail	3.4	Blackrock Area parking on Skyline Dr. to *Trayfoot Mtn. Trail* R, after 1.4 mi. straight ahead to end at Madison Run Fire Rd.; moderate; *Furnace Mtn. Summit Trail* (0.5 m) (2,657 ft.); scenic views; w access is SR 663 E of Grottoes; 3.3 mi. in wilderness
84.7	Trayfoot Mtn. Trail	5.4	Blackrock Area parking on Skyline Dr. to Blackrock, past junction of *Furnace Mtn. Trail* to *Paine Run Trail* (h) (3.7 mi.); strenuous; Blackrock scenic views, rock outcrops; use of *Paine Run Trail* and *AT* is circuit of 10 mi.
87.4	Paine Run Trail	3.7(h)	**Blackrock Gap trailhead (P)** on Skyline Dr. (W) to park boundary; moderate; stream, spring, 3.6 mi. in wilderness (W); access on SR 614, E of Harriston
87.4	Moormans River Fire Rd.	6.9(h)	**Blackrock Gap trailhead (P)** (E) on Skyline Dr. (North Fork and South Fork) to Jarman Gap on Skyline Dr. 96.8 mp; moderate to strenuous; stream, wildlife
90.0	Riprap Trail	4.4	**Riprap trailhead (P)** on Skyline Dr. (W) to park boundary; moderate to strenuous; scenic, stream, wildflowers, 4.2 mi. in wilderness; 0.4 mi. on *AT* to trailhead, Calvary Rocks, Chimney Rock; junction with *Wildcat Ridge Trail* (2.5 mi.) for return to Wildcat Ridge parking Skyline Dr. 92.1 mp, loop of 7.1 mi. with *AT* to origin 9.8 mi.
92.1	Wildcat Ridge Trail	2.5	Wildcat Ridge parking area on Skyline Dr. (W) to *Riprap Trail*; strenuous; views, 2.3 mi. in wilderness (see connection with *Riprap Trail* and *AT*, above)

mp	Trail Name	Mileage	Termini and Brief Description
94.1	Turk Mtn. Trail	0.9	From Turk Gap parking area on Skyline Dr. (0.2 mi. s on *AT*) to summit of Turk Mtn. (2,981 ft.); easy; wildflowers, superb view, geology, 0.9 mi. in wilderness
94.1	Turk Gap Trail	1.6(h)	From Turk Gap parking area on Skyline Dr. (W) to park boundary; moderate; old manganese mine, 1.4 mi. in wilderness
94.1	Turk Branch Trail	2.5(h)	From Turk Gap parking area on Skyline Dr. (E) to South Fork of *Moormans River Fire Rd.*; moderate; 1.7 mi. in wilderness; circuit can be made s on fire road to Jarman Gap 96.7 mp and return on the *AT*, 7.5 mi.

6 : National Battlefield Parks

On Fame's eternal camping ground,
 their silent tents are spread,
and glory guards with solemn round,
 the bivouace of the dead.
—*Theodore O'Hara*

Colonial-Era Trails

COLONIAL NATIONAL HISTORIC PARK
York and James City Counties

Yorktown is best known for the Yorktown Battlefield, the location of the last major battle of the American Revolution. It was on October 19, 1781, in the home of Augustine Moore, near the banks of the York River, that peace commissioners ratified the terms by which Lord Cornwallis surrendered to Washington's allied French and American forces. Jamestown Island is best known as the location of the first permanent English settlement, founded in 1607. Both of these historic sites, plus a 23-mile parkway connecting them through Colonial Williamsburg and the Cape Henry Memorial, are components of the 9,833-acre Colonial National Historic Park. The park was designated by an act of Congress in 1930. Since then two historic trails in the park have been established, sponsored in part by the Peninsula Council of Boy Scouts. These are the *Yorktown Battlefield Trail* and the *Jamestown Colony Trail*.

Access: To reach Yorktown Battlefield, turn off US 17 onto the Colonial Parkway and go 0.6 miles to the visitor center parking area. To reach Jamestown, follow the Colonial Parkway west from Yorktown for 23 miles. Otherwise, turn off I-64, exit 242, on VA 199 (west) to VA 31 and follow the signs to Jamestown.

550 **Yorktown Battlefield Trail**
Length and Difficulty: 12.5 miles (20 km); easy
Features: battlefield history, museum, bicycling
Trailhead: Yorktown Battlefield Visitor Center
Description: At the visitor center examine the exhibits and request a trail map from the information desk. (The trail can be hiked or cycled with or without the 3.5-mi. French Artillery Park Loop.) When leaving the visitor center look for the sign "Hornwork," the main British defense line, on the left, and follow over the earthworks to a 5-point road junction. Cross the road, turn left, and continue walking on VA 238 east until reaching Surrender Road, SR 704 junction. Turn right and go 0.2 miles to yellow-marked Goosley Road. Proceed on Goosley Road to W. Tour Road; turn left and reach reconstructed redoubt, an outer line of defense, at 1.2 miles. Continue ahead to the French Loop, marked by a brown sign, right, at 2.9 miles. (The French Artillery Park Loop through the French

encampment is 3.5 mi.) On returning, continue ahead to Washington's Head-quarters area at 7.9 miles. From there, follow the road over Beaver Dam Creek bridge, cross under US 17, and reach Surrender Field Pavilion at 10.2 miles. Here swords were formally exchanged by General O'Hara and Gen. Benjamin Lincoln to signify the end of the war. From the parking lot follow the red-arrow tour across the road and through a wooded area; go to junction at SR 704. Cross road to Grand French Battery. From here, cross through the Second Siege line (and cross VA 238) to redoubts of the British line #9 and #10. Visitor center is ahead, left, at 12.5 miles.

Jamestown Colony Trail

Length and Difficulty: 5.5 miles (8.8 km); easy

Feature: colonial history

Description: Visit the visitor center before beginning the hike, then go to the monument behind the center and proceed around the Jamestown site, as a preliminary to the longer loop trail. Hike the Island Loop Drive on the grassy shoulder facing traffic, examining the exhibits along the way. Subjects include colonial shipbuilding, agriculture, Indian trade, winemaking, medicine, household supplies, and brick making.

USGS map: Surry

Address and Information: Colonial National Historic Park, P.O. Box 210, Yorktown, VA 23690; phone: 804-898-3400 (in Yorktown) and 804-229-1282 (in Jamestown). Available for free are brochures and other handouts; books are on sale.

Civil War–Era Trails

There are seven Civil War battlefield parks in Virginia, at least 28 historic attractions, and more than 250 sites designated by state historical markers along the highways. They commemorate four years (July 21, 1861–April 12, 1865) of tragedy in 1,000 battles, engagements, skirmishes, and encounters; 60 percent of the war was fought in Virginia. (During the Civil War the number of men in battle was 4,137,304—1 in 8 of the population—and more than 617,000 died. In contrast, more than 120,000 died in World War I and 400,000 in World War II.) To hike the trails in these battlefields is to retrace and recount the heroic bravery and valor of the Confederate and Union soldiers. For the hiker to choose the season of the year in which the battles were fought provides an additional emotional awareness.

MANASSAS NATIONAL BATTLEFIELD PARK
Prince William County

The First Battle of Manassas was fought here on July 21, 1861, when Union general Irvin McDowell attacked a strategic east-to-west railroad junction over a stream called Bull Run. During this famous battle on Henry Hill, Confederate general Barnard Bee of South Carolina, in an attempt to rally his Third Brigade, used Gen. Thomas J. Jackson's brigade as an anchor. "Form, form," said General Bee, "there stands Jackson like a stone wall, rally behind the Virginians." A few minutes later General Bee was killed by Union gunfire. The battle ended in a rout for General McDowell's troops and a Confederate victory. The Second Battle of Manassas, August 28–30, 1862, secured a place in history for Gen. Robert E. Lee as he defeated the 75,000 Union troops with his 48,327 Confederates. In the two battles the South lost 11,456 men and the North 17,170. These battles are commemorated in the 3,200-acre Manassas National Battlefield Park. There are 50 miles of walking routes, including a 20-mile bridle trail in the park. It is recommended that hikers stop at the visitor center before their tours.

   Access: From I-66, exit 47, turn on VA 234 (north) (Sudley-Manassas Rd.), and go 0.6 miles to park entrance and visitor center on right. From US 29 turn on VA 234 (south) and go 0.4 miles to park entrance on left.

Henry Hill Trail (1.2 mi.), **Stone Bridge Trail** (5.5 mi.),
552–54   **Deep Cut Trail** (6.5 mi.)
Length and Difficulty: 13.2 miles (21.1 km); easy
Feature: battlefield history
Trailhead: At parking space at visitor center; or at parking lot on US 29 at Prince William and Fairfax county line, 1.3 miles east of VA 234 junction with US 29; or from parking lot on SR 622, 0.9 miles from US 29 and 1.4 miles east on US 29 from junction of VA 234
Description: From the visitor center begin on the 1.2-mile *Henry Hill Trail*. It has interpretive signs, artillery positions, and four push-button stations explaining in detail the fight to control the hill in the First Battle of Manassas. For a more detailed look at the First Battle of Manassas, take the blue-blazed *Stone Bridge Trail* from either of two access points on the *Henry Hill Trail*. If turning at the first right (east), pass Jackson's Guns and the site of the Van Pelt House; cross the Stone Bridge (the first was destroyed by the Confederates, the second was built about 1870); reach the Farm Ford across Bull Run; and pass the Carter House ruins and the Stovall Marker. At marker #7 is Matthews Hill, a slope facing Henry Hill, where the armies clashed and General McDowell thought the Union forces had won the war. Parallel the Sudley Road and arrive at the Stone House, a Union field hospital after the fighting was over. Cross US 29 to marker #9, the Henry House, a significant point because the battle here left the Union forces in retreat. Return to the *Henry Hill Trail* and to the visitor center.

   If hiking the *Deep Cut Trail*, which has two spur routes of 2.3 and 2.5 miles, hikers can save distance by crossing the Sudley Road highway after Matthews Hill. Follow the green (X) markers to a picnic area. This tour focuses on the third and last day of the Second Battle of Manassas, August 30, 1862. At stop B there is an unfinished railroad where General Jackson deployed his wing of troops in an excellent defensive position. (Here is a parking lot on SR 622 [Featherbed Lane] and a 2.3-mi. side trail, right, on the railroad bed to Sudley Church, Sudley Rd., and Bull Run.) At stop C is Groveton Monument. (Here a loop side trail for 2.5 mi. circles Battery Heights and the Brawner Farm.) Cross Featherbed Lane and parallel it to the historic Dogan House at stop D. Here is the Groveton Confederate Cemetery, where repose two known and between 250 and 500 unknown Confederate soldiers. Cross the highway, US 29, to monuments honoring the 5th and 10th New York Infantry. Union troops were driven off the ridge at the battle for Chinn Ridge at stop F. Before the trail crosses Chinn Branch, there is a monument to Col. Fletcher Webster, who was killed here. (He was the only son of U.S. senator Daniel Webster.) Following the retreat from the ridge, the Union forces clustered at Sudley Road (near stop G) bank for protection (bank is barely visible today). It rained during the night and all the next day, and during the darkness the Union troops retreated across Bull Run; the battle was over. Maj. Gen. John Pope's army suffered 10,000 killed and wounded, and 4,000 missing. Gen. Robert E. Lee's army suffered about 8,500 killed and wounded and only a few missing.

USGS maps: Manassas, Gainesville

Address and Information: Manassas National Battlefield Park, 12521 Lee Highway, Manassas, VA 22110; phone: 703-361-1339. Available for free are brochure and flyers; trail guide and books are on sale.

FREDERICKSBURG AND SPOTSYLVANIA NATIONAL MILITARY PARK
Spotsylvania and Orange Counties, City of Fredericksburg

This military park comprises 5,644 acres and seven major historic sites, including four major battlegrounds: Fredericksburg (December 11–13, 1862); Chancellorsville (April 27–May 6, 1863); Wilderness (May 5–6, 1864); and Spotsylvania Court House (May 8–21, 1864). No other theater of war in America has had such fierce fighting and slaughter. The Union army lost more than 65,000 men, and the South lost at least 35,000.

The Fredericksburg Visitor Center and the Chancellorsville Visitor Center have exhibits, slide shows, and displays to acquaint the visitor with the history of the Civil War action. Hikers should stop at these centers before taking the hikes. Two interpretive trails at the visitor center in Fredericksburg are the *Sunken Road Trail* and the *Lee Drive Trail*. The 0.2-mile *Sunken Road Trail* begins behind the visitor center and parallels Sunken Road (Telegraph Rd.) to six markers, the last being at the Kirkland Monument. Confederates were entrenched behind this wall. By darkness on December 13, 1862, more than 7,500 Federal troops lay dead or wounded on the open space between the wall and the river. During the night, Sgt. Richard Kirkland from South Carolina responded to the anguished pleas for water from the wounded Union soldiers. His humanitarian act of distributing water at the risk of his life gave him the title "Angel of Marye's Heights." A walk from the visitor center accesses Marye's Heights and the Fredericksburg National Cemetery. Here are graves for 15,243 men, of which 12,770 are unknown. The verses of Theodore O'Hara's "The Bivouac of the Dead" (written to honor Kentuckians in the Mexican War) are on metal plaques here.

The dark blue-blazed 5.2-mile *Lee Drive Trail* is an easy route to Prospect Hill, with information markers along the way. It can be an auto route or a walking route. Two vehicles are necessary unless backtracking. To reach the trail from the visitor center, take US 1 south for 0.6 miles and turn left into Battlefield Park. At 0.2 miles farther is a paved foot trail, 350 yards, right, to General Lee's command post. From here go 0.4 miles to Howison Hill parking area and exhibit; the trail begins behind the artillery site. At 0.5 miles pass behind the park maintenance area; cross Lee Drive and reach a picnic area at 1.2 miles. Cross the road again, following the well-graded trail through oaks and scattered pines with holly and dogwood forming a light understory. Cross Deep Run at 1.7 miles, ascend on a gentle terrain to a road, and follow the shoulder to Lansdowne Valley Road, SR 638. Reenter the woods, right, at 2.9 miles and arrive at Prospect Hill exhibit area near General Lee's

555–56   defense line at 5.2 miles.

     USGS maps: Fredericksburg, Guinea

     Access to Fredericksburg Visitor Center: On US 1, Lafayette Boulevard between Sunken Road and Willis Street, or from US 1A, take VA 3, William Street, east for 0.3 miles to Hanover Street. After another 0.8 miles turn right at Littlepage Street and continue 0.3 miles to Lafayette Boulevard. Turn right and go 0.1 mile to parking area.

557–59   **Chancellorsville Battlefield**

The next major battle after Fredericksburg occurred the following spring, April 27–May 6, 11 miles west on the Orange Turnpike (now VA 3) at Chancellorsville crossroads. Some historians claim General Lee achieved his greatest military victory here. This battle is also where he lost Gen. "Stonewall" Jackson, who General Lee claimed was a "right arm" military leader. There are three trails here for a comprehensive tour of what happened in dozens of square miles of forest thickets. The *Jackson Trail* (east and west) is a 10.9-mile hike or auto tour. The *Chancellorsville History Trail* is a 4-mile loop from the Chancellorsville Visitor Center on the northern side of the turnpike, and the 1-mile *Hazel Grove Fairview Trail* leads to the battle sites on the southern side of the turnpike.

     For the *Jackson Trail*, prepare by examining the exhibits and audiovisuals at the Chancellorsville Visitor Center. If hiking, a second vehicle should be at the Jackson flank attack marker west on VA 3. Otherwise, for the vehicle route, drive north from the visitor center on Bullock Road for 0.8 miles to the apex of General Hooker's last line at Ely's Ford Road, SR 610. Turn right and go 0.7 miles to Chancellorsville Inn ruins, an area captured from General Hooker in an incredible victory by the Confederates on May 3, 1863. Cross VA 3, and go 1.1 miles on SR 610 to the Lee-Jackson Bivouac. Here, on the night of May 1, 1863, the Confederate leaders planned the battle of Chancellorsville. General Lee would never see Jackson again. From here the hiker, history buff or not, can hike or ride the road following General Jackson's famous and risky flank march along Furnace Road. Reach Catharine Furnace remains at 1.4 miles, turn left on *Jackson Trail* (east) and reach Brock Road, SR 613, at 4.2 miles. (Here Jackson turned south as part of the plan to deceive

Gen. Joseph Hooker's scouts.) After 0.3 miles turn right on *Jackson Trail* (west). Cross the small stream, a significant spot to pause and imagine what this trail in the wilderness must have been like with a 7-mile column of thirsty horses and men stopping for water. Rejoin SR 613 at 6.7 miles, cross Orange Plank Road, SR 621, at 7.9 miles and reach VA 3 at 9.4 miles. Turn east on VA 3 for 1.5 miles to the site where on May 2 General Jackson surprised the Union army with a flank attack. The victorious march ended in tragedy for General Jackson when that night he was mistakenly shot by his own troops. He died of pneumonia eight days later at Chandler Plantation at Guinea Station, south of Fredericksburg. Taking General Jackson's place was cavalry officer J. E. B. Stuart, who on the morning of May 3 proved his leadership ability at the decisive battle at Fairview. Access to this point is by trail or vehicle from Stuart Drive south of the visitor center.

USGS maps: Chancellorsville, Brokenburg

Access to Chancellorsville Visitor Center: From I-95, exit 130, in Fredericksburg, drive west on VA 3 for 8 miles.

Wilderness Battlefield

560

A year almost to the day after Chancellorsville, the premier Civil War leaders, Confederate general Robert E. Lee and Union lieutenant general Ulysses S. Grant, led in their first battle with each other, May 5–6, 1864. Fought in a dense thicket of scrubby trees known as the Wilderness, the battle was a draw; but Union casualties numbered more than 17,000, and Confederate losses were about 11,000. General Grant broke the stalemate by repositioning at Spotsylvania Court House to the southeast. There is a 2-mile foot trail loop, the *Jordan Flank Attack Trail*, at an exhibit shelter.

Access to the Wilderness Battlefield: From Chancellorsville Visitor Center drive west 4.3 miles on VA 3 and turn left on VA 20. Continue for 2 miles to trailhead, right.

Spotsylvania Court House Battlefield

561–64

Two days after the Wilderness battle, there were two weeks of battle northwest of Spotsylvania Court House that ended without a decisive victory for either side. More than 25,000 soldiers fell during May 8–21, 1864. But the loss to General Lee is considered greater because he had fewer men in reserve. General Grant's battle plan was to push on to Richmond, 50 miles south, but the Confederates stopped the effort on May 8, 1864.

The *Spotsylvania Battlefield Trail* is 7 miles. Begin the hike at Sedgwick Monument and exhibit shelter on SR 613. The blue-blazed loop trail goes north and parallels Grant Drive. Cross the road at 0.6 miles along Upton's trace, and turn left over Doles' Salient at 0.9 miles. Cross Bloody Angle Drive to McCoull Spring and to the McCoull House ruins at 1.6 miles. Turn left here through woods, and parallel Gordon Drive left to Bloody Angle Drive. Here is the *Bloody Angle Loop Trail* at 2.5 miles. On May 12 this area was the scene of the most intense and desperate hand-to-hand combat of the war in 20 hours of rain, mud, and blood. After hiking the short, blue-blazed *Bloody Angle Loop Trail*, return to the McCoull House ruins at 4.2 miles. From here the red-blazed *McCoull/Harrison Loop Trail* goes 1.5 miles and passes the Harrison House ruins on its southern approach to crossing Gordon Drive again. Reach SR 613 at 5.5 miles. Here a connecting trail, the white-blazed *Laurel Hill Loop Trail*, goes to Hancock Road after passing the Maryland Monument. Cross Hancock Road and return to the exhibit shelter at 7 miles. The trail is a national recreation trail.

USGS maps: Spotsylvania, Brokenburg, Chancellorsville

Access to Spotsylvania Court House Battlefield: From the Wilderness area at VA 3, drive southeast 10 miles on Brock Road, SR 613, to Spotsylvania Exhibit Shelter. From Fredericksburg drive south on US 1 for 3 miles and turn right on VA 208 for 6 miles to Spotsylvania Court House. Turn right on SR 613 for 2 miles.

Address and Information: Fredericksburg and Spotsylvania National Military Park, 120 Chatham Lane, Fredericksburg, VA 22405; phone: 703-373-4461.

RICHMOND NATIONAL BATTLEFIELD PARK
Chesterfield, Hanover, and Henrico Counties

An area of 763 acres, the Richmond National Battlefield Park commemorates battlegrounds and other sites in the drive to capture the Confederate capital during the Civil War. Six sites were associated with Gen. George McClellan's campaign in 1862 (Chickahominy Bluff, Beaver Dam Creek, Gaines's Mill, Glendale Malvern Hill, and Drewry's Bluff). In 1864 Gen. Ulysses Grant led campaigns at Cold Harbor, Fort Harrison, and Parker's Battery. Other nearby battlefields, such as Fair Oaks, White Oak Swamp, and Savage Station, are not within the park system but were part of McClellan's campaigns. A loop drive of 100 miles from the Chimborazo Visitor Center is necessary to visit all the historic battle areas, restored houses, cemeteries, and other park facilities scattered in a three-county area. Five designated hiking trails are in the park, a total of 3.6 miles. Before visiting or hiking, go to the Chimborazo Visitor Center in Richmond for historical information and detailed maps on the motor routes. Also, each major battlefield has interpretive facilities, and both Cold Harbor and Fort Harrison have visitor centers.

Access: Southbound on I-95 in downtown Richmond, take exit 74B to Franklin Street (west); go one block to 14th St. and turn left. At the first traffic light turn right on east Broad; Chimborazo Visitor Center is at 3215 E. Broad Street. Northbound I-95 traffic should take exit 74C (east) to E. Broad Street and follow directions as above.

Cold Harbor Trail (1.1 mi.), **Breakthrough Point Trail** (0.2 mi.), **Fort Harrison Trail** (0.1 mi.), **Fort Brady Trail** (0.4 mi.), **Fort Darling Trail** (0.5 mi.)

565–69

Length and Difficulty: 2.3 miles (3.7 km); easy

Features: battlefield history, James River overlook

Trailheads: See information at each trail.

Description: The *Cold Harbor Trail* is 1.1 miles, a loop trail through Confederate and Federal earthworks involved in the battle of Cold Harbor, May 31–June 13, 1864. The battle cost the Federal army thousands of casualties in a few hours and was Gen. Robert E. Lee's last major victory. (Cold Harbor is on VA 156 northeast of I-295 and SR 615 junction.) *Breakthrough Point Trail*, a short loop trail of 0.2 miles, is near the Watt House. It follows a portion of the Seven Days Battle line to the point where Confederate forces broke through Federal defenses at the Battle of Gaines's Mill, June 27, 1862. (Access via a spur road from VA 156 at Cold Harbor.)

The *Fort Harrison Trail* is 0.1 mile, a loop with exhibits describing construction techniques and soldier life at Civil War field fortifications. The *Fort Brady Trail* is farther downriver on the park road to Fort Brady. (Access is off VA 5 [New Market Rd.] south of Richmond at Battlefield Park Rd.)

Across the James River (west) at Drewry's Bluff is the site of Fort Darling and the Confederate Naval/Marine Training Center. The *Fort Darling Trail* loops 0.5 miles to an overlook of the James River where Confederate artillery stopped a Federal fleet, including the ironclad *Monitor*, from steaming upstream to attack Richmond. (Access from the James River Bridge in Richmond on I-95 south to 64A and the junction with SR 613 [Willis Rd.]. Go right [north] at junction with US 301/1 for 0.8 mi. to Bellwood Rd., SR 656, on right. After taking SR 656, go under I-95 and make a sharp left on Fort Darling Rd.)

Address and Information: Richmond National Battlefield Park, 3215 E. Broad St., Richmond, VA 23223; phone: 804-226-1981. Available are brochures and flyers.

NEW MARKET BATTLEFIELD HISTORICAL PARK
City of New Market

The 280-acre New Market Battlefield Park and Hall of Valor is a registered national historic landmark. It is administered by Virginia Military Institute as a nonprofit educational facility and was made possible by a gift from VMI alumnus George Randall Collins. The area honors the 257 teenage cadets under the command of Gen. John C. Breckinridge, who with other batteries and companies on May 15, 1864, courageously forced the Federal units to retreat. Before hiking the *New Market Battlefield Trail*, visit the park museum for information and audiovisuals. The 1-mile loop trail from the parking lot at the Hall of Valor leads to the historic Bushong Farm, where Confederate wounded were treated after the battle. Among the 43 Confederates killed, 10 were VMI cadets. Pass exhibit markers around the "field of lost shoes" to Federal lines and scenic overlooks 200 feet above the North Fork of the Shenandoah River. Return along the cliffs through a border of cedar and redbud.

570

Access: From I-81, exit 264, junction of VA 211, follow signs. (Open daily 9–5.)

Address and Information: New Market Battlefield Historical Park, New Market, VA 22844; phone: 703-740-3102.

PETERSBURG NATIONAL BATTLEFIELD
Prince George County and City of Petersburg

Established as a national military park in 1926, the site of the Petersburg siege was designated a national battlefield in 1962. Its 2,700 acres extend to Fort Lee on the east, to US 460 and VA 109 on the south, and to US 301 on the west, with VA 36 running through the northern edge. A 16-mile auto tour of the siege lines around Petersburg begins at the junction of US 301, Crater Road, and the park's Siege Road. The route includes four of the major forts General Lee maintained during the 10-month siege, June 15, 1864, to April 2, 1865.

After General Lee's army defeated General Grant's army at Cold Harbor on June 3, 1864, Grant said that the key to taking Richmond was Petersburg, but a series of Union fumbles on June 15 and 18 cost him 10,000 men and a long delay in the capture of the city. The delay became 10 months, the longest siege in American warfare. More than 70,000 soldiers died. During this time General Grant's Army of the Potomac, with 100,000 men, was well armed and supplied from the City Point (Hopewell) Military Railroad, on which 500,000 tons of material were transported. In contrast, General Lee's army of 60,000 men was far less well equipped for the battle of Fort Stedman. Finally, with his defenses crumbling, General Lee evacuated Petersburg on the night of April 2, 1865.

Besides the siege lines, the auto tour at the Petersburg National Battlefield includes Poplar Grove National Cemetery, a tract of 8.7 acres southwest of Fort Wadsworth. From early June to late August the park has a living history program of artillery demonstrations and live exhibitions of soldier life of the Civil War. Comprehensive displays and audiovisuals are at the visitor center. There are 14 miles of trails, including spurs and paved interpretive routes, of which 10.3 miles are part of the *Petersburg Battlefield National Recreation Trail*.

Access: From I-95 in Petersburg, turn at signs on VA 36 east, E. Washington Street (and US 301 south and US 460 east), and go 1.8 miles to park entrance on right.

571–79   **Petersburg Battlefield National Recreation Trail**
Length and Difficulty: 7 miles (11.2 km) combined, round-trip; easy
Feature: battlefield history
Trailhead: Parking area on VA 109, Mahone Ave. junction with A Ave., 1.2 miles
   south from VA 36, and 1.6 miles northeast from junction of US 460 and VA 109.
Description: Designated a national recreation trail in 1981, this loop trail has two
   optional spurs. The wide trail is exceptionally well designed and marked. Its
   surface is chiefly beds of pine needles, with spots of blacktop or gravel. The first
   major historic stop is at Meade Station, one of the key supply points for Grant's
   military railroad. At 0.5 miles turn left on Jordon Point Road, go 125 yards, and
   turn right on the *Branch Trail* to Siege Road at 1.1 miles. (On the right is the
   Battery 5 Spur Trail, which proceeds right along the multiuse lane to the visitor
   center and to the site of the famous 17,000-lb. Union mortar, the "Dictator."

Petersburg National Battlefield Park. (Courtesy Virginia Division of Tourism)

Backtrack for a round-trip total of 1.7 mi. Along the way, near the park entrance from VA 36, is the *Battery 7 Trail*, a round-trip side trail of 1.3 mi.)

After returning to *Branch Trail* follow it across Siege Road to Fort Friend and the *Friend Trail*. Cross Harrison Creek and reach a junction, left, with Fort Stedman at 2.7 miles from the beginning of the *Petersburg Battlefield Trail*. (At this point those who wish to hike the *Short Loop Trail* should bear left to Fort Stedman exhibit, cross Siege Rd., and go to the *Encampment Trail*; turn right. After 50 yds. turn left, cross Harrison Creek, and follow the *Harrison Creek Trail* for 0.6 mi. to Attack Rd. Turn left, and reach Union Camp at Siege Rd. Turn right on old Prince George Courthouse Rd., returning to parking area for a total of 4.7 mi.)

Continue on the *Petersburg Battlefield Trail* to Colquitt's Salient and to Fort Haskell at 3.9 miles. Here is an excellent example of the well-preserved fortifications. Cross and parallel Siege Road past the Taylor House site to the railroad at 4.5 miles. (Here the *Crater Spur Trail* continues across the railroad to the site of the ironic and incredible plans of the 48th Pennsylvania Infantry to tunnel under the Confederate line. After a loop of 1.3 mi. return to the *Petersburg Battlefield Trail*.) Follow the *Petersburg Battlefield Trail* east to the *Encampment Trail*, cross Taylors Creek, pass the junction with the *Short Loop Trail* at 5.6 miles, and return to trailhead and parking area for a total of 7 miles. (If spur trails are hiked the total round-trip is 11.3 mi.)

Address and Information: Petersburg National Battlefield, P.O. Box 549, Petersburg, VA 23804; phone: 804-732-3531.

APPOMATTOX COURT HOUSE
NATIONAL HISTORICAL PARK
Appomattox County

After the Federal victory on April 1, 1865, at Five Forks, southwest of Petersburg, General Lee realized the siege of Petersburg was over. The next day both Petersburg and Richmond were evacuated, and a western retreat began. Lee made a skillful withdrawal but counted on supplies arriving at Amelia for his tired and starving army. The supplies never came, and valuable time was lost foraging for food. Furthermore, 8,000 of his men, one-fourth of his army, were wounded, killed, or captured on April 6 in the swampy bottom of Sayler's Creek (now Sailor's Creek Battlefield Historical Park on SR 617, 2 mi. north of VA 307 near Rice. The park has an auto tour to designated stops identifying the sequence of the battle.) General Lee set up his headquarters about 1 mile east of the Appomattox River on the old Richmond-Lynchburg Stage Road. (The trail described next follows General Lee's route from his headquarters to other significant points in the final days of the Confederacy.)

After the end of the Civil War, the Appomattox Court House village was neglected for 65 years—the former McLean House was dismantled, the courthouse burned in 1892, and other buildings were in decay. Even the bill passed by Congress in 1930 to build a monument was never honored. Finally, in 1934 the NPS recommended complete restoration of the village, and in 1935 Congress passed a bill authorizing it as a national historical monument. In 1954 it was also designated a national historical park. The park has 1,323 acres and 13 major buildings that have been meticulously restored.

Access: From the town of Appomattox go east on VA 24 for 3 miles to entrance on left. From US 60 at Mt. Rush, go west on VA 24 for 17 miles to entrance on right.

580–81   **Appomattox History Trail**
Length and Difficulty: 6 miles (9.6 km); easy
Features: battlefield history, McLean House
Trailhead: Visitor center
Description: A recommended beginning point for the hike is the visitor center at Appomattox Court House, following east by the jail to Surrender Triangle on the Old Richmond–Lynchburg Road, where approximately 22,000 Confederates laid down their arms on April 12, four years to the day after the first shots were fired at Fort Sumter. Descend on a grassy ridge following trail arrow sign to the Appomattox River Wayside at 0.6 miles. Cross a bridge by the marker honoring Joel Walker Sweeney, the inventor of the 5-string banjo, and reach the site of the Apple Tree. Here, General Lee waited on April 9 for a response from General Grant to Lee's offer of surrender. Pass the *Appomattox National Environmental Study Area Trail* on the right and follow VA 24 to the site of General Lee's last field headquarters at 1.5 miles. Here General Lee held his last council of war on the night of April 8. From this point follow the trail onto a woods road at 1.8 miles, enter a Virginia pine stand for 0.2 miles, and reach an open field at

Alexander Sweeney's Prizery. Again enter the woods, cross the Appomattox River at 2.4 miles, and follow it upriver for 0.4 miles to a sharp left uphill. Reach Prince Edward Court House Road, SR 627, at 3.8 miles. Cross the road and continue through a hardwood forest with mountain laurel and huckleberry.

At 5 miles reach the North Carolina Monument honoring troops who distinguished themselves in three major battles—Big Bethel, Gettysburg, and Chickamauga—and who fired the final Confederate shots at Appomattox. Go 0.2 miles to VA 24. (A spur of 0.5 mi. on the left along the highway leads to the site of General Grant's headquarters.) Turn right to a Confederate cemetery at 0.3 miles and follow the old coach route to McLean House. Here, at 1:30 P.M. on Palm Sunday, April 9, General Lee met with General Grant to surrender in dignity and honor the Army of Northern Virginia. (When General Lee mounted his horse "Traveller" to return to his men, General Grant and his officers lifted their hats to him in respect. General Grant immediately ordered rations issued for the hungry men in gray and ordered paroles to be printed.) Complete the hike to the visitor center at 6 miles.

USGS maps: Appomattox, Vera

Addresses and Information: Appomattox Court House National Historical Park, P.O. Box 218, Appomattox, VA 24522; phone: 804-352-8987. (For Boy Scout credit on history trails, contact Blue Ridge Mtn. Council, Boy Scouts of America, 2131 Valley View Blvd., Roanoke, VA 24012; phone: 703-265-0656.) Available for free are brochures and flyers; books are on sale.

7 : National Historical Parks

On the dark and bloody ground to Kentucky went Daniel Boone.
—R. G. Thwaites

CUMBERLAND GAP NATIONAL HISTORICAL PARK
Lee County, Virginia; Bell County, Kentucky;
and Claiborne County, Tennessee

Before the American Indians made use of it along the "Warrior's Path," Cumberland Gap had been the pass for buffalo and deer that trampled across it in large herds seeking new pastures. It was the main pass on the wilderness trail that became the Wilderness Road, marked by Daniel Boone from Virginia to Kentucky in 1775. By 1792 more than 100,000 pioneers had crossed the gap for Kentucky and beyond. Subsequently the route became a significant artery of migration, trade, and transportation to the West. In both the American Revolution and the Civil War it was an important military objective. In the twentieth century the gap became a traffic funnel for US 58 in Virginia and US 25E from Tennessee. During the 1990s the highway will become four lanes. With such a rich history, the area was deemed appropriate for designation as a national shrine. Accordingly, in 1940 Congress authorized Cumberland Gap National Historical Park; it has 20,270 acres, 7,526 of which are in Virginia.

The park's headquarters and visitor center are on the Kentucky side of the gap, at the edge of Middlesboro; the town of Cumberland Gap is in Tennessee; and the Wilderness Road Campground is in Virginia. From the visitor center is Pinnacle Road, a winding 4-mile motor ascent to Pinnacle Overlook (2,440 ft.) with panoramic views. At this point is the southeastern trailhead of scenic 16.6-mile *Ridge Trail*, a state boundary line route on Cumberland Mountain. On the Kentucky side is picturesque SR 988 (Sugar Run Rd.). It goes 2.5 miles to a picnic area with moss-covered rocks, dense hemlocks, and access to the 2.2-mile *Sugar Run Trail* by cascading Sugar Run. With interpretive help from the visitor center a motor route can be planned to Cubbage, Kentucky, for penetrating Brush Mountain to the Hensley Settlement. Once a high and hardy pioneer community, it was abandoned in the early 1950s, but the NPS has restored a few buildings. It is easily accessible by foot from the remote *Ridge Trail*.

For access to Tri-State Peak (1,990 ft.), there is a parking area on US 25E (0.9 mi. west of the US 58/25E junction). The *Tri-State Trail*, a moderate, 0.9-mile, well-graded and popular trail, passes the site of Fort Foote to Tri-State Pavilion and exhibit. On the return is appealing 0.8-mile *Wilderness Road Trail*, which descends to Iron Furnace, near the CSX Railroad tunnel under the gap. The combined length of both trails is 3.4 miles. Another historic area, outside the park, is 9.5 miles east of the US 58/25E junction. Near here in October 1773, Boone was leading his own family and several other families to Kentucky, but the pioneer attempt failed

Cumberland Gap National Historical Park. (Courtesy Virginia Division of Tourism)

when his teenage son, James, and five other youths were tortured and murdered by Shawnee Indians at Indian Creek. (A state historical marker is near the junction of US 58 and SR 684 at Ewing.) Within the park is the large Wilderness Road Campground on US 58, 1.3 miles east of the US 58/25E junction. It has trailer and tent sites (no hookups), comfort stations, waste disposal unit, picnic area, amphitheater, and nature trails. The *Green Leaf Nature Trail*, 0.7 miles, begins at the amphitheater. To the left the trail dips into a valley with tall hardwoods. It makes a figure eight in combination with 1.1-mile *Honey Tree Trail* that loops on a slope. Other trails that access the campground are described below. The campground is open year round.

582–85

Length and Difficulty: 16.6 miles (26.6 km); strenuous

Connecting Trails: *Sugar Run Trail* (2.2 mi.), *Lewis Hollow Trail* (1.8 mi.), *Gibson Gap Trail* (4.8 mi.), *Hensley Trail* (0.4 mi.), *Chadwell Gap Trail* (2.1 mi.), *Ewing Trail* (2.4 mi.)

Features: scenic outcrops, historic site, caves, wildlife, wildflowers

Trailheads: The southwestern trailhead is at the Pinnacle Overlook. For the northeastern trailhead, take SR 724 from US 58 at Ewing and go 1 mile to Civic Park for parking. This is the southern trailhead of 2.4-mile *Ewing Trail*, an access trail to 16.6-mile *Ridge Trail* for a hiking total of 19 miles.

Description: If overnight camping is planned, first secure a backcountry use permit from the park office. Begin the hike at the Pinnacle parking area, ascend to the ridge, and follow an old fire road on the crest. Occasional rock outcroppings provide views into Kentucky and Virginia. The *Ridge Trail*'s forest cover is chiefly oak, hickory, black locust, and black birch with an understory of mountain laurel, dogwood, chestnut sprouts, and buckberry. Frequent patches of woodland sunflower, purple phlox, red fire pink, and blue Virginia spiderwort provide colorful trail borders. Wildlife is less abundant, but deer, grouse, squirrel, and chipmunk may be sighted. There are no bears, but there are rattlesnakes. At 1.7 miles is a junction with the *Lewis Hollow Trail* (also called the *Skylight Cave Trail*), right, and the *Sugar Run Trail*, left. (The *Lewis Hollow Trail*, with high traffic volume, descends 0.5 mi. to Skylight Cave. [A flashlight is necessary to examine the ceiling.] The trail parallels Lewis Hollow, passes the Wilderness Road Campground picnic area, and ends inside the campground entrance station at 1.8 mi.) (The *Sugar Run Trail* descends southwest to the headwaters of Sugar Run, and at 1.5 mi. provides a fork at the confluence of Sugar Run and a tributary. To the right is a descent to Sugar Run Picnic Area; to the left the trail descends to SR 988, 0.9 mi. south of the picnic area.)

At 5.1 miles approach a primitive campsite and a junction with the *Gibson Gap Trail*, right. (It descends to a long, sweeping switchback before crossing Station Creek at 2.3 miles. It then stays on the mountainside for a number of coves, descends on switchbacks, and crosses Station Creek twice more before reaching the campground. Also used as a horse trail, it provides access to a parking area at US 58 near the campground.) At 10.5 miles is Indian Rock, with good views. At 11 miles and 11.7 miles are short, steep trails on the left to Hensley Settlement, and at 1.4 miles is Chadwell Gap (3,385 ft.), with a primitive campsite. Reach another side trail at 12.6 miles that leads 0.2 miles left to Martins Fork campsite with water. The *Ridge Trail* meets the *Chadwell Gap Trail* on the right at 12.8 miles. (It descends 2.1 mi. on 16 switchbacks to a trailhead near private homes. Along the way, at 0.1 mi., are caves and cement steps. In the coves are black cohosh and meadow rue. At the parking area it is 0.4 mi. on SR 688 and 1.7 mi. on SR 690 [Caylor Rd.] to US 58, 10.9 mi. east of the campground.)

The *Ridge Trail* makes a junction with the *Ewing Trail*, right, at 15.6 miles.

This connection has high horse traffic, but ahead, at 16.4 miles, there is a foot trail, right, to the *Ewing Trail.* At this junction is White Rocks primitive campground 0.2 miles down the steep mountain on the Kentucky side. Ahead the *Ridge Trail* reaches its northeastern terminus at 16.6 miles at White Rocks. Here is a spectacular view of the three states from spots of rock and huckleberries. On the *Ewing Trail* descend steeply on switchbacks for 0.5 miles on a footpath to the old road with horse traffic. Follow it on switchbacks for 1.9 miles to Civic Park (which has a stream and a shelter). From here it is 1 mile on SR 724 to Ewing on US 58, 4 miles east of SR 690.

USGS Maps: Middlesboro south and north, Varilla, Ewing

Address and Information: Cumberland Gap National Historical Park, Box 1848, Middlesboro, KY 40965; phone: 606-248-2817; headquarters is off US 25E at the eastern edge of town. Available for free are a brochure and map of the park, and flyers for campground and backcountry camping; books are on sale at the visitor center. For equestrian information, phone 703-926-6964.

8 : National Wildlife Refuges

Where plants and animals can't survive,
soon the same environment won't be fit for people.
—Jay R. Hair

Under the U.S. Fish and Wildlife Service of the Department of Interior is the National Wildlife Refuge System; its purpose is to manage the preservation of wildlife. The system was established in 1903 when President Theodore Roosevelt authorized the first refuge on Pelican Island, Florida. By the 1990s the nation had set aside more than 90 million acres of lands and waters for this purpose. In Virginia there are fourteen refuge locations, six of which offer visitor opportunities: Back Bay, Chincoteague, Eastern Shore of Virginia, Dismal Swamp, Mason Neck, and Presquile. The Dismal Swamp and MacKay Island have acreage in both Virginia and North Carolina. Emphasis is on management benefits for waterfowl, but the protection of all species is provided. Where compatible with wildlife management plans, recreational use is allowed. Examples are hunting, fishing, hiking, bicycling, picnicking, boating, swimming, and nature study.

The three smaller refuges are described here, and the three larger ones with trail networks are described separately. The Eastern Shore of Virginia NWR has 651 acres. Its visitor center is accessed on the first right turn, SR 600, after crossing the Chesapeake Bay Bridge-Tunnel on US 13 to Kiptopeke. The *Eastern Shore Nature Trail* is a 0.5-mile loop to an observation deck for viewing waterfowl in Magathy Bay. From here the islands of Skidmore and Smith can be seen in the Atlantic Ocean.

593

Mason Neck NWR is in Fairfax County, only 18 miles south of Washington, D.C. It was established in 1960 for the primary purpose of protecting the national symbol, the bald eagle. But more than the bald eagle is protected by this blend of upland forest, bogs, and Potomac River front marsh. Thousands of waterfowl use the 285-acre Great Marsh on the Atlantic flyway. With a total of 2,276 acres the refuge is host to more than 211 bird species. Deer roam freely in the forest. The refuge has a high traffic volume on the 3-mile loop *Woodmarsh Trail*, which forks after 0.8 miles. Interpretive points are described in a trail brochure guide at the parking area. The bay area has yellow pond lilies and rose mallow. From US 1, travel on VA 242 (near Lorton) for 4.3 miles to High Point Road, right. Turn at the sign and go

594

0.7 miles on a gravel road to a parking area on the left. *USGS map* is Fort Belvoir.

In Chesterfield County is Presquile NWR, established in 1952 with 1,329 acres, of which 279 are uplands, with the remaining acreage in tidal swamp and marsh. The uplands are on Turkey Island, an island of folklore and intrigue in an oxbow bend of the James River. From its visitor center is the 0.7-mile *Presquile Nature Trail*, which describes the island's history, flora, and fauna. Access is limited to government-owned ferry or private boat. Visitors should make prior arrangements for ferry use with the refuge office (see Addresses and Information, below).

To reach the dock from VA 10 (across the Appomattox River from Hopewell), travel on SR 827 for 3.4 miles.

595

Addresses and Information: Eastern Shore NWR, 5003 Hallett Circle, Cape Charles, VA 23434; phone: 804-331-2760. Mason Neck NWR, 14416 Jefferson Davis Highway, Suite 20A, Woodbridge, VA 22191; phone: 703-339-5278. Presquile, Box 620, Hopewell, VA 23860; phone: 804-458-7541. Available are trail brochures and information leaflets.

BACK BAY NATIONAL WILDLIFE REFUGE
City of Virginia Beach

Established in 1938, the 5,568-acre Back Bay NWR has been set aside primarily to protect the habitat of migrating waterfowl on the Atlantic flyway. It is located between Little Island Park in Sandbridge and False Cape State Park. On the east is Atlantic Ocean frontage, on the west is a marginal section of mainland, and in the center are many islands, including Long Island and Ragged Island in the bay. The refuge does not allow camping but does permit hiking and biking through the refuge to enter False Cape State Park, which does allow camping. Camping permits are required, and applications must be made in person at Seashore State Park in northern Virginia Beach. (See Addresses and Information, below, and Seashore State Park and Natural Area in Chapter 11.)

The refuge and the park share a number of natural environment management policies, but they differ in some of the recreational opportunities. An agreement between them allows for highly restricted use of the refuge dike road (*Back Bay Dike Trail*) by motorized vehicles. As a result hikers may see vehicles transporting nature study groups through the refuge to the park's Environmental Education Center. A day-use area only, the refuge charges an entrance fee and requires all vehicles left overnight for backpacking into the park to be parked at Little Island Park, a Virginia Beach facility outside the refuge's entrance gate.

Nearly 300 avian species have been recorded in the refuge, including 30 species of waterfowl such as geese, ducks, and swans. The peak of fall migration is in December, and the migratory peak for songbirds and shorebirds is in the spring. There are three endangered species in the refuge: bald eagle, loggerhead sea turtle, and peregrine falcon. Among the regular mammals are deer, raccoon, gray fox, mink, and otter. Turtles include the eastern mud, red-bellied, and snapping. In addition to water and black rat snakes there is the poisonous cottonmouth moccasin. The feral swine are from domesticated stock and are considered trespassers. Some of the common vascular plants are coastal gaillardia (*Gaillardia pulchella*), marsh mallow, meadow beauty, spikerushes, beach holly, yaupon, wax myrtle, maple, live oak, pine, and red cedar.

Bay Trail (0.4 mi.), **Seaside Trail** (0.2 mi.), **Dune Trail** (0.2 mi.),
Back Bay Dike Trail (3.8 mi.), **Outdoor Classroom Trail** (0.1 mi.)
596–600
Length and Difficulty: 9.3 miles (14.9 km) combined, round-trip; easy
Connecting Trail: Barbour Hill Interpretive Trail (2.4 mi.)

Features: wildlife, wild plants, refuge, beach, waterfowl, historic site

Trailhead: Refuge visitor center in the daytime, or if parked overnight, 1.5 miles north at Little Island Park near the refuge entrance gate

Introduction: The trails provide an exciting coastal experience for hiking and biking. The experience is enhanced when the trails in False Cape State Park are used for an extended retreat to the coastal backcountry. Planning for either or both requires different schedules and equipment, but it is essential to bring water to both refuge and park, neither of which has a supply. All water must be carried in, and one gallon per day per person is recommended. In addition, insect repellent and sun lotion should be taken. The most comfortable seasons and the best times to see wildlife are spring, fall, and winter. Summer is unpleasant because of humidity and insects. The refuge is closed (and so is the park) from the first to the second Saturday in October for hunting. Also, the refuge may have other seasonal closings to protect waterfowl. (Call in advance if planning long trips.)

Directions: Begin from the visitor center on the *Dike Trail* (road) at the trail network signboard. To the right is the *Bay Trail*, which follows a wide trail 0.4 miles among yaupon, wax myrtle, live oak, and cordgrass to an observation deck at Buck Island Bay. A side feature is Sunset point, part of a boardwalk trail called Outdoors Classroom. It also has an observation deck to encounter bay-edge biological habitats. It connects with an access to the visitor center parking area. To the left of the *Dike Trail* is short *Seaside Trail*, an all-sand treadway to the ocean. (The first 2.7 mi. of the *Dike Trail* are without shade trees.) After 280 yards the trail forks left to follow the East Dike. At 0.3 miles is the *Dune Trail*, a boardwalk trail, left, to the ocean. (A loop can be made by turning left on the beach to turn left again on the *Seaside Trail* for a return of 1 mi.)

Continuing on the *Dike Trail* pass closed crossover dikes of the impoundments at 0.6 miles, 1.5 miles, and 1.7 miles on the right. At 2.2 miles turn right on a crossover dike between the freshwater lakes; enter a forest at 2.7 miles and reach a junction with the West Dike road. Turn left in a grove of maple, willow, and pine. Exit the forest at 3.3 miles, and reach a junction on the right with the western side of the False Cape State Park's *Barbour Hill Interpretive Trail* (road) at 3.5 miles. (There may not be a trail sign here.) Continue ahead and turn right at the entrance to False Cape State Park at 3.8 miles. Backtrack. (The *Barbour Hill Interpretive Trail* continues on the right into the park. Proceed first to an observation deck on the left to view waterfowl, and continue 0.7 miles farther to the park's contact station. Another 0.7 miles, right, leads to a campsite. Return to the *Dike Trail* [described above] after a loop of 2.1 mi. to make a day's round-trip back to the visitor center at 9.7 mi.)

USGS maps: North Bay, Knotts Island

Access: From the southern end of us 60 (Pacific Ave.) at the beach in Virginia Beach, cross the bridge and drive south 4.7 miles on General Booth Boulevard. Turn left on sr 615 (Princess Anne Rd.), go 0.8 miles and turn left on Sandbridge Road. After 5.4 miles turn right on Sandpiper Road and continue 3.7

miles to Little Island Park. Access to Back Bay NWR entrance is 0.2 miles, and it is another 1.3 miles to the visitor center and parking area. If coming from I-64 in western Virginia Beach, take VA 407, exit 286 (Indian River Rd.) southeast to cross Princess Anne Road at Pungo at 12 miles. Cross the road, and after 1.1 miles turn left on New Bridge Road and follow it 1.2 miles to Sandbridge Road. Follow it 3.1 miles to Sandpiper Road and turn right. Follow it as described above.

Addresses and Information: Back Bay NWR, 4005 Sandpiper Rd. (P.O. Box 6286), Virginia Beach, VA 23456; phone: 804-721-2412. Available are information brochures and bird list. False Cape State Park (mailing address only), 4001 Sandpiper Rd., Virginia Beach, VA 23456; phone: 804-426-7128. Available are brochures with maps and permit and camping information. Seashore State Park and Natural Area (for False Cape camping permits), 2500 Shore Dr., Virginia Beach, VA 23451; phone: 804-481-2131; Little Island Park (a city park near refuge entrance), phone: 804-426-7200.

CHINCOTEAGUE NATIONAL WILDLIFE REFUGE
Accomack County

The northernmost of Virginia's barrier islands is also one of the most fascinating. Assateague Island, 37 miles long and spanning the Maryland/Virginia line, was designated a national seashore in 1965. The Virginia portion consists of Chincoteague NWR and a small NPS facility near the southern tip of the island. As part of an interagency agreement, the NPS administers, as an agent of the Fish and Wildlife Service, a portion of the beach for surfing, swimming, and fishing. Established in 1943, the refuge area is managed for migratory birds, endangered species, and other native animals. Over 300 species of birds use the refuge for at least a portion of the year, including geese, ducks, swans, herons, hawks, egrets, ibises, gulls, and terns. The wild ponies have made the island nationally famous with the "Pony Swim" and auction the last Wednesday in July. During Thanksgiving week the refuge holds "Waterfowl Week" for observing the waterfowl at their peak in numbers. This is the only time the gated 7.5-mile Service Road is open to private vehicles. The refuge has another road, the 3.2-mile Wildlife Loop, which is used by hikers, bikers, and birders around freshwater Snow Goose Pool. From 3 P.M. to dusk motor vehicles are allowed on the road. To begin, take the first left turn on the Service Road behind the refuge visitor center. After 1 mile the loop turns right and crosses the pool on a dike to enter a wooded area. At 1.9 miles is a junction on the left with 1.2-mile *Swan Cove Trail.* (It is a side trail for walking and bicycling from Toms Cove visitor center of the NPS.) The loop route turns west and then north to pass right of other freshwater impoundments before returning to the refuge visitor center.

Another trail is the *Lighthouse Trail,* a short (less than 0.3 mi.) walk to the 124-foot-tall Assateague Lighthouse, an active facility of the U.S. Coast Guard. It is diagonally west across Beach Road from the refuge visitor center. The most popular walk in the refuge is the 1.6-mile *Woodland Trail* (formerly the *Pony Trail*). It is a

601

hiking and biking loop from a parking area on Beach Road between the refuge and the NPS visitor center. Through pine and water oak the trail passes an open area and observation deck near a marsh. Here the ponies frequently graze. The area is also known for the Sika elk and white-tailed deer roaming freely in the refuge. Additionally, the endangered Delmarva fox squirrel (*Sciurus niger cenereus*) nests and feeds here. At the beach, across from the NPS amphitheater, is 0.6-mile *Toms Cove Nature Trail*, an interpretive trail about coastal wildlife and such flora as glasswort and sea oxeye.

The refuge's most remote and challenging walk is the 7.5-mile (15 miles round-trip) Service Road from the visitor center to a cul-de-sac at Wash Flats. Among dunes, wetlands, and marshes the road was created from a dike when freshwater impoundments were made. The road provides an excellent opportunity to observe waterfowl. To reach it from the visitor center, go north on the Wildlife Loop for 1 mile to the road's gate. Camping or straying from the road is not allowed. Although the road is not a trail, backpackers may hike the 25 miles between Toms Cove north to Oceanside Campground or nearby Assateague State Park in Maryland. Because camping is not allowed in the Virginia section, backpackers must plan to hike 13.5 miles to the first campsite 1 mile over the state line. Beyond that point there are other campsites on the beach and on the bayside at campsites shared with canoeists. All drinking water must be carried. Permits and reservations are necessary and may be acquired from the visitor center at either Toms Cove in the south or Barrier Island in the north. (See Addresses and Information, below.)

USGS maps: Chincoteague east and west, Boxiron

Access: From US 13 junction with VA 175, go 10.5 miles east on VA 175 to Chincoteague. Turn left on N. Mair Street and continue 4 blocks, then turn right on Maddox Boulevard and go 2.2 miles to refuge visitor center, left. For Toms Cove Visitor Center (NPS), continue another 2 miles to the beach. For Barrier Island Visitor Center (NPS), take highway 376 for 4.2 miles east of Berlin, turn right on highway 611, and go 3 miles, right.

Addresses and Information: Chincoteague NWR, P.O. Box 62, Chincoteague VA, 23336; phone: 804-336-6122. Assateague Island National Seashore, P.O. Box 38, Chincoteague, VA 23336; phone: 804-336-6577. In Maryland, Assateague State Park, Rt. 2, Box 293, Berlin, MD 21811; phone: 301-641-2120. Assateague Island National Seashore headquarters, 7206 National Seashore Lane, Berlin, MD 21811; phone: 410-641-1441. Available are brochure with maps, bird list, information flyers on camping permits for NPS, and other materials.

GREAT DISMAL SWAMP
NATIONAL WILDLIFE REFUGE
Cities of Suffolk and Chesapeake

Few places in Virginia invoke such legends and mystery as the Great Dismal Swamp. George Washington once owned a share of it, calling it a "glorious paradise." Col. William Byrd II cursed it as a "vast body of dirt and nastiness." He is said

Great Dismal Swamp National Wildlife Refuge. (Courtesy Virginia Division of Tourism)

to have given the swamp its name, having nearly lost his life surveying the state line through it in 1728. Earlier, in 1664, William Drummond, a governor of North Carolina, had discovered the lake that bears his name, but made no claim for it. In 1763 George Washington organized a draining and logging company, and one of the ditches bears his name. Eventually all the timber was cut from the vast swamp, and 140 miles of roads were created for access, thus leaving the ditches. The result was the destruction of the swamp's natural hydrology and the decline of plant and animal diversity. In 1973, climaxing years of efforts by conservationists to preserve the swamp, the Union Camp Corporation donated 49,100 acres of land to the Nature Conservancy. This land was then conveyed to the Department of the Interior, and the refuge was officially established through the Dismal Swamp Act of 1974. The refuge currently covers 131,770 acres, 82,150 of which are in Virginia, and 49,620 are in North Carolina.

Lake Drummond, in the heart of the swamp, is a 3,100-acre circular natural lake kept pure by the tannic acid from the cypress and juniper. Its average depth is 5 feet. The swamp is unique because it is not a depressed marshland. Instead it is a "perched bog," with the lake at its highest point and streams slowly draining from it. Peat bogs near the lake and elsewhere may be as deep as 18 feet. Access to the lake by boat is from Feeder Ditch off US 17, 3.5 miles north of the North Carolina state line. The U.S. Army Corps of Engineers maintains a campground on this route. (For information, call 804-421-7401.) Hiking and biking access is on Washington Ditch. Among the flora and fauna are 8 species of turtles, 14 species of frogs, 15 species of snakes (including copperhead, canebreak rattlesnake, and cottonmouth moccasin), 48 species of trees, 29 species of shrubs, 20 species of vines, and 209 species of birds. Bear, bobcat, and deer inhabit the swamp, and crappie and perch are in the lake. An endangered animal in the swamp is the short-tailed shrew (*Sorex longirostris fisheri*). Birding is best in the spring during migration and when the flowers are in bloom. This is also the best time for hiking because the insects are less troublesome. Some of the wildflowers to look for are dwarf trillium, silky camellia, climbing hydrangea, swamp azalea, sheep laurel, and swamp rose. A rare fern is the log fern, found in the swamp more than elsewhere.

The refuge is open to hiking, biking, nature study, fishing, and boating year round during daylight hours. Because the refuge is meant to protect and manage the swamp's unique ecosystem, there are portions of the refuge closed to public use. Some of the ditch roads are maintained; others have become impassable. The best two hiking routes are described below.

605–7
Jericho Ditch Trail (5.9 mi.), **Dismal Town Boardwalk Trail** (0.9 mi.), **Washington Ditch Trail** (4.5 mi.)
Length and Difficulty: 20.7 miles (32.4 km) combined, round-trip; easy
Features: swamp, Lake Drummond, wildlife, wildflowers, historic site
Trailheads: See refuge access at end of description.
Description: The *Jericho Ditch Trail* (road) is the longest and most exploratory toward the center of the swamp. At 1.8 miles it intersects with Hudnell Ditch (east) at Five Points. To the immediate right (south) is Lynn Ditch, and to the southeast is Jericho Ditch. At 5.3 miles (after making the only turn in the long straight trail) the trail turns more to the south, passes Camp Ditch, left, and at 5.9 miles reaches Middle Ditch, right. Beyond this point the *Jericho Ditch Trail* is not passable. Backtrack, or use Middle Ditch and Lynn Ditch for a loop of 14.7 miles to SR 642 via Jericho Lane to point of origin.

At the parking entrance to the *Washington Ditch Trail* is the *Dismal Town Boardwalk Trail* and a directional signboard. The first 0.8 miles on the loop nature trail are on an elaborate elevated boardwalk. Side trails extend to observation points in a forest of red maple, swamp black gum, elm, and ash. Parts or all of the swamp may be dry, depending on the season of the year. The trail returns to the signed *Washington Ditch Trail.* To the left the *Washington Ditch Trail* goes straight for 4.5 miles to Lake Drummond; to the right it is 0.1 mile to the parking area. Hikers to Lake Drummond should carry drinking water and insect repellent and wear strong, protective footwear. Round-trip is 9 miles.

USGS maps: Suffolk, Corapeake, Lake Drummond, Lake Drummond NW

Access: For access to the *Jericho Ditch Trail,* begin at junction of US 13/VA 32/VA 337 in downtown Suffolk. Drive east 0.7 miles on US 13/VA 337 to right fork on SR 642 (White Marsh Rd.). Follow it south for 0.8 miles to Jericho Ditch Lane on the left. (The other two trails can be accessed 4.5 mi. farther south on SR 642; make a left turn to the parking area.) Another access is from the courthouse in downtown Suffolk on US 13/VA 32 south for 3.4 miles to fork. Follow signs on VA 32 (Carolina Rd.) for 4.4 miles to SR 675 (Cypress Chapel Rd.). Turn left for 0.5 miles to SR 642 (White Marsh Rd.). After 1.8 miles reach a junction with SR 604 (Desert Rd.), where to the right is the refuge office (closed on weekends), and straight ahead (northeast) 1 mile is the Washington Ditch entrance road, right.

Address and Information: Dismal Swamp NWR, P.O. Box 349, Suffolk, VA 23434; phone: 804-986-3705. Available are brochure of bird species, brochure of Dismal Swamp with map outline, and leaflets on flora and fauna.

9 : Other Trails in the National Park System

The woods, my Friends, are round you roaring,
Rocking and roaring like a sea.
—William Wordsworth

ASSATEAGUE ISLAND NATIONAL SEASHORE
Accomack County, Virginia, and Worcester County, Maryland

With 39,630 acres, the 37-mile Assateague barrier island is a haven for migratory waterfowl, wild ponies, and students of nature. Of the island's total acreage, 17,377 acres are federal property, with 6,897 in Maryland and 10,479 in Virginia. For hiking opportunities, see (in Chapter 8) Chincoteague NWR.

Access: From the town of Chincoteague at junction of VA 175 and SR 2113, follow SR 2113 for 2.2 miles to Refuge Information Center.

Address and Information: Assateague Island National Seashore, 7206 National Seashore Lane, Berlin, MD 21811; phone: 410-641-1441.

BOOKER T. WASHINGTON NATIONAL MONUMENT
Franklin County

This national monument honors Booker T. Washington (1856–1915), who was born a slave on the James and Elizabeth Burroughs plantation. The story of his life, in *Up From Slavery*, is one of childhood poverty and illiteracy and an adulthood that included graduation from Hampton Institute, the founding of the Tuskegee Institute, and distinction as an American educator whose advice was sought by Presidents William McKinley, Theodore Roosevelt, and William H. Taft. The monument area has a visitor center, living historical farm, picnic area, and hiking trails. The set of trails was designated a national recreation trail in 1981. The park is open year round.

The 0.5-mile *Plantation Trail* begins at the parking area of the visitor center and follows a wide trail to the reconstructed kitchen cabin, tobacco barn, pigpen, hen house, and horse barn. After this loop, return to the junction with the *Jack-O-Lantern Branch Trail* south of the tobacco barn. For 1.5 miles the trail has interpretive markers and makes a loop. For the first 0.8 miles it follows Jack-O-Lantern Branch among wildflowers such as orchid, soapwort, and mandrake. Some of the trees are Virginia pine, black walnut, and sycamore. After turning right near Gill Creek the trail passes a small cemetery on its return to the tobacco barn. It is believed the Jack-O-Lantern Branch received its name from foxfire, an eerie phosphorescent light caused by a luminous fungus in decaying wood. It is visible along the stream at night.

608–9

Access: From Rocky Mount junction of US 220 Bypass and VA 40, go 1.1 miles east on VA 40 to VA 122. Turn left on VA 122 and go 12.3 miles to entrance of the monument on the right.

Address and Information: Booker T. Washington National Monument, Rt. 3, Box 310, Hardy, VA 24101; phone: 703-721-2084. Available are brochure with map, trail guide, and information flyers.

GEORGE WASHINGTON BIRTHPLACE NATIONAL MONUMENT
Westmoreland County

Pope's Creek Plantation, which the Washington family acquired in 1718, was the first home of George Washington, who was born there February 22, 1732. After 3 ½ years his father, Augustine, and his mother, Mary Ball, moved the family to the Little Hunting Creek Plantation—later named Mount Vernon. Four years later they moved near Fredericksburg. George was eleven when his father died. His half brother, Augustine II, inherited Pope's Creek Plantation, but young George frequently returned for stays at his birthplace.

In 1858 the commonwealth acquired the area, but the Civil War delayed restoration. With the assistance of the Wakefield National Memorial Association in 1923 and John D. Rockefeller in 1931, the commonwealth was able in 1932, the 200th anniversary of Washington's birth, to officially transfer the 394 acres with buildings to the federal government. It is open daily, except December 25 and January 1. (To reach Monroe Hall, the birthplace of James Monroe, drive west 2.8 mi. on VA 3 to Oak Grove, then take VA 205 to the historic site.)

There are two significant trails of interest to the visitor. From the visitor center take the easy, 1-mile *Washington Historic Trail* on a gravel path along the edge of the cliffs to the birthplace site. On the way pass through an exceptionally large grove of aging cedars. Circle by the kitchen house, memorial house, barn, and farm area to complete the loop. The 1-mile *Washington Nature Trail* is at the picnic area, accessible by driving back to the granite monument and turning right. Follow the trail signs in a loop to interpretive plaques about the trees, shrubs, flowers, animal life, and history of the area.

USGS map: Colonial Beach South

Access: From US 301 junction with VA 3 (36 mi. from I-95 in Fredericksburg), go east 12.5 miles on VA 3 to left turn on VA 204.

Address and Information: George Washington Birthplace National Monument, Washington's Birthplace, VA 22575; phone: 703-224-0196. Available for free are brochures and flyers; books are on sale at the visitor center.

GEORGE WASHINGTON MEMORIAL PARKWAY
Arlington and Halifax Counties and City of Alexandria in Virginia

Established in 1930, the George Washington Memorial Parkway administers 7,142 acres on the Potomac shores in Virginia and Maryland. On the Virginia side is the 28-mile, landscaped riverfront, limited access parkway from Mount Vernon to the American Legion Memorial Bridge (1-495); Fort Hunt; Jones Point Lighthouse; Arlington House, Roosevelt Island; Turkey Run Park; and Great Falls National

Park. In addition there are other recreational, natural, and historical facilities. (Mount Vernon, the colonial mansion and estate of George and Mary Washington, is not part of the NPS. It has been owned and maintained by the Mount Vernon Ladies' Association since 1858.) Of particular interest for recreation are the 18-mile *Mount Vernon Trail* and 10.1-mile *Potomac Heritage Trail*, both of which parallel the parkway and the river, and the 13 miles of trail network in Great Falls National Park.

Access to Mount Vernon Trail: Parking area at Mount Vernon and parking area at Roosevelt Island.

612–16   **Mount Vernon Trail**

Length and Difficulty: 18 miles (28.8 km); easy

Connecting Trails: Dyke Marsh Trail (1 mi.), Jones Point Trail (0.5 mi.), Potomac Heritage Trail (10.1 mi.)

Features: hike and bike paved trail, scenic views, historic site, urban adventure, waterfowl

Trailheads: Parking lot at Mount Vernon for south on VA 235 (Mount Vernon Hwy.); parking lot for north at Roosevelt Island by parkway

Description: This limited access trail for bikers, hikers, joggers, and strollers begins at the last parking lot for recreational vehicles at Mount Vernon. Descend in a forest to Little Hunting Creek at 1 mile. Here is Riverside Park, a place to fish and picnic. At 2.9 miles cross the parkway; on the left is a trail diversion to Forest Hunt Park for picnic area, rest rooms, drinking water, and telephone. Continue on the left side of the parkway 5 miles to Alexandria Avenue and cross over to the riverside. Enter the 240-acre Dyke Marsh at 5.6 miles, where 250 species of birds have been seen. Water and rest rooms are available at Belle Haven, another picnic area, at 7.2 miles. From here the *Dyke Marsh Trail* goes 1 mile on a road to the Dyke Marsh shoreline. Cross Hunting Creek bridge and go under I-95 on South Street. (To the right is the *Jones Point Trail*, which goes 0.5 mi. round-trip partly through woods and a meadow to Jones Point Light-house, named in honor of a fur trader whose cabin was here in 1692.)

At 8.9 miles leave the wooded area and enter the historic city of Alexandria (with a citywide network of bike trails). Continue to 11.4 miles, where the 107-acre Daingerfield Island begins. Picnicking, sailing, fishing, and a restaurant are here. After crossing Four-Mile Run there is a junction, left, with the *Four Mile Run Trail* (hike and bike). (It follows 2.2 mi. upstream to Shirlington Road [past I-395] to join the *Washington and Old Dominion Railroad Trail* [hike and bike].) Pass by the western side of the National Airport from 12.6 miles to 14.3 miles. Reach Gravelly Point at 14.5 miles for an excellent view of the nation's capitol. Follow along the edge of the Potomac past hardwoods, shrubs, and white pines to the Lyndon B. Johnson Memorial Grove at 15.9 miles. Food, water, rest rooms, and telephone are here. At 16.5 miles is Memorial Bridge. (To the right across the river is Lincoln Memorial and upstream from there is the *Rock Creek Trail*. It connects with the *C and O Canal Trail*, which follows the Potomac

River to the *AT* in Harpers Ferry, West Virginia.) Continue along the parkway, pass under the Theodore Roosevelt Memorial Bridge, and reach the parking area and causeway to Roosevelt Island at 17.6 miles. At 18 miles the trail ends but connects with the *Custis Trail* (hike and bike), left. (It parallels I-66 to Bon Air Park, where it connects with the *Four Mile Run Trail* and the *W&OD Railroad Trail* ahead and to the left. See Chapter 10.) At the parkway, where the *Mount Vernon Trail* ends, is the southern trailhead of the *Potomac Heritage Trail* for foot travel only.

USGS maps: Mount Vernon, Alexandria, Washington west

Turkey Run Park   617–22

The George Washington Memorial Parkway's headquarters is at Turkey Run Park, a developed and landscaped area between the parkway and the Potomac River near I-495. A day-use area, it also has a visitor center, three picnic areas, rest rooms, telephone, and four short trails. On the eastern side is 75-yard *River Trail* from parking and picnic area A to the *Potomac Heritage Trail*. From this picnic area west is 0.7-mile *Woods Trail*, which parallels the park road to picnic area C. From here a loop is made with the *Big Switchback Trail* (110 yds.), the *Turkey Run Trail* (0.5 mi.), and a few yards of the *Potomac Heritage Trail*. The 10-mile, blue-blazed *Potomac Heritage Trail* is a foot trail only, and no camping is allowed. It meanders between the parkway and the Potomac River through a hardwood forest of river birch, sycamore, beech, oak, and witch hazel. Spots of the terrain are rocky high bluffs, floodplains, and slippery creek crossings. A national scenic trail, it is maintained by the PATC and is part of a long trail proposed through three states and the District of Columbia by the Potomac Heritage Trail Association.

At the stream crossing of Turkey Run the *Potomac Heritage Trail* goes 1.6 miles through floodplain sections northwest to its trailhead at I-495, and 8.4 miles southeast to Roosevelt Island. Access to the northwestern trailhead is from I-495 (Capital Beltway), exit 13, on VA 193 (Georgetown Pike) east at Balls Hill Road north. At the fourth block, turn left (over I-495) on Live Oak Drive to its cul-de-sac and trailhead. Downriver from Turkey Run follow the trail 0.7 miles to a rocky area and at 0.9 miles to a concrete tower for river gauging and yellow-blazed *River Trail*, an access to picnic area C. Continue downriver, pass under VA 123 bridge and over ramps to arrive at Marcy Park at 3.6 miles. Follow the *Battery Trail* briefly to the parking area and then follow an old road. Cross rocky Pimmit Run and under Chain Bridge at 4.2 miles. Cross the *Gulf Branch Nature Trail* in a steep damp area at 4.8 miles and *Donaldson Run Trail* at 5.3 miles. Cross the *Windy Run Trail* at 6.7 miles (see Arlington County in Chapter 12 for details on the latter three trail crossings). Continuing between the parkway and the river, pass through a forested floodplain in sections, cross Spout Run, pass under Key Bridge, and reach a junction with the *Custis Trail* (hike and bike) at a grassy area at 8.2 miles. After 0.2 miles is the southeastern trailhead at Roosevelt Island parking area and pedestrian bridge. Here is the northern trailhead of the *Mount Vernon Trail*.

USGS maps: Falls Church, Washington west

Access: From I-495, exit 14 (Capital Beltway), on the George Washington Memorial Parkway southeast 2 miles. From 14th Street Bridge (Memorial Bridge) on the parkway northwest 7 miles.

Address and Information: George Washington Memorial Parkway, NPS, Turkey Run Park, McLean, VA 22101; phone: 703-285-2606/2591. Available are brochures and maps of Turkey Run Park and other properties the park service administers.

GREAT FALLS PARK

The Great Falls Park on the shore of the Potomac River is the most northern of the George Washington Memorial Parkway properties. It is northeast of Reston and is bordered on the north by Riverbend Park, a Fairfax County recreational park. Formed from the clear cascades high in the West Virginia mountains, the Potomac River puts on its dramatic finale of thundering white water here, a feature that gives the park its name. This spectacular natural area had a trading post on its riverbanks for Native Americans and early colonists, and later it was a shipping point to pioneers moving upriver. In 1784 the Patowmack Company was formed to navigate the falls with canals and locks, which were completed in 1802. During this time the town of Matildaville (now in ruins) developed as a central trading post. In 1828 the Chesapeake and Ohio Canal Company purchased the Patowmack Company but constructed the new canal and locks on the Maryland side of the river.

Park facilities include a visitor center, picnic areas, a snack bar, and trails (including a short access trail for the physically disabled to a river overlook) for hiking, biking, and horseback riding. Rock climbing and fishing are allowed, but camping is not. There is no boat access. Visitors are warned to stay away from the slippery edges of the jagged rocks along the shoreline. (Each year there are fatalities from falls or hazardous water sports in the park.)

Access: From I-495 (Capital Beltway), exit 13, take VA 193 west (Georgetown Pike) for 3.9 miles to junction with SR 738, and turn right into the park.

623–32

River Trail (1.5 mi.), **Patowmack Canal Trail** (1.3 mi.), **Ridge Trail** (1.5 mi.), **Old Carriage Road Trail** (1.6 mi.), **Swamp Trail** (0.9 mi.)

Length and Difficulty: 5.1 miles (8.2 km) combined, round-trip; easy

Connecting Trails: *Matildaville Trail* (1.1 mi.), *Mine Run Trail* (0.5 mi.), *Riverbend Equestrian Trail* (0.4 mi.), *Heritage Trail* (1.7 mi.), *Upland Trail* (2 mi.), *Difficult Run Trail* (3.1 mi.) (the latter three trails are in adjoining parks in Fairfax County)

Features: scenic views, waterfalls, historic site, canal ruins

Trailhead: Visitor center

Introduction: Combined distance of one-way trails, including spurs, is about 13 miles, but round-trips can double the distance of some trails. The *River Trail,* the *Patowmack Canal Trail,* and the *Swamp Trail* are foot trails only. The *Matildaville Trail* is foot and horse only. If planning a long trip, a park trail map is recommended. Also, the park offers guided tours. Described below is an example of a loop using a combination of multiple-use trails and hiking trails only.

Great Falls Park, George Washington Memorial Parkway. (Photograph by Allen de Hart)

Description: At the parking area at the visitor center examine the trail diagram board. If beginning on the blue-blazed *River Trail*, turn left or right. (To the left it is 0.7 mi. to the boundary with Riverbend Park and its 1.7-mi. *Heritage Trail*.) Turn right and cross Patowmack Canal site to scenic overlooks of waterfalls and Falls Island. Pass through a picnic area and connector trails to the canal near Mather Gorge among walnut, oak, and sycamore. Pass spur to Sandy Landing and arrive at Cow Hoof Rock, a scenic area, at 1.4 miles. Ahead the foot trail ends at the *Ridge Trail*, left or right, which is a hike, bike, and horse trail at 1.6 miles. (To the right it is 0.3 mi. to a connection with the *Old Carriage Road Trail* and a return to the visitor center for a loop of 3 mi.) Continue left in a forest of oak, ash, river birch, and elm; pass a picnic area and at 2.2 miles reach a junction with the *Difficult Run Trail*. (It goes right to Difficult Run Park in Fairfax County.) Turn left and continue 0.2 miles to a riverview, and backtrack. Also backtrack to the junction with the *River Trail* at 3.2 miles. Turn left, and after 0.3 miles reach a junction with the *Matildaville Trail*, right, and the *Old Carriage Road Trail*, right, both of which lead back to the visitor center. Continue left, then right on the *Ridge Trail* for 0.2 miles to a right turn on the *Swamp Trail* at 3.7 miles. (The *Ridge Trail* continues northwest for 0.4 mi. to the park road.) The 0.9-mile foot trail is through a forested, flat, low area with markers about wildlife and wild plants. At 4.6 miles is a junction with the *Old Carriage Road Trail*, right and left. Turn left, and after 0.2 miles there is a connector, right, with the *Matildaville Trail* to the town ruins. Continue north on the *Old Carriage Road Trail* to the visitor center at 5.1 miles. (If continuing on the *Old Carriage Road Trail*, cross the park road, and near Clay Pond connect with the *Mine Run Trail*, the *River Trail*, the *Upland Trail*, and the *Riverbend Equestrian Trail* for a total round-trip of 3.4 mi.)

USGS maps: Seneca, Vienna, Falls Church, Rockville

Address and Information: Great Falls Park, NPS, P.O. Box 66, Great Falls, VA 22066; phone: 703-285-2964. Available are park brochure and trail map.

PRINCE WILLIAM FOREST PARK
Prince William County

A forested watershed of Quantico Creek, the 18,571-acre park is shaped like a sweet birch leaf with the tip near the town of Independent Hill and the stem base at the town of Triangle. In the southeastern corner of the county, the park is bordered on the south and southwest by SR 619 (Joplin Rd.), on the south by Quantico Marine Corps Base, on the north by VA 234 (Dumfries Rd.), and on the east by I-95 and the town of Dumfries. The park is rapidly becoming a prized oasis of woodland in a metropolitan environment 32 miles south of Washington, D.C., and 23 miles north of Fredericksburg. A significant feature of the park is the physiographic divide of the piedmont plateau with its hilly ridges in the west, and a drop at the fall line to the coastal plain province in the east. Granite, schist, and quartzite are part of its geology, and Catoctin greenstone (also found in high elevations of the Blue Ridge Mountains) is at the confluence of Quantico Creek and its South

Fork. Pyrite was mined here in the early part of the twentieth century. The park's unconsolidated soils were subjected to severe erosion during the two centuries the park was farmland.

Its terrestrial community of 95 plant species is dominated by hardwoods and scattered Virginia pines. Its plant diversity is enhanced by the transition from northern to southern climate ranges and the eastern and western physiographic provinces. Some plants are rare; for example, the whorled pogonia (*Isotria verticillata*), a yellow-green wild orchid can be seen here. With diverse topography there is diverse wildlife. Deer, turkey, grouse, fox, beaver, raccoon, and squirrel are most common. There are 152 species of birds, including the great horned owl, cuckoo, brown creeper, and scarlet tanager. The lakes have trout, bass, bluegill, and perch.

Archaeological research traces the area's cultural resources to as early as 4500 B.C. Potomac Indians may have had villages in the park area as early as A.D. 700. English settlement and tobacco plantations were here after 1650, and by 1731 Prince William County was formed. Between 1899 and 1920 pyrite mining was a major industry. In the meantime, the soil was so depleted the farmers had difficulty maintaining a livelihood. The U.S. government purchased the area, with closed mines and poor farms, for reclamation and recreation under the National Industrial Recovery Act. It was named the Chopawamsic Recreation Demonstration Area. Visitors today will notice part of that history in the cabin camps, lakes, and trails constructed by the CCC from 1934 to 1940. During World War II the U.S. Army used the park for a top secret military installation, and in 1948 the park was returned to the NPS and renamed Prince William Forest Park. The park has also played significant roles in other wars. During the Revolutionary War local militia repaired Telegraph Road for Gen. George Washington's troops to pass through on their way to defeat the British at Yorktown in 1781. There are 35 cemeteries in the park where men of both sides of the Civil War are buried. In World War I the pyrite mines produced ingredients used in gunpowder.

Public facilities today include five cabin camps for groups, two tent camps (Turkey Run Ridge and Oak Ridge), a concessionaire campground with hookups for trailers and recreational vehicles (Travel Trailer Village on VA 234), a primitive backcountry campground (Chopawamsic, which requires a permit), ponds for fishing, picnic areas, visitor center, and 35 miles of trails. Bicycling is allowed on the paved roads and some of the fire roads. Hunting is prohibited. Among the 16 trails three are interpretive. The shortest and easiest is 0.2-mile *Pine Grove Forest Trail* at the visitor center. It is popular with children and is easy for the physically impaired. The *Geology Trail* is a 2-mile loop that uses other trails such as the *Quantico Falls Trail*, part of the *North Valley Trail*, all of the *Cabin Branch Trail*, part of Pyrite Mine Road, and a short piece of the Scenic Road. Access is from parking lot D or E. The other trail about natural science is the *Farms to Forest Trail*. It is a double-loop, with the first loop 1.1 miles. Yellow-blazed, it is keyed to markers about trees, birds, and topography. Halfway around the loop a 1.7-mile extension begins. It goes deeper into the forest and passes by a tributary to Quantico Creek. Active or former beaver ponds are prominent on this trail. Access is at

633–38 Oak Ridge Campground entrance.

There are a number of short loop options. The most popular is the *Laurel Trail*. It is a 1.3-mile, yellow-blazed loop north of the visitor center, which partly uses the *Birch Bluff Trail* on the eastern side of the loop. At the northwestern corner of the trail is an access bridge over South Fork to the *South Valley Trail*. (Because there is no bridge at the northern end of the *Birch Bluff Trail*, it is not recommended for a loop to the pyrite mine site.) Another short loop is the *Little Run Trail*, a 0.7-mile, yellow-blazed loop at Turkey Run Ridge Campground, off Park Central Drive.

A loop of 2 miles can be made to the pyrite mine site. Begin at parking lot D on Park Central Drive and follow Pyrite Mine Road to a junction with orange-blazed *Cabin Branch Mine Trail*. Turn left, and after 0.3 miles turn right on the *North Valley Trail* to the mine site. Continue downstream and make another right to return on the Pyrite Mine Road.

Another 2-mile loop is *Chopawamsic Trail*. Formerly called the *Deer Ridge Trail* and the *Bobcat Ridge Trail*, it circles the campsites in a 430-acre tract reserved for backpack camping. All water must be carried in; trash must be carried out; and no pets are allowed. A permit is necessary for camping in this area, and during the winter hunting season the area is closed. Access is 2.1 miles west on SR 619 from the visitor center. Turn left on Breckenridge Road and go 0.7 miles to the parking lot. Below is a description of the park's longest trail, the *South Valley Trail*, with its options for shorter or longer loops. It, as with all other trails in the park's main

639–41 area, are for day use only.

Access: From I-95, exit 150, at SR 619, turn west to the park entrance road on the right near I-95 ramps.

642–47 **Laurel Trail** (1.3 mi.), **South Valley Trail** (9.7 mi.)

Length and Difficulty: 9.2 miles (14.7 km) combined; easy to moderate

Connecting Trails: *Turkey Run Ridge Trail* (1.4 mi.), *High Meadows Trail* (2.1 mi.), *Oak Ridge Trail* (1.6 mi.), *Farms to Forest Trail* (2.8 mi.)

Features: historic site, stream, lake, wildflowers, wildlife

Trailheads: Visitor center or Oak Ridge Campground

Description: Begin at the visitor center on the western side of the yellow-blazed *Laurel Trail* loop. After 0.4 miles intersect with Orenda Road, and cross the bridge over South Fork to white-blazed *South Valley Trail*, right and left. (To the right it goes 0.9 mi. to Pyrite Mine Rd. and the *North Valley Trail*.) Turn left, leave the road, and continue upstream. (On Orenda Rd. north it is 1 mi. to Park Central Dr. and parking area D for a junction with Pyrite Mine Rd.) Cross Mary Bird Branch and at 1.4 miles reach a junction with the *Turkey Run Ridge Trail* coming from the right. (It goes north 1.4 mi. to Turkey Run Campground and connects with 0.5-mi. *Mary Bird Branch Trail* and 2.1-mi. *High Meadows Trail*.) At 1.6 miles cross Park Central Drive near parking lots A and B. Ahead, in an oxbow of the creek is a 0.1-mile spur to parking lot C of Park Central Drive. Intersect with Park Central Drive again at 3 miles, meet Taylor Farm Road on the right, and cross Park Central Drive near parking lot I. (The Taylor Farm Rd. goes 0.6 mi. north to intersect with the *High Meadows Trail* and Turkey Run Ridge Campground.) The main trail parallels the stream, passes gneiss rocks, and continues through a forest of tall hardwoods.

At 5 miles reach a junction with the *High Meadows Trail*, right. (It goes 2.1 mi. to Turkey Run Ridge Campground.) A few yards beyond, the trail crosses the creek, but there may not be a bridge. Farther upstream, on the approach to Lake #5, is an arched bridge over the creek. Cross the stream at the intersection with Mawavi Road at 6.7 miles. (The road goes 0.5 mi. left to Camp #2 and right 0.4 mi. to Park Central Dr. and parking lot G.) Continue ahead through a forest of oak, poplar, birch, and wild azalea to the last crossing of South Fork (where there may not be a bridge). The trail then skirts close enough to SR 619 to allow traffic to be heard, but it soon veers northeast to reach a junction with the *Oak Ridge Trail* at 9 miles.

(To make a loop back to the visitor center, turn right on yellow-blazed *Oak Ridge Trail*, hike 0.5 mi., cross Mawavi Rd., and at 1.6 mi. reach Black Top Rd. Turn right, cross Taylor Farm Rd. at 2.4 mi., and arrive at Turkey Run Campground at 3.3 mi. From there hike on the *Turkey Run Ridge Trail* for 1.4 mi. to the *South Valley Trail* for a return to the visitor center at 6.2 mi., a round-trip total of 15.2 mi.) Continue ahead 0.2 miles to Old Ridge Road, Oak Ridge Campground on the left, and the *Farms to Forest Trail* at 9.2 miles.

USGS maps: Joplin, Quantico

Address and Information: Prince William Forest Park, P.O. Box 209, Triangle, VA 22172; phone: 703-221-7183. Available are free brochures with park map.

III : State Managed Trails

10 : Wildlife Management Areas

Deer walk upon our mountains, and the quail
Whistle about us their spontaneous cries;
Sweet berries ripen in the wilderness;
And in the isolation of the sky . . .
—*Wallace Stevens*

Of Virginia's 25.5 million acres of land, 4 million acres are public lands, and this includes 170,000 acres in 27 WMAs. The following WMA descriptions primarily emphasize trail usage, though some other facilities are listed as well. Only the WMAs with named or specifically designated trails are described in this chapter, and those with a network of trails are described in more detail. The Virginia agency responsible for developing and preserving these public hunting lands is the Department of Game and Inland Fisheries. From the mountains to the sea, the state has lands of diversity for both game and nongame wildlife. The areas are a source of pleasure and education to hunters, fishermen, naturalists, hikers, campers, birders, and others who love the outdoors. Primitive camping, unless otherwise posted, is permitted for a maximum of seven days, with no more than three camp units for a group. Camping is prohibited within 100 yards of boat ramps or fishing lakes. Hiking and camping are not recommended during hunting season, and hikers must wear a blaze orange cap and jacket. If poaching is observed, report the violation to 1-800-237-5712. Because facilities and regulations vary at each WMA, it is recommended that hikers call in advance about hunting seasons and potential campsites. A few of the WMAs have given special attention to singular trails; they are collectively described in this introduction. Gated roads are open from the first Saturday in October to the second Saturday in February, and from the second Saturday in April to the third Saturday in May.

The Gathright WMA is a showplace of conservation and recreation in the rugged Alleghany Highlands bordering West Virginia. Three government agencies have been responsible for the management of the area since Congress authorized the Gathright Dam on the Jackson River in 1947. Finally in 1965 the U.S. Corps of Engineers began construction; the dam was completed in 1981, and recreational use began in 1982. In 1978 Congress renamed the 2,530-acre lake in honor of Benjamin Moomaw, an area citizen whose efforts made the project possible. The WMA's original 18,000 acres became 13,428 when the GWNF became responsible for the lake and its shoreline. Gathright's 2-mile *Sweet Acron Trail* follows an old woods road, spot bordered with scenic wildlife grazing fields, on the spine of Bolar Mountain. (No camping is allowed.) Access is 3 miles north of the entrance to Lake Moomaw Campground on SR 600 to gated *Bolar Ridge Fire Trail*, right. It is 1.5 miles up a steep, scenic road to the trailhead, right. Address: Gathright WMA, Rt. 2, Box 648, Hot Springs, VA 24445; phone: 703-839-2635. 648–49

Ragged Island WMA has 1,537 acres in Isle of Wight County. It has three canoe trails into one of the largest undisturbed brackish marshes remaining on the James River. One of the state's 300 watchable wildlife areas, it has 220 species of birds and

38 species of fish. The 0.5-mile, round-trip *Ragged Island Trail* is a path from a parking area at the southwestern end of James River Bridge on US 17/US 258/VA 32 (northeast of Bartlett). The surprisingly pleasant and worthwhile walk with a 400-yard boardwalk goes through loblolly pine, cordgrass, saltgrass, and sea lavender to an observation deck at the river. (No camping is allowed.) For information, call 804-357-5224 or 804-367-1000.

650

Formerly known as Apple Manor WMA, reflecting the orchard on the property and other nearby orchards, the G. Richard Thompson WMA has 4,160 acres on the Blue Ridge Mountains. It is the only WMA with the *AT* weaving through its boundaries. East of Front Royal it is between I-66 north to the border of Sky Meadows State Park and US 50. Access near Linden from VA 55 is on SR 638, which has a number of gated access routes to the *AT*, and at the first access to the *Ted Lake Trail*. The *Ted Lake Trail* can also be accessed from SR 688, 1.2 miles north from VA 55 near Markham. If accessing the blue-blazed trail from SR 638, follow it 1 mile to its intersection with the *AT* at a spring and Manassas Gap Shelter. It then descends on a ridge to SR 688. The WMA has a lake stocked with bass and sunfish on SR 688, and its moist, rich hollows have especially large zones of trillium. Address: Thompson WMA, P.O. Box 349, Sperryville, VA 22740; phone: 703-825-3653.

651

White Oak WMA's 2,712 acres are in Pittsylvania County, 12 miles northeast of Danville. It borders the quietly flowing Banister River for 4.5 miles. It has eleven ponds for fishing, horse trails, and 1.1-mile, unique *Hiawatha Nature Trail* with thirty-three interpretive posts. The trail is maintained by the Pittsylvania County school system. On its path by the river are trout lilies and river birch, and on its rocky bluffs by the river is mountain laurel. Access is from SR 832, 3.9 miles east from US 29 in Chatham to SR 649 for 1.6 miles. Another route is from Danville north on US 29 to SR 640 on the right. Turn and go 7.8 miles to SR 649 on the left, and go 0.9 miles to parking area on the right. Address: White Oak WMA, Rt. 1, Box 76-G, Chatham, VA 24531; phone: 804-432-1377.

652

Address and Information: Virginia WMA, 4010 W Broad St. (Box 11104) Richmond, VA 23230; phone: 804-367-1000. Available for free are *Virginia Wildlife Watcher's Guide*, a tabloid about all the places to observe wildlife; *Virginia Hunting Guide*, a tabloid about all the WMAs, hunting and fishing seasons, and map sources; and leaflets and brochures on bird lists and endangered species. A fee is charged for *Virginia Wildlife*, an excellent subscription journal dedicated to the conservation of Virginia's wildlife and natural resources.

AMELIA WILDLIFE MANAGEMENT AREA
Amelia County

With more than 3 miles of frontage along the Appomattox River, ponds, and considerable diversity of vegetation, the Amelia WMA is an excellent wildlife habitat. The adjoining lands of Westvaco and Chesapeake Corp significantly expand its recreational opportunities. The 2,217 acres of state land, purchased in 1967, include 100 acres of water and 850 acres of fields. Anglers can expect bass, bluegill, crappie, and walleye pike. All of its trails are easy. The *Woodcock Trail* is 4 miles round-trip and follows an old winding trail partly along a small stream to the Appomattox River for backtracking. Its access is at the entrance parking lot on SR 652. Access to 2.5-mile *Lake Trail* is at the boat ramp parking area, off SR 652 and under huge oaks. The 2.5-mile loop may not be maintained at all points, but at the beginning take a left, and follow the lake boundary south. After 1.4 miles cross the *Bunny Trail*, which goes 0.7 miles left, to SR 692. This is a serene environment. Follow the lake boundary to the dam and return through the woods to the parking area. The *Marsh Point Trail* is a 1-mile ridge route that splits at 0.7 miles. Both legs then lead down the hill to the bottomland and the banks of the Appomattox River. Backtrack to its start, which was at the main parking area on the ridge of SR 652.   653–56

USGS map: Chula

Access: From US 360 east of Amelia, take SR 604 north and go 7 miles to Masons Corner. Turn left on SR 616; continue 1.5 miles and turn right on SR 652 to the WMA entrance.

Address and Information: Amelia WMA, c/o Hunting Information, HC06, Box 46, Farmville, VA 23901; phone: 804-367-1000.

CLINCH MOUNTAIN WILDLIFE MANAGEMENT AREA
Smyth, Russell, Tazewell, and Washington Counties

The 25,477-acre Clinch Mountain WMA, the state's largest, is scenic, remote, high, and rugged. Laurel Bed Lake, a 300-acre man-made lake, is excellent for trout fishing. Adjacent to the lake is a unique stand of black cherry that has been designated a natural area by the Society of Foresters. The trees in the cove are more than 3 feet in diameter and more than 85 feet high. Big Tumbling Creek, heavily stocked with trout, forms falls and pools through deep gorges to the North Fork of the Holston River, west of Saltville. Activities include picnicking, horseback riding, boating, canoeing, birding, hiking, and berry picking. Camping is allowed at the designated site on Little Tumbling Creek. It is open from the third Saturday in March to Labor Day. The campground has water, fireplace, firewood, and vault rest rooms (and is part of the Division of State Parks).

The WMA has several administrative access roads that are developed, gated, and closed to vehicles. They make exciting hiking routes in Twin Hollows and Short Mountain (4,020 ft.). Both are 3 miles each and are accessed from the main entrance road. Also, hunters have made a 3-mile loop that ascends from Jackson Gap above the campground to White Rocks, right, along the ridgetop to Panther Lick Cove, and descends to follow Brian Cove Creek back to the campground. To access the lake and campground, follow the same directions as under trailhead for the *Clinch Mountain Trail*, below.

Clinch Mountain Trail   657
Length and Difficulty: 2.4 miles (3.8 km); strenuous
Features: scenery, wildlife, black cherry grove, ruggedness
Trailhead: To reach the WMA from I-81 at VA 91 (Glade Spring exit 29) go north on

VA 91 for 5.2 miles into Saltville. In the center of Saltville take SR 634 on the left; cross the Holston River bridge and proceed to the junction with SR 613. Turn left on SR 613, drive 4 miles to SR 747, and turn right up Tumbling Creek Road and continue 2 miles to entrance in the WMA.

Description: Cross below the dam from the parking area to the trail junction. Continue ahead up the mountain at the edge of the Black Cherry Natural Area. (The right and left trails follow the Laurel Bed Creek.) Ascend steeply for 1 mile to ridge crest (3,800 ft.), then descend on switchbacks to Little Tumbling Creek and the campground road at 2.4 miles. Backtrack, or have a car waiting. It is 1.5 miles, left, on the road to the campground.

USGS map: Saltville

658   **Red Branch Trail**
Length and Difficulty: 8.4 miles (13.4 km) round-trip; moderate to strenuous
Features: wildlife, scenic wildflowers, seclusion
Trailhead: After entering the WMA on SR 747, park at the trout holding pond.
Description: Begin on the western side of the road and follow up the hollow. Ascend gradually, then enter the Red Branch Hollow at 2.6 miles. Follow Red Branch, steep in places, for another 1.6 miles to the edge of the WMA boundary. Directly west is the top of Beartown Mountain (4,700 ft.). Remote and rugged, hikers may wish to hike to the top of the mountain to see a number of plant species, including red spruce, normally found much farther north or on higher elevations. Backtrack.

USGS map: Saltville
Address and Information: Clinch Mountain WMA, Rt. 2, Box 569, Saltville, VA 24370; phone: 703-944-3434.

GOSHEN/LITTLE NORTH MOUNTAIN
WILDLIFE MANAGEMENT AREA
Rockbridge and Augusta Counties

The Goshen WMA to the south, the Little North Mountain WMA to the north, and Goshen Pass Natural Area in between form a 34,000-acre tract of state-owned land stretching 35 miles from White Rock Mountain west of Lexington to Buffalo Gap west of Staunton. A scenic area of sandstone and limestone, rugged mountain terrain, and an abundant variety of flora and fauna, this large forest offers hikers alluring trails and roads for solitude and scenic views. Some trails are unnamed. An example is a trail network across the Goshen Pass swinging footbridge. Trails meander to an overlook of the river and outside the Goshen Pass Natural Area to a BSA camp at Lake Merriweather and up to the ridgetop of Little North Mountain WMA. There are at least eight campsites on the named trails. (See introduction to this chapter for information on camping and opening of gated roads.) In addition to hunting in the WMAs, there is fishing, canoeing, and kayaking in the white water of the Maury River.

Access to Goshen Pass Area: From I-81 exit 195, at junction of US 11 north of Lexington, take US 11 north for 1 mile to junction with SR 716 west, and turn left. Go under I-81 on SR 716 and proceed 3.5 miles to VA 39. Turn right on VA 39 and go 6.4 miles to Laurel Run Picnic Area in Goshen Pass by the Maury River. (Goshen Pass swinging bridge is 1.7 mi. farther upriver on the right.)

Access to Little North Mountain Area: See trailhead access below.

Laurel Run Trail

659

Length and Difficulty: 4.2 miles (6.7 km) round-trip; moderate
Features: cascades, rhododendron groves
Trailhead: In Goshen Pass at the junction of the stream, Laurel Run, and VA 39, a few yards downriver from the picnic area
Description: After parking at the Laurel Run Picnic Area, cross the road and walk downriver to a gated hunter's 4WD road on the right by the stream. Ascend on the road by a tumbling creek in a channel of rosebay rhododendron, oaks, maples, hemlock, and witch hazel to the end of the road at 2.1 miles. Backtrack.
USGS map: Goshen

Guy's Run Trail (4.2 mi.), Piney Mountain Trail (2 mi.), Meadow Ground Trail (2.1 mi.)

660–62

Length and Difficulty: 23.6 miles (37.6 km) combined, round-trip; moderate to strenuous
Features: streams, scenic views, wildlife, seclusion
Trailhead: From Laurel Run Picnic Area drive upriver on VA 39 for 3.3 miles to Guy's Run Access Road and entrance gate on the left (0.6 mi. beyond junction with SR 601). (The gated small roads across the road from a parking area at SR 601 are not on WMA property.)
Description: If camping on this potentially long hike, use care that vehicles do not block access roads. Begin *Guy's Run Trail* at the gated road from the parking area. At 2 miles an old road extends left. (It crosses the stream, traverses Forge Mountain, and crosses other tributaries for about 1.5 mi. to the bluffs over the Maury River and Goshen Pass. Backtrack to *Guy's Run Trail*.)

Continue upstream among hardwoods, hemlock, and rhododendron. At 2.3 miles meet the *Piney Mountain Trail* on the right. (It leads steeply right of Piney Branch for 2 mi. to the top of Bratton Mountain [3,000 ft.].) Backtrack to *Guy's Run Trail* and continue upstream along Guy's Run. Ford the stream several times and observe the potential campsites on the way. At 4.2 miles the *Meadow Ground Trail* and a campsite are on the right at a trail fork. The right fork leads 2.1 miles to the top of a beautiful mountain gap called the Mohla Loop, 6.3 miles from VA 39. Backtrack. The left fork steadily ascends east on ridges, makes a junction with SR 627 on the southern side of Coopers Knob, and ascends steeply to Big Butt (4,400 ft.). Here is the site of a former fire tower. Backtrack 7.8 miles to VA 39 (except during the seasons when the gates are open).
USGS maps: Goshen, Millboro

663　Little North Mountain Trail

Length and Difficulty: 12.8 miles (20.5 km); moderate

Features: wildlife, scenic views, geological formations, wildflowers

Trailheads: To reach the southern trailhead from Guy's Run access area on VA 39, drive northeast on SR 601 across the bridge of Calfpasture River. Follow SR 601 for 11.2 miles to a junction with SR 682 and turn right. Ascend on SR 682 for another 3.8 miles to TV/radio relay towers and trailhead. If approaching from Augusta Springs, turn off VA 42 on SR 811, go 0.3 miles, and turn left on SR 601. Follow SR 601 3.9 miles to SR 682.

For the northern trailhead on VA 42, drive southeast 2.2 miles from the junction of VA 254 and VA 42 in Buffalo Springs (9 mi. west of Staunton on VA 254). On the left of the highway is a trail sign; on the right side of the highway is roadside parking. (It is 6 mi. southwest on VA 42 to Augusta Springs.)

Description: (It is recommended that this trail be hiked from southwest to northeast. Contact the WMA office before hiking and inquire about any changes, trail route closures, or relocations.) Wildlife on the mountain includes bear, deer, grouse, and turkey. From near the TV/radio relay towers, go north 450 feet to an old woods road on the left and follow the ridge. (There may or may not be white blazes, and the trail may be overgrown in sections.) West are views of Little Calfpasture River and Elliott Knob on the Great North Mountain range. Views to the east are of dairy farms in the Shenandoah Valley and the Blue Ridge Mountains farther east. (Blazes may disappear after about 2 mi.) Descend to cross SR 603 after a forest gate at Pond Gap (and near the wildlife boundary) at 4.8 miles.

Pass under a power line and descend to Jackson Hunter Access Road at 5.5 miles. Turn right and ascend to Pig Path Gap, a scenic area. Continue ascending on the road and turn right on a foot trail at 8.1 miles. At 8.7 miles is a trickling stream (which may be dry in the summer). Ascend, follow the ridge, and descend to King Mountain Gap at 10 miles. (Ignore white or colored blazes to the left or right.) Ascend on a fire road and follow it for 1.7 miles to an overgrown foot trail on the left. Descend steeply and cross a small stream at 12.2 miles. Reach the C&O Railroad at 12.4 miles at a signal box. (Some of the trains that pass through here have retained those lonesome steam-whistle type sounds, fitting for the backcountry.) Turn left on the railroad track and follow it to an old woods road on the right. Turn right and descend about 150 yards to the trailhead sign at 12.8 miles. Backtrack, or have a second vehicle waiting.

USGS maps: Goshen, Augusta Springs, Churchville

Address and Information: Goshen/Little North Mountain WMA, 50 Lori Lane, Churchville, VA 24421; phone: 703-248-9360.

HIDDEN VALLEY WILDLIFE MANAGEMENT AREA
Washington County

Hidden Valley WMA is a scenic, high mountain area, excellent for hiking. It has a 60-acre lake nestled in the headwaters of Brumley Creek (3,600 ft.) and filled with trout. Except during hunting season, few people are seen on the trails. Camping is permitted around the lake. The lake has a boat ramp.

Brumley Creek Trail (3 mi.), **Long Arm Hollow Trail** (2.5 mi.), **Brumley Rim Trail** (4.7 mi.)   664–66

Length and Difficulty: 9.5 miles (15.2 km) combined, round-trip; easy to strenuous
Features: lake, stream, wildlife, serenity
Trailhead: In Abingdon take US 19/58A northwest for 10.3 miles to SR 690, right, and go 2 miles up a steep but paved road to Hidden Valley and lake parking area.
Description: If hiking the *Brumley Creek Trail* from the parking area by the lake, follow the trail to the end of the lake, pass the dam, and take the trail to the left at the fork. (The *Long Arm Hollow Trail* goes right.) Follow downstream through oak, hickory, maple, birch, locust, cherry, and hemlock to a junction at 2.3 miles, right, with the *Brumley Rim Trail*. Continue ahead to a connection with Little Brumley Creek at 3 miles, and a picturesque waterfall on the left. Backtrack to the lake or take the *Brumley Rim Trail* for a loop.

For the *Long Arm Hollow Trail*, from the parking lot follow the trail to the dam and take the right fork below the dam. Ascend, following the creek, for 2.5 miles to the ridge top. Several trails converge. (The trail to the right runs to an FAA tower at 0.5 mi. Farther ahead the trail descends for another 1.3 mi. to the entrance road, and from there it takes a right and goes 1 mi. back to the parking area.) The *Brumley Rim Trail* turns left, following the ridge for 3 miles. Turn left at trail junction and descend to Stagger Hollow for 1.7 miles. When you reach the *Brumley Creek Trail*, turn left and, after another 2.3 miles, return to the parking area. (A number of other unnamed trails descend from the *Brumley Rim Trail* toward Poor Valley; if hikers are unfamiliar with the area, topographical maps are advised.)
USGS map: Brumley

HIGHLAND WILDLIFE MANAGEMENT AREA
Highland County

The Highland WMA encompasses some of the best high mountain land in this remote corner of the state. The 14,284 acres are divided into two large tracts, plus a smaller one. The largest tract lies on Jack Mountain and includes 4,400-foot Sounding Knob, the best-known landmark in the county. The mountaintop includes a grazed open area, maintaining a bald appearance. The other large tract is scenic Bullpasture Mountain, bordering the edge of Bath County and the Bullpasture Gorge.

Access to Sounding Knob: From Staunton take US 250 west to McDowell, and after 2 miles turn left on SR 615. Continue on SR 615 to the *CCC Fire Trail* shortly beyond Davis Run.

Access to Bullpasture Mountain: Take US 250 to McDowell and turn left on SR 678 to the Bullpasture Gorge parking area. From the south, take VA 39 from I-81 north of Lexington; from VA 39 take SR 625 to Williamsville, then SR 678 through Bullpasture Gorge to the parking area.

667   **CCC Fire Trail**
Length and Difficulty: 10 miles (16 km) round-trip; strenuous
Features: Sounding Knob, scenic views, wildlife
Trailhead: See above for Sounding Knob.
Description: This fire road is open to motor traffic only during hunting seasons, but it is open to hikers year round. Follow on left of Davis Run for 1 mile. (At this point a 2-mi. exceptionally steep trail leads left, ascending to the western slope of Buck Hill and into remote Jack Mountain.) Continue on the road to a gap in the ridge; turn right, following the ridge (a private road comes in from the left side of the mountain), and go north to Sounding Knob. As the road skirts the knob, take a side trail to the left at 1 mile from the gap, ascending steeply to the knob. Return and continue to WMA boundary at 5 miles. Backtrack.
USGS maps: Monterey southeast, Williamsville

668   **Bullpasture Mountain Trail**
Length and Difficulty: 7 miles (11.2 km) round-trip; moderate
Features: wildlife, stream, seclusion
Trailhead: See above for Bullpasture Mountain.
Description: In the Bullpasture Gorge explore this area by crossing the river from the parking area and following the gated trail along the river and up the mountain. At 2 miles an optional trail to the right leads up a hollow to the top of Bullpasture Mountain and, at approximately 2 miles, to SR 614 on the other side. Back on the *Bullpasture Mountain Trail*, at 3.5 miles another trail on the left leads across the mountain, also connecting with SR 614. It roughly parallels the other trail for approximately 2.5 miles. Backtrack (unless crossing the mountain for vehicle shuttle at SR 612, 613, or 614).
USGS maps: Monterey Southeast, Williamsville
Address and Information: Highland WMA, HC03, Box 70, Monterey, VA 24465; phone: 703-468-2419.

HOG ISLAND WILDLIFE REFUGE
Surry and Isle of Wight Counties

Acquired in 1953, the 3,200 acres of Hog Island have become one of the prime waterfowl areas along the James River. In recent years some 10,000 Canada geese and 15,000 ducks have been on the refuge at peak times, plus herons, egrets, and dozens of other species. The waterfowl benefit from an intensive management program of the Virginia Game Commission. The controlled ponds are drained in the spring, and millet is grown through the summer. As the fall waterfowl migration starts, the areas are flooded. The spectacle of birds coming in to feed in the refuge is impressive. Woodlands in the area are chiefly loblolly pine. Hiking in this area is allowed only during the daytime; no camping.

Access: From VA 10 at Bacon's Castle, take SR 650 to entrance gate, having passed VEPCO's Surry nuclear power plant and the Carlisle Tract on the right.

There are at least four loop trails, with parking areas at the beginning of each. The first trail reached on the refuge road leads a short distance—0.3 miles—into the woods. The loops are 1.7 miles, 3 miles, 4.2 miles, and 3.2 miles, in combinations of trails around the lakes. Also, at the refuge headquarters, a 0.6-mile trail extends northwest to the edge of the James River. All the trails are unnamed.

Address and Information: Hog Island WMA, RFD, Surry, VA 23883; phone: 804-357-5224.

POWHATAN WILDLIFE MANAGEMENT AREA
Powhatan County

This 4,415-acre tract 30 miles west of Richmond, on the rolling central piedmont plateau, is ideal for the hiker. Dispersion is easy with thirteen trails dipping into copses, winding around lazy brooks, and rising on gentle ridge crests. The area is 75 percent forest, with fields near the six stocked lakes. Hunting for turkey, dove, and quail is popular. Bluegill, bass, and catfish are in the lakes. Powhatan Lakes, two of the WMA's largest, are north of US 60 with entry on SR 625. Around the perimeter of the southern tract, between US 60 and VA 13, are seven access points at which to park and begin the trails. Short to long circuits can be made on the trails. A few need to be backtracked. The combination described below includes all the trails.

Access: For main access point drive 1.5 miles south of US 60 on SR 627 (4 mi. west of US 60/522 junction), then turn left and go 0.5 miles to parking area on Deer Lane, SR 622.

Fescue Trail (2.1 mi.), **Squirrel Ridge Trail** (0.4 mi.), **Nature Trail** (0.6 mi.), **Arrowhead Trail** (2.8 mi.), **Holly Trail** (0.7 mi.), **Pine Trail** (1.1 mi.), **CCC Trail** (1.5 mi.), **Dogwood Trail** (1.5 mi.), **Franklin Trail** (0.6 mi.), **Red Bud Trail** (0.4 mi.), **White Oak Trail** (0.7 mi.), **Red Oak Trail** (0.6 mi.), **Power Line Trail** (0.8 mi.)   669–81

Length and Difficulty: 15.6 miles (25 km) combined, partial round-trip; easy
Features: wildlife, stream, wildflowers
Trailhead: See main entrance to WMA at end of description.
Description: No trails are blazed, and some are not marked by signs. The *Fescue Trail* trailhead is on the left, 0.25 miles after entry on SR 622, Deer Lane. This trail runs 0.7 miles to a crossing of Sallee Creek, making a junction at 1.7 miles with the *CCC Trail* and ending at Salmon Creek at 2.1 miles. Backtrack, or turn left on the return at the *CCC Trail* for connections to other trails in making a loop. Begin this labyrinth of trails by descending from the parking area between the two lakes, right. Follow grassy open space to a stand of large oaks on a knoll on the left. (Grassy road to right goes 0.5 mi. to parking area across the road, SR 627, from the Cozy Acres Campground.) From the knoll on the *Squirrel Ridge Trail* descend and ascend through open area to forest road. Here is part of the

Nature Trail. After 0.4 miles meet the *Arrowhead Trail* and take the left on a wide avenue, partially open, bordered with a magnificent display of redbud. At 1.2 miles is a junction with the *Holly Trail*, which goes right.

At the junction of the *Arrowhead* and the *Holly* trails, there are three options. The shortest is to go left on the *Arrowhead*, bearing left at the clearing near Sunfish Pond; cross the dam at 1.4 miles among fennel, sumac, and alder; and follow the *Pine Trail* to parking area for a loop of 2.1 miles.

Option two is to follow the *Arrowhead Trail* east, without taking the shortcut to the lake. This route will cross Sallee Creek, reach a junction with the *CCC Trail* at 1 mile, and offer two choices of a loop back to the parking area. If turning right on the *CCC Trail*, go 0.5 miles to the *Dogwood Trail*, take another right for 0.8 miles, and turn right again at the junction with the *Holly Trail*. From this junction go another 0.8 miles back to the *Arrowhead*, follow the directions across the dam, and return to the parking area for a total of 5.2 miles. Or, if turning left on the *CCC Trail*, the hiker can follow for 1.1 miles to a junction of the *Fescue Trail*. Turn left here and return to parking area on the *Fescue Trail* for a total of 5.5 miles.

For the third option for routes from the junction of the *Holly Trail* and the *Arrowhead Trail*, bear right on the *Holly Trail*, and go 0.8 miles to a junction with the *Dogwood Trail*. Turn left, cross Sallee Creek, pass the *Franklin Trail* on the right, and reach a fire road after another 0.8 miles. (To the right is an access road and the game-manager residence, and to the left is access to the *CCC Trail* and the short *Redbud Trail*.) Continue straight ahead across the fire road, entering on the *White Oak Trail*, which after 0.7 miles becomes the *Red Oak Trail*. Follow the *Red Oak Trail* for 0.6 miles to another fire road, and turn left on the *Arrowhead Trail*. Follow the *Arrowhead Trail* straight west to its original junction with the *Holly Trail* (crossing only the *CCC Trail*) for 1.8 miles. Backtrack, or go right across the Sunfish Pond and turn left on the *Pine Trail* to the parking area at the original trailhead. Total loop is 6 miles. (The *Power Line Trail* extends from a parking area on SR 601, 0.5 mi. from the junction of US 60 and SR 684.) Combined mileage of all options is 15.6 miles. No camping on these trails.

Access: For the main access point, drive 1.5 miles south of US 60 on SR 627 (4 mi. west of US 60/522 junction), then turn left and go 0.5 miles to parking area on SR 622 (Deer Lane).

Address and Information: Powhatan WMA, HC06, Box 46, Farmville, VA 23901; phone: 804-367-1000

RAPIDAN WILDLIFE MANAGEMENT AREA
Greene and Madison Counties

The 9,000-acre Rapidan WMA has eight separate tracts, chiefly in Madison County north of Standardsville and approximately 25 miles southwest of Culpepper. Four of the parcels are mortised into the Shenandoah National Park, with Fork, Doubletop, and Bluff Mountains being the most popular for hiking. It is a scenic, rugged, and forested area, and the Rapidan River cascades between two parcels of the WMA. Near its beginning is the confluence of Mill Prong and Laurel Prong. The major trails originate in the Shenandoah National Park. (For descriptions of the *Staunton River Trail*, the *Jones Mountain Trail*, the *Laurel Prong Trail*, the *Doubletop Mountain Trail*, and fire roads, consult the *Shenandoah National Park Appalachian Trail Guide*, published by the PATC, 118 Park St., SE, Vienna, VA 22180; phone: 703-242-0315.) Also, see Chapter 5 in this guide. Other recreation in the WMA is fishing for brook trout and hunting for bear, deer, and wild turkey.

Access to the Rapidan River Area: From Criglersville take SR 670 1 mile to SR 649, turning left. Go for 3 miles to Shenandoah National Park boundary, and continue to a junction with SR 622; turn right, following SR 622 up the river.

Address and Information: Rapidan WMA, 1320 Belman Rd., Fredericksburg, VA 22401; phone: 703-899-4169.

11 : Parklands

Peace is here in every season
a quiet beauty.
The sky falling about me
evenly to the compass . . .
—Anne Spencer

Virginia's park system was created in 1936 for the purpose of managing and protecting diverse land and water resources and cultural history, and to offer the public a natural environment for outdoor recreation. From the original six to the forty parks, historic sites, and natural areas of today, the natural legacy remains strong. Virginians voted their approval of the park system in 1993 when they passed a $93 million bond referendum to acquire four more parks and ten natural areas. In addition, existing parks are slated to receive renovations and improvement of facilities. The 65,000-acre park system is administered by the Division of State Parks, which has four division branches: information, administration and management, maintenance and operation, and design and construction. As a unit it is part of the Department of Conservation and Recreation. To catalog the parks geographically, the division lists them in Mountain, Piedmont, and Coastal regions. They are described in that order, alphabetically, in this chapter.

In 1994 the state had forty-two public parks and natural areas (and more in planning and construction stages) with varied titles: thirty parks (of which four are historical parks and one is both a park and a natural area), one museum, one WMA, and ten natural areas. Nine of the properties do not have trails. Among the developing natural areas are Bethel Beach, Bush Mill Stream, North Landing River, Pinnacle, and Poor Mountain.

Bethel Beach Natural Area (50 acres) is in Mathews County and is an excellent place for birding (90 species) at a beach, dune, and marsh area. Access is off VA 14 at Port Haywood onto SR 608 and to SR 609. Follow the latter road 4.8 miles to the beach and along the northern boundary of Winter Harbor. Call 804-786-7951 for information.

Bush Mill Stream Natural Area (110 acres) is developing 0.6-mile *Deep Landing Trail* near a tidal area where the stream empties into Great Wicomico River. Access is off VA 201 on SR 642, about 0.6 miles east of the Howland intersection. Call 804-786-7951 for information.

North Landing River Natural Area (1,886 acres) has a short interpretive trail into a pocosin and freshwater tidal marsh in Virginia Beach. Access is on the eastern side of Blackwater Road about 1 mile north of the Pungo Ferry Road intersection. Call 804-786-7951 for information.

Pinnacle Natural Area Preserve is developing a network of signed trails that ascend from the parking lot to the top of Cooper Ridge. The 68-acre tract was formerly owned by the Nature Conservancy, and trails, including the *Cooper Ridge Trail*, were developed by the YACC to Big Falls and scenic overlooks in 1978. Spectacular views are of the Pinnacle, east, and the Clinch River area, north. Access from Lebanon in Russell County is 1 mile north on VA 82 to follow SR 640, right, for 4.4 miles to a left turn on SR 721. After 1 mile is the low-water bridge of Big Cedar Creek. Call Hungry Mother State Park (703-783-3422) for information.

Another natural area is being developed on Poor Mountain in Roanoke County. It is accessible on Poor Mountain Road from US 11/460 at Glenvar. Call 804-786-7951 for information.

Because of the diverse locations of the parklands, hikers can choose parks with trail networks at high elevations, such as Grayson Highlands, or near sea level, such as Seashore State Park and Natural Area. Among primitive and remote areas are Clinch Mountain deep in the Appalachian range and False Cape at the Atlantic Ocean. Trail features and other facilities are described here, but some details about fees for campgrounds; swimming pools; boat, horse, or bicycle rentals; and picnic shelter or cabin reservations are not listed because of unpredictable changes. All fees are low or moderate, with cabin rentals being the most expensive. For cabin and campground reservation applications and fee information, call park headquarters or campgrounds for a brochure titled "Reservations and Fees Guide." The park system has used Ticketron or Ticketmaster for reservations, but in the future each park may be responsible for its own rentals. If in doubt, call the park office.

Here are a few introductory facts about the parks. Camping rates are nightly, and cabin rates are weekly, except at Westmoreland, which has both nightly and weekly rates for camping and cabin rentals. No firearms or alcohol are allowed. Pets must be on leashes, but they are allowed in cabins and campgrounds. Fishing permits, according to state law, are required for individuals over age sixteen. No wildlife or plant life can be removed from the parks, and no hunting is allowed except at specific parks were there is an overpopulation (False Cape is an example).

Lodges are at Breaks Interstate and Douthat; cabins are at Claytor Lake, Douthat, Fairy Stone, Hungry Mother, Seashore, Staunton River, and Westmoreland. Parks with electrical and water hookups at campgrounds are Bear Creek, Claytor Lake, Fairy Stone, Hungry Mother, Kiptopeke, Occoneechee, and Westmoreland (with the bond referendum, expect more to have these services). Campgrounds with all other services are at Douthat, Grayson Highlands, Natural Tunnel, Twin Lakes, Holliday Lake, Pocahontas, Staunton, and Seashore. False Cape and Sky Meadows have primitive campgrounds year round. False Cape is the only park where motorized vehicles are prohibited (walk in for 3.5 mi. or travel 6 mi. by boat). Seven parks have environmental education centers: Douthat, Sky Meadows, Smith Mountain, False Cape, Mason Neck, Seashore, and York. Group use facilities with overnight conference rooms and accommodations are at Twin Lakes' Cedar Crest Center and Hungry Mother's Hemlock Haven Conference Center. Groups conducting environmental education or research are at False Cape's Wash Woods Environmental Education Center. Five parks have restaurants: Breaks Interstate, Douthat, Hungry Mother, Fairy Stone, and Westmoreland. Twin Lakes and Pocahontas have organized group cabins and camps. Group camping is at Breaks Interstate, Douthat, Pocahontas, Staunton, Seashore, and Westmoreland.

Almost all the parks have a foot trail system. Those with bridle trails are Claytor

Lake, Grayson Highlands, Hungry Mother (may be the only one with horse rentals), Shot Tower/New River, Sky Meadows, Westmoreland, and York. Bicycle trails are at Breaks Interstate, Shot Tower/New River, Fairy Stone, Twin Lakes, Pocahontas (with rentals), Chippokes Plantation (with rentals), False Cape, Seashore (with rentals), and York. There are 307 miles of hiking trails, 24 miles of self-guiding trails, 93 miles of bridle trails, 87 miles of bicycle trails, and 39 miles for the physically handicapped. Some parks are expanding their trail systems, and others have trails in the planning stage. Most of the natural areas do not have named trails, but Caledon is an exception. Natural areas are for day use only; an inquiry should be made to the Richmond office for updated information on new areas.

Address and Information: Virginia State Parks, 203 Governor St., Suite 306, Richmond, VA 23219; phone: 804-786-1712. Available are brochures, leaflets, and a booklet, *Virginia State Parks*. For Division of Planning and Recreation Resources, phone 804-786-2556.

Mountain Division

BREAKS INTERSTATE PARK
Dickenson County

In 1954 the 4,500-acre Breaks Interstate Park was created by joint action of the Kentucky and Virginia legislatures to protect controlled areas of natural beauty and to open them for recreational use. An allotment of land with legend, history, and spectacular scenery, the park also has complete facilities. Among them are an Olympic-size swimming pool; forest campsites with full services; grounds designated for picnicking, hiking, and bridle trails; cabins; a motor lodge; a restaurant; a visitor center with exhibits; and a playground. One area is for horseback riding. Other activities include fishing and nature studies. Some of the facilities and activities are open year round, but the regular schedule is from Memorial Day to Labor Day. The Russell Fork River has carved out what is often called the "Grand Canyon of the South," a 1,600-foot-deep gorge extending 5 miles, leaving the "Towers"—natural sandstone skyscrapers. All trails are marked and blazed. The forest is chiefly hardwoods, with abundant wildflowers, ferns, lichens, and mosses on the forest floor.

Access: From Haysi in Virginia take VA 80 north for 8 miles and turn left to entrance. From Elkhorn in Kentucky take KY 15, then VA 80 for 7 miles to entrance on right.

Ridge Trail (0.5 mi.), **Geological Trail** (0.4 mi.), **Grassy Overlook Trail** (0.5 mi.), **Overlook Trail** (0.7 mi.), **Towers Trail** (0.2 mi.), **Tower Tunnel Trail** (0.2 mi.)

684–89

Length and Difficulty: 5.2 miles (8.3 km) combined, round-trip; easy
Trailhead: Any of the overlook parking areas
Description: All of these are blazed rim trails designed to provide scenic views of

the canyon's river, rock formations, faults, and vegetation. They can be interconnected among themselves and with the following two sets of trails. Some of the trails must be backtracked. For an educational tour make a ridge loop with the *Geological Trail*, with information about trees, shrubs, wildflowers, rock outcrops, caves, fossils, rock faults, and rock formations.

USGS map: Elkhorn City

Center Creek Trail (0.4 mi.), **Grassy Creek Trail** (0.5 mi.), **Laurel Branch Trail** (1.3 mi.), **Loop Trail** (0.4 mi.), **Prospectors Trail** (1.5 mi.), **River Trail** (1 mi.)   690–95

Length and Difficulty: 9.1 miles (14.6 km) combined, round-trip; moderate to strenuous

Trailhead: At the visitor center, or Stateline Overlook parking areas, or at Tower Tunnel parking

Description: Each of the three trailheads offers connection to any of these trails. It is recommended the hiker secure a trail map from the visitor center. On descent, parts of the trails are steep; exceptions are part of the *Laurel Branch Trail* and the *Loop Trail*. The following is a challenging loop trail arrangement: Park at the Stateline Overlook, hike the *Ridge Trail* for 0.5 miles to the Notches, descend for a few yards to the *Prospectors Trail*, make a left turn on it and go another 0.8 miles. Turn right on the exceptionally steep *River Trail*, and descend for another 0.3 miles. Turn right, following the riverbank for 0.3 miles to the confluence of the Russell River and Grassy Creek. Turn right, ascend slightly, and reach the *Laurel Branch Trail* 0.4 miles farther. (The *Center Creek Trail* turns left here to the Center Creek Picnic Area.) Turn right; ascend steeply for 0.5 miles to the Notches. From here turn right on the *Geological Trail* for 0.4 miles to the Stateline Overlook for a total loop of 3.2 miles. Distance for all trails combined is 9.1 miles.

USGS map: Elkhorn City

Lake Trail (0.5 mi.), **Cold Spring Trail** (0.4 mi.)   696–97

Length and Difficulty: 2 miles (3.2 km) combined, round-trip; easy

Trailhead: Visitor center parking area

Description: These trails connect and provide entry to the Laurel Lake area, which has a swimming pool, or connect via the *Laurel Branch Trail* with the other trails in the two preceding entries. The *Cold Spring Trail* may be wet and rocky.

USGS map: Elkhorn City

Deer Trail (0.4 mi.), **Beaver Trail** (0.3 mi.)   698–99

Length and Difficulty: 1.1 miles (2.7 km) combined, round-trip; easy

Trailhead: Parking area near cottages

Description: Begin on the *Deer Trail* at the grassy shoulder of the parking lot. Descend into the forest of hardwoods, filberts, and running cedar. Join the *Beaver Trail* at the lake for a circuit and backtrack.

USGS map: Elkhorn City

Address and Information: Breaks Interstate Park, Breaks, VA 24607; phone: 703-865-4413

CLAYTOR LAKE STATE PARK
Pulaski County

Claytor Lake State Park, established in 1948, has 472 acres, of which 350 acres are wooded. The park is located on a portion of the 4,500-acre Claytor Lake. Activities and facilities include boating, water skiing, and fishing from a modern marina; swimming at a sand beach with bathhouse; and camping with full services, or in vacation cabins. Other activities include nature study, horseback riding, picnicking, and hiking.

Access: From exit 101 on I-81 between the towns of Radford and Dublin, take SR 660 southeast for 2 miles to the park entrance.

700   **Claytor Lake Trail**
Length and Difficulty: 1.6 miles (2.6 km); easy
Trailhead: Marina parking area
Description: The blue-blazed trail begins at the woodline across the road from the
  marina parking lot. Look for the trailhead display. The trail passes through a
  mixed hardwood and pine forest and offers several views of Claytor Lake.
  Return to the starting point through a portion of the campground. Vegetation
  includes pine, sycamore, yellow poplar, locust, oak, and hickory.
USGS map: Dublin

701   **Shady Ridge Trail**
Length and Difficulty: 0.6 miles (0.9 km); easy
Trailhead: Picnic area parking lot
Description: This is a self-guiding, interpretive trail with eight posts keyed to the
  brochure rack at the beginning of the trail. Ascend steeply at first; after forking
  for a loop at the ridge crest, the wide trail is easy. There is an exposure to the
  history of the area, ecology, flora and fauna, and lichens and mosses. Among
  the birds is the eastern phoebe.
USGS map: Dublin
Address and Information: Claytor Lake State Park, Rt. 1, Box 267, Dublin, VA 24084;
  phone: 703-674-5492. Available are brochures of the park and of the *Shady
  Ridge Trail.*

DOUTHAT STATE PARK
Bath and Alleghany Counties

Deep in the Allegheny Mountains, Douthat State Park has 4,493 acres of scenic high ridges, more miles of hiking trails than any of the state's other parks, and a 50-acre lake stocked with trout. Its facilities include a visitor center with exhibits, a restaurant, a camp store, vacation cabins, and a swimming beach with bathhouse.

Activities include boating, fishing, picnicking, camping, nature study, and hiking. Trails are color coded and generally in good condition. A hiking map from the visitor center is recommended for long hikes. The campgrounds are open from the Monday nearest April 1 to the Monday nearest December 1.

There are 24 trails, ranging in length from 0.3 miles to 4.5 miles, in the park system. Most of these are clustered near Douthat Lake, where they connect for circuits. For example, use 1 mile of the *YCC Trail* (which parallels the highway and lake) and a spur across the road to include 1.2 miles of the *Wilson Creek Trail* for a loop of 2.4 miles to the visitor center and back. Or make a circuit from campground A or B with the *Backway Hollow Trail* to join the *Huff's Trail* at 0.4 miles or 0.7 miles. Then swing onto the mountainside with the *Laurel View Trail* to include a slice of the *Blue Suck Trail* for a loop of 4.5 miles or 5.2 miles, depending on which campground was the starting point. This could be extended by using the *Middle Hollow Trail* and the *Pine Tree Trail*. A short walk on the *Heron Run Trail* for about 0.7 miles is popular for views of the western side of the lake. Another short trail, the 0.3-mile *Buck Lick Interpretive Trail*, is on the eastern side of the lake near the restaurant. It has markers about geology, forest succession, and flora and fauna. Whether choosing a single trail or a combination, hikers will find the park's network to be scenic and worthwhile. Described below are two circuit hikes that extend to the most remote and challenging areas of the park. For hikers who wish backpacking excursions into the adjoining GWNF from these circuits, see Warm Springs Ranger District in Chapter 2. 702–7

Access: From Clifton Forge at the junction of I-64@/US 60 and SR 629, go north 5.5 miles on SR 629 to the visitor center.

Stony Run Trail (4.5 mi.), **Tuscarora Overlook Trail** (0.9 mi.),
Middle Mountain Trail (2 mi.), **Salt Stump Trail** (2.5 mi.),
Backway Hollow Trail (0.9 mi.), **Huffs Trail** (1.2 mi.), **Blue Suck Trail** (3 mi.) 708–16
Length and Difficulty: 15 miles (24 km) combined, round-trip; moderate to strenuous
Features: wildlife, scenic views, geological formations
Trailhead: Visitor center
Description: These trails are on the western side of Wilson Creek, forming a connecting system for a long loop that ascends to Middle Mountain Ridge (and a network of trails in the GWNF) and descends on the northern end of the park, where connecting trails south provide a return to the campgrounds and visitor center.

Begin from the visitor center, hiking down the road 0.5 miles to the trailhead for orange-blazed *Stony Run Trail* on the right. (Or take the *Beards Gap Hollow Trail*, which is closer to the visitor center.) Ascend; at 1.4 miles pass a junction with the *Locust Gap Trail* on the right. Continue ahead for another 1.1 miles to Stony Run Falls on the left. For the next 2 miles ascend on switchbacks to a junction with the *Middle Mountain Trail* and the yellow-blazed *Tuscarora Overlook Trail* at 4.5 miles. Take the right fork on the *Tuscarora Overlook Trail* to a scenic view at 5 miles. At 5.9 miles make a sharp left turn, and after a few yards make a sharp turn right to be on the white-blazed *Middle Mountain Trail*. (A right turn at the 5.9-mi. junction, on the *Blue Suck Trail*, leads down the mountain for 3 mi. to the visitor center.)

Follow the ridge trail to the edge of the park boundary at 7.7 miles to begin the *Salt Stump Trail*. Descend, passing the *Pine Tree Trail* on the right at 8.7 miles, and reach the *Backway Hollow Trail* on the right at 10.3 miles. (A second vehicle could be arranged near here at the campground.) Follow the *Backway Hollow Trail* for 0.7 miles to the junction on the right with the *Huffs Trail*. Take the *Huffs Trail*, passing the *Laurel View Trail* on the right and then the *Middle Hollow Trail* intersection, and reach the *Blue Suck Trail* at 12.2 miles. Turn left on the *Blue Suck Trail*, pass the *Tobacco House Ridge Trail* on the right and then the group camping area, and return to the visitor center at 13.1 miles. Forest cover along the trails is chiefly hemlock, oak, Virginia pine, white pine, poplar, maple, beech, and birch. Some of the understory is redbud, dogwood, sassafras, mountain laurel, rhododendron, buckberry, and sourwood. Wildflowers and berries are plentiful.

USGS map: Healing Spring

Brushy Hollow Trail (3.5 mi.), **Mountain Top Trail** (2.3 mi.),
717–23 **Ross Camp Hollow Trail** (0.8 mi.), **Wilson Creek Trail** (1.4 mi.)
Length and Difficulty: 8 miles (12.8 km) combined, round-trip; easy to strenuous
Features: stream, scenic views, wildlife, wildflowers
Trailhead: Visitor center parking area
Description: These trail combinations are on the eastern side of Wilson Creek. Use a vehicle to the trailhead for the *Brushy Hollow Trail* near Wilson Creek. Inquire of trail adviser at the visitor center for the best area in which to park, as space is limited. Hikers must ford the creek (actually a river; if the water is high, a better route would be to take the *Beards Gap Trail* from the visitor center).

Begin the trail across Wilson Creek, and after 1 mile begin a long series of switchbacks northeast and north extending to a junction with the *Beards Gap Trail* on the left at 3.2 miles. (The *Beards Gap Trail* descends steeply for 1.1 mi. to the visitor center.) Continue ahead, passing excellent overlooks west into the Wilson Creek valley. At 3.5 miles pass a junction on the left with the *Buck Hollow Trail*, which has an outstanding overlook 0.5 miles west on its 1-mile descent to the *Wilson Creek Trail*. Continue ahead a few yards to a junction with the *Mountain Side Trail* on the left and the *Mountain Top Trail* on the right. (The *Mountain Side Trail* goes 1.4 mi. north on the western side of the slope to rejoin the *Mountain Top Trail*.) Turn right on the *Mountain Top Trail*, ascending switchbacks, and pass scenic views at 5.2 miles. Turn sharply left at park boundary and from the junction of the *Beards Mountain Trail* in the GWNF. Descend and pass a junction with the *Mountain Side Trail* on the left at 5.8 miles. At 6.6 miles, near the last rental cabin, veer right and take either the *Guest Lodge Trail* or the *Ross Camp Hollow Trail* to the *Wilson Creek Trail*. Continue on the *Wilson Creek Trail*, paralleling the park road—SR 629—and passing a picnic area and, on the right at 7.5 miles, a junction with the *Buck Lick Interpretive Trail*. Immediately beyond the junction is the *Buck Hollow Trail* on the left, mentioned previously. Continue ahead on the *Wilson Creek Trail* to the amphitheater and to the visitor center at 8 miles.

USGS map: Healing Spring

Address and Information: Douthat State Park, Rt. 1, Box 212, Millboro, VA 24460; phone: 703-862-7200

GOSHEN PASS NATURAL AREA
Rockbridge County

At one of Virginia's most scenic spots for white water, the turbulent Maury River twists and cuts its way through Goshen Pass in North Mountain. Highway 39 turns with the river, providing exciting views. Picnicking is allowed, but parking space is along the highway, and limited. At the *Laurel Run Trail* site where Laurel Run joins the Maury River, for example, vehicles should be parked so as not to block the trail or the road. The *Laurel Run Trail* is 4 miles round-trip and easy to follow. (See Goshen Wildlife Management Area, Chapter 10.) At the western end of the gorge a 150-foot suspension bridge for pedestrians crosses the Maury River on *Goshen Pass Trail* so hikers can explore the Round Mountain area. With the natural area and the WMA the state has a total of 33,000 acres in the Little North Mountain range. Adjoining national forest land adds more recreational opportunities.   724

The Maury River was named after the famous oceanographer Matthew Fontaine Maury, the first man to chart the seas of the world. He retired in Lexington, and upon his death his body was carried through Goshen Pass before burial, as he had requested, by VMI cadets.

Access: From the junction of VA 39 and VA 252 (9 mi. north of Lexington), go west on VA 39 for 5.5 miles to Goshen Pass.

Address and Information: Virginia State Parks, 203 Governor St, Suite 306, Richmond, VA 23219; phone: 804-786-1712

GRAYSON HIGHLANDS STATE PARK
Grayson County

Virginia's highest state park (5,090 ft.) is a 4,935-acre preserve amid rugged peaks of igneous rock, alpine meadows, waterfalls, and spruce-fir forests. An area of mountain grandeur, it borders the crest zone of Mount Rogers, whose mile-high peak is the center of attraction for both the state park and the adjacent Mount Rogers National Recreation Area (see Chapter 1). Solitude is easy to find in this park. Facilities in the park include campgrounds, rest rooms and hot showers, horse trails, hiking trails, and a visitor center with exhibits. Activities include hiking, hunting, horseback riding, picnicking, and nature study.

There are three loop trails at separate locations in the park. The *Rock House Ridge Trail* (1.8 mi.) is an easy route from the picnic area to an example of a pioneer homestead and cemetery. The trail follows a low saddle around a knoll and receives its name from a huge leaning shelter-type rock formation. The *Cabin Creek Trail* can be accessed from Massie Gap near the entrance to the equestrian campground. Moderate in difficulty, it descends 0.6 miles to Cabin Creek, named for pioneers who settled in the hollow. Near the base are big-toothed aspens, whose leaves are known for quivering in the breeze. At 1 mile is a 25-foot waterfall. The trail is completed on an old railroad grade after 1.9 miles. Another moderate loop is accessed from the parking area at the visitor center at the end of the highest road. The *Listening Rock Trail* descends from the parking area to Buzzard Rock and Listening Rock for views of the valley below. To complete the 1.8-mile route, return to the road and make a right to the parking area. At the parking area entrance, right, is a 200-foot trail to Wildcat Overlook (4,935 ft.), a jumble of boulders and with a magnificent view of North Carolina and Tennessee. Described below is a combination of trails, including a scenic section of the *AT*, for a remarkable

725–27 diversity of topography.

Access: On US 58 7.7 miles west from Volney and 25 miles east from Damascus to park entrance on VA 362.

Wilson Creek Trail (1.8 mi.), *AT* (4.6 mi.), **Rhododendron Trail** (0.5 mi.),
Big Pinnacle Trail (0.4 mi.), **Twin Pinnacles Trail** (1.6 mi.),
728–31 **Stampers Branch Trail** (1.7 mi.)

Length and Difficulty: 10.6 miles (17 km) combined, round-trip; easy to strenuous
Features: waterfall, grazing fields, scenic views, rock formations, wildlife, wild-
    flowers
Trailhead: Campground or Massie Gap parking area
Description: This connecting-trail arrangement is recommended for a hike of a full
    day; take a day pack with lunch, a camera, and rain gear. Park regulations
    require all hikers to be off the trails at sundown.
    From the campground follow the *Wilson Creek Trail* sign, descending to
    Wilson Creek in a forest of red maple, beech, and yellow and black birch, with
    an understory of striped maple and ferns at 0.6 miles. Follow upstream with
    cascades on right, and reach a 25-foot waterfall at 1 mile. Ash and rhodo-
    dendron decorate the area. At road junction turn sharply right, follow old
    logging road, and cross Quebec Branch at 1.3 miles. Pass through open meadow,
    reaching the *AT* near Wilson Creek at 1.7 miles. Turn left, cross stile, and follow
    white-blazed *AT* through thick grass spotted with flame azalea, mountain lau-
    rel, and large sweet blueberry bushes. Cross Quebec Branch again at 2.7 miles
    and ascend to rocky ridge crest at 3.4 miles. At 3.9 miles is a sign on the left to
    the Massie Gap parking area. Continue ahead, following an old open cattle
    road; cattle and ponies may be grazing nearby.
    Cross stile at 4.4 miles, leaving Grayson Highlands State Park. Follow the *AT*,
    veering left at fork with blue-blazed *Rhododendron Trail* at 4.5 miles. After 1.1
    miles more, come to a junction with the *Rhododendron Trail* again on a huge
    rocky peak of Wilburn Ridge. (From here it is 2 mi. on the *AT* to the summit of

Mount Rogers [5,729 ft.], Virginia's highest mountain. The summit has no view and is covered with the only spruce-fir forest in the state. Fog often surrounds its green and fragrant beauty.) Follow the blue-blazed trail right to an enormous array of boulders with a 360° view at 5.9 miles. Vegetation, stunted by strong winds, is rhododendron, mountain ash, azalea, and conifer. Descend to a junction with the *AT* at 6.8 miles, and follow the *Rhododendron Trail* to the Massie Gap sign at 7.2 miles. Continue the descent to the Massie Gap parking area at 7.7 miles.

Cross the parking area and begin the steep climb—gaining 400 feet in elevation—on the *Big Pinnacle Trail* to the summit of Big Pinnacle (5,068 ft.) at 8.1 miles. Views are spectacular, the sights including Mount Rogers and White Top Mountain (Virginia's second highest peak) and the valleys of Virginia, North Carolina, and Tennessee. Wildflowers, ferns, and lichens are abundant. From here continue through dense grass, scattered spruce, and hawthorn bushes on the *Twin Pinnacles Trail* to Little Pinnacle (5,089 ft.) for more scenic views at 8.6 miles. Descend to a junction with the *Stampers Branch Trail* at 8.9 miles and turn left, but not before a visit to the visitor center nearby. Continue descent on the *Stampers Branch Trail*, crossing main road, Stampers Branch, and Wilburn Branch, and reaching a log cabin near the campground for a complete loop of 10.6 miles.

USGS maps: Whitetop Mountain, Troutdale, Park, Grassy Creek

Address and Information: Grayson Highlands State Park, Rt. 2, Box 141, Mouth of Wilson, VA 24363; phone: 703-579-7092. Available for free are park brochure of information with map and leaflets; there is a fee for detailed map, "Mount Rogers High Country and Wildernesses."

HUNGRY MOTHER STATE PARK
Smyth County

Excellent mountain scenery, a picturesque lake, and well-planned trails make the 2,180-acre Hungry Mother State Park a popular recreation area. More than 12 miles of trails make hiking very pleasurable. The paths were largely established by the CCC in the 1930s. Most of the park is a designated natural area. Facilities include campgrounds, vacation cabins, a visitor center, and a restaurant. Hiking, horseback riding, picnicking, swimming, paddleboating, fishing, and nature study are popular activities. The park's name honors Molly Marley from a legend that she and her child escaped from Indian capture. Molly collapsed, but the child wandered downstream to a pioneer home, where the child said the mother was hungry. The search party found Molly had died.

In addition to the longer combination of trails described below, there is a double loop with the *Raider's Run Trail* (1.5 mi.) and scenic *Old Shawnee Trail* (1 mi.). Access is from the parking area between the information center and the store.

732–33

Access: Take I-81 at VA 16 into Marion. Follow the signs and proceed 3 miles north of Marion on VA 16 to the park entrance.

Molly's Pioneer Trail (0.6 mi.), **Molly's Knob Trail** (1.6 mi.), **CCC Trail** (1 mi.), **Lake Trail** (3.1 mi.), **Middle Ridge Trail** (1.1 mi.), **Ridge Trail** (0.7 mi.)

Length and Difficulty: 10.5 miles (16 km) combined, round-trip; easy to moderate

Features: scenic views, historic site, wildlife, wildflowers

Trailhead: Parking area near visitor information beyond the rental cabins

Description: All these trails connect, but backtracking is necessary to connect one to another in order to form loops. *Molly's Pioneer Trail* is a short loop of 0.6 miles, red blazed and interpretive in nature, to educate about the wild animals, trees, shrubs, and flowers. Halfway around this trail *Molly's Knob Trail* (1.6 mi.) begins. Follow *Molly's Knob Trail* to the summit (3,270 ft.) for views of Marion, Mount Rogers, and White Top Mountain to the southwest. Backtrack, or descend to a junction with the *CCC Trail*, orange blazed, for 1.1 miles to Campground D. This route requires vehicle shuttle. Another route from *Molly's Knob Trail* can be made by taking the *CCC Trail* to a junction with the *Lake Trail* (3.1 mi.) and looping back to the visitor center. Or, to make yet another loop, take the *Middle Ridge Trail* (1.1 mi.) from *Molly's Knob Trail* to the *Lake Trail*. A shorter route from Molly's Knob can be taken by picking up the *Ridge Trail* (0.7 mi.) on the left 0.8 miles from the knob and then connecting with the *Lake Trail*. Whatever the loop arrangements, a trail map from the visitor center will assist in planning and can prevent extra climbing or unexpected, long connections. Signs are posted at the intersections. Wildlife in the area includes deer, raccoon, fox, squirrel, grouse, and wild turkey. Flora includes pines—Virginia, pitch, shortleaf, and white—and the usual southern Appalachian hardwoods, with banks of wintergreen and trailing arbutus, wildflowers, ferns, and Indian pipe amid the forest-floor duff.

USGS maps: Marion, Chatham Hill

NATURAL TUNNEL STATE PARK
Scott County

The 527-acre park has a natural tunnel that William Jennings Bryant declared the eighth (natural) wonder of the world. Probably formed during the early Pleistocene epoch of at least 1 million years ago, the enormous cave developed from groundwater in Hunter Valley. It had carbonic acid that dissolved the section of limestone and dolomitic bedrock. Since then Stock Creek has flowed through to join the Clinch River. Paralleling the creek, with room to share in the tunnel, is Southern Railroad, first constructed in 1882 by Southern, Ohio, and Atlantic Railroad companies. It is reported that Daniel Boone in 1769 was the first white man to explore this immense karst formation. The park has a visitor center with railroad artifacts, a chairlift and 0.3-mile *Tunnel Trail* to the gorge and tunnel, a modern swimming complex, a picnic area, a campground with hot showers, and rim trails.

Access: On US 23 at Clinchport go north for 2 miles, turn right on SR 871, and go 0.6 miles to park entrance.

Lover's Leap Trail (0.4 mi.), **Tunnel Hill Trail** (0.7 mi.), **Center Trail** (0.2 mi.),
Gorge Ridge Trail (0.3 mi.), **Purchase Hill Trail** (1.1 mi.) 741–45

Length and Difficulty: 2.8 miles (4.5 km) combined, round-trip; moderate
Features: scenic views, wildflowers, lichens, geological formations
Trailhead: Visitor center
Description: Begin the *Lover's Leap Trail* at the visitor center. Honor all signs about
    extreme danger. (After 0.2 mi. the *Tunnel Hill Trail* begins left for 0.7 mi. to the
    swimming pool and picnic parking area.) At 0.4 miles is Lover's Leap overlook.
    Here are views of the gigantic chasm with a rim of about 3,000 feet and a depth
    of 400 feet. (After the overlook, the *Center Trail* is on the left and connects with
    the *Tunnel Hill Trail.*) Continue on the *Gorge Ridge Trail,* which goes to the
    campground, but after 0.2 miles the *Purchase Hill Trail* goes right. It follows the
    chasm rim 1.1 miles through hardwoods of oak, dogwood, and ash, with black
    cohosh and may apples on the forest floor, to a knoll. Backtrack to the visitor
    center for a total of 2.8 miles.
    On the banks of the steep *Tunnel Hill Trail* are ash, walnut, poplar, colum-
    bine, and ladies' tresses. From the base chairlift there is a 500-foot boardwalk
    upstream to an observation deck at the tunnel's mouth. Entrance into the
    tunnel is prohibited. Backtrack, or take the chairlift to the visitor center.
USGS map: Clinchport
Address and Information: Natural Tunnel State Park, Rt. 3, Box 250, Duffield, VA
    24244; phone: 703-940-2674. Available are park brochure and map.

SHOT TOWER AND NEW RIVER TRAIL STATE PARK
Carroll, Grayson, Pulaski, and Wythe Counties

This is Virginia's longest state park. It is unique in mineralogy, topography, and
human history. Except for the Shot Tower tract and former railroad stations, the
park's width averages 80 feet for its 57.3 miles. In December 1986 Norfolk Southern
Corporation donated the railroad corridor to the Division of State Parks. As a
result the way opened for developing a rails-to-trails avenue, the *New River Trail,*
from termini in the south at Galax and Fries to a northern terminus in Pulaski. It
parallels 39 miles of the spectacular New River, which geologists claim to be one of
the oldest rivers (350 million years) in the world. It has carved its riverbed from a
much higher plateau during the millenia and has exposed rich deposits of iron ore,
lead, zinc, and limestone.

The New River Valley's archaeological history reveals that Native Americans
were here about 10,000 B.C., more as transients than long-term settlers. Shawnee
and Cherokee had settlements in the area at the time European explorers and pioneers came after the mid-eighteenth century. European family names frequently
became the names of the villages, industries for the natural resources, streams, and
mountains. Some industries have lasted 200 years, indicating how the railroad was
part of their marketing success. As each new town developed upriver, a new
railroad branch was extended from the main line. Now that most of the industries
have closed and the rails and ties have been removed, this historic railroad con-

tinues to serve the public in a way never imagined by the immigrant laborers. They would be less surprised about use of the river. Never navigable for industrial use, the river today is popular for the white-water sports of canoeing, kayaking, and rafting. Concentrated rapids are near Fries, the Shot Tower, and Bertha, and class 3–4 rapids are at Foster Falls, downriver from the Shot Tower.

The park's most southern trailhead is in the town of Galax, north of US 58 at Chestnut Creek. After 12 miles the trail meets a 5.5-mile branch from the other southern trailhead in the town of Fries by the New River. After joining, the trail follows the railroad bed north to the eastern edge of Pulaski. Because the northern trailhead is at mile marker #2, the actual combined hiking distance is 55.3 miles. Along the route are 29 trestles, 3 bridges, 2 tunnels, 2 dams, a lake, and stretches of white water. In addition to the 3 trailheads, there are 9 major access points for parking. They are Cliffview, Gambetta, Chestnut Yard, Byllesby, Ivanhoe, Austinville, Shot Tower, Allisonia/Hiwassee, and Draper. Since some of the trestles have been renovated and a smooth passageway has been constructed on all trestles, the trail accommodates horseback riding, hiking, bicycling, cross-country skiing, jogging, and strolling.

The Shot Tower section of the park was formerly Shot Tower Historical State Park, opened to the public in 1968 after extensive renovation. The property was a gift to the commonwealth by the Lead Mines Ruritan Club in 1964. Its early history began in 1807 when Thomas Jackson, a joint owner of a lead mining company in Austinville, constructed a 75-foot-high stone tower with a 75-foot-deep shaft in the earth where an access was from the bank side of the New River. The tower was constructed for the purpose of making lead bullets. At the tower are picnic tables, rest rooms, the park headquarters, and 0.7-mile *Shot Tower Historical Trail* on the northern side of the tower. A fee is charged for climbing the tower, and tours may be arranged with the park rangers.

746

Access to Park Headquarters: At exit 24, I-77, turn east at Poplar Camp on VA 69 to US 52. Turn left and drive 1.5 miles to park entrance, left.

Access to Galax Trailhead: From I-77, exit 14, on US 58 west, drive 10.5 miles to parking area right (across the bridge) at junction of East Stuart Street and Railroad Drive.

Access to Fries Trailhead: From I-77, exit 14, on US 58 west, drive 9.5 miles, turn right on Hanes Road, and follow signs to Cliffview and SR 721. From Cliffview follow SR 721 (and old SR 606) 5.8 miles to Fries. From I-81, exit 80, at Fort Chiswell, turn south on US 52. After 1.3 miles, turn right on VA 94. (If coming from the Shot Tower, cross the New River bridge on US 52 north and take the first left [SR 619] to Porters Crossroads. Turn left on VA 94.)

Access to Pulaski Trailhead: From I-81, exit 94, north on VA 99, drive 2 miles to Xaloy Drive, right.

747   **New River Trail**
Length and Difficulty: 55.3 miles (88.5 km); easy to moderate
Features: scenic views, geological formations, historic site, wildlife, wildflowers, trestles, riverside, multiple uses

New River State Park Trail. (Courtesy Virginia Division of Tourism)

Trailheads: See directions above.

Introduction: The trail is described from Galax to Pulaski in mile points, but the 5.5 miles from Fries to Fries Junction are included as linear distance. For the first 45.5 miles the route is downriver, but after crossing Claytor Lake the trail soon begins an ascent to Pulaski. Hikers will notice the original mile markers begin from Pulaski. Where intact, the markers can serve for distance counting for hikers going southwest. Unless backtracking, two cars will be needed. If planning a through-hike, advance arrangements will be necessary for camping. At the time of this writing there are no state or national forest campsites on the trail, but they are being planned. A few private campgrounds exist near the trail. Information about them can be obtained from the park office. Because there are so many historic sites to visit and scenic areas to observe, through-hikers may wish to allow 3–4 days. (If the Foster Falls section is closed, hikers should consult the park office about alternate hiking routes.) To enhance the trail's intrigue topographical maps may be helpful.

The park has a few regulations designed to benefit all trail users. No motor vehicles are allowed, and no parking is permitted in front of gates. There is to be no trespassing on private property, no littering, no firearms, and no alcohol. Pets must be leashed. All group excursions must have a permit. Equestrians and bicyclists must follow the courtesy and safety rules regarding passing, speed, and dismounting.

Nearby convenience stores are located in Galax, Fries, Ivanhoe, Austinville, and Draper. Water fountains are at Cliffside and Shot Tower, and rest rooms are at Cliffside, Fries, near Byllesby Dam, Shot Tower, and Draper. Accommodations for the physically impaired are at Ivanhoe and Cliffside.

Description: From the parking lot and trail information sign in Galax, follow the trail downstream, cross two bridges, and at 0.7 miles notice original railroad mile marker 51. Reach Cliffview at 2.3 miles. Here is a parking area, a substation office for a ranger, a picnic area, rest rooms, and across SR 721 the Cliffview Trading Post. It provides camping (no hookups), bicycle rentals, and trail supplies. To the northwest is "Cliffside," a mansion built in 1902 by state senator Thomas Felts. (For highway access here from US 58, see access directions above to Fries. For access to the next parking area, Chestnut Yard, follow SR 721 north to junction with SR 607, right, and follow it to Chestnut Creek. To reach the Gambetta parking area go 1 mi. on SR 607 from the SR 721 junction and turn left on SR 793.)

Continue from Cliffside into a forest with white pine, hardwoods, wild rose, and filberts. At 5.4 miles is Chestnut Creek waterfalls with a large pool. Ahead are banks of rhododendron. After a gate there is a bike rack and horse tie-up at the Chestnut Yard parking area at 6.4 miles. Ahead at 6.7 miles is a clearing where the Chestnut Yard railroad turntable was used to switch engine direction. There are pastures at 6.9 miles and a 190-foot trestle at 8.3 miles. Reach Gambetta parking area, left, at SR 793 at 9.5 miles. At 10.5 miles is an oxbow turn between Toby Knob (west) and Bald Rock (east) in an isolated area. Chestnut Tunnel, 195 feet long, is at 11.2 miles. The trail crosses its longest trestle, 1,089 feet, over the New River at Fries Junction, where at 12 miles it joins the Fries trail section. (From the Fries trailhead there is an N&W Railroad caboose that serves as a town information center, with rest rooms, water, and a telephone.) Hiking downstream, cross trestles at 0.6 miles, 1.5 miles, 2 miles, 2.5 miles, 3.7 miles, and 4.8 miles. Wood ducks and Canada geese may be near the river islands, and from 2.6 miles to 4.7 miles are continuous river rapids.

After Fries Junction the trail crosses a trestle at Brush Creek, which flows from Mount Rogers National Recreation Area of the JNF. At 13.2 miles is the site of an old health spa, now a rest stop with a picnic table and rest room. Arrive at Byllesby Dam and SR 602 at 14.5 miles. The access road ascends 3.7 miles to VA 94, where it goes right to Ivanhoe and left to Fries. At 17.1 miles is Buck Dam, which, as with Byllesby, was constructed in the early years of the century for electrical energy. Between the dams are rapids. Waterfowl and songbirds are frequently seen here. Cross Big Branch trestle and arrive at the parking lot in Ivanhoe at 19 miles. Here is a store, a telephone, and water. (Access from VA 94 is on SR 639 in the town.) At 20.2 miles is the remains of an enormous rock crusher, a 1901 model used for early industries in Ivanhoe. After the quarry area the trail leaves the riverside, turns left, and cuts more directly to cross the river on a 670-foot-long trestle. Reach the historic Austinville Lead Mines at 22.8 miles. Although closed in 1981, it served the area's industrial life for nearly 200 years. Cross SR 636 in the community of Austinville at 23 miles. (Access here is right on SR 636, which becomes VA 69 and goes 4.5 mi. east to I-77, exit 24.) The famous Austin family homestead is at 24.1 miles, the birthplace of Stephen Austin, founder of Texas, and son of Moses Austin, who owned the local lead mines. For the next 2 miles are a few old abandoned buildings on the right and a 135-foot-long tunnel. Soon the gentle sounds of the river rapids are replaced by the rumble of I-77 traffic high on the New River Bridge. After passing under the bridge, there is a side trail to the Shot Tower (described above) at 26.2 miles. Here is park headquarters on the southern slope of the hill. Picnic tables and a rest room are near the tower. A few yards ahead on the trail is US 52 and Jackson Bridge, the site of Jackson's Ferry and named for the same Englishman who built the tower. The ferry operated until 1931.

The trail may be temporarily closed for the next 5 miles because of a land dispute through the Foster Falls area. Contact the park manager for trail conditions. Otherwise, drive south from the bridge on US 52 for 1.5 miles and turn left on SR 607 (0.2 mi. north of I-77, exit 24, junction with US 52 from VA 69), and follow it 5.1 miles to VA 100. Turn left and go 2.5 miles to Barren Springs Station, the location of a former iron furnace, and trail crossing. Here is mile point 34.4. On the right it is 4.9 miles on the trail to the parking lot in Allisonia. (For road access to Allisonia from VA 100, continue on SR 607 for 2.4 mi.; make a sharp turn right and descend on Boone Furnace Road to a junction with SR 693 at 4.1 mi. Turn left, and after 1 mi. reach the railroad parking lot, right. Here is mile point 39.3.) Historic Allisonia has a number of buildings with turn-of-the-century architecture; the train depot is also preserved. Continue northeast on the trail and at 41.3 miles cross SR 693. To the right is Hoover Color Corporation, which produces iron oxide ores for color pigments.

Cross the 970-foot-long bridge, which offers great views of the river/lake, and enter a forested canopy of ash, locust, and maple. At 42.6 miles (1 mi. from the bridge) is a side trail, left, to Horseshoe Campground and General Store. The trail ascends slightly through groves of redbud and offers splendid views of the lake area. Cross 420-foot-long Delton Trestle at 43.8 miles, where nearby is a foundation for a former railroad engine water tank. Cross two other long trestles and leave the forest and enter farmland. At 45.7 miles is Draper parking area. Here are picnic tables, a rest room, a telephone, a signboard, and Bryson Store across the road. (For egress to I-81, go northwest by a few historic buildings on SR 658 to VA 76, and turn left for 1 mi. to exit 24. If returning to Allisonia, turn right on VA 76 [Possum Hollow Rd.] to SR 672 [Lowmans Ferry Rd.], turn right, and cross Claytor Lake, reach a junction with SR 693 [Julia Simpkins Rd.], turn right, and go to Hiwassee and Allisonia, a distance of 12.6 mi.)

The scenery now changes to rolling farm hills, cattle, and patches of yellow stalk. To the northwest is cone-shaped Draper Mountain. At 48 miles the trail crosses VA 76 on a trestle. The hum of I-81 traffic is heard. Pass under I-81 at 48.3 miles. As if a sign for the trail to end, there is a lone original railroad crossing signal, right, at 49.3 miles. Cross a 476-foot-long trestle over Peak Creek, and arrive at Dora Junction, the northern trailhead parking area at 49.8 miles. This whistle stop is named for an iron furnace and Pulaski Iron Company. Ahead it is 2 miles on the closed railroad grade to the Pulaski depot. Access here is on Xaloy Way, off VA 99, and 2 miles south to I-81, exit 94. If returning to Draper, drive under I-81 to VA 76 (Possum Hollow Rd.) and turn right.

USGS maps: Galax, Austinville, Max Meadows, Fosters Falls, Hiwassee, Duplin, Pulaski

Addresses and Information: Shot Tower and New River Trail State Park, Rt. 1, Box 81x, Austinville, VA 24312; phone: 703-699-6778 (Cliffview substation: 703-236-8889); Cliffview Trading Post, Rt. 4, Box 163, Galax, VA 24333; phone: 703-744-7720. Available are brochures, flyers, and map of the trail and shot tower.

SKY MEADOWS STATE PARK
Clarke and Fauquier Counties

This historic property is part of a 7,883-acre tract purchased by Capt. James Ball from Lord Fairfax in 1713. Descendants sold and divided the property until in 1966 a housing development was plotted for this farm of mountain and valley meadows. But Paul Mellon prevented it from materializing and gave 1,132 acres to Virginia State Parks in 1975. The park opened in 1983. In 1987 another 248 acres were added that contain 3.6 miles of the *AT*. In 1991 Mellon gave an additional 462 acres. Hikers do not have to go far on this preserve to appreciate the donor's generosity. The stone house on a hilltop was constructed by Isaac Settle about 1810. He gave it to his son Abner, who named it Mount Bleak. From this house visitors receive information on the park. The park has a lake for fishing; two bridle trails (*Sherman's Mill Trail* [1 mi.] and *Lost Mountain Trail* [3 mi.], with a staging area); a

748–49   picnic area; farm buildings; a primitive, hike-in campground; and trails.

Access: From US 50, drive south on US 17 for 1.2 miles to park entrance on SR 170. From I-66, exit 18, drive north on US 17 for 6.4 miles.

Piedmont Overlook Trail (0.7 mi.), **North Ridge Trail** (1.7 mi.),
750–54   **Gap Run Trail** (1.2 mi.), **South Ridge Trail** (1.6 mi.), **Snowden Trail** (1.1 mi.)

Length and Difficulty: 5.3 miles (8.5 km) combined, round-trip; moderate to strenuous

Connecting Trail: AT (3.6 mi.)

Features: scenic views, historic site, wildflowers

Trailhead: From the visitor center west on service road

Description: Short and long loops can be made on these connecting trails. The longest loop is described here. At the service road ascend on the *Piedmont Overlook Trail* in a field of clover and wildflowers. Views are of Lost Mountain and Gap Run Valley toward the east. At 0.5 miles join the *North Ridge Trail* and reach a junction with the *Gap Run Trail* at Gap Run at 1 mile. Here is a rocky area with papaw, spicebush, and jack-in-the-pulpit. (The trail descends to the primitive campground.) Continue upstream on the *North Ridge Trail* to a junction with the *South Ridge Trail* at 1.6 miles. (To the right is a spur trail that ascends steeply for 0.3 mi. to the *AT*, where a resting bench is appreciated. The *AT* goes left to Thompson WMA and I-66, and right to Ashby Gap and US 50. Backtrack.) The *South Ridge Trail* follows an old woods road and at 2.6 miles goes through a stile to grassy pastures and scenic views. The *Gap Run Trail* is left at 2.9 miles. (It is 0.6 mi. to the shelter and campsites.) To the right on the service road is access to the *Snowden Trail,* a loop in a forest with interpretive signs. Return 0.6 miles on the service road for a loop of 5.3 miles (not counting the *Gap Run Trail* or side trails).

USGS map: Upperville

Address and Information: Sky Meadows State Park, Rt. 1, Box 540, Delaplane, VA 22025; phone: 703-592-3556. Available are brochures and flyers on history and trail outline.

Piedmont Division

BEAR CREEK LAKE STATE PARK
Cumberland County

Centered in the heart of the Cumberland State Forest, this peaceful and serene 150-acre park was established in 1939. Activities include boating (boat rentals are available), fishing (for blue gill, bigmouth bass, and pickerel), picnicking (reservations are available if desired), hiking (around the lake and side trails), swimming (in the lake near beach and bathhouse), and camping (with electrical and water hookups). The nearby 15.2-mile *Willis River Trail* can be accessed from SR 666, the park entrance road, near the campground and beach. (See Cumberland State Forest at the end of this chapter.)

Access: From the town of Cumberland drive east 0.5 miles on US 60 and turn left on SR 622. Drive 3.3 miles to SR 629 and turn left; turn left again on SR 666.

Lakeside Trail (0.8 mi.), **Running Cedar Trail** (0.2 mi.), **Lost Barr Trail** (1.5 mi.), **Circumferential Trail** (1.5 mi.), **Pine Knob Trail** (0.5 mi.)   755–59

Length and Difficulty: 4.5 miles (7.2 km) combined, round-trip; easy

Features: lake, wildflowers, fishing, wildlife

Trailhead: Parking loop in picnic area

Description: From the picnic area hike downstream (northwest) on the orange-blazed *Lakeside Trail.* After 0.3 miles reach a junction with blue-blazed *Running Cedar Trail,* right, which connects to Campground C. (It passes through beds of running cedar [clubmoss] and under tall tulip poplars.) Pass other side trails to Campground A and reach the lake's dam at 0.8 miles. Around the dam to the other side of the lake is the *Lost Barr (Bear) Trail.* It is an interpretive, self-guiding loop trail with 10 stations keyed to a descriptive brochure. At 0.8 miles at a road bridge it connects with white-blazed *Circumferential Trail.* Follow it to cross Bear Creek road bridge, pass through lowlands, and cross Little Bear

Creek footbridge to rejoin the *Lakeside Trail* at 3 miles. (To the right is an access trail to the *Willis River Trail*.) Turn left and reach a junction, right, with the *Pine Knob Trail*, which can be used for returning to Campground C on SR 666 or back to the picnic area for a loop. Continue on the *Lakeside Trail* to the picnic area for a total of 3.2 miles around the lake.

USGS map: Gold Hill

Address and Information: Bear Creek Lake State Park, Rt. 1, Box 253, Cumberland, VA 23040; phone: 804-492-4410. Available is a leaflet with map.

FAIRY STONE STATE PARK
Patrick and Henry Counties

Fairy Stone State Park, established in 1936, is a 4,570-acre natural preserve in the foothills of the Blue Ridge Mountains. It has a 168-acre lake fed by Goblintown Creek, which flows into the adjoining Philpott Reservoir. The park is named for the famous lucky hexagonal crystals found in the southern tip of the park boundary. The crystals, called staurolite, are composed of iron aluminum silicate in small tan-brown and gray-blue forms of the Roman, Maltese, and St. Andrew's crosses. They have been formed by intense heat and pressure during the folding and crumpling of the Appalachian mountain chain.

A wide range of facilities include those for swimming, boating, fishing, hiking, bicycling, nature study, and tent and trailer camping. Also, housekeeping cabins are rented on a weekly basis from Monday to Monday and are exceptionally popular. The park has a number of short, easy to moderate hiking trails, three of which connect. A separate one is the *Dam Spillway Trail*, a 1-mile, easy, round-trip path on the edge of the lake through a mixed forest. It is accessed from the nature center. For the physically impaired there is 0.1-mile *Handicapped Trail* 0.9 miles
760–61 north on SR 623. It is a cement-paved trail to a picnic area in a cove by the lake.

Access: From Bassett go 9 miles west on VA 57 and turn right on VA 346. After 1 mile is the park entrance and information center. (VA 57 continues west to VA 8, leading south to Stuart, and north to Woolwine.)

762 **Oak Hickory Trail**

Length and Difficulty: 1.3 miles (2.1 km) round-trip; easy to moderate

Trailhead: Picnic area near the park entrance

Description: Where the road crosses the stream, look for a red-blazed trail sign and go right or left on the loop. Large trees include beech, oak, poplar, white pine, and maple. Parts of this serene path are mossy, with a rhododendron canopy. Deer are often seen in this area.

Iron Mine Trail (1 mi.), **Stuart's Knob Trail** (1.7 mi.),
763–65 **Whiskey Run Trail** (2 mi.)

Length and Difficulty: 4.7 miles (7.5 km) combined, round-trip; easy to moderate

Features: iron mines, wildflowers, geological formations, scenic views

Trailhead: Access on SR 623, 0.7 miles from park entrance, left.

Description: Ascend on a well-graded trail through periwinkle beds, fire pink, redbud, and a young mixed forest. At 0.2 miles is a junction with blue-blazed *Whiskey Run Trail*. Continue left through remains of iron mines and pass junction with orange-blazed *Stuart's Knob Trail* at 0.5 miles. At 0.7 miles is a superb view of the park beach and lake. At 0.9 miles reach an open-shaft mine near a return to parking area. On *Stuart's Knob Trail* ascend steeply to a rocky knob. Heavy vegetation prevents scenic views. Return to the *Iron Mine Trail*. The *Whiskey Run Trail* branches off the *Iron Mine Trail*. It circles the base of Stuart's Knob for 1.5 miles before rejoining the *Iron Mine Trail* at a park overlook. Descend on the *Iron Mine Trail* to the parking lot.

USGS maps: Charity, Philpott Reservoir

Address and Information: Fairy Stone State Park, Rt. 2, Box 723, Stuart, VA 24171; phone: 703-930-2424. Available are brochures and flyers on history of the fairy stone legend and park outline with trails.

HOLLIDAY LAKE STATE PARK
Buckingham and Appomattox Counties

Established in 1939, the peaceful, 250-acre Holliday Lake State Park lies within the Buckingham-Appomattox State Forest. The park's major attraction is a 150-acre lake, offering boating and fishing as well as swimming at a spacious beach area. Canoes, rowboats, and paddleboats can be rented. Other facilities are a campground (no utility hookups), store and concessions, picnic areas, visitor center, bathhouse, and lake trail for hiking.

Access: On VA 24 east of the town of Appomattox and US 460, go 8 miles to SR 626, right. Follow SR 626 for 3.5 miles, turn left on SR 640 for 0.3 miles, and then right on SR 692 for 2.9 miles.

Lakeshore Trail (4.7 mi.), Saunders Creek Trail (0.3 mi.)   766–67

Length and Difficulty: 5 miles (8.0 km); easy

Features: scenic views, lake, wildlife, fishing

Trailhead: Parking area near boat dock

Description: From the boat dock and bathhouse area begin the *Lakeshore Trail* either left or right for a loop. If hiking left, follow the initial dark-blue marker with subsequent orange arrow signs around the lake. Vegetation includes Virginia pine, shortleaf pine, oak, hickory, poplar, mountain laurel, red cedar, alder, white pine, green ash, dogwood, and numerous wildflowers. Reach lake overview at 0.4 miles on exceptionally well graded trail. At 0.6 miles pass an access trail to Campground B (now closed). Cross small streams at 0.8 miles and 1 mile. At 1.1 miles a shortcut bridge over Forbes Creek is on the right. (Trail upstream goes for 0.4 mi. to a point where rock-hopping the stream allows for a circle back to the bridge.)

After crossing the bridge, continue right to clearing and views of lake on right at 1.5 miles, and at forest road junction at 1.6 miles go straight ahead. Cross a small tributary, and reach rocky bluff with huckleberries at 2.7 miles.

Descend steeply to a scenic cement bridge over the dam at 2.8 miles. Cross small stream in a cove, and follow upstream for 0.2 miles. Turn away from stream bank and reach paved gated road at 3.9 miles (right is entrance to 4-H Educational Center). Climb steps across road, descend to stream bank, follow through mature forest with beds of running cedar, and reach a bridge at the lake at 4.5 miles. Here is the *Saunder's Creek Trail*, an orange-blazed path left to the campground and right to the lake. Turn right and follow along lakeshore for another 0.2 miles to parking area.

USGS map: Holliday Lake

Address and Information: Holliday Lake State Park, Rt. 2, Box 622, Appomattox, VA 24522; phone: 804-248-6308.

LAKE ANNA STATE PARK
Spotsylvania County

The 2,058-acre park is on a northside peninsula of Lake Anna, a large lake on the North Anna River in Louisa and Spotsylvania counties southwest of Fredericksburg. The park opened to the public in 1983. Its land, and the land under the water, has been home to European settlers and their descendants since the early eighteenth century. They cut the trees from the sloping hills, farmed, and mined for iron, lead, and gold. Before them were the Maannahoack Sioux, fierce natives who held the colonists at bay for a century. The area is in the gold pyrite belt where in 1829 gold was found along Pigeon Run. A foundation site of the 1790s Goodwin Gold Mine still exists. Iron ore had been discovered early, and mining began in the 1720s. There are many historic sites to visit here, and at the park's visitor center are exhibits and displays of the area's natural and human history. Near the visitor center is an 0.3-mile interpretive loop trail around a preserved pond built by a former landowner. Access to the pond is easy for those who are physically handicapped, and a sheltered deck provides a place to observe waterfowl. Attractions are boating and fishing, swimming at a beach with bathhouse, a picnic area, and summer nature programs on the network of trails. A singular trail, the *Fisherman's Trail*, makes a 1-mile loop into the woods and fields near the lake. Access is from the boat launch and picnic parking area.

768

Access: From I-95, exit 118, take SR 606 west at Thornburg to VA 208. After about 11 miles turn right on SR 601 and go 3.3 miles to park entrance, left. From US 522 it is about 8 miles east on VA 208 to a left turn on SR 601.

Turkey Run Trail (1.5 mi.), **Mill Pond Trail** (0.6 mi.),
Cedar Run Trail (0.7 mi.), **Big Woods Trail** (1.1 mi.),
769–74   **Glenora Trail** (1.7 mi.), **Railroad Ford Trail** (1.5 mi.)

Length and Difficulty: 8.2 miles (13.1 km) combined, round-trip; easy
Features: scenic views, historic site, geological formations, wildlife, wildflowers
Trailhead: Parking area 1.8 miles from SR 601 on park entrance road
Description: At the parking area begin on the yellow-blazed *Turkey Run Trail* on a wide and easy route through a mature forest. At 0.4 miles reach a junction with

the *Mill Pond Trail*, left. (It descends to the lake and the site of Hailey's gristmill in the last century. Backtrack.) At 0.6 miles is the *Cedar Run Trail*, left. (White blazed, it makes a turn at the lake and returns to the *Turkey Run Trail* after 0.7 mi. In a grassy area at the lake there are good lake views. Cedar, walnut, and blackgum are near old homesites.) At 0.8 miles on the *Turkey Run Trail*, the *Big Woods Trail* begins on the right, and the *Turkey Run Trail* continues ahead to dead-end at the lake. Backtrack, and follow the *Big Woods Trail* for 1.1 miles. Along the way it crosses a bridge built by Eagles Scout Troop 97. After following an old woods road it intersects with the *Glenora Trail*, right and left. After a left turn, it is 0.2 miles to the lake and past the ruins of the early 1800s plantation home called "Glenora." Remains of the old smokehouse and other buildings are on the left. There are excellent views of the lake beyond the buildings. Backtrack and continue on the *Glenora Trail* for 1.1 miles to the *Railroad Ford Trail*, left. Turn here on a red-blazed trail that goes to the end of the peninsula and loops back to the *Glenora Trail* near the visitor center. Part of the trail is on an old railroad grade where lead and zinc were transported for armaments during World War I. At 0.7 miles are lake views and large beech trees. After returning to the green-blazed *Glenora Trail*, turn left, where along the lakeside and on the hillside are fritillary butterflies and wildflowers in the summer. Ahead are the pond and visitor center for a total of 8.2 miles. (Lesser distances are 3.8 mi., 5.9 mi., and 6.6 mi.) From the visitor center walk, the entrance road 0.7 miles to make a complete loop to the parking area at the *Turkey Run Trail*.

USGS map: Lake Anna West

Address and Information: Lake Anna State Park, 6800 Lawyers Rd., Spotsylvania, VA 22553; phone: 703-854-5503. Available are brochure of park and trails, "Fortune's Wheel" history brochure.

OCCONEECHEE STATE PARK
Mecklenburg County

Leased from the U.S. Army Corp of Engineers in 1968, the 2,690-acre Occoneechee State Park adjoins the John H. Kerr Reservoir near Clarksville. The park is named after the powerful Occoneechee Indians, who lived in the area from 1250 to 1676. They, like the Saponi and Tutelo Indians, traded furs from now-inundated islands until colonial rebels led by Nathaniel Bacon in 1676 massacred many of them, thereby breaking their stronghold. The survivors scattered into what is now North Carolina. Facilities include 142 campsites, and popular activities are picnicking, boating, hiking, and summer interpretive programs. Bass fishing is a popular sport in the reservoir. Park camping facilities for tents and trailers are open from Memorial Day through Labor Day. Bathhouse, water, and electric hookups are available.

Access: From the junction of US 58/15 and VA 49, across the bridge from Clarksville, go east on US 58 for 0.6 miles and turn right at park sign. Follow VA 364 for 0.5 miles to the park headquarters.

775–78   **Plantation Trail**
Length and Difficulty: 0.8 miles (1.3 km) round-trip; easy
Connecting Trails: *Mossy Creek Trail* (0.7 mi.), *Warrior's Path Trail* (0.2 mi.), *Big Oak Trail* (0.6 mi.)
Features: historic site, nature study
Trailhead: Terrace Garden parking area 0.1 mile south of park office
Description: Follow the red-blazed *Plantation Trail* by the site of the Occoneechee plantation home of Dempsey Crudup into a forest of black and honey locust, black walnut, maple, oak, and cedar. At 0.2 miles pass the *Mossy Creek Trail*. (It extends right for 0.7 mi. to a large white oak stand, and to the park office.) On the *Plantation Trail* follow a stream near beech and pine to a junction with the *Warrior's Path Trail*. (It leads 0.2 mi. right to parking area at the lakeshore.) After another 0.1 mile pass a junction with yellow-blazed *Big Oak Trail*, right. (It crosses the road near Campground B, and after a few yards it leaves the road at a huge white oak. It ascends to end near the entrance to Campground C in a group of large red and white oaks.)
USGS maps: Clarksville north and south, Tungsten
Address and Information: Occoneechee State Park, Rt. 1, Box 3, Clarksville, VA 23927; phone: 804-374-2210. Available is a brochure on park and fishing regulations.

POCAHONTAS STATE PARK
Chesterfield County

Pocahontas State Park is southwest of Richmond and was established in 1946. It has 7,604 acres with 27 miles of roads for hiking. A 156-acre lake fed by Swift Creek is used for boating and fishing. Also provided are a large swimming pool, a bathhouse, areas for camping and picnicking, bicycle trails, hiking trails, wildlife exhibits, a visitor center, and a playground. Camping facilities are seasonal, but full services are between Memorial Day and Labor Day.

Access: From the junction of VA 10 and SR 655 at Chesterfield Courthouse follow the park signs and go west on SR 655 for 3.8 miles, then turn right into park entrance on SR 780. Park office and parking area are another 1.5 miles away. (Access via I-95 is from exit 61; go west 7 mi. on VA 10 to Chesterfield Courthouse and SR 655.)

779–82   **Beaver Lake Nature Trail**
Length and Difficulty: 2.6 miles (4.2 km) round-trip; easy
Connecting Trails: *Ground Pine Nature Trail* (1.2 mi.), *Third Branch Trail* (0.2 mi.), *Awareness Trail* (0.3 mi.)
Features: historic site, lake, wildlife, wildflowers
Trailhead: Park visitor center
Description: Follow the blue-blazed trail down to Beaver Lake, which is bordered with tag alder; at 0.1 mile turn right and hike through a forest of large poplar, loblolly pine, oak, beech, and holly, with a groundcover of periwinkle. Pass old

spring at 0.2 miles; a junction with yellow-blazed *Ground Pine Nature Trail*, extending right, is at 0.3 miles.

Continue through beds of ground pine and running cedar to lake overlooks at 0.5 miles and 0.7 miles. Cross boardwalk near large walnut, poplar, and sycamore stand at 0.8 miles. At 1.3 miles reach the *Third Branch Trail* and Old Mill Site. Turn left, cross stream, and continue circuit of the lake through a mixed forest. Arriving at the picturesque dam and spillway at 2.3 miles, descend, and cross footbridge below the dam. From there, a return to the visitor center can be made on the 0.3-mile *Awareness Trail*, which is marked in red, paved, and graded for wheelchair use (but may not have a sign). Return can also be made on the 0.1-mile spillway route to the junction with the *Beaver Lake Nature Trail*.

Another route, for a circuit of 3.8 miles to include half of the *Beaver Lake Nature Trail*, follows the trail signs for *Beaver Lake Nature Trail* from the visitor center to the junction with the *Ground Pine Nature Trail* at 0.3 miles. Turn right on the *Ground Pine Nature Trail* and go 0.2 miles to Crosstic Road, a bicycle trail. Turn left and follow the green-blazed bicycle trail across a cut left to Horner Road. Turn left again on Bottoms Road and, 2.2 miles from the visitor center, turn left off the bicycle trail onto the *Third Branch Trail*. Go 0.2 miles and make connections with the *Beaver Lake Trail*. At that point turn right or left for the return to the visitor center.

USGS maps: Chesterfield, Beach

Address and Information: Contact Park Superintendent, Pocahontas State Park, 10300 Park Rd., Chesterfield, VA 23832; phone: 804-796-4255. Available are brochures and maps of the park and road network.

SMITH MOUNTAIN LAKE STATE PARK
Bedford County

Smith Mountain Lake (20,500 acres) is the state's second largest lake. Constructed in the early 1960s the lake backs up the Roanoke and Blackwater Rivers for 40 miles in length and about 550 miles of shoreline in Franklin, Pittsylvania, and Bedford counties. On the northern side of the lake is 1,506-acre Smith Mountain Lake State Park, which has four major peninsulas. Old tobacco barns and young forests attest to the farm life of the past. Water enthusiasts find the lake ideal for boating, skiing, and fishing. Each March the Smith Mountain Ruritans Bass Fishing Tournament is held here. The park offers a campground (electric hookups but no hot showers), a picnic area, a boat launch and rentals, and nature programs.

At the visitor center and parking area are two short trails. The 1-mile, yellow-blazed *Lake View Trail* makes a loop at the end of the peninsula near the shoreline. The 0.6-mile, blue-blazed *Tobacco Run Trail* passes a tobacco barn near the road before crossing to end at the lake. In the campground, near the park office, is the 0.5-mile, gold-blazed *Beech Wood Trail* loop.

783–85

Access: From Bedford on US 460 drive south 13 miles on VA 122 to Moneta and take SR 608 for 6 miles. Turn right on SR 626 into the park. From US 29 in Altavista drive west on VA 342 for 15 miles to Woodford Corner and turn left on SR 626. Follow it directly 14 miles to the park.

786–87   **Chestnut Ridge Trail** (1.7 mi.), **Turtle Island Trail** (1.3 mi.)
Length and Difficulty: 3 miles (3.8 km) combined, round-trip; easy
Features: wildlife, lake, scenic views, historic site
Trailhead: Parking area between park office and visitor center
Description: Begin across the road on the red-blazed *Chestnut Ridge Trail*. It makes a double loop, the first after 0.3 miles and again at 0.8 miles to the lakeside. In a forest of locust and sourwood among mountain laurel there are reminders of early farms, particularly tobacco. Begin the green-blazed *Turtle Island Trail* loop at the parking area. This interpretive trail is marked with posts and keyed to a trail guide. Hikers will see a forest succession study area, a soil nutrient cycle, a changing shoreline, a senescent forest, plant life, and animal habitats. Among the Virginia pine and redbud are Saint-John's-wort. At 0.6 miles is a footbridge to Turtle Island.
USGS map: Smith Mountain Dam
Address and Information: Smith Mountain Lake State Park, Rt. 1, Box 41, Huddleston, VA 24104; phone: 703-297-6066. Available are brochure of park facilities and map, and trail guide for *Turtle Island Trail*.

STAUNTON RIVER STATE PARK
Halifax County

Containing 1,287 acres of forest, meadows, and shorelines, the Staunton River State Park forms a peninsula into the 48,000-acre John H. Kerr Reservoir (also called Buggs Island Lake). By boat, it is about 15 miles upstream from the Occoneechee State Park. The park's history is associated with the Occoneechee Indians, who once controlled the area but were almost all annihilated or driven into North Carolina by Nathaniel Bacon in 1676. Bacon's marauders were taking revenge on Indians in general because some Indians had murdered colonists on his estate near Richmond. Also in the park area, on June 25, 1864, a Union attack on the Richmond-Danville Railroad at the Staunton River Bridge was defeated by a Confederate group of old men and boys. In the late 1880s the Christian Social Colony settled on the peninsula, but it failed to find the expected utopia. Rich in history, the park was established in 1936, one of the six original state parks formed during the Great Depression. The park and river are named in honor of Capt. Henry Staunton, who commanded a company of soldiers to protect the early settlers from Indian attacks before the Revolutionary War.

In addition to deer, raccoon, wild turkey, and squirrel, the park also has several varieties of snakes; the copperhead is the only poisonous one. Snapping turtles and eastern box turtles also are seen in the park. During the early spring evenings a hiker can hear an orchestra of frogs—pickerel, bullfrogs, gray treefrogs, and spring peepers. Several species of waterfowl and wading birds, including geese, puddle ducks, diving ducks, osprey, and occasionally a great blue heron, can be seen. Multiple facilities include campsites, vacation cabins, an Olympic-size swimming pool, bathrooms, boat rentals and ramps, playgrounds, a visitor center, and nearly 10 miles of hiking trails. Activities include picnicking, fishing, tennis, interpretive tours, and nature study.

Access: From US 58 and US 360 junction in eastern South Boston, go north on VA 360 for 5.3 miles to SR 613. Turn right on SR 613 and go 2.8 miles to Scottsburg. Turn right on VA 344 and go 8 miles to the park entrance.

River Bank Trail   788–94
Length and Difficulty: 7.3 miles (11.7 km) round-trip; easy to moderate
Connecting Trails: *Tutelo Trail* (0.1 mi.), *Crow's Nest Trail* (0.4 mi.), *Robin's Roost Trail* (0.5 mi.), *Loblolly Trail* (0.6 mi.), *Campground Trail* (0.1 mi.), *Capt. Staunton's Loop Trail* (0.5 mi.)
Features: waterfowl, scenic views, lake, wildflowers
Trailhead: Parking area near the end of the peninsula
Description: From the entrance of the park, drive 1.7 miles to parking area in picnic area near the end of the peninsula. Begin hike on the blue-blazed *River Bank Trail* toward the tip of the park at 0.3 miles. Views of the lake and shoreline are outstanding in all seasons. Follow the blazes right on a wide trail along the Dan River side of the lake through walnut, pine, locust, sourwood, hickory, cedar, and sweet gum. Spring and summer wildflowers flourish.

At 1.3 miles pass the *Tutelo Trail* on right (which leads 0.1 mi. to a parking area and information center). At 1.4 miles and 1.8 miles pass through picnic areas. At 2.3 miles pass the *Crow's Nest Trail* on right (which leads 0.4 mi. to VA 344 in the center of the park). At 2.8 miles pass the *Robin's Roost Trail* on right (which leads 0.5 mi. through a stand of pines to VA 344 in the park). The trail curves away from the lake at 3.3 miles, crosses VA 344 at 4.8 miles, and reaches a junction with the *Loblolly Trail* at 5.5 miles. (The *Loblolly Trail* goes right for 0.6 mi. to VA 344.) Continue ahead east along the Staunton River side of the lake at 6.2 miles, and pass a junction with the *Campground Trail* on the right (which leads 0.1 mi. to Campground A). At 6.4 miles pass the *Capt. Staunton's Loop Trail,* with white markers (which goes right for 0.5 mi. to loop's trailhead at VA 344). Continue along scenic riverbank to park water plant and boat dock at 7.1 miles. Cross road, and return to parking area where hike began at 7.3 miles.
USGS map: Buffalo Springs
Address and Information: Staunton River State Park, Rt. 2, Box 295, Scottsburg, VA 24589; phone: 804-572-4623. Available are campground and park maps, brochures of park.

TWIN LAKES STATE PARK
Prince Edward County

Located in the state's central piedmont, the double-lake, 349-acre Twin Lakes State Park adjoins the Gallion–Prince Edward State Forest. Goodwin Lake with 15 acres and Prince Edward Lake with 36 acres provide a tranquil area where the hiker can circle either body of water or, with a connector trail, hike both. Wildlife is chiefly deer, quail, raccoon, beaver, squirrel, and wild turkey. Oak, hickory, and maple predominate in a mixed forest. The park has a campground, a swimming beach, a bathhouse, and group-use facilities. There are areas for boating, fishing, picnicking, nature study, and hiking. One of the trails, the *Dogwood Hollow Trail,* is a self-guided interpretive trail with 7 stops. From the park office the blue-blazed trail crosses the road and descends among mixed woods, ferns, and wildflowers. Recross a small stream and complete the loop after 1 mile. Another 1-mile loop trail is the *Goodwin Lake Nature Trail.* Access is at the parking area of the concession stand. It follows blue markers to the head of the lake, where there is likely to be evidence of beavers. Cross two bridges at 0.5 miles and 0.6 miles, cross the dam, and return to the picnic area and trail origin. (A *Connector Trail,* 0.3 mi., goes to

795–97 *Otter's Path Trail.*)

Access: From the junction of US 460/360 at Burkeville, go 4 miles southwest on US 360 to SR 613 and turn right. Go 1.5 miles on SR 613 to a junction of SR 629, where a large park sign gives directions to the park. Proceed right for 0.5 miles to the entrance of the day-use area.

798   Otter's Path Trail
Length and Difficulty: 4 miles (6.4 km) round-trip; moderate
Features: cascades, wildlife, wildflowers
Trailhead: Prince Edward Lake boat launch
Description: In either direction follow the orange markers around the lake. The trail winds around coves, up and down steep banks, and over mossy patches. If hiking right from the ramp, cross a cascading stream at 1.1 miles. At 2.1 miles cross a bridge near an active beaver dam and stroll through a white pine stand. Make a right at a barricade into a mature hardwood stand of maple, hickory, and beech along a small stream. At 2.8 miles return to the lake's edge, follow the trail through a mixed forest, and cross the dam and wooden walkway back to the parking area. (A *Connector Trail,* 0.3 mi., goes to the *Goodwin Lake Nature Trail.*)
Address and Information: Twin Lakes State Park, Rt. 2, Box 70, Green Bay, VA 23942; phone: 804-392-3435. Available for free are brochure and flyers; there is a fee for brochure on *Dogwood Hollow Trail.*

Coastal Division

BELLE ISLE STATE PARK
Lancaster County

This 733-acre tract was the first to be purchased with funds from the state's 1992 Parks and Recreation bond referendum. On the lower Northern Neck peninsula, it is on the northern side of the Rappahannock River. It is almost an island, with

Mulberry Creek on the northwest and Deep Creek on the southeast. The park has eight types of wetlands. It was inhabited by Powhatan Indians before English settlers came to farm the area in the seventeenth century. There are plans to develop the park fully, but at present it has picnicking, bicycling, hiking, and birding. It is not open year round; thus visitors should call ahead. There are two trails on old farm roads. The *Watch House Trail* (0.5 mi.), one-way, signed red, is near the site of an old house used for guards to prevent poachers from stealing oysters. The *Neck Fields Trail* (1.2 mi.), one-way, signed green, is another river access trail through former farmlands.

799–800

Access: From the junction of VA 354 and SR 683 (3 mi. south of junction of VA 354 and VA 3) turn onto SR 683 to parking area.

Address and Information: Belle Isle State Park, Rt. 3, Box 550, Lancaster, VA 22503; phone: 304-462-5030. Available is an information flyer.

CALEDON NATURAL AREA
King George County

Bordered on the northern side by the Potomac River, this 2,579-acre preserve was donated to the commonwealth by Ann Hopewell Smoot in 1974. Designated a national natural landmark, the park and nearby area are a summer home to a large concentration of the noble-looking bald eagle. At the Smoot home, part of which is now a visitor center, are exhibits on the eagle and the park's history. Preservation of the eagle's habitat is the park's primary focus. Tours of the park can be arranged from mid-June to the first week in September. The park is closed on Mondays and Tuesdays. Picnicking and hiking are allowed in the recreational zone of the park.

Access: From US 301 drive west on VA 218 for 3.6 miles and turn right to park entrance.

Fern Trail (0.9 mi.), **Poplar Grove Trail** (0.8 mi.), **Laurel Glen Trail** (0.7 mi.), **Benchmark Trail** (1.1 mi.), **Cedar Ridge Trail** (1.1 mi.)

801–5

Length and Difficulty: 4.6 miles (7.4 km) combined, round-trip; easy to moderate
Features: old growth forest, birding, serenity
Trailhead: From the visitor center parking area
Description: These five, color-coded, signed trails are connecting loops in the order listed. They surprisingly ascend and descend on forested hills close to marshlands and slow-moving creeks. The delightful trails weave through a forest of oak, beech, hickory, and tulip poplar among fern beds and mosses. Hawks, warblers, woodpeckers, chickadees, and goldfinches are among the bird species on the trails. Osprey and herons are in the eagle habitat.
USGS map: King George
Address and Information: Caledon Natural Area, Rt. 5, Box 1124, King George, VA 22485; phone: 703-663-3861. Available are park map and nature adventure brochure.

CHIPPOKES PLANTATION STATE PARK
Surry County

Chippokes Plantation State Park was established in 1967, but its 1,683 acres across the James River from Jamestown have an agricultural history of more than 350 years. When Capt. William Powell first patented the land, in 1619, he named the area in honor of an Indian chief, Choupouke, who had befriended the Jamestown settlers. Through the centuries the plantation area has retained its original boundaries and plantation atmosphere. In 1990 the Farm and Forestry Museum opened to the public. It features artifacts to describe the history of Virginia's farm environment. The park fronts the James River and has more than 500 acres of cultivated and grazing lands. The large antebellum mansion on the property was constructed in 1854. Facilities include a visitor center, historic buildings, formal gardens, a swimming pool, a picnic area, trails, and a fishing area. At the mansion parking area are two bicycle trails, one to the beach for 1.3 miles, and the 0.5-mile *James River Trail*. There is also a 0.4-mile walking path on the *James River Trail* to the river. Another walking path is the 1-mile lower *Chippokes Creek Trail* through farm and forest that must be backtracked.

806–7

USGS maps: Surry, Hog Island

Address and Information: Chippokes Plantation State Park, Rt. 1, Box 213, Surry VA 23883; phone: 804-294-3625. Available are map of the park brochure, Farm and Forestry Museum brochure.

FALSE CAPE STATE PARK
City of Virginia Beach

The 4,321-acre False Cape State Park (and the adjoining Pocahontas/Trojan WMA and Back Bay NWR) is one of the few remaining undeveloped and undisturbed areas on the Atlantic Coast. A haven for waterfowl, the park is part of the Atlantic flyway, which aids a huge migratory bird population in winter. Located at the southeastern tip of the state between Back Bay NWR and the North Carolina state line, the park is a milewide barrier spit between the Atlantic Ocean and shallow Back Bay. There are 6 miles of pristine beach with dunes, maritime forests, and marshes. Although isolated, it is not totally undisturbed. There is a gravel road running through the park, particularly for Wash Woods Environmental Education Center. It can accommodate up to 22 people overnight for the purpose of ecological studies. The park offers tours on a pontoon boat for aquatic studies in Back Bay, guided hikes, bike tours, and a loggerhead sea turtle program. Other programs are offered in union with Virginia Marine Science Museum and the Virginia Institute of Marine Science. To manage the deer and feral hog population the park is closed one week (beginning the first Saturday) in October for the exclusive use of hunters. Recreational activities include fishing (crappie, perch, and bass in Back Bay), primitive camping, hiking, biking, and beachcombing.

Access: From the southern end of US 60 (Pacific Ave.) at the beach in Virginia Beach, cross the bridge, and at 0.8 miles pass the Virginia Marine Science Museum

False Cape State Park. (Courtesy Virginia Division of Tourism)

on General Booth Boulevard. At 4.7 miles turn left on SR 615 (Princess Anne Rd.), go 0.8 miles, and turn left on Sandbridge Road. After 5.4 miles turn right on Sandpiper Road and continue 3.7 miles to Little Island Park. It is another 0.2 miles to the entrance of the Back Bay NWR and another 1.3 miles to the refuge visitor center and parking area. From here it is 3.8 miles to the park entrance by hiking or biking. (From I-64 in west Virginia Beach take VA 407, exit 286 [Indian River Rd.] southeast to cross Princess Anne Rd. at Pungo at 12 mi. Cross the road, and after 1.1 mi. turn left on New Bridge Rd., and follow it 1.2 mi. to Sandbridge Rd. Follow it 3.1 mi. to Sandpiper Rd. and turn right. Follow it as described above.) By boat, continue south from Pungo on Princess Anne Road for 11.8 miles to Public Landing Road, left, to a boat dock. It is about 6 miles across Back Bay to park dock landings at Barbour Hill, False Cape, and Wash Woods.

> **False Cape Main Trail** (4.2 mi.), **Barbour Hill Interpretive Trail** (2.4 mi.),
> **Barbour Hill Beach Trail** (0.7 mi.), **False Cape Landing Trail** (0.4 mi.),
> **Wash Woods Beach Trail** (0.6 mi.), **Wash Woods Interpretive Trail** (0.7 mi.),
> **Wash Woods Cemetery Trail** (0.5 mi.), **Dudley Island Trail** (3 mi.)   808–15

Length and Difficulty: 22 miles (35.2 km) combined, round-trip; easy
Connecting Trail: *Back Bay Dike Trail* (3.8 mi.)
Features: bay, Atlantic beach, wildlife, fishing, isolation
Trailheads: Three boat docks (see Access, above), and *Back Bay Dike Trail* (See
   Back Bay NWR in Chapter 8.)

Introduction: Virginia State Parks literature describes this park as a paradise, but without some advance planning for staying overnight, it could be paradise lost. Request a brochure about overnight camping, preparations, and regulations before leaving home (see Addresses and Information, below). Call about campsite availability. Free permits are required, and they must be picked up in person at the visitor center in Seashore State Park, 2500 Shore Drive in north Virginia Beach. (Visitor center hours vary; call in advance.) If not accessing the park by boat across Back Bay, hikers may park their vehicles (for a fee) at Little Island Park at Sandbridge Beach. Backpack 5.3 miles from Little Island Park to the entrance of the state park through the refuge. Assigned campsites may be another 1.5 miles to 3 miles. Because the campsites are primitive, all water must be carried in and all trash carried out. Open fires are not permitted. Insect repellent, sunscreen, and a shade tarp are essential in hot weather. Permits are not required for day use.

Description: If planning to hike all the trails in the park and the *Back Bay Dike Trail* through the refuge and back, add 10.6 miles for a total of 32.6 miles. Beginning at the refuge visitor center and entering the park, follow the *Barbour Hill Interpretive Trail* for 0.7 miles to the park's contact station. At the park entrance is an observation deck for viewing wildfowl. At the contact station is a primitive rest room and information about the park. A ranger is usually stationed here, and the *Barbour Hill Interpretive Trail* continues right (west). At 0.7 miles a spur trail goes left to Barbour Hill campsite and boat dock, and the interpretive trail bends right to make a loop back to the *Back Bay Dike Trail* (0.3 mi. from the park's entrance). From the contact station the *False Cape Main Trail* (road) goes left 280 yards and turns right. Ahead is the *Barbour Hill Beach Trail* and beach campsite. Follow the main trail through the park, which is primarily forested with live oak, pine, wax myrtle, and yaupon. At 1 mile is an open area with a bog on the left and pleasant views of the bay on the right. After another 1 mile is an intersection where to the right is False Cape Landing campsite in a grassy field, and a boat dock by the bay. To the left it is 0.4 miles on the *False Cape Landing Trail* to another campsite near the beach. (False Cape received its name from mariners who falsely identified the slight curve in the beach for Cape Henry at Chesapeake Bay.) These are the last campsites on the journey south.

Continue on the main trail for 1.2 miles to another intersection. Here is a 0.3-mile road to the right to the ranger's quarters, and the 0.6-mile *Wash Woods Beach Trail* to the ocean on the left. Ahead on the main trail it is 0.1 mile to the *Wash Woods Interpretive Trail* left. It goes 0.2 miles over a high sand dune to an observation deck from which the bay and ocean can be seen with the woods and dunes in between. To the right is a junction with the *Cemetery Trail*, and ahead the interpretive trail goes 0.5 miles over dunes to the ocean. On the main trail it is 80 yards to a fork in the road. To the right it is 0.2 miles to the Wash Woods Environmental Educational Center, 8.2 miles from the refuge visitor center. Except for summer students involved in research at the center's dorms and classrooms, this area is usually quiet, almost ghostly. In this area a human settlement once developed, known mainly for its fishing and hunting. (Wash Woods received its name from the practice of using wood from shipwrecks to construct buildings.)

The most remote part of the park is ahead. From the left fork of the main trail begins the *Dudley Island Trail;* it is 0.4 miles in sand to the *Cemetery Trail,* which crosses the *Dudley Island Trail.* To the right it is 100 yards to the ruins of a Methodist church and a cemetery heavily shaded with live oaks and pine. To the left the *Cemetery Trail* passes over dunes to join the *Wash Woods Interpretive Trail.* The *Dudley Island Trail* continues ahead 2.6 miles to the Atlantic Ocean at the Virginia/North Carolina state line. Bicycles and motor vehicles are not allowed on the trail. On a route of sand, shrub, and solitude the trail passes Sheep House Hill and Stormonts Pond. A return loop can be made by hiking the beach to access the *Wash Woods Beach Trail* for a distance of 6.7 miles.

USGS map: Knotts Island

Addresses and Information: False Cape Park, 4001 Sandpiper Rd., Virginia Beach, VA 23456; phone: 804-426-7128 (this is a mailing address, not a park office). Wash Woods Environmental Education Center phone: 804-426-2610; pay phone: 804-721-9925. Seashore State Park and Natural Area (for False Cape camping permits), 2500 Shore Dr., Virginia Beach, VA 23451; phone: 804-481-2131. Back Bay NWR, 4005 Sandpiper Rd. (P.O. Box 6286), Virginia Beach, VA 23456; phone: 804-721-2412. Available are park and refuge map brochures, camping information.

GUNSTON HALL
Fairfax County

Gunston Hall, the colonial home and plantation of George Mason (1725–1792), is famous for its splendid architectural beauty. Its Palladian room, designed by William Buckland, has been called "the most beautiful room in America." The historic site also includes a number of service buildings, a schoolhouse, and formal gardens. The house and 556 acres were deeded to the commonwealth by Mr. and Mrs. Louis Hertle. Since 1950 it has been open to the public, and in 1961 it became listed on the National Register of Historic Places. Mason is the "Father of the Bill of Rights" for the U.S. Constitution; he drafted a number of documents that have influenced human rights internationally. In the Virginia Declaration of Rights in 1776 he stated "That all men are by nature equally free and independent and have certain inherent rights." Although not listed among the official state parks and natural areas, it receives state technical support services from the Department of Conservation and Recreation and educational services from the Department of Education. The facility is managed by the National Society of the Colonial Dames of America. Adjoining the preserve is Pohick Bay Regional Park on the northwest, and to the south are Mason Neck NWR and Mason Neck State Park.

The historic preserve has an interpretive nature trail accessible west of the gardens. From there it follows signs around Deer Park, and after 0.4 miles in the forest on the *Barn Wharf Trail* it takes a right to the wharf overlook at Gunston

Cove at the Potomac River. Among the flora are cedar, oak, maple, walnut, persimmon, and wildflowers. Wildlife includes mink, otter, turkey, deer, bald eagle, and songbirds. Birding is a feature of the trail. After a return to the nature trail and back to the formal gardens the round-trip hike is an easy 1.7 miles.

816

USGS map: Fort Belvoir

Access. From US 1 turn east on VA 242 (near Lorton) and drive 3.5 miles to Gunston Hall, left.

Address and Information: Gunston Hall, Lorton, VA 22079; phone: 703-550-9220. Available are information brochures.

KIPTOPEKE STATE PARK
Northampton County

One of Virginia's newest and evolving state parks, Kiptopeke (meaning "Big Water" in the language of the Accawmack Indians) has 375 acres, purchased in 1992. At the site of the former Virginia Beach to Eastern Shore Ferry, there is nearly 1 mile of Chesapeake Bay beach frontage. The park has a campground with hook-ups, a picnic area with shelters, a store, an 1,800-foot-long fishing pier, a swimming area and bathhouse, and a planned trail system. One trail, scenic 1-mile *Baywood Trail*, is complete. It is across the road from the campground southeast to the beach, in primary and secondary dunes and forest to a hawk observation deck. Nearby is the Virginia Society of Ornithology migratory bird banding station and

817 fields of songbirds and butterflies.

Access: On US 13, 4 miles north of the northern end of the Chesapeake Bay Bridge-Tunnel, turn west on SR 704 (0.2 mi. on SR 645), opposite Cedar Grove.

Address and Information: Kiptopeke State Park, 3540 Kiptopeke Dr., Cape Charles, VA 23310; phone: 804-331-1040. Available are leaflet and park map.

LEESYLVANIA STATE PARK
Prince William County

Leesylvania, meaning "Lee's Woods," is the ancestral homesite of Henry Lee II and his wife, Lucy Grimes Lee. Here they farmed on a plantation, served as gracious colonial hosts, reared eight children, and were buried on one of the farm's mossy knolls. They were the grandparents of Robert E. Lee, whose father, Henry Lee III, was born here in 1756. He is best known as "Light Horse Harry" Lee. He was a member of the Continental Congress, governor of Virginia, and a member of the U.S. Congress. He is also known for his penned eulogy of his friend George Washington, "first in war, first in peace, and first in the hearts of his countrymen."

Today visitors will see only the ruins of the buildings at this noble estate, but its soil is secure, thanks to preservationists Don Curtis and Eleanor Lee Templeman. In 1978 the estate owner, philanthropist Daniel K. Ludwig, donated a large share of the property to the commonwealth for a state park, which opened in 1992. The park is located on a peninsula facing the Potomac River. On the northern side is Occoquan Bay, and on the southern side is Powell's Creek. Across the Potomac is

Cornwallis Neck in Maryland. The park has picnic grounds, a boat launch for boating and fishing, and trails. A short 0.4-mile loop, the *Bushey Point Trail*, is a stroll among ferns and spicebush to a sandy overlook at the Potomac River. It is near a parking area between the railroad and the boat launch. Another forest trail is 1.4-mile *Powell's Creek Trail*. At the trail entrance is a 150-million-year-old petrified stump. On the interpretive loop the trail descends to a scenic overlook of Powell's Creek at 0.7 miles. The forest understory has papaw, mountain laurel, black cohosh, and cut-leaved toothwort. Access is at a parking lot, right, after the park entrance. A longer trail is described below.   818–19

Access: From I-85, exit 156, south of Woodbridge, and the junction of SR 638 east, drive 1.6 miles to US 1. Turn right, go 0.2 miles, turn left on SR 610 (Neabsco Rd.) for 1.4 miles, and turn right to park entrance. The end of the road is 2.4 miles farther.

Lee's Woods Trail   820

Length and Difficulty: 2 miles (3.2 km); easy
Features: scenic views, historic site
Trailhead: Parking area at the end of the road near picnic area
Description: Pass a monument in honor of Henry Lee III, father of Robert E. Lee, and approach the wide trail on a hillside. (If there is a pamphlet about the trail at a display box, take one for assistance in understanding the marker numbers.) At 0.2 miles is Freestone Point, a high bluff by the Potomac River. Here was an artillery battery used by the Confederates in the Civil War. Algonquian Indians first used the river bluff to view hostile or friendly traffic. The trail passes views of Occoquan Bay on a side trail. Then, straight, it goes to marker #5, the homesite of John Fairfax. The home burned in 1910. At 1 mile is the homesite of Henry and Lucy Lee's plantation home that burned in the 1790s. Beyond here and the Lee's gravesite is a descent to the 200-year-old Escaped Gardens. At 1.4 miles is a side trail to view hills cut by a railroad line in 1872. From here complete the loop on a wide trail.
USGS maps: Quantico, Indian Head
Address and Information: Leesylvania State Park, 16236 Neabsco Rd., Woodbridge, VA 22191; phone: 703-670-0372. Available are flyer of park information and map, pamphlets "A Potomac Legacy" and "A History of Leesylvania."

MASON NECK STATE PARK
Fairfax County

Once the hunting and fishing grounds of Dogue Indians, this historic area's recorded history began in 1755, where George Mason, father of the Bill of Rights of the U.S. Constitution, constructed Gunston Hall, a colonial home. In the 1960s Friends of Mason Neck organized to preserve the peninsula from commercial and residential development. The result was a purchase of 5,000 acres by the Nature Conservancy, from which the park's 1,804 acres were purchased by the state in 1969. Adjoining the park on the northeast is Mason Neck NWR (see Chapter 8).

Other adjoining property are Pohick Bay Regional Park and Gunston Hall Historical Facility. On the southwestern side are Occoquan Bay and Belmont Bay. In addition to the habitat for bald eagle, the park accommodates at least 200 species of songbirds. Other wildlife includes deer, bobcat, and fox. The park has a visitor center, a picnic area, a canoe launch, and trails. The visitor center provides interpretive programs, children's programs, and canoe trips.

Access: From US 1, junction with VA 242 (east to Gunston Hall), drive 4.3 miles to High Point Road, right. Pass the Mason Neck NWR parking lot after 0.7 miles and continue to the visitor center after another 2.9 miles.

Beach Trail (0.3 mi.), **Bay View Trail** (1 mi.), **Wilson Spring Trail** (0.7 mi.),
821–24 **Kane's Creek Trail** (1 mi.)

Length and Difficulty: 3 miles (4.8 km) combined, round-trip; easy
Features: scenic views, birding, canoeing
Trailhead: Parking area at visitor center
Description: At the visitor center stroll on the *Beach Trail* for a view of Belmont Bay, then head to the south for hiking red-blazed *Bay View Trail*, an interpretive loop. At the fork choose the right and cross elevated boardwalks in the marsh, an excellent place for birding. At 0.5 miles make a small loop at a scenic bluff before curving north. Some of the vascular plants are papaw, mountain laurel, and blueberries. On the return, right, is yellow-blazed *Wilson Spring Trail*. Follow it through a hardwood forest of oak, ash, beech, and pine. Some of the trees are dead because of the gypsy moth. Cross the entrance road and reach a junction with the blue-blazed *Kane's Creek Trail*. It also makes a loop but has a side trail that requires about 0.2 miles of backtracking from a scenic view of Kane's Creek. Deer may be seen on this trail. Complete the loop through holly, ash, maple, and oak on a parallel with the entrance road to the visitor center.
USGS maps: Fort Belvoir, Indian Head
Address and Information: Mason Neck State Park, 7301 High Point Rd., Mason Neck, VA 22079; phone: 703-550-0960. Available are flyer of park facilities and map.

SEASHORE STATE PARK AND NATURAL AREA
City of Virginia Beach

Established in 1936 as one of the six original parks in the state system, the Seashore State Park and Natural Area leads in the number of visitors. Remarkably preserved, it is a natural area and a national natural landmark and has national recreation trails. Set in a metropolitan environment, it offers respite for those who wish a campsite in the dunes by the Chesapeake Bay or a cabin in the pines and oaks with tree frogs and songbirds. Rich in ecological succession, the 2,700-acre park has more than 600 species of plants. Many of its animal species are found in the mid-Atlantic states as well as the Carolinas. The area around the park has an impressive history. Near the park's campground are Cape Henry Memorial Landing Place, where the English landed in 1607 before settling in Jamestown, and the

Old Cape Henry Lighthouse, the first built by the federal government in 1791. Both are in the Fort Story Military Reservation. On the beach area near the park is the city's Life-Saving Museum of Virginia and Virginia Marine Science Museum. The park includes facilities for boating, fishing, hiking, picnicking, bicycling, and nature study. There is a visitor information center, a large area of 235 campsites for tents and trailers, housekeeping cabins, and a grocery store. The visitor center is open from 9 A.M. to 6 P.M. in the summer. (Contact the center for hours during other seasons.) The park has a labyrinth of hiking trails, one of which, the *Cape Henry Trail*, is central to all the others. It extends the entire length of the park to a contact station on 64th Street, 0.2 miles from US 60.

Access: From the junction of US 60 and US 13 near the Chesapeake Bay Bridge-Tunnel go east on US 60 (Shore Dr.) for 4.5 miles. At a traffic signal turn right on VA 343, the park entrance, or turn left if entering the campground. If coming from the beach area of the city, go north on US 60 on Atlantic Avenue to Shore Drive.

Cape Henry Trail (6 mi.), **Bald Cypress Trail** (1.5 mi.), **Osmanthus Trail** (3.1 mi.), **Fox Run Trail** (0.3 mi.), **Long Creek Trail** (4 mi.), **High Dune Trail** (0.2 mi.), **Kingfisher Trail** (0.6 mi.), **White Hill Lake Trail** (1.4 mi.), **Osprey Trail** (1.2 mi.)

825–33

Length and Difficulty: 18.3 miles (30 km) combined, round-trip; easy
Features: scenic views, marsh, swamp, wildlife, wildflowers
Trailheads: Parking lot at the visitor center, or contact station on 64th Street of Atlantic Avenue at the beach
Description: All trails can be accessed from the visitor center, but the immediate ones are the *Cape Henry Trail* and the *Bald Cypress Trail*. Connecting trails can be used to form loops of various distances. Camping is not allowed on any trail, and only the *Cape Henry Trail* is open for bicycling. One section of the dark-green-blazed *Cape Henry Trail* goes north and northwest from the visitor center to Broad Bay for 1.1 miles. Backtrack. The second section goes southeast from the visitor center, passing intersections with the *High Dune Trail*, right at 0.2 miles; the *Bald Cypress Trail* (for the second time), right and left at 0.4 miles; the *Kingfisher Trail*, right at 1.2 miles; and the *White Hill Lake Trail*, right at 2.4 miles. It reaches the contact station on 64th Street at 3.5 miles. Here is drinking water and a rest room. The last section crosses the road, turns right, meanders, but parallels with 64th Street to a parking area at Narrows boat ramp to complete the trail at 6 miles. Backtrack, or have a second vehicle waiting. On this wide, busy trail the treadway is usually dry. It is forested by oak, loblolly pine, sweet gum, ash, and holly.

The self-guiding, red-blazed *Bald Cypress Trail* begins at the visitor center at a large trail display sign. Markers along the trail explain the uniqueness of the water forest, lagoons, plants, fish, birds, reptiles, and dunes. Visitors will hear spring peepers on spring nights, bullfrogs and the shrill of kingfishers in the summer, and chattering squirrels almost any season. At 0.3 miles the trail makes a junction with the blue-blazed *Osmanthus Trail* (which makes a loop and returns to the *Bald Cypress Trail* 0.2 mi. to the right). The *Osmanthus Trail* is wide, and sections are heavily draped with Spanish moss, an epiphyte. The trail goes deeply into the park and undulates on the dunes and swales. Some of the flora is the same as that on the *Bald Cypress Trail* and the *Cape Henry Trail*. Upon returning to the *Bald Cypress Trail* there will be more swamp and stately cypress. The trail is completed after crossing the wide *Cape Henry Trail*, passing the white-blazed *High Dune Trail*, and connecting with the yellow-blazed, leg-stretching *Fox Run Trail* to make a right turn for returning to the visitor center.

The orange-blazed *Long Creek Trail* does not loop; it is a linear route, as is the *Cape Henry Trail*, to 64th Street. The trail begins on the entrance road, makes a junction with the *Fox Run Trail* at 0.4 miles, and at 1.4 miles makes a junction with the *Kingfisher Trail*, left. (The 0.6-mi. *Kingfisher Trail* serves as an excellent option for making a loop back to the visitor center via the *Cape Henry Trail* for 3.6 mi.) At 1.6 miles the trail joins pink-blazed *White Hill Lake Trail*. (It goes 1.4 mi. ahead to a junction with the *Cape Henry Trail* for another loop option of 5.7 mi. to the visitor center.) The *Long Creek Trail* turns right and crosses a cement bridge to pass between White Lake on the left and Broad Bay on the right. In this scenic area are sweet pepperbush, sensitive ferns, and wax myrtle. At 2.3 miles is a junction with green-blazed *Osprey Trail*, right. (The *Osprey Trail* descends steeply to a boardwalk and low level by the bay. From here are views of the us 60 bridge, northwest. To the left is a swamp and another boardwalk crossing with views of the bay. The trail meets the *Long Creek Trail* after 1.2 mi.) Continue on the *Long Creek Trail* on a wide old road and pass a damp area at 3.4 miles. Reach a junction with the *Osprey Trail* at 3.5 miles. On this trail and the *Osprey Trail* are multiple cuts through the forest made by bicyclists. Pass a gate and reach 64th Street at 4 miles. It is 0.6 miles left to the contact station, where a loop of 8.3 miles can be made by returning to the visitor center on the *Cape Henry Trail*.

USGS map: Cape Henry

Address and Information: Seashore State Park and Natural Area, 2500 Shore Dr., Virginia Beach, va 23451; phone: 804-481-2131/491-5190. Available for free are flyer with map and campground information, trail pamphlet. Books are on sale at visitor center.

WESTMORELAND STATE PARK
Westmoreland County

The 1,295-acre Westmoreland State Park is located on the northern edge of the Northern Neck, a peninsula between the Rappahannock and Potomac Rivers in the coastal plain. The area is rich in geological history, beginning about 127 million years ago, with remains of ancient marine life fossils found in the beach sediments. The area is also rich in political history. Adjoining the park on the east is Stratford, home of some of the Lee family and the birthplace of Robert E. Lee (see Leesylvania State Park in this chapter). Eight miles west in Wakefield is the birthplace of George Washington. Early owners of the park property were Nathaniel Pope, about 1650, and Thomas Lee, in 1716. The park was established in 1936, one of the original six in the state's park system.

Facilities include a visitor center, a nature center, campgrounds with hookups, primitive cabins in a campground, vacation cabins, an amphitheater, a bathhouse and swimming pool, a picnic area, playgrounds, rowboat and paddle boat rentals, a boat ramp, a grocery store, a restaurant (with superb views of the Potomac), group camps, bridle and hiking trails, and some facilities for the physically impaired. Some of the trails connect, and others serve as connectors between one facility and another. For example, the 0.5-mile, yellow-blazed beach trail goes from near the camp store to the beach and swimming pool area. The 0.4-mile, white-blazed *River Trail* connects west cabins with the west picnic area. The *Laurel Pond Trail*, a 1.4-mile, orange-blazed trail goes from the parking area on the entrance road (across from Campground C) to the boat ramp. After 0.5 miles at Rock Spring Pond, the 0.5-mile, green-blazed *Rock Spring Trail* connects from the entrance road (across from the *Turkey Neck Trail*).   834–36

Access: From junction of US 301 and VA 3, drive 17.5 miles east on VA 3 to VA 347, and turn left on park road.

Big Meadow Trail (0.6 mi.), **Turkey Neck Trail** (3.1 mi.), **Beaver Trail** (0.4 mi.)   837–39
Length and Difficulty: 4 miles (6.4 km) combined, round-trip; easy
Features: scenic views, fossils, marsh, wildlife, geological formations
Trailheads: Parking area near nature center, and on entrance road near campground B
Description: The red-blazed *Big Meadow Trail* has changed names and distance over the years, but it gets its most recent name from a large low area, partly marsh from beaver dams, on the eastern side of the park. Currently the trail is an interpretive route with markers keyed to a park brochure. It begins east of the visitor center at a median in the road to the east cabins. It descends on an old logging road, once an area whose floor was in a Miocene sea. In recent years the forest has become broadleaf with cherry, oak, beech, and tulip poplar. Its understory is dogwood, holly, sassafras, and papaw. At the last marker the trail turns left in a descent to the Potomac River and a sandy beach at 0.6 miles. Here are views of the jagged profile of Horsehead Cliffs. Backtrack to the main trail and continue ahead over a bridge to an observation deck in the meadow, also called Yellow Swamp, a name used because of its yellow hue in the summer. Here are shorebirds, and flowering plants such as white mallow, arum, and water rose. The blue-blazed *Turkey Neck Trail* begins here right and left. It makes a 2.3-mile loop but also has a spur west to pass a campground and exit at the entrance road. The loop is bisected by the 0.4-mile *Beaver Trail*. If taking the left, follow the edge of the meadow and beaver dams and cross occasional boardwalks. Turkeys or hawks may be seen or heard in the area. If not making the complete loop, turn left at the first left and pass a spur to Campground C at 1.7 miles. Continue ahead to the entrance road, turn right, and walk back to the point of origin for a total of 4 miles.

USGS map: Stratford Hall

Address and Information: Westmoreland State Park, Rt. 1, Box 600, Montross, VA 22520; phone: 804-493-8821. Available are brochure with park map and *Big Meadows Trail* brochure.

YORK RIVER STATE PARK
James City County

York River State Park has 2,505 acres of a valuable and sensitive estuarine environment where bluffs rise from a mixture of salt and fresh water. The area has valuable Native American history of interest to archaeologists. For centuries the area has been upper farmland bordered with hardwood forests and low brackish creeks. The park's northern border is the York River; through the center of the park is Taskinas Creek. Activities are boating and fishing (with access to the river on SR 605 (Croaker Landing Rd.) off SR 607 (Croaker Rd.) on the northwestern corner of the park. There are picnic areas near the visitor center, a freshwater pond nearby, and a trail network for hiking, biking, and horseback riding. (There is no campground.) There are three equestrian trails, the longest of which is 2.6-mile *Meh-Te-Kos Trail*, and four trails are multiple-use for hiking and biking, the longest of which is 1.3-mile *Backbone Trail*. All the trails connect, and some are short and clustered, which provides distance options for visitors. The park is spacious, serene, and uncrowded.

840

Access: From I-64, exit 231 (11 mi. north of Williamsburg), take Croaker exit north on SR 607 for 0.7 miles. Turn right on SR 606, go 1.6 miles, and turn left on SR 696 (York River State Park Rd.) for 1.9 miles to visitor center.

Woodstock Pond Trail (1.3 mi.), **Beaver Trail** (0.6 mi.),
Mattaponi Trail (1.4 mi.), **Backbone Trail** (1.3 mi.),
Laurel Glen Trail (0.4 mi.), **Pamunkey Trail** (0.8 mi.),

841–48

Powhatan Forks Trail (1.4 mi.), **Majestic Oak Trail** (1 mi.)

Length and Difficulty: 9.7 miles (15.5 km) combined, round-trip; moderate

Features: scenic views, marsh, fossils, wildlife, historic site

Trailhead: Parking area near visitor center

Description: From the visitor center, walk north to views of the river, then turn right, downhill to the pond on the *Woodstock Pond Trail*, a physical fitness trail. It crosses the dam for a circle of the pond, but it also connects to the backcountry trails. The pond is a popular freshwater impoundment for blue gill and largemouth bass. A short trail, closer to the lake, is the *Beaver Trail*. At the eastern end of the dam begin the *Mattaponi Trail*. It affords excellent views of the river and provides access to an area of beach where the Yorktown formation regularly exposes 5-million-year-old marine fossils. The trail curves south in woodlands and crosses a bridge in a pocket marsh. At 1.7 miles the trail ends, but it picks up a short piece of the *Woodstock Pond Trail* before connecting with the *Backbone Trail* on an old woods service road. At 2 miles is a junction with *Laurel Glen Trail*, left, which makes a 0.8-mile loop in a community of ferns and

York River State Park. (Courtesy Virginia Division of Tourism)

mountain laurel. Continue on the *Backbone Trail* (which is used by both hikers and bikers) through woods and fields to the *Pamunkey Trail*, left, at 3.7 miles. Follow it 0.8 miles on top of a ridge and a descent to the edge of York River. An observation tower provides scenic views of marsh and river. Backtrack to a spur trail left at 5.2 miles. Follow the spur 0.2 miles to an intersection for the *Majestic Oak Trail*, left and right, and the *Powhatan Forks Trail* straight ahead. Take the left, which like the *Pamunkey Trail*, is on a ridgeline. It ends near a large white oak at the river and connects with the northern fork of the *Powhatan Forks Trail* over a 200-foot-long boardwalk in a tidal marsh. Follow the *Powhatan Forks Trail* south to its eastern fork, left, for another view of the river. Backtrack on the fork to the main *Powhatan Forks Trail* and turn left. It connects with the *Majestic Oak Trail* at 8 miles. Turn left for a quick access to the *Backbone Trail*, right and left. Take the right, follow it to the *Woodstock Pond Trail*, take a left to parallel the entrance road, and return to the visitor center at 9.7 miles.
USGS map: Gressitt

Taskinas Creek Trail

849

Length and Difficulty: 1.6 miles (2.6 km) round-trip; moderate
Features: marsh, wildlife, wildflowers, birding
Trailhead: Parking area at visitor center
Description: This is a self-guiding trail with a brochure keyed to 18 emphasis stops. Quiet hikers may see deer, songbirds, herons, and hawks. After 0.2 miles on an old road, parallel to the main entrance road and through a field, turn right into

the forest. At 0.4 miles are two huge twin oaks, and at 0.6 miles is a kiosk about the wildlife and brackish water of Taskinas Creek. Cross a 280-foot-long boardwalk through marsh cordgrass. Here, as at all tidal marshes, part of the area changes from aquatic to terrestrial twice daily because of the tides. Ascend and reach a scenic overlook of the marsh at 0.8 miles. Begin a climb and curve south to return through mountain laurel, galax, and open hardwood forest.

USGS map: Gressitt

Address and Information: York River State Park, 5526 Riverview Rd., Williamsburg, VA 23188; phone: 804-566-3036. Available are brochure on facilities and trail map, "Life on Edge" brochure for trail guide.

State Forests

Virginia has eleven state forests with a total of 50,636 acres. They are managed for the purpose of multiple usage to include timber production, hunting, fishing, wildlife control, watershed protection, and forestry research. Within four of the forests are state parks for other recreational activities such as camping, hiking, picnicking, and swimming. The parks are Holliday Lake in Appomattox-Buckingham State Forest (19,535 acres); Twin Lakes in Prince Edward-Gallion State Forest (6,970 acres); Pocahontas in Pocahontas State Forest (5,783 acres); and Bear Creek Lake in Cumberland State Forest (16,233 acres). Although the forests have many gated roads for day hikes, only the Cumberland has focused on a major trail, the *Willis River Trail*, described below. Another forest, 278-acre Zoar State Forest in King William County, has a 1-mile interpretive trail among old growth trees by the Mattaponi River. To reach it from US 360 at Aylett, go north 1.6 miles on SR 600 to a parking area on the right.

CUMBERLAND STATE FOREST
Cumberland County

850 **Willis River Trail**
Length and Difficulty: 15.2 miles (24.3 km); moderate
Features: wildlife, streams, historic site, wildflowers, scenery
Trailheads: For the northern trailhead, leave the town of Cumberland (at US 60) and go north on SR 622 for 1.8 miles. Take the right fork on SR 623 and go 2.6 miles; bear right on SR 624 for 1.2 miles to SR 608. After 2.2 miles look for a narrow dirt road on the right, and go 0.4 miles to the parking area. For the southern trailhead go west 3.1 miles on US 60 from the town of Cumberland and turn right on SR 629. Follow it 3 miles to a parking and picnic area on the right at Winston Lake.
Introduction: A joint project by the Virginia Department of Forestry and the Old Dominion Appalachian Trail Club, the trail is marked by white blazes and usually receives annual maintenance. It is entirely on state property, but camping is not permitted. However, the trail has a short connector to Bear Creek

Lake State Park, which does have a campground. State roads bisect the trail at six places, thus making short hikes an option. In a forest of hardwoods and pine, hikers are likely to see wildlife.

Description: Across the river from the parking area at the northern end is a swinging footbridge, but this is not in the trail's direction. Instead, go right from the parking area through patches of clubmoss and by large groves of mallow near the river marsh. At 0.7 miles reach SR 615. Turn left, cross Reynolds Creek bridge, and turn right off the road. Ascend and descend on low ridges and coves among squirrel cups, Christmas fern, and tall beech trees. At 1.7 miles rock-hop the creek in a scenic area, and slightly ascend. Pass near the stream again at 2.1 miles and 2.4 miles, then follow an old logging road to gravel SR 224 at 2.9 miles. Turn right and follow the road for 0.6 miles to turn left at a forest road gate. Enter a flat damp area with ferns and honeysuckle, cross Bonbrook Creek, and arrive at paved SR 224 at 4.8 miles. (Parking space is nearby.)

Descend on a gentle path to Willis River at 5.3 miles. Go upstream on an alluvial floodplain among oak, river birch, spicebush, sycamore, and papaw (which has ripe edible fruit in early September). Follow the boundary line of 27-acre Rock Quarry Natural Area. At 6.3 miles reach a grassy road turnaround. Turn left to Rock Quarry Road. (Here is an exit, left, for 0.4 mi. to SR 623.) Turn right on the grassy road and follow the trail 0.2 miles to another cul-de-sac. Enter the forest and descend through oaks and beech to a bluff and Willis River at 6.8 miles. Bear left, leaving the river edge, and go 0.4 miles before returning to the riverbank. Again bear left from the river; pass an enormous oak, and go through a floodplain with light understory for 0.1 mile to the riverbank. Follow upstream, turn left on grassy road, go 180 yards, turn right off road at 7.7 miles, and reach Horn Quarter Creek. Follow along the edge of the scenic rocky stream to a crossing. Ascend to a cul-de-sac of seeded road. Turn left and follow road past a large oak and grazing field on the right and a deep pit on the left. Turkey, deer, pheasant, dove, and quail are often seen here. Turn right off road with pines at 8.3 miles, onto an overgrown road. Reach SR 622 at 9 miles. Turn left for 65 yards to a junction of SR 622 and SR 623.

Follow SR 622 (or under a power line if not overgrown) for 0.5 miles to a junction with SR 629 (Oak Hill Rd.) at 9.5 miles. (Here SR 629 leads 0.8 mi. right to Bear Creek Lake State Park and 2.1 mi. farther south on SR 629 to the southern trailhead at Winston Lake.) Follow the trail into a stand of pine and cross a forest road at 10.2 miles. (To the right on the forest road it is 0.3 mi. to Bear Creek Lake State Park campground at paved road. From here it is 0.3 mi. left, downhill, on the road to the beach and concession stand. To the right is the campground, with showers, and 0.3 mi. to the park's entrance off SR 629 at the lake's dam.)

Continuing on the *Willis River Trail*, reach a junction with a spur trail, right, at 10.7 miles. (The spur trail is 0.4 mi. from the park's beach, parking area, and concession stand, accessed by either the park's *Lakeside Trail* or part of the *Pine Knob Trail*. On the way it passes the park's *Circumferential Trail*.) The *Willis*

River Trail crosses a small stream and at 10.8 miles begins a parallel with the Little Bear Creek, to cross it at 11.4 miles. The area has a number of patches of pinesap, ladies tresses, and papaw. Large river birch and sycamore are prominent. Raccoon, deer, squirrel, and songbirds are in the area. Follow around a steep bluff, return to edge of Little Bear Creek, turn right, and pass an open spring under large beeches at 12.1 miles. At 12.2 miles cross Bear Creek Forest Road. (On this road it is 1.8 mi. right to SR 629.)

Cross Bear Creek at 12.4 miles, where large bunches of liverwort are on the rock ledges. Follow open gated forest road to Booker Forest Road, turn left, and follow it to cross paved SR 628 at 13.3 miles. (It is 2 mi. left on SR 628 to US 60, and 1.2 mi. right to SR 629 and entrance to Cumberland State Forest office.) Descend gradually to a damp area with patches of yellow root and cardinal flowers near a brook at 13.6 miles. At 14.6 miles cross a stream in a rocky area near an old field of young saplings and gentian. Proceed left (south) of the 10-acre Winston Lake on a slope through acres of clubmoss in a mixed forest. At a junction with old CCC walkway turn right (there is a parking area across the road, left); descend on steps, and cross a footbridge to a parking and picnic area at 15.2 miles at exit to SR 629. (It is 3 mi. left [south] to US 60, and 1.1 mi. right [north] to SR 628. Another 1 mi. north on SR 629 is park entrance.)

Addresses and Information: Cumberland State Forest, Rt. 1, Box 139, Cumberland, VA 23040; phone: 804-492-4121; access is at the intersection of SR 628 and SR 629. Zoar State Forest, P.O. Box 246, Aylett, VA 23009; phone: 804-769-2655/2962; access is on SR 608, 0.2 miles northwest of intersection of US 360 and SR 600. Virginia Division of Forestry, Box 3758, Charlottesville, VA 22903; phone: 804-977-6555.

IV : County and Municipality Trails

12 : County Parks and Recreation Areas

I see weather-beaten trees as a metaphor for humanness. Like people,
they are vulnerable to forces of nature.
—Paul Cunningham

Of Virginia's ninety-five counties, seventy-four have parks and recreation departments. Locally operated, they are usually administered by a county board of commissioners, supervisors, or other government agencies. In planning their parks and recreation areas they may request assistance from the state's Division of Planning and Recreation Resources. The division can provide help with water conservation, environmental regulations, greenways, grants, and programs. Depending on funding and demographics, the counties may have a single park with basic facilities or multiple parks with multiple facilities and services, such as the 300 parks in Fairfax County. A few counties and towns combine their resources, such as Floyd County. Another combination, though governed separately, is the multiple parks of Richmond and Henrico County in a metropolitan environment. About 25 percent of the county parks have trail systems—trails other than physical fitness or connector trails between facilities. They are described in this chapter. For a directory of the state's county and city recreation departments, call the Department of Conservation and Recreation in Richmond, 804-786-2556.

Albemarle County

Albemarle County has six parks: Chris Greene, Beaver Creek, Totier Creek, Walnut Creek, Rivanna, Mint Springs Valley, and Ivy Creek Natural Area. The latter is described under Charlottesville in Chapter 13. Mint Springs Valley has a well-developed trail system, and Walnut Creek has plans for trails.

MINT SPRINGS VALLEY PARK

The valley, with a series of three small, terraced lakes, is surrounded by mountains on three sides. The water supply for the town of Crozet flowed from this valley until 1971, when Beaver Creek Reservoir was constructed. Since then the park has become an excellent area for hiking the serene old mountain roads through orchards and by ruins of old cabins. Activities at the park include swimming, fishing, boating, and nature study.

Access: From I-64, exit 107, at US 250, go 1.7 miles to VA 240. Turn left and go 1.4 miles to Crozet. Pass under railroad bridge, turn left, and go 1.8 miles on SR 788, which becomes SR 684 to reach the park, left.

Lake Trail (0.5 mi.), **Fire Trail** (1.8 mi.), **Big Survey Trail** (0.8 mi.), **Hollow Trail** (0.5 mi.)

Length and Difficulty: 3.6 miles (5.8 km) combined, round-trip; moderate

Features: scenic views, wildlife, historic site, tranquility, wildflowers

Trailhead: Behind the beach area

Description: The loop *Lake Trail* from the picnic shelter passes to the south of all three lakes. For the *Fire Trail*, begin northwest of the beach area and ascend on a wide trail past cottonwood trees and an old stone chimney. At 0.5 miles is a junction with the *Big Survey Trail*, right. (It loops up a rocky slope of Bucks Elbow Mountain and rejoins the Fire Trail.) Continue ahead on two saddles and a knoll to another junction of the *Big Survey Trail* and begin a descent. Reach a junction with the *Hollow Trail* at 1.1 miles. (The *Hollow Trail* connects from the picnic area along a stream between Bucks Elbow Mountain and Little Yellow Mountain.) Continue to 1.4 miles, where a sharp descent begins for a return to the picnic area. Vascular plants in the area are wildflowers, locust, walnut, cherry, maple, and tree of heaven.

USGS map: Crozet

Address and Information: Albemarle County Parks and Recreation, 401 McIntire Rd., Charlottesville, VA 22901; phone: 804-296-5844. Available is a trail leaflet with map.

Arlington County

Arlington County, the state's smallest (26 sq. mi.), formed in 1920, is land that was ceded to the federal government as part of the District of Columbia in 1789, then retroceded to Virginia in 1846. It is notable for its history and national landmarks: Arlington House, Arlington National Cemetery, Fort Myer, Washington National Airport, the Pentagon, and George Washington Memorial Parkway. It also has outstanding recreational areas. There are two northern Virginia regional parks and more than ninety-four county parks, forty of which have designated hike/bike trail systems with a 7.5-mile bicycle trail along Four Mile Run (see Chapter 9). Additionally, a portion of the *Washington and Old Dominion (W&OD) Trail* follows Four Mile Run from Alexandria through the county to the city of Falls Church and beyond. There is also a 5.5-mile bicycle trail along I-66 that joins the *W&OD Trail*. (It is recommended that hikers unfamiliar with the parks and trail network in Arlington first go to the Lubber Run Community Center office at 300 N. Park Dr. for orientation with the public open-space map. The office also has current information on area campgrounds.) The first three trails described below end at the Potomac River.

USGS maps: Falls Church, Washington West, Annandale, Alexandria

GLEBE ROAD PARK

Gulf Branch Nature Center is here, an excellent educational facility. The *Gulf Branch Nature Trail* extends 1.3 miles in a 37-acre, dense forest with tall poplar and oak along Gulf Branch to the Potomac River (0.5 mi. southeast of the Chain Bridge). This is a serene area amid the continual sounds of jetliners, where chipmunks, squirrels, raccoons, owls, and songbirds ignore the noise pollution. Wildflowers are prominent.

Access: From the junction of US 29 (Lee Highway) and Military Road, follow Military Road north to 3608 Military Road; phone: 703-558-2340.

ZACHARY TAYLOR PARK 856

The 1.1-mile *Donaldson Run Trail* leads under tall hardwoods, along a stream valley, to the Potomac River. The 44-acre park has a 1.5-mile hiking/biking trail that extends from Military Road west to Yorktown Boulevard. The forest has an understory of haw, maple, and spicebush. (Adjoining the park near the river is Potomac Overlook Regional Park. See Chapter 14.)

Access: From junction of US 29 (Lee Highway) and Military Road, follow Military Road to 30th Street. Turn right on 30th Street to the parking area.

WINDY RUN PARK 857

In a park of 13 acres the 1.4-mile *Windy Run Trail* descends to the Potomac River, only 1.5 miles upriver from Key Bridge. A remarkable trail, it begins from the parking area in a cul-de-sac of Kenmore Street. It crosses a stream three times under large oak, poplar, and beech. Wild hydrangea, spicebush, and goat's-beard adorn the trail border. A surprise awaits the hiker at the river, where a glistening stream of water falls 45 feet in a flume. A descent can be made on the right of the stream by a railing to an enchanting part of the forest below.

Access: From the George Washington Memorial Parkway take Spout Run Parkway to Lorcom Lane and go 3 blocks to Kenmore Street, right.

GLENCARLYN PARK 858–60

Long Branch Nature Center is here. Within 98 acres, the *Long Branch Nature Trail* and the *Glencarlyn Park Trail* connect and provide 1.5 miles of trail to the 8-mile *Arlington County Bicycle Trail*. (The bicycle trail can also be hiked along Four Mile Run to facilities such as picnic areas, lighted tennis courts, and comfort stations in other parks—Barcroft, Bluemont, Bon Air, and East Falls Church.)

Access: From Arlington Boulevard (US 50) turn south to 625 South Carlin Springs Road, between Northern Virginia Doctors' Hospital and Glencarlyn Elementary School; phone: 703-558-2742.

Address and Information: Arlington County Parks and Recreation, #1 Courthouse Plaza, Suite 414, 2100 Clarendon Blvd., Arlington, VA 22201; phone: 703-358-4747.

Campbell County

LONG ISLAND PARK

Away from the noise of interstate highways and the smog of the cities is Long Island Park on the banks of the Staunton River. Only the occasional zephyric sound of an N&W train competes with the gurgling rapids below a basin of still water. Families come here to fish, picnic at shelters (which can be reserved), and play games in a grassy meadow. From a parking area near the highway the 1.2-mile *Long Island Trail* follows the riverside to Hill Creek. A return can loop past a railroad trestle and garlands of honeysuckle on red cedar and redbud to the picnic area and riverside for a total of 2.4 miles. This bucolic park is a joint project of the Virginia Game and Inland Fisheries, Virginia Commission on Outdoor Recreation, and Campbell County Recreation Department.

USGS map: Long Island

Access: From Gladys on US 501 follow SR 761 south for 6.6 miles; from Brookneal on US 501 follow SR 633 west for 7.6 miles; from Cody on VA 40 follow SR 640 north for 5 miles to a turn left on SR 639 for 0.8 miles, and right on SR 761 for 1.8 miles.

Address and Information: Campbell County Recreation Department, P.O. Box 369, Rustburg, VA 24588; phone: 804-332-5161.

Chesterfield County

HENRICUS HISTORICAL PARK

In 1986 the resurrection of the Citie of Henricus on the James River began with the establishment of Henricus Historical Park. It was financed by Chesterfield County, Henrico County, Henrico Doctors' Hospital, the city of Richmond, Tarmac-LoneStar Inc., and others. With a wealth of history the 1.3-mile *Henricus Trail* is a wide, scenic route from Dutch Gap boat launch to the high bluff of Henricus. Sir Thomas Dale and his crew built an outpost here in 1611. The next year he established Mount Malady, a forty-bed hospital (retreat) for the colonists. He also planned a university, but all his dreams were lost in the Indian massacre of 1622. The trail, with occasional elevated walkways, is shaded by river birch and sycamore to observation decks, interpretive signs, monuments, and superior views of the river. Backtrack for a total of 2.6 miles.

USGS maps: Dutch Gap, Drewrys Bluff

Access: From I-95, exit 61, at VA 10 (toward Hopewell) go 0.2 miles on VA 10 (first traffic light) and turn left on SR 732 (Old Stage Rd.) and go 2 miles to parking area by the river.

POINT OF ROCKS PARK

Opened in 1980, the park has 182 acres of diverse natural areas and historical significance. The area has been the site of Native American villages, a colonial plantation, a customs wharf, major Civil War encampments, and red ocher mining. It now provides multiple recreational facilities for fall fields and courts, picnicking, and heritage and nature study of the Ashton Creek Marsh.

Access: From I-95, exit 61, at VA 10 (toward Hopewell) take VA 10 east for 5 miles to SR 746. Turn right and go 2 miles to the park.

Ashton Creek Trail (0.5 mi.), **Woodthrush Trail** (0.7 mi.),
Cobbs Wharf Trail (1.3 mi.)   863–65
Length and Difficulty: 2.5 miles (4 km) combined, round-trip; easy
Features: historic site, marsh, wildlife, wildflowers
Trailhead: At visitor cabin from nearest picnic parking area
Description: Begin at the homestead display and enter the forest at the trail signs. The *Ashton Creek Trail* is a self-guiding nature study trail and crosses Cobblestone Creek where there are quartzite stones. It connects with a loop of the *Woodthrush Trail*, after which it connects with the *Cobbs Wharf Trail*, right and left. (To the right the trail ends at Ruffin Mill Rd.) Follow the trail left to Ashton Creek Marsh. A spur trail is on boardwalks to an observation deck in the marsh of arum, cattails, and cordgrass. Return to the main trail, reach another observation deck at 0.8 miles with views of the marsh, and again at 1.3 miles. To the right is a Civil War battery site, and ahead are views of the Appomattox River. Return by a meadow on the left.
USGS maps: Chester, Hopewell

ROCKWOOD PARK   866

The 162-acre Rockwood Park, Chesterfield County's first park, opened in 1975. Its facilities are expansive with multiple picnic areas, ball courts and fields, and a unique area for community vegetable garden plots. In the undeveloped natural area of the park there is wildlife in a mixed hardwood forest and a swamp area along Falling Creek. The park staff provides extensive programs for nature study. The *Rockwood Nature Trail* is actually a network of easy, color-coded paths. Entrance is at the trails parking area. Follow the YCC sign on white blazes. At 0.1 mile is a blue-marked trail to the left and a green-marked trail on the right. The white-blazed trail ends at 0.3 miles, and an orange-blazed trail goes left and right through mature hardwoods. There are clubmosses, ferns, and wildflowers. If taking the right, follow the edge of the lake and reach a paved road near a physical fitness area at 0.7 miles. Follow the road, right, back to the lake and pick up the orange-marked trail at 1.2 miles. Pass a marsh, explore three side trails to the left, and reach a gravel road at 1.9 miles. Return to the parking area at 2.1 miles. Mileage for all connecting trails is a total of 3.4 miles.
USGS map: Chesterfield
Access: From US 360 and SR 653 junction, southwest of Richmond, take SR 653 north for 0.1 mile and turn right to park entrance. Continue for 0.4 miles to parking area for trail entrance.
Address and Information: Chesterfield County Parks and Recreation, P.O. Box 40, Chesterfield, VA 23832; phone: 804-748-1623. Available are brochures and maps on all parks.

Fairfax County

The Fairfax County Park Authority maintains 350 parks and recreational facilities (including five nature/visitor centers and seven indoor recreation centers) for one of the finest county park systems in Virginia and in the nation.

In 1950, when the Virginia General Assembly passed the Park Authorities Act, the Fairfax County Board of Supervisors began immediately to adopt a resolution for creating a park authority. Since then more than 16,000 acres have been acquired to provide the best in services to the citizens of the metropolitan area. In addition to the usual sports facilities and bicycle routes, there are cultural centers, parks with a working farm of the 1930s, an indoor ice rink, restored landmarks, and historic sites. In addition to an incomparable record of wise and effective management, the county has developed a master plan for facilities to serve future generations. Hikers may wish to examine the master plan and the *Annual Register of Parks and Facilities* at the park authority's headquarters. Each quarter of the year the county publishes *Parktakes*, a magazine of more than 100 pages about park classes, programs, and events as varied as aquatics, garden and farm workshops, fencing, roller hockey tournaments, boat races, and concerts.

Descriptions of the county's numerous parks would fill a volume. For this guidebook some short and long trails suggested by the park authority are described to reflect trail, facility, and camping variety. Covered in the regional parks section of this guidebook, Chapter 14, under the Northern Virginia Regional Park Authority (of which Fairfax County is a member), are the *W&OD Trail* (also called the *W&OD Railroad Trail*), Bull Run–Occoquan Regional Park trails, Fountainhead Park trails, and Pohick Bay trails. The Great Falls Park trails and the *Mount Vernon Trail* are listed with national park trails in Chapter 9. (Not covered, by request, are 24 trails under the aegis of 93 private clubs and organizations in the county with recreational facilities.) The county's five nature/visitor centers are at Annandale Community Park (see entry, below); Riverbend Park (see entry, below); Hidden Pond Park (8511 Greeley Blvd., Springfield, VA 22150, phone: 703-451-9588); Ellanor C. Lawrence Park (see entry, below); and Huntley Meadows Park (see entry, below).

Access to park authority headquarters: From I-495, exits 9-A or 9-C, take I-66 west to US 50 (Lee Jackson Memorial Highway) and turn east. Immediately turn left on Waples Mill Road, and after one block turn right on Pender Drive. Continue to headquarters on right at 3701 Pender Drive, Fairfax, VA 22030; phone: 703-246-5700.

867   ANNANDALE COMMUNITY PARK

In addition to recreational facilities, the park has the Hidden Oaks Nature Center and the 0.3-mile loop, interpretive *Old Oak Nature Trail*. The trailhead is on the approach to the right of the nature center, through large white oaks and by a small steam with scattered gum, pine, mountain laurel, and wildflowers.

Access: From I-495, exit 6, at Little River Turnpike (VA 236), east to the left at the first traffic light at Hummer Road. Take Hummer Road for 3 blocks to Royce Street, turn left, and go to the nature center parking on the left at the corner of Linda Lane.

Address and Information: Annandale Community Park, 4030 Hummer Rd., Annandale, VA 22003; phone: 703-941-1065.

BRADDOCK PARK   868

At present there is a 3.2-mile natural service trail, *Braddock Park Trail*, for equestrians and hikers; there are plans for additional trails as the 58-acre park is developed. Terrain is gentle, and most of the forest is young hardwood. The trailhead is at the parking area on Braddock Road (SR 620), near a sign forbidding unauthorized vehicles.

Access: From SR 620, 1.5 miles southeast from US 29 in Centreville, go to 13241 Braddock Road (between Union Mill Rd. and Clifton Rd., which is SR 645).

Address and Information: Braddock Park, 13241 Braddock Rd., Clifton, VA 22024; phone: 703-378-2671.

BURKE LAKE PARK

In the 894-acre Burke Lake Park there are trails, facilities for tent or trailer camping, fishing (for musky, bass, walleye, and sunfish), and boating in the 218-acre lake. Also, there is picnicking, golfing, and bicycling. The park is open all year, but camping is seasonal (check with the park for spring opening and autumn closing).

Access: From I-495, exit 5, go west on Braddock Road to left on Burke Lake Road. Turn left on Ox Road and go to park entrance on the left. Another access is from I-95 and Occoquan junction; take VA 123, Fox Road, for 8 miles.

Burke Lake Trail (4.7 mi.), **Beaver Cove Nature Trail** (0.7 mi.)   869–70
Length and Difficulty: 6.1 miles (9.8 km) combined, round-trip, easy
Features: scenic views, wildlife, wildflowers, fishing
Trailhead: Family campground or the marina
Description: From the park entrance and information center, follow the road left for 1.2 miles to the end of the road, and park at camp store visitor parking. Take the *Beaver Cove Nature Trail*, hiking 0.7 miles to a junction with the lake trail. If turning right, proceed along the lake border through poplar, oak, beech, aspen, and beds of ferns among partridge berry. Pass the family campground and begin a gravel physical fitness trail, which ends, or begins, east of the par-three golf course. Cross a stream near Burke Lake Road at 1.8 miles and continue around the lake, reaching the marina at 2.9 miles. Follow the trail to the dam at 3.8 miles. After crossing the dam continue to follow along the lake edge in and out of coves and through hardwoods with scattered pine. Complete the *Burke Lake Trail* at 5.4 miles and return to the trailhead on the *Beaver Cove Nature Trail* for a total of 6.1 miles.

USGS map: Fairfax

Address and Information: Burke Lake Park, 7315 Ox Rd., Fairfax Station, VA 22039; phone: 703-323-6600. Available is a brochure with park facilities, map, and campground sites.

871   SCOTTS RUN NATURE PRESERVE

Halfway between the Arlington County line and Great Falls Park on the Potomac River is Scotts Run Nature Preserve, with 337 acres. Mainly a conservation area, its major activities are fishing, hiking, and nature study. It has easy, round-trip, 2.9-mile *Scotts Run Trail*. Access to it is at the parking area. Follow it on a frequently used path downstream near river birch, sumac, dogwood, and locust with spots of tag alder and redbud. Rock-hop the stream, but notice that the trail can be hiked on either side. Approach a defile with rocky terrain and a steep ascent to the ridge on the left for an excellent view of the Potomac River. Descend to a rocky gorge with pools and cascades. Under a heavy cover of hemlock, mountain laurel, and witch hazel, the mosses and lichens give the ambience of a Blue Ridge Mountains glen. Wildflowers bloom between the base of the cascades and the narrow Potomac River beach. Backtrack to parking area.

USGS map: Falls Church

Access: From I-495, exit 13, VA 193 (Georgetown Pike), go west on Georgetown Pike for 0.7 miles to parking entrance on the right. (Exit from the parking area into traffic is dangerous.)

Addresses and Information: Scotts Run Nature Preserve, 7400 Georgetown Pike, McLean, VA 22102; phone: 703-759-3211. (For information, contact Riverbend Nature Center, 8814 Jeffery Rd., Great Falls, VA 22066; phone: 703-759-3211.)

872   ELLANOR C. LAWRENCE PARK

Formerly the Walney Farm, this exceptionally beautiful 640-acre park was donated to the county in 1971 by Ellanor C. Lawrence and her husband David Lawrence, the founder and publisher of *U.S. News and World Report*. In accordance with Mrs. Lawrence's wishes, the park offers a visitor center, ballfields, fitness trail, historic buildings, archaeological sites, and educational programs. A short interpretive *Nature Trail* is near the amphitheater.

Access: From I-495, exit 9/9A, go west on I-66 for 11 miles to exit 53 on VA 28. Turn right (north) on Sully Road to first right, Walney Road. Cabell's Mill is 0.5 miles on the right and the visitor center is 1 mile on the left.

Address and Information: Lawrence Park, 5040 Walney Rd., Chantilly, VA 22021; phone: 703-631-0013.

873–75   HUNTLEY MEADOWS PARK

Nestled in Fairfax County's Hybla Valley, this park is a natural island in the vast suburban sea of northern Virginia. Its 1,261 acres harbor majestic mature forests, wildflower-speckled meadows, and acres of wetlands bursting with life. It is ideal wildlife habitat for beavers, otters, herons, ducks, deer, and many songbird and butterfly varieties as well as a host of other animals. Facilities include a visitor center with exhibits and an auditorium, a 0.6-mile boardwalk wetland trail known as the *Heron Trail*, and 2-mile *Hike-Bike Trail*. The *Heron Trail* is an interpretive trail that meanders through the park with signs about the natural habitats of plants and animals and has a side trail, the 0.4-mile *Pond Trail*. There is also a wildlife observation tower for viewing waterfowl.

Access: From I-495, exit 1, go south 3.5 miles on US 1 (Richmond Hwy.) to Lockheed Boulevard and turn right. Go 0.5 miles to park entrance on the left at Harrison Lane.

Address and Information: Huntley Meadows Park, 3701 Lockheed Blvd., Alexandria, VA 22306; phone: 703-768-2525.

LAKE FAIRFAX PARK 876–77

Another of the county's excellent parks for camping is Lake Fairfax Park, with 479 acres, including a 30-acre lake. Although the park is open year round, the campground is seasonal, usually from March to November (check with the office for dates). There are 135 campsites, 76 of which have hookups. Other facilities are an Olympic-size swimming pool and areas for fishing, picnicking, and sports on athletic fields. Entrance to the 0.8-mile *Lake Fairfax Nature Trail* begins at campsite c21. Additionally, part of the 5-mile *Rails to River Trail* passes through the park. (This equestrian trail connects south to the W&OD Regional Park trail at Michael Faraday Court, and north from Lake Fairfax Park across Hunter Mill Rd. at Colvin Run Creek to Leesburg Pike [VA 7] near Colvin Run Mill. For more information, contact Colvin Run Stream Valley Park, 10017 Colvin Run Dr., Great Falls, VA 22066; phone: 703-759-2771.)

Access: From I-495, exit 10-B, take Leesburg Pike (VA 7) west for 6.5 miles to left on Baron Cameron Avenue (SR 606). Go 0.5 miles and turn left on Fairfax Drive to park entrance.

Address and Information: Lake Fairfax Park, 1400 Lake Fairfax Dr., Reston, VA 22090; phone: 703-471-5414.

MASON DISTRICT PARK 878–79

This 121-acre park is centrally located in Fairfax County and is unique because of its historic landmarks. It has ballfields and courts, a picnic area, and forests and meadows with a history of 400 years of land use. The park's trails have been designed to preserve the land features. The 1.3-mile *Mason District Trail* is mostly through the forest but connects with the *Nature Trail* and a 0.6-mile jogging/exercise trail.

Access: From I-495, exit 6, take VA 236 (Little River Tpk.), east for 2 miles to turn left on John Marr Drive, and right on VA 244 (Columbia Pike) to park entrance on the right.

Address and Information: Mason District Park, 6621 Columbia Pike, Annandale, VA 22003; phone: 703-941-1730.

RIVERBEND PARK

The 409-acre Riverbend Park is an outstanding preserve for maintaining the natural beauty of the Potomac River shoreline. It has a visitor center overlooking the river and a nature center tucked back in the forest. All trails can begin or make connections at the nature center.

Access: From I-495, exit 13, take VA 193 (Georgetown Pike), west for 5 miles and turn right on Riverbend Road. Go 2 miles on Riverbend Road to Jeffery Road, turn right, and proceed 1.5 miles to the nature center entrance.

Paw Paw Passage Trail (1.2 mi.), **Potomac Heritage Trail** (1.7 mi.),
880–84   **Upland Trail** (1 mi.), **Center Trail** (0.3 mi.), **Duff and Stuff Trail** (0.2 mi.)
Length and Difficulty: 5.5 miles (8.8 km) combined, round-trip; easy
Features: scenic views, wildlife, wildflowers, fishing
Trailheads: From the nature center
Description: The *Paw Paw Passage Trail* is a loop from the nature center connecting with the *Potomac Heritage Trail*. Go left at the sign, descending to a spur trail on the right for an exhibit area and overlook. Pass the pond, turn sharply right, and follow the *Potomac Heritage Trail* down the river for 1.7 miles. Along the floodplain grow huge beech, poplar, elm, basswood, birch, and sycamore. In the understory are large patches of papaw (also spelled *pawpaw*), holly, iron-wood, and spicebush. Wildflowers and ferns are commonplace. The springtime display of trilliums and bluebells is exceptional.

    Pass the visitor center and picnic area on the way to a junction with the *Upland Trail*, right. It can be followed back to the nature center on rolling terrain among tall trees and by a number of spur trails right and left. Or continue another 1 mile on the *Potomac Heritage Trail* to a junction with the *Center Trail* and its 0.3 miles to the nature center. (The *Potomac Heritage Trail* connects with the *River Trail* at the boundary of Great Falls Park. It does not connect with a trail by the same name downriver in the George Washington National Memorial Parkway.) Back at the nature center is the *Duff and Stuff Trail*, which is paved, self-guiding, and useful for the physically disabled. Other natural surface trails in the forest can be used for horseback riding.

USGS maps: Seneca, Rockville
Address and Information: Riverbend Park, 8814 Jeffery Rd., Great Falls, VA 22066; phone: 703-759-3211. Available are brochures and trail maps.

WAKEFIELD AND LAKE ACCOTINK PARKS

These two parks are connected only by the *Accotink Stream Valley Trail*, which passes by Accotink Creek under the Braddock Road bridge west near I-495. Wakefield Park's 290 acres provide an exceptionally broad list of outdoor and indoor activities, including athletic fields, tennis courts, bicycle and hiking trails, picnic areas, and facilities for the physically disabled. At Lake Accotink, which has 482 acres and is south of Wakefield, facilities emphasize outdoor water sports, picnicking, and hiking. The bike/hike trails provide a linear route in Wakefield Park and a loop around the lake in Lake Accotink Park.

Access: To Wakefield Park, leave I-495, exit 5, on sr 620 (Braddock Rd.) west for 0.2 miles to park entrance on the right. For Lake Accotink Park, leave I-495, exit 5, on sr 620 (Braddock Rd.) east for 0.5 miles and turn right on Heming Avenue to park's rear entrance. Or, from I-95, exit 169 (south of its intersection with I-495), turn west on sr 644 (Old Keene Mill Rd.), and at end of access ramps turn right on Backlick Road. Follow it to Highland Street and make a left to the marina entrance.

Accotink Stream Valley Trail 885

Length and Difficulty: 4 miles (6.4 km); easy

Features: scenic area, waterfowl, wildflowers, fishing, historic site

Trailheads: Parking lot at Wakefield Recreation Center, or parking lot at Lake Accotink Park marina

Description: If entering from Wakefield Park, follow the trail by the recreation building to the parking area and into the forest on a wide trail. Go downstream and under the Braddock Road bridge to parallel the Accotink Creek south. The forest is chiefly river birch, sycamore, oak, ash, basswood, and wildflowers. Pass a marsh and follow the trail near the edge of the lake. Join a physical fitness trail for the last 0.7 miles to the marina area at Lake Accotink park.

USGS map: Annandale

Addresses and Information: Wakefield Park, 8100 Braddock Rd., Annandale, va 22003; phone: 703-321-7080. Lake Accotink Park, 7500 Accotink Park Rd., Springfield, va 22152; phone: 703-569-3464. Available are brochures and maps of bicycle and canoe trails and park facilities.

WOLFTRAP STREAM VALLEY PARK 886

This park is a forest corridor with Wolftrap Creek running through it. On the northern end of the park are Wolf Trails Park and Springlake Park, both small areas, but together the parks provide a beautiful and peaceful area for 4-foot-wide, asphalt *Wolftrap Stream Valley Trail* (formerly *Waverly/Wolftrap Trail*). It begins at the Creek Crossing Road west of Westwood Golf Course in Vienna. The trail meanders north for 1 mile to sr 677 (Old Courthouse Rd.). (The park is near to and south of Wolftrap Farm Park, and southeast of Meadowlark Gardens Regional Park.)

Access: From I-495, exit 11, go west on va 123 into Vienna and turn right on sr 675 (Beulah Rd.). Go 2 blocks and turn right on Creek Crossing Road to park entrance. Or, continue north on Beulah Road to Abbotsford Drive and turn right.

Address and Information: Wolftrap Stream Valley Park, 1801 Abbotsford Dr., Vienna, va 22180; phone: 703-281-0182.

Gloucester County

887 TINDALL'S POINT PARK

From the parking area at Gloucester Point follow the trail signs to display stations on easy, 0.5-mile *Tindall's Point Trail*. Here is information on the Revolutionary War and Civil War fortifications at a scenic overlook of the York River. A picnic area adjoins the trail.

USGS map: Claybank

Access: From Yorktown cross the Coleman Memorial Bridge on US 17 north and enter Gloucester County. Park on the left at the end of the bridge.

Address and Information: Gloucester County Parks and Recreation, P.O. Box 157, Gloucester, VA 23061; phone: 804-693-2355.

Hanover County

888–89 POOR FARM PARK

The Poor Farm Park is located in the South Anna District near Stagg Creek, behind Patrick Henry High School and Liberty Middle School. The gate at the end of SR 810 is locked except for day use. The picnic area with shelters is on a grassy hill, where large trees provide a forest cover. Other facilities are soccer fields, volleyball courts, an archery range, horseshoe pits, an amphitheater, a *Nature Trail*, and a trail for mountain bikes. The *Patrick Henry Cross-County Trail* and other unnamed trails connect for a total of 2.8 miles, plus at least 2 miles of old logging roads near Stagg Creek. The forest is mixed hardwoods and pines with an understory of shrubs and wildflowers.

Access: From junction of I-95, exit 92, and VA 54 go west on VA 54 for 4.8 miles to SR 810 and turn left. Gated road is at the end of SR 810.

Address and Information: Hanover County Parks and Recreation, 200 Berkley St., Ashland, VA 23005; phone: 804-798-8062.

Henrico County

There are twenty-five parks spread over the county, but most are in the heavily populated suburbs of the city of Richmond. In a successful bond referendum in 1989 the park system renovated many of its parks and constructed an outstanding nature center and aquarium, nature pavilions, more tennis courts, a skateboard park, and two new parks; it also made plans for other new parks. Some of the parks have trails that focus on natural history. They are described below from northwest to north and northeast on grids 9, 15, 17, and 18 if using an ADC street map of Richmond. (See Chapter 13 for trails inside Richmond's city limits.)

DEEP RUN PARK

A day use 167-acre facility with two lakes, picnic area, sport fields, and a pleasant 2.4 miles *Deep Run Trail*, makes this park desirable for hikers and bikers. The paved trail loops around the lakes and through the woods of a young forest.

Access: From I-64, exit 180, turn south on Gaskins Road. After 1.2 miles turn west (R) on Ridgefield Parkway for 0.4 miles R.

ECHO LAKE PARK

With an 8-acre stocked lake and pier for fishing, this 24-acre day-use park has picnic areas, a playground, and 0.7-mile *Echo Lake Trail* around the lake. The trail has a nature observation blind and footbridges; lake and grassy shore have mallards and Canada geese.

Access: From I-295, exit 49, turn south on US 33 (Staples Mill Rd.) for 0.4 miles, and turn west (right) on Springfield Road for 0.5 miles left.

CRUMP MEMORIAL PARK

Half of this 150-acre day-use park is Meadow Farm Museum, a living history site. There is a nineteenth-century farmhouse, an 1850 doctor's office, a smokehouse, an orchard, a barn, farm animals, a blacksmith shop, and a family cemetery. (The park is open year round, but the museum is closed on Mondays, and December through February. For information on Old Fourth of July Festival and Harvest Festival, call 804-672-5106 or 1367.) At the parking area east, downstream, is 0.3-mile *River Birch Trail*, a loop among knobby white oaks and around North Run Creek. To access the 0.5-mile loop, self-guiding *North Run Creek Trail*, walk up the hill to the farm barn and go left. The forest is mixed hardwood and pine. At marker #9 is a side trail to a field of wild roses.

Access: From I-295, exit 45, turn south on Woodman Road to first street on the right, Mountain Road, and follow it 1.7 miles to park entrance on the right.

THREE LAKES PARK

The 18 acres of lakes are next to each other and separated by earthen dams. *Three Lakes Trail* makes loops around the lakes for 1.5 miles. There is an observation deck for lake views. Nearby is a play equipment area and picnic shelters. Unique to this 90-acre day-use park is a nature center with one of the largest outdoor aquariums in Virginia. The park is open daily, but the nature center is closed Mondays and December through February (call 804-262-4822 for more information).

Access: From I-95, exit 82, turn northeast on US 301 (Chamberlayne Rd.); go 0.8 miles, turn right on Wilkinson Road, and go 0.9 miles south to Sausiluta Drive, right.

Echo Lake Park, Henrico County. (Photograph by Allen de Hart)

895   VAWTER STREET PARK

In this 352-acre, day-use park is Glen Lea Recreation Area, which has a picnic area and ballfields. The park's special feature is the 0.8-mile *Chickahominy River Trail*. It begins at the southeastern corner of the parking lot, then drops suddenly into a forest of tall trees and fern beds with a deep ravine on the right. After 0.2 miles it reaches a field and crosses under a power line to follow the margin of the forest for about 0.2 miles. It turns left into wetland woods, follows a small dike ridge, crosses a boardwalk, and forks. Either fork goes about 250 yards to the marshy edge of the Chickahominy River and the raucous squawk of surprised waterfowl. Backtrack.

USGS map: Richmond

Access: From us 360 intersection, go west on E. Laburnum Avenue and turn right on Vawter Avenue, or from va 627 (Richmond-Henrico Tpk.) go east 0.8 miles and turn left. It is 0.7 miles to the parking area, right.

Address and Information: Henrico County Recreation and Parks, 8600 Dixon Power Dr. (P.O. Box 27032), Richmond, va 23273; phone: 804-672-5100. Available are parks brochure, flyers with park maps.

Isle of Wight County

CARROLLTON NIKE PARK   896

The 0.8-mile *Nike Park Nature Trail* follows a trail sign through a forest of tall trees with wax myrtle understory to an observation deck over a marsh to view waterfowl. Facilities at this park are ballfields, picnic areas, and a ramp for boating and fishing.

Access: From junction of us 258 and va 10/32 at Benns Church, go northeast on us 258 to park sign. Turn left on sr 665 to Carrollton and go 3.2 miles; turn left on sr 669 and go 1 mile to park entrance on the left.

FORT BOYKIN HISTORIC PARK   897

This tranquil and scenic historic site sits on a high cliff by the James River and is named in honor of Maj. Francis Boykin of the American Revolution. The fort was a strategic military post from 1623, when Capt. John Smith constructed a star-shaped salient, to 1862, when the fort was shelled and burned by Union gunboats. For the next forty-six years the fort lay in ruins, entangled with vines and briars. From 1908 to 1978 it changed private ownership at least five times. Each owner, including the late sisters Ella, Elizabeth, and Susan Jordan, landscaped or cared for the historic shrine. The sisters willed the property to the commonwealth, which in turn leased it to the county for fifty years.

From the parking area, follow the signs on the 0.5-mile *Fort Boykin Trail*. Go over the salient and turn right to the second largest black walnut tree in the state. Meander to the other interpretive markers, to magazine sites, a chimney plinth, Greer Gardens, and magnificent views of the James River. The park is open from 9 A.M. to dusk Wednesdays through Sundays.

Access: From the Pagan River bridge in downtown Smithfield, drive north on va 10 (Church St.) for 1.5 miles to a fork and take sr 674 (Blount's Corner Rd.) for 1.1 miles to sr 673 (Morgart's Beach Rd.), and turn right. Go 1 mile to parking area on the left.

Address and Information: Isle of Wight County Public Recreational Facilities Authority, Rt 2., Box 4, Carrollton, VA 23314; phone: 804-357-2291; resident managers, 804-357-5956. Available is a brochure with map.

King George County

898   BARNESFIELD PARK

This park is in Mathias Point Neck with its eastern boundary at the Potomac River. It has a 3.4-mile round-trip, backcountry road-trail and 0.2-mile *Wayside Trail* from the parking area at the eastern end of the ballfields. Osprey have built nests in the park, and usually a family is at the top of a ballfield lighting pole. The *Wayside Trail* meanders through a dense growth of saplings and honeysuckle, crosses a service road, enters a pine grove, and descends on banks of shells to the shore of the Potomac River. From this point are views of the river and the Nice Memorial Bridge spanning the river to Maryland. A hike on the dead-end road-trail to a lake offers a quiet area for birding and observing wildlife. The park also has other unnamed paths, one of which follows an old former highway west from the entrance road.

USGS map: Dahlgren

Access: On US 301, north side, at approach to the Potomac River Bridge (Nice Memorial), 3.1 miles east of VA 206 crossroads.

Address and Information: King George County, P.O. Box 71, King George, VA 22485; phone: 703-775-4FUN.

Lancaster County

899   HICKORY HOLLOW TRAIL

Lancaster County is a coastal farming area bordered by the Rappahannock River on the south and known for its scenic bays, branches, and breezy beach points. It has only one public trail, the easy, 4-mile *Hickory Hollow Trail*. It is an exceptionally good example of a trail prepared for educational purposes. It has 45 different signs describing with an unusual degree of detail the species of trees, shrubs, and wildflowers near Western Branch. Some of the trees are oak, hickory, elm, black gum, green ash, and red maple. At 0.2 miles the trail forks left to make the long loop.

USGS map: Lancaster

Access: From the town of Lancaster, drive 0.6 miles east; on VA 3, pass the school and turn left on SR 604 for 0.3 miles left to parking area.

Address and Information: Public Works Department, P.O. Box 167, Lancaster, VA 22503; phone: 804-462-5129.

Loudoun County

The *W&OD Railroad Trail* goes 22.4 miles from Herndon in Fairfax County to Purcellville in Loudoun County. The Red Rock Wilderness Overlook Regional Park offers the *Loblolly Trail*, a loop route, also in the county. See descriptions for both of these under Northern Virginia Regional Park Authority in Chapter 14.

Address and Information: Loudoun County Parks and Recreation, 18 N. King St., Leesburg, VA 22075; phone: 703-777-0343.

Northampton County

INDIANTOWN PARK   900

The 52-acre Indiantown Park, on Virginia's Eastern Shore, is a converted U.S. government camera site. The historic area is adjacent to an old Native American village and the Pocahontas Farm. Financial assistance from public and private sources and volunteer work made it possible for the county's first park to open. Among its facilities are a recreational center, a swimming pool, ballfields, picnic areas, and 1.5-mile *Indiantown Nature Trail*. It begins between the parking lot and the softball field. Forming a loop, the trail passes an Indian burial ground among hardwoods and pines.

USGS map: Cheriton
Access: From US 13 at Eastville, go east on SR 631 for 2 miles to park entrance.
Address and Information: Northampton County Parks and Recreation, P.O. Box 847, Eastville, VA 23347; phone: 804-678-5179.

Prince William County

The Prince William County Park Authority, created in 1977 from the previous parks and recreation agency, has forty recreational parks with 2,672 acres. Additional recreational areas are associated with the public school system and with Manassas. Two parks have trails that focus on nature study.

VETERANS' MEMORIAL PARK   901

The easy, 0.8-mile *Veterans' Memorial Nature Trail* has twenty-three interpretive points with two decks for observing migratory and local waterfowl, forest succession, wetland plants, flowers, and wildlife. White marsh mallow and water lilies are prevalent in the summer.

USGS map: Occoquan
Access: In Woodbridge at junction of US 1 and SR 636 (Featherstone Rd.) (at Featherstone Shopping Center) go east 1.9 miles on Featherstone Road to Veterans' Drive and parking area, left.
Address and Information: Veterans' Memorial Park, 14300 Featherstone Rd., Woodbridge, VA 22191; phone: 703-491-2183.

The 778-acre day-use park has a lake, a golf course, a marina with boat rentals, ballfields and tennis courts, picnic areas, playgrounds, and two loop trails. Access to *Locust Shade Trail* is at the fourth parking lot, left, after the park entrance. Ascend on a hill as part of a nature trail near a fence of I-95, descend, pass side trail right to ballfield, and go under a power line. Cross a footbridge at 0.5 miles, and 200 feet farther is a bridge, right, which is part of the loop. Continue ahead, upstream in a peaceful forest away from the sound of I-95 traffic. At 1.2 miles curve right within the sound of SR 619 traffic. Begin descent from hill at 1.6 miles and cross the wooden footbridge at 2.2 miles to complete the loop. Return to fourth

902   parking lot at 2.8 miles.

Another easy trail is the forested *South Trail*, a 1.4-mile loop whose trailhead is at the far end of the second parking area (closer to the park's entrance). After 0.1 mile it divides. If going right, cross a footbridge, ascend to a ridge, and follow its crest. Descend, cross a stream in a beech grove, and at 0.7 miles turn left on an old road for a return to the parking area. (At the trailhead there is a 0.2-mi. connecting

903   trail to the fourth parking lot.)

USGS map: Quantico

Access: From I-95, exit 151, go east on SR 619 (Joplin Rd.) for 0.4 miles, turn right on US 1, and after 1.3 miles turn right into park.

Addresses and Information: Locust Shade Regional Park, 4701 Locust Shade Dr., Triangle, VA 22172; phone: 703-221-8579. County office: Prince William County Park Authority, 14420 Bristow Rd., Manassas, VA 22111; phone: 703-335-7060.

Roanoke County

Roanoke County has forty-eight parks, spread widely throughout the county on a total of 827 acres. The Department of Parks and Recreation has a combined park system with the Roanoke County School Board and the Roanoke County Board of Supervisors. The resulting recreational areas have 51 tennis courts, 22 basketball courts, 55 ballfields, 21 football/soccer fields, and many picnic areas. Some parks emphasize preservation and natural areas. Those with trails are described below.

904   GLEN COVE PARK

The 0.5-mile, self-guiding *Nature Trail* loops through a 16-acre forest and by a stream. Emphasis here is on herbaceous plants and small mammals.

Access: In northwestern Roanoke, follow either Cove Road or Peter's Creek Road east off VA 419 between US 460 and I-81.

905–6   HAPPY HOLLOW GARDENS

Hilly Hiking Trail is a 1-mile walk through hardwoods and white and Virginia pines on the mountainside with both loops and linear paths. The park also has a short *Nature Trail* through azaleas for the physically handicapped to a picnic table.

Access: Take sr 7600 (Mount Chestnut Rd.) off us 211 (Bent Mountain Rd.) and go 2.3 miles up the mountain. Turn left at the park entrance. (Mount Chestnut Rd. is 0.3 mi. south of Poages Mill Church of the Brethren, or 4.3 mi. south on us 221 from va 419 junction in Roanoke.)

Rockbridge County

LAKE ROBERTSON PARK

Named in honor of Senator A. Willis Robertson, a devoted conservationist, this park has 581 acres of hills and meadows and a 31-acre lake stocked with bass and sunfish on the eastern slopes of North Mountain. The park has a swimming pool and bathhouse, tennis courts, ballfields, picnic areas, a campground (with hook-ups), and a boat ramp. Hunting is allowed during fall and spring game seasons outside the developed areas. The trail network has two shelters. (One of the sponsoring agencies for the county is the Virginia Commission of Game and Inland Fisheries.)

Access: From us 11 junction with va 251 in Lexington, drive west on va 251 for 10.6 miles. Turn left on sr 770 in Collierstown, and after 1.3 miles turn right on sr 652 to the park.

South Boundary Trail (1.6 mi.), **Branch Trail** (1 mi.), **Ridge Trail** (1.5 mi.),
North Boundary Trail (1.7 mi.), **Lake Trail** (1.5 mi.)   907–11

Length and Difficulty: 7 miles (11.2 km) combined, round-trip; moderate
Features: scenic views, wildlife, wildflowers, lake
Trailheads: From campground, picnic area, or boat house
Description: From the camping area pass through sites 25 and 26 to the children's
    playground, where trail signs give direction. Ascend on the *South Boundary
    Trail* for 1.1 miles to a shelter. Turn right, pass a junction on right with the
    Branch Trail (which leads 1 mi. to the *Ridge Trail*), and reach a second shelter at
    1.7 miles at the *Ridge Trail*, right. Continue on the *North Boundary Trail* (or
    return to campground 1.5 mi. on the *Ridge Trail*) to a junction with the *Lake
    Trail* at 2.8 miles and a second junction with the *Lake Trail* near the dam at 3.4
    miles. A loop can be completed by taking the *Lake Trail* in either direction to
    the campground entrance. Among the vascular plant species are Virginia pine,
    hardwoods, red raspberry, redbud, and lavender bee balm.
Address and Information: Lake Robertson Park and Rockbridge County Parks and
    Recreation, Rt. 2, Box 251, Lexington, va 24450; phone: 703-463-4164.

Stafford County

CURTIS MEMORIAL PARK   912

The 565-acre Curtis Memorial Park, dedicated to property donors Jesse and Emma Curtis, is Stafford County's answer to recreational needs for its citizens. The park is exceptionally well landscaped and meticulously maintained. Its facilities include an Olympic-size swimming pool, picnic areas, tennis courts, ballfields, and a 91-acre lake stocked for fishing. The county has seventeen other parks, some affiliated with the public school system. Behind the park office parking area is easy, 0.4-mile *Cedar Path Nature Trail*. It has an outstanding display of vascular plants: hardwoods, pine and cedar, wild orchids and azaleas, huckleberry, ferns, lichens, and clubmoss.

Access: From I-95 in Fredericksburg drive west on US 17 for 5.2 miles to SR 612. Turn right for 2 miles to the park entrance.

Address and Information: Stafford County Parks and Recreation, 58 Curtis Ln., Hartwood, VA 22406; phone: 703-752-5632.

13 : Municipal Parks and Recreation Areas

We shall never understand the natural environment
until we see it as a living organism.
—Paul Brooks

The Old Dominion map has names of nearly 1,000 communities, towns, and cities, of which 188 are incorporated towns and 41 are independent cities. Some places, like Dot in Lee County, are small, unincorporated communities, but some names only mark a crossroad or historic site where villages once existed. The smallest incorporated town is Duffield in Scott County, and the largest city is Virginia Beach (population 393,069 in the 1990 census). Virginia Beach is part of the Hampton Roads area, which has a population of 1 million, but the North Virginia portion of the Washington, D.C., metro area has more than 1,733,000 inhabitants. The largest city in acreage is Suffolk. Jonesville is the state's farthest west incorporated town, Chincoteague is in the east, and Lovettsville is in the north (the latter is as far north as Baltimore).

Parks and recreation departments are in 68 towns and cities. Under city government they usually have a supervisor, manager, or director with a budget approved by a city council or other government body. Towns may not be as independent because of county government jurisdiction or combination policies or programs. Planning assistance for the parks is available from the state's Division of Planning and Recreation Resources. The assistance includes water conservation, environmental regulations, grants, greenways, and recreational programs. Parks that have trail systems, other than physical fitness or service trails between facilities, are described in this chapter. For a directory of the state's town, city, and county parks and recreation departments, call 804-786-2556 at the Department of Conservation and Recreation in Richmond.

Alexandria

The area was settled in 1670, but its historic townhouses and Potomac River waterfront shops did not develop until surveyors John West, Jr., and George Washington laid out streets and equal-size blocks in 1749. In 1789 the town was ceded to the District of Columbia, as was adjoining Arlington County. In 1846 Alexandria was returned to Virginia at the citizens' request. Walks in the historic district can begin at the visitor bureau at the William Ramsay House, the city's oldest (1724). It is at 221 King and Fairfax streets. The city has more than forty-five parks and a network of bicycle trails. Some are walking trails that connect for a 7.5-mile continuous hike from Ramsay Nature Center at the western edge of the city east to the Potomac River.

DORA KELLY NATURE PARK

The Ramsay Nature Center, at the western end of the William Ramsay School on Sanger Avenue, is the western trailhead for the easy 1.5-mile *Dora Kelly Trail.* The center has information about the 28 numbered interpretive posts on the trail. Begin at the western end of Sanger Avenue and descend to rocky Holmes Run to turn left. Continue along the stream on a paved bike/hike trail. The guideposts identify trees, shrubs, flowers, and animals among tall oaks and hickories. Cross the creek near a scenic rocky area and then cross Beauregard Street into the Holmes Scenic Easement.

Access: From Shirley Memorial Highway, I-395, exit 4, go northwest on Seminary Road to Beauregard Street. Turn left and go 0.8 miles to Sanger Avenue, right, for entrance to the parking area at the Ramsay Nature Center and end of Sanger Avenue.

914 BROOKVALLEY PARK AND HOLMES RUN

The *Dora Kelly Trail* connects here with the 1.8-mile *Holmes Run Trail* under I-395. The trail continues southeast, crosses under Duke Street, and continues along Holmes Run to Eisenhower Avenue. Most of this easy trail meanders through a predominantly residential neighborhood featuring a variety of views and vistas, play equipment for children, and picnic areas. The trail also includes Alexandria's Bicentennial Tree, a 200-year-old willow oak.

Access: From Ramsay School follow Sanger Avenue southeast to cross Beauregard Street and I-395 to Van Dorn Street. Turn right and after 1 block turn left on Taney Street, then right on Ripley Street to Holmes Run Parkway and the western trailhead. For the eastern trailhead continue south on Van Dorn Street 1.6 miles (from Taney St.) to Eisenhower Street. Turn left and follow it 1.7 miles into Hensley Park and across the stream to Cameron Run Regional Park and trail intersection.

915 CAMERON RUN REGIONAL PARK

From here the 3.8-mile *Cameron Run Trail* passes through a forested area, crosses a bridge at Lake Cook, crosses Eisenhower Avenue, and parallels the road. After 1.4 miles pass the cloverleaf of Telegraph Road, which intersects with the noise pollution of I-95/495. Pass the Eisenhower Avenue metro station and at 2.4 miles enter a gated trail to a vacant area before arriving at Payne Street and another gate. Turn north to Wilkes Street and make a right to descend to the waterfront area at Pomander Park. Here is a junction right and left with the *Mount Vernon Trail* (see Chapter 9). The *Jones Point Trail* is 0.5 miles on the right.

Access: From Cameron Run Regional Park drive east on Eisenhower Avenue to Holland Lane. Turn left to a right turn on Duke Street. Follow it to Union Street and turn right to the Marina and Pomander parks.

Addresses and Information: Department of Recreation, Parks and Cultural Activities, 1108 Jefferson St., Alexandria, VA 22314; phone: 703-838-4343. Available are trail and bike maps. Ramsay Nature Center, 5700 Sanger Ave., Alexandria, VA 22311; phone: 703-838-4829.

Blacksburg

Blacksburg is a university city with more than 23,000 students in Virginia Polytechnic Institute and State University (founded 1872). It houses the Museum of Geological Sciences. Off us 460 near the university entrance is Smithfield Plantation (1773), the home of three state governors: James P. Preston, John Buchanan, and John Floyd. Framed in the Great Valley with sweeping pastoral surroundings, the city has a complementary backdrop with Brush Mountain in the JNF. Among the facilities operated by the city's parks and recreation department are a nature center at its headquarters and trails elsewhere. One special trail is the 1-mile hike and bike *Huckleberry Line Trail*, located on the railroad bed of the abandoned Huckleberry Line. It extends from the junction of Harrell and Miller streets to South Gate Drive. (Plans are to increase the distance.) 916

Another trail is the *Ellett Valley Nature Trail*, an easy, 2-mile double loop. From its parking area on Jennell Road the trail enters a gate and soon forks for a 1-mile loop or a 2-mile loop. It is self-guiding with interpretive markers and has 3 side loops named the *Earth Awareness Trail*, the *Micro Trail*, and the *Cycle of Life Trail*. The forest has oak, tulip poplar, black locust, hickory, and maple in climax groves. The trail passes an old farm site and a spring. (For group hikers, a tour guide is available from the park office.) 917–20

USGS map: Blacksburg

Access: To reach the *Ellett Valley Nature Trail* take SR 642 (Jennell Rd.) off us 460 and follow it 2.3 miles to a narrow entrance on the right. Also, from us 460B (South Main St.) take SR 603 (Ellett Rd.) to Jennell Road and turn right. Go 0.2 miles to trail entrance, left.

Address and Information: Department of Parks and Recreation, 725 Patrick Henry Dr., Blacksburg, VA 24060; phone: 703-961-1135. Available is a brochure and map of trails. Museum of Geological Sciences phone: 703-231-6029.

Buena Vista 921

At the edge of the Shenandoah Valley, east of Lexington, the town's eastern boundary adjoins the GWNF, and only 5 miles east is the BRP. In the forest the *Indian Gap Trail* and the *Reservoir Hollow Trail* have termini in the town. These trails lead to the *Elephant Mountain Trail* for an outstanding view of Buena Vista (meaning "good view"). (See Chapter 2, Pedlar Ranger District.) In addition, the town has its own trail in 315-acre Glen Maury Park. The 2.2-mile, easy *Glen Maury Nature Trail* follows an interconnecting system of sloping, woodland, and grassy bald trails. The trail begins from the parking area at the multipurpose building and extends to the Maury River. Other activities at the park are swimming in an Olympic-size pool, picnicking, fishing, camping (with full service), and horseback riding. There are also ballfields, playgrounds, and a mountaintop pavilion with a grand view of the town.

Access: In downtown Buena Vista take 10th Street west from Magnolia Avenue (US 501) for 0.3 miles to park entrance across the Maury River bridge.

Address and Information: Glen Maury Park (and Buena Vista Department of Parks and Recreation), 2039 Sycamore Ave., Buena Vista, VA 24416; phone: 703-261-7321.

Charlottesville

Almost in the center of the state, the area is the birthplace of Thomas Jefferson, whose accomplishments include the design and founding of the University of Virginia (1819). Having examined the classical architecture of Europe, he combined the styles to create an academic quadrangle with lawns, white colonnaded buildings, serpentine walls, gardens, and the inimitable rotunda. His home, Monticello, 3 miles east of the university, illustrates one of America's most classic architectural designs. Jefferson's interest in the natural environment is illustrated by his initiation and planning of the epic Lewis and Clark Expedition in 1804–6. (George Rogers Clark was born 2 mi. north of the city. A memorial is on W. Main St. east of the university.) One of the city's major parks is Pen Municipal Park, a 285-acre tract in a bend of the Rivanna River. It has an 18-hole golf course, tennis courts, ballfields, picnic shelters, a children's playground, and a 3-mile network of unnamed trails. It is located off SR 631 on the northern edge of the city. The city's flagship of trail networks is described below.

IVY CREEK NATURAL AREA

Charlottesville's Department of Parks and Recreation and the Albemarle County Department of Parks and Recreation jointly hold in perpetuity the 215 acres of Ivy Creek Natural Area for free use by the public. In addition, the private, nonprofit Ivy Creek Foundation assists the city and county in planning and protecting the preserve. There are more than 400 species of plants and 80 species of birds. Garden and civic clubs provide community support for landscaping, an information kiosk, a reference library, and birdhouses.

Access: From US 29 north in Charlottesville, take SR 743 (Hydraulic Rd.), west for 2.3 miles to the entrance, left.

922–35   **Ivy Creek Nature Trail**
Length and Difficulty: 5.7 miles (9.1 km) combined, round-trip; combined; easy
Features: historic site, streams, lake, wildlife, wildflowers
Trailhead: Parking area
Description: The trail system is graded, well designed, and carefully mowed in the open fields. It has 13 interconnecting short trails that make loops within loops. Among the tree species are maple, oak, walnut, beech, cherry, and poplar. Conifers include cedar, pine, and hemlock. Birding is popular here. For the

quiet enjoyment of all visitors, pets are not allowed. From the parking area begin the hike by following the signs at a kiosk (and Virginia's first public solar composting rest rooms) to a restored farm barn. (To the right is 0.1-mi. *Wheelchair Trail*.) Hike straight ahead on the *Blue Trail* (0.5 mi.), partly in a field and in hardwoods. Pass a spring and connect with the *White Trail* (0.4 mi.), which goes left to the barn and right to cross cascading Martin's Branch at 0.8 miles. After hiking the *Yellow Trail* (0.4 mi.) loop, which is partly beside South Rivanna Reservoir, return to the *White Trail*, turn right, and connect with the *Orange Trail* (0.9 mi.) at 1.4 miles. (To the left is the *Red Trail*.) Turn right and follow the trail at the edge of the field until meeting the *Alternate Trail* (0.2 mi.). (It connects with the *Yellow Trail*, curves through the forest to a cove at the lake and reconnects with the *Orange Trail*.) Here the hiker has an option. To the right is the *Peninsula Trail* (0.7 mi.), which makes a loop through a mature forest to the lake. To the left the *Orange Trail* continues to meander in a circle until it rejoins the *White Trail* and the *Red Trail* (0.9 mi.) at 3.2 miles. (Along the way on the *Orange Trail* is the picturesque *Green Trail* [0.2 mi.], a circle and a shortcut to the *Red Trail*.)

Continue on the *Red Trail*, cross a stream, and at a pipeline clearing fork left to stay on the *Red Trail*, or go right to follow the *Woods Trail* (0.7 mi.). (It goes through a forest to cross the headwaters of Martin's Creek before returning to the *Red Trail*.) After crossing Martin's Creek and a tributary reach the *Field Trail* (0.4 mi.). (It ascends to near SR 743, passes a forest succession plot, and returns to the parking lot. Along the way the *School Trail* [0.3 mi.] is on the left. It goes to the *Watchable Wildlife Trail* [0.1 mi.] for a return to the parking lot.) Continue on the *Red Trail* to its junction at 5.6 miles with the *White Trail*. Turn right and complete the trail at the barn.

USGS maps: Charlottesville West and East

Addresses and Information: Charlottesville Department of Parks and Recreation, P.O. Box 911, Charlottesville, VA 22902; phone: 804-971-3260. Available is a brochure and map of parks. Ivy Creek Foundation, P.O. Box 956, Charlottesville, VA 22902; phone: 804-973-7772. Available are brochure and information on Ivy Creek Natural Area and free guided tours.

Chesapeake

In 1963 the city of South Norfolk and Norfolk County became the new city of Chesapeake. With 353 square miles it became the second largest city in acreage in the state. It adjoins Portsmouth and Norfolk on the northern boundary, Virginia Beach on the east, North Carolina on the south, and the city of Suffolk on the west. More than half of the Great Dismal Swamp NWR and most all of Lake Drummond are within the city's boundaries, and the intracoastal waterway passes through the eastern edge of the refuge and the northeastern corner of the city. Waterways crisscross the entire city, whose elevation is an average of 12 feet. From the western swamps and marshes originates the Northwest River; it leaves the southeastern corner of the city and flows into Currituck Sound of North Carolina.

NORTHWEST RIVER PARK

Where Indian Creek flows into the Northwest River is the location of the city's 763-acre Northwest River Park. Carefully planned to protect the natural environment and to provide a variety of outdoor recreation for the entire family, it is set apart from urban demographics. A quiet place (except for noise from naval aircraft flights), it is an extraordinary laboratory for nature study. There are 160 species of birds, 150 species of herbaceous plants (including 7 species of wild orchids), 136 species of ferns, clubmosses, shrubs, trees, and vines. Wild mammals are chiefly deer, squirrel, mink, nutria, raccoon, and otter. There are 18 species of snakes (including 3 species of poisonous reptiles) and 16 species of fish. Activities include fishing, hiking, nature study, and boating (a ramp is provided). There are equestrian trails, picnic shelters, a children's playground, canoe rentals, facilities for camping (tents and recreational vehicles), and a visitor center. On the eastern side of the visitor center is 210-yard *Fragrance Trail*. It is a loop that has Braille signs for the visually impaired. Among the more than 40 plants are dwarf wild azalea,
936 sweet bay, silky camellia, fragrant sumac, and bigleaf snowbell.

Access: From the junction of I-64, exit 290, and VA 168, drive south on VA 168 (Battlefield Blvd. and Great Bridge Bypass) 11.8 miles to Indian Creek Road on the left (at food mart). Turn left and go 4.1 miles to the park entrance on the right.

Indian Creek Trail (1.9 mi.), **Shuttle Trail** (1.3 mi.), **Deer Island Trail** (0.8 mi.), **Otter Point Trail** (0.8 mi.), **Wood Duck Slough Trail** (0.3 mi.),
937–43 **Molly Mitchell Trail** (1.3 mi.), **Rein Memorial Trail** (0.2 mi.)
Length and Difficulty: 6.6 miles (9.6 km) combined, round-trip; easy
Features: waterfowl, wetlands and marsh, wildlife, wildflowers
Trailhead: Visitor center
Description: These trails connect for short or long loops. The longest loop is
    described here. From the visitor center, facing the lake, follow the left side of the
    lake to a grassy knoll and trail sign for the *Indian Creek Trail*. (To the left of the
    trail entrance is the flower garden and the *Shuttle Trail*. The *Shuttle Trail* is a
    dead-end road used for hiking or vehicular traffic to Southern Terminal, the
    southern end of the *Indian Creek Trail*.) After entering the woods, cross a bridge
    over the lake and reach a junction with the *Deer Island Trail*, left and right, at
    0.2 miles. (The *Deer Island Trail* follows an old road left for 0.7 mi. to the *Shuttle
    Trail*. It passes a walk-in backcountry camping area and canoeing access and
    crosses a scenic footbridge. To the right it goes 0.1 mi. to the park's recreational
    vehicle campground.

    Continuing on the *Indian Creek Trail* (25 yds. right on the *Deer Island Trail*
    and off to the left), pass through a forest of sweet gum, maple, poplar, oaks, and
    beech. There are large patches of Christmas fern and wild ginger. Cross a bridle
    trail at 0.7 miles, a boardwalk at 1 mile, and another at 1.6 miles in Moonshine

Meadow. At 1.8 miles is a view of a long boardwalk, but bear left to cross a small stream and exit at the *Shuttle Trail* near a pond and picnic shelter at 1.9 miles, the end of the trail. To the right it is 0.1 mile to a beautiful grassy area and a view of Northwest River. Here is a picnic area and a building for canoe rentals. To the right is 0.2-mile *Rein Memorial Trail*, a long boardwalk into the marsh of Indian Creek.

To complete the long loop, continue on 0.8-mile *Otter Point Trail* (30 yds. north of the southern terminus of the *Indian Creek Trail* on the *Shuttle Trail*) to Smith Creek, but turn away from the creek to reconnect with the *Shuttle Trail* at 2.7 miles. Turn right, and after a few yards turn right on 0.3-mile *Wood Duck Slough Trail* to a bridge in a damp area with cypress, trout lily, and pennywort. Cross Blue Heron Bridge and reach a junction with the *Molly Mitchell Trail* at 3 miles. Pass through a forest of large beech and sweet gum with an understory of switchcane. After crossing three more bridges arrive at picnic area #4 at 4.1 miles. Reach the northern trailhead at the parking area at 4.2 miles and the visitor center at 4.3 miles.

USGS map: Moyock

Addresses and Information: Department of Parks and Civic Center, P.O. Box 15225, Chesapeake, VA 23320; phone: 804-547-6411, or Northwest River Park System, 1733 Indian Creek Rd., Chesapeake, VA 23322; phone: 804-421-7151/3145. Available are brochures and leaflets on park flora and fauna, and park map.

Falls Church

The *W&OD Railroad Trail* goes 1.3 miles through Falls Church on its route from Arlington to Purcellville. (See Northern Virginia Regional Park Authority, Chapter 14.) The city also has a short trail in Berman Park.

Address and Information: Department of Recreation and Parks, 223 Little Falls St., Falls Church, VA 22046; phone: 703-241-5077.

Fredericksburg

The city of Fredericksburg, halfway between Richmond and Washington, D.C., is on the southern side of the Rappahannock River. It was authorized to be developed by the general assembly in 1727 and to be named in honor of Frederick, Prince of Wales, the eldest son of King George II. (Frederick's eldest son, George III, was king during the American Revolution.) During the Civil War the town was caught in the center of battles, but many of the buildings were not destroyed. Today, the historic district is maintained, and a 1-mile walking tour is worthwhile. In the space of about eight by five blocks there are at least twenty historic sites. Among them are the Mary Washington house and grave and the James Monroe Museum (see Chapter 6 for national military parks). Begin the walk at the city visitor center at 706 Caroline Street.

The city shares administrative jurisdiction with Stafford County for three parks across the river in Falmouth. They are Falmouth Waterfront Park, St. Claire Brooks Memorial Park, Old Mill Park, and John Lee Pratt Memorial Park. These day-use parks have facilities for picnicking and fishing, tennis courts, ballfields, and unnamed trails between facilities. One trail, the 1.2-mile *St. Brooks Trail*, begins at the northern corner of the parking area for picnic area B. It goes to the corner of the woods under a power line and crosses a wide bridge. It descends into a deep ravine near a stream where a heavy canopy is formed by tall beech, tulip poplar, and a variety of oaks. Part of a light understory contains skunk cabbage, papaw, and mountain laurel. The trail exits at River Road near a parking area. Backtrack, or make a loop by walking upriver on a 0.5-mile trail in a forest of ash, elm, and sycamore to a parking area and softball field. Cross the road, ascend to picnic area A, turn right, and walk right of the baseball field to picnic area C parking area. Turn left in the parking lot to the point of origin. Access to the park is off US 1 in Falmouth east on Prince Street, which becomes Butler Road, and park entrance, right.

944–45

The city has its own parks, such as Motts Run Reservoir Park, Canal Park, Snowden Park, Riverside Drive Park, and Alum Spring Park. In the 40-acre Alum Spring Park is picnicking and unique 0.3-mile *Alum Spring Trail* to explore the sandstone cliffs. Water dripping from under the cliffs carries alum, deposited in crystalline pink, white, and yellow layers on the ground. During the revolutionary period alum was used to preserve meat. A pedestrian swing bridge is over Hazel Run. Access from US 1 on VA 3 is 0.1 mile east to Greenbrier Drive, right, for 0.4 miles. Other city parks with trails are described below.

CANAL PARK, OLD MILL PARK, AND RIVERSIDE DRIVE PARK

Although these parks are near each other and focus on different facilities and services, they are all water oriented and provide an exciting loop trail through a historic section of the city. The first 1.3 miles of the wide, paved trail follow a canal and are designed for bikers, hikers, birders, joggers, and strollers. The remainder of the route is on sidewalks or grassy paths of the other parks.

Access: From US 1 take Fall Hill Avenue west 0.7 miles to the parking lot, left, at VEPCO Canal bridge.

946   **Canal Park Trail**
Length and Difficulty: 3.2 miles (5.1 km); easy
Features: canal, waterfowl, scenic views, historic sites, wildflowers
Trailhead: Parking lot at VEPCO Canal bridge
Description: Begin at the trail bridge over the canal and follow beside the canal through overhanging willow, elm, and ash. White mallow and cattails are on the right side in marshes. At 0.3 miles is a connector bridge and access right and left to residential and office areas. Pass under US 1 at 0.7 miles and by an access ramp. Pass another access footbridge at 0.9 miles. There is a lake to the right

with waterfowl and songbirds. Cross Washington Street at 1.2 miles. (To the right on Washington St. in the second block is the Mary Washington Monument and Grave.) Cross Canal Street and a footbridge at 1.3 miles. Reach Princess Anne Street (us 1/17B) at 1.6 miles.

The canal goes underground here, and the trail turns right to immediately turn left on Ford Street to Caroline Street for a left turn. Follow Caroline Street past markers and at 2 miles pass the entrance to Old Mill Park, right. (The park offers day-use facilities for picnicking and fishing and children's playgrounds.) At 2.3 miles pass under us 1/17 (which accesses Caroline St.). Enter Riverside Park and pass historic markers of old mills, one of which is the Francis Thorton Mill at 2.6 miles. Here is also the legendary Indian punch bowl and scenic views of and foot access to the Rappahannock River. Continue upriver and cross Hill Avenue to the sidewalk at 3.1 miles for a return to the parking lot. (Across the road from the parking lot is the Rappahannock Outdoor Educational Center, which provides rentals, sales, and classes in canoeing, tubing, rafting, and kayaking.)

USGS map: Fredericksburg

Addresses and Information: Fredericksburg-Stafford County Park Authority, Saint Clair Brooks Park, P.O. Box 433, Fredericksburg, VA 22404; phone: 703-373-7909. Available is a brochure with map of the parks. Fredericksburg Recreation Department, 408 Canal St., Fredericksburg, VA 22401; phone: 703-372-1158. Rappahannock Outdoor Educational Center, 3219 Fall Hill Ave., Fredericksburg, VA 22401; phone: 703-371-5085. Fredericksburg Visitor Center, 706 Caroline St., Fredericksburg, VA 22401; phone: 703-373-1776.

Front Royal

94/

Front Royal is an ideal town for hikers. Not only does the town have excellent parks, recreation facilities, and hiker amenities, it is surrounded by trails and natural areas. It is the northern gateway to lofty Skyline Drive and the *Dickey Ridge Trail* in the Shenandoah National Park. On its western edge is white water on the South Fork of the Shenandoah National Park; on the northeastern corner of the GWNF is the long *Massanutten Mountain Trail*, and to the east for 3.2 miles on us 522 is the *AT*. For an underground trail, on the southern edge of town there is Skyline Caverns, with its rare, flowerlike calcite crystal formations. On the northern edge of town is I-66 on its route from Washington, D.C., to nearby I-81 at Strasburg.

A historic town with shrines, museums, and cemeteries related to the Civil War, it has also honored its citizens after its founding in 1788. Its park services include recreational, social, and cultural activities for all ages. Its largest of ten parks is Municipal Park, which has the Bing Crosby Stadium on 8th Street. Across Happy Creek from the stadium is the imaginative Happy Creek Fantasyland for children. Trails by the creekside lead to a castlelike, multilevel wooden structure with interconnecting tunnels, slides, bridges, and ladders. Upstream, on Commerce Avenue for 1 mile, is the *Happy Creek Trail,* a 0.7-mile scenic paved bike and hike trail among flowering shrubs, arched bridges, and an arboretum. Entrance is at Prospect Street or Front Street from E. Main Street. Another fine park is described below.

948   LEACH'S RUN WILDLIFE HABITAT PARK

The park is located at the northeastern edge of town with soccer fields, picnic shelters, and 0.8-mile loop *Leach's Run Trail.* It is designed in a rustic place for an educational and pleasant experience. Deer frequent the fields and near the old apple trees. Begin the trail from the parking area in the meadow near soccer field #4. Enter the woods at the far edge of the field and ascend through sycamore, locust, oak, and honeysuckle. Exit the forest and pass picnic shelter #6 at 0.4 miles. Cross the road and enter the woods to follow left on an old road. Pass picnic shelter #7 and a field bordered with sumac and wild rose. In July the area is lavender and pink with bee balm, thistle, and sensitive briar. Pass through an area of young trees and shrubs to return to the road and parking area.

USGS map: Front Royal

Access: From Commerce Avenue go east on 6th Street to follow Sycamore Drive, descend, and turn right at 1 mile. The gate is 0.2 miles farther.

Address and Information: Parks and Recreation Department, P.O. Box 1560, Front Royal, VA 22630; phone: 703-635-7750. Available is a brochure on seasonal activities. For Skyline Caverns, call 703-635-4545.

949   Hampton

The historic city of Hampton was settled in 1610 in Kecoughtan Indian territory. Its survival and continuous functioning makes the city the oldest location in America where English is spoken. Strategically located at the mouth of the James River on the Chesapeake Bay, it was vulnerable to the wars of 1776, 1812, and 1861, but it survived them all. Historic sites are at Casement Museum and Fort Monroe at the end of US 258.

At Grandview Preserve is a 4.5-mile round-trip walk on the *Grandview Preserve Trail.* This easy and scenic route from the Chesapeake Bay to the Back River offers views of waterfowl and wetlands filled with sumac, wax myrtle, cattail, and switchcane. It passes Hawkins Pond, right, on a wide access trail to the beach at 0.4 miles. Turn left and walk on the beach toward the Back River and the end of the beach and sand dunes. Backtrack.

Access: From I-64, exit 268, drive northeast on Mallory Street 0.5 miles to Mercury Boulevard and turn left. Go 0.3 miles and turn right on Old Buckroe Road. Follow it to Silver Isles Boulevard, turn right, and after 0.1 mile turn left on Beach Road. Go 2.6 miles and turn left on State Park Drive. (Observe parking signs.)

Addresses and Information: Department of Parks and Recreation, City Hall, Hampton, VA 23669; phone: 804-727-6347. For Fort Monroe: Department of the Army, HHC Fort Monroe Bldg., Fort Monroe, VA 23551; phone: 804-727-2092.

Herndon

950

The *W&OD Railroad Trail* has a 2.4-mile stretch through Herndon on its way from Arlington to Purcellville. (See Northern Virginia Regional Park Authority, Chapter 14.) The 0.7-mile *Sugarland Run Trail* connects SR 606, Elden Street, to the *W&OD Railroad Trail.*

Address and Information: Herndon Parks and Recreation, 814 Ferndale Ave. (P.O. Box 427), Herndon, VA 22070; phone: 703-435-6868.

Lexington

Founded in 1777, Lexington is the county seat of Rockingham County in the Shenandoah Valley. In its historic residential and downtown districts is a 16-block section of homes, churches, museums, burial shrines, shops and stores, and universities. It is the home of Washington and Lee University (founded in 1749), the nation's sixth oldest, where Robert E. Lee served as president from 1865 until his death in 1870. It is also the home of Virginia Military Institute (founded in 1839), the nation's oldest state-supported military college. Here Thomas J. "Stonewall" Jackson taught military tactics and math for ten years before the Civil War. Both of these Confederate heroes are buried in Lexington. The city has three diverse trails: one is a sidewalk trail in the historic districts, another is semiurban by a stream, and the longest is in the countryside with its origin in the city. It is the *Chessie Nature Trail*, described in Chapter 16. The other trails are described here.

Lee-Jackson and VMI-Marshall Tour Trail

951

Length and Difficulty: 2 miles (3.3 km) combined, round-trip; easy
Features: historic site, museums, churches, gardens
Trailhead: Visitor parking lot on Washington Street
Description: From Main Street go 1 ½ blocks east on Washington Street to the visitor information center and parking lot. After receiving guide maps, follow 8 blocks of historic Lexington on the Lee-Jackson route to Lee's and Jackson's homes, universities, churches, and burial shrines. Pass the front campus of Washington and Lee University, regarded as one of the most beautiful campuses in the nation. Continue on the hike to VMI's George C. Marshall Museum and the parade ground to form a loop back to Washington Street. In addition, a 16-block hike tracing 215 years of American history can continue (see guide map) in the residential and business area. (Approximate time for combined urban hike is 4 hrs.)

USGS map: Lexington

Address and Information: Lexington Visitor Center, 102 E. Washington St., Lexington, VA 24450; phone: 703-463-3777. Available are brochures and maps.

WOODS CREEK PARK

A day-use park, it is partly city public property and partly the grounds of Washington and Lee University and Virginia Military Institute. It is a tranquil greenway with a diversity of woodlands, meadows, songbirds, squirrels, spring peepers, bluets and meadow violets, and sections of an old railroad grade. It is favored by hikers, joggers, strollers, and picnickers.

Access: For the northeastern trailhead, turn off US 11/11B at its fork at the southern end of Maury River Bridge on short Moses Mill Road (which becomes short Jordan's Point Rd. to the parking area, right). For the southwestern trailhead, take Jordan Street northwest from US 11B (downtown Main St.) to Pendleton Place, left, at the parking lot of Waddell School.

952   **Woods Creek Trail**
Length and Difficulty: 2.1 miles (3.4 km); easy
Features: historic sites, scenery, geological formations, wildlife, wildflowers
Trailheads: See access above.
Description: If hiking from Jordan's Point Road (also known as VMI Island), hike
    back 90 yards from the parking area to a service road, right. The road divides
    here, and if there is not a trail sign, take the left fork, which is also part of a
    physical fitness section. To the left is Woods Creek. At 0.4 miles pass right of
    VMI tennis courts, and at 0.6 miles cross a paved road to follow an old railroad
    grade. Turn left from a parking area and descend to creekside. Here are tall
    maple, sycamore, and tulip poplar with scattered papaw in the understory. At
    1.2 miles go under an old railroad culvert, close to the stream. Pass through part
    of Washington and Lee campus and under US 60 bridge, cross a low footbridge,
    and slightly ascend into white pines at 1.5 miles. At 1.6 miles cross Lime Kiln
    Road and bridge over Woods Creek. To the left are playfields, picnic areas, and
    open fields. The trail now becomes asphalt with pine bark and gravel on side
    trails. Cross Jordan Street, pass a small dam to the right, and cross a stream at
    1.9 miles. Reach the end of the trail on crafted stone steps at the corner of
    Stonewall Street and Ross Road at 2.1 miles. It is 0.1 mile left to Waddell
    Elementary School and parking area.

    Backtrack, or follow an alternate street route to northeastern trailhead: Walk
    east on Jordan Street one block and turn left on Jackson Street. Follow it to
    Preston Street, turn right, then left on Lee Avenue to Washington Street. Turn
    left and go around the Lee Episcopal Church onto the front lawns of Washington and Lee campus. Pass the Lee Chapel, come onto Letcher Avenue, and
    enter the campus of VMI. Follow straight on VMI Parade Street to Richardson
    Hall, pass other halls, and curve right to a junction with Institute Hill Street,
    left. Follow it past the VMI Hospital, turn left on the next street, and descend to
    join Moses Hill Road for a left.

Addresses and Information: Lexington Public Works, Shop Rd., Lexington, VA 24450; phone: 703-463-3154; or Lexington Visitor Center (see above). Available are brochures of city and Woods Creek Park.

Lynchburg

Lynchburg was settled in 1759 and was named for John Lynch, who built the first commercial buildings, a ferryhouse and a tobacco warehouse, by the James River. It was the beginning of what is today the state's second largest city west of Richmond and a center for business, industry, and commerce in central Virginia. The city is 15 miles southeast of the BRP, the GWNF, and the AT. To these great attractions from Lynchburg is VA 130, a scenic state byway. To the southwest of the city is magnificent Smith Mountain Lake, and to the east is Buckingham-Appomattox State Forest. A historic city of museums, mansions, colleges, and Civil War shrines, it is also near the restored Thomas Jefferson personal retreat, Poplar Forest, begun in 1806. (Access is southwest of the city off US 221 on SR 661.) While the city treasures its human history, it also preserves its natural history. With a citywide system of diverse parks, it has set aside more than 900 acres. One of the oldest city parks is Riverside Park on Rivermont Avenue. Here is 0.3-mile *Alpine Trail* to the Miller-Clayton House (1791) and the packet boat *Marshall*. The city's largest park is Blackwater Creek Natural Area with 288 acres and 12 miles of trails. Plans are to extend the trail system upstream to Sandusky Park and downstream to the riverfront, and across the James River by Percival's Island on a footbridge.

BLACKWATER CREEK NATURAL AREA

This carefully planned and constructed area for preserving the natural environment is located in the heart of the city. A basically undisturbed area, it is a day-use facility for hiking, bicycling, horseback riding, and picnicking. Within the area is the 115-acre Ruskin Freer Nature Preserve. It provides a good example of forestry succession. (Access to it from US 29 and US 501B is 0.8 mi. northwest on US 501B to Tate Spring Rd. Turn right, go 0.2 mi., and turn left to the end of the street. Access to the trailheads is described below.) Along the creekside and on the high bluffs of the gorge are hardwoods such as oak, tulip poplar, hickory, beech, sycamore, and ironwood. The understory has dogwood, redbud, mountain laurel, Scotch broom, ferns, and wildflowers. Deer and wild turkey may be seen.

Blackwater Creek Trail

954–57

Length and Difficulty: 5.8 miles (9.3 km); easy to moderate
Connecting Trails: *Bike Trail* (3.4 mi.), *Ruskin Freer Lower Trail* (0.4 mi.), *Ruskin Freer Upper Trail* (0.7 mi.)
Features: stream, gorge, historic site, wildflowers, scenery

Trailheads: The park has multiple accesses, but to reach the northeastern trailhead from US 29, downtown, drive northwest on US 29B (Main St.), which becomes Rivermont Drive. Cross the Blackwater Creek Bridge and turn left on Bedford Avenue at the top of the hill. After 0.7 miles turn left again on Hollins Mill Road and go 0.7 miles to Blackwater Creek Natural Area parking lot at Hollins Mill dam. The southern trailhead is at Blackwater Creek Athletic Area on Monticello Avenue. Access from US 29 and US 501B/406B is on US 501B west for about 0.5 miles on Langhorne Road to Murrell Road. Turn left and look for Monticello Avenue right after about 0.3 miles. Or continue ahead to Lynchburg College and turn right on Old Forest Road to a right on Monticello Avenue.

Description: (At the Hollins Mill Rd. parking area is 1 mi. of the *Bike Trail* downstream on the western side to exit at Cabell St. The other 2.4 mi. are described below.)

Begin the *Blackwater Creek Trail* and the *Bike Trail* together upstream from the parking area on a wide, paved trail. At 0.3 miles the *Bike Trail* goes left and the *Blackwater Creek Trail* goes right into a meadow. (The *Bike Trail* ascends to cross the Blackwater Creek gorge on an old railroad trestle, and at 0.7 mi. turns left to follow the western side of the gorge. At 1.5 mi. is a junction with East Randolph St., for access, and at 2.4 mi. is a dead end. The city's park department plans to extend the trail 0.2 mi. for a western trailhead at Langhorne St.)

On the *Blackwater Creek Trail* pass under a railroad trestle at 0.5 miles and another trestle at 0.6 miles. Large sycamores are near the trail and on the creek banks. In this area the trail is wide and is used by park service personnel. At 1 mile on the left is an access to Jefferson Park (reached by car from Langhorne Rd. on Caroline St. [opposite the intersection with Murrell Rd.] to Park Dr., left.) At 2 miles is a swinging bridge, right, over the creek, for the *Ruskin Freer Lower Trail* and the *Ruskin Freer Upper Trail*. Both make interloops and are easily accessible from Thomson Drive access at 2.3 miles, left. At 2.5 miles cross the creek on a swinging bridge and turn left to leave the loop trails. Ascend on a narrow footpath among wildflowers such as hepatica and saxifrage at 3 miles. At 3.3 miles is an unofficial trail access right to the *Bike Trail*.

Cross a swinging footbridge over Ivy Creek at 3.4 miles, near the confluence with Blackwater Creek. Follow a narrow path up Blackwater Creek, and at 3.9 miles arrive at a meadow. Pass autumn olives and cedar to cross a footbridge over the creek. Turn right and cross a narrow boardwalk against a rocky wall of the gorge. Christmas fern are prominent in the rich soil between the rocks. On the approach to Langhorne Road, cross a footbridge on a pipeline to go under the street bridge at 4.2 miles. At 4.9 miles the trail descends left to cross a cement bridge for a right turn under Hill Street. (If water is too high on the trail bridge, use the Hill St. bridge and descend right to the creekside.) The remainder of the trail follows a wide gravel road for 0.5 miles before opening into a large, grassy meadow and picnic area. To the left is the parking area of Blackwater Creek Athletic Area.

USGS map: Lynchburg

Address and Information: Lynchburg Park and Recreation Department, 301 Grove St., Lynchburg, VA 24501; phone: 804-847-1640. Available is a park brochure with map.

Newport News

The city is the base for the Newport News Shipbuilding Company (1886), the largest in the world. With Norfolk and Portsmouth, two cities across the James River from Newport News, the three cities constitute the port of Hampton Roads, one of the world's finest deep and natural harbors. The first settlers on this part of the peninsula were David Gookin and about sixty other Irishmen in either 1619 or 1621. The site's name, "Newportes Newes," had preceded them. One historical claim is that Capt. Christopher Newport's arrival with supplies, news from England, and additional colonists to the James River was good news. In the city are the Wars Memorial Museum of Virginia (documents and artifacts from 1775 to the present); the Virginia Living Museum (zoology); the Mariners' Museum (maritime history, photography, and the 5-mi. *Noland Trail*); and the Newport News Park (claimed to be the largest municipal park in the nation).

NEWPORT NEWS PARK

The 8,065-acre park has more than 200 campsites; laundry facilities; picnic shelters; two golf courses; playgrounds; boat ramps; boat and bike rentals (no swimming); bike, equestrian, and hiking trails; 25 miles of fire roads (which can be used for hiking); an arboretum; horse shows; concerts and other cultural activities; fishing; and children's programs. In addition to the trails described below there is an 0.8-mile *Lakeside Nature Trail* that can be accessed from the parking lot for the fishing area concessions at the second entrance on the left after entering the park. The park is popular for nature study and birding. There are more than 190 species of birds, 30 species of mammals, and more than 30 species of amphibians and reptiles. The park is open year round. (It adjoins the Colonial National Historical Park.)

958

Access: From SR 105 (Fort Eustis Blvd.), crossing of parallel routes I-64 and SR 143, turn north on SR 143 (Jefferson Ave.), to the park entrance on the right.

White Oak Trail (2.8 mi.), **Wynn's Mill Historical Trail** (1.1 mi.),
Twin Forts Trail (0.7 mi.)

959-61

Length and Difficulty: 4.6 miles (7.4 km) combined, round-trip; easy
Features: waterfowl, swamp, wildflowers, historic site, lake
Trailhead: From the Interpretive Center
Description: From the parking area secure a trail guide pamphlet, which lists 23 stations, from the Interpretive Center. Cross the entrance road and follow the signs for 0.1 mile to dam #1 bridge over the 380-acre Lee Hill Reservoir. At the northern end of the bridge is a junction with the 0.7-mile *Twin Forts Trail* on

White Oak Trail, Newport News Park. (Photograph by Mike Poplawski)

the left. (It makes a loop to examples of well-preserved Confederate earthworks, many with descriptive signage.) Continue right and pass through a hardwood forest of oak, elm, red mulberry, persimmon, hornbeam, and hazel alder. Among the ferns and clubmosses are closed gentian, orange-fringed orchid, and pink lady's-slipper. Deer, red foxes, salamanders, and squirrels frequent the area. At 1.3 miles is an old homesite and fire road. The *Wynn's Mill Historical*

Trail goes straight across the fire road and returns near the swamp bridge. (The loop trail is 1.1 mi. and has some of the largest Confederate earthworks in the park. A water-powered gristmill once operated here. Some of the vascular plants on this trail are Indian pipe and devil's walking stick. It is also a heron rookery.)

Continue on the *White Oak Trail* and at 1.7 miles cross the swamp bridge. Nearly 600 feet long, it weaves through a marsh with white ash, sycamore, and wild rose. Woodpeckers, kingfishers, herons, and hawks may be seen here. At 2.1 miles cross a bridge over Deer Creek and return to the parking lot at 2.8 miles on the *White Oak Trail* (or 4.6 mi. for all trails).

USGS map: Yorktown

Address and Information: Newport News Park, 13560 Jefferson Ave., Newport News, VA 23603; phone: 804-886-7911 or 247-8451. Available are brochures and maps of the park facilities and trails.

Norfolk

Norfolk's location at the world's largest natural harbor made it an ideal place for English settlers in the 1630s. In 1682 the Virginia general assembly purchased 50 acres on the Elizabeth River, a tidal estuary, from Nicholas Wise, a carpenter and early settler. The purpose was to start a new town for manufactured products and commerce. By 1736 it was Virginia's largest town, and by the end of the nineteenth century it was a prosperous industrial city. Norfolk and its sister city, Portsmouth, became the headquarters of the Atlantic fleet. Fulfilling its early purpose, Norfolk has since become the oldest naval port in the United States and, with the U.S. naval base, houses the largest naval installation in the world. Norfolk, Newport News, and Portsmouth are known worldwide as Hampton Roads. But Norfolk is more than a major commercial and industrial seaport; it is also the cultural hub of Hampton Roads. Easily accessible by land, sea, and air, it provides museums (such as the Chrysler Museum, with art treasures of the past 5,000 years), historic houses, monuments, performing arts centers, recreational areas, the Virginia Zoological Park, and the Norfolk Botanical Gardens.

NORFOLK BOTANICAL GARDENS   962–63

Unsurpassed in beauty, scope, and design, the 175-acre Norfolk Botanical Gardens has been home for the annual International Azalea Festival since 1954. There are more than thirty special gardens here, with 12 miles of colorful intertwining trails. Moderate year-round temperatures encourage horticulturists to grow a wide range of plants found in both northern and southern climates. As a result there are a quarter-million azaleas of every known variety, 900 varieties of camellias, and 150 varieties of rhododendron. The gardens were established in 1931 and were expanded in 1958. A Japanese garden was created in 1962; a rose garden with more than 250 varieties and 4,000 plants was dedicated in 1976; and in 1992 a pavilion of tropical plants was added.

In addition, the gardens are a mecca for horticultural activities, including a botanical library, educational programs, and the Norfolk Public Schools Center for Horticulture. Regional and local garden and nature clubs contribute to projects, sponsor floral shows, and maintain a *Fragrance Garden Trail* for the visually impaired. There are also the *R. W. Cross Nature Trail* and trails to the shoreline of Lake Whitehurst and Mirrow Lake. At least 145 species of birds have been sighted, either as residents or as migratory fowl. In addition to the trails there are boat tours. Hours of operation are weekdays 8:30 A.M. to 5:00 P.M., and weekends and holidays 10:00 A.M. to 5:00 P.M. A small fee is charged.

Access: Turn off I-64, exit 279, at Northview Avenue (east) and go 1 mile to Azalea Gardens Road, VA 192, on the left. After 0.6 miles turn right into the Botanical Gardens. Access is also from US 60; turn off on VA 170, Little Creek Road, and go 1.1 miles. Turn left on Azalea Gardens Road, VA 192.

Address and Information: Department of Parks and Recreation, 501 Boush St., Norfolk, VA 23510; phone: 804-441-2400. For Botanical Gardens general information, phone: 804-640-6879; for administrative office, phone: 804-441-5830. Available are brochures and list of seasonal blooming periods.

964   ## Poquoson

The city of Poquoson is on the Virginia Peninsula. It is bordered by Plum Tree Island NWR on the east at Chesapeake Bay; the Langley Air Force Base, the NASA Research Center, the Back River, and the city of Hampton on the south; and the Poquoson River with coves, bays, and islands on the north. Poquoson City Park has an excellent swimming pool facility, plus areas for picnicking, ball games, and nature study on the 0.5-mile *Poquoson Nature Trail*. It is a serpentine pea-gravel loop through a forest of gums, oaks, and pines.

Access: From I-64, exit 256, take VA 171 for 3 miles to an intersection with Wythe Creek Road. Proceed ahead and VA 171 becomes Little Florida Road. Follow it 1 mile, turn left on Cedar Road, go 0.2 miles, and turn left on Municipal Drive. The park is to the left.

Address and Information: Poquoson Parks and Recreation, 830 Poquoson Ave., Poquoson, VA 23662; phone: 804-868-9745.

Radford

Between Radford University and downtown Radford is 35-acre Wildwood Park, a preserve for nature study and hiking. Through the park's center is Connellys Run, which provides a moist environment for a diversity of vascular plants. Here and on the hillsides are wildflowers such as bee balm, wild phlox, and coltsfoot. Prominent species of trees are oak, tulip poplar, yellow buckeye, locust, white ash, mulberry, and red maple. In 1980 four trails were constructed by a local YACC with a grant from the Virginia Commission of Outdoor Recreation in cooperation with the city's Department of Parks and Recreation. In 1993 plans were begun to renovate the trail system by altering their directions and changing their names. It is a project of Radford University's Department of Recreation and Leisure Services, the city's Department of Parks and Recreation, and other community support. One of the new trails will be designed for the physically impaired. (Contact the park office for progress in the renovation project.)

During the summer, usually mid-June through August, the city presents an outdoor historical drama, *The Long Way Home* by Earl Hobson Smith. It is the story of Mary Draper Ingles, a survivor of the Draper's Meadow Massacre by Shawnee Indians in 1755. Captured, imprisoned, and taken to Big Bone Lick in Boone County, Kentucky, she escaped and made a dangerous 500-mile return journey through the forests near the Ohio, Kanawha, and New Rivers.

Access: From I-81 and VA 177 junction, exit 109, go north 4.2 miles on VA 177 to US 11 in downtown Radford. Turn left and go a few blocks to the park on the left, behind Charter Federal Bank.

Addresses and Information: Department of Parks and Recreation, 29 First St., Radford, VA 24141; phone: 703-731-3633/3677; about 0.2 miles west of Wildwood Park. Information on outdoor drama: P.O. Box 711, Radford, VA 24141; phone: 703-639-0679.

Richmond

The capital of Virginia, Richmond, is preeminently historic. In 1607, soon after the Jamestown landing, Capts. Christopher Newport and John Smith, with a party of nineteen other men, sailed up the James River to the falls, the present site of Richmond. Thomas Stegg established a trading post here in 1637, and by 1644 Fort Charles was built to protect the English settlers from Indian attacks. The fort's name was changed to Richmond in 1733. By 1737 William Byrd II had a town laid out on what is now Church Hill (east of the present capital). It was incorporated in 1742. It was at St. John's Church on Church Hill in 1775 that Patrick Henry made his famous challenge, "Give me liberty or give me death." When Virginia seceded from the Union in 1861, the seat of the Confederate government was moved from Montgomery, Alabama, to Richmond. As a result the city became a major military objective of the Union forces for the next four years.

A modern city of skyscrapers, Richmond continues its historic leadership in commerce, marketing, industry, banking, medicine, and transportation. An educational center, it has distinguished universities, two of which are Virginia Commonwealth University and Medical College of Virginia, and the University of Richmond. Its cultural heritage and emphasis is exemplified in museums, churches, historic districts, monuments, shrines, libraries, art centers, and government buildings (the design for the capitol building was selected by Thomas Jefferson.) Attention is also given to parks and recreation. There are more than sixty areas set aside for preservation, sports activities, and enjoyment of natural beauty. Some parks have trails, and outside the parks are some historic sidewalk trails. Both types of trails are described below. (See Henrico County, Chapter 12, for parks adjoining the city.) Also of interest are gardens in or near the city. Two examples are Ginter Botanical Gardens (off I-95, exit 80, on Lakeside Ave. north [SR 161]), and Bryan Park (at the same exit, on Hermitage Rd., south to Bellevue Ave., then right to the park).

JAMES RIVER PARK

The James River Park property is in five sections. The Main Section is between the Robert E. Lee Bridge (US 1/301) and Powhite Parkway Bridge on the south side; Belle Isle Section is partly under the Lee Bridge; Texas Avenue Section is partly under the Boulevard Bridge on the north side; Pony Pasture Section is upriver on Riverside Drive on the south side near the Huguenot Bridge; and farther northwest is Huguenot Woods Section, partly under Huguenot Bridge on the south side. (The Texas Ave. Section, east of Maymont Park, has a parking area at the end of the street. Undesignated trails, such as fishermen's paths, go across the railroad to the river.) Trails on the other four sections are described below. The James River Park has a diversity of wildlife and botanical species; fishing is excellent; hiking is easy; and the quality of white-water sports in a metropolitan area is unparalleled in the nation. Picnic facilities are provided, but camping and fires are not permitted. A visitor center, accessible by foot, is halfway between 22nd Street and 42nd Street on Riverside Drive.

Access: From junction of Lee Bridge, US 1/301 south, and Riverside Drive, go west on Riverside Drive 0.3 miles to parking area on the right at 22nd Street.

Geology Interpretive Trail (0.8 mi.), **Riverside Trail** (0.8 mi.), **Meadow Trail** (0.6 mi.), **Buttermilk Trail** (1.4 mi.)

965–68

Length and Difficulty: 3.6 miles (5.8 km) combined, round-trip; easy
Features: scenic views, riverside, historic site, waterfowl
Trailhead: See access above.
Description: Begin on the eastern end of the parking area; ascend steps to pedestrian bridge over the Southern Railway, and descend steps at 0.1 mile. To the left is the *Riverside Trail* and to the right is the *Geology Interpretive Trail*. (On the geology trail are cement walkways in places. At 0.4 mi. the trail ends at the former railroad bridge to Belle Isle. Backtrack.) To continue on the *Riverside Trail* cross a canal bridge at 0.3 miles, and at 0.8 miles turn right on gravel park service road to the visitor center. The well-maintained *Meadow Trail* loops the visitor center.

   Continue ahead and enter a forest at 1 mile, pass a picnic area at 1.3 miles, and climb the cement steps to the pedestrian bridge at 1.4 miles on the left. (The trail to the right continues to a picnic area at 0.3 mi. and to the Boulevard Park Drive Bridge [Nickle Bridge] at 0.5 mi.)

   After crossing the pedestrian bridge, turn right and enter the *Buttermilk*

Trail. (A climb up the rock steps leads to the 42nd Street parking area.) Follow the *Buttermilk Trail* by the old Netherwood Granite Quarry at 1.7 miles and cross the park service road at 2 miles. Continue through a mature hardwood forest, cross Reedy Creek, pass Buttermilk Spring on the right, and complete the loop of 2.8 miles at the 22nd Street parking area. Some of the vascular plants hikers will see on these trails are red elm, green ash, papaw, oak, hackberry, periwinkle, clubmosses, and tree of heaven.

USGS map: Richmond

Belle Isle Trail 969

This is an easy, 1-mile loop trail on an old road around the edges of Belle Isle. Another 0.2 miles is necessary to arrive on the island by the elevated footbridge under the Robert E. Lee Bridge. After descending from the footbridge, pass the remains of the Old Dominion Iron and Steel Factory and the area of the notorious Civil War prison for Federal enlisted men. Keep right on the old road, pass white-water rapids, some class 4 and 5, and pass an old quarry pit lake. An old picnic area is here and a spur trail left, up the hill, leads to a good view of the area. Curve around the end of the island and pass the remains of an old VEPCO hydropower plant. Oak, gum, papaw, soapwort, and sensitive ferns are along the trail. At 0.8 miles is the remains of an 1815 snuff factory. Come out of the woods, bear left for a completion of the loop, and begin the return on the footbridge at the sign and kiosk. Access to the island is closed at night.

USGS map: Richmond

Access: If on the Downtown Expressway going east, take Byrd Street exit to 7th Street. Turn right and go to Tredegar Street and turn right to parking area. If going west on the expressway, take Canal Street and turn left on 10th Street to Tredegar Street. Otherwise take 5th Street south to Byrd Street, turn left, go 2 blocks and turn right on 7th Street to Tredegar Street.

Pleasant Creek Trail 970–73

The *Pleasant Creek Trail* with side trails is in the Pony Pasture Section of the James River Park. It is a popular area for sunbathing, fishing, hiking, nature study, birding, and tubing (at gentle rapids upriver from the parking lot). This area is considered the best birding location in metropolitan Richmond. Additionally, here is a good place for wildflower field trips into biotic zones, and aquatic biology study. Rest rooms and drinking water are at the ranger station. The easy, 1.3-mile loop is from the parking lot on a wide trail. Pass a side trail, left, the *Quiet Woods Trail*, at 0.4 miles. Continue ahead in a mature forest of sycamore, tulip poplar, and river birch to the James River at 0.7 miles. Turn left on a side trail, the *Forest Trail*, at 0.9 miles for a return on a wide trail in the Pony Pasture to the *River Access Trail* (a spur to the river), and to the parking lot.

USGS map: Bon Air

Access: From the junction of Huguenot Road at the Huguenot Bridge and Riverside Drive take Riverside Drive east, downriver for 1.8 miles to the parking lot on the left.

Belle Isle Trail, Richmond. (Photograph by Allen de Hart)

974   **Huguenot Woods Trail**

The 1-mile round-trip *Huguenot Woods Trail* is in the Huguenot Woods Section of the James River Park, the farthest section upriver. This section has a boat ramp and an access to riverside fishing. From the parking lot walk out to an observation point, then follow the river's edge downriver through a mature floodplain forest for 0.5 miles to Rattlesnake Creek. Backtrack. There is also a 0.2-mile side trail halfway along the trail.

Access: From the Huguenot Bridge descend the ramp to Riverside Drive (southern end of bridge) and go upriver to Southampton Street parking area. Parking is also possible downriver opposite Oxford Parkway.

FOREST HILL PARK   975

Forest Hill Park adjoins James River Park's Main Section on the north, and Forest Hill Avenue and us 60 on the south. Forest Hill is one of Richmond's famous seven hills. The park has a lake, a picnic area with pavilions, a tennis court, and a nature study area. Some unmarked trails extend along Reedy Creek, which flows through the park. The 1-mile round-trip *Reedy Creek Trail* follows an old road below the dam to Riverside Drive, where a connection can be made with the *Buttermilk Trail.* The park has large tulip poplar and beech trees, with banks of wildflowers and shrubs. Vehicles are not allowed in the park.

USGS map: Richmond

Address and Information: Richmond Department of Recreation and Parks, City Hall, 900 E. Broad St., Richmond, VA 23219; phone: 804-780-5695. Available are brochures and maps of the city parks.

MAYMONT PARK   976-79

Formerly Crenshaw's Dairy Farm, the 105 acres on the edge of Richmond purchased by Maj. James H. Dooley in 1886 became his estate, which he renamed in honor of his wife, the former Sallie O. May. At the death of the Dooleys in 1925 this magnificent English country estate was willed to the city of Richmond for "the pleasure of its citizens." It is operated by the private, nonprofit Maymont Foundation and is free to the public. There are four distinctive trails in the park, totaling approximately 4 miles. The *Historic Walk* has seven major points of interest, beginning at the carriage entrance and including the Dooley Mansion. On the *Garden Walk* are fifteen major areas, which include the Italian garden, the Japanese garden, and the wildflower garden. More than fifty trees are labeled on the *Tree Walk*, and the *Animal Walk* includes an aviary, a small and large mammal habitat, and other zoo features. A detailed map and walking-tour guide is available at the nature center information desk at the entrance from Hampton Street.

Access: From the boulevard, VA 161, in Byrd Park, follow the signs to Hampton Street and go south to the park entrance on the left. (Trail entrances begin here.) There is also the Spottswood entrance from Shirley Street off the Boulevard in Byrd Park.

Address and Information: Maymont Park, Maymont Foundation, 1700 Hampton St., Richmond, VA 23220; phone: 804-358-7166. Available are brochures and map of the park.

CAPITOL SQUARE AREA

Richmond has two downtown sidewalk trails with a common focus on Capitol Square. The *Old Dominion Trail*, the oldest, is a linear trail of 7.5 miles designed by the Robert E. Lee Council of the Boy Scouts. The *Richmond Walking Trail* has been designed by the Chamber of Commerce to loop around the Capitol Square at ten historic sites.

Access: From any of the expressways, such as I-95, I-64, I-195, or I-295, turn off at the proper interchange that has signs for downtown. Follow signs to Broad Street and Capitol Square.

980   **Old Dominion Trail**

Length and Difficulty: 7.5 miles (12 km); easy to moderate
Features: historic site, architecture, art, gardens
Trailhead: Corner of 24th Street and Broad Street
Description: Begin at the St. John's Church (est. 1741) at 24th Street and Broad. (In this church, in 1775 when George Washington, Thomas Jefferson, and other patriots were assembled at the Virginia Convention to discuss independence, Patrick Henry made his famous "liberty or death" speech.) After visiting inside the church hike west on Broad Street to 12th Street at 0.9 miles, and turn right to Marshall Street, where a right turn leads half a block to the Egyptian Building (the only architecture of its type in America). Backtrack to the junction of 12th Street, proceed on Marshall Street to 11th Street, and take a left to Capitol Square. Reach the governor's mansion at 1.2 miles. After leaving the mansion enter the capitol building at 1.3 miles. Visit the Old Bell Tower at 1.6 miles, and leave the capitol grounds by the side gate, which exits on 9th Street.

Leaving the capitol grounds, turn left and proceed down 9th Street to Main Street. Turn right and hike on Main Street to Monroe Park at 2.4 miles. From Monroe Park pass the mosque and turn left on S. Cherry Street. Follow S. Cherry Street to the entrance of Hollywood Cemetery at 3 miles. Visit the burial sites of James Monroe, John Tyler, and Jefferson Davis. Backtrack to Main Street and turn left at 5 miles. Follow Main Street to the boulevard, and turn left on the boulevard at 6.3 miles. Stay on the boulevard (VA 161) past the carillon, through Byrd Park, and to Shirley Street. Turn left on Shirley Street at 7.4 miles and turn right for entry into Maymont Park parking area at 7.5 miles. Backtrack or have second vehicle.

981   **Richmond Walking Trail**

This loop walk through midtown can take 2 hours, visiting the ten historic sites and walking from the origin, at the state capitol, to the John Marshall House. Circle east on Governor Street and to the James River and return by way of St. Paul's Episcopal Church on E. Grace, for approximately 1.5 miles. The detailed information and map from the state's visitor bureau is a must for this urban hike.

Address and Information: Contact Richmond Convention and Visitor Bureau, 201 E. Franklin St., Richmond, VA 23219; phone: 804-649-373.

Suffolk

In 1974 Nansemond County and the city of Suffolk merged as Suffolk City, making its 430 square miles the largest city acreage in the state, but twelfth in population. The city boundary on the east includes part of the Great Dismal Swamp NWR. There are other swamps without drainage in the southern part of Suffolk's boundaries. Examples are Cypress, Moss, Quake, and Dragon swamps. North of the original city are Lake Meade, Western Branch Reservoir, and the Nansemond River, whose mouth is at the James River. These bring waterways to the old city limits and through half of the old county boundaries. In the northern area the city has two major parks.

BENNETT'S CREEK PARK 982

This day-use park is a former U.S. Army Nike missile installation. It now features picnic areas with shelters, boat ramp access to the Nansemond and James Rivers, fishing, crabbing, a children's playground, and a scenic nature trail. Although the park is open year round, it is closed on Mondays and Tuesdays. The 0.9-mile *Florida Maple Trail* is an easy hike from the parking area and pier along Bennett's Creek. It crosses footbridges to a grove of beautiful Florida maples. Other trees are sycamore, locust, and ash. There are two lookouts to the marsh for viewing waterfowl. At 0.4 miles backtrack or turn left to exit in a field of clover for a return to the parking area.

USGS map: Chuckatuck

Access: From US 17, 2 miles west of Belleville, take SR 626 (Shoulder Hill Rd.) south for 0.9 miles and turn right on SR 757 to the park.

LONE STAR LAKES PARK 983–86

The eight man-made Lone Star Lakes are the focus of a water resource and recreation project acquired by the city in 1975 from Lone Star Industries. The day-use park has 490 acres of lakes and 682 acres of land surface. Developed from marl mining pits, the lakes have freshwater fish such as largemouth bass, bluegill, and crappie. In addition to fishing, other activities are boating (no swimming), picnicking, bicycling, horseback riding, birding, and hiking. There are four short trails and 10 miles of unpaved back roads for hiking and viewing wildlife. The park is open year round but is closed on Mondays and Tuesdays.

To hike the 0.1-mile *Nature Trail*, turn left after entering the gate at the park office, then turn right to a parking area up from an embankment. Follow the sign through the woods and descend to Butler Lake. Backtrack or follow the paved road for a return. For the 0.1-mile *Cedar Creek Trail*, turn right on the road after the park entrance and look for a trail sign on the left. Constructed by a troop of Eagle Scouts the trail loops through an embankment of hardwoods and vines. Drive ahead and take a fork left for 0.5 miles to a picnic area beside the lake to 0.3-mile *Southern Lakes Trail*. It crosses a footbridge and winds through a damp lakeside before crossing a low ridge among hardwoods such as willow oak. It ends at a parking area on the alternate road from the fork. Backtrack. After another 0.5 miles on the road, park at a picnic area with 0.6-mile, double loop *Lone Star Lake Trail*. The first loop is at the base of large marl banks, but the second loop undulates over the banks near Cedar Creek. Tall beech, ash, and locust are over sections of wax myrtle.

USGS map: Chuckatuck

Access: From Suffolk follow VA 10/32 north from the junction of US 58/460 for 6.7 miles to Chuckatuck. Turn right to Bob House Parkway and to the park entrance after 0.5 miles.

Address and Information: Department of Parks and Recreation, 301 N. Main St. (P.O. Box 1858), Suffolk, VA 23439; phone: 804-925-6325; ranger station for Bennett's Creek Park, 804-484-3984; ranger station at Lone Star Lakes, 804-255-4308.

Vienna

The *W&OD Railroad Trail* goes 2 miles through Vienna in Fairfax County. (See Northern Virginia Regional Park Authority, Chapter 14.)

Address and Information: Department of Parks and Recreation, Vienna Community Center, 120 Cherry St., SE, Vienna, VA 22180; phone: 703-255-6360.

Virginia Beach

Virginia's largest city in population, it is one of the most popular beach areas on the nation's East Coast. Its history is traced to the first landing of the Jamestown colonists at Cape Henry. In 1963 it merged with Princess Anne County, creating 255 square miles of land and 57 square miles of water with 290 miles of shoreline. It is know for its 28 miles of public beaches (particularly on the Atlantic Coast), boardwalks, water sports, and fishing on piers, bays, lakes, and reefs as well as Atlantic deep-sea fishing. Lynnhaven Bay and Rudee Inlet are popular for catching blue crabs, oysters, speckled trout, and flounder; Back Bay is known for freshwater fishing. The state sponsors the Virginia Saltwater Fishing Tournament from April to November. On General Booth Boulevard is the Virginia Marine Science Museum, with major exhibits of the state's marine environment. At the northeastern corner of the city is Seashore State Park, and at the southeastern corner is False Cape State Park (see Chapter 11). The city has 134 parks, most of which are community oriented with regular sports activities. Red Wing Park has gardens and a nature trail.

987 RED WING PARK

One of the city's oldest parks, it is also among the most beautiful. Red Wing Gardens has special sections for roses, azaleas, natural areas, and a Japanese Garden. In the center of the park are multiple ballfields, and at the eastern end of the loop road are sheltered picnic areas. From the parking area is the triple-loop, 0.8-mile *Red Wing Nature Trail*. Color coded, it weaves through the pine, ash, elm, and maple forest to a swamp with lizard tails and royal and sensitive ferns.

USGS map: Virginia Beach

Access: At the junction of Oceana Boulevard and General Booth Boulevard (3 mi. south from US 60 at the beach on General Booth Blvd.), go east into the park.

Addresses and Information: Department of Parks and Recreation, 2150 Lynnhaven Parkway, Virginia Beach, VA 23456; phone: 804-471-5827 (administrative); 804-473-5251 (parks information office). Virginia Marine Science Museum, 717 General Booth Blvd., Virginia Beach, VA 23451; phone: 804-437-4949.

Williamsburg

Settled in 1633 and known as Middle Plantation, its name was changed to Williamsburg in 1699 when it became the state's capital. It remained the seat of government until 1780, when the capital was moved to Richmond. During that colonial period of 81 years it was the center of the state's political power, social charm, and cultural advancement. It had the nation's second oldest college, the College of William and Mary (1693), Virginia's first printing press and newspaper, and the philosophical and intellectual seeds of independence with George Mason's Declaration of Rights. For nearly 150 years after the capital was changed, it remained a quiet college town with many of its historic buildings in decay or decline. In 1926 Williamsburg's lifestyle and future dramatically changed under the influence of W. A. R. Goodwin, rector of Bruton Parish Church, and the financial backing of John D. Rockefeller Jr. to restore the capital area. Today there is a restored section, Historic Area, 1 mile long by a half-mile wide, a popular national attraction. The city is between the James and the York Rivers, and between Jamestown and Yorktown on the Colonial Parkway. Highway 5 from here to Richmond is one of Virginia's scenic byways. Visitors will find more than restoration; there are museums, gardens, and parks. The major park is Waller Mill Park.

WALLER MILL PARK   988–90

With nearly 3,000 acres, of which 365 acres are dual lakes, the day-use park is a haven for wildlife. Located at the northern edge of the city, it provides boating (no gasoline powered), fishing (for bass, crappie, pike, and bluegill), canoeing (rentals available), picnicking, bicycling, nature study, and hiking from the first weekend of March to mid-December. One unique feature is a Seniors Walking Course with fourteen stretching-exercise stations near the upper parking lot. There is also the 3.2-mile *Dogwood Trail*, mainly for bicycling, across the road.

The park has 1.5-mile *Bayberry Nature Trail*, which is self-guiding with seventy-five interpretive markers about plants, wildlife, mosses, and vines. It begins from the parking lot on a floating bridge and continues to a fork for making a loop.

Another loop is the 2.6-mile *Lookout Tower Trail*. It begins from the lower end of the parking lot and follows trail signs. It crosses an old railroad grade to the edge of the lake. After 0.3 miles there is an observation deck. At the trail's fork either direction may be taken for the loop completion. Deer and turkey may be sighted on the trail, and vascular plants include ironwood, black and sweet gum, oaks, hazelnut, red maple, and loblolly pine.

USGS map: Williamsburg

Access: At junction of I-64, exit 243, and SR 143, turn west and immediately turn right on Rochambeau Drive. Go 1.2 miles, turn left on SR 645 (Airport Rd.), and go 0.4 miles to entrance on left. (SR 645 connects with US 60.)

Addresses and Information: Department of Parks and Recreation, 202 Quarter-path Rd., Williamsburg, VA 23185; phone: 804-220-6170. Available are leaflet about facilities and pamphlet trail guide. Visitor Center at Colonial Parkway and VA 132, phone: 800-HISTORY, or 804-220-7645.

v : Regional, Military, College, and Private Trails

14 : Regional Parks

Where urban facilities are compact,
walking still delights.
—Lewis Mumford

Northern Virginia Regional Park Authority

Arlington, Fairfax, and Loudoun Counties,
and Cities of Alexandria, Fairfax, and Falls Church

The Northern Virginia Regional Park Authority (NVRPA) is the result of combined efforts in the 1950s of a group of conservationists, the Northern Virginia Planning District Commission, and local governments of Fairfax and Arlington counties and the city of Falls Church. They united to protect some of the natural heritage from suburban encroachment, and their remarkable wisdom and foresight led to organizing the regional park system in 1959 under the Virginia Park Authorities Act. Since then Loudoun County and the cities of Fairfax and Alexandria have been added. Functioning under a twelve-member board, the park authority plans, acquires, develops, and operates regional parks and other sites in nineteen locations. With good management it uses revenue-producing sources for 72 percent of its annual budget. Management employs a professional staff of 90 and more than 200 part-time employees.

The park authority provides an extraordinary variety of public recreational, educational, and cultural activities. In more than 9,000 acres there are historic homes; gardens; swimming pools; campgrounds; picnic areas; golf courses; club and conference centers; ballfields; playgrounds; lakes and streams for boating, canoeing, fishing, and kayaking; bridle paths; concert halls; nature trails; the 45-mile W&OD Railroad Trail, and many other facilities and activities. The parks that have named trails are described below.

Access to NVRPA Headquarters: From I-66 junction with VA 123 in the city of Fairfax, go 4.3 miles on VA 123 (Ox Rd.), south, to junction with SR 654 (Popes Head Rd.). A sign is at the corner, right. From I-95, exit 160, go north on VA 123 (at first Gordon Blvd., but becomes Ox Rd. before crossing the Occoquan River bridge) for 11.5 miles.

Address and Information: NVRPA, 5400 Ox Rd., Fairfax Station, VA 22039; phone: 703-352-5900. Available are magazines, brochures, flyers for all parks, and calendar of events.

BULL RUN–OCCOQUAN REGIONAL PARKS

The 5,000-acre park and recreational complex of Bull Run-Occoquan is northern Virginia's largest park system. It includes six separate (but sometimes with adjoining property lines) areas: Bull Run Regional Park, Hemlock Overlook Regional Park, Bull Run Marina, Fountainhead Regional Park, Sandy Run Regional Park, and Occoquan Regional Park stretching more than 25 miles. Among the facilities are those for hiking and nature study, plus about 30 miles of shoreline for fishing, boating, lake cruises, and rowboat rentals. There are picnic grounds, visitor centers, playgrounds, a swimming pool, indoor archery range, historic sites, bike and bridle trails, and many cultural and educational programs. Camping with electrical and water hookups and an outdoor concert center are at Bull Run Regional Park. These connecting parks along the creeks and rivers offer more than the above recreational opportunities; they have forests and marshes for the preservation of wildlife and a water supply for many of the residents in this area.

Bull Run Regional Park

This large park is best known for its wide range of activities. Its spacious fields can accommodate thousands of people for activities such as country music jamborees, contests, or soccer tournaments. It has a family campground with 150 sites, plus all amenities. There are campgrounds for Scouts and children's playgrounds. It has Virginia's only public skeet and trap shooting center and indoor archery range. It has one of the largest all-breed dog shows in the United States, and its trails pass through hundreds of acres of Virginia bluebells. Its season is from the first of March through November, but the swimming pool is open from Memorial Day through Labor Day weekend.

991   The 1.5-mile, yellow-blazed *Bull Run Nature Trail* may be the most beautiful wildflower trail in Virginia, particularly in mid-April, when the Virginia bluebells (*Mertensia virginica*) carpet the forest floor. Many other wildflowers are in profusion in the open forest of birch and ash. The trail begins at the visitor center and forms a loop by Cub Run and Bull Run. It touches another loop trail, the 1.8-mile, white-blazed trail that circles the campground pool and azalea garden. Also, it connects with the blue-blazed *Bull Run-Occoquan Trail* described below.

992   **Bull Run-Occoquan Trail**
Length and Difficulty: 17.7 miles (38.3 km); moderate
Features: wildlife, wildflowers, streams, historic site
Trailheads: Parking area near group camps B and C in Bull Run Regional Park for northwestern trailhead, and parking area at Fountainhead Regional Park for the southeastern end
Introduction: In addition to the two trailheads, there are three access points in between. This long trail has an intriguing name, which is part English for nontide waters ("runs" or "rundles"), and part Taux or Doag Indian for "end of the water." The trail is also called the *BROT* and the *Blue Trail* (not to be confused with the *Big Blue Trail*). The trail passes through a sanctuary for deer, doves, bullfrogs, and bald eagles; a forest of tall beech and birch; and beds of bluebells and bluets. Its treadway is in hemlock groves and on flood plains, muddy ravines, hillsides, rock formations, and patches of ferns and mosses. There are reminders of the Civil War and remnants of pioneer home sites. Camping and

campfires are not allowed, except at Bull Run Regional Park, which is open from mid-March through November. Although horseback riding is permitted, hunting, bicycling, and use of motorized vehicles are prohibited. Hikers are requested to carry plenty of potable water and a map (available from the visitor center) and to hike with a companion.

Description: Begin the hike downstream. Soon after the start there is a unique joining of two large sycamores on the streambank. Other trees in the area are locust, ash, and elm. Cross Cub Run on a footbridge, follow close to Bull Run, and go under Ordway Road bridge. At 1.7 miles reach a year-round parking access at VA 28 (Centreville Rd.). (Access from I-66, exit 53, in Centreville is south on VA 28 to the last road on the right before the Bull Run bridge. If driving north on VA 28, the route is from Manassas.) At Little Rocky Run, Johnny Moore Creek, and Popes Head Creek, cross large stepping-stones if bridges are absent. Pass through a rocky section and reach Hemlock Overlook Regional Park at 6.6 miles. Here is a year-round access point from SR 615 (Yates Ford Rd.). (Yates Ford Rd. is from SR 641 [Kincheloe Rd.] south of the town of Clifton.) George Mason University operates an environmental education center here.

At 11.3 miles is Bull Run Marina, where SR 641 (Kincheloe Rd.) joins SR 612 (Old Yates Ford Rd.). The boat ramp is on the northern side of the road. Clifton is north and Manassas is southwest on SR 612. Accessibility here is seasonal (contact George Mason University, 703-830-9252, for open days from April to November and for boat and canoe rentals). Continue ahead and cross Wolf Run and Stilwell Run. Complete the trail in Fountainhead Regional Park at 17.7 miles. Access here is on SR 727, which is off SR 647 (Hampton Rd.). Accessible season is from mid-March to mid-November, with boat launching facilities, boat rentals, picnic area, rest rooms, and telephone. (Plans are for continuing the trail to Sandy Run Regional Park downstream at the end of Van Thompson Rd., off SR 647 [Hampton Rd.]).

USGS Maps: Manassas, Independence Hill, Occoquan

Access: From junction of VA 28 and US 29 in Centreville, go west 3 miles on US 29 to Bull Run Park sign on Bull Run Post Office Road, left, and go 2 miles to park entrance.

Address and Information: Bull Run Regional Park, 7700 Bull Run Dr., Centreville, VA 22020; phone: 703-631-0550 (or 703-352-5900). Available is a park brochure and trail map.

Hemlock Overlook Regional Park

This park has limited facilities for the public unless reserved for group programs through the George Mason University Environmental Education Center. All trails, however, are open without prior arrangement. There are five short trails here for a total of 3 miles. One extends from the parking lot past the pond. Others, on steep terrain, are spurs from the blue-blazed *Bull Run-Occoquan Trail* at the riverside, and another trail connects from Yates Ford Road to the old power plant and dam site.

Access: From the town of Clifton go south on SR 645 (Clifton Rd.) for 0.7 miles and turn right on SR 615 (Yates Ford Rd.) to the park.

Address and Information: Hemlock Overlook Regional Park, 13220 Yates Ford Rd., Clifton, VA 22024; phone: 703-830-9252 (or 703-352-5900).

Bull Run Marina

The park has three unnamed but blazed trails. One is a joint 1.3-mile route with the blue-blazed *Bull Run-Occoquan Trail*; another is a 1.3-mile, orange-blazed trail from the Kincheloe Road junction with Old Yates Ford Road parking area; and the other is a 1.2-mile, yellow-blazed trail forming a loop from the visitor center. Both orange- and yellow-marked trails connect with the *Bull Run-Occoquan Trail*. Here, as at other places near Bull Run, is evidence of deer, beaver, turkey, raccoon, and wildfowl. The park is operated by George Mason University, and during April to early November boats and canoes can be rented. There are also a snack bar, rest rooms, and telephone. Because the facilities may not be open every day of the week, call for information (703-830-9252).

Access: From the junction in the city of Fairfax with VA 236 (Main St.) and VA 123 (Chain Bridge Rd., which becomes Ox Rd., S) drive south on VA 123. Go 8 miles to SR 643 (Henderson Rd.) and turn right. Go 5 miles to Old Yates Road, turn left on SR 612, and go 1 mile to the park.

Address and Information: Bull Run Marina, 12619 Old Yates Ford Rd., Clifton, VA 22024; phone: 703-830-9252.

Fountainhead Regional Park

A seasonal park, it is open from mid-March to mid-November. There is a tackle and bait store, a place for boat launching and boat rentals, a place for picnicking, rest rooms, and a telephone. The park is the southeastern terminus of the *Bull Run-Occoquan Trail*. Other trails here are a 1-mile, yellow-blazed trail and a 2-mile, white-blazed trail. The first goes left from the parking lot, and the latter goes right; both are circular paths and are self guiding. Hikers can take the yellow-blazed trail entry to the *Bull Run-Occoquan Trail* for 3 miles over hillsides, sometimes through rocky areas with hemlock, rhododendron, ferns, mountain laurel, and clubmosses.

Access: See directions above for Bull Run Marina, except after 1.9 miles on SR 643 (Henderson Rd.) turn left on SR 647 (Hampton Rd.), and turn right after 1.7 miles to reach the park.

Address and Information: Fountainhead Regional Park, 10875 Hampton Rd., Fairfax Station, VA 22039; phone: 703-250-9124 (or 703-352-5900).

993 ### Occoquan Regional Park

One of six parks along Bull Run, Occoquan Reservoir, and the Occoquan River, this 400-acre historic park is diagonally across the river from the town of Occoquan. The park's entrance lane is lined with sycamores, and the entrance to the ballfields is lined with golden raintree. Near soccer fields #3 and #4 is an old brick kiln that was operated by inmates of a prison that used to be in the park area. The paved, 2-mile *Occoquan River Trail* parallels the entrance road and passes picnic areas en route to the riverside. It then ascends to the ballfields and circles a batting cage. The park has an excellent dock with a boat ramp and year-round boat storage. There is a snack bar and visitor center, and it is open from mid-March through November.

USGS Map: Fort Belvoir

Access: From I-95, exit 160 (south of the Occoquan River bridge), take VA 123 north for 1.6 miles to park entrance on the right. (From Fairfax, drive south on VA 123 to the park entrance on the left.)

Address and Information: Occoquan Regional Park, 9520 Ox Rd., Lorton, VA 22079; phone: 703-690-2121 (or 703-352-5900). Available is a park brochure and map.

MEADOWLARK GARDENS REGIONAL PARK   994–95

Paved and mulched trails lead the visitor through 95 acres of natural and landscaped gardens in this magnificent park. Quiet and classic in design, the main *Meadowlark Gardens Trail* has a number of side trails in its 1.2-mile circuit that starts from and returns to the visitor center. Along the way are the native tree collection, the hosta garden, the daylily collection (with hybrids of tan-pink, salmon, brilliant red, and deep burgundy), the azalea woods, the herb garden, the cherry collection, Siberian iris, and the lilac gardens. There are three gazebos (one in each lake) and grassy hillsides of open space to sit on benches and watch birds. Near the visitor center to the left is 0.3-mile *Nature Trail*, which enters the forest of Virginia pine, maple, oak, and dogwood on a wide gravel path to a large gazebo. The park is open daily.

USGS Map: Vienna

Access: From I-495, exit 10, take the Leesburg Pike, VA 7, northwest 4.5 miles to SR 702 (Beulah Rd.), and turn left. After crossing a bridge over the Washington Dulles Expressway (no access here) the highway becomes SR 675. After 1.6 miles from VA 7 the park is on the right.

Address and Information: Meadowlark Gardens Regional Park, 9750 Meadowlark Gardens Ct., Vienna, VA 22182; phone: 703-255-3631. Available for free are newsletter and brochures; books are on sale at visitor center.

POHICK BAY REGIONAL PARK   996–98

The park is open all year, and the large swimming pool is open from Memorial Day weekend to Labor Day weekend. On the Pohick Bay (Pohick is the Algonquin Indian word for "water place") of the Mason Neck peninsula, this beautiful area has an excellent family campground with full service. There are facilities for boating, sailing, birding, golfing, picnicking, horseback riding (4 mi. trail), and nature study (see Chapter 8 for nearby Mason Neck NWR, and Chapter 11 for Mason Neck State Park). There are two trails here, plus connectors. The *Yellow Trail* is 1.4 miles and begins near the park gatehouse. It makes a junction with the *Blue Trail*, which goes 1.6 miles to boat ramp and visitor center. The *Orange Trail* is 0.6 miles from the junction of the *Yellow Trail* and the *Blue Trail* to campsites #118/119 and to the entrance road parking area.

USGS Map: Fort Belvoir

Access: From US 1 junction with VA 242, near Lorton, go 3.2 miles east on VA 242 to Pohick Bay Drive park entrance, left.

Address and Information: Pohick Bay Regional Park, 6501 Pohick Bay Dr., Lorton, VA 22079; phone: 703-339-6104.

999–1001   POTOMAC OVERLOOK REGIONAL PARK

Open all year for day use only, the 100-acre park has a nature center with archaeological and wildlife displays. The park is between the George Washington Memorial Parkway (no access) on the east, Donaldson Run on the northwest and Zachary Taylor Park on the southwest (see Chapter 12). Near the picnic area and comfort station is the 0.6-mile, green-blazed *Nature Trail* entrance. It makes a loop to the Potomac palisades for views of Georgetown and downriver to the Washington Monument 5 miles away. The 1.1-mile *Blue Trail* connects with the *Nature Trail*, makes a loop around the visitor center, and connects with the 0.3-mile *Donaldson Trail*. It connects with the *Donaldson Run Trail* left to Zachary Taylor Park, and right to the *Potomac Heritage Trail*. These trails have large oak, maple, and tulip poplar trees with an understory of haw and dogwood.

USGS Map: Washington West

Access: From the George Washington Memorial Parkway (northwest at Key Bridge), exit at Spout Run Parkway, turn right on Lorcom Lane, and go 5 blocks to turn right on Military Road. After 3 blocks on Military Road turn right on Marcey Road and into the park.

Address and Information: phone: 703-528-5406 (see NVRPA address, above)

RED ROCK WILDERNESS OVERLOOK
1002–7   REGIONAL PARK

This 67-acre sanctuary is on the bank of the Potomac River near Leesburg in Loudoun County, near Harrison Island. Open all year, it is a tranquil preserve of forest and flowers and away from the noise of traffic. From the parking area the *Loblolly Trail* has five connecting trails: the *Hemlock Trail*, the *Holly Trail*, the *Spruce Trail*, the *White Pine Trail*, and the *Sweetbay Trail* for a total of 3 miles. They follow ridges and converge at Cattail Branch, which flows into Goose Creek. At the northeastern point of the *Loblolly Trail* are three overlooks from the sheer cliffs of the Potomac to the river and into the hills of Maryland.

USGS Map: Leesburg

Access: From US 15 in Leesburg go 1.5 miles east on SR 773 (Edwards Ferry Rd.) to parking area on left.

Address and Information: phone: 703-352-5900 (see NVRPA address, above)

Entry to the 1-mile *Upton Hill Trail* can be either east of the reflecting pool or east of the swimming pool complex, in the 26-acre park. In a densely populated area the tall poplars and oaks provide a forest oasis. The reflection pool has beautiful gardens and a gazebo over the water. The park is open all year, but the swimming pools are open from Memorial Day weekend to Labor Day weekend.

Access: From I-95, exit 8, drive east 3.6 miles on US 50 (Arlington Blvd.) to Seven Corners (southeastern edge of Falls Church), and turn left on Wilson Boulevard. Drive 0.6 miles and turn right on Patrick Henry Drive at 6060 Wilson Boulevard.

Address and Information: phone: 703-534-3437 (see NVRPA address, above)

WASHINGTON & OLD DOMINION RAILROAD
REGIONAL PARK   1009

Dramatically different from any other park in the regional system, this is a 100-foot-wide corridor 45 miles long from Alexandria northwest to Purcellville. Its remarkable feature is the *W&OD Trail*, constructed on the railroad bed of the former Washington and Old Dominion Railroad, which operated from 1859 to 1968. It was severely damaged during the Civil War but was rebuilt. Passengers gave the railroad the sobriquet of "The Virginia Creeper" (not to be confused with another "Virginia Creeper" in the JNF). The reality of this trail did not come easily. It took money and years of negotiating to retain the right-of-way. Actually, the corridor has two trails. The 8-foot- or 10-foot-wide asphalt route is for strollers, joggers, hikers, and bikers in a shadeless passage. Parallel to it on natural surface, which receives some shade in the summer, is 30.5 miles for equestrians and hikers. This trail is shorter because it begins in Vienna on its northwestern route. The paved trail begins at the city limits of Alexandria, passes through Arlington County, Falls Church, Fairfax County, Vienna, Reston, Loudoun County, Herndon, and Leesburg to Purcellville.

The regional park system is continuing its safety programs. An example is a bridge over major traffic arteries such as VA 28 near Dulles Airport and VA 7 in Falls Church. Other changes have been the construction of a trail that links the *W&OD Trail* with a wayside park for trail users in the city of Fairfax. (There is a dream to link the *W&OD Trail* to the *AT* with a 9-mile foot trail.) Trail scenery is diverse: high-rise condominiums, shopping centers, suburban homes and lawns, gardens, ponds, streams, bridges, meadows, cattle crossings, farms, forests, and the interminable power line. There are more than 450 species of wildflowers and about 100 species of birds seen on the trail. A rare and treasured trail, it is a gift the citizens have given to themselves. Their creeper and cinders has become the hikers' and bikers' Champs Élysées.

Hikers unfamiliar with the trail and its metro environment should at least have the REI map, distributed free from the *W&OD Trail* office or the park authority office. If planning an all-day trip or a through-hike, purchase the 54-page detailed guidebook with maps (see Addresses and Information, below). The guide has information on how to prepare for the trip, safety and security, street accesses, mile posts, courtesy for multiple-use trail traffic, fast food restaurants, rest rooms, telephones, and emergency aid. For bikers there is a list of repair shops, and for equestrians, water sources and accesses. Request a list of places to stay overnight (no camping on the trail). There are motels, hotels, and bed and breakfast inns, but campgrounds are rare. At 16.5 miles is one option. At the intersection of Sunset Hills Road and Wiehle Avenue in Reston, go north on Wiehle Avenue for about 1.3 miles to turn right on North Shore Drive. Follow it right around Ring Road to Hunt Club Road, and follow it to a right turn on Lake Fairfax Drive into Lake Fairfax Park and campground for a total of about 3 miles (see Information, below).

Access: The southeastern trailhead is at the intersection of Shirlington Road and Four Mile Run Drive. Take exit 6 off I-395 and go north two short blocks (each with a traffic light) on Shirlington Road. The trail parallels Four Mile Run Drive northwest. (Here at the trailhead the *W&OD Trail* connects southeast with the *Anderson Bikeway* [also called *Four Mile Run Bike Trail*] at the pedestrian overpass of I-395 for another downstream connection with the NPS *Mount Vernon Trail* [see Chapter 9]). The northwestern trailhead for the *W&OD Trail* in Purcellville is one block off Main Street (VA 7) on 21st Street (SR 690) to O Street.

Addresses and Information: NVRPA, 5400 Ox Rd., Fairfax Station, VA 22039, phone: 703-352-5900. Available are free brochures and calendar of events, brochures on individual parks with maps, and *Discover Your Regional Parks* magazine. There is a nominal charge for the *W&OD Trail Guide*. W&OD Trail Office, 21293 Smiths Switch Rd., Ashburn, VA 22011, phone: 703-729-0596. Available are free brochures with maps about the *W&OD Trail*; there is a nominal charge for the *W&OD Trail Guide*. Lake Fairfax Park, 1400 Lake Fairfax Dr., Reston, VA 2290; phone: 703-471-5414 for camping information (see Fairfax County Parks in Chapter 12).

Upper Valley Regional Park Authority

Augusta County

The Upper Valley Regional Park Authority was formed in 1966 between the city of Harrisonburg and the counties of Augusta and Rockingham. The city of Staunton was included the following year. The first acquisition was Natural Chimneys in 1970, followed by the Grand Caverns in 1974. The parks operate independently because of different facilities and activities. User fees make them almost self-supporting.

1010   GRAND CAVERNS REGIONAL PARK

These limestone caverns were formerly known as Cave Hill and later as Weyer's Cave. There are three major entrances on the hillside at the southwestern edge of the town of Grottoes, but only one entrance is open to the public now. It is not known who discovered the first cave in the 1780s, but it was on the property of John Madison, a friend of Thomas Jefferson, who explored it and drew a map of the interior. In 1804 Bernard Weyer, a 17-year-old trapper, discovered the Grand Caverns, the entrance open today, and in 1835 the Fountain Cave was discovered by Edmund Weast. The subterranean 0.7-mile trail passes gigantic stalactites and stalagmites into chambers as large as the 5,000-square-foot Grand Ballroom. The caverns are one of only fourteen caves in the nation designated natural landmarks by the Department of the Interior. Guided tours begin every 30 minutes daily from 9 A.M. to 5 P.M. from April 1 through October, weekends in March, and by group reservations from November through February.

At a small stone wall, near the inclined walkway to the caverns, is white-blazed *Grand Caverns Nature Trail*. It ascends through basswood, redbud, locust, and wildflowers such as goat's-beard and Virginia bluebells. There are overlooks at 0.3 miles and 0.4 miles of the South Fork of the Shenandoah River and the Blue Ridge Mountains beyond. Backtrack for a total distance of 0.9 miles. The park also has a swimming pool, a ballfield, and a picnic area. From picnic shelter #4 is a hike-bike trail around the perimeter of the park.

USGS Map: Grottoes

Access: From I-81, exit 235, and US 11, go east 6 miles on VA 256 to the town of Grottoes, and right on SR 825. The park is on the right; cross the bridge to the parking area. Access also from US 340 in Grottoes; go west on VA 256 and turn left on SR 825.

NATURAL CHIMNEYS REGIONAL PARK 1011

The 134-acre park is at Mt. Solon, southwest of the town of Bridgewater, and northwest of Grand Caverns. Its spectacular natural beauty is a group of seven limestone chimneys ranging from 65 to 120 feet high. More than 500 million years old, the chimneys contain iron, magnesium, and chert on the top. Because the chimneys appear castlelike, they inspired a jousting tournament on the meadow at the base of the chimneys in 1821. It has become the Natural Chimneys Jousting Tournament, America's oldest continuously held sports event, and is staged each year on the third Saturday in August. Held the third Saturday in June is the annual National Jousting Hall of Fame Tournament. Excellent for birdwatching, the park has 125 species of birds. The park is open year round.

There is 3-mile, easy *Natural Chimneys Nature Trail* in the park. It begins from the visitor center parking area, follows a sign to the right, and ascends a graded treadway. It passes a shelter and an access road and reaches chimneys overlook at 1.5 miles. It descends to a picnic shelter and parking area. From here it turns right to follow through and around the chimneys, where six exhibit signs explain the unique rock formations. The return is on the road from the parking area to the visitor center. The park has full camping services from March through November and limited services the other months. There are hookups for electricity and water. There are also biking trails, picnic shelters, a camp store, a laundry, a swimming pool, and playgrounds.

USGS Map: Parnassus

Access: From I-81, exit 240, go 3.5 miles west on VA 257 to Bridgewater. Turn left on VA 42 for 3.8 miles to SR 747. Turn right, go 3.5 miles to Mt. Solon, and then right on SR 731 for 0.6 miles to park entrance.

Addresses and Information: Grand Caverns Regional Park, P.O. Box, 478, Grottoes, VA 24441; phone: 703-249-5705. Natural Chimneys Regional Park, Mt. Solon, VA 22843; phone: 703-350-2510. For information on both parks, call 703-249-5729. Available is a brochure with map.

15 : U.S. Army Corps of Engineers and Military Areas

U.S. Army Corps of Engineers

JOHN W. FLANNAGAN RESERVOIR
Dickenson County

Completed in 1964, the reservoir retains rainfall from a 221-square-mile watershed and stores the waters of the Cranesnest and Pound Rivers. The dam is 250 feet high and 916 feet long, creating a 1,145-acre lake, 40 miles of shoreline and 7,130 acres surrounding the lake. Its northwestern border adjoins the Clinch Ranger District of the JNF and is within sight of Pine Mountain, the divide between Virginia and Kentucky. It is named for a congressman who served the Ninth Virginia District from 1931 to 1949 and who was influential in flood control of the Appalachian highlands. There are fourteen recreation areas, all near the water. These include two campground, five boat launch areas, and five picnic areas. There are two trails, both on the northern side of the lake, but a new trail system is under study on the southern side near the Cranesnest Campground.

Lower Twin Area   1012–13

The Lower Twin Campground is a peaceful hollow with a dock, a boat ramp at the lake, hot showers (no hookups), a waste disposal unit, and a picnic area. Two trails begin here. The easy, 0.8-mile loop *Trail of Trees* begins at a sign near campsite #15. It crosses a footbridge, follows upstream, ascends, and returns from a ridgeside. Along the way are oak, beech, hemlock, rhododendron, and a closed coal mine. The other trail, 1.7-mile *Twin Eagle Trail,* is a moderate, linear trail between the Lower Twin Branch and the Upper Twin Branch. It begins on the side of the hill on the approach to the dock from the campground. It traverses a hillside among redbud, basswood, locust, and oak. At 1.5 miles it descends steeply to cross a branch over a footbridge. It enters a field, the site of an old campground. After 115 yards it reaches an old paved road, where it turns right. Follow it to a gate and parking space on SR 611. Backtrack or use a second car.

USGS maps: Haysi, Clintwood

Access: To access the dam from the town of Haysi and VA 80, go west 3.4 miles on VA 63 and turn right on SR 614. After 0.5 miles turn right on SR 739 and follow it 3.3 miles to a junction with SR 611. (Along the way are the dam crossing and the reservoir office on the left.) (On SR 611 right it is 0.9 mi. to a mountain grocery store and another 10 mi. to Breaks Interstate Park.) On SR 611, turn left and after 0.7 miles southwest turn left on SR 683. Go 0.4 miles to the Lower Twin Campground gate. It is another 0.3 miles to the dock. To reach the western end of the

Twin Eagle Trail, return to SR 611, turn left, and after 1.2 miles park at the gate on the left.

Address and Information: Flannagan Reservoir, Rt. 1, Box 268, Haysi, VA 24256; phone: 703-835-9544. Available is a brochure with map and facilities list.

JOHN H. KERR RESERVOIR
Mecklenburg and Charlotte Counties

This large, 50,000-acre reservoir has 37,500 acres in Virginia and 12,500 acres in North Carolina. It was completed in 1953. Its watershed is 9,580 square miles of the entire Roanoke River (Staunton) basin, and it has 800 miles of shoreline. Its dam is 2,786 feet wide and 189 feet high. A popular lake for boating, fishing, and water skiing, it has thirteen boat ramp areas with fishing piers at some of the docks. North Bend Park and Marina is an example, and it also has a pier for the physically disabled. There are nine picnic areas and five campgrounds (some with hookups) with hot showers. (There are campgrounds and other facilities on the North Carolina side, south of the dam, also. In addition, there are two state parks up-river—Occoneechee State Park and Staunton River State Park. See Chapter 11.) Below the dam is 169-acre Bugg's Island, named for Samuel Bugg and family, who were early settlers. Before English settlement the river basin was dominated by the Occoneechee Indians from 1250 to 1676, when they were killed or scattered by Nathaniel Bacon and his followers. Although called Bugg's Island Dam by many Virginians, the reservoir was named in honor of a North Carolina congressman who was influential in federal funding of the reservoir project.

The reservoir area has two trails. An easy, round-trip trail, the *Liberty Hill Trail*, is 0.7 miles. It is accessible at the parking area of Liberty Hill Cemetery on the southern end of the dam. It follows 15 interpretive signs down to the riverbank through a forest of hickory, pine, gum, and oak. Scenic views of Bugg's Island and the river channel below the dam to Lake Gaston are part of the appeal of the trail.

1014   The other trail is described below.

1015   **Eagle Point Trail**
Length and Difficulty: 7.4 miles (11.8 km); easy
Features: lake views, historic site, wildlife
Trailheads: Access to eastern trailhead: From US 58 at the western edge of Boydton, go 0.2 miles on Jefferson Street (SR 756) and turn right. Stay on SR 705 for 7 miles to parking area on right at BSA Camp Eagle Point. (It is 0.4 mi. ahead to Eagle Point boat ramp and scenic shore area.) Access to western trailhead: Same as above, except after 4.4 miles on SR 705 from SR 756 turn right on SR 823 and drive 2 miles to parking area on left.
Description: The white-blazed trail follows the northern edge of Kerr Lake, in and out of coves, and skirts the slopes of peninsulas. The forest is mature hard-woods with scattered Virginia pine and cedar. Wildlife is mainly deer, raccoon, squirrel, fox, snakes, and some wild pigs. The hardwoods offer fine fall colors. If beginning at the eastern trailhead, descend, pass a large oak, and go under

power lines at 0.5 miles, 1.1 miles, and 1.3 miles. At 1.8 miles is an open view of the lake and a picnic area. Cross a number of small streams between rolling hills and cross the last stream at 3.6 miles. (Trail distance may vary 0.2 mi. here because of choice of stream crossing, depending on water levels.) Ascend among patches of running cedar. Cross an old road at 4 miles and pass a white oak with a 13.5-foot circumference. Cross another old road at 4.2 miles. At 5.1 miles to the right is the old cabin of Dr. William C. Hutcheson (not easily seen in dense full forest foliage). Descend to remnants of an old springhouse. Enter the edge of a field, cross an old road at 5.5 miles, and arrive at a historic cemetery at 6 miles. Pass through the edge of a field, turn left, and follow an old road past two huge post oaks for a turn left. Follow the road, which is also a good equestrian trail, to the gate and the western trailhead at 7.4 miles. Backtrack, or have a second vehicle.

USGS maps: Kerr Dam, Tungsten

Address and Information: John H. Kerr Reservoir, Rt. 1, Box 76, Boydton, VA 23917; phone: 804-738-6143 or 738-6143.

PHILPOTT LAKE
Franklin, Henry, and Patrick Counties

The 10,000 acres of Philpott Lake and surrounding lands were authorized by Congress in 1944 to be developed for flood control, hydroelectric power, and recreation. Construction by the U.S. Army Corps of Engineers began in 1948, and the project was completed for full operation in 1953. The clear, blue-green lake encompasses 3,000 acres and has a shoreline of 100 miles. A total of 5,000 acres are leased to the Virginia Commission of Game and Inland Fisheries for wildlife management purposes. Fairy Stone State Park adjoins the boundary on the west, and nearby, downriver and southeast, are the community of Philpott and the town of Bassett. Public facilities include boat launching ramps, nature trails, and areas for fishing, water skiing, picnicking, camping, hunting, and nature study. Camping is allowed in eight of the fifteen recreational areas. The campgrounds are open from April 1 through October, unless otherwise stated below.

Philpott Park and Overlook   1016–17
This area offers the most spectacular views of the gorge, dam, and lake. One of the islands seen upriver is Turkey Island, west of the larger Deer Island. There are two trails here. To follow the *Smith River Trail*, follow the sign at the scenic overlook parking area. Descend on switchbacks for 0.1 mile to the top of the dam. Continue descending the switchbacks, reaching the base of the dam at 0.3 miles. Follow the twenty-one interpretive trail signs down the Smith River with a guide booklet provided by the resource manager's office. Reach the trail's end at 0.7 miles at a large, nine-pronged sycamore. Other vegetation on the trail includes hemlock, beech, poplar, and rhododendron. Backtrack for a moderate to strenuous ascent.

The other trail is 1.6-mile round-trip *Fishing Barge Trail*. It leaves the overlook parking area west, passing the rest rooms on the left. Descend to a parking area at

0.1 mile. Reach the boat launching site at 0.2 miles, and follow right, along the lake, on a steep slope in a white pine stand. Reach the end of the trail at a group campsite at 0.6 miles, but continue another 0.2 miles to the Group Camp Swim Area. Backtrack. (Camping at this park requires reservations.)

USGS map: Philpott Reservoir

Access: From downtown Bassett go west on VA 57 for 2 miles to junction with SR 904. Turn right on SR 904 and go 1.2 miles to resource management center and visitor exhibit, and parking area at the overlook.

1018   *Goose Point Park*

This area has public boat ramps, a campground, picnicking, swimming, hot showers, and a nature trail. The *Goose Point Trail* is an easy 0.5-mile hike from the campground along the lake to the amphitheater. The forest is mixed with hardwoods and pines, and there is a scenic view from the peninsula. Except for the campground the park is open year round. (Camping reservations are not required here.)

USGS map: Philpott Reservoir

Access: From downtown Bassett go west on VA 57 for 7.5 miles to SR 822 and turn right. Follow it for 5.3 miles to Goose Point Park.

1019   *Jamison Mill Park*

The 0.7-mile *Jamison Mill Trail* is an easy round-trip that begins in the picnic area near the entrance. In addition to a picnic area there is a fishing area and a campground with hot showers. Begin the hike across the road on the right side of the river against a rocky bluff. Cross a small bridge in an area of trout lilies, spring beauty, mayapples, and ground cedar. Ascend through a hemlock forest and at 0.2 miles join an old road. Turn left for an excellent view of the campground below. At 0.4 miles reach a paved area for camping; return to the bridge over the river and to the picnic area parking at 0.7 miles. (Camping reservations are not required here; open from Memorial Day through Labor Day.)

USGS map: Philpott Reservoir

Access: From the town of Ferrum take SR 623 southwest for 3.8 miles to junction with SR 605 and turn left. Drive 1.2 miles to junction with SR 780 and turn right. Follow it 1.9 miles to Jamison Mill.

1020   *Salthouse Branch Recreation Area*

This beautiful area is on the eastern side of the lake near a peninsula and Deer Island. Secluded, it has a good family campground with hot showers. It also has a picnic area, a boat launch, and a place to swim. Vascular plants are oak, maple, tulip poplar, beech, pine, and rhododendron. *Salthouse Branch Nature Trail* is a 0.5-mile interpretive trail with twenty stops on an easy loop. Access to it is from the campground at the trail signs. It crosses three streams. (Camping reservations are not required here. Portions of the park are open all year, but not the campground.)

USGS map: Philpott Reservoir

Access: From the town of Henry drive west on SR 605 for 1.7 miles to junction with SR 798. Take SR 798 on the left for 1.4 miles to junction with SR 773 and follow it 0.4 miles to enter the recreation area.

Address and Information: Resource Management Center, Philpott Lake, Rt. 6, Box 140, Bassett, VA 24055; phone: 703-629-2703. Available are brochure with map and recreation facilities.

Military Installations

Virginia has 372,692 acres of military lands, of which 174,198 are seasonally available for public hunting, fishing, and hiking. Another 1,141 acres are designated for other recreational activities. Fort A. P. Hill, one of the largest of nine U.S. Army installations in the state has outstanding space for Boy Scout camping. Similar arrangements can be made at Quantico marine base. (Trails for hiking or field trips for nature study are no longer provided at Fort Pickett Military Reservation.) For information on camping, trails, travel, and recreational activities on Virginia's military bases, request the *Armed Forces Recreation Areas Travel Guide*, DOD PA-15, from any of the addresses below.

FORT A. P. HILL MILITARY RESERVATION
Caroline County

The A. P. Hill Military Reservation, named in honor of Civil War general Ambrose Powell Hill, includes a 212-acre tract of land set aside for the Boy Scouts of America. In this area, hiking is permitted once requests to use the facility are approved. Group participation in hiking exercises is allowed in designated areas during specific times of the year, if such activities do not interfere with training of military personnel. Written requests are mandatory. The request should state the desired dates and purpose, and hikers must be self-sufficient. If desired, long hikes can be arranged outside the BSA area. A former nature trail at Beaverdam Pond is being constructed by a group of Eagle Scouts.

USGS maps: Rappahannock Academy, Port Royal, Bowling Green

Access: From junction of VA 2 and US 301 in Bowling Green go northeast 2.2 miles on US 301 to main entrance, left.

Address and Information: Commander: Attn: DPTMS, Hq. Fort A. P. Hill, Bowling Green, VA 22427; phone: 804-633-8333 (main office, 804-633-8710); FAX: 804-633-8406.

FORT BELVOIR
Fairfax County

The 1,300-acre Accotink Bay Wildlife Refuge and Nature Study Area has about 7 miles of trails open to the public. The preserve's wildlife is abundant, accountable in part to the adjoining protected areas of Mason Neck NWR, Pohick Bay Regional

Park, and the Gunston Hall Plantation. Hikers are likely to see deer, beaver, mink, or osprey. Hiking is allowed in daylight only. Outside the refuge is a campground on the base large enough to accommodate 750 Boy Scouts in groups. Camping is also provided for active-duty and retired military personnel as well as civilians working for the military services.

Access: One access point is off US 1, 8 miles south of Alexandria. Another is east of Lorton from I-95; take US 1 north for 4 miles.

Address and Information: Public Relations Branch, Fort Belvoir, VA 22060; phone: 703-545-6700; for camping: 703-806-5007.

QUANTICO MARINE BASE
Stafford, Prince William, and Faquier Counties

The Quantico Marine Base has 61,000 acres of woodlands and 807 acres of lakes. Designated areas around the lakes and open fields can accommodate from 200 to 1,800 campers in groups. The campers must be self-sufficient; it is not a camp for recreational vehicles. There are 15 miles of streams open to the public for fishing, and hunting is also allowed with proper licenses. Trails are unnamed and are within the designated areas. It is advisable to call in advance about services and restrictions.

Access: Off I-95, exit 147, turn east across US 1 on SR 619 (near Triangle) into base and sentry gate.

Address and Information: Marine Corps Development and Education Command, Quantico, VA 22134; phone: 703-640-2121.

16 : Colleges and Universities

Only the educated are free.
—Epictetus

College of William and Mary

The nation's second oldest college (founded 1693) has three self-guiding tours, which provide short walks on the campus for botanical observation. The college plant tour begins at the Sir Christopher Wren Building, on the corner of Richmond and Jamestown roads, and takes a clockwise direction around the quadrangle. At plant label #31, a left turn leads across Blair Road to Wildflower Refuge, and opposite the refuge across Old Campus Road is John Millington Hall, which houses the Department of Biology. On the roof of this building is a self-guiding tour of plants in the greenhouse. Other unnamed walks are around the wooded area of Lake Matoaka, west of the Commons.

Access: From I-64, exit 238, take VA 143 west 0.5 miles to VA 132 right and go 2.2 miles to Duke of Gloucester Street. Turn right, and the college is directly ahead.

Address and Information: Office of Communication, College of William and Mary, Williamsburg, VA 23185; phone: 804-253-4000.

New River Community College
1021

Well designed for hiking and jogging, the 0.8-mile *New River Community College Trail* makes a loop through large oak, hickory, and white pine in a forest on the campus. The understory is dogwood, maple, and wildflowers such as black cohosh, mayapple, and large beds of Virginia creeper.

Access: From US 11 in Dublin, go 0.4 miles west on VA 100 to the campus entrance on the left. At the parking area the sign should be to the right, across the entrance road.

Address and Information: Information Center, New River Community College, Box 1127, Dublin, VA 24084; phone: 703-674-4121.

Rappahannock Community College, South
1022

The *Rappahannock Community College Nature Trail* is a 0.9-mile easy loop through hardwoods and pines. A carpet of leaves and pine needles makes this a pleasant hike. The understory has dogwood, blueberry, and wildflowers. Campus access is from the parking area, within the gate of the recreational area. Trail may be unmarked.

Access: From the town of Glenns on VA 33, go west 0.7 miles from the junction with US 17. On campus turn left near the main building and enter the gate of the recreational area.

Address and Information: Recreation Department, Rappahannock Community College, South, Saluda, VA 23149, phone: 804-758-5324.

1023   ## University of Virginia

In 1975 Mary Hall Betts designed and compiled a guide for a 0.6-mile walking tour on the grounds of Thomas Jefferson's "Academic Village" of 1819. The *University of Virginia Academic Walk* covers twenty-two major points of academic and architectural interest. Among them are the Rotunda; the Lawn, formed by two parallel rows of buildings connected by the Colonnades and the five Pavilions on each side; the ten formal gardens, each designed differently but enclosed by the serpentine walls behind the Ionic, Doric, or Corinthian Pavilions; and the East and West Ranges, where student rooms are connected with a series of arches framing a covered walkway. The walk begins at the south portico of the Rotunda and turns left between Pavilions II and IV. A loop is formed by touring the East Range and gardens and the statue of Homer near Cabell Hall, with a return on the West Range. Request a guide map in the Rotunda.

Access: From I-64, exit 118, turn north on US 29 to US 29B and turn right. At the junction with W. Main Street, turn right to the Rotunda.

Address and Information: Office of Information Services, University of Virginia, Charlottesville, VA 22903; phone: 703-924-0311.

Virginia Military Institute

Of all the college and university trails in Virginia, the 7.3-mile *Chessie Nature Trail* is the longest and most unique. It has been owned and maintained by the VMI Foundation, Inc., an independent endowment agency for VMI since 1979. The Chessie was developed by the foundation with the assistance of the Virginia Environmental Endowment, the Chesapeake and Ohio Railroad, the Commission on Outdoor Recreation, VMI, the Rockbridge Area Conservation Council, and many individual citizens. A day-use trail, it is used for hiking, birding, jogging, fishing, cross-country skiing, and picnicking. Bicycles, horses, and vehicles are not permitted. Sections of the trail are arbored with ash, sycamore, and mulberry, and other sections pass through open grassy meadows. Deer, fox, and many species of birds are likely to be seen.

1024   ### Chessie Nature Trail
Length and Difficulty: 7.3 miles (11.7 km); easy
Features: scenic views, historic site, river, wildflowers, geological formation

Trailheads: For the western trailhead in Lexington, turn off Main Street at junction with fork of US 11/11B at the southern end of Maury River bridge onto short Moses Mill Road (which becomes short Jordan's Point Rd.), and follow it to the parking area on VMI Island. (This is also the parking area for the northeastern trailhead of the *Woods Creek Trail*.) At the eastern trailhead, park by the river near the junction of US 60 bridge and SR 608 in Buena Vista.

Description: From the parking area in Lexington follow the signs, cross a pedestrian bridge over the Maury River, and pass under US 11 bridge. Before crossing the Mill Creek bridge there is a wye site where the trains turned around. At 1 mile the high cliffs are pocketed with bloodroot, trillium, columbine, fire pink, and meadow rue in the spring. Pass under I-81 bridge at 2.5 miles. Cross a small bridge at 2.7 miles, and then pass through gates three times between 2.8 miles and 4 miles in a pastoral valley. At 4.1 miles is South River Lock on the right, the site of an old canal. Cross South River on a skillfully constructed 235-foot footbridge with C&O trusses. After 5.4 miles enter a field of wildflowers such as Virginia bluebells, chicory, soapwort, and nodding onions. On the right at 5.9 miles are remnants of the Ben Salem Lock. Pass cliffs of limestone veined with calcite and quartz (formed about 500 million years ago). At 6.6 miles pass the Zimmerman's Lock site, and cross a road at 6.9 miles. At 7.3 miles reach a junction with US 60 and SR 608, the completion of the trail. Backtrack or use a second vehicle.

USGS maps: Lexington, Glasgow, Buena Vista

Address and Information: VMI Foundation, P.O. Box 932, Lexington, VA 24450; phone: 703-464-7287. Available is a brochure with map. Information is also available from the Lexington Visitors Bureau; phone: 703-463-3777.

17 : Private and Special Holdings

If you have a garden and a library,
you have everything you need.
—Cicero

There are hundreds of trails on private property in Virginia, most of which are short walks in natural or formal gardens. Some are open to the public during annual April Historic Garden Week (usually the last week of April). Others are longer treks in forests or on farms for hunting, fishing, horseback riding, or viewing scenic points of interest. A few are at large industrial research corporations or forest products companies. In addition, there are well-maintained trails at private resorts, where hikers are expected to be paying guests or have permission to be on the premises. Examples are The Homestead, where scenic trails blend into the 16,000-acre estate (P.O. Box 2000, Hot Springs, VA 24445; phone: 703-839-5500); Wintergreen Resort with 13,000 acres near Reeds Gap and 30 miles of trails (P.O. Box 706, Wintergreen, VA 22958; phone: 804-325-2200 [reservations 1-800-325-2200]); and the 11,000-acre Mountain Lake Resort (Mountain Lake, VA 24136; phone: 703-626-7121). The following listed properties have trails open to the public, with restrictions as described.

Forest Products Companies

Virginia has seven major forest-industry companies that manage lands intensively to produce lumber and fiber. Additionally, the lands provide desirable wildlife habitat and recreational opportunities. Designated areas allow hunting, fishing, hiking, and nature study. A few offer limited backpacking and primitive camping. One of the largest such corporations is Union Camp, with 345,000 acres in Virginia and North Carolina. The company has designated forest roads open to the public for hiking, though the roads are not named as trails. (Contact Land Manager, Union Camp Corp., Franklin, VA 23851; phone: 804-569-4321.) Another land-managing corporation is Owens-Illinois, with hundreds of miles of logging roads in seven counties that can be used for hiking. Permits and fees are necessary for hunting or fishing. Hiking without firearms does not require a permit. (Contact Forest Management, Owens-Illinois, Big Island, VA 24526; phone: 804-299-5911.) The Glatfelter Pulp Wood Company also allows hiking on designated wildlife tracts and firelines. Hunters must pay fees and have a permit. (Contact Glatfelter Pulp Wood Company, P.O. Box 868, Fredericksburg, VA 22404; phone: 703-373-9431.) Two companies have public trail systems; they are described here.

CHESAPEAKE FOREST PRODUCTS COMPANY

This company owns and cares for over 350,000 acres of woodlands located in Virginia, Maryland, and Delaware. Three well-designed trail systems have been constructed and are open to the public from dawn to dusk every day. The trails, all in Virginia, are located in New Kent, Lancaster, and Prince Edward counties.

Lancaster County Nature Trail 1025

This beautiful trail winds and loops through a 1,000-acre woodland on the eastern bank of the Western Branch of the Carrotoman River, a tributary of Chesapeake Bay. The two-loop, easy, 1.6-mile, self-guided trail passes wetlands of big cordgrass and arrow arum, and upland oaks and pines with twenty-eight marked stops. Among the wildflowers are atamasco lily (*Zephyranthes atamasco*) and showy orchid (*Orchis spectabilis*). At 0.2 miles and 0.5 miles are splendid views of the river. On the ridge at 1.1 miles is an example of forest succession, and at 1.3 miles the trail begins a descent on an old road for a return to the parking area.

USGS map: Lancaster

Access: At Lancaster Courthouse, go 0.5 miles west on VA 3 to a parking area on the left.

New Kent Nature Trail 1026

In a 565-acre forestland, this 3.1-mile, easy to moderate trail has three color-coded loops (red-blazed, 0.9 mi.; white-blazed, 0.7 mi.; orange-blazed, 1.5 mi.). It is a self-guiding educational trail with forty-nine markers, which describe trees, shrubs, flowers, and historic sites. Among the tree species are oak, hackberry (known for its "witches'-switch," a thick cluster of twigs), hickory, and pine. Flowers include columbine, blueflag iris, and trailing arbutus. Deer have been seen near the stream and field in the third loop. If beginning on the red-blazed loop go right at the first fork. At 0.3 miles is a description of the life cycle of loblolly pine. At 0.5 miles is a fork to return to the parking area for 0.9 miles or to continue on the white-blazed trail for another 0.7 miles. Continue ahead to where the white-blazed trail turns left, but a longer trail, orange blazed, stays right. At 1.3 miles the orange-blazed trail passes under a power line and at 1.4 miles crosses a small stream. It ascends to the site of Warreneye Church, then to a scenic view. It passes under the power line again, descends to a field, and reaches a junction with the red-blazed trail at 2.5 miles for a return to the parking area at 2.7 miles.

USGS map: West Point

Access: From I-64, exit 220 (east of Richmond), take VA 33 east for 3.8 miles to the parking area on the right.

Prince Edward County Nature Trail 1027

This easy, 1.7-mile, double loop, self-guided trail is in a 75-acre forested tract near the Briery Lake Reservoir and the Briery Creek WMA. There are twenty-six interpretive markers in the first 0.6-mile loop of a mature forest, and there are some lowland hardwoods on the second 1.1-mile loop. There is also an old mill site dated about 1820 near a stream.

USGS map: Hampden Sydney

Access: From Farmville drive south on US 15 for 8 miles to the marked parking area on the right.

Addresses and Information: Chesapeake Forest Products Company, P.O. Box 450, Keysville, VA 23947; phone: 804-736-8505. Main office: Chesapeake Forest Products Company, P.O. Box 311, West Point, VA 23181; phone: 804-843-5000. Available are brochures at signboards of the trails with map and marker numbers.

1028   WESTVACO

When it comes to wildflower pilgrimages, no one does it better than Westvaco (West Virginia Pulp and Paper Company). An example is the company's group tour in April on the *Buffalo Creek Trail*. Otherwise, visitors hike on their own to see about seventy-five species of wildflowers on the 1.6-mile, easy loop. The flowers peak from mid-April to mid-May. Among them are green and gold (*Chrysogonum virginianum*) and yellow lady's-slipper (*Cypripedium calceolus*). There are both lowland and upland hardwoods and conifers such as hemlock and white pine. Wildlife includes turkey, woodcock, deer, and songbirds. The trail begins near the creek, turns left of the field, and passes to the right of a hemlock forest. Its loop is mainly in the forest. In addition to the nature trail there are another 3 miles of old forest roads for hiking. The Buffalo Creek Nature Area of 125 acres is registered with the Virginia Native Plant Registry. (In addition to the forests here in Campbell and Bedford counties, Westvaco has forests in twenty-three other counties for a total of nearly 245,000 acres. Contact the company for information on fees and specific locations to hunt, fish, or hike.)

USGS map: Lynch Station

Access: From US 29 go west 6.2 miles to Evington on VA 24. From Evington continue west for 2.5 miles to the county line and parking area on the left near Buffalo Creek bridge. (It is 19.3 mi. west to US 460 in Bedford.)

Address and Information: Westvaco, Rt. 4, Box 134, Appomattox, VA 24522; phone: 804-352-7132. Available is a brochure with map and botanical list.

Mariners' Museum Park

The Mariners' Museum Park in Newport News is the state's foremost museum of nautical history. There are displays and exhibits in galleries that chronicle the development of ship building, navigation, and oceanography. Among the exhibits are artifacts representing 3,000 years of maritime science. The museum is a nonprofit educational facility developed in the 1930s and made possible by philanthropists Archer and Anna Hyatt Huntington (for whom the 2,500-acre Huntington Beach State Park in South Carolina is named). Within the park's 550 acres is 167-acre Lake Maury, named for Matthew F. Maury, U.S. naval officer and hydrographer from Spotsylvania County. Around the lake is the *Noland Trail*, the state's finest private trail open to the public. It passes through a mature forest of jack pine, sweet gum, oak, maple, and magnolia and is home to more than 435 species

Noland Trail, Mariners' Museum Park. (Photograph by Allen de Hart)

of vascular plants. There are more than 110 species of birds. The museum is open daily except Christmas Day.

Noland Trail

1029–30

Length and Difficulty: 5 miles (8 km); easy
Features: scenic views, lake, wildflowers, historic site
Trailheads: Parking lot at the museum

Description: The *Noland Trail* was completed in 1991 and was made possible by the financial generosity of Lloyd Noland Jr., a local businessman. The trail is well designed and has fourteen bridges crossing quiet coves. There is a granite mileage marker every 0.5 miles, and parts of the trail are useful for the physically impaired. Begin the trail from the entrance road at the northern side of the museum's parking area. At 0.2 miles is an overlook of the lake and the museum buildings before crossing a curved bridge at 0.4 miles. There is another overlook of the lake at 0.6 miles near tall pines and an understory of dogwood, mountain laurel, and blueberry. Pass a wildlife meadow and then cross a service road at 1.3 miles. There is a large white oak near a side trail, the *Indian File Trail*, at 1.8 miles. The side trail rejoins the main trail at an overlook at 2 miles. Another side trail goes to an overlook on a peninsula a few yards ahead. At 3.1 miles the trail leaves a grassy area and crosses the lake's dam at Museum Drive. On the western side is a parking lot and a large spreading water oak. This area offers scenic views of both the lake and the James River. Ascend on a grassy knoll to historic monuments and reenter the forest. There is another fine view of the lake at 3.5 miles. For the next 1.5 miles the trail crosses three more bridges in lowlands with bayberry and buttonwood. There are also beds of jewelweed, mandrake, galax, and wild petunia. Complete the trail at the southern edge of the museum and parking area.

USGS map: Mulberry Island

Access: From I-64, exit 258-A, drive 3 miles west on US 17 (Clyde Morris Dr.), cross VA 143 to SR 312, and at US 60 (Warwick Blvd.), cross to Museum Drive.

Address and Information: Mariners' Museum Park, Museum Dr., Newport News, VA 23601; phone: 804-595-0368. Available for free is a trail brochure and map; books are on sale in gift shop.

Pinnacles of Dan Hydro Development

The 3,640-acre Pinnacles of Dan Hydro Development, near the BRP, is owned by the city of Danville and is under city, state, and federal regulation. Two dams— Talbott and Townes—on the Dan River are 75 miles west of the city in Patrick County. At the Townes Dam a pipeline channels water over trestles and through a sealed tunnel on the western side of the gorge to the power plant downriver. Between the pipeline's tunnel and the river are three pinnacles with breathtaking, panoramic views of the gorge. As recently as the early 1950s the route of the *AT* was through the gorge and over these sharp peaks. The route, and the Devil's Stairsteps on the eastern side of the gorge, had been chosen by Myron Avery and other Appalachian Trail Conference officials. When Earl Shaffer, the first through-hiker, hiked from Georgia to Maine in the summer of 1948, he wrote, "This couple of miles was probably the most rugged and most spectacular segment of the Trail."

Although the property is publicly owned, its description is placed in a special property category in this book because of its uniqueness. The public should be aware that the city of Danville allows fishing, hiking, backpacking, camping, and nature study as a voluntary public service and not by public mandate. To preserve this rugged wilderness-type area and to provide safety for all visitors, there are some necessary restrictions. First, a free written permit is required and must be carried by the visitor at all times. Permits may be acquired in Danville or at the site of the hydro development. In Danville, permits can be obtained at the Electric Department, Utilities Service Building, 1040 Monument Street (phone: 804-799-5270), Monday through Friday from 8 A.M. to 5 P.M. At the site, the preferred location to obtain a request is the power plant on SR 648 (Kibler Valley Rd.) for 24-hour-a-day service. Permits are also available from a ranger at the top of the canyon rim parking area gate to the Townes Dam each day at about 7:15 A.M. and 2:45 P.M. (If the ranger is not at the gate because of other unexpected work, visitors should drive down the mountain on SR 614 to the power plant [see *Access*, below].) Prohibited are campfires, hunting, firearms, fireworks, alcohol and illegal drugs, damage to plants and animals, swimming, littering, bicycles, motorcycles, ATVs, and pets. Fishing boats must be small and are limited to 5 hp. Visitors are reminded that they enter the gorge at their own risk.

Aqueduct Trail (3 mi.), **Pinnacle Trail** (1.4 mi.)   1031–32
Length and Difficulty: 7.4 miles (10.8 km) combined, round-trip; strenuous
Features: outstanding views, wildflowers, wildlife, rugged terrain
Trailheads: Parking area at the end of SR 602 for northern trailhead; parking area at
    end of SR 648 for southern trailhead (See Access, below.)
Description: From the parking area at the northern trailhead descend on the steep and narrow paved road for 0.7 miles to Townes Dam. Descend the steps below the dam to the *Aqueduct Trail*. Follow the aqueduct to a long and high trestle over Barnard Creek at 1.7 miles. After crossing, continue on a descent before climbing over a rocky area for ascension to a ridge and a junction left with the *Pinnacle Trail* at 2.1 miles. (From here the *Aqueduct Trail* descends on switchbacks to Kibler Valley and the power plant at 3 miles. Backtrack, or have a two-car arrangement.) Follow the *Pinnacle Trail* on the ridge to a low saddle and begin to climb steeply over precipitous rocks. There may be faint white blazes, a reminder of the *AT*'s original route over the peaks. Reach the highest pinnacle (2,662 ft.) at 0.3 miles. Growing in the crevices of the rocks are scrub pine, mountain laurel, bleeding hearts, galax, serviceberry, ferns, mosses, and lichens. Vultures soar on the updrafts, and unless the sound of the river rises from the gorge, there is silence. Ice and snow make this trail exceptionally dangerous. Backtrack.

If hiking farther east, descend, staying on the ridge spine and climbing over large boulders to the Dan River at 0.7 miles. Elevation loss from the highest peak is 1,100 feet. Backtrack. (The old *AT* crossed the river here and ascended on a steep, rocky spine called the Devil's Stairsteps to the top of the mountain, which is private property.)

USGS map: Meadows of Dan

Access: For the northern trailhead, drive south from US 58 in Meadows of Dan (near the BRP) on SR 614 for 3.8 miles to a junction with SR 602. Turn left on SR 602 and go 1 mile to a parking area at the gate to Townes Dam. For the southern trailhead, drive north from VA 103 at Claudville on SR 773 for 1.5 miles to SR 648 (Kibler Valley Rd.) and follow it 5.8 miles to its end at the power plant. (For a road connection between the trailheads, continue south on SR 614 for 3.6 mi. to the community of Bell Spur. Descend 5.5 mi. to junction with SR 773 in the community of Carters Mill. Turn left, east, 3.3 mi. to junction with SR 648 and turn left. Drive 5.8 mi. to the power plant.)

Address and Information: Pinnacles of Dan Hydroelectric Station, Rt. 1, Box 65A-1, Ararat, VA 24053; phone: 703-251-5141.

The Nature Conservancy

Formed in 1950, the Nature Conservancy is a private conservation organization with more than 600,000 members dedicated to the preservation of natural environments. Through its action and cooperation with public and private agencies, it maintains more than 2 million acres of natural diversity in more than 1,600 natural sanctuaries in all fifty states, the Virgin Islands, Canada, and elsewhere. The conservancy acquires funding from individual contributors, foundation grants, corporate gifts, and investments. It publishes the *Nature Conservancy News*.

The Virginia chapter was established in 1960, and since then its members have been active in acquiring and protecting forests, islands, wetlands, and significant wildlife sanctuaries. In 1995 there were thirty preserves in more than 10,000 acres of rare habitats. Some of the preserves offer a variety of hiking and naturalist activities for day use only. Before visiting or hiking the areas, permission is necessary from the Virginia field office (see Addresses and Information, below).

Addresses and Information: Virginia Chapter, 1110 Rose Hill Dr., Suite 200, Charlottesville, VA 22903; phone: 804-295-6106. Virginia Field Office, 2126 North Rolfe St., Arlington, VA 22209; phone: 703-528-4952. Available are permission and brochures or flyers about the preserves.

ALBEMARLE COUNTY

Fernbrook Preserve

This 63-acre preserve has 2 miles of light hiking trails through a second growth forest and the scenic bluffs of the Rivanna River.

Ivy Creek Preserve

A beautiful natural area of woods and meadows near Charlottesville, this 81-acre preserve offers short hikes and self-guided walks in a pristine environment.

FAIRFAX COUNTY

Fraser Preserve
On the Potomac River, 25 miles northwest from Washington, D.C., is this peaceful and magnificent 220-acre preserve.

FAUQUIER COUNTY

Wildcat Mountain Preserve
This 655-acre preserve is 30 miles northwest from Washington, D.C., on the northern reaches of the Blue Ridge Mountains. The hiking trails are through second growth forests and fields and provide excellent areas for birders.

MONTGOMERY COUNTY

Bottom Creek Gorge
This spectacular 1,500-acre preserve is nestled in the Blue Ridge Mountains and protects four rare fish in the creek forming the headwaters of the Roanoke River. The preserve claims the state's second highest waterfall. Self-guided nature walks are available.

Falls Ridge Preserve
Comprising 655 acres, the preserve is split by the geological Salem Fault. The two resulting soil types, shale/sandstone and limestone, sit side by side and support widely varying plant life. The preserve has an unusual travertine falls that builds out by laying down lime deposits over time.

VIRGINIA BEACH

North Landing River Preserve
The 6,000-acre preserve protects a unique freshwater wind tide marsh surrounding the North Landing River. Many rare plants and unusual birds make the marsh their home. The preserve is accessible by small boat or canoe and by foot along the boardwalk nature trail.

Virginia Living Museum   1033

In Newport News, the Virginia Living Museum was formerly the Peninsula Nature and Science Center. It has expanded its focus on natural science to include wildlife and plant life in a natural living habitat. Among the animal species are river otter, deer, bobcat, skunk, fox, raccoon, beaver, and bald eagle—all native to Virginia. They are seen on 0.5-mile *Living Museum Nature Trail*, which passes through upland and lowland species of trees, shrubs, ferns, and a wildflower garden. In addition there are an indoor and an outdoor aviary, aquariums, a planetarium with daily shows, displays, educational programs, and a butterfly garden. There is a nominal admission charge, and the museum is open daily except Christmas, Thanksgiving, and New Year's Day.

Access: From I-64, exit 258A, take the J. Clyde Morris Boulevard (US 17) south 2 miles and turn left at the museum entrance. (Ahead and on the boulevard across US 60 is Mariners' Museum.)

Address and Information: Virginia Living Museum, 524 J. Clyde Morris Blvd., Newport News, VA 23601; phone: 804-595-1900.

1034–35   Westmoreland Berry Farm

There are other outstanding berry farms in Virginia, but none on such a grand scale beside the Rappahannock River with a trail network as this one. A historic 1,600-acre site, it was originally patented in 1641. By 1803 it was known as Leesville Plantation, with sweeping views from a hill to the lowland fields and the river. The current management raises sixteen different crops, including black, red, and purple raspberries; strawberries; blackberries; blueberries; peaches; and apricots. Fresh or preserved fruit is sold, and there is also a pick-your-own policy.

Request permission to hike the trails at the open-air market. From here descend on the farm road to the peach orchard, turn left at a brown shed on a smaller road, and go to the end of the road at a dam at 0.7 miles. Begin the *Main Trail* over a small berm beside an oak tree and cross the dam and stream to a field. Keep right in grasses and pink meadow beauty on an old road. At 0.2 miles turn right on the *Troy Creek Trail*. It follows an old road under tall oaks and beech with holly, laurel, and ferns in the understory. Hushed, remote, and reposeful, the area has large mounds in the earth and scenic bluffs by Troy Creek. At 0.9 miles pass a marsh with waterfowl and songbirds. Reach a fork at 1.4 miles. (To the left the hiker can return to the dam at the edge of the field for a distance of 2 mi.) Continue right in a deep forest, stay right at a fork with the *Main Trail*, and reach a cabled gate at 2 miles. Backtrack, but go straight from the fork on the left. Pass a timber cut and reach a junction with the *Troy Creek Trail* at 2.6 miles. Follow the edge of the field for a return to the dam at 3.1 miles.

USGS map: Rollins Fork

Access: From VA 3 (0.3 mi. east of the King George and Westmoreland counties boundary) turn right on SR 634 and drive 0.9 miles. Turn right on SR 637 and drive 1.5 miles to sign and road on the right for 0.2 miles to the farm.

Address and Information: Westmoreland Berry Farm, Highway 637, Box 1121, Oak Grove, VA 22443; phone: 804-224-8967.

Maps

Virginia's Department of Conservation and Recreation, Division of Planning and Recreation Resources, has divided the Commonwealth into 11 regions, determined by urban/rural and physiographic distinctions. Beginning in 1995 this will change to seven regions. But because seven regions would require larger single maps that would not fit on one or two pages in this book, the older 11-region division is retained here for convenience. In addition, there is an index map showing regions and counties and two municipal maps for northern Virginia and the Richmond area.

In the department's 1989 *Virginia Outdoors Plan* one can find descriptions, plates, diagrams, and tables for each region and the 22 planning districts within the regions. Covering 26 outdoor recreational activities, the plan also projects future public needs. For more information on the plan, call 804-786-2556. In the Virginia Division of Tourism's *Virginia Travel Guide*, the state is divided into six regions, similar to those in the plan but without maps.

In the maps that follow, trail numbers correspond with those in the margins of the pages where the trails are described. The trail numbers are also found in the index along with the trail names and page numbers. A few trail numbers will appear more than once if the trail is long, for example the Appalachian Trail or the New River State Park Trail. Such trails are also shown by dotted lines. The maps are not detailed for lack of space but instead provide general orientation. As recommeded in the Introduction, hikers should have an official Virginia highway map, an atlas (such as the *Virginia Atlas and Gazetteer* by De Lorme Mapping Company or an ADC Street Map), and topographic maps for wilderness areas. Although the state highway map uses a small rectangle for secondary roads, the actual road signs are a black-and-white circle. For a complete legend to the maps, see page 360.

Abbreviations Used on Maps

HP	– Historic Park	NS	– National Seashore
NA	– National Area	NWR	– National Wildlife Refuge
NB	– National Battlefield	RA	– Recreation Area
NBP	– National Battlefield Park	RP	– Regional Park
NF	– National Forest	SF	– State Forest
NHP	– National Historic Park	SP	– State Park
NM	– National Monument	WMA	– Wildlife Management Area

THE COUNTIES
AND REGIONS OF VIRGINIA

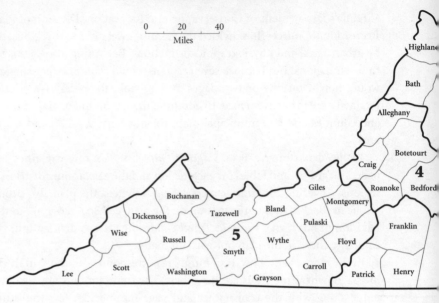

N

Frederick
Clarke
Loudoun
Warren
Arlington
Shenandoah
Fauquier
Fairfax
Rappahannock
Prince
William
6
Page
Madison   Culpeper
Stafford
Rockingham
King
George
1
Greene
Westmoreland
Augusta
Orange   Spotsylvania
Northumberland
Albemarle
7
Caroline
Richmond
Louisa
Essex
Rockbridge
Fluvanna
Hanover
8
King and Queen
Nelson
Goochland
King William
Middlesex
Lancaster
10
Accomack
Amherst
Buckingham
Cumberland
Powhatan
Henrico
New Kent
2
Gloucester
Appamattox
Amelia
Chesterfield
Charles
City
Northampton
Campbell
Prince
Edward
Nottoway
Prince
George
York
James
City
Mathews
Charlotte
Dinwiddie
9
Surry
Hampton
3
Lunenburg
Sussex
Isle of
Wight
Pittsylvania
Greensville
Chesapeake
Virginia
Beach
11
Halifax
Brunswick
Southampton
Suffolk
Mecklenburg

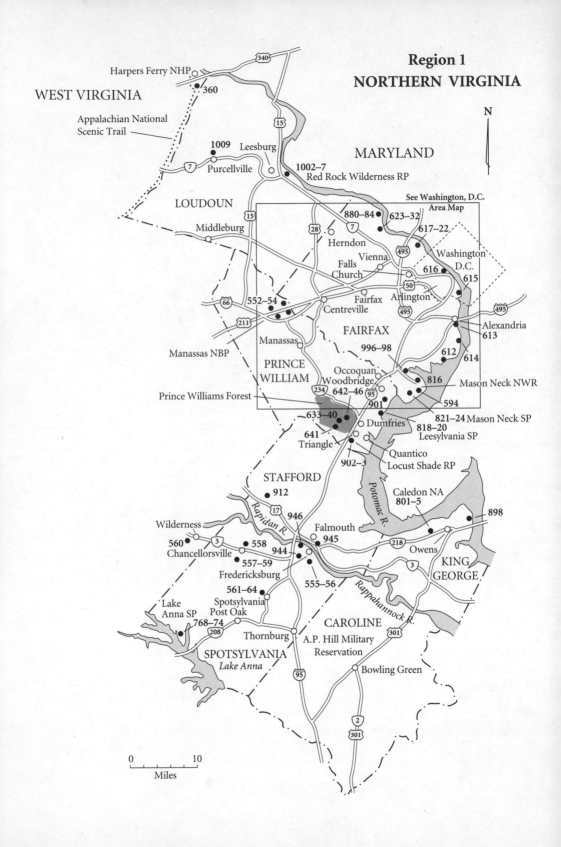

Region 1
NORTHERN VIRGINIA

N

Harpers Ferry NHP
360

WEST VIRGINIA

Appalachian National
Scenic Trail

1009 Leesburg
Purcellville
1002–7
Red Rock Wilderness RP

MARYLAND

LOUDOUN

Middleburg

See Washington, D.C.
Area Map

880–84 623–32

617–22

Herndon

Vienna

495

Washington
D.C.

Falls
Church

616

615

552–54

Fairfax
Centreville

50

Arlington

495

495

Alexandria
613

FAIRFAX

Manassas

996–98

612

614

Manassas NBP

PRINCE
WILLIAM

Occoquan
Woodbridge

816

Mason Neck NWR

Prince Williams Forest

234 642–46

901

95

594

633–40

Dumfries

821–24 Mason Neck SP

641
Triangle

902–3

818–20
Leesylvania SP

Quantico
Locust Shade RP

STAFFORD

912

946

Caledon NA
801–5

Wilderness

Rapidan R.

17

Falmouth

Potomac R.

898

560
Chancellorsville

3

558
557–59

944
945

218

Owens

3

KING
GEORGE

Fredericksburg

561–64

555–56

Rappahannock R.

Lake
Anna SP

768–74

Spotsylvania
Post Oak

208

Thornburg

CAROLINE

A.P. Hill Military
Reservation

301

SPOTSYLVANIA
Lake Anna

95

Bowling Green

2

301

0   10
Miles

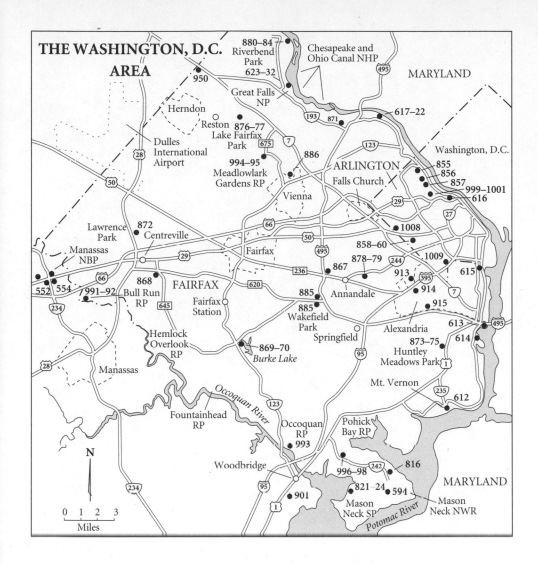

THE WASHINGTON, D.C. AREA

880–84
Riverbend Park
623–32

Chesapeake and
Ohio Canal NHP

MARYLAND

950

Great Falls
NP

Herndon

193   871

617–22

Reston   876–77
Lake Fairfax
Park   675

7

Dulles
International
Airport

Washington, D.C.

123

886

855
856
857
999–1001
616

ARLINGTON

Falls Church

994–95
Meadowlark
Gardens RP

29

27

Vienna

66

1008

Lawrence
Park   872
Centreville

50

858–60

Manassas
NBP

495

878–79

1009

867

244
913   395

615

236

868

FAIRFAX

620

914

552 554   991–92
Bull Run
RP   645

Fairfax
Station

885

Annandale

915

885
Wakefield
Park

Alexandria

613
873–75   614

234

Hemlock
Overlook
RP

Springfield

Huntley
Meadows Park

495

1

28

Manassas

869–70
Burke Lake

95

Mt. Vernon

235

612

Occoquan River

123

Fountainhead
RP

Occoquan
RP
993

Pohick
Bay RP

N

Woodbridge

996–98
242

816

MARYLAND

95

821–24   594

234

1

901

Mason
Neck SP

Mason
Neck NWR

Potomac River

0   1   2   3
Miles

Legend

(29) Federal highways

(85) Interstate highways

(8) State primary highways

[605] State secondary highways

▨ National Parks, forests, lakes, and rivers

• 652   Trail numbers

— ·· —   County line

— ··· —   State line

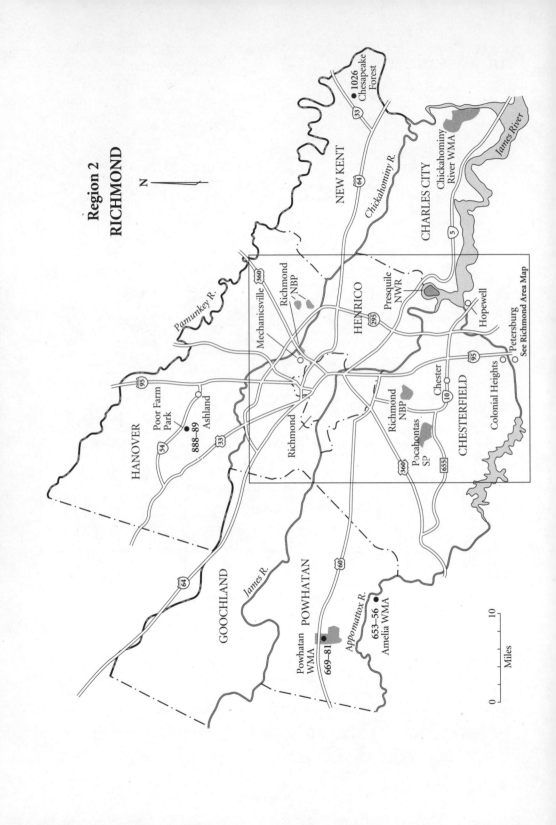

N

Chesapeake
Forest
1026

NEW KENT

33

Chickahominy R.

64

CHARLES CITY

Chickahominy
River WMA

James River

5

Pamunkey R.

Mechanicsville

Richmond
NBP

360

HENRICO

295

Presquile
NWR

Hopewell

Petersburg
See Richmond Area Map

Poor Farm
Park

Ashland

888–89

HANOVER

54

33

95

Richmond

Richmond
NBP

Chester

10

95

Petersburg

Colonial Heights

CHESTERFIELD

Pocahontas
SP

360

655

GOOCHLAND

James R.

64

POWHATAN

60

Powhatan
WMA

669–81

Appomattox R.

653–56
Amelia WMA

0   10
Miles

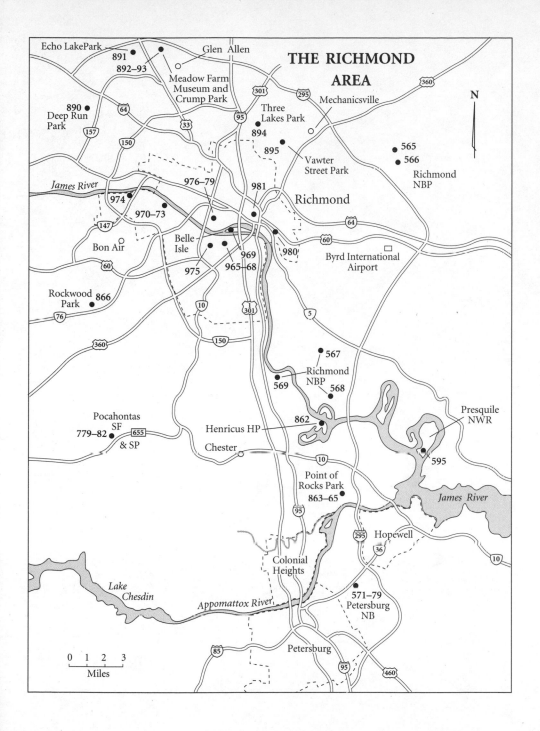

THE RICHMOND
AREA

N

Echo LakePark
891
892–93
Glen Allen
Meadow Farm
Museum and
Crump Park
301
295
Mechanicsville
890
Deep Run
Park
64
33
95
Three
Lakes Park
894
895
565
566
Richmond
NBP
157
150
Vawter
Street Park
James River
976–79
981
Richmond
974
970–73
64
147
Belle
Isle
969
980
60
Byrd International
Airport
Bon Air
975
965–68
60
Rockwood 866
Park
76
10
1
301
5
150
567
779–82
Pocahontas
SF
& SP
655
569
Richmond
NBP
568
Henricus HP
862
Presquile
NWR
Chester
10
595
Point of
Rocks Park
863–65
95
James River
295
36
Hopewell
10
Colonial
Heights
Lake
Chesdin
Appomattox River
571–79
Petersburg
NB
0 1 2 3
Miles
85
Petersburg
95
460

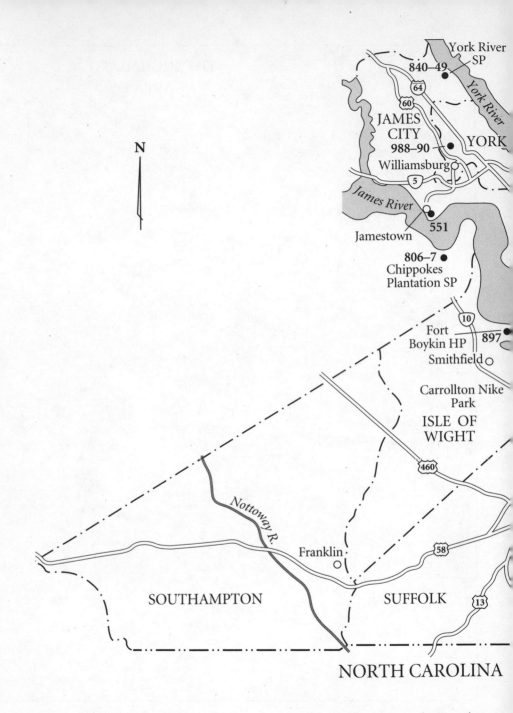

N

York River SP

840–49

64

60

JAMES CITY

988–90

YORK

Williamsburg

5

James River

551

Jamestown

806–7
Chippokes
Plantation SP

10

Fort
Boykin HP   897

Smithfield

Carrollton Nike
Park

ISLE OF
WIGHT

460

Nottoway R.

58

Franklin

SOUTHAMPTON

SUFFOLK

13

NORTH CAROLINA

Region 3

HAMPTON ROADS

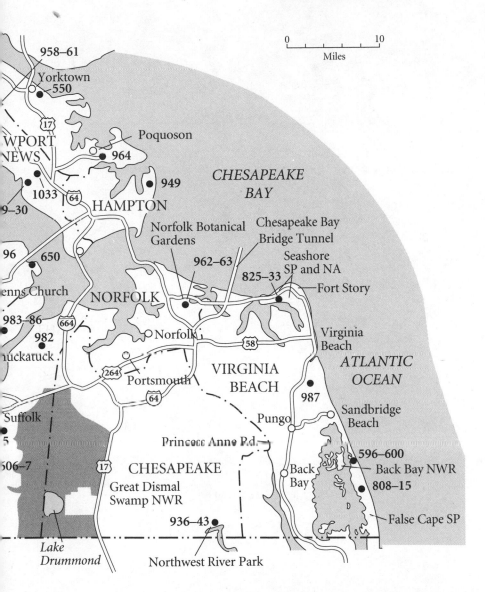

0   10
Miles

958–61

Yorktown
550

17

WPORT
NEWS

Poquoson

964

949

*CHESAPEAKE
BAY*

1033

64

HAMPTON

9–30

Norfolk Botanical
Gardens

Chesapeake Bay
Bridge Tunnel

96   650

962–63

Seashore
SP and NA

825–33

enns Church

NORFOLK

Fort Story

983–86

664

Norfolk

58

Virginia
Beach

982

*ATLANTIC
OCEAN*

huckatuck

264

Portsmouth

VIRGINIA
BEACH

64

987

Suffolk

Pungo

Sandbridge
Beach

5

Princess Anne Rd.

06–7

17

CHESAPEAKE

Back
Bay

596–600

Back Bay NWR

Great Dismal
Swamp NWR

808–15

936–43

False Cape SP

*Lake
Drummond*

Northwest River Park

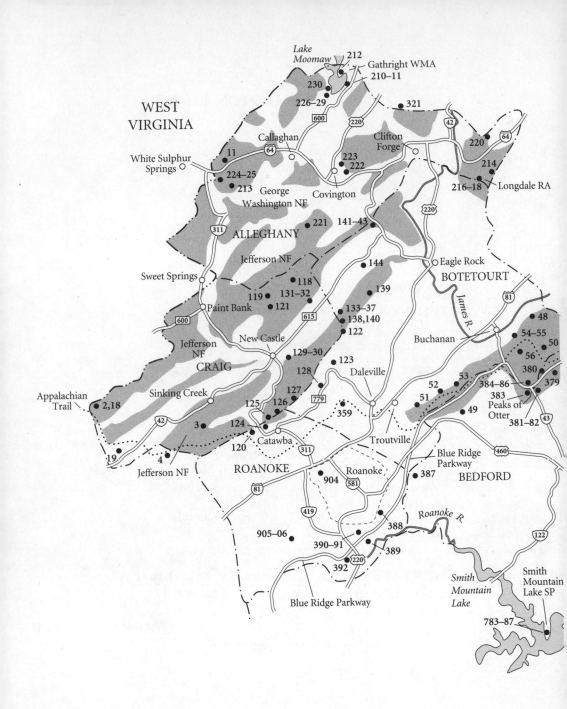

WEST
VIRGINIA

Lake
Moomaw

212

Gathright WMA
210–11

230

226–29

600   220

321

42   64

220

Callaghan

Clifton
Forge

223
222

220

White Sulphur
Springs

64

11

224–25

213   George
Washington NF   Covington

214

216–18   Longdale RA

311

ALLEGHANY

221   141–43

220

Jefferson NF

144   Eagle Rock   BOTETOURT

81

Sweet Springs

118   139

James R.

81

119   131–32

121   133–37

615   138,140

122   Buchanan

48

54–55

50

600   Paint Bank

Jefferson
NF   New Castle   129–30   123   Daleville

56

380

384–86   379

CRAIG

128   53   383

127   779   52   Peaks of
Otter

381–82   43

Appalachian
Trail   2,18   Sinking Creek   125   126   51   49

359

123   Troutville

Blue Ridge
Parkway   BEDFORD

460

122

3   124

42   120   Catawba

311

19   4   ROANOKE

81   904   Roanoke   387

Jefferson NF   581

419

905–06   388   Roanoke R.

390–91   389

392   220

Smith
Mountain
Lake

Smith
Mountain
Lake SP

Blue Ridge Parkway

783–87

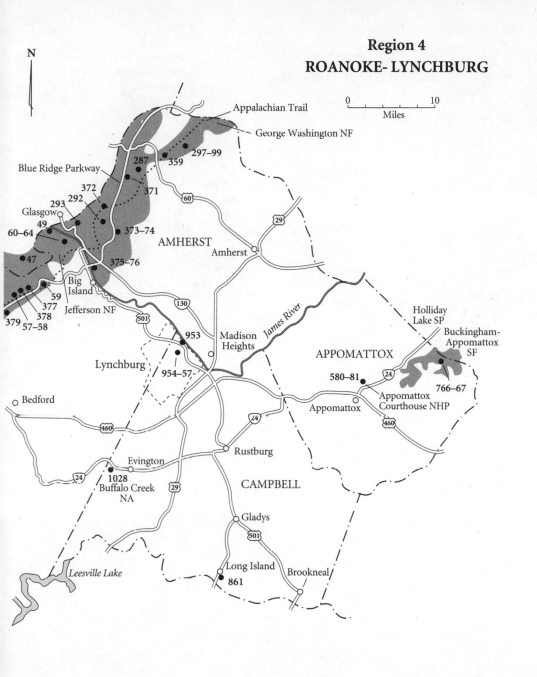

Region 4
ROANOKE- LYNCHBURG

N

Appalachian Trail

George Washington NF

0   10
Miles

297–99

287   359

Blue Ridge Parkway

372
293 292   371

Glasgow   60

60–64   49

47   373–74

375–76   AMHERST

Amherst

Big
Island

59
377   Jefferson NF

379   378
57–58

953

Madison
Heights

Lynchburg

954–57

Bedford

James River

Holliday
Lake SP

APPOMATTOX

Buckingham-
Appomattox
SF

580–81

766–67

Appomattox
Courthouse NHP

Appomattox

Evington

1028
Buffalo Creek
NA

Rustburg

CAMPBELL

Gladys

Leesville Lake

Long Island   Brookneal
861

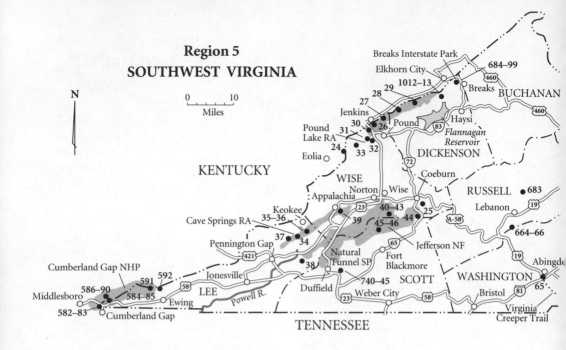

Region 5
SOUTHWEST VIRGINIA

N

0   10
Miles

KENTUCKY

Breaks Interstate Park
Elkhorn City
Breaks
684–99
BUCHANAN
460
1012–13
29
28
27
Jenkins
30
31
26 Pound
Pound Lake RA
24
33 32
Eolia
Haysi
Flannagan Reservoir
83
DICKENSON
72
Coeburn
RUSSELL
683
WISE
Norton Wise
Appalachia
23
40–43
25
Lebanon
19
Keokee
Cave Springs RA
35–36
39
45–46 44
A-58
664–66
37 34
45–46
Jefferson NF
19
Pennington Gap
421
65
Abingdo
Cumberland Gap NHP
592
Natural Tunnel SP
Fort Blackmore
WASHINGTON
591
Jonesville
Duffield
740–45 SCOTT
81 65
586–90
58
Bristol
582–83
584–85
Ewing
LEE Powell R.
38
Weber City
23
58
Virginia Creeper Trail
Middlesboro
Cumberland Gap
TENNESSEE

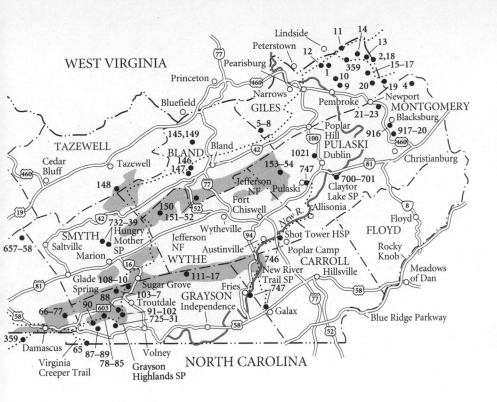

WEST VIRGINIA

Lindside
Peterstown
Pearisburg
Princeton
Bluefield
Narrows
GILES
5–8
Pembroke
Poplar Hill
Bland
BLAND
145,149
146,
147
Cedar Bluff
Tazewell
TAZEWELL
148
150
151–52
732–39
42
Hungry Mother SP
SMYTH
Saltville
Marion
657–58
Glade Spring
108–10
88
90
66–77
603
359
Damascus
Virginia Creeper Trail
65
87–89
78–85
Volney
Grayson Highlands SP
NORTH CAROLINA

11 14
12 13
1 359 2,18
10 15–17
9 20 19 4
Newport
MONTGOMERY
21–23 Blacksburg
916 917–20
PULASKI
1021
Dublin
Christianburg
153–54
747
Jefferson NF
Pulaski
Fort Chiswell
700–701
Claytor Lake SP
Allisonia
Floyd
Wytheville
Jefferson NF
Austinville
Shot Tower HSP
Poplar Camp
746
CARROLL
Hillsville
FLOYD
Rocky Knob
Meadows of Dan
WYTHE
111–17
Sugar Grove
103–7
Troutdale
91–102
725–31
GRAYSON
Independence
Fries
New River Trail SP
747
Galax
Blue Ridge Parkway

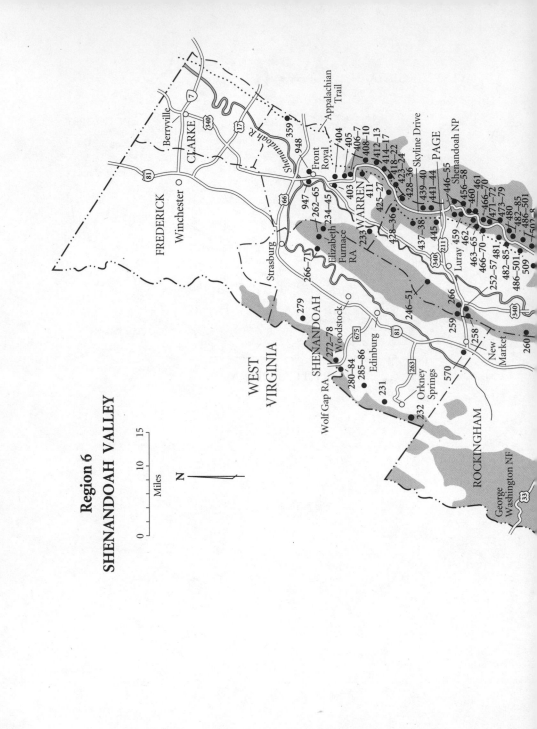

Region 6
SHENANDOAH VALLEY

N

Miles
0   10   15

FREDERICK

Winchester

Berryville

CLARKE

Appalachian Trail

Shenandoah R.

359
948
Front Royal

404
405
406–7
408–10
412–13
414–17
418–22
423–24
428–36
Skyline Drive
PAGE
439–40
441–44
446–55
456–58
460
461
466–70
471–72
473–79
480
482–85
486–501
502–8

947
262–65
234–45
403
411
425–27
WARREN
428–36
233
445
437–38
Luray
462
459
463–65
466–70
252–57
482–85
486–501
509
Shenandoah NP

Elizabeth Furnace RA

Strasburg

266–71

279

SHENANDOAH

272–78
Woodstock
280–84
285–86
Edinburg
231

Wolf Gap RA

246–51

259
266
258
New Market
260

Orkney Springs
232

570

WEST VIRGINIA

ROCKINGHAM

George Washington NF

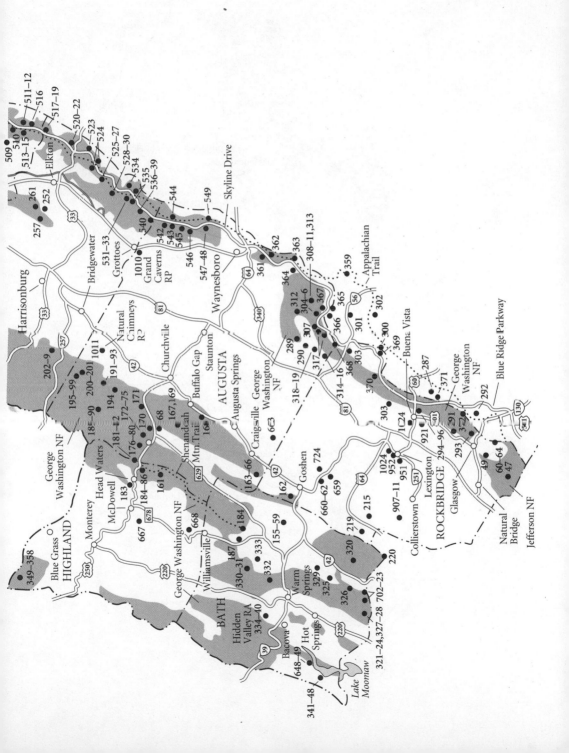

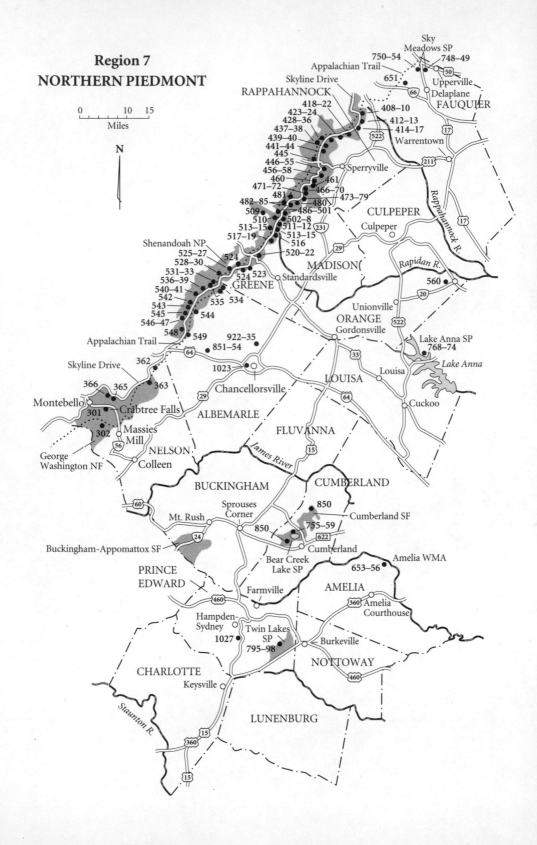

Region 7
NORTHERN PIEDMONT

0   10   15
Miles

N

RAPPAHANNOCK
Appalachian Trail
Skyline Drive
Sky
Meadows SP
750–54   748–49
651
Upperville
Delaplane
FAUQUIER
418–22
423–24
428–36
437–38
439–40
441–44
445
446–55
456–58
460
461
471–72
466–70
481   473–79
482–85   480
509   486–501
510   502–8
513–15   511–12
517–19   513–15
516
525–27   520–22
Shenandoah NP
528–30
531–33   524
536–39
540–41   524 523
542   Standardsville
543   535   534
545   GREENE
546–47   544
548   549
Appalachian Trail   922–35
851–54
Skyline Drive   362   1023
366   365   363
Montebello   Chancellorsville
301
302   Crabtree Falls
Massies
Mill
George
Washington NF   56
Colleen   NELSON

408–10
412–13
414–17
Warrentown
522
Sperryville
CULPEPER
Culpeper
MADISON
231
29   Rapidan R.
560
20
Unionville
ORANGE   522
Gordonsville
Lake Anna SP
768–74
Lake Anna
LOUISA
64
Louisa
Cuckoo
17
Rappahannock R.
211
17

ALBEMARLE   FLUVANNA
James River
15

BUCKINGHAM   CUMBERLAND
850
Sprouses   755–59
Corner   622
Mt. Rush   850   Cumberland SF
24   Cumberland
Buckingham-Appomattox SF   Bear Creek   Amelia WMA
Lake SP   653–56
PRINCE   Farmville   AMELIA
EDWARD   360   Amelia
Courthouse
Hampden-
Sydney   Twin Lakes   Burkeville
1027   SP
795–98   NOTTOWAY
460
CHARLOTTE
Keysville
Staunton R.   LUNENBURG
15
360
15
60

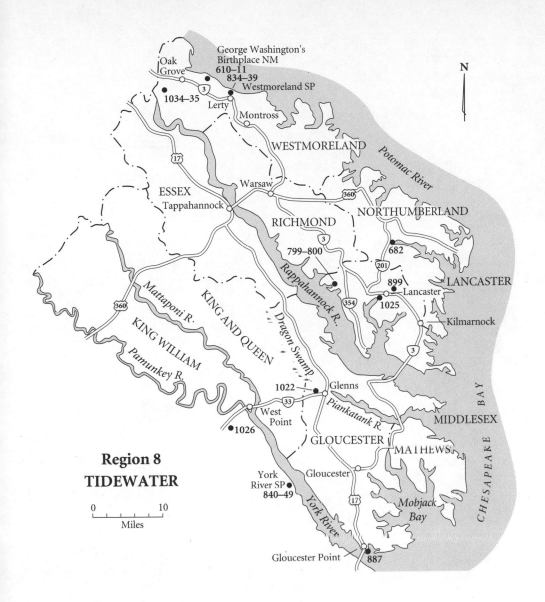

George Washington's
Birthplace NM
610–11
834–39
Westmoreland SP

Oak
Grove

1034–35
Lerty

Montross

WESTMORELAND

Potomac River

17

Warsaw

ESSEX
Tappahannock

RICHMOND

NORTHUMBERLAND

3

799–800

682

201

354

899
Lancaster

LANCASTER

1025

Kilmarnock

3

Mattaponi R.

KING AND QUEEN

Rappahannock R.

360

KING WILLIAM

Pamunkey R.

Dragon Swamp

1022
Glenns

Piankatank R.

MIDDLESEX

BAY

33
West
Point

1026

GLOUCESTER

MATHEWS

Region 8
TIDEWATER

York
River SP
840–49

Gloucester

17

Mobjack
Bay

CHESAPEAKE

York River

0   10
Miles

Gloucester Point

887

N

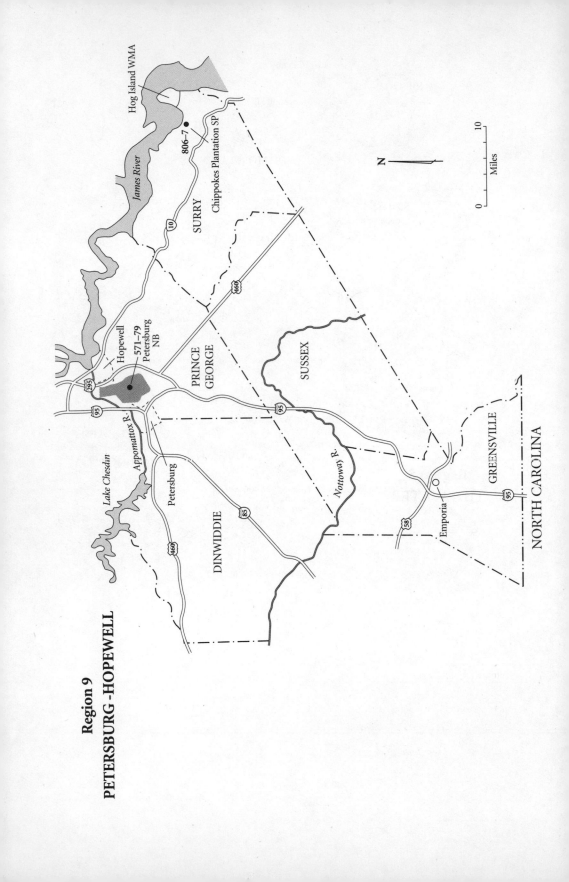

Region 9
PETERSBURG-HOPEWELL

Hog Island WMA

James River

806–7

Chippokes Plantation SP

10

SURRY

Hopewell

571–79
Petersburg
NB

PRINCE
GEORGE

SUSSEX

295

95

Appomattox R.

Lake Chesdin

Petersburg

Nottoway R.

DINWIDDIE

85

460

58

Emporia

95

GREENSVILLE

NORTH CAROLINA

N

10

Miles

0

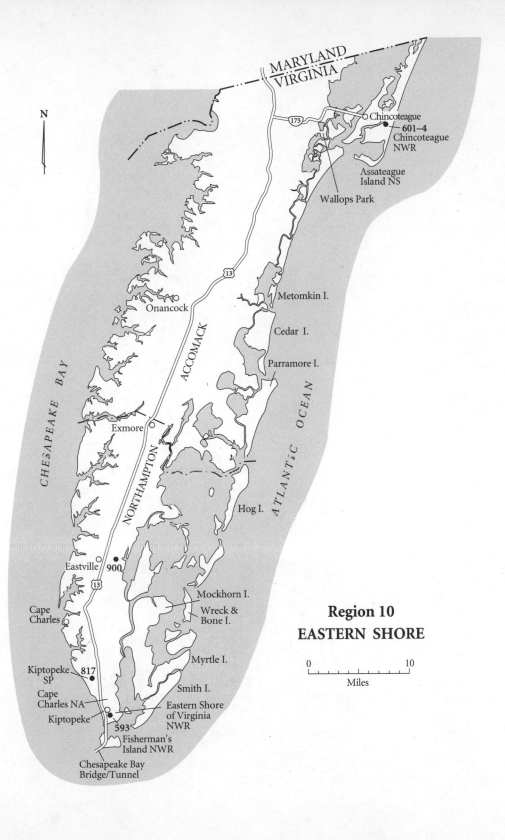

N

MARYLAND
VIRGINIA

175

Chincoteague
601–4
Chincoteague
NWR

Assateague
Island NS

Wallops Park

13

Metomkin I.

Onancock

ACCOMACK

Cedar I.

Parramore I.

CHESAPEAKE BAY

ATLANTIC OCEAN

Exmore

NORTHAMPTON

Hog I.

Eastville   900

13

Mockhorn I.

Cape
Charles

Wreck &
Bone I.

Region 10
EASTERN SHORE

Myrtle I.

0   10

Miles

Kiptopeke
SP   817

Smith I.

Cape
Charles NA

Eastern Shore
of Virginia
NWR

Kiptopeke

593

Fisherman's
Island NWR

Chesapeake Bay
Bridge/Tunnel

Region 11
SOUTHERN PIEDMONT

0   10   15
Miles

N

Nottoway R.

85

58

BRUNSWICK

Lake Gaston

South Hill

85

1

MECKLENBURG

1014

Boydton

1015

775–78   1015

John H. Kerr Res.
(Buggs Island Lake)

15

360

344

788–94

Clarksville

Occoneechee SP

HALIFAX

Scottsburg

501

Staunton River SP

South Boston

Roanoke (Staunton) R.

Dan R.

Danville

29

White Oak WMA   • 652

Chatham

PITTSYLVANIA

58

NORTH CAROLINA

Smith Mountain Lake

Smith Mountain Lake SP   786–87

Roanoke R.

608–9   783–85

122

FRANKLIN

220

Philpott Res.

1016–17

Bassett

Martinsville

40

1019

1020

605

57

HENRY

220

220

Rocky Mount

Booker T. Washington NM

Ferrum   393

760–65

Fairy Stone SP   1018

Stuart SP

58

Blue Ridge Parkway

Woolwine   397   8

394–95   8   103

Mabry Mill   398

Meadows of Dan   1031–32   PATRICK

Pinnacles of Dan   399

Claudville

APPENDIX A
Sources of Information

The addresses of national, state, and local forests, parks, recreation areas, historic sites, gardens, and other areas are provided in the text. The following agencies, organizations, and clubs are also valuable sources of information.

U.S. Congress

Committee on Agriculture (House)
Longworth House Office Bldg., Rm. 1301
Washington, DC 20515
(Phone: 202-225-2171)

Committee on Agriculture, Nutrition, and Forestry (Senate)
Russell Bldg., Rm. 328-A
Washington, DC 20510
(Phone: 202-224-2035)

Committee on Energy and Natural Resources (Senate)
Dirksen Bldg., Rm. SD-364
Washington, DC 20510
(Phone: 202-224-4971)

Committee on Environment and Public Works (Senate)
Dirksen Bldg., Rm. SD-458
Washington, DC 20510
(Phone: 202-224-6167)

Committee on Interior and Insular Affairs (House)
Longworth House Office Bldg., Rm. 1324
Washington, DC 20515
(Phone: 202-225-2761)

Committee on Merchant Marine and Fisheries (House)
Longworth House Office Bldg., Rm. 1334
Washington, DC 20515
(Phone: 202-225-4047)

Environmental and Energy Study Conference (House)
H2-515 Ford House Office Bldg.
Washington, DC 20515
(Phone: 202-226-3300)

U.S. Government/Executive Branch

Army Corps of Engineers
Pulaski Bldg.
200 Mass Ave. NW
Washington, DC 20314
(Phone: 202-272-0010)

   District Office (Flannagan)
   502 Eighth St.
   Huntington, WV 25701

   District Office (Philpott & Kerr)
   P.O. Box 1890
   Wilmington, NC 28402

Council on Environmental Quality
722 Jackson Place NW
Washington, DC 20503
(Phone: 202-395-5750)

Department of Agriculture
Fourteenth St. and Independence Ave. sw
Washington, DC 20250
(Phone: 202-720-8732)

   Forest Service
   P.O. Box 96090
   Washington, DC 20090
   (Phone: 202-205-0957)

   Forest Service Regional Office
   Suite 800, 1720 Peachtree Rd. NW
   Atlanta, GA 30367
   (Phone: 404-347-4177)

   Soil Conservation
   P.O. Box 2890
   Washington, DC 20013
   (Phone: 202-447-4543)

   Soil Conservation State Biologist
   Federal Bldg., Room 9201
   400 N 8th St.
   Richmond, VA 23240

Department of Commerce
National Oceanic and Atmospheric
   Administration
Hoover Bldg., Rm. 5128
14th and Constitution Ave. NW
Washington, DC 20230
(Phone: 202-377-3384)

Department of the Interior
1849 C St. NW
Washington, DC 20240
(Phone: 202-208-1100)

   Bureau of Land Management
   (Phone: 202-208-5717)

   Bureau of Mines
   (Phone: 202-501-9649)

   National Park Service
   Interior Bldg.
   P.O. Box 37127
   Washington, DC 20013
   (Phone: 202-208-6843)

      Regional Director (Southeast)
      75 Spring St. sw
      Atlanta, GA 30303
      (Phone: 404-331-5185)

   U.S. Fish and Wildlife Service
   Washington, DC 20240
   (Phone: 202-208-4131)

      Regional Office (Northeast,
         Region 5)
      One Gateway Ctr., Suite 700
      Newton Corner, MA 02158
      (Phone: 617-965-5100)

U.S. Government/Independent Agencies

Advisory Council on Historic
   Preservation
1100 Pennsylvania Ave. NW, #809
Washington, DC 20004
(Phone: 202-786-0503)

Environmental Protection Agency
401 M St. sw
Washington, DC 20460
(Phone: 202-260-2090)

National Regional Commissions

Appalachian Regional Commission
1666 Connecticut Ave. NW
Washington, DC 20235
(Phone: 202-673-7893)

Atlantic State Marine Fisheries
   Commission
1400 Sixteenth St. NW
Washington, DC 20036
(Phone: 202-387-5330)

Interstate Commission on the Potomac
  River Basin
6110 Executive Blvd., Suite 300
Rockville, MD 20852
(Phone: 301-984-1908)

Marine Mammal Commission
1825 Connecticut Ave. NW, Rm. 512
Washington, DC 20009
(Phone: 202-606-5504)

Migratory Bird Conservation
  Commission
Interior Bldg.
Washington, DC 20240
(Phone: 703-358-1716)

National and Regional Organizations

American Bass Association, Inc.
886 Trotters Trail
Wetumpka, AL 36092
(Phone: 205-567-6035)

American Birding Association
P.O. Box 6599
Colorado Springs, CO 80934
(Phone: 719-634-7736)

American Camping Association, Inc.
5000 State Rd., 67N
Martinsville, IN 46151
(Phone: 317-342-8456)

American Cave Conservation
  Association
131 Main and Cave Sts.
Horse Cave, KY 42749
(Phone: 502-786-1466)

American Federation of Mineralogical
  Societies, Inc.
Central Office, 920 SW 70th St.
Oklahoma City, OK 73139

American Fisheries Society
5410 Grosvenor Lane, Suite 110
Bethesda, MD 20814
(Phone: 301-897-8616)

American Forests
1516 P St. NW
Washington, DC 20005
(Phone: 202-667-3300)

American Geographical Society
156 Fifth Ave., Suite 600
New York, NY 10010
(Phone: 212-242-0214)

American Hiking Society
P.O. Box 20160
Washington, DC 20041
(Phone: 703-385-3252)

American Littoral Society
Sandy Hook
Highlands, NJ 07732
(Phone: 201-291-0055)

American Rivers
801 Pennsylvania Ave. SE, Suite 400
Washington, DC 20003
(Phone: 202-547-6900)

Appalachian Mountain Club
5 Joy St.
Boston, MA 02108
(Phone: 617-523-0636)

Appalachian Trail Conference
P.O. Box 807
Harpers Ferry, WV 25425
(Phone: 304-535-6331)

Boy Scouts of America (National)
P.O. Box 152079
Irving, TX 75015
(Phone: 214-580-2000)
(Call for information on state chapters.)

Camp Fire, Inc.
4601 Madison Ave.
Kansas City, MO 64112
(Phone: 816-756-1950)

Center for Marine Conservation
1725 DeSales St. NW, Suite 500
Washington, DC 20036
(Phone: 202-429-5609)

Chesapeake Bay Foundation, Inc.
162 Prince George St.
Annapolis, MD 21401
(Phone: 410-268-8816)

Clean Water Action
1320 Eighteenth St. NW
Washington, DC 20036
(Phone: 202-457-1286)

Cousteau Society
870 Greenbrier Circle, Suite 402
Chesapeake, VA 23320
(Phone: 804-523-9335)

Defenders of Wildlife
1244 Nineteenth St. NW
Washington, DC 20036
(Phone: 202-659-9510)

Ducks Unlimited, Inc.
One Waterfowl Way
Long Grove, IL 60047
(Phone: 708-438-4300)

Environmental Defense Fund, Inc.
257 Park Ave. South
New York, NY 10010
(Phone: 212-505-2100)

Friends of the Earth
218 D St. SE
Washington, DC 20003
(Phone: 202-544-2600)

Friends of the Blue Ridge Parkway
2301 Hendersonville Rd.
Arden, NC 28704
(Phone: 1-800-228-7275)
and
3536 Brambleton Ave. SW
Roanoke, VA 24018
(Phone: 703-772-7900)

Girl Scouts of the U.S.A.
420 Fifth Ave.
New York, NY 10018
(Phone: 212-852-8000)
(Call for information on state chapters.)

National Arbor Day Foundation
100 Arbor Ave.
Nebraska City, NE 68410
(Phone: 402-474-5655)

National Audubon Society
700 Broadway
New York, NY 10003
(Phone: 212-797-3000)

National Boating Federation
P.O. Box 4111
Annapolis, MD 21403
(Phone: 301-280-1911)

National Geographic Society
Seventeenth and M Sts. NW
Washington, DC 20036
(Phone: 202-856-7000)

National Parks and Conservation
   Association
1015 Thirty-first St. NW
Washington, DC 20007
(Phone: 202-944-8530)

National Speleological Society
Cave Ave.
Huntsville, AL 35810
(Phone: 605-745-4366)

National Wildlife Federation
1400 Sixteenth St. NW
Washington, DC 20036
(Phone: 202-797-6800)

   Mid-Atlantic Office
   (Phone: 202-797-6693)

The Nature Conservancy
1815 North Lynn St.
Arlington, VA 22209
(Phone: 703-841-5300)

   Southeast Regional Office
   P.O. Box 270
   Chapel Hill, NC 27514
   (Phone: 919-967-5493)

North American Family Campers
  Association
P.O. Box 328
Concord, VT 05824
(Phone: 802-695-2563)

Rails-to-Trails Conservancy
1400 Sixteenth St. NW, Suite 300
Washington, DC 20036
(Phone: 202-797-5400)

Sierra Club
730 Polk St.
San Francisco, CA 94109
(Phone: 415-776-2211)

   Appalachian Field Office
   1116 #C West St.
   Annapolis, MD 21401
   (Phone: 410-268-7411)
   (See Virginia Agencies for chapter
   information.)

Smithsonian Institution
1000 Jefferson Dr. SW
Washington, DC 20560
(Phone: 202-357-2700)

Trout Unlimited
800 Follin Lane SE, Suite 250
Vienna, VA 22180
(Phone: 703-281-1100)

Izaak Walton League of America, Inc.
1401 Wilson Blvd. (Level B)
Arlington, VA 22209
(Phone: 703-528-1818)

The Wilderness Society
900 Seventeenth St. NW
Washington, DC 20006
(Phone: 202-833-2300)

Virginia Agencies

Council on the Environment
202 N. Ninth St., Suite 900
Richmond, VA 23219
(Phone: 804-786-4500)

Department of Conservation and
  Recreation
203 Governor St., Suite 302
Richmond, VA 23219
(Phone: 804-786-2121)

   Division of Natural Heritage
   203 Governor St., Suite 402
   Richmond, VA 23219
   (Phone: 804-786-4554)

   Division of Planning and Recreation
     Resources
   203 Governor St., Suite 326
   Richmond, VA 23219

   Division of Soil and Water
     Conservation
   203 Governor St., Suite 206
   Richmond, VA 23219
   (Phone: 804-786-2064)

Division of State Parks
203 Governor St., Suite 306
Richmond, VA 23219
(Phone: 804-786-2132)

Department of Game and Inland
  Fisheries
4010 W. Broad St. (Box 11104)
Richmond, VA 23230
(Phone: 804-367-1000)
(Publishes *Virginia Wildlife*)

Department of Highways and
  Transportation
1401 E. Broad St. (Central Office); also
  1221 E. Broad St.
Richmond, VA 23219
(Phone: 804-786-2702)
(Highway Helpline for road conditions:
  instate 1-800-367-7623; out of state:
  804-786-3181)

Department of Mines, Minerals, and
  Energy
2201 West Broad St.
Richmond, VA 23220
(Phone: 804-367-0330)

Fish and Wildlife Information Exchange
2206 S. Main St., Suite B
Blacksburg, VA 24060
(Phone: 703-231-7348)

Marine Resources Commission
P.O. Box 756
Newport News, VA 23607
(Phone: 804-247-2200)

Northern Virginia Hiking Club
12803 Longfellow Ct.
Woodbridge, VA 22192

Piedmont Environmental Council
P.O. Box 460
Warrenton, VA 22186
(Phone: 703-347-2334/804-977-2033)

Potomac Backpackers Association
P.O. Box 256
Arlington, VA 22210

Public Employees for Environmental
    Responsibility
(Phone: 202-408-0041)

Sierra Club (Virginia chapter)
P.O. Box 14648
Richmond, VA 23221
(Phone: 804-256-4541; call this number
    for information on the groups listed
    below)

    Blue Ridge (Faber)
    Chesapeake Bay (Virginia Beach)
    Falls of the James (Richmond)
    Great Falls (Vienna)
    Highlands (Bristol)
    Mount Vernon (Alexandria)
    New River (Blacksburg)
    Piedmont (Charlottesville)
    Roanoke River (Roanoke)
    Shenandoah (Harrisonburg)
    Thunder Ridge (Lynchburg)
    York River (Gloucester)

State Extension Services
School of Forestry and Wildlife
VPI & SU
Blacksburg, VA 24061
(Phone: 703-231-8844)

State Water Control Board
4900 Cox Rd. (P.O. Box 11143)
Richmond, VA 23230
(Phone: 804-527-5000)

Trout Unlimited (Virginia council)
211 Shady Oak Lane
Forest, VA 24551
(Phone: 804-526-6004)

Virginia Division of Forestry
P.O. Box 3758
Charlottesville, VA 22903
(Phone: 804-977-6555)

Virginia Division of Tourism
1021 E. Cary St. (Tower II)
Richmond, VA 23219
(Phone: 804-786-2051)
(Publishes *Virginia Travel Guide*, free)
(Write or call the Virginia Division of
    Tourism for an address list of
    Virginia's many local bicycle clubs.)

Virginia Museum of Natural History
1001 Douglas Ave.
Martinsville, VA 24112
(Phone: 703-666-8000)

Izaak Walton League of America
    (Virginia Division)
506 Stone Gate Dr.
Blacksburg, VA 24060
(Phone: 703-552-0227)

Virginia Citizens' Organizations

Appalachian Trail Conference
P.O. Box 807
Harpers Ferry, WV 25425
(Phone: 304-535-6331)

Kanawha A.T. Club
P.O. Box 4474
Charleston, WV 25364

Mount Rogers A.T. Club
Route 7, Box 345
Abingdon, VA 24210

Natural Bridge A.T. Club
P.O. Box 3010
Lynchburg, VA 24503

Old Dominion A.T. Club
P.O. Box 25283
Richmond, VA 23260

Piedmont A.T. Hikers
P.O. Box 4423
Greensboro, NC 27404

Potomac A.T. Club
118 Park St. SE
Vienna, VA 22180
(Phone: 703-242-0693)

Roanoke A.T. Club
P.O. Box 12282
Roanoke, VA 24024

Tidewater A.T. Club
P.O. Box 8246
Norfolk, VA 23503

Virginia Tech A.T. Club
P.O. Box 538
Blacksburg, VA 24060

Bike Virginia, Inc.
P.O. Box 203
Williamsburg, VA 23187
(Phone: 804-229-0507)

Canoe Cruiser Association
P.O. Box 572
Arlington, VA 22216

Capital Hiking Club
3324 Glenmore Dr.
Falls Church, VA 22041

Coastal Canoeists
P.O. Box 566
Richmond, VA 23204

Virginia Forestry Association
1205 E. Main St.
Richmond, VA 23219
(Phone: 804-644-8462)

Virginia Horse Council
P.O. Box 1191
Middleburg, VA 22117
(Write for information on riding clubs.)

Virginia Native Plant Society
P.O. Box 844
Annandale, VA 22003

Virginia Society of Ornithology
7495 Little River Turnpike, #201
Annandale, VA 22003
(Phone: 703-308-2285/256-8275)

Virginia Trail Association
12 West Maple St.
Alexandria, VA 22310
(Phone: 703-548-7490)

Virginia Wildlife Federation
4602 D West Grove Ct.
Virginia Beach, VA 23455
(Phone: 804-464-3136)

Virginia Wilderness Committee
Route 1, Box 250
Staunton, VA 24401

Wanderbirds Hiking Club
10416 Adel Rd.
Oakton, VA 22124

Wildlife Center of Virginia
P.O. Box 98
Weyers Cave, VA 22980
(Phone: 703-234-9453)

Wildlife Society (Virginia chapter)
Route 2, Box 173-C
Buchanan, VA 24066
(Phone: 703-857-7705)

Federal and State Endangered and Threatened Species in Virginia

An endangered species is one that is in danger of extinction throughout all or a significant portion of its range. A threatened species is one that is likely to become an endangered species within the foreseeable future throughout all or a significant portion of its range. In this table, F = Federal, S = State, E = Endangered, and T = Threatened.

FAUNA

Amphibians

Frogs

Barking treefrog	*Hyla gratiosa*	ST

Salamanders

Eastern tiger salamander	*Ambystoma tigrinum*	SE
Mabee's salamander	*Ambystoma mabeei*	ST
Shenandoah salamander	*Plethodon shenandoah*	FE

Birds

Bachman's sparrow	*Aimophila aestivalis*	ST
Bald eagle	*Haliaeetus leucocephalus*	FT
Bewick's wren	*Thryomanes bewickii*	SE
Gull-billed tern	*Sterna nilotica*	ST
Henslow's sparrow	*Ammodramus henslowii*	ST
Loggerhead shrike	*Lanius ludovicianus*	ST
Peregrine falcon	*Falco peregrinus*	FE
Piping plover	*Charadrius melodus*	FT
Red-cockaded woodpecker	*Picoides borealis*	FE
Roseate tern	*Sterna dougallii*	FE
Upland sandpiper	*Bartramia longicauda*	ST
Wilson's plover	*Charadrius wilsonia*	SE

Freshwater Crustaceans

Lee County Cave isopod	*Lirceus usdagulun*	FE
Madison Cave amphipod	*Stygobromus stegerorum*	ST
Madison Cave isopod	*Antrolina lira*	FT

Freshwater Fishes

Blackbanded sunfish	*Enneacanthus chaetodon*	SE
Carolina darter	*Etheostoma collis*	ST

Duskytail darter	*Etheostoma sp.*	SE
Emerald shiner	*Notropis atherinoides*	ST
Greenfin darter	*Etheostoma chlorobranchium*	ST
Longhead darter	*Percina macrocephala*	ST
Orangefin madtom	*Noturus gilberti*	ST
Paddlefish	*Polyodon spathula*	ST
Roanoke logperch	*Percina rex*	FE
Sharphead darter	*Etheostoma acuticeps*	SE
Shortnose sturgeon	*Acipenser brevirostrum*	FE
Slender chub	*Erimystax cahni*	FT
Spotfin chub	*Cyprinella monacha*	FT
Steelcolor shiner	*Cyprinella whipplei*	ST
Tennessee dace	*Phoxinus tennesseensis*	SE
Tippecanoe darter	*Etheostoma tippecanoe*	ST
Variegate darter	*Etheostoma variatum*	SE
Western sand darter	*Ammocrypta clara*	ST
Whitemouth shiner	*Notropis alborus*	ST
Yellowfin madtom	*Noturus flavipinnis*	FT

Mammals

Delmarva Peninsula fox squirrel	*Sciurus niger cinereus*	FE
Dismal Swamp southeastern shrew	*Sorex longirostris fisheri*	FT
Eastern big-eared bat	*Plecotus rafinesquii macrotis*	SE
Eastern cougar	*Felis concolor couguar*	FE
Gray bat	*Myotis grisescens*	FE
Indiana bat	*Myotis sodalis*	FE
Northern flying squirrel	*Glaucomys sabrinus*	FE
Rock vole	*Microtus chrotorrhinus*	SE
Snowshoe hare	*Lepus americanus*	SE
Virginia big-eared bat	*Plecotus townsendii virginianus*	FE
Water shrew	*Sorex palustris*	SE

Marine Mammals

Blue whale	*Balaenoptera musculus*	FE
Fin whale	*Balaenoptera physalus*	FE
Florida manatee	*Trichechus manatus*	FE
Humpback whale	*Megaptera novaeangliae*	FE
Northern right whale	*Eubalaena glacialis*	FE
Sei whale	*Balaenoptera borealis*	FE
Sperm whale	*Physeter catodon*	FE

Millipedes

Ellett Valley pseudotremia	*Pseudotremia cavernarum*	ST
Laurel Creek xystodesmid	*Sigmoria whiteheadi*	ST

Mollusks

Freshwater and Land Snails

Brown supercoil	*Paravitrea septadens*	ST
Rubble coil	*Helicodiscus lirellus*	SE
Shaggy coil	*Helicodiscus diadema*	SE
Spiny riversnail	*Io fluvialis*	ST
Spirit supercoil	*Paravitrea hera*	SE
Unthanks Cave snail	*Holsingeria unthanksensis*	SE
Virginia coil	*Polygyriscus virginicus*	FE

Freshwater Mussels

Appalachian monkeyface mussel	*Quadrula sparsa*	FE
Atlantic pigtoe mussel	*Fusconaia masoni*	ST
Birdwing pearlymussel	*Lemiox rimosus*	FE
Black sandshell mussel	*Ligumia recta*	ST
Brook floater mussel	*Alasmidonta varicosa*	SE
Cracking pearlymussel	*Hemistena lata*	FE
Cumberland bean mussel	*Villosa trabalis*	FE
Cumberland combshell mussel	*Epioblasma brevidens*	SE
Cumberland monkeyface mussel	*Quadrula intermedia*	FE
Deertoe mussel	*Truncilla truncata*	SE
Dromedary pearlymussel	*Dromus dromas*	FE
Dwarf wedge mussel	*Alasmidonta heterodon*	FE
Elephant-ear mussel	*Elliptio crassidens*	SE
Fanshell mussel	*Cyprogenia stegaria (= irorata)*	FE
Fine-rayed pigtoe mussel	*Fusconaia cuneolus*	FE
Fragile papershell mussel	*Leptodea fragilis*	ST
Green blossom mussel	*Epioblasma torulosa gubernaculum*	FE
James spiny mussel	*Pleurobema collina*	FE
Little-wing pearlymussel	*Pegias fabula*	FE
Ohio pigtoe mussel	*Pleurobema cordatum*	SE
Oyster mussel	*Epioblasma capsaeformis*	SE
Pimpleback mussel	*Quadrula pustulosa pustulosa*	ST
Pink mucket mussel	*Lampsilis abrupta (= orbiculata)*	FE
Pink pigtoe mussel	*Pleurobema rubrum*	SE
Purple bean mussel	*Villosa perpurpurea*	SE
Purple lilliput mussel	*Toxolasma lividus*	SE
Rough pigtoe mussel	*Pleurobema plenum*	FE
Rough rabbitsfoot mussel	*Quadrula cylindrica strigillata*	ST
Sheepnose mussel	*Plethobasus cyphyus*	ST
Shiny pigtoe mussel	*Fusconaia cor*	FE
Slabside pearlymussel	*Lexingtonia dolabelloides*	ST
Slippershell mussel	*Alasmidonta viridis*	SE
Snuffbox mussel	*Epioblasma triquetra*	SE
Spectaclecase mussel	*Cumberlandia monodonta*	SE
Tan riffleshell mussel	*Epioblasma florentina walkeri*	FE
Tennessee heelsplitter mussel	*Lasmigona holstonia*	SE

Reptiles

Lizards

Eastern glass lizard	*Ophisaurus ventralis*	ST

Snakes

Canebrake rattlesnake	*Crotalus horridus atricaudatus*	SE

Turtles

Atlantic green sea turtle	*Chelonia mydas*	FT
Bog turtle	*Clemmys muhlenbergii*	SE
Eastern chicken turtle	*Deirochelys reticularia*	SE
Hawksbill sea turtle	*Eretmochelys imbricata*	FE
Kemp's Ridley sea turtle	*Lepidochelys kempi*	FE
Leatherback sea turtle	*Dermochelys coriacea*	FE
Loggerhead sea turtle	*Caretta caretta*	FT
Wood turtle	*Clemmys insculpta*	ST

FLORA

Addison's leatherflower	*Clematis addisonii*	SE
Chaffseed	*Schwalbea americana*	FE
Eastern prairie fringed orchid	*Plantanthera leucophaea*	SE
Ginseng	*Panax quinquefolius*	FT
Harper's fimbristylis	*Fimbristylis prepusilla*	FE
Leo's clover	*Trifolium calcaricum*	SE
Long-stalked holly	*Ilex collina*	FE
Mat-forming water hyssop	*Bacopa stragula*	SE
Millboro leatherflower	*Clematis viticaulis*	SE
Nestronia	*Nestronia umbellula*	FE
Northeastern bullrush	*Scirpus ancistrochaetus*	FE
Peters mountain mallow	*Iliamna corei*	FE
Piratebush	*Buckleya distichophylla*	FE
Seabeach pigweed	*Amaranthus pumilus*	FT
Sensitive joint-vetch	*Aeschynomene virginica*	SE
Shale barren rock-cress	*Arabis serotina*	FE
Small anthered bittercress	*Cardamine micranthera*	FE
Small whorled pogonia	*Isotria medeoloides*	FE
Smooth coneflower	*Echinacea laevigata*	FE
Sun-faced coneflower	*Rudbeckia heliopsidis*	FE
Swamp pink	*Helonias bullata*	SE
Variable sedge	*Carex polymorpha*	FE
Virginia round-leaf birch	*Betula uber*	FE
Virginia sneezeweed	*Helenium virginicum*	SE
Virginia spiraea	*Spiraea virginiana*	SE

APPENDIX C
Trails for Special People

The following lists of trails are offered as examples of trails that are particularly suited for three categories of special people: adventurous backpackers (rugged, secluded, wilderness-type trails of moderate to strenuous difficulty); families with young children (short walks of 0.1 mi. to 1.5 mi. on easy terrain offering scenic views and emphasizing animals and plants); and people with disabilities (PWD) (easy, short, usually paved trails for enjoying scenery, plant life, and fishing). Hikers and backpackers will notice many more trails in these and other categories throughout the book.

Adventurous Backpackers

Allegheny Trail (three sections, 36.5 mi., linear)

Appalachian National Scenic Trail (544.6 mi., linear)

Big Blue Trail (55.3 mi., linear)

Chief Benge/Little Stony Creek Trails (19.3 mi., linear)

Cumberland Mountain Trail (22.8 mi., linear)

Dike/False Cape Trails (32.6 mi., round-trip)

Fore Mountain/Middle Mountain Trails (18.8 mi., linear)

Iron Mountain Trail (50.6 mi., linear)

Little Wilson Creek Wilderness Trails (24.1 mi., circuit and backtrack)

Massanutten Mountain Trails (60 mi., linear)

New River State Park Trail (55.3 mi., linear)

North Mountain (North)/Crawford Mountain Trails (22.3 mi., linear)

North Mountain (South)/Lick Branch Trails (17.9 mi., linear)

Oliver Mountain/Brushy Lick Trails (15.7 mi., circuit and backtrack)

Ramsey Draft/Bald Ridge Trails (17.9 mi., circuit)

Rich Hole/White Rock Tower Trails (12 mi., linear)

Ridge/Ewing Trails (19 mi., linear)

Ridge/Saddle/Old Rag Fire Road/AT/Nicholson Hollow Trails (19.5 mi., circuit)

Rock Castle Gorge Trail (10.6 mi., circuit)

Shenandoah Mountain Trail (30.7 mi., linear)

Virginia Creeper Trail (34.1 mi., linear)

Whetstone Ridge Trail (11.4 mi., linear)

Wild Oak Trail (25.7 mi., circuit)

Willis River Trail (15.2 mi., linear)

Families with Young Children

Alpine Trail

Alum Spring Trail

Animal Trail

Ashton Creek Trail

Bald Cypress Trail

Barn Wharf Trail

Bayberry Nature Trail

Baywood Trail

Belle Isle Trail

Big Spy Mountain Trail

Boston Trail
Braley Pond Trail
Buck Lick Interpretive Trail
Buffalo Creek Trail
Bull Run Nature Trail
Cock's Comb Trail
Cycle of Life Trail
Dismal Town Boardwalk Trail
Dune Trail
Dyke Trail
Eastern National Children's Forest Trail
Eastern Shore Nature Trail
Echo Lake Trail
Elk Run Trail
Fenwick Nature Trail
Fisherman's Trail
Fort Boykin Trail
Fragrance Garden Trail
Goodwin Lake Nature Trail
Green Leaf Nature Trail
Greenstone Trail
Guest River Gorge Trail
Heron Trail
Hiawatha Nature Trail
Indian Gap Trail
James River Trail
Lancaster County Nature Trail
Lake Trail
Limberlost Nature Trail

Living Museum Nature Trail
Long Island Trail
Mountain Farm Trail
Mountain Industry Trail
Meadowlark Garden Trail
Meadow Spring Trail
Molly's Pioneer Trail
New Market Battlefield Trail
Pandapas Pond Trail
Pass Mountain Nature Trail
Phillips Creek Trail
Pig Iron Trail
Ragged Island Trail
Roaring Run Falls Trail
River Loop Trail
R. W. Cross Nature Trail
Ruskin Freer Trails
Salthouse Branch Nature Trail
Stony Fork Nature Trail
Three Lakes Trail
Trail of Trees
Tree Walk Trail
Todd Lake Trail
Tunnel Trail
Watchable Wildlife Trail
Whispering Water Trail
Whiteoak Trail
Woodland Trail

People with Disabilities (PWD)

Awareness Trail
Bark Camp Lake Trail (fishing)
Beartree Lake Trail (fishing)
Discovery Way Trail
Duff and Stuff Trail
Fenwick Wetlands Trail (fishing)
Fragrance Garden Trail (Braille)
Fragrance Trail
Handicapped Trail

Happy Creek Trail
Lake Anna State Park (trail to the lake)
Limberlost Nature Trail
Lion's Tale Trail (Braille)
Massanutten Story Book Trail
Nature Trail (map number 906)
Pine Grove Forest Trail
Wheelchair Trail

Bibliography

Manuscripts

Abstracts and Transcripts from Original Colonial Papers, I–X. Virginia Public Library, Richmond.

Anderson, Robert, and William Nelson. Letterbooks. Alderman Library, University of Virginia, Charlottesville.

British Colonial Papers (1625). Library of Congress, Washington, D.C.

Colonial Papers, 1710–1720. Archives Division, Virginia State Library, Richmond.

Virginia Miscellaneous Papers, 1606–1863. Manuscripts Division, Library of Congress, Washington, D.C.

Maps

Maps Division, Alderman Library, University of Virginia, Charlottesville. Includes the *John Smith Map of 1608, Nova Virginia Tabula Map of 1671*, and the *W. E. Myer Map of 1928*.

Municipal and County Maps (current). Various publishers, coverage, and scale. Examples are *Street Map of the Virginia Peninsula* (Hampton–Newport News–Yorktown–Poquoson–York County–James City County and Williamsburg), Dolph Map Co.; *Street Map of Richmond and Petersburg*, Rand McNally; County of Fairfax Public Parks, Fairfax County Park Authority; *ADC's Street Map of Richmond and Vicinity, Prince William County, Northern Virginia*, and others, Langenscheidt Publishing Group. Local chambers of commerce usually have street maps of towns, cities, and counties.

NPS. Maps of the Blue Ridge Parkway. Scale is based on mileposts.

——. Maps of Shenandoah National Park. Published by Potomac Appalachian Trail Club. Best maps are North, Central, South (nos. 9, 10, and 11), and a general map of the park published by the NPS. Scale: 5/16 inch = 1 mile.

USFS. District maps of Virginia and West Virginia. District headquarters. Scales: 1 inch = 1 mile or 1 inch = 1.3 miles (current).

——. Maps of the Appalachian Trail (recreation guides). Maps 1, 2, 3, 4, and 5 cover the trail from Mount Rogers National Recreation Area to the northern end of the BRP near Waynesboro.

——. Maps of Virginia and West Virginia. USFS Headquarters, Roanoke and Harrisonburg. Scale: 1:126,720 (current).

USGS. Maps of Virginia. (Also, modified USFS topographical maps, which show boundaries.) There are 788 maps listed. 1:24,000 scale of 7½-minute series.

Virginia Atlas and Gazetteer Map. LeLorme Mapping Company of Freeport, Maine. Full state map with topographical scale.

Virginia Department of Transportation. Official highway map (current) and 95 county maps (current). Richmond.

Public Documents

Commonwealth of Virginia. Department of Conservation and Economic Development, for the Division of Parks and Recreation. *Outdoor Plan.* Richmond, 1994.
GWNF. *Comments and Responses of the EIS for the Revised Land and Resource Management Plan.* Harrisonburg, Va.
——. *George Washington National Forest Final Revised Land and Resource Management Plan.* Harrisonburg, Va.
——. *Record of Decision of the Final Environment Impact Statement.* Harrisonburg, Va.
——. *A Summary of the Final EIS.* Harrisonburg, Va.
JNF. *Final Environmental Impact Statement.* Roanoke, Va.
——. *Jefferson National Forest Land and Resource Management Plan.* Roanoke, Va.

Books, Theses, and Articles

Allied Recreation

Bowen, John. *Adventuring in the Chesapeake Bay Area.* San Francisco: Sierra Club Books, 1990.
Corbett, H. Roger. *Virginia Whitewater.* Rockville, Md.: Seneca Press, 1988.
Gooch, Bob. *Virginia Fishing Guide.* Charlottesville: University Press of Virginia, 1992.
Porter, Randy, and Nancy Sorrells. *A Cyclist's Guide to the Shenandoah Valley.* Staunton, Va.: Shenandoah Odysseys, 1994.
Skinner, Charlie, and Elizabeth Skinner. *Bicycling the Blue Ridge.* Birmingham, Ala.: Menasha Ridge Press, 1990.

Flora and Fauna

Angier, Bradford. *Field Guide to Edible Wild Plants.* Harrisonburg, Pa.: Stackpole, 1974.
Bailey, John W. *Mammals of Virginia.* Richmond: William Sprint, 1946.
Bull, John, and John Farrand Jr. *The Audubon Society Field Guide to North American Birds: Eastern Region.* New York: Alfred A. Knopf, 1977.
Catlin, David T. *A Naturalist's Blue Ridge Parkway.* Knoxville: University of Tennessee Press, 1984.
Cunningham, Paul. "The Gentle Melancholy of Trees," *American Artist,* June 1994.
Gupton, Oscar W., and Fred W. Swope. *Wildflowers of the Shenandoah Valley and Blue Ridge Mountains.* Charlottesville: University Press of Virginia, 1979.
Harvill, A. M., Charles Stevens, and Donna M. E. Ware. *Atlas of the Virginia Flora.* Vols. 1–2. Farmville, Va.: Virginia Botanical Association, 1977–81.
Linzey, Donald W., and Michael J. Clifford. *Snakes of Virginia.* Charlottesville: University Press of Virginia, 1981.
Martof, Bernard S., William M. Palmer, Joseph R. Bailey, and Julian R. Harrison. *Amphibians and Reptiles of the Carolinas and Virginia.* Chapel Hill: University of North Carolina Press, 1980.

Petrides, George A. *A Field Guide to Trees and Shrubs.* Boston: Houghton Mifflin, 1988.

Radford, Albert E., Harry E. Ahles, and C. Ritchie Bell. *Manual of the Vascular Flora of the Carolinas.* Chapel Hill: University of North Carolina Press, 1986.

Schmutz, Ervin M., and Lucretia B. Hamilton. *Plants That Poison.* Flagstaff, Ariz.: Northland, 1989.

Simpson, Marcus B. Jr. *Birds of the Blue Ridge Mountains.* Chapel Hill: University of North Carolina Press, 1992.

Stokes, Donald W. *The Natural History of Wild Shrubs and Vines.* New York: Harper and Row, 1989.

Strausbaugh, P. D., and Earl L. Core. *Flora of West Virginia.* Vols. 1–4. 2d ed. Morgantown: West Virginia University Books, 1973.

Virginia's Birdlife. Rev. ed. Lynchburg: Virginia Society of Ornithology, 1979.

Webster, William David, James F. Parnell, and Walter C. Biggs. *Mammals of the Carolinas, Virginia, and Maryland.* Chapel Hill: University of North Carolina Press, 1985.

White, Christopher. *Endangered and Threatened Wildlife of the Chesapeake Bay Region.* Centerville, Md.: Tidewater, 1982.

History

Abernethy, Thomas Perkins. *The South in the New Nation.* Baton Rouge: Louisiana State University Press, 1961.

——. *Three Virginia Frontiers.* Baton Rouge: Louisiana State University Press, 1940.

Alvord, Clarence W., and Lee Bidgood. *The First Explorations of the Trans-Allegheny Region of the Virginians, 1650-1674.* Cleveland: Arthur Clark, 1912.

Bartram, William. *The Travels of William Bartram, 1791.* Naturalist's ed. Edited by Francis Harper. New Haven: Yale University Press, 1958.

Beverley, Robert. *The History and Present State of Virginia.* Edited by Louis B. Wright. Chapel Hill: University of North Carolina Press, 1947.

Briceland, Alan. *Westward from Virginia: Exploration of Virginia-Carolina Frontier.* Charlottesville: University Press of Virginia, 1987.

Brooks, Maurice. *The Appalachians.* Boston: Houghton Mifflin, 1965.

Cooke, John Esten. *Virginia: A History of the People.* Edited by Horace Scudder. Boston: Houghton Mifflin, 1887. Reprint, New York: AMS Press, 1973.

Dabney, Virginius. *Virginia: The New Dominion.* Garden City, N.Y.: Doubleday, 1971.

de Hart, Allen. "Colonial History of Prince George County, Virginia." M.A. thesis, University of Virginia, Charlottesville, 1957.

Heatwole, Henry. *Shenandoah National Park and Guide to Skyline Drive.* Luray, Va.: Shenandoah Natural History Association, 1990.

Jolley, Harley E. *The Blue Ridge Parkway.* Knoxville: University of Tennessee Press, 1969.

Lederer, John. *The Discoveries of John Lederer.* 1672. Reprint, edited by William P. Cumming, Charlottesville: University Press of Virginia, 1958.

Lord, William G. *Blue Ridge Parkway Guide.* Asheville, N.C.: Hexagon, 1976. Flora and fauna included in addition to history.

Raeburn, Paul. "Can This Man Save Our Forests?" *Popular Science,* June 1994.

Rountree, Helen C. *Pocahontas's People: The Powhatan Indians of Virginia through Four Centuries*. Norman: University of Oklahoma Press, 1990.

———. *Powhatan Foreign Relations, 1500–1722*. Charlottesville: University Press of Virginia, 1993.

———. *The Powhatan Indians of Virginia: Their Traditional Culture*. Norman: University of Oklahoma Press, 1989.

Williams, Ted. "Can the Forest Service Heal Itself?" *Wildlife Conservation*, September/October 1994.

Trail Gear and Supplies

Axcel, Claudia, Diana Cook, and Vikki Kinmont. *Simple Foods for the Pack*. San Francisco: Sierra Club Books, 1986.

Fletcher, Colin. *The Complete Walker III*. New York: Alfred A. Knopf, 1987.

Gorman, Stephen. *Winter Camping*. Boston: Appalachian Mountain Club Books, 1991.

Greenspan, Rick, and Hal Kahn. *The Camper's Companion*. San Francisco: Foghorn Press, 1991.

McHugh, Gretchen. *The Hungry Hikers Book of Good Cooking*. New York: Alfred A. Knopf, 1993.

Pahlow, Mannfried. *Living Medicine: The Healing Properties of Plants*. Translated by Linda Sontag. Wellingborough: Thorsons, 1980.

Randall, Glenn. *The Modern Backpacker's Handbook*. New York: Lyons and Burford, 1993.

Trail Guides

Adkins, Leonard M. *Walking the Blue Ridge: A Guide to the Trails of the Blue Ridge Parkway*. Chapel Hill: University of North Carolina Press, 1991.

Appalachian Trail Guide. Vol. 6, *Maryland and Northern Virginia*. Edited by Michael T. Shoemaker. Vienna, Va.: Potomac Appalachian Trail Club, 1989.

———. Vol. 7, *Shenandoah National Park*. Edited by Jean Golightly. Vienna, Va.: Potomac Appalachian Trail Club, 1991.

———. Vol. 8, *Central and Southwest Virginia*. Edited by Jack Albright. Harpers Ferry, W.Va.: Appalachian Trail Conference, 1991.

Beale, B. De Roy. *Tucker Trails through Southside Virginia*. Richmond: B. D. Beale, 1986.

de Hart, Allen. *Hiking the Mountain State: The Trails of West Virginia*. Boston: Appalachian Mountain Club, 1986. Includes trails of Jefferson and George Washington national forests in West Virginia.

de Hart, Allen, and Bruce Sundquist. *Monongahela National Forest Hiking Guide*. Charleston, W.Va.: West Virginia Highlands Conservancy, 1993. Includes topographical maps of trails connecting to Virginia trails.

Denton, James W. *Circuit Hikes in Shenandoah National Park*. Vienna, Va.: Potomac Appalachian Trail Club, 1986.

Garvey, Edward B. *Hiking Trails in the Mid-Atlantic States*. Chicago: Great Lakes Living Press, 1976.

Golightly, Jean. *Guide to Circuit Hikes in Virginia, West Virginia, Maryland, and Pennsylvania*. Vienna, Va.: Potomac Appalachian Trail Club, 1986.

Hogarth, Paul. *Walking Tours of Old Washington and Alexandria*. McLean, Va.: EPM, 1985.

Johnson, Elizabeth. *The Big Blue*. Vienna, Va.: Potomac Appalachian Trail Club, 1984.

Wilderness

Hart, John. *Walking Softly in the Wilderness*. San Francisco: Sierra Club Books, 1984.

Hampton, Bruce, and David Cole. *Soft Paths: How to Enjoy the Wilderness without Harming It*. Harrisonburg, Pa.: Stackpole, 1988.

Hodgson, Michael. *The Basic Essentials of Minimizing Impact on the Wilderness*. Merrillville, Ind.: ICS, 1991.

Simer, Peter, and John Sullivan. *The National Outdoor Leadership School's Wilderness Guide*. New York: Simon and Schuster, 1985.

Schimelpfenig, Tod, and Linda Lindsey. *Wilderness First Aid*. Lander, Wyo.: National Outdoor Leadership School, 1991.

General Index

Accomack County, 207–8, 212
Accotink Bay NWR, 345
Albemarle County, 281–82, 356
Alleghany County, 240–42
Allegheny Mountain, 108, 110–14, 124
Allegheny Mountain Area, 113–14
Allegheny Trail. *See* Trail Index
Amelia County, 226–27
Amelia WMA, 226–27
Amherst County, 129–32
Animals, 14–16; poisonous, 17–18. *See also* Hunting; Wildlife; Appendix B
Annandale Community Park, 286–87
Appalachian National Scenic Trail, 1, 7–8, 151–59. *See also* Trail Index
Appalachian Trail Clubs, 29, 54, 129, 132–33, 152, 276. *See also* Appendix A
Appalachian Trail Conference, 55–56, 152
Appamattox County, 198–99, 255–56
Appamattox Court House National Historical Park, 198–99
Arlington County, 213–14, 282–83, 331–38
Arthur, Gabriel, 5–6
Assateague Island National Seashore, 207, 212
Augusta County, 86–89, 90–94, 98, 102–3, 136–39, 228–29, 338–40
Augusta Springs Conference Center, 86
Austin, Stephen, 251
Austinville Lead Mines, 250

Back Bay NWR, 205–7
Bacon's Rebellion, 6, 257, 260
Bald Mountain, 137–38
Barbours Creek Wilderness, 69, 83, 111, 107
Bark Camp Recreation Area, 38
Barnesfield Park, 296
Bath County, 86, 94, 114–15, 141–47, 240–42

Batts, Captain Thomas, 5–6
Bealer's Ferry Pond, 84
Bear Creek Lake State Park, 253–54, 277
Beards Mountain, 137–38
Beartown Mountain, 228
Beartown Wilderness, 2, 79–80
Beartree Lake, 59
Beartree Recreation Area, 56, 59
Bedford County, 16, 59, 259–60
Belle Isle (Richmond), 321
Belle Isle State Park, 262–63
Bennett's Creek Park, 325
Berkley, Governor William, 4–7
Bicycling, 1, 20–21, 29, 56, 59, 69, 84, 214–15, 216–17, 248, 252, 258, 263–66, 270–72, 274, 282–83, 289, 291, 293, 302, 308, 327, 333, 337–38. *See also Chapters 13 and 14 for paved hike-bike trails*
Big Ben Picnic Area, 79
Big Butt Mountain, 229
Big Meadows Campground and Lodge, SNP, 157, 174
Big Pinnacle, 245
Big Tumbling Creek, 227
Big Walker Mountain, 70–89, 86
Big Walker Mountain Scenic Byway, 79
Birding, 15, 35, 47, 53, 71, 73, 75, 81, 99, 120, 168, 173, 205, 207, 219, 232, 263–64, 268, 270, 277, 285, 289, 297, 304, 306, 308, 315, 318, 323, 325, 339, 348. *See also* Wildlife
Black Cherry Natural Area, 228
Blacksburg Nature Center, 303
Blackwater Creek Natural Area, 313–14
Blowing Springs Campground, 140
Blue Hole Picnic Area, 98
Blue Ridge Parkway, 45, 48, 50, 52, 128–29, 132, 135, 127, 160–71
Boating, 29, 41–42, 44, 46, 83, 97–98, 107, 114–15, 136, 140, 146, 161, 204, 227, 233,

240, 253–62, 264–68, 273–75, 281, 286, 299–300, 315, 326–27, 331, 334, 341–44. *See also* Canoeing and Kayaking

Bolar Flats Picnic Area, 98

Bolar Mountain Recreation Area, 146–47

Booker T. Washington National Monument, 212

Boone, Daniel, 200, 246

Botetourt County, 16, 48–49, 71, 75–76, 77–78, 108–10

Bottom Creek Gorge, 357

Boy Scouts, 99, 199, 342, 345–46

Braddock Park, 287

Braley Pond Picnic Area, 85

Breaks Interstate Park, 238–39

Briery Creek WMA, 351

Brook Valley Park, 302

Bryan Park, 320

Buckingham/Appamattox State Forest, 255, 276

Buckingham County, 255–56

Buffalo Creek Nature Area, 352

Bugg's Island, 342

Bull Pasture Gorge, 231–32

Bull Run Marina, 334

Bull Run Occoquan Regional Parks, 331–35

Bull Run Regional Park, 332–333

Burke Lake Park, 287

Burke's Garden, 79

Bush Mill Stream Natural Area, 236

Buzzard Rock, 118

Byrd, Harry F., 160

Caledon Natural Area, 263

Cameron Run Regional Park, 302

Campbell County, 284

Campgrounds, 55, 61, 65, 68–69, 101, 141, 161, 169. *See also names of specific recreation areas*

Camp Roosevelt, 116–20

Canal Park, 308–9

Cane Patch Campground, 38, 41

Canoeing and Kayaking, 1, 20, 116, 143, 225, 228, 243, 269–70, 305–7, 315, 320, 331. *See also* Boating

Cape Henry Memorial Landing, 270

Capital Square (Richmond), 323–24

Caroline County, 345

Carroll County, 55, 67–68, 247–52, 284–85

Carrolton Nike Park, 295

Cascades Recreation Area, 31, 36

Catawba Mountain, 71

Cave Mountain Recreation Area, 46

Cave Spring Recreation Area, 41–42

Chancellorsville Battlefield, 192–93

Charlotte County, 343–43

Cherokee National Forest, 25, 56

Chesapeake Forest Products Company, 226, 350–52

Chesterfield County, 194–95, 258–59

Chestnut Creek Waterfalls, 250

Chestnut Tunnel, 250

Chincoteague NWR, 207–8

Chippokes Plantation State Park, 264

Chopawamsic Campground, 219

Civilian Conservation Corps, 91, 119, 152, 219, 231, 234, 246

Civil War, 36, 90–95, 116, 122–23, 189–99, 269, 284–85, 295, 307, 311, 313, 319

Clark County, 252–53

Claytor Lake State Park, 240, 249

Clinch Mountain WMA, 227–28

Cold Mountain Area, 132–33

Coles Mountain Picnic Area, 107

College of William and Mary, 327, 347

Colonial National Historic Park, 188–89

Congressional Acts, 25–26, 46, 83, 152, 160, 172

Cowpasture River, 85, 96–97, 141, 143

Crabtree Falls, 83, 128, 134–35

Craig County, 34, 36, 73, 75–76

Craig Creek Recreation Area, 69, 78

Cranesnest Campground, 341

Crockett Cove Valley, 81

Crump Memorial Park, 293

Cumberland County, 253–54, 276–78

Cumberland Gap National Historical Park, 200–203

Cumberland State Forest, 276–78

Currin Valley Opportunity Area, 80

Curry Creek Area, 48

Curtis Memorial Park, 229–300

Daniels, Josephus, 160
Dan River, 261, 354–55
Dark Horse Hollow Picnic Area, 79
Deep Run Park, 293
Deerfield Valley, 87–88
Devil's Bathtub, 46
Devil's Fork Area, 45
Devil's Hole Mountain, 115
Devil's Marbleyard, 52
Dickenson County, 39, 238–39, 241–42
Dismal Creek Area, 31
Dora Kelly Nature Park, 302
Douthat State Park, 141–43, 240–42
Doyle, Warren, 151
Draper Mountain, 251
Drummond, William, 209

Eastern Continental Divide, 30, 36
Eastern Shore of Virginia NWR, 204
Echo Lake Park, 293
Elephant Mountain Area, 131–32
Elizabeth Furnace Recreation Area,
    116–17, 122–23
Elkhorn Lake, 84, 89, 93, 97–100
Elkwallow Wayside, 174
Ellanor C. Lawrence Park, 286, 288
Elliott Knob, 85, 87
Eyes of Wildlife (Watchable Wildlife), 84

Fairfax County, 267–70, 281, 286–91,
    331–38, 345–46, 357
Fairy Stone State Park, 254–55
Fallam, Robert, 5
Falls Ridge Preserve, 357
False Cape State Park, 205–7, 264–67
Fat Mountain, 128
Fauquier County, 252–53, 346, 359
Feathercamp Mountain, 60
Fenwick Mines Recreational Complex,
    70
Fernbrook Preserve, 356
Fishing, 15, 21, 31, 33, 29, 37, 42, 47, 54,
    56–57, 59, 65, 67, 78–79, 80, 84–85,
    90–91, 98, 102, 111–12, 114, 128, 136, 140,
    144–46, 165, 168, 214–16, 226–27, 231,
    237, 240–41, 245, 253, 255, 258–62, 271,
    287–88, 289, 303, 327, 242, 348, 335

Flat Top Mountain, 31
Flatwoods Group Picnic Area, 38
Floyd County, 161, 281
Fore Mountain Area, 111–12
Forest Hill Park, 323
Fort A. P. Hill Military Reservation, 345
Fort Belvoir, 345–46
Fort Boykin Historical Park, 295
Fountainhead Regional Park, 334
Fox Creek Horse Camp, 55
Franklin County, 212, 343–45
Fraser Preserve, 357
Fredericksburg and Spotsylvania
    National Military Park, 193–94
Fridley Gap, 22
Fullers Rocks, 131

Gatewood, (Grandma) Emma, 151
Gathright WMA, 225
George C. Marshall Museum, 311
George Mason University Environmen-
    tal Education Center, 333
George Washington Birthplace National
    Monument, 213
George Washington Memorial Parkway,
    213–16
Giles County, 31, 33–36
Ginten Botanical Gardens, 320
Glebe Road Park, 282–83
Glencarlyn Park, 283
Glen Cove Park, 298
Glen Lea Recreation Area, 294
Glen Maury Park, 303
Gloucester County, 292
Goose Point Park, 344
Goshen Pass, 228
Goshen Pass Natural Area, 242
Goshen WMA, 85, 228–29, 243
Grand Caverns Regional Park, 338–39
Grandview Preserve, 310
Grayson County, 56, 59, 61–62, 243–45,
    247–52
Grayson Highlands Campground, 64
Grayson Highlands State Park, 61–62,
    243–45
Great Dismal Swamp NWR, 208–11, 325,
    305

Great Falls Park, 216–18
Great North Mountain, 115, 125
Green Cove Station, 57
Greene County, 234–35
Green Pond, 138
Greenwood Point Campground, 147
G. Richard Thompson WMA, 226
Grindstone Campground, 61–62, 66
Gulf Branch Nature Center, 282
Gunston Hall, 267–68

Hale Lake, 68
Halifax County, 213–16, 260–61
Hammond Hollow Area, 48–49
Hanging Rock Raptor Migration Observatory, 34
Hanover County, 194–95, 292
Hardscrabble Knob, 91
Hazzard Mill Canoe Camp, 116
Health and safety, 16–20
Hearthstone Lake Area, 102–3
Hemlock Overlook Regional Park, 333–34
Henrico County, 194–95, 281, 292–93
Henricus Historical Park, 284
Henry County, 254–55, 343–45
Hensley Settlement, 202
Hickory Hollow Gardens, 298
Hidden Oaks Nature Center, 286
Hidden Pond Park, 286
Hidden Valley Area, 145–46
Hidden Valley Recreation Area, 84
Hidden Valley WMA, 231–32
High Cliff Campground, 116
High Knob Recreation Area, 38, 44
Highland County, 90–94, 147–48, 231–32
Highlands Scenic Tour, 107–8
Hog Camp Gap, 132
Hog Island WMA, 222–23
Holliday Lake State Park, 255–56
Homestead, The, 350
Hone Quarry Recreation Area, 97, 105–6
Honey Spring Picnic Area, 31
Hopper Creek Group Camp, 47
Horseback riding, 21, 28, 39, 47, 49–52, 54–69, 84, 111, 176–87, 216–17, 226, 238, 243, 245, 248–52, 272–74, 337–38

Horseshoe Campground, 251
Huckleberry Ridge Area, 35
Humpback Rock Recreation Area, 161, 163
Hungry Mother State Park, 245–46
Hunting, 4, 7, 14–16, 20, 29–30, 34, 37, 39, 41, 43, 51, 53, 59, 67, 70–71, 75, 77, 81, 84, 87–89, 102, 109, 114, 116, 139, 162, 205–11, 225–35, 243, 299, 352. *See also* Wildlife
Huntley Meadows Park, 288–89
Hurricane Campground, 65
Hussy Mountain Horse Camp, 55
Hypothermia, 18

Indians. *See* Native Americans
Indiantown Park, 297
Interior Picnic Area, 30
Iron Mountains, 59–61, 65–68
Isle of Wight County, 222–23, 295–96
Ivey Creek Natural Area, 304
Ivey Creek Preserve, 356

James City County, 188–89, 274–76
James River, 164, 232–33, 264, 295, 315, 320–21, 327, 354
James River Face Wilderness, 46, 51
James River Gorge, 131
James River Park, 320–22
James River Recreation Area, 51–52
Jamison Mill Park, 344
Jennings Creek Area, 49–50
Jerkemtight Creek, 96
Jerry's Run Area, 112–13
John H. Kerr Reservoir, 257, 342–43
Johns Creek and Mountain Area, 36–37
John W. Flannagan Reservoir, 341–42
Jones Point Lighthouse, 213

Kennedy Park, 119
Kids Fishing Day, 84
Kimberling Creek Wilderness, 79
King George County, 263, 296
King William County, 276
Kiptopeke State Park, 268
Knights of the Golden Horseshoe, 7

Lake Anna State Park, 256–57
Lake Drummond, 210–11
Lake Fairfax Park, 289
Lake Keokee Recreation Area, 42
Lake Maury, 352
Lake Moomaw, 83, 107, 114–15, 139–40, 146, 225
Lake Moomaw Campground, 225
Lake Robertson Park, 299
Lancaster County, 296, 351
Lancaster County State Park, 262–63
Lanum, Henry (Hank), Jr., 132–33
Laurel Bed Lake, 227
Laurel Fork Area, 147–48
Laurel Run Picnic Area, 299
Leach's Run Wildlife Habitat, 310
Lederer, John, 5–6, 83
Lee Chapel, 311–12
Lee County, 41, 200–203
Leesylvania State Park, 268–69
Lewis Fork Wilderness, 54, 63–64
Lewis Mountain Campground, 157, 171, 184
Little Dry Run Wilderness, 54
Little Fort Campground, 116
Little North Mountain WMA, 228–30
Little Walker Mountain, 80–82
Little Wilson Creek Wilderness, 54, 63–65
Locust Shade Regional Park, 298
Locust Springs Recreational Area, 140
Lott Mountain Campground, 157, 174
Lone Star Lakes Park, 325–26
Longdale Recreation Area, 108–10
Long Island Park, 284
Loudoun County, 297, 331, 336
Lovingston Spring Area, 133–34
Lower Twin Area and Campground, 341–42
Lubber Run Community Center, 282
Luther Hassinger Memorial Bridge, 57
Lyndon B. Johnson Memorial Grove, 214

Mabry Mill, 161–62, 171
Mackaye, Benton, 151
Madison County, 234–35

Manassas National Battlefield Park, 189–91
Marcy Park, 215
Mariners Museum Park, 352–54
Mason District Park, 289–90
Mason Neck NWR, 204, 207
Mason Neck State Park, 267, 269–70
Massanutten Mountain Area (East), 117–20
Massanutten Mountain Area (South), 120–22
Massanutten Visitor Center, 116, 120–21
Massie Gap, 244–45
Mathews Arm Campground, 117, 172–73, 178
Mathews County, 236
Maury River, 128, 243, 303, 312, 349
Maury River Valley, 132
Maymont Park, 320, 323
Meadow Farm Museum, 293
Meadowlark Gardens Regional Park, 335
Mecklenburg County, 342–43, 257–58
Middle Creek Picnic Area, 47
Middle Mountain Area, 141–43
Mill Mountain Area, 86
Mill Mount Torry Furnace, 137
Mills Creek Reservoir, 138
Minerals, 16, 28, 63, 183, 218, 247, 254, 339
Monongahela National Forest, 25, 70–71, 83, 97, 107, 113, 139
Monroe Hall, 213
Monster Rock, 79
Montgomery County, 37, 357
Morris Hill Recreation Area, 107–8
Mountain House Picnic Area, 85, 91, 94–95
Mountain Lake (and Resort), 30, 33, 36, 350
Mountain Lake Wilderness, 32, 35–37
Mountains (over 4,000 ft): Flat Top (JNFPF), 31; Bald Knob, 36; Wind Rock, 36; High Knob, 44; Apple Orchard, 48; Mount Rogers, 53; Pine Mountain, 53; White Top, 53; First Peak, 64; Second Peak, 64; Third Peak, 64; Elliott Knob, 86; Hardscrabble Knob, 92; Redish Knob, 97; Little Bald

Knob, 99; Big Bald Knob, 100; Flag-
pole Knob, 105; Big Knob, 112; Cold
Mountain, 128; Mount Pleasant, 128;
Pompey Mountain, 133; Rocky Moun-
tain, 134; Paddy Knob, 138; Chester
Flats, 154; Chestnut Knob, 154; Elk
Garden, 154; Flat Top (BRP), 166;
Hawkbill, 172; Stony Man Mountain,
174; Short Mountain, 227; Beartown,
228; Big Butt, 229; Sounding Knob,
231; Wildcat, 244; Big Pinnacle, 245;
Little Pinnacle, 245
Mount Malady, 284
Mount Pleasant, 132–33
Mount Rogers, 28–29, 53, 61, 68, 243
Mount Rogers National Recreation Area,
53–68
Mount Rogers NRA Headquarters and
Visitor Center, 79
Mount Rogers Scenic Byway, 55–56, 61
Mount Vernon, 214

Narrowback Mountain, 102–3
National Chimneys Regional Park,
339–40
Native Americans, 3–7, 54, 79, 200–201,
216, 245, 247, 256, 263, 268–69, 284, 297
Nature Conservancy, The, 209, 236,
356–57
Needham, James, 5–6
Nelson County, 133–35
New Market Battlefield Historical Park,
195
New Market Gap Picnic Area, 119, 121
New River Community College, 347
New River Trail. *See* Trail Index
Northampton County, 268
North Anna River, 256–57
North Creek Recreation Area, 47, 49–50
North Creek Special Management Plan,
47
North Fork of Pond Reservoir, 41
North Landing River Preserve, 357
North Mountain and Crawford Moun-
tain Area, 27–90
North Mountain Lick Branch Area,
71–73

North Mountain (North) Area, 125–26
North Mountain (South) Area, 127–28
North River Campground, 97–99, 102

Oak Ridge Campground, 220
Occoneechee State Park, 257–58
Occoquan Bay, 270
Occoquan Regional Park, 334
Occoquan River, 331, 334–35
Old Mill Park, 308–9
Old Rag Mountain, 172–75, 181
Oliver Mountain Area, 114–15
Orange County, 193–94
Otter Creek Recreation Area, 101, 161–62,
164–65

Page County, 117–22
Patrick County, xi, 161, 168–71, 254–55,
343–45, 354–55
Patterson Mountain Area, 70, 75–78
Peak Creek Opportunity Area, 80
Peaks of Otter Recreation Area and
Lodge, 46, 161–62, 165–67
Pearis Mountain, 33
Pen Municipal Park, 304
Petersburg National Battlefield, 196–97
Peters Mountain, 30, 33–36, 69, 111–12
Peters Mountain Area, 70–71
Philpott Lake (Reservoir), 343–45
Pine Mountain Area, 39–40
Pines Campground, The, 69
Pines Recreation Area, 69
Piney Mountain Area, 143–45
Pinnacle Natural Area Preserve, 236–37
Pinnacles of Dan Hydro Development,
354–56
Plants, 14–16; poisonous, 17–18, 29. *See
also* Appendix B
Plum Tree NWM, 318
Pocahontas State Forest, 276
Pocahontas State Park, 258–59
Pohick Bay Regional Park, 335–36
Point of Rocks Park, 284–85
Pompey Mountain, 133
Pony Pasture, 321
Poor Farm Park, 292
Poor Mountain Natural Area, 237

Poplar Forest, 313
Poquoson City Park, 318
Potomac Appalachian Trail Club, 26,
  122–23, 157–58, 174–75, 183, 215
Potomac Overlook Regional Park, 336
Potomac River, 147, 159, 214–15, 268, 272,
  283, 288, 290, 296, 301, 336
Potts Mountain, 36–39, 69–71
Potts Valley Area, 110–11
Powell Mountain, 123–25
Powhatan County, 233–34
Powhatan WMA, 233
Presquile NWR, 204
Price Mountain Area, 75–76
Priest, The, 128
Prince Edward County, 261–62
Prince Edward/Gallion State Forest, 276
Prince George County, 196–97
Prince William County, 189–91, 218–21,
  268–69, 297–346
Prince William State Forest, 218–21
Pulaski County, 81, 240, 247–52

Quantico Marine Base, 346
Quebec Branch, 64, 244

Raccoon Branch Campground, 65–67
Ragged Island WMA, 225–26
Ramsay Nature Center, 302
Ramseys Draft Wilderness, 83, 85, 90–94,
  97
Rapidan WMA, 234–35
Rappahannock Community College
  (South), 347–48
Rappahannock River, 262, 272, 296, 307,
  309
Raven Cliff Horse Camp, 55, 68
Reddish Knob, 97–98, 103–4
Red Rock Wilderness Overlook Park, 336
Redwing Park, 326–27
Revolutionary War, 118, 188–89, 219, 295,
  319
Rich Hole Wilderness, 83, 107–8, 140
Richmond National Battlefield Park,
  194–95
Riverbend Park, 286, 290
Riverside Drive Park, 308–9

Riverside Park, 214, 313
Roads and highways, 10
Roanoke County, 71, 167–68, 298–99
Roanoke Mountain Recreation Area, 161
Roanoke River, 162, 167, 259
Roaring Run Furnace Area, 77–78
Rockbridge County, 51, 86, 108–10,
  120–22, 228–29, 243, 299
Rock Castle Gorge, 169–71
Rockingham County, 104–6, 129–36
Rockwood Park, 285
Rocky Knob Recreation Area, 161,
  168–70
Rocky Mountain, 134
Rocky Row Area, 129–31
Rogers, William Barton, 54
Roosevelt Island, 215
Rough Mountain Wilderness, 140
Ruskin Freer Nature Preserve, 313–14
Russell County, 237, 227–28
Russell Fork River, 30–40, 238

Saint Mary's Waterfall, 138
Saint Mary's Wilderness, 83, 129, 138–39
Salthouse Branch Recreation Area,
  344–45
Salt Pond Mountain Area, 35
Salt Springs Mountain, 104–5
Scott County, 44–45, 246–47
Search and rescue, 19–20
Seashore State Park and Natural Area,
  270–72
Settlers Museum of Southwest Virginia,
  79
Shady Mountain Disabled Hunters Area,
  84
Shaffer, Earl, 151, 354
Shawvers Run Wilderness, 69, 83, 111
Shenandoah County, 117–18, 120–28
Shenandoah Mountain Area, 90–94,
  95–96
Shenandoah Mountains, 85, 97, 106
Shenandoah National Park, 115, 128, 160,
  172–87, 234–35, 309
Shenandoah Picnic Area, 97–98
Shenandoah River, 96–97, 115–16, 118,
  123–24, 159, 172

Shenandoah Valley, 5, 83, 97, 109, 122–23, 126, 164, 166, 172, 303, 311
Sherando Lake Recreation Area, 128–29, 136–38
Shot Tower and New River Trail State Park, 247–52. *See also* Trail Index
Signal Corps Knob, 95
Signal Knob, 115–16, 122–23
Skulls Gap Picnic Area, 55
Skyland Lodge, 174, 180
Skyline Drive (SNP), 172–87
Sky Meadows State Park, 226, 252–54
Smart View Recreation Area, 161
Smith Mountain Lake State Park, 259–60
Smith River, 343
Smyth County, 61–62, 68, 227–28, 245–46
Snow Goose Pool, 207
Snow skiing, 29, 55, 94, 161, 174, 229, 248
Sounding Knob, 231
Spotswood, Governor Alexander, 7
Spotsylvania County, 191–99, 256–57
Spotsylvania Court House Battlefield, 193–94
Stafford County, 299–300, 346
Staunton River State Park, 260–61
Steel Bridge Recreation Area, 69
Stony Fork Recreation Area, 79–80
Stony Run Area, 77–78
Sugar Camp Farm, 34
Sugar Run Picnic Area, 202
Surry County, 222–23, 264

Tamahawk Pond Picnic Area, 116
Tazewell County, 227–28
Three Lakes Park, 293
Three Top Mountain, 123–25
Thunder Ridge Area, 51
Thunder Ridge Wilderness, 46
Tindall's Point Park, 292
Track Fork Area, 81–82
Trail of the Lonesome Pine, 38
Trails, 1; early history, 3–7; titles and numbers, 8; length, difficulty, and features, 9; descriptions, addresses, information and support facilities, blazes,

and maps, 10–12; wilderness, 13–14; trail courtesy, 21; trails of the future, 22. *See also* Appendix C; Trail Index
Tri-State Peak, 200
Turkey Run Park, 215–16
Turkey Run Recreation Area, 220–21
Twin Lakes State Park, 261–62
Twin Springs, 134
Tye River Area, 134–35

University of Virginia Biological Station, 35–36
University of Virginia Ranges and Gardens, 348
Upper Twin Branch, 341
Upton Hill Regional Park, 337

Vawter Street Park, 294–95
Veterans' Memorial Park, 297
Virginia Creeper Trail Club, 57
Virginia Institute of Marine Science, 264
Virginia Living Museum, 315, 357–58
Virginia Marine Science Museum, 264, 326
Virginia Military Institute Foundation, 348–49
Virginia Tech Outing Club, 80

Wakefield and Lake Accotink Parks, 290–91
Waller Mill Park, 327–28
Walnut Flats Campground, 30
Waonaze Peak, 125
Warren County, 117–20
Warwick House, 145
Washington and Old Dominion Railroad Regional Park, 337–38
Washington County, 56, 59, 227–28, 230–31
Washwoods Environmental Education Center, 266
Waterfalls, 29, 31–32, 44, 47, 50, 56, 63, 65, 77, 129, 134, 136, 138, 163, 165–66, 169, 172, 176–79, 181–82, 184–86, 250
Weather, 19
Westmoreland Berry Farm, 358
Westmoreland County, 213, 272–74, 358

Westmoreland State Park, 272–73
Westvaco, 226, 352
West Virginia Scenic Trail Association, 34
Whetstone Ridge, 135
Whetstone Visitor Center, 161–62
White Oak WMA, 226
White Pine Horse Camp, 31
White Rock Branch Area, 34
White Rocks, 203
White Rocks Campground, 30
Whitetop Picnic Area, 55
Wildcat Mountain Preserve, 357
Wilderness Battlefield, 193
Wilderness Road Campground, 201–2
Wildflowers. *See Feature sections under trail headings*
Wildlife. *See especially Chapters 1, 2, 3, 5, 8, 10, and 11*
Wildlife Center of Virginia, 84
Wildwood Park, 318

Willis River, 277–78
Windy Run Park, 283
Wintergreen Resort, 350
Wise County, 39, 44
Wolf Creek Picnic Area, 79
Wolf Gap Campground, 125–27
Wolftrap Stream Valley Park, 291
Wood, Abraham, 5–6
Woods Creek Park, 312–13
Woodstock Lookout, 123–24
Wythe County, 67–68, 80–81, 247–52

Xaloy Way, 252

York County, 188
York River, 292, 327
York River State Park, 274–76
Yorktown Battlefield, 188

Zachary Taylor Park, 336
Zoar State Forest, 276

Trail Index

All trails mentioned in the book are listed below, whether they are merely connectors, have limited usage, or receive a full descriptive treatment. Boldface numbers refer to the trail numbers that appear in the outside margins of the text, next to the trail descriptions; these correspond with the same numbers on the maps. Trail names not followed by boldface numbers are either older names (now superseded), historic trails not in current use, ORV trails, or connecting trails that originate outside Virginia.

Accotink Stream Valley Trail, 290–291; **885**

Allegheny Trail, 7–8, 12, 33–34, 69, 70–71, 84, 108, 113–14, 140, 155; **11**

Alpine Trail, 313; **953**

Alternate Trail, 305; **929**

Alum Spring Trail, 308; **945**

Anderson Bikeway, 338

Animal Walk, 323; **979**

Anthony Knobs Trail, 109; **218**

Appalachian National Scenic Trail, 7–8, 12–14, 20–22, 25, 29–30, 33, 46, 48–67, 69–71, 79–80, 84, 116, 118, 129, 131–135, 162, 165, 167, 172, 176, 187, 226, 244–245, 253. *See especially 151–59 for a condensed listing of all major milepoints of interest and facilities*; **359**

Appalachia Trail, 43–44; **39**

Apple Orchard Falls Trail (NPS), 50, 165; **378**

Apple Orchard Falls Trail (USFS), 50; **57**

Appomattox History Trail, 198–99; **580**

Appomattox National Environmental Study Area Trail, 198–99; **581**

Aqueduct Trail, 355–56; **1031**

Arlington County Bicycle Trail, 283; **860**

Arrowhead Trail, 233–34; **672**

Ashton Creek Trail, 285; **863**

Austin Gap Trail, 39–40; **27**

Austin Mountain Trail, 185–86; **538**

Awareness Trail, 258–59; **782**

Back Bay Dike Trail, 205–7, 265–66; **599**

Backbone Ridge Trail, 47; **50**

Backbone Trail, 274–75; **844**

Back Draft Trail, 86; **156**

Backway Hollow Trail, 241–42; **711**

Bailey Gap Trail, 30

Balcony Falls Trail, 46, 51; **60**

Bald Cypress Trail, 271–72; **826**

Bald Knob Trail, 30

Bald Mountain Trail, 138–39; **317**

Bald Ridge Trail, 89–90, 99–100; **173**

Barbour Hill Beach Trail, 265–66; **810**

Barbour Hill Interpretive Trail, 205–6, 265–66; **809**

Bark Camp Lake Trail, 44–45; **42**

Barn Wharf Trail, 267–68; **816**

Batlick Mountain Trail, 112–13; **225**

Battery Trail, 215; **622**

Battery 5 Spur Trail, 196; **573**

Battery 7 Trail, 197; **574**

Bayberry Nature Trail, 327–28; **989**

Bay Trail, 205–6; **596**

Bay View Trail, 270; **822**

Baywood Trail, 268; **817**

Beach Trail, 270; **821**

Bear Cliff Trail, 30

Bear Draft Trail, 99–101; **193**

Bearfence Loop Trail, 183; **513**

Bearpen Trail, 63–65; **97**

Bear Rock Trail, 143–44; **330**

Bear Trap Trail, 123–24; **271**

Beartree Gap Trail, 59–60; **70**

Beartree Lake Trail, 59–60; **71**

Bearwallow Run Trail, 147–48; **358**
Beards Gap (Hollow) Trail, 142, 241–43; **714**
Beards Mountain Trail, 141–43, 242; **326**
Beaver Cove Nature Trail, 287; **870**
Beaver Lake Nature Trail, 258–59; **779**
Beaver Trail, 239; **699**
Beaver Trail, 273; **839**
Beaver Trail, 274; **842**
Beecher Ridge Trail, 178; **432**
Beech Grove Trail, 59–61; **77**
Beech Wood Trail, 259; **785**
Belfast Trail, 46, 52; **62**
Belle Cove Trail, 129–31; **291**
Belle Isle Trail, 321; **969**
Benchmark Trail, 263; **804**
Benson Run Trail, 86; **161**
Berry Hollow Fire Road, 175, 181; **402**
Betty's Rock Trail, 181; **481**
Big Blue/Bear Wallow Trail, 123; **264**
Big Blue Spur Trail, 122–23; **259**
Big Blue Trail, 84, 116–18, 123–26, 158, 172, 177; **235**
Big Devils Stairs Trail, 177; **414**
Big Hollow Trail, 104; **204**
Big Meadows Horse Trail, 181; **483**
Big Meadow Trail, 273; **837**
Big Oak Trail, 258; **778**
Big Pinnacle Trail, 244–45; **729**
Big Ridge Trail, 100
Big Run Loop Trail, 185; **535**
Big Run Portal Trail, 184–85; **532**
Big Schloss Trail, 125–26; **273**
Big Spy Mountain Trail, 164; **368**
Big Survey Trail, 282; **853**
Big Switchback Trail, 215; **620**
Big Wilson Creek Trail, 8, 63–65; **96**
Big Woods Trail, 256–57; **772**
Bike Trail, 313–14;,**955**
Birch Bluff Trail, 220; **639**
Bird Knob Trail, 120–21; **253**
Black Ridge Trail, 169; **396**
Black Rock Trail, 182; **493**
Blackwater Creek Trail, 313–15; **954**
Bloody Angle Loop Trail, 193–94; **562**
Blueberry Trail, 105–6; **208**
Blue Loop Trail (A), 136–38; **308**

Blue Loop Trail (C), 137; **313**
Blue Spur Trail, 122; **263**
Blue Suck Trail, 109; **217**
Blue Trail, 305; **924**
Blue Trail, 332
Blue Trail, 335–36; **997**
Blue Trail, 336; **1000**
Bluff Trail, 176–77; **412**
Bobcat Ridge Trail, 220
Bobs Gap Trail, 39–40; **28**
Bogan Run Trail, 145–46; **340**
Bolar Ridge Fire Trail, 225; **649**
Boss Trail, 80; **146**
Boston Knob Trail, 162, 164; **370**
Braddock Park Trail, 287; **868**
Braley Branch Trail, 90; **175**
Braley Pond Trail, 86, 89–90; **172**
Branch Trail, 196; **572**
Branch Trail, 299; **908**
Breakthrough Point Trail, 195; **566**
Bridge Hollow Trail, 90–91; **174**
Broad Hollow Trail, 179; **452**
Brown Mountain Trail, 184–85; **528**
Brown's Gap Fire Road, 185–86; **537**
Browntown Trail, 177; **417**
Brumley Creek Trail, 231; **664**
Brumley Rim Trail, 231; **666**
Brush Mountain Horse Trail, 38; **23**
Brushy Hollow Trail, 142, 242; **717**
Brushy Lick Trail, 114–15; **227**
Brushy Ridge Trail, 86; **157**
Brushy Ridge Trail, 141–42; **322**
Buchanan Trail, 49–50; **54**
Buck Hollow Trail, 179; **446**
Buck Hollow Trail, 242–43; **721**
Buck Lick Interpretive Trail, 143, 241, 243; **707**
Buck Mountain Trail, 168; **392**
Buck Ridge Trail, 179; **448**
Buck Run Spur Trail, 147–48; **355**
Buck Run Trail, 147–48; **349**
Buckwheat Mountain Jeep Trail, 100
Buffalo Creek Trail, 352; **1028**
Bullpasture Mountain Trail, 232; **668**
Bull Run Nature Trail, 332; **991**
Bull Run/Occoquan Trail, 332–34; **992**
Bunny Trail, 227; **655**

Burke Lake Trail, 287; **869**

Bushy Point Trail, 269; **818**

Buttermilk Trail, 320–21, 323; **968**

Buzzard Rock Trail, 117–18; **236**

Cabin Branch Mine Trail, 219–20; **637**

Cabin Creek Trail, 244; **726**

Caldwell Road Trail, 69

California Ridge Trail, 98, 102–3; **198**

Cameron Run Trail, 302; **915**

Campground #1 Spur Trail, 146; **348**

Campground Trail, 261; **793**

Camp Hoover Trail, 182; **498**

Canal Park Trail, 308–9; **946**

Canoe Camp Trail, 116; **233**

Cape Henry Trail, 271–72; **825**

Capt. Staunton's Loop Trail, 261; **794**

Cascades Trail, 30–33; **9**

Catawba Creek Trail, 71–72; **128**

Cat Knob Trail, 183; **512**

Catlett Mountain Trail, 179; **454**

Catlett Spur Trail, 179; **453**

ccc Fire Trail, 231–32; **667**

ccc Trail, 233–34; **675**

ccc Trail, 246; **736**

Cedar Creek Trail, 125–26; **279**

Cedar Creek Trail, 325–26; **984**

Cedar Path Nature Trail, 300; **912**

Cedar Ridge Trail, 263; **805**

Cedar Run Trail, 174, 180–81; **482**

Cedar Run Trail, 256–57; **771**

Cellar Mountain Trail, 139; **318**

Center Creek Trail, 239; **690**

Center Trail, 247; **743**

Center Trail, 290; **883**

Chadwell Gap Trail, 202–3; **591**

Chancellorsville History Trail, 192; **558**

Channel Rock Trail, 79–80; **150**

Charcoal Passage Creek Trail, 117; **245**

Charlie Thomas Trail, 182; **497**

Chessie Nature Trail, 311, 348–49; **1024**

Chestnut Flat Spring Trail, 87–88; **165**

Chestnut Ridge Trail, 59–60; **73**

Chestnut Ridge Trail, 99–100

Chestnut Ridge Trail, 162, 168; **390**

Chestnut Ridge Trail, 260; **786**

Chestnut Trail, 35–36; **15**

Chickahominy River Trail, 294; **895**

Chief Benge Scout Trail, 44–45; **40**

Chimney Hollow Trail, 88–89; **168**

Chippokes Creek Trail, 264; **807**

Chopawamsic Trail, 220; **641**

Christian Run Trail, 147–48; **354**

Circumferential Trail, 253–54, 277; **758**

Claylick Draft Trail, 140

Claytor Lake Trail, 240; **700**

Cliffside Trail, 61–62; **80**

Cliff Trail, 98, 104–6; **207**

Cliff Trail, 137; **311**

Clinch Mountain Trail, 227; **657**

Cobbler Mountain Trail, 145–46; **337**

Cobbs Wharf Trail, 285; **865**

Cock's Comb Trail, 109; **215**

Cold Harbor Trail, 195; **565**

Cold Springs Run Trail, 147–48; **352**

Cold Spring Trail, 87; **164**

Cold Spring Trail, 139; **319**

Cold Spring Trail, 239; **697**

Coles Trail, 107; **212**

Comers Creek Fall Trail, 65–66; **105**

Comers Creek Trail, 65–66; **106**

Compton Gap Fire Road, 176; **410**

Compton Peak Trail, 176; **408**

Connector Trail, 262; **797**

Conservancy Trail, 31–33; **10**

Conway River Fire Road, 183; **511**

Cooper Ridge Trail, 236–37; **683**

Corbin Cabin Cutoff Trail, 180; **460**

Corbin Hollow Trail, 181; **477**

Corbin Mountain Trail, 181; **476**

Cornelius Creek Trail, 47, 50; **58**

Cotoctin Trail, 163; **363**

Counts Cabin Trail, 39–40; **29**

Cove Branch Trail, 69; **119**

Cove Mountain Trail, 49–50; **55**

Crabtree Falls Trail, 134–35; **301**

Craig Creek Trail, 78; **144**

Crane Trail, 141; **320**

Crater Spur Trail, 197; **579**

Crawford Knob Trail, 88; **169**

Crawford Mountain Trail, 87–88; **167**

Crescent Rocks Trail, 181; **480**

Crest Trail, 63–64; **98**

Cross Rock Trail, 166; **382**

Crow's Nest Trail, 261;, 790
Crusher Ridge Trail, 180; 462
Cumberland Mountain Trail, 39–40; 26
Curry Creek Trail, 48–49; 51
Custis Trail, 215; 616
Cycle of Life Trail, 303; 920

Dam Spillway Trail, 254; 760
Dam Trail, 137–38; 309
Dark Hollow Falls Trail, 174, 182; 491
Deadening Nature Trail, 185; 533
Deep Cut Trail, 190–91; 534
Deep Landing Trail, 236; 682
Deep Run Trail, 293; 890
Deer Island Trail, 306–7; 939
Deer Ridge Trail, 220
Deer Trail, 71–71; 125
Deer Trail, 239; 698
Devil's Fork Loop Trail, 45–46; 45
Dickey Gap Trail, 65–66; 103
Dickey Knob Trail, 66–67; 108
Dickey Ridge Trail, 176, 309; 403
Dickinson Gap Trail, 8, 30; 1
Difficult Run Trail, 216, 218; 632
Discovery Way, 121; 258
Dismal Branch Trail, 35
Dismal Town Boardwalk Trail, 210–11;
    606
Divide Trail, 68; 115
Dixon Branch Trail, 35
Dogwood Hollow Trail, 262; 795
Dogwood Trail, 233–34; 676
Dogwood Trail, 327–28; 988
Donaldson Run Trail, 215, 283; 856
Donaldson Trail, 336; 1001
Dora Kelly Trail, 302; 913
Doubletop Mountain Trail, 235
Dowells Draft Trail, 88–89, 99–100;
    170
Doyles River/Jones River Trail, 185; 534
Doyles River Trail, 174, 185; 527
Dragon's Tooth Trail, 69, 71; 120
Dry Run Fire Road, 184; 521
Dry Run Trail, 111–12; 223
Dudley Island Trail, 265–67; 815
Duff and Stuff Trail, 290; 884
Duncan Hollow Trail, 117, 119–21; 247

Dune Trail, 205–6; 598
Dyke Marsh Trail, 214; 614

Eagle Point Trail, 342–43; 1015
Earth Awareness Trail, 303; 918
Eastern National Children's Forest Trail,
    110; 221
Eastern Shore Nature Trail, 204; 593
Echo Lake Trail, 293; 891
Elephant Mountain Trail, 131–32, 303;
    296
Elkhorn Lake Trail, 98; 188
Elk Run Trail, 166; 384
Elkwallow Trail, 178; 431
Ellett Valley Nature Trail, 303; 917
Elmore Trail, 75–76; 137
Encampment Trail, 197; 577
Ewing Trail, 202–3; 592

Fallingwater Cascades Trail, 166; 380
Falls Hollow Trail, 86; 160
Falls Ridge Trail, 127–28; 284
False Cape Landing Trail, 265–66; 811
False Cape Main Trail, 265–67; 808
Farms to Forest Trail, 219–21; 638
Fat Mountain Trail, 128; 286
Feathercamp Branch Trail, 59–61; 72
Feathercamp Ridge Trail, 59–60; 75
Fee Booth Spur Trail, 146; 344
Fenwick Nature Walk, 73–74; 131
Fenwick Wetlands Trail, 73; 132
Fern Trail, 263; 801
Ferrier Trail, 71–73; 130
Ferris Hollow Trail, 87–88; 166
Fescue Trail, 233–34; 669
Field Trail, 305; 933
Fire Trail, 282; 853
First Peak Trail, 8, 63–64; 94
Fisherman's Trail, 256; 768
Fishing Access Trail, 114; 230
Fishing Barge Trail, 343–44; 1017
Flat Peter Loop Trail, 35
Flattop Trail, 61–62, 66; 82
Flat Top Trail, 166; 381
Florida Maple Trail, 325; 982
Fore Mountain Trail, 111–12, 142; 222
Forest Nature Trail, 182; 494

Forest Trail, 321; 972
Fork Mountain Trail, 177; 429
Fork Mountain Trail, 183; 503
Fort Boykin Trail, 295; 897
Fort Brady Trail, 195; 568
Fort Darling Trail, 195; 569
Fort Harrison Trail, 195; 567
Fort Mountain Fire Road, 183; 507
Fortney Branch Trail, 107; 210
Four Mile Run (Bike) Trail, 214–15; 615
Fox Hollow Nature Trail, 176; 404
Fox Run Trail, 271–72; 828
Fragrance Garden Trail, 317–18; 962
Fragrance Trail, 306; 936
Franklin Trail, 233–34; 677
Fridley Gap Trail, 120–22; 257
Friend Trail, 197; 575
Furnace Mountain Summit Trail, 186; 541
Furnace Mountain Trail, 185; 540
Furnace Spring Horse Trail, 180; 469

Gap Creek Trail, 119–20; 248
Gap Run Trail, 184; 526
Gap Run Trail, 252–53; 752
Garden Walk, 323; 977
Geological Trail, 238–39; 685
Geology Interpretive Trail, 320; 965
Geology Trail, 219; 634
George's Cut Trail, 30
Gibson Gap Trail, 202; 589
Gillam Run Trail, 141–43; 325
Glass House Trail, 123; 265
Glencarlyn Park Trail, 283; 859
Glen Maury Nature Trail, 303; 921
Glenora Trail, 256–57; 773
Glenwood Horse Trail, 29, 47–50, 52; 549
Goodwin Lake Nature Trail, 262; 796
Goose Point Trail, 344; 1018
Gorge Ridge Trail, 247; 744
Goshen Pass Trail, 243; 724
Grand Caverns Nature Trail, 339; 1010
Grandview Preserve Trail, 310; 949
Grassy Creek Trail, 239; 691
Grassy Overlook Trail, 238–39; 686
Graves Mill Trail, 183; 508
Great Indian Warpath, 7

Green Leaf Nature Trail, 201; 584
Greenstone Trail, 163; 364
Green Trail, 305; 931
Greenwood Point Trail, 146–47; 341
Grooms Ridge Trail, 99–100; 192
Groundhog Trail, 34, 155; 12
Ground Pine Nature Trail, 258–59; 780
Grouse Trail, 71–72; 126
Guest Lodge Trail, 242; 723
Guest River Gorge Trail, 38–39; 25
Gulf Branch Nature Trail, 215, 282, 283; 855
Gunter Ridge Trail, 46, 52; 63
Guy's Run Trail, 229; 660

Habron Gap Trail, 117, 119; 242
Hale Lake Trail, 67–68; 111
Hammond Hollow Trail, 48–49; 53
Handicapped Trail, 254; 761
Hankey Mountain Trail, 99
Hannah Run Trail, 179; 456
Happy Creek Trail, 310; 947
Hardscrabble Trail, 90–92; 180
Hardwood Cove Trail, 169; 397
Harkening Hill Trail, 166–67; 385
Harris Hollow Trail, 177; 416
Harrison Creek Trail, 197; 578
Harvey Hollow Trail, 30
Hawksbills Trail, 181–82; 484
Hazel Grove Fairview Trail, 192; 559
Hazel Mountain Trail, 179–80; 447
Hazel River Trail, 179; 450
Heartbreak Trail, 104; 202
Heiskell Hollow Trail, 178; 434
Helms Trail, 75–76; 135
Helton Creek Spur Trail, 62–63; 89
Helton Creek Trail, 62–63; 88
Hemlock Trail, 336; 1003
Henley Hollow Trail, 68; 113
Henricus Trail, 284; 862
Henry Hill Trail, 190–91; 552
Henry Lanum Trail, 132–33; 297
Hensley Trail, 202; 590
Heritage (Potomac) Trail, 216–18
Heron Run Trail, 241; 706
Heron Trail, 288–89; 873
Hiawatha Nature Trail, 226; 652

Hickerson Hollow Trail, 176; **407**
Hickory Hollow Trail, 296; **899**
Hidden Valley Trail, 146
High Dune Trail, 271–72; **830**
High Knob Lake Shore Trail, 44; **41**
High Knob Trail, 44
High Meadows Trail, 220–21; **645**
High Tree Rock Trail, 63–64; **101**
High Water Trail, 80; **147**
Hike-Bike Trail, 288–89; **874**
Hilly Hiking Trail, 298; **905**
Historic Walk, 323; **976**
Hogback Spur Trail, 177; **423**
Hollow Trail, 282; **854**
Holly Trail, 233–34; **673**
Holly Trail, 336; **1004**
Holmes Run Trail, 302; **914**
Hone Quarry Ridge Trail, 104–5; **203**
Honey Tree trail, 201; **585**
Hoof and Hill Trail, 31; **8**
Hoop Hole Trail, 77; **143**
Horse Heaven Trail, 68; **117**
Hot Mountain/Short Mountain Trail,
    180; **457**
Huckleberry Line Trail, 303; **916**
Huckleberry Loop Trail, 35; **14**
Huffs Trail, 241–42; **712**
Huguenot Woods Trail, 322; **974**
Hull Branch Trail, 177; **419**
Hull School Trail, 177–78; **441**
Humpback Rock Trail, 163; **362**
Hunkerson Gap Trail, 116; **232**
Hunting Creek Trail, 48, 51; **59**
Hurricane Creek Trail, 65–66; **104**
Hurricane Knob Nature Trail, 65; **109**

Indian Creek Trail, 306–7; **937**
Indian File Trail, 354; **1030**
Indian Gap Trail, 131–32, 303; **294**
Indian Gap Trail, 164; **371**
Indian Grave Ridge Trail, 117, 119; **241**
Indian Run Trail, 181; **475**
Indiantown Nature Trail, 297; **900**
Iron Mine Trail, 254–55; **763**
Iron Mountain Trail, 29, 54, 56, 59–61,
    65–68, 154; **68**
Iron Ore Trail, 77–78; **142**

Island Overlook Trail, 146–47; **347**
Ivy Creek Nature Trail, 304–5; **922**

Jack-O-Lantern Branch Trail, 212; **609**
Jackson River Gorge Trail, 145–46; **339**
Jackson Trail, 114–15; **229**
Jackson Trail, 192–93; **557**
James River Trail, 165; **375**
James River Trail, 264; **806**
Jamestown Colony Trail, 189; **351**
Jamison Mill Trail, 344; **1019**
Jenkins Gap Trail, 176; **411**
Jeremys Run Trail, 174, 178; **437**
Jericho Ditch Trail, 210–11; **605**
Jerry's Run Trail, 90–94; **178**
Jerry's Run Trail, 112–13; **224**
Johns Creek Mountain Trail, 36–37; **19**
Johns Creek Trail, 37
Johnson Farm Loop Trail, 166–67; **386**
Johns Run Trail, 129; **290**
Jones Mountain Trail, 183, 235; **505**
Jones Point Trail, 214, 302; **613**
Jones River Trail, 177, 185; **528**
Jordan Flank Attack Trail, 193; **560**
Jordan River Trail, 177; **415**

Kabel Trail, 8, 63–64; **95**
Kane's Creek Trail, 270; **824**
Kelly Trail, 75–76; **139**
Kennedy Peak Trail, 117, 119; **243**
Kennedy Ridge Trail, 129; **289**
Keyser Run Trail, 177; **418**
Kingfisher Trail, 271–72; **831**
Kitchen Rock Trail, 44–45; **43**
Knob Mountain Cutoff Trail, 178; **438**
Knob Mountain Trail, 178; **435**

Lake Fairfax Nature Trail, 289; **876**
Lake Keokee Loop Trail, 41–42; **36**
Lakeshore Trail, 255–56; **766**
Lakeside Nature Trail, 315; **958**
Lakeside Trail, 41; **32**
Lakeside Trail, 137; **310**
Lakeside Trail, 253–54, 277; **755**
Lake Trail, 227; **654**
Lake Trail, 239; **696**
Lake Trail, 246; **737**

Lake Trail, 282; **851**
Lake Trail, 299; **911**
Lake View Trail, 259; **783**
Lancaster County Nature Trail, 351; **1025**
Lands Run Gap Trail, 176; **406**
Lantz Mountain Trail, 140
Laurel Branch Trail, 239; **692**
Laurel Fork Trail, 41; **31**
Laurel Fork Trail, 147–48; **351**
Laurel Glen Trail, 263; **803**
Laurel Glen Trail, 274–75; **845**
Laurel Hill Loop Trail, 194; **564**
Laurel Pond Trail, 273; **835**
Laurel Prong Trail, 182–83, 235; **499**
Laurel Run Trail, 127; **282**
Laurel Run Trail, 229, 243; **659**
Laurel Spur Trail, 127–28; **285**
Laurel Trail, 220–21; **642**
Laurel View Trail, 241; **703**
Leach's Run Trail, 310; **948**
Leading Ridge Trail, 180; **459**
Lee Drive Trail, 191–92; **556**
Lee-Jackson and vmi-Marshall Trail,
    311–12; **951**
Lee's Creek (Horse) Trail, 70; **123**
Lee's Woods Trail, 269; **820**
Lewis Fork Trail, 61–62; **81**
Lewis Hollow Trail, 202; **580**
Lewis Mountain Trail, 184; **516**
Lewis Peak Trail, 186; **539**
Lewis Springs Falls Trail, 182; **492**
Liberty Hill Trail, 342, **1014**
Lick Branch Trail, 70–73; **129**
Lighthouse Trail, 207; **602**
Limberlost Nature Trail, 181; **473**
Lion's Tale Trail, 119; **246**
Lipes Branch Horse Trail, 69; **118**
Listening Rock Trail, 244; **727**
Little Cove Mountain Trail, 49–50; **56**
Little Devils Stairs Trail, 177; **422**
Little Dry Run Trail, 68; **114**
Little Mare Mountain Spur Trail, 141,
    143; **328**
Little Mare Mountain Trail, 141–43; **324**
Little North Mountain Trail, 230; **663**
Little River Trail, 98, 102–3; **199**
Little Rocky Row Run Trail, 129–31; **293**

Little Run Trail, 220; **636**
Little Sluice Mountain Trail, 125–26; **276**
Little Stony Creek Trail, 38, 44–45; **44**
Little Stony Creek Trail, 125–26; **275**
Little Stony Man Trail, 180; **463**
Little Wilson Creek Trail, 63–64; **102**
Living Museum Nature Trail, 357–58;
    1033
Loblolly Trail, 261; **792**
Loblolly Trail, 336; **1002**
Locust Gap Trail, 241–42; **715**
Locust Shade Trail, 298; **902**
Locust Spring Run Spur Trail, 147–48;
    357
Locust Spring Run Trail, 147–48; **350**
Lone Star Lake Trail, 325–26; **986**
Long Arm Hollow Trail, 231; **665**
Long Branch Nature Trail, 283; **858**
Long Creek Trail, 271–72; **829**
Long Island Trail, 284; **861**
Lookout Mountain Trail, 99, 101
Lookout Tower Trail, 327–28; **990**
Loop Trail, 75–76; **136**
Loop Trail, 146; **343**
Loop Trail, 239; **693**
Lost Barr Trail, 253–54; **757**
Lost Mountain Trail, 252; **749**
Loudoun Heights Trail, 159; **360**
Lover's Leap Trail, 247; **741**
Lovingston Spring Trail, 133–34; **300**
Lower Cherokee Path, 5
Lower Lost Woman Trail, 143; **334**
Lum Trail, 59–61; **67**
Lupton Trail, 123–24; **269**

McAllister Fields Trail, 108; **213**
McCoull/Harrison Loop Trail, 194; **563**
McDaniel Hollow Trail, 183; **506**
Madison Run Fire Trail, 185; **536**
Mad Sheep Trail, 140
Main Trail, 358; **1034**
Majestic Oak Trail, 274–75; **848**
Mare Run Trail, 143
Marshall Draft Trail, 86, 95–96; **186**
Marsh Point Trail, 227; **656**
Martin Bottom Trail, 122; **261**
Mary Bird Branch Trail, 220; **647**

Mason District Trail, 289; **878**
Mathews Arm Trail, 178; **433**
Matildaville Trail, 216, 218; **628**
Mattaponi Trail, 274–75; **843**
Massanutten Mountain East Trail, 84,
    116–20, 309; **234**
Massanutten Mountain South Trail, 84,
    119–22; **252**
Massanutten Mountain West Trail, 84,
    122–25; **266**
Massanutten Story Book Trail, 121; **259**
Mayking Loop Trail, 38; **24**
Meadow Ground Trail, 229; **661**
Meadowlark Gardens Trail, 336; **994**
Meadow School Trail, 183; **514**
Meadow Spring Trail, 179; **455**
Meadow Trail, 320; **967**
Medden Hollow Trail, 114–15; **228**
Meh-Te-Kos Trail, 274; **840**
Micro Trail, 303; **919**
Middle Hollow Trail, 241–42; **704**
Middle Mountain Trail, 111–12, 141–43,
    241–42; **321**
Middle Mountain Trail, 119–20; **250**
Middle Mountain Trail, 147–48; **353**
Middle Ridge Trail, 246; **738**
Milford Gap Trail, 117–18; **239**
Mill Creek Trail, 30
Mill Creek Trail, 64
Millers Head Trail, 181; **472**
Mill Mountain Trail, 86–87; **162**
Mill Mountain Trail, 117, 125; **272**
Mill Mountain Trail, 140
Mill Pond Trail, 256–57; **770**
Mill Prong Horse Trail, 182; **496**
Mill Prong Trail, 183; **502**
Mills Creek Trail, 129, 137–38; **312**
Mills Creek Trail (A), 137–38; **312**
Mine Bank Creek Trail, 138; **316**
Mine Bank Mountain Trail, 129; **288**
Mine Gap Trail, 123–24; **268**
Mine Run Trail, 216, 218; **629**
Molly Mitchell Trail, 306–7; **942**
Molly's Knob Trail, 246; **734**
Moorman's River Fire Road, 186; **544**
Morgan Run Trail, 120–21; **256**
Morris Hill Trail, 107; **211**

Mossy Creek Trail, 258; **776**
Mountain Farm Trail, 163; **361**
Mountain Fork Trail, 44
Mountain Industry Trail, 171; **398**
Mountain Lake Horse Trail, 36; **18**
Mountain Side Trail, 142, 143, 242; **722**
Mountain Top Trail, 141–43, 242; **718**
Mount Marshall Trail, 176–77; **413**
Mount Pleasant Trail, 132–33; **298**
Mount Rogers Spur Trail, 61–62; **83**
Mount Rogers Trail, 55, 61–62; **78**
Mount Vernon Trail, 214–15, 302, 338; **612**
Muddy Run Trail, 145–46; **338**
Mud Pond Gap Trail, 105–6; **209**
Mullins Branch Trail, 66–67; **110**

Naked Top Trail, 182
Narrowback Trail, 102–3; **200**
Natural Chimneys Nature Trail, 339–40;
    1011
Nature Trail, 233–34; **671**
Nature Trail, 288; **872**
Nature Trail, 289; **879**
Nature Trail, 292; **888**
Nature Trail, 298; **904**
Nature Trail, 298; **906**
Nature Trail, 325; **983**
Nature Trail, 335; **995**
Nature Trail, 336; **999**
Neck Fields Trail, 263; **800**
Neighbor Mountain Trail, 178; **443**
Nelson Draft Trail, 95–96; **185**
New Kent Nature Trail, 351; **1026**
New Market Battlefield Trail, 195; **570**
New River Community College Trail,
    347; **1021**
New River Trail, 8, 22, 248–52; **747**
Nicholson Hollow Trail, 174, 179–80;
    461
Niday Trail, 30
Nike Park Nature Trail, 295; **896**
Noland Trail, 22, 315, 352–54; **1029**
North Boundary Trail, 299; **910**
North Fork Trail, 30
North Mountain Trail, 127–28; **281**
North Mountain Trail (Central), 108–9;
    214

North Mountain Trail (North), 87; **163**
North Mountain Trail (South), 71–72; **124**
North Ridge Trail, 252–53; **751**
North River Gorge Trail, 98, 101–2; **194**
North Run Creek Trail, 293; **843**
North Valley Trail, 219–20; **636**

Oak Hickory Trail, 254; **762**
Oak Ridge Trail, 220–21; **646**
Occoneechi Path (Trail), 5–6
Occoquan River Trail, 334–35; **993**
Old Carriage Road Trail, 216, 218; **626**
Old Dominion Trail, 323–24; **980**
Old Hotel Trail, 132–33; **299**
Old Oak Nature Trail, 286–87; **867**
Old Orchard Trail, 62; **86**
Old Rag Fire Road, 175, 181; **474**
Old Shawnee Trail, 245; **733**
Olinger Gap Trail, 41–42; **35**
Oliver Mountain Trail, 114–15; **226**
One Mile Run Trail, 184; **527**
Onion Mountain Loop Trail, 165; **379**
Orange Trail, 305; **927**
Orange Trail, 335–36; **998**
Orkney Springs Trail, 116; **23**
Osmanthus Trail, 271–72; **827**
Osprey Trail, 271–72; **833**
Otter Creek Trail, 164–65; **373**
Otter Lake Trail, 164–65; **374**
Otter Point Trail, 306–7; **940**
Otter's Path Trail, 262; **798**
Outdoor Classroom Trail, 205–6; **600**
Overall Run/Beecher Ridge Trail, 177; **427**
Overall Run Trail, 177; **476**
Overlook Trail, 238–39; **687**

Paddy Knob Trail, 140
Paine Run Trail, 186; **543**
Pamunkey Trail, 274–75; **846**
Pandapas Pond Trail, 30, 37–38; **21**
Panther Falls Trail, 129; **287**
Passamaquoddy Trail, 180; **465**
Pass Mountain Nature Trail, 179; **445**
Pass Mountain Trail, 179; **444**
Patowmack Canal Trail, 216, 218; **624**

Patrick Henry Cross-Country Trail, 292; **889**
Patterson Mountain Trail, 75–76; **133**
Patterson Ridge Trail, 185; **531**
Paw Paw Passage Trail, 290; **880**
Payne Branch Trail, 41, 43; **37**
Pearis Thompson Horse Trail, 31; **6**
Peer Trail, 125–26; **274**
Peninsula Trail, 305; **930**
Petersburg Battlefield Trail, 196–96; **591**
Phillips Creek Trail, 41; **33**
Picnic Area Spur Trail, 146; **346**
Piedmont Overlook Trail, 252; **750**
Pig Iron Trail, 117; **244**
Pine Grove Forest Trail, 219; **633**
Pine Hill Gap Trail, 179–80; **458**
Pine Knob Trail, 253–54, 277; **759**
Pine Mountain Trail, 39
Pine Mountain Trail, 61–62; **79**
Pine Trail, 233–34; **674**
Pine Tree Trail, 241–42; **705**
Piney Branch Trail, 177; **420**
Piney Mountain Trail, 143–44; **332**
Piney Mountain Trail, 229; **661**
Piney Ridge Trail, 46, 51–53; **64**
Piney Ridge Trail, 177; **428**
Pinnacle Trail, 355–56; **1032**
Pitt Spring Lookout Trail, 121; **260**
Pitt Springs Trail, 120–21; **255**
Plantation Trail, 212; **608**
Plantation Trail, 258; **775**
Pleasant Creek Trail, 321; **970**
Pocosin Hollow Fire Road, 184; **517**
Pocosin Hollow Trail, 184; **519**
Pocosin Horse Trail, 184; **518**
Pole Bridge Link Trail, 177; **421**
Polecat Trail, 81–82; **154**
Pompey/Mount Pleasant Loop Trail, 132
Pond Knob Trail, 98; **206**
Pond Trail, 289; **875**
Pony Trail, 207
Poplar Grove Trail, 263; **802**
Poquoson Nature Trail, 318; **964**
Possum Rest Trail, 176; **409**
Potomac Heritage Trail, 214–15, 336; **618**
Potomac Heritage Trail, 290; **881**
Potts Arm Trail, 69; **121**

Potts Mountain Trail, 30; 2
Poverty Creek Horse Trail, 38; 22
Powell Mountain Trail, 124
Powell Mountain Trail, 183; 510
Powell's Creek Trail, 269; 819
Power Line Trail, 233–34; 681
Powhatan Forks Trail, 274–75; 847
Presquile Nature Trail, 204; 595
Price Mountain Horse Trail, 70; 122
Price Mountain Trail, 72, 75–77; 130
Priest (Overlook) Trail, The, 162–63; 365
Prince Edward County Nature Trail, 351;
    1027
Prospectors Trail, 239; 694
Purchase Hill Trail, 247; 745

Quantico Falls Trail, 219; 635
Quiet Woods Trail, 321; 971

Raccoon Branch Trail, 66–67; 109
Ragged Island Trail, 226; 650
Raider's Run Trail, 245; 732
Railroad Ford Trail, 256–57; 774
Rails to River Trail, 289; 877
Ramsey's Draft Trail, 90–94; 176
Rapidan Fire Road, 182; 495
Rappahannock Community College
    Nature Trail, 347; 1022
Red Branch Trail, 228; 658
Red Bud Trail, 233–34; 678
Red Fox Trail, 40; 30
Red Gate Fire Road, 182; 490
Red Oak Trail, 233–34; 680
Red Trail, 305; 915
Red Wing Nature Trail, 326–27; 987
Reedy Creek Trail, 323; 975
Rein Memorial Trail, 306–7; 943
Reservoir Hollow Trail, 131–32, 303; 295
Rhododendron Trail, 244–45; 728
Ribble Trail, 31; 5
Rich Hole Trail, 109–10; 219
Richmond Walking Trail, 324; 981
Ridge Trail, 174–75; 401
Ridge Trail, 200, 202, 203; 586
Ridge Trail, 216, 218; 625
Ridge Trail, 238–39; 684
Ridge Trail, 246; 739

Ridge Trail, 299; 909
Riprap Trail, 186; 545
River Access Trail, 321; 973
River Bank Trail, 261; 788
Riverbend Equestrian Trail, 216, 218; 630
River Birch Trail, 293; 892
River Loop Trail, 145; 336
Riverside Trail, 146; 345
Riverside Trail, 320–21; 966
River Trail, 215; 617
River Trail, 216, 218; 623
River Trail, 239; 695
River Trail, 273; 834
Road Hollow Trail, 90–92; 177
Roanoke Mountain Summit Trail, 167;
    389
Roanoke River Trail, 167; 388
Roanoke Valley Horse Trail, 162, 168; 391
Roaring Fork Trail, 80; 148
Roaring Run Falls Trail, 77; 141
Roaring Run Trail, 120–21; 254
Robertson Mountain Trail, 181; 478
Robin's Roost Trail, 261; 791
Rock Castle Gorge Trail, 162, 169–71; 394
Rock Creek Trail, 214
Rock House Ridge Trail, 243–44; 725
Rock Shelter Trail, 146
Rock Spring Trail, 273; 836
Rockwood Nature Trail, 285; 866
Rocky Branch Trail, 178; 442
Rocky Mountain/Brown Mountain Trail,
    185
Rocky Mountain Run Trail, 185; 529
Rocky Mount Trail, 184; 525
Rocky Run Trail, 84
Rockytop Trail, 185; 530
Ronk Trail, 30
Rose River Fire Road, 182; 486
Rose River Loop Trail, 182; 487
Ross Camp Hollow Trail, 143, 242; 719
Round Meadow Creek Trail, 171; 399
Running Cedar Trail, 253–54; 756
Rush Trail, 59–60; 74
Ruskin Freer Lower Trail, 313–14; 956
Ruskin Freer Upper Trail, 313–14; 957
R. W. Cross Nature Trail, 317–18; 963

Saddleback Mountain Trail, 184; **522**

Saddle Gap Trail, 129–31; **292**

Saddle Trail, 175, 181; **479**

Saint Brooks Trail, 308; **944**

Saint Mary's Gorge Trail, 138; **315**

Saint Mary's Trail, 138–39; **314**

Salamander Trail, 182; **485**

Salthouse Branch Nature Trail, 344–45;
    1020

Salt Pond Ridge Trail, 141–42; **323**

Salt Stump Trail, 142, 241–42; **710**

Sam Ramsey Hunter Access Trail, 86; **159**

Sams Ridge Trail, 179; **451**

Sand Spring Mountain Trail, 102–3; **196**

Sandy Gap Trail, 141–42; **327**

Saponi Trail, 5–7

Sartain Trail, 37; **20**

Sarver Trail, 30

Saunders Creek Trail, 255–56; **767**

Scales Trail, 8, 63–64; **93**

School Trail, 305; **934**

Scothorn Gap Trail, 119–20; **249**

Scotts Run Trail, 288; **871**

Seaside Trail, 205–6; **597**

Seven Bar None Trail, 123–24; **270**

Seven Sisters Trail, 79–80; **152**

Shady Ridge Trail, 240; **701**

Shapiro Trail, 63–64; **100**

Sharp Top Trail, 166; **383**

Shaw Gap Trail, 59–60; **69**

Shawl Gap Trail, 117–18; **237**

Shaws Ridge Trail, 86, 94   95; 183

Shenandoah Mountain Trail (North),
    84–85, 90–94, 98; **181**

Shenandoah Mountain Trail (South),
    84–85, 95–96, 98; **184**

Sherman's Mill Trail, 252; **748**

Shoe Creek Trail, 135; **302**

Short Loop Trail, 197; **576**

Short Ridge Trail, 86; **158**

Shot Tower Historical Trail, 248; **746**

Shuttle Trail, 306–7; **938**

Signal Knob Trail, 122–23; **262**

Simmons Gap Fire Road, 184; **524**

Sinclair Hollow Trail, 94; **182**

Skyland/Big Meadow Horse Trail, 180,
    182; **467**

Skyland Trail, 180; **468**

Skylight Cave Trail, 202

Slabcamp Run Trail, 147–48; **356**

Slacks Overlook Trail, 136–37; **304**

Slate Springs Trail, 98, 104–6; **205**

Slaughter Trail, 183; **515**

Smart View Loop Trail, 168; **393**

Smith River Trail, 343; **1016**

Smith Roach Gap Trail, 184; **523**

Snead Farm Loop Trail, 176; **405**

Snowden Trail, 252–53; **754**

South Boundary Trail, 299; **907**

Southern Lakes Trail, 325–26; **985**

South Ridge Trail, 252–53; **753**

South River Falls Trail, 174, 184; **520**

South Trail, 298; **903**

South Valley Trail, 220–21; **643**

Spec Mines Trail, 48–49; **52**

Spotsylvania Battlefield Trail, 193; **561**

Springhouse Ridge Trail, 92

Spruce Trail, 336; **1005**

Squirrel Ridge Trail, 233–34; **670**

Stack Rock Trail, 127; **283**

Stampers Branch Trail, 244–45; **731**

Standrock Branch Horse Trail, 31; 7

Staunton River Trail, 182, 235; **504**

Stephens Trail, 119

Stewarts Knob Trail, 167; **387**

Stone Bridge Trail, 190–91; **553**

Stone Mountain Trail, 41–43; **34**

Stony Fork Nature Trail, 80; **151**

Stony Man Horse Trail, 180; 166

Stony Man Nature Trail, 180; **464**

Stony Mountain Trail, 182; **488**

Stony Run Trail, 141–42, 241–42; **708**

Straight Branch Trail, 59; **66**

Straight Fork Ridge Trail, 45–46; **46**

Stuart's Knob Trail, 254–55; **764**

Sugar Hollow Trail, 146–47; **342**

Sugarland Run Trail, 311; **950**

Sugarload Trail, 177; **424**

Sugar Maple Trail, 62–63; **87**

Sugar Run Trail, 200–202; **587**

Sulphur Ridge Trail, 75–77; **140**

Sulphur Springs Gap Trail, 125–26; **277**

Sulphur Springs Trail, 46, 51–53; **61**

Sunken Road Trail, 191; **555**

Swamp Trail, 216, 218; **627**
Swan Cove Trail, 207; **601**
Sweet Acron Trail, 225; **648**
Sweetbay Trail, 336; **1007**

Tanners Ridge Horse Trail, 182; **500**
Tanners Ridge Trail, 182; **501**
Taskinas Creek Trail, 275–76; **849**
Tearjacket Trail, 90–92, 99–100; **179**
Ted Lake Trail, 226; **651**
Third Branch Trail, 258–59; **781**
Third Peak Trail, 63–64; **99**
Thompson Hollow Trail, 177; **425**
Thornton Hollow Trail, 178; **440**
Thornton River Trail, 178; **439**
Three Lakes Trail, 293; **877**
Thunder Ridge Trail, 165; **377**
Tibbet Knob Trail, 127–28; **280**
Tillman Trail, 103; **201**
Timber Ridge Trail, 102–3; **195**
Tindall's Point Trail, 292; **887**
Tobacco House Ridge Trail, 242; **716**
Tobacco Run Trail, 259; **784**
Todd Lake Trail, 98; **189**
Tolliver Trail, 117, 119; **240**
Tom Cove Nature Trail, 208; **604**
Torry Ridge Trail, 136–39; **307**
Tower Hill Mountain Trail, 143–44; **333**
Towers Trail, 238–39; **688**
Tower Tunnel Trail, 238–39; **689**
Traces Nature Trail, 178; **430**
Track Fork Trail, 81–82; **153**
Trail of the Lonesome Pine, 38
Trail of Trees, 165; **376**
Trail of Trees, 341; **1012**
Trayfoot Mountain Trail, 186; **542**
Tree Walk, 323; **978**
Trimble Mountain Trail, 98–99; **190**
Tri-State Trail, 200; **582**
Troy Creek Trail, 9, 358; **1035**
Tub Run Trail, 69
Tucker Trail, 75; **134**
Tunnel Hill Trail, 247; **742**
Tunnel Trail, 246; **740**
Turk Branch Trail, 187; **549**
Turkey Neck Trail, 273; **838**
Turkey Pen Ridge Trail, 129, 138

Turkey Run Ridge Trail, 220; **644**
Turkey Run Trail, 215; **621**
Turkey Run Trail, 256–57; **769**
Turkey Trail, 71–72; **127**
Turk Gap Trail, 187; **548**
Turk Mountain Trail, 187; **547**
Turtle Island Trail, 260; **787**
Tuscarora Overlook Trail, 142, 241–42; **709**
Tutelo Trail, 261; **789**
Twin Eagle Trail, 341; **1013**
Twin Forts Trail, 315–17; **961**
Twin Pinnacles Trail, 244–45; **730**

Unaka Nature Trail, 67–68; **112**
University of Virginia Academic Walk, 348; **1023**
Upland Trail, 216, 218; **631**
Upland Trail, 290; **882**
Upper Dark Hollow Trail, 182; **489**
Upper Lost Woman Trail, 145; **335**
Upton Hill Trail, 337; **1008**

Veach Gap Trail, 117–18; **238**
Veterans' Memorial Nature Trail, 297; **901**
Virginia Creeper Trail, 8, 54–56, 59, 154; **65**
Virginia Highlands Horse Trail, 29, 54, 62–68; **90**
Virginias' Walk, 34; **13**

Wagon Road Trail, 123–24; **267**
Walker Mountain Trail, 86; **155**
Wallace Tract Trail, 96–97; **187**
Wallen Ridge Trail, 43; **38**
Walton Tract Trail, 141, 143; **329**
War Branch Trail, 30
Warm Springs Mountain Trail, 143–44; **331**
Warrior's Path, 7
Warrior's Path Trail, 258; **777**
War Spur Connector Trail, 35–36; **17**
War Spur Trail, 35–36; **16**
Washington and Old Dominion Railroad Trail, 215, 282, 286, 297, 307, 311, 326, 331, 337–38; **1009**

Washington Ditch Trail, 210–11; **607**
Washington Historic Trail, 213; **610**
Washington Nature Trail, 213; **611**
Wash Woods Beach Trail, 265–67; **812**
Wash Woods Cemetery Trail, 265–67; **814**
Wash Woods Interpretive Trail, 265–67; **813**
Watchable Wildlife Trail, 305; **935**
Watch House Trail, 263; **799**
Waterfall Mountain Trail, 119–20; **251**
Waverly-Wolftrap Trail, 291
Wayside Trail, 296; **898**
Weakley Hollow Fire Road, 174–75, 181; **400**
Weddlewood Trail, 178; **436**
West Augusta Trail, 90
West Naked Creek Trail, 183; **509**
Wheelchair Trail, 305; **923**
Whetstone Ridge Trail, 135–36; **303**
Whiskey Run Trail, 254–55; **765**
Whispering Water Trail, 61; **84**
White Hill Lake Trail, 271–72; **832**
White Oak Canyon Horse Trail, 181; **470**
White Oak Canyon Trail, 174, 180–81; **471**
White Oak Draft Trail, 89, 99–100; **171**
White Oak Flats Trail, 164; **372**
White Oak Trail, 233–34; **679**
White Oak Trail, 315–17; **959**
White Pine Trail, 336; **1006**
White Rock Falls Trail (GWNF), 136; **305**
White Rock Falls Trail (BRP), 162–63; **366**
White Rock Gap Trail (GWNF), 136–37; **306**
White Rock Gap Trail (BRP), 163; **367**
White Rocks Trail, 179; **449**
White Rock Tower Trail, 109–10; **220**

White Rock Trail, 125–26; **278**
Whitetail Trail, 47; **48**
White Trail, 305; **925**
Wilburn Ridge Trail, 55, 62; **85**
Wildcat Mountain Trail, 46; **47**
Wildcat Ridge Trail, 186; **546**
Wilderness Road Trail, 200; **583**
Wilderness Trail, 7
Wild Oak Trail, 12, 89–92, 99–102; **191**
Willis River Trail, 253–54, 276–78; **850**
Wilson Creek Horse Trail, 63–64; **92**
Wilson Creek Trail (Douthat SP), 143, 241–43; **720**
Wilson Creek Trail (JNF and Grayson SP), 63–65, 244; **91**
Wilson Spring Trail, 270; **823**
Windy Run Trail, 215, 283; **857**
Wolf Creek Nature Trail, 80; **149**
Wolf Creek Trail, 79; **145**
Wolf Ridge Trail, 102–3; **197**
Wolftrap Stream Valley Trail, 291; **886**
Woodcock Trail, 226–27; **653**
Wood Duck Slough Trail, 306–7; **941**
Woodland Trail, 169; **395**
Woodland Trail, 207–8; **603**
Woodmarsh Trail, 204; **594**
Woods Creek Trail, 312–13, 349; **952**
Woodstock Pond Trail, 274–75; **841**
Woods Trail, 215; **619**
Woods Trail, 305; **932**
Woodthrush Trail, 285; **864**
Wright Hollow Trail, 59–60; **76**
Wynn's Mill Historical Trail, 315–17; **960**

YACCer's Run Trail, 108–9; **216**
Yankee Horse Trail, 164; **369**
YCC Trail, 241; **702**
Yellow Trail, 305; **926**
Yellow Trail, 335–36; **996**
Yorktown Battlefield Trail, 188–89; **550**